# Dictionary of Literary Biography

## *Dictionary of Literary Biography Documentary Series*

# Dictionary of Literary Biography Yearbooks

**1980** edited by Karen L. Rood, Jean W. Ross, and Richard Ziegfeld (1981)

**1981** edited by Karen L. Rood, Jean W. Ross, and Richard Ziegfeld (1982)

**1982** edited by Richard Ziegfeld; associate editors: Jean W. Ross and Lynne C. Zeigler (1983)

**1983** edited by Mary Bruccoli and Jean W. Ross; associate editor Richard Ziegfeld (1984)

**1984** edited by Jean W. Ross (1985)

**1985** edited by Jean W. Ross (1986)

**1986** edited by J. M. Brook (1987)

**1987** edited by J. M. Brook (1988)

**1988** edited by J. M. Brook (1989)

**1989** edited by J. M. Brook (1990)

**1990** edited by James W. Hipp (1991)

**1991** edited by James W. Hipp (1992)

**1992** edited by James W. Hipp (1993)

**1993** edited by James W. Hipp, contributing editor George Garrett (1994)

**1994** edited by James W. Hipp, contributing editor George Garrett (1995)

**1995** edited by James W. Hipp, contributing editor George Garrett (1996)

**1996** edited by Samuel W. Bruce and L. Kay Webster, contributing editor George Garrett (1997)

**1997** edited by Matthew J. Bruccoli and George Garrett, with the assistance of L. Kay Webster (1998)

**1998** edited by Matthew J. Bruccoli, contributing editor George Garrett, with the assistance of D. W. Thomas (1999)

**1999** edited by Matthew J. Bruccoli, contributing editor George Garrett, with the assistance of D. W. Thomas (2000)

**2000** edited by Matthew J. Bruccoli, contributing editor George Garrett, with the assistance of George Parker Anderson (2001)

**2001** edited by Matthew J. Bruccoli, contributing editor George Garrett, with the assistance of George Parker Anderson (2002)

**2002** edited by Matthew J. Bruccoli and George Garrett; George Parker Anderson, Assistant Editor (2003)

# Concise Series

**Concise Dictionary of American Literary Biography,** 7 volumes (1988–1999): *The New Consciousness, 1941–1968; Colonization to the American Renaissance, 1640–1865; Realism, Naturalism, and Local Color, 1865–1917; The Twenties, 1917–1929; The Age of Maturity, 1929–1941; Broadening Views, 1968–1988; Supplement: Modern Writers, 1900–1998.*

**Concise Dictionary of British Literary Biography,** 8 volumes (1991–1992): *Writers of the Middle Ages and Renaissance Before 1660; Writers of the Restoration and Eighteenth Century, 1660–1789; Writers of the Romantic Period, 1789–1832; Victorian Writers, 1832–1890; Late-Victorian and Edwardian Writers, 1890–1914; Modern Writers, 1914–1945; Writers After World War II, 1945–1960; Contemporary Writers, 1960 to Present.*

**Concise Dictionary of World Literary Biography,** 4 volumes (1999–2000): *Ancient Greek and Roman Writers; German Writers; African, Caribbean, and Latin American Writers; South Slavic and Eastern European Writers.*

# Twentieth-Century Spanish Fiction Writers

Dictionary of Literary Biography® • Volume Three Hundred Twenty-Two

# Twentieth-Century Spanish Fiction Writers

Edited by
Marta E. Altisent
*University of California Davis*
and
Cristina Martínez-Carazo
*University of California Davis*

A Bruccoli Clark Layman Book

THOMSON
GALE

Detroit • New York • San Francisco • San Diego • New Haven, Conn. • Waterville, Maine • London • Munich

# THOMSON

## GALE

Dictionary of Literary Biography
**Volume 322: Twentieth-Century Spanish Fiction Writers**
Marta E. Altisent and Cristina Martínez-Carazo

**Editorial Directors**
Matthew J. Bruccoli and Richard Layman

**LIBRARY OF CONGRESS CATALOGING-IN-PUBLICATION DATA**

Twentieth-century Spanish fiction writers / edited by Cristina Martínez-Carazo and Marta Altisent.
        p. cm. — (Dictionary of literary biography ; v. 322)
    "A Bruccoli Clark Layman book."
    Includes bibliographical references and index.
    ISBN 0–7876–8140–7 (hardcover : alk. paper)
    1. Spanish fiction—20th century—Dictionaries. 2. Spanish fiction—20th century—Bio-bibliography—Dictionaries. 3. Spanish fiction—20th century—Biography—Dictionaries.
I. Title: 20th century Spanish fiction writers. II. Martínez-Carazo, Cristina. III. Altisent, Martha Eulalia, 1950- IV. Series.

    PQ6144.T94  2005
    863'.609'03—dc22

                                                                2005023690

Printed in the United States of America
10 9 8 7 6 5 4 3 2 1

*In memory of Professor Ricardo Gullón, our mentor, teacher, and friend*

# Contents

# Plan of the Series

The advisory board, the editors, and the publisher of the *Dictionary of Literary Biography* are joined in endorsing Mark Twain's declaration. The literature of a nation provides an inexhaustible resource of permanent worth. Our purpose is to make literature and its creators better understood and more accessible to students and the reading public, while satisfying the needs of teachers and researchers.

To meet these requirements, *literary biography* has been construed in terms of the author's achievement. The most important thing about a writer is his writing. Accordingly, the entries in *DLB* are career biographies, tracing the development of the author's canon and the evolution of his reputation.

The purpose of *DLB* is not only to provide reliable information in a usable format but also to place the figures in the larger perspective of literary history and to offer appraisals of their accomplishments by qualified scholars.

The publication plan for *DLB* resulted from two years of preparation. The project was proposed to Bruccoli Clark by Frederick G. Ruffner, president of the Gale Research Company, in November 1975. After specimen entries were prepared and typeset, an advisory board was formed to refine the entry format and develop the series rationale. In meetings held during 1976, the publisher, series editors, and advisory board approved the scheme for a comprehensive biographical dictionary of persons who contributed to literature. Editorial work on the first volume began in January 1977, and it was published in 1978. In order to make *DLB* more than a dictionary and to compile volumes that individually have claim to status as literary history, it was decided to organize volumes by topic, period, or

genre. Each of these freestanding volumes provides a biographical-bibliographical guide and overview for a particular area of literature. We are convinced that this organization—as opposed to a single alphabet method— constitutes a valuable innovation in the presentation of reference material. The volume plan necessarily requires many decisions for the placement and treatment of authors. Certain figures will be included in separate volumes, but with different entries emphasizing the aspect of his career appropriate to each volume. Ernest Hemingway, for example, is represented in *American Writers in Paris, 1920–1939* by an entry focusing on his expatriate apprenticeship; he is also in *American Novelists, 1910–1945* with an entry surveying his entire career, as well as in *American Short-Story Writers, 1910–1945, Second Series* with an entry concentrating on his short fiction. Each volume includes a cumulative index of the subject authors and articles.

Between 1981 and 2002 the series was augmented and updated by the *DLB Yearbooks*. There have also been nineteen *DLB Documentary Series* volumes, which provide illustrations, facsimiles, and biographical and critical source materials for figures, works, or groups judged to have particular interest for students. In 1999 the *Documentary Series* was incorporated into the *DLB* volume numbering system beginning with *DLB 210: Ernest Hemingway*.

We define literature as the *intellectual commerce of a nation:* not merely as belles lettres but as that ample and complex process by which ideas are generated, shaped, and transmitted. *DLB* entries are not limited to "creative writers" but extend to other figures who in their time and in their way influenced the mind of a people. Thus the series encompasses historians, journalists, publishers, book collectors, and screenwriters. By this means readers of *DLB* may be aided to perceive literature not as cult scripture in the keeping of intellectual high priests but firmly positioned at the center of a nation's life.

*DLB* includes the major writers appropriate to each volume and those standing in the ranks behind them. Scholarly and critical counsel has been sought in deciding which minor figures to include and how full their entries should be. Wherever possible, useful references are made to figures who do not warrant separate entries.

Each *DLB* volume has an expert volume editor responsible for planning the volume, selecting the figures for inclusion, and assigning the entries. Volume editors are also responsible for preparing, where appropriate, appendices surveying the major periodicals and literary and intellectual movements for their volumes, as well as lists of further readings. Work on the series as a whole is coordinated at the Bruccoli Clark Layman editorial center in Columbia, South Carolina, where the editorial staff is responsible for accuracy and utility of the published volumes.

One feature that distinguishes *DLB* is the illustration policy—its concern with the iconography of literature. Just as an author is influenced by his surroundings, so is the reader's understanding of the author enhanced by a knowledge of his environment. Therefore *DLB* volumes include not only drawings, paintings, and photographs of authors, often depicting them at various stages in their careers, but also illustrations of their families and places where they lived. Title pages are regularly reproduced in facsimile along with dust jackets for modern authors. The dust jackets are a special feature of *DLB* because they often document better than anything else the way in which an author's work was perceived in its own time. Specimens of the writers' manuscripts and letters are included when feasible.

Samuel Johnson rightly decreed that "The chief glory of every people arises from its authors." The purpose of the *Dictionary of Literary Biography* is to compile literary history in the surest way available to us—by accurate and comprehensive treatment of the lives and work of those who contributed to it.

The *DLB* Advisory Board

# Introduction

The aim of *DLB 322: Twentieth-Century Spanish Fiction Writers* is to introduce the reader to the variety and excellence of the authors who shaped the development of Spanish fiction in the twentieth century. The entries focus on the interconnections between life and writing and trace the writers' personal response to the cultural, intellectual, and political concerns of the day, as well as to the traditions and literary styles that shaped their imagination.

Designed for the scholar, the student, and the nonspecialist alike, *DLB 322* provides a condensed assessment of the authors' aesthetic and personal preferences as shown through their fiction and nonfiction. The editors have provided an up-to-date list of primary and selected secondary publications. The strength of the volume lies in the contributors, most of whom are recognized critics and professors of Spanish literature well acquainted with the need for a reliable and accessible study guide to complement their students' readings.

For reasons of space, younger established authors, such as Luis Landero, Marina Mayoral, Paloma Díaz Más, and Almudena Grandes, could not be included. Also omitted were most Catalan, Galician, and Basque novelists whose original works did not appear in Spanish at the time of publication, with the notable exceptions of Mercé Rodoreda, Montserrat Roig, and Carme Riera, authors who achieved early nationwide recognition and have become part of high-school and college curricula in Spain. This criterion also leaves out masterful bilingual prose writers such as Josep Pla, Llorenç Villalonga, Sebastiá Juan Arbó, Alvaro Cunqueiro, Rafael Dieste, Bernardo Atxaga, and Manuel Rivas, who are typically excluded by the uniform-language requirements of anthologies and textbooks of Spanish literature. It is anticipated that future, more-extensive guides will be able to represent the multilingual nature of the Spanish literary scene after the 1970s, when the expansion of the publishing market and local governmental subsidies contributed to the flourishing of other vernacular literatures in the peninsula.

The Spanish-American War marks the beginning of the twentieth century in the literary history of Spain. The loss of the Atlantic and Pacific colonies after four centuries of Spanish domination, followed by the defeat in Cuba, brought about a new social and political climate and a growing awareness of the waning role of Spain in world events. The defeat of 1898 had an acute psychological impact on Spanish intellectuals. A group of writers labeled the Generación del 1898 (Generation of 1898), led by Angel Ganivet and Miguel de Unamuno and including Azorín (José Martínez Ruiz), Antonio Machado, Pío Baroja, Ramón del Valle-Inclán, and Ramiro de Maeztu, articulated their moral and ideological concerns for a national destiny that was to embrace the past greatness of Spain along with all the controversial legacies. They advocated a national regeneration that must start with self-knowledge and a critical view of the history of Spain. Their novels were no longer a mirror of the major social transformations of the moment, as had been the case for the realist writers of the Restoration (the twenty-five-year period following the restoration of the Spanish monarchy in 1874), such as Benito Pérez Galdós, Juan Valera, Armando Palacio Valdés, Emilia Pardo Bazán, and Leopoldo Alas, but an instrument for self-reflection as well as a vehicle for diagnosis of the stagnant values of Spanish contemporary society that had led to cultural and political decline.

Unamuno and Ganivet's propositions were philosophical rather than political. They adapted mainstream European thought to the crisis of Spain, which they saw as a "psychological ailment," without touching on the underlying social and economic factors, as Herbert Ramsden notes in *The 1898 Movement in Spain* (1974). Their deterministic pattern of thought and feeling was not exclusively Spanish but peculiar to the age, inspired by the post-Darwinist historicism of Hippolyte Taine and by the ideas of Arthur Schopenhauer, Friedrich Nietzsche, Edmund Husserl, and Sigmund Freud.

The Generación del 1898 took various strident positions against the status quo, exemplified by the young Azorín's anarchist spirit, Valle-Inclán's vitriolic satires of the court of Queen Isabel II, and Unamuno's personal enmity toward the dictator Miguel Primo de Rivera and King Alfonso XIII. Most of these writers, however, with the exception of Maeztu and Valle-Inclán, abandoned the political dissent of their youth. Lacking a consistent political commitment or adherence to a specific cause, their legacy was limited to the invention of a national identity based on the spiritual and aesthetic heritage of the Spanish classics, as well as on the indigenous traditions and collective beliefs that remained intact in the heart of the Spanish countryside, an innate cultural essence that Unamuno defined as *intrahistoria* (intrahistory). A symbolic and metaphysical transcendence was attributed to Castile, with its barren highlands and limpid skies, as the material core of the Spanish spirit. The writers of the periphery saw in the Castilian *meseta* (central plateau) the natural center of the regional diversity of Spain and the root of all its spiritual quests.

The year 1902 might be considered a landmark in the renovation of Spanish fiction, with the publication of groundbreaking works such as Valle-Inclán's *Sonata de Otoño* (translated as "Autumn Sonata," 1924), Vicente Blasco Ibáñez's *Cañas y barro* (translated as *Reeds and Mud,* 1928), and Unamuno's *Amor y pedagogía* (Love and Pedagogy). The first two works display vestiges of the symbolist and naturalist tradition, while in his humorous novel Unamuno embraced the antirealist experimentation of Anglo-European modernist fiction, characterized by stream of consciousness, internal ironies, fragmentary plots, self-reflective or self-conscious narrative, metafiction, intellectual humor, absurdist parody, and musical and lyrical structures, features that led to a redefinition of the genre from *novela* to *nivola* (antinovel or unnovel). In Valle-Inclán's four *Sonata* novellas (1902–1905) art for art's sake reached its pinnacle, while his satirical *esperpentos* (works that intentionally exaggerate the ugliness of reality, usually targeting traditional Spnish values and institutions) anticipated the acerbic pessimism of expressionist and absurdist drama. Baroja's fiction evolved from a type of social determinism to Surrealist trends, as in *El hotel del cisne* (1946, The Hotel of the Swan). Unamuno also called his novels *dramas del alma* (tragedies of the soul), establishing the foundation for an existential and confessional tone that blended poetic, autobiographical, philosophical, and dramatic elements. The immediacy of his style broke away from two persistent traits of nineteenth-century realist prose: rhetoricism and *casticismo* (pure or authentic Spanishness).

The early avant-garde efforts of the Generación del 1898 overlapped with those of subsequent literary groups in the pre–Spanish Civil War years, the Generación de 1914 and the Grupo poético de 1927 (Poetic Group of 1927). Writers such as Gabriel Miró, Eugenio d'Ors, Ramón Pérez de Ayala, Benjamín Jarnés, and Ramón Gómez de la Serna followed the precepts of José Ortega y Gasset's dehumanized art and opened the novel to a higher degree of abstraction and literary self-consciousness. Disengaged from the pressing historical realities of Europe, their art was soon to be eclipsed by a return to socially conscious preoccupations brought about by the reformist spirit of the Second Republic (1931–1936) and the turbulent political events that were to follow shortly thereafter.

The neutrality of Spain in World War I did not prevent ideological schisms among Spanish intellectuals, some of whom sided with either the Allies or the German-backed Central Powers, becoming *aliadófilos* or *germanófilos,* respectively. At both ends of the political spectrum one can find the axiological divisions that were to polarize the nation at the onset of the Second Republic and during the Civil War (1936–1939). The momentary triumph of the Left in April 1931 suppressed the emergent *falangista* (Falangist) movement that later reemerged and served as an ideological foundation for Francisco Franco's military insurrection.

The progressive spirit of the Second Republic culminated in one of the most productive and cosmopolitan periods of Spanish arts and letters, with personalities such as Federico García Lorca, Salvador Dalí, Pablo Picasso, Manuel de Falla, and Luis Buñuel, whose formative years coincided with Primo de Rivera's dictatorship (1923–1930) and who had won international recognition by the early 1930s. In this period, referred to as the Edad de Plata (Silver Age) of Spanish letters, three generations of writers engaged in a fecund dialogue with mainstream European intellectual thought as avid readers, translators, and commentators on Freud, Søren Kierkegaard, Nietzsche, Schopenhauer, Johan Huizinga, Oswald Spengler, Henri Bergson, and Husserl. Their works shaped the increasingly cultivated and receptive audience that the poet Juan Ramón Jiménez referred to as *la inmensa minoría* (the vast minority).

Even though the Second Republic was short-lived, its impact nurtured a whole generation of intellectual dissenters who were compelled to flee after the Civil War. The triumph of the Frente Popular (People's Front) in 1936 gave impetus to the reemergence of the social-realist and engagé novels of Ramón Sender, Andrés Carranque de Ríos, Max Aub, and Arturo Barea, authors who were committed to anarchist, socialist, or communist ideals and dared to denounce the broad inequities and repression imposed on the working class by both political sides.

The Civil War gave way to a testimonial genre that transcended languages and nationalities and served as the mode best suited to report the excesses and contradictions of the conflict from a subjective standpoint. Semi-autobiographical accounts of battle, survival in concentration camps, and partisan resistance by André Malraux, George Orwell, Ernest Hemingway, Sender, Barea, and Rodoreda had an authenticity transcending the inevitably propagandistic subtexts. These testimonies were first published abroad and republished by mainstream Spanish publishers in the late 1960s, after thirty years of censorship.

For the writers who remained in Spain, Francoist censorship was harsh but not powerful enough to suppress all creativity. References to the war and its consequences had to be made obliquely or diverted into extemporal, existential concerns. *Tremendismo* was an overtly graphic and stylized literary response to the abjection, violence, and mental illness brought about by the war, a self-conscious literary dissection of the cruelty of life by way of metaphor and stylization. As a trend, *tremendismo* aimed at the destruction of poetic tenderness by overstimulation of the senses and excessive use of the grotesque. The degradation of family values and the spirit of vigilance and mistrust that Franco's regime helped to foster are depicted in Camilo José Cela's *La familia de Pascual Duarte* (1942; translated as *Pascual Duarte's Family*, 1946, and as *The Family of Pascual Duarte*, 1964) and Carmen Laforet's *Nada* (1945, Nothingness; translated as *Nada*, 1958, and as *Andrea*, 1964), two fictional paradigms of *tremendismo*, with its emphasis on the horrid, exposing the emotional and physical traumas that were haunting the survivors of the war in the city and in the countryside.

In the 1950s Italian neorealist literature and cinema helped to consolidate social realism. The fiction of Vasco Pratolini and Elio Vittorini and the movies of Vittorio De Sica and Roberto Rossellini depicted postfascist Italian society in the process of reconstruction, a situation with which the Spanish people could identify. Political schisms, regional rivalries, clerical superstitions, unemployment, lottery wins, the festive spirit of local customs, and melodramatic sentimentality were issues that disguised everyday miseries. The self-deprecation, black humor, caricature, and tenderness in Italian neorealism were soon adopted by Spanish movie directors such as Luis García Berlanga and writers

such as Francisco García Pavón, Ignacio Aldecoa, Daniel Sueiro, Medardo Fraile, Jesús Fernández Santos, Luis and Juan Goytisolo, and Juan Marsé.

Novels and short stories depicted the miserable economic conditions that kept Spain in the shadow of industrial Europe, uncovering what the press did not dare to expose. Novels by Miguel Delibes, Jesús López Pacheco, Sueiro, Alfonso Grosso, and Juan García Hortelano dealt with the destitution and impoverished conditions in postwar cities, as well as with the rural misery hidden behind Franco's official propaganda of enduring peace and prosperity. Peasant communities desolated by the migration of the young to the city and abroad, the dispossession of villages by hydroelectric projects, and labor accidents in mines and power plants became the epic dramas of a nation being reworked.

The second wave of Spanish social realism lacked the terse, testimonial style of the first wave. It incorporated psychoanalytic, existential, and Marxist concerns and shifted the perspective from alienated peasants or factory workers to the young, educated, urban middle class that had conformed to Franco's totalitarian rule in order to maintain its privileges. At the same time, Spain was rapidly developing new socio-economic structures and becoming part of a southern European belt of capitalist development.

In *Novela española de nuestro tiempo* (1975, Spanish Novel of Our Time) Gonzalo Sobejano uses the term *realismo dialéctico* (dialectical realism) to define the dynamic confrontation of the evolving self with a rapidly changing environment that defies explanation in terms of simple materialistic causation. The literary hero is no longer an opinionated or impassive observer but an active participant, full of self-doubt, who feels the futility of his involvement in a repressive system and ends up withdrawing from history and regressing to a *tiempo de silencio* (time of silence), as in Luis Martín-Santos's 1961 novel of that title (translated as *Time of Silence*, 1964). In *Tiempo de silencio* a young doctor abandons his career in Madrid for an obscure life in the provinces after being falsely accused of performing a fatal abortion on a gypsy girl impregnated by her father. Martín-Santos's ambitious stream-of-consciousness work opened the way to a myriad of novels that experimented with time, space, and the role of the narrative voice, such as Juan Benet's *Volverás a Región* (1967, Return to Región), Juan Goytisolo's *Revindicación del Conde Don Julián* (1970, Vindication of Count Julian; translated as *Count Julian*, 1974), and Cela's *oficio de tinieblas 5* (1973, Office of Darkness 5).

The Spanish novel of the late 1960s explored the self-conscious processes of writing in search of language-sustained fictional worlds. Reality was mediated by myth or was subordinated to the literary self. Writers such as Juan Pedro Aparicio, Luis Mateo Díez, Marina Mayoral, Soledad Puértolas, Jorge Martínez Reverte, Vicente Molina-Foix, Raúl Guerra Garrido, Alvaro Pombo, and Eduardo Mendoza were not committed to the political concerns of the radical Left and embraced a variety of aesthetic influences. Some followed the French theories of structuralism set forth in the literary review *Tel Quel,* some incorporated psychoanalytic discourse, and some integrated myth and fantasy in the depiction of the everyday, as in Latin American magic-realist fiction.

A common denominator among the leftist authors emerging around 1968–including Luis Goytisolo, Manuel Vázquez Montalbán, Fernando Savater, Marsé, Félix de Azúa, Roig, Lourdes Ortiz, and Rosa Montero–is the denunciation of the declining values of the counterculture and the eclipse of Marxist and feminist convictions in the wake of the hedonistic society of post-Franco Spain. The accelerated development of the northern regions went hand in hand with a will to forget the past, as the proletariat entering the middle class and the intellectuals already integrated into the Socialist Party no longer wished to be reminded of their revolutionary aspirations. Montero, Guerra Garrido, Vázquez Montalbán, and Ortiz voiced less-privileged or silenced perspectives, minor dissensions that the capitalist order had now made mainstream.

Writers engaged in the anti-Franco resistance created satirical portraits of the new Spanish technocratic and political elites. Writers such as Miguel Espinosa, Terenci Moix, Luis Goytisolo, Vázquez Montalbán, Ortiz, Eduardo Mendicutti, and Mercedes Soriano also targeted the bourgeoisie and the sentimental education that had molded it by transcending the portrayal of the personal journey of sexual discovery in order to express the collective need to exorcise guilt and suffocating parochial mores.

After Franco's death in 1975, new freedoms made political gossip and speculation much more exciting than fiction. The public was more interested in learning about the secrets and scandals of the leaders of recent history than in any fictional account of the past, so the political and sociological essay took precedence over fiction. Santos Sanz Villanueva states that "el clima de libertad de opinión de la etapa de la transición política indujo la falsa esperanza de un resurgimiento literario a cargo de los textos que los mecanismos de control de la dictadura habían impedido publicar" (the climate of freedom of speech during the period of political transition to democracy induced the false hope of a literary revival owing to the writings released by the regime's censorship machinery).

The quantity and quality of Spanish prose increased in the 1980s, with lively publications by established and young writers alike reconnecting with a wide readership that had the pleasure of reading as its main goal. Several generations overlapped on the best-seller lists, with writers creating imaginative plots that broke the impasse left by the hermetic fiction of the *Novísimos.* Later works by Cela, Delibes, Gonzalo Torrente Ballester, Juan Goytisolo, José Manuel Caballero Bonald, and Carmen Martín Gaite still surprise readers with relevant contemporary messages full of humor, acid wit, irony, and autobiographical wisdom. The stories of Mendoza, Javier Tomeo, Landero, Pombo, Antonio Muñoz Molina, Riera, Francisco Ayala, and Manuel Vicent surprise readers with anecdotes taken from preposterous events reported in the daily press. Vázquez Montalbán, Azúa, Marsé, and Guerra Garrido seek foremost to capture the reader's attention, writing in genres such as the detective novel, the historical novel, the erotic novel, and the fantastic as frameworks within which to insert a clever critique of postindustrial social values and customs or to parody obsolete sentimental conventions. The critic José Maria Castellet announced readers' new participation in the literary text, which now reclaimed their attention from the media and offered relief from the everyday through a deceptively light alternative form of entertainment.

At the end of the Franco dictatorship the issue of Basque, Catalan, and Galician nationalism emerged in a backlash against the suppression of political autonomy and the imposition of Spanish over the languages of these regions. In the case of the Catalan language, the revival of the flourishing vernacular literature of the 1920s and 1930s became the basis for reconstructing an interrupted historical identity. Most monolingual Catalan writers continued publishing in Spanish (for example, Villalonga and Pla), while some, such as Salvador Espriu, Carles Riba, Josep Carner, and Rodoreda, opted for Catalan as a sign of resistance, thereby limiting their audience to the cultured minority. After 1970 the Catalan language was widely used in literary and critical works alike, although it was still common practice to write academic articles and journalism in Spanish to reach a larger audience, a phenomenon evident in the works of Roig, Riera, and Pere Gimferrer, who faced the challenge of bringing Catalan to a contemporary cultural context without the aid of linguistic models. Most Barcelona-born writers who received their primary and secondary education in the postwar period (for example, Juan and Luis Goytisolo, Marsé, Vázquez Montalbán, Mendoza, and Azúa) chose Spanish as their creative language but reflected the bilingual nature of the city in their works, interspersing Catalan words and expressions in the speech of their characters, just as the bicultural settings of Barcelona dominate their works. Others, such as Moix, switched to Spanish when their mother tongue ceased to be a dissenting language and became a reminder of the confining provincialism they wanted to leave behind. Three novels of this generation are unsurpassed epics of the city: Luis Goytisolo's *Recuento* (1973, A Retelling), Mendoza's *La ciudad de los prodigios* (1986; translated as *The City of Marvels*, 1988), and Moix's *Lleonard, o, El sexe dels àngels* (1992, Leonard, or The Gender of Angels). The first is a generational chronicle set at the end of the Franco dictatorship; the second is a foundational novel that depicts the two apotheoses that transformed Barcelona into a modern European capital, foretelling the splendors of 1992, the year the city hosted the Summer Olympics. The International Exposition of 1899 and the World's Fair of 1929 appear as historical climaxes that parallel the unscrupulous ascendancy of a self-made man, Onofre Bouvila, who becomes one of the forefathers of the entrepreneurial class of the city. Moix's work is a roman à clef that targets the Catalan petit bourgeois mentality and cultural politics during the emergent nationalism of the mid 1960s.

Another continuing subject of modern Spanish literature is the Civil War. Franco's censorship could not obliterate the heroic accounts told from varying perspectives, both within and outside of Spain. Real-life chronicles written in the trenches, such as those by Sender and Barea, and accounts written during the aftermath were published abroad and became accessible to Spanish readers after the 1970s. Ayala's *La cabeza del cordero* (1949, The Lamb's Head), Sender's *Réquiem por un campesino español* (originally published as *Mosén Millán*, 1953; translated as *Requiem for a Spanish Peasant*, 1960), Barea's three-volume autobiography *La forja de un rebelde* (translated as *The Forge*, 1941; *The Track*, 1943; and *The Clash*, 1946; collected as *The Forging of a Rebel*, 1946; original Spanish version published, 1951), Aub's story "El cojo" (1944, The Lame Man; translated, 1980), and Rodoreda's novel *La plaça del diamant* (1962, Diamond Square; translated as *Pigeon Girl*, 1967, and as *The Time of the Doves*, 1980) were instant best-sellers.

Before these works were published, writers who remained in Spain offered personal accounts that avoided political statements, emphasizing existential or moral concerns. José María Gironella's *Los cipreses creen en Dios* (1953; translated as *The Cypresses Believe in God*, 1955) and Augustín de Foxá *Madrid de corte a checa* (1962, Madrid from Court to Prison) are sentimental dramas that mark the eclipse of a careless bourgeois lifestyle set against the harsh realities of the war, told from the winners' perspective.

The Franco dictatorship also inspired oblique political tales of totalitarian domination set in a dystopic future, as in Delibes's *Parábola del náufrago* (1969, Parable of a Castaway; translated as *The Hedge*, 1983), or in an invented tropical republic, as in Ayala's *Muertes de perro* (1958; translated as *Death as a Way of Life*, 1964), a novella that takes up the paradigm of the Latin American *novela de dictador* (dictator novel). Ayala also resorted to other periods of Spanish history to offer a critique of Franco's totalitarian rule. Retrospective memories dominated by nostalgia, pain, or shame for the collective loss of innocence are found in Cela's *Víspera, festividad y octava de San Camilo del año 1936* (1969, Eve, Feast and Octave of St. Camillus's Day in the Year 1936; translated as *San Camilo, 1936*, 1991), in which he exorcises his political guilt by portraying himself as a cowardly young man hiding in the midst of Madrid's heroic Republican resistance, thinking only of making love to his fiancée. In García Pavón's *Cuentos Republicanos* (1961, Republican Stories) and *Los liberales* (1965, The Liberals) and in Caballero Bonald's *Dos días de setiembre* (1962, Two Days of September), the Civil War marks the end of an idyllic lifestyle, destroying the communal spirit of southern villages such as Jérez and Tomelloso, where the authors grew up as sons of entrepreneur landowners. In *Primera memoria* (1960, First Memory; translated as *School of the Sun* and as *Awakening*, 1963) Ana María Matute duplicates the social divisions of the war in the betrayal by two adolescent cousins of their *chueta* (Majorcan of Jewish descent) friend, whom one of them falsely accuses of stealing. Civil War themes continue to fascinate the Spanish public, as the successes of Juan Iturralde's *Dias de llamas* (1979, Day of Flames), Julio Llamazares's *Luna de lobos* (1985, Wolf Moon), and Javier Cercas's *Soldados de Salamina* (2001; translated as *Soldiers of Salamis*, 2004) attest. Cercas's novel, part fiction and part biography, narrates the story of how a Republican soldier spared the life of a *falangista* soldier, Rafael Sánchez Mazas, who had fled a prisoner-of-war camp in north Girona. After the war Rafael becomes an impassive high functionary of the government, haunted by the memory of the soldier whose generosity he can never reciprocate.

After the death of Franco, Spanish fiction became progressively detached from local, provincial, and bourgeois themes and increasingly open to urban and cosmopolitan issues. Although several novelists have reflected upon the moral and political sequels to the dictatorship, the dominant trend has been the tendency to erase national particularities and the sense of victimhood in favor of a progressive image of Spain as a country worthy of member status in the European Union (achieved in 1982), having more in common with its European neighbors than with its own cultural past. This cosmopolitan impulse does not imply the erasure of distinctive Iberian traits of identity but rather a tendency to universalize the cultural legacy of Spanish achievements and to inscribe them within an international artistic discourse. Part of this tendency arises from the novelist's preference for the urban medium, both as a subject and a setting. The term *postmodern* can be applied to a contemporary aesthetic of Spanish fiction that is characterized by the dissolution of barriers between high and low culture, the hybridization of genres, the lack of political or ideological commitment, and the writer's conscious disavowal of any moral conviction. These common denominators of the new democratic novel do not exclude old categories. If the realist novel focused on the individual conscience as a narrative center, introspection and emotional density now address the emptiness of the technocratic world rather than metaphysical questions. In *De postguerra: 1951–1990* (1994, On the Postwar Period: 1951–1990) critic José-Carlos Mainer points to a revival of the sentimental novel, ready to embrace the "obscenity of feelings" displaced by the new eroticism.

Novels are no longer self-sufficient textual worlds but rather subsidiaries of cinema, painting, music, the essay, autobiography, and bioscience; language experimentation and playfulness have been replaced by the accelerated rhythms, improvisation, chaos, and chance that govern urban life. Authors such as Enrique Vila-Matas, Juan José Millás, and Javier Marías seek the complicity of an extinct reader with whom they can engage in creating imaginary worlds amid the noise and distraction of the mass media. At the same time, images from cinema, photography, painting, and comics have become integrated into the literary text to an unprecedented extent in the generation that includes writers such as Lucía Etxebarria, Angela Vallvey, and José Angel Mañas. The interrelation between audiovisual and verbal discourses corresponds to the disappearance

of barriers between popular and high culture and to the reinstatement of movies and television programs as fully legitimate artistic media. Novels incorporate forms and messages from a wide range of sources, including popular music ( jazz, rock, and rap), video clips, advertisements, self-help guides, tabloids, and Internet chats, which reclaim readers' attention. The extensive presence of such forms and the use of virtual reality, together with a lack of literary referents and psychological depth, are common in the works of Generation X writers, whom leading literary critics have censured for their inability to create complex and memorable characters and their constant borrowing from movie and television narrative structures. The need to comply with market demands constrains young and established authors alike. In some cases the production schedule imposed on writers limits both experimentation and research as they resort to the more commercially secure forms sought by publishers and readers. This commercial orientation risks the loss of cultural values in fiction, which is transformed from an uncompromising object of art into a commodity. Still, there are some benefits: newly emerging writers connect with a wider audience attracted to best-selling novels that are more accessible to the general public. Bestseller lists, the impact of the media on cultural production, and extensive marketing campaigns providing greater visibility for new writers have helped to create readers loyal to "launched" authors, even if these readers are less inclined to enjoy classic literary works. The novel in Spain is now less an instrument of moral or social change than a tool for measuring dissent and contradictions within modern society without fully exploring aspects of social unrest, including solitude, uprooting, financial insecurity, loss of communal memory, the absence of moral standards, the need for instant gratification, and collective boredom. As a consequence of widespread unrest, plots are centered on the individual conscience rather than on collective concerns. The great causes, such as communism, ecology, militant feminism, and liberation theology, have lost their vigor, having been replaced with more-modest and viable proposals. The legitimation of previously marginalized positions, such as women's rights, multiple sexual orientations, interracial coexistence, and multiculturalism, is expanding a belief system no longer shared universally. This new horizon does not preclude the relevance of works exploring the universal and timeless subjects of enduring love, thwarted ambitions, and journeys to one's origins.

A constant feature of postmodern Spanish literature is nostalgia as a feeling that emphasizes a private, subjective past over the collective present and that allows writers to enhance common and trivial experiences without losing sight of the fleeting nature of their evocations. The present is perceived as a deceptive stage of adult life, incapable of fulfilling youthful expectations, a dissatisfaction reflected in the ironic ruminations of Vázquez Montalbán's Catalan detective character Pepe Carvalho and in many of Muñoz Molina's lucid *perdedores* (losers or failures), as well as in the retreat of authors to a land of their childhood that no longer exists, as is seen in the travel chronicles of Llamazares and in the imaginary regions conjured up by José María Merino and Díez from the legends of the León countryside.

There are distinctive differences in the works of the last two generations of twentieth-century Spanish fiction writers. Those who enjoyed recognition and honors in the 1980s, including Marías, Muñoz Molina, Millás, Marsé, Llamazares, Ortiz, Montero, Puértolas, Arturo Pérez-Reverte, Riera, Esther Tusquets, and Vila-Matas, conceive of writing as an act of solitary, almost solipsistic reflection, but they do so from two different moral preconceptions. Marías's aloof characters lack moral commitment or clear programmatic principles of behavior, while Muñoz Molina's protagonists are more historically grounded *agonistas* (self-questioning characters). The engagement of Muñoz Molina's heroes with the past and their awareness of Franco's social legacy make them appear tense, anguished, and incapable of distinguishing their personal fate from collective amnesia. The emotional intensity of these protagonists contrasts with the unaffected and Apollonian demeanor of Marías's narrators, who, lacking definite direction and convictions, surrender to their present circumstances without judging them.

Marías's empathy with the British cultural elite and cosmopolitan settings, explicit in *Todas las almas* (1989; translated as *All Souls,* 1992), contrasts with the localism of Muñoz Molina's provincial heroes, limited by daydreaming and alienation. Beyond these divergent attitudes and contexts, both authors have distanced their fiction from transcendental concerns, attempting only to expose basic civic values in their characters' decisions, thus reclaiming what an increasingly impulsive and selfish society has done away with. In depicting interpersonal relations, everyday commitments, and family affairs, their first-person narratives do not aspire to change the social or moral order but rather to articulate a sensible judgment of the world that confines them, remaining conscious of their arbitrary and inconclusive explorations.

Writers born after 1960, such as Mañas, Ray Loriga, Suso de Toro, Etxebarria, Juan Manuel de Prada, Benjamín Prado, David Trueba, Roger Wolfe, and Vallvey, share an indifference toward common enterprises for collective well-being and a basic self-centeredness. The adolescent-like conflicts they expose tend to run deeper than they appear, while remaining obscure and unarticulated. Their characters are shallow antiheroes, disconnected from social reality, irresponsible, irreverent, restless, and capable of cruelty and self-destructive impulses. Mañas's *Historias del Kronen* (1994, Stories from the Kronen) has become a paradigm for this type of social novel, in which disregard for form and style in favor of everyday speech struck a chord of truthfulness and spontaneity. The banal and venal conversations of a group of youths drinking, flirting, and yelling in their neighborhood bar, the Kronen, are interrupted only when the sole youth among them with homosexual tendencies dies after a bout of drinking that he was incited to engage in by the others as a demonstration of his virility. The group meets in the Kronen the next evening as if nothing has happened, a routine symptomatic of a generation out of touch with the past and the future. Written during the decline of the Socialist Party government, *Historias del Kronen* may lead the reader to infer the degradation of a society in which ideals had succumbed to power, money, and instant gratification, a society in search of palliatives to fill the vacuum left by a former way of life regulated by family, religion, and secure work, all of which the conformist majority has begun to miss. Dissent, lack of purchasing power, and political indifference keep the customers of the Kronen excluded from the more glamorous consumerist fiesta goers; the bar patrons learn to escape from apathy and audiovisual solipsism through the more socializing stimulants of alcohol, drugs, and violence. The dispossessed youth labeled Generation X by Douglas Coupland might include these sons of the Spanish establishment who seem as ready to practice aggression to ease their pain as their American peers.

Best-selling authors such as Mañas and Etxebarria have given voice to the young urban subculture by integrating urban speech, colloquial expressions, anglicisms, and generational tics into their narratives. Their impoverished and terse linguistic mannerisms point to a symbolic level of generalized impotence and morbidity. Nevertheless, their writing differs greatly from that of contemporaries such as Belén Gopegui, Blanca Riestra, and Prada, who have opted for a return to the literary novel by means of a baroque and metaphorical discourse rich in classical references. Unashamed of his canonical models, Prada demonstrates in his works a return to a high style, evoking many influences and reassessing the craftsmanship of the storyteller, often replacing visual or oral mimesis by the autonomous work of art as a sustained effort of metalanguage and self-referential creation.

—*Marta E. Altisent and Cristina Martínez-Carazo*

## Acknowledgments

This book was produced by Bruccoli Clark Layman, Inc. Philip B. Dematteis was the in-house editor. He was assisted by Tracy Simmons Bitonti, Charles Brower, Penelope M. Hope, and R. Bland Lawson.

Production manager is Philip B. Dematteis.

Administrative support was provided by Carol A. Cheschi.

Accountant is Ann-Marie Holland.

Copyediting supervisor is Sally R. Evans. The copyediting staff includes Phyllis A. Avant, Caryl Brown, Melissa D. Hinton, Philip I. Jones, Rebecca Mayo, and Nancy E. Smith.

Pipeline manager is James F. Tidd Jr.

Editorial associates are Elizabeth Leverton, Dickson Monk, and Timothy C. Simmons.

In-house vetter is Catherine M. Polit.

Permissions editor is Amber L. Coker. Permissions assistant is Crystal A. Gleim.

Layout and graphics supervisor is Janet E. Hill. The graphics staff includes Zoe R. Cook and Sydney E. Hammock.

Office manager is Kathy Lawler Merlette.

Photography editor is Mark J. McEwan.

Digital photographic copy work was performed by Joseph M. Bruccoli.

Systems manager is Donald Kevin Starling.

Typesetting supervisor is Kathleen M. Flanagan. The typesetting staff includes Patricia Marie Flanagan and Pamela D. Norton.

Library research was facilitated by the following librarians at the Thomas Cooper Library of the University of South Carolina: Elizabeth Suddeth and the rare-book department; Jo Cottingham, interlibrary loan department; circulation department head Tucker Taylor; reference department head Virginia W. Weathers; reference department staff Laurel Baker, Marilee Birchfield, Kate Boyd, Paul Cammarata, Joshua Garris, Gary Geer, Tom Marcil, Rose Marshall, and Sharon Verba; interlibrary loan department head Marna Hostetler; and interlibrary loan staff Bill Fetty and Nelson Rivera.

# Twentieth-Century Spanish Fiction Writers

# Dictionary of Literary Biography

# Max Aub
*(2 June 1903 – 22 July 1972)*

Sebastiaan Faber
*Oberlin College*

BOOKS: *Los poemas cotidianos* (Barcelona: Omega, 1925);

*Narciso: Teatro* (Barcelona: Altés, 1928);

*Geografía* (Madrid, 1929; enlarged edition, Mexico City: Era, 1960);

*Teatro incompleto* (Barcelona: Omega, 1931);

*Fábula verde* (Valencia: Tipografía Moderna, 1932);

*"A" (poemario)* (Valencia: Tipografía Moderna, 1933);

*Luis Alvarez Petreña* (Valencia: Miracle, 1934; enlarged edition, Mexico City: Joaquín Mortiz, 1965); enlarged as *Vida y obra de Luis Alvarez Petreña* (Barcelona: Seix Barral, 1971);

*Espejo de avaricia: Caracter, en tres actos y siete cuadros* (Madrid: Cruz y Raya, 1935);

*Proyecto de estructura para un teatro nacional y escuela nacional de baile: Dirigido a su Excelencia el Presidente de la República, don Manuel Azaña y Díaz* (Valencia: Tipografía Moderna, 1936);

*Campo cerrado: Novela* (Mexico City: Tezontle, 1943);

*"San Juan": Tragedia* (Mexico City: Tezontle, 1943);

*Diario de Djelfa, con seis fotografías* (Mexico City: Unión Distribuidora de Ediciones, 1944; enlarged edition, Mexico City: Joaquín Mortiz, 1970);

*Morir por cerrar los ojos: Drama en dos partes* (Mexico City: Tezontle, 1944);

*No son cuentos* (Mexico City: Tezontle, 1944)–includes "Santander y Gijón," translated by Caroline Muhlenberg as "At Santander and Gijón," in *Spanish Writers in Exile*, edited by Angel Flores (Sausalito, Cal.: B. Porter, 1948), pp. 76–80; and "El Cojo," translated by Alan A. Gonzalez-Arauzo as "El Cojo," in *The Humanities: Cultural Roots and Continuities*, edited by Mary Ann Frese Witt, volume 2 (Lexington, Mass.: Heath, 1980), pp. 298–307;

*La vida conyugal, drama en tres actos* (Mexico City: Letras de México, 1944);

*Campo de sangre: Novela* (Mexico City: Tezontle, 1945);

*Discurso de la novela española contemporánea* (Mexico City: Colegio de México, 1945);

*El rapto de Europa; o, Siempre se puede hacer algo: Drama real en tres actos* (Mexico City: Tezontle, 1946);

*Cara y cruz: Drama en tres actos* (Mexico City: Sociedad General de Autores de México, 1948);

*De algún tiempo a esta parte* (Mexico City: Tezontle, 1949);

*Deseada: Drama en ocho cuadros* (Mexico City: Tezontle, 1950; revised and enlarged edition, Mexico City: Ecuador 0 0 0", 1967);

*Campo abierto* (Mexico City: Tezontle, 1951);

*No* (Mexico City: Tezontle, 1952);

*La prosa española del siglo XIX*, 3 volumes (Mexico City: Antigua Librería Robredo, 1952–1962);

*Yo vivo* (Mexico City: Tezontle, 1953);

*Algunas prosas* (Mexico City: Los Presentes, 1954);

*Las buenas intenciones: Novela* (Mexico City: Tezontle, 1954);

*La poesía española contemporánea* (Mexico City: Imprenta Universitaria, 1954);

*Ciertos cuentos* (Mexico City: Antigua Librería Robredo, 1955)–includes "La gabardina," translated by Annella McDermott as "The Raincoat," in *The Dedalus Book of Spanish Fantasy*, edited by McDermott and Margaret Jull Costa (Sawtry, U.K.: Dedalus, 1999), pp. 31–41; "La lancha," translated by Elizabeth Mantel as "The Launch," in *Great Short Stories of the World* (Pleasantville, N.Y.: Reader's Digest Association, 1972), pp. 740–745; and "La Espina," translated by Will Kirkland as "The Fishbone," *Pequod*, 16–17 (1984): 151–155;

*Max Aub (© Colita/CORBIS)*

*Cuentos ciertos* (Mexico City: Antigua Librería Robredo, 1955)–includes "Manuscrito Cuervo: Historia de Jacobo," translated by Kirkland as "The Manuscript of a Crow: Jacob's Story," *New Directions in Prose and Poetry,* 45 (1982): 3–21; and "Uba-Opa," translated by Kirkland, *Hambone,* no. 3 (1983): 118–122;

*Tres monólogos y uno solo verdadero* (Mexico City: Tezontle, 1956);

*Crímenes ejemplares* (Mexico City: Juan Pablos, 1957);

*Heine* (Mexico City: Juan Pablos, 1957);

*Una nueva poesía española (1950–1955)* (Mexico City: Imprenta Universitaria, 1957);

*Jusep Torres Campalans* (Mexico City: Tezontle, 1958); translated by Herbert Weinstock as *Jusep Torres Campalans* (Garden City, N.Y.: Doubleday, 1962);

*Cuentos mexicanos, con pilón* (Mexico City: Imprenta Universitaria, 1959)–includes "El caballito," translated by George D. Schade as "El caballito," *Image of Spain,* special issue of *Texas Quarterly,* 4, no. 1, edited by Ramón Martínez López (1961): 174–180;

*Del amor* (Mexico City: Agosta, 1960);

*Obras en un acto,* 2 volumes (Mexico City: Universidad Nacional Autónoma de México, 1960);

*Poesía mexicana, 1950–1960* (Mexico City: Aguilar, 1960);

*La verdadera historia de la muerte de Francisco Franco y otros cuentos* (Mexico City: Libro Mex, 1960);

*La calle de Valverde* (Xalapa, Mexico: Universidad Veracruzana, 1961);

*Campo del moro* (Mexico City: Joaquín Mortiz, 1963);

*El Zopilote y otros cuentos mexicanos* (Barcelona: EDHASA, 1964);

*Campo francés* (Paris: Ruedo Ibérico, 1965);

*Historias de mala muerte* (Mexico City: Joaquín Mortiz, 1965);

*Las vueltas* (Mexico City: Joaquín Mortiz, 1965);

*Manual de historia de la literatura española,* 2 volumes (Mexico City: Pormaca, 1966);

*Hablo como hombre* (Mexico City: Joaquín Mortiz, 1967);

*Pruebas* (Mexico City: Ciencia Nueva, 1967);

*Campo de los almendros* (Mexico City: Joaquín Mortiz, 1968);

*El cerco* (Mexico City: Joaquín Mortiz, 1968);

*Teatro completo* (Mexico City: Aguilar, 1968);

*Enero en Cuba* (Mexico City: Joaquín Mortiz, 1969);

*Guía de narradores de la Revolución Mexicana* (Mexico City: Fondo de Cultura Económica, 1969);

*Poesía española contemporánea* (Mexico City: Era, 1969);

*Retrato de un general, visto de medio cuerpo y vuelta hacia la izquierda* (Mexico City: Joaquín Mortiz, 1969);

*El desconfiado prodigioso, Jácara del avaro, Discurso de la plaza de la Concordia, Los excelentes varones, Entremés de "El Director," La madre* (Madrid: Taurus, 1971)–includes *El desconfiado prodigioso,* translated by Cory Reed as *The Remarkable Misanthrope, Modern International Drama,* 19, no. 2 (1986): 5–23;

*La gallina ciega: Diario español* (Mexico City: Joaquín Mortiz, 1971)–excerpts translated anonymously as "From *Blind Man's Buff: A Spanish Diary*," *Review: Latin American Literature and Arts,* 59 (1999): 24–31;

*Los muertos* (Mexico City: Joaquín Mortiz, 1971);

*Pequeña y vieja historia marroquí* (Madrid: Papeles de Son Armadans, 1971);

*Subversiones* (Madrid: Helios, 1971);

*Versiones y subversiones* (Mexico City: Alberto Dallal, 1971);

*El teatro español sacado a la luz de las tinieblas de nuestro tiempo: Discurso leído por su autor en el acto de su recepción académica el día 12 de diciembre de 1956, contestación de Juan Chabás y Martí* (Madrid: Academia Española, 1956 [i.e., Mexico City, 1971]);

*Ensayos mexicanos* (Mexico City: Universidad Nacional Autónoma de México, 1974);

*Imposible Sinaí* (Barcelona: Seix Barral, 1982); excerpts translated by Kirkland as "Impossible Sinai," *New Orleans Review,* 13, no. 4 (1986): 24–42;

*Max Aub y la vanguardia teatral: Escritos sobre teatro, 1928–1938,* edited by Manuel Aznar Soler (Barcelona: Universitat de València, 1993);

*Diarios (1939–1972),* edited by Aznar Soler (Barcelona: Alba, 1998; enlarged edition, 2 volumes, Mexico City: Conaculta, 2000, 2003);

*De Max Aub a Unamuno* (Segorbe: Fundación Max Aub, 1998);

*De Max Aub a Cervantes* (Segorbe: Fundación Max Aub, 1999);

*De Max Aub a Benito Pérez Galdós* (Segorbe: Fundación Max Aub, 2000);

*Cuerpos presentes,* edited by José-Carlos Mainer (Segorbe: Fundación Max Aub, 2001).

**Editions and Collections:** *Mis páginas mejores* (Madrid: Gredos, 1966);

*Ultimos cuentos de la guerra de España* (Caracas: Monte Avila, 1969);

*Novelas escogidas,* prologue by Manuel Tuñón de Lara (Mexico City: Aguilar, 1970);

*La uña y otras narraciones* (Barcelona: Picazo, 1972);

*Los pies por delante y otros cuentos* (Barcelona: Seix Barral, 1975);

*La calle de Valverde,* edited by José Antonio Pérez Bowie (Madrid: Cátedra, 1985);

*Antología de relatos y prosas breves de Max Aub* (Mexico City: Universidad Nacional Autónoma Metropolitana, Unidad Azcapotzalco, 1993);

*Escribir lo que imagino: Cuentos fantásticos y maravillosos,* edited by Ignacio Soldevila Durante and Franklin B. García Sánchez (Barcelona: Alba, 1994);

*Enero sin nombre: Los relatos completos del Laberinto Mágico* (Barcelona: Alba, 1995);

*Yo vivo,* edited by Pilar Moraleda (Segorbe: Fundación Max Aub, 1995);

*Geografía; Prehistoria, 1928,* edited by Soldevila Durante (Segorbe: Fundación Max Aub, 1996);

*No,* edited by Ana I. Llorente Gracia (Segorbe: Fundación Max Aub, 1997);

*San Juan: (Tragedia),* edited by Manuel Aznar Soler (Valencia: Pre-Textos, 1998);

*Manuscrito cuervo: [Historia de Jacobo],* edited by Pérez Bowie, epilogue by José María Naharro-Calderón (Segorbe: Fundación Max Aub, 1999);

*Campo de los almendros,* edited by Francisco Caudet (Madrid: Castalia, 2000);

*Heine,* edited by Mercedes Figueras (Segorbe: Fundación Max Aub, 2000);

*Obras completas,* 11 volumes projected, 10 volumes published to date, edited by Joan Oleza Simó and others (Valencia: Generalitat Valenciana, Conselleria de Cultura i Educació, Direcció General del Llibre, Arxius i Biblioteques, 2001– );

*Hablo como hombre,* edited by Gonzalo Sobejano (Segorbe: Fundación Max Aub, 2002);

*Imposible Sinaí,* edited by Eleanor Londero (Segorbe: Fundación Max Aub, 2002).

PRODUCED SCRIPTS: *Sierra de Teruel/L'espoir,* motion picture, screenplay by Aub, Denis Marion, and André Malraux, Corniglion-Molinier, 1939;

*Los olvidados,* motion picture, screenplay by Luis Buñuel and Luis Alcoriza, additional dialogue by Aub, Ultramar, 1950.

OTHER: *Antología traducida,* edited and translated by Aub (Mexico City: Universidad Nacional Autónoma de México, 1963; enlarged edition, Barcelona: Seix Barral, 1972; edited by Pasqual Mas i Usó, Segorbe: Fundación Max Aub, 1998).

SELECTED PERIODICAL PUBLICATION–UNCOLLECTED: "Héroes: De Byron a Malraux," *Vanguardia* (Barcelona), 19 March 1938, p. 2.

Max Aub has been recognized belatedly as one of the most important writers among the hundreds who left Spain after General Francisco Franco defeated the republican (Loyalist) government in the Spanish Civil War of 1936 to 1939. With more than fifty books published in exile–including plays, short stories, novels, poetry, and essays–he was also one of the most prolific of those writers. Although his works were prohibited in Franco's Spain, he was well known and respected in Mexico, where he lived for thirty years and wrote most of his works. Aub thought of

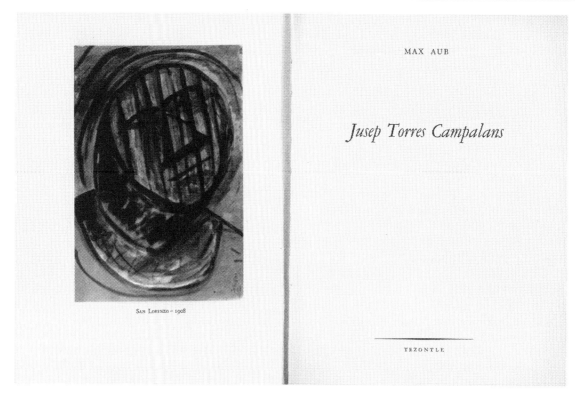

SAN LORENZO ~ 1908

MAX AUB

*Jusep Torres Campalans*

TEZONTLE

*Frontispiece and title page for Aub's hoax "biography" (1958) of a fictitious Cubist painter who disappeared from Paris at the beginning of World War I. Torres Campalan's purported artworks, which were exhibited in connection with the publication of the book, were actually by Aub himself (Thomas Cooper Library, University of South Carolina).*

himself primarily as a playwright, but he is most widely recognized as the author of "El laberinto mágico" (The Magical Labyrinth), a series of five novels and a screenplay written between 1938 and 1968 that constitute a compelling chronicle of the civil war and its aftermath of persecution and exile. Outside the Spanish-speaking world Aub is best known as the author of *Jusep Torres Campalans* (1958; translated, 1962), a work of fiction that is presented as the biography of an unknown avant-garde painter. This literary hoax is his only major work to be translated into English.

Most of Aub's books were first printed in Mexico in small, badly distributed runs that were sometimes paid for by the author himself. While he wrote for a Spanish audience, by the time the Franco censorship was lifted most of his books were out of print, and Aub was known only by a handful of specialists. Since Franco's death in 1975 and Spain's transition to democracy three years later, his prestige in Spain has steadily grown. In 1998 the leading Spanish novelist Antonio Muñoz Molina heralded Aub as an exemplary literary and political figure, and many new editions of his works have appeared in Spain.

Max Aub Mohrenwitz was born in Paris on 2 June 1903. His father, Friedrich Wilhelm Aub, a jewelry wholesaler, was German; his mother, Suzanne Mohrenwitz Aub, a merchants' daughter, was a French citizen but was also of German descent. Aub's parents were agnostic Jews, although Aub seems not to have learned of his Jewish heritage until he was eighteen. Aub spoke German and French as a child and did not begin to learn Spanish until the family, fearing that Friedrich Aub would be arrested in France because he was a German citizen, fled to Valencia after World War I broke out in 1914. In 1920, instead of going to college, Aub joined his father's business and became a traveling jewelry salesman. Until the mid 1930s he spent part of every year trekking across Spain and dedicated the remaining months to reading and writing.

Aub wrote his first play, *Crimen* (Crime), in 1923; never produced, it was first published in his *Teatro completo* (Complete Plays) in 1968. At the end of that year he made his first trip to Madrid and read his poetry in the Ateneo, the city's principal cultural center. Two years later he published *Los poemas cotidianos* (The Daily Poems). Through his contacts in

Madrid, his subscriptions to European cultural magazines, and a three-month stay in Germany in 1924 he kept abreast of literary and artistic developments in Spain and abroad. In 1925 he wrote two more plays: *El desconfiado prodigioso* (The Remarkable Misanthrope) and *Una botella* (A Bottle). Neither was ever produced; *El disconfiado prodigioso* was published in 1926 in the journal *Alfar,* and both appeared in the collection *Teatro incompleto* (1931, Incomplete Plays). Also, in 1925 he became a regular contributor to avant-garde journals such as *Azor, La Gaceta Literaria,* and the prestigious *Revista de Occidente,* founded and directed by the philosopher José Ortega y Gasset.

Ortega was Spain's most important theoretician and promoter of the avant-garde, a movement to which Aub's early novellas *Geografía* (1929, Geography) and *Fábula verde* (1932, Green Tale) belong: they are short, dense texts in which poetic language, particularly metaphor, takes precedence over plot or dialogue. In *La deshumanización del arte* (1925; translated as *The Dehumanization of Art,* 1948) Ortega argued that to be pure, art and literature should avoid realism and melodrama and be as far removed as possible from social and political reality. He also argued that true art and literature could and should be appreciated only by an aesthetically sensitive minority. The popularity of these views among Spanish writers and artists coincided with the first years of the dictatorship of Miguel Primo de Rivera, who took power in 1923 and initially met with little resistance from Spanish intellectuals. Toward the end of the decade, however, discontent with the dictator and the monarchy grew, and the intelligentsia became increasingly politicized.

Aub married Perpetua Barjau Martín in 1926. In 1929 he joined the Spanish Socialist Party. The Second Republic was proclaimed in April 1931. During this period Aub was gradually moving away from Ortega's "dehumanized" aesthetics in favor of a more realistic style and explicitly ethical and political content, although his work continued to bear the stylistic marks and the transgressive spirit of the avant-garde. *Luis Alvarez Petreña* (1934), for instance, is presented as a nonfiction series of letters between an avant-garde poet and his lover; at the same time, the book underscores the ethical crisis of avant-gardism: realizing that his life and work are without value, Alvarez Petreña commits suicide.

Aub began putting his creative work expressly at the service of politics in early 1936 by writing plays for the electoral campaign of the Popular Front. The outbreak of the Civil War, following a failed military coup in July 1936 against the newly elected Popular Front government, further convinced him of the need for a politically committed literature. For Aub, such engagement did not mean submitting his material to the dictates of a political party; instead, it implied a profound commitment to realism—to recording and explaining social and political reality with the goal of changing that reality for the better. In March 1938 he wrote a long essay for the Loyalist newspaper *La Vanguardia* in which he argued that the writer "cannot . . . attempt any more to let History serve as a pedestal for him; on the contrary, it is he who has to begin serving History. He does not organize a fantastic world, but attempts to reflect it. He does not let himself be carried away by inspiration; he takes notes. . . . Today's novelist does not invent, he writes commentary."

During the civil war Aub edited the Socialist-Communist newspaper *Verdad* and directed a university theater company. From November 1936 to July 1937 he served as cultural attaché in Paris, helping to prepare the Spanish pavilion for the International Exhibition. He commissioned a painting for the exhibition from Pablo Picasso; the result was *Guernica,* painted in response to the destruction of the Basque city of that name by German bombers under Franco's command on 26 April 1937. Returning to Valencia, Aub was appointed secretary of the National Theater Council. Throughout 1938 he worked with the French novelist André Malraux on the screenplay for the movie *Sierra de Teruel* (Mountains of Teruel), based on Malraux's Civil War novel *L'espoir* (1937; translated as *Man's Hope,* 1938). In February 1939, as Franco's forces were poised to defeat the republic, Aub and the rest of the movie crew joined the five hundred thousand Spanish refugees who had already fled to France.

Aub spent the first year of his exile in Paris, feverishly writing about the Civil War. He finished the novel *Campo cerrado* (1943, Closed Field) in five months. Publication of the work was delayed when Aub was arrested by the French police in April 1940 on charges of being a Communist. Although the charge was false—Aub had many Communist friends but had always maintained a critical distance from the party—he spent the following two years in concentration camps, separated from his wife and three daughters (María Luisa, born in 1927; Elena, born in 1931; and Carmen, born in 1936). He was first held in France and then in Djelfa, Algeria, where he performed hard labor in the desert. Throughout this period he wrote poems and ideas for novels and short stories on scraps of paper that he kept in his pockets; some of the poems were later published in *Diario de Djelfa* (1944, Djelfa Diary). Thanks to the intervention of a Mexican diplomat, he was released in the

MAX AUB

*Campo del Moro*

PQ
6601
.U2

C357

*Title page for Aub's 1963 novel (Field of the Moor), about the military coup against Republican prime minister Juan Negrín in 1939 and the ensuing civil war within the Civil War (Thomas Cooper Library, University of South Carolina)*

summer of 1942. After three months in Casablanca, he embarked by ship for Mexico, which had taken in tens of thousands of Republican refugees since 1938. On the voyage he drafted the novel *Campo francés* (1965, French Camp).

Aub survived during his first years in Mexico by taking occasional jobs as a translator, teacher, reviewer, and scriptwriter. In July 1943 he published at his own expense the play *"San Juan,"* a tragedy about Jewish refugees trapped on a boat in the Mediterranean. *Campo cerrado* appeared later that year; the manuscript had been smuggled into Mexico by a friend of Aub's. In the preface Aub explains that the work is the first in a five-volume series about the Civil War titled *"El Laberinto Mágico."* The first chapter describes a folkloric ritual in a small town

near Valencia in which a bull with his horns on fire is chased through a maze of narrow streets. The image of a raging bull caught in a labyrinth, based on the Greek myth of the minotaur, signifies the Civil War, in which all of Aub's characters, and the author, seem to have lost their way. Equally labyrinthine are the characters' conversations, which are rife with misunderstandings, dead ends, and unbridgeable differences of opinion. In a more general sense, the labyrinth stands for life itself. The working-class protagonist of *Campo cerrado,* Rafael López Serrador, joins the popular resistance against the right-wing military rebels in Barcelona after several years of aimless drifting. The novel ends shortly after the outbreak of the Civil War.

In 1943 Aub began teaching cinema theory at the Mexican Cinematographic Institute; a year later he was appointed secretary of Mexico's National Committee of Cinematography. Also in 1944 he published his first collection of short stories, *No son cuentos* (They Are Not Stories), all of which deal with the Civil War and its aftermath.

The second novel in the "Laberinto mágico" series, *Campo de sangre* (Field of Blood), appeared in 1945. Set between December 1937 and March 1938, it describes rearguard life in Barcelona and the fierce battle for Teruel, which the Republican forces lost. While *Campo cerrado* is conventionally structured around a single main character, *Campo de sangre* consists of a complex series of loosely connected episodes without a central protagonist. This labyrinthine structure is characteristic of Aub's remaining Civil War novels: together they introduce hundreds of characters who, between and during the battles, engage in discussions of politics, Spain, aesthetics, and the social role of intellectuals. The series has been described by Manuel Tuñón de Lara as a great epic tapestry of the Civil War whose real protagonist is the war itself.

In 1945 Aub published *Discurso de la novela española contemporánea* (Discourse of the Contemporary Spanish Novel). He defends Spain's realist tradition, which he says is most genuinely represented by Benito Pérez Galdós and Pío Baroja, and condemns Ortega's avant-garde aesthetics for having "castrated" a generation of novelists by teaching them to despise realism.

In 1946 Aub's wife and daughters joined him in Mexico. After publishing three major plays in four years—*El rapto de Europa* (1946, The Abduction of Europa), *Cara y cruz* (1948, Heads and Tails), and *Deseada* (1950, Desired)—Aub brought out *Campo abierto* (1951, Open Field), the third volume to appear in the "Laberinto mágico" series but chronologically the second. Covering the first five months of the war, it is set in Valencia and Madrid in Republican Spain and in Burgos in Francoist territory. More than half of the novel is a description of the defense of Madrid against the advancing Francoists.

Aub's fourth novel, *Las buenas intenciones* (1954, Good Intentions), is not part of "El laberinto mágico," even though it is set in Madrid between 1924 and 1939 and shares some characters with the Civil War novels. Structurally, however, *Las buenas intenciones* is much more conventional than those works. Clearly inspired by Galdós, to whom it is dedicated, the novel features a straightforward plot: it is the sad tale of Agustín Alfaro, who believes that good intentions are all that one needs to succeed in life and who is shot to death just as he is about to recover a lost love.

In 1955 Aub obtained Mexican citizenship and published two collections of short stories. Almost all of the texts in *Ciertos cuentos* (Certain Stories) belong to the fantasy genre—a relatively undeveloped vein of Aub's oeuvre. *Cuentos ciertos* (True Stories) includes more civil war material than *Ciertos cuentos;* "Manuscrito Cuervo: Historia de Jacobo" (translated as "The Manuscript of a Crow: Jacob's Story," 1982), for example, mixes the fantastic with historical realism and satire in a story about a pedantic crow named Jacob who attempts to understand life in a French concentration camp full of Spanish Civil War refugees.

Much of Aub's work is hard to classify in terms of genre. His Civil War novels are a mélange of fact and fiction, although fact always takes precedence: Aub's goal is to tell the truth about the war and refute the distortions of history propagated by the Franco regime. The collection *Crímenes ejemplares* (1957, Exemplary Crimes) is a different kind of hybrid: here Aub claims to present authentic, though anonymous, interviews with eighty-seven murderers in which they explain their motives—or lack thereof—for killing. In 1958 Aub again surprised his readers with what appeared to be another work of nonfiction: *Jusep Torres Campalans,* the biography of a Cubist painter who had mysteriously disappeared from Paris at the beginning of World War I. The book is painstakingly documented and profusely illustrated and was published in conjunction with an exhibition at a prestigious Mexico City gallery of the painter's work, which was as unknown and surprising as the man himself; the publication of the English translation in 1962 was accompanied by a similar art show in New York City. According to his "biographer," Torres Campalans had been an important member of the Spanish avant-garde, a friend of Picasso's, and, possi-

*Paperback cover for Aub's 1965 novel, about a World War II concentration camp in France (Thomas Cooper Library, University of South Carolina)*

bly, the first Cubist. He was a pure invention, and the artworks were painted by Aub.

Following *Cuentos mexicanos* (1959, Mexican Stories), Aub published *La verdadera historia de la muerte de Francisco Franco y otros cuentos* (1960, The True History of the Death of Francisco Franco and Other Stories). In the title story a waiter becomes so fed up with the Spanish exiles who patronize his Mexico City café that he travels to Spain and kills Franco. The following year Aub published his sixth novel, *La calle de Valverde* (Valverde Street). Set in Madrid in the 1920s, during Primo de Rivera's dictatorship and the cultural renaissance known as Spain's Silver Age, it is a prequel to the Civil War novels and shares their episodic structure.

As the Civil War series progressed, Aub's style became less ornate and more elliptical, relying less on description and more on action and dialogue. *Campo del moro* (1963, Field of the Moor), one of his leanest novels stylistically, describes the early days of March 1939, the last month of the war, when a group of Republican officers led by Colonel Segismundo Casado López overthrew Prime Minister Juan Negrín: while Negrín refused to consider capitulation, Casado believed that he could negotiate an acceptable surrender for the Republic. The coup led to a civil war within the Civil War in which the Republicans, on the brink of defeat, spent several days arresting and shooting each other. For Aub, who had been a friend of Negrín's, Casado's rebellion amounted to treason. The theme of betrayal, present in the entire "Laberinto mágico" series, pervades this novel on all levels. *Campo del moro* is about the betrayal of Spain by Casado, Franco, and the Western democracies but also about personal betrayals committed out of human weakness.

In 1960 Aub was appointed director of the radio and television division of the Universidad Nacional Autónoma de México (Autonomous National University of Mexico). In 1965 he published the fifth volume of "El laberinto mágico" novel, *Campo francés* (French Camp), a screenplay set in concentration camps in France before and during the German occupation of the country. *Hablo como hombre* (1967, I Speak Like a Man) is a collection of essays summarizing Aub's political position, a "third way" aiming at a socialist economy under a liberal government. Aub refused to accept the Cold War choice between East and West, declaring that he would never be either a Communist or an anti-Communist; while he admired the Communists' struggle against fascism, he rejected their dogmatism and dictatorial tendencies.

*Campo de los almendros* (1968, Field of Almonds), the last and longest of the Civil War novels, is also the most dramatic work in the series. During the final days of the war thousands of Loyalist men, women, and children, surrounded by Francoist and Italian troops in the port city of Alicante, wait for British and French boats to come to their rescue. As it becomes clear that the boats will never arrive, many commit suicide; the rest are captured and killed or imprisoned.

Since the 1950s Aub had made regular trips to Europe, although for some years France had denied him a visa because of his police record from the 1940s. In 1969 he was allowed to visit Spain. His two and a half months there were laced with disappointments that are recorded in *La gallina ciega: Diario español* (1971, Blindman's Buff: Spanish Diary). Although Aub had been aware of the long-term effects of Francoist propaganda and censorship on Spanish life, his firsthand observations shocked him. The Spaniards he met struck him as passive, apolitical, and shamelessly consumerist. Especially difficult for him to accept was that hardly anyone knew who he was, let alone read any of his work.

In the spring of 1972 Aub made a second trip to Spain to collect material for a novel about his friend, the movie director Luis Buñuel. His heart had always been weak, and by then he had been diagnosed with diabetes, as well. He died on 22 July, a week after returning from Spain.

While Max Aub is gradually being recognized as one of Spain's most important twentieth-century writers, his rediscovery—and that of other Spanish Civil War exiles—is still hampered by the legacies of Francoist censorship and the "pact of oblivion" that accompanied Spain's transition to democracy. Aub believed that much of the damage done to Spanish arts and letters by the Civil War and its aftermath was irreparable. Six months before his death he added one last hoax to his oeuvre, publishing the acceptance speech he would have given if the Civil War had never happened and he had been admitted to the Spanish Royal Academy of Language in 1956. The pamphlet, in a style and format that were a perfect imitation of the academy's publications, was more than a joke: by imagining what Spanish cultural life would have been like if the Republic had prevailed, Aub illustrated the loss the Civil War and the Franco dictatorship had inflicted on his country, his fellow intellectuals, and himself.

**Letters:**

*Epistolario del exilio: Max Aub (1940–1972),* edited by Miguel A. González Sanchís (Segorbe: Fundación Caja Segorbe, 1992);

*Max Aub, Francisco Ayala: Epistolario, 1952–1972,* edited by Ignacio Soldevila Durante (Segorbe: Fundación Max Aub, Biblioteca Valenciana, 2001).

**Interviews:**

María Embeita, "Max Aub y su generación," *Ínsula,* 253 (December 1967): 1, 12;

Emir Rodríguez Monegal, "Max Aub (I)" and "Max Aub (II)," in his *El arte de narrar: Diálogos* (Caracas: Monte Avila, 1968), pp. 21–48;

Ricardo Domenech and José Monleón, "Entrevista con el exiliado Max Aub en Madrid," *Primer Acto,* 130 (March 1971): 44–51;

Antonio Núñez, "Encuentro con Max Aub," *El Urogallo,* 16 (1972): 33–39;

Lois A. Kemp, "Diálogos con Max Aub," *Estreno,* 3, no. 2 (1977): 8–11, 15–19;

Elena Poniatowska, "Max Aub," in her *Todo México,* volume 4 (Mexico City: Diana, 1998), pp. 151–160.

**Bibliographies:**

Miguel Angel González Sanchís, "Max Aub, bio-bibliografía," in Aub, *San Juan* (Barcelona: Anthropos, 1992), pp. 107–121;

Ignacio Soldevila Durante, "Maxaubiana (ensayo bibliográfico)," in *Actas del Congreso Internacional "Max Aub y el Laberinto Español,"* volume 2, edited by Cecilio Alonso (Valencia: Ayuntamiento de Valencia, 1996), pp. 947–976;

Soldevila Durante, "Bibliografía," in his *El compromiso de la imaginación: Vida y obra de Max Aub* (Segorbe: Fundación Max Aub, 1999), pp. 223–312;

Arie Vicente, "Max Aub," in *Modern Spanish Dramatists: A Bio-bibliographical Sourcebook,* edited by Mary Parker (Westport, Conn.: Greenwood Press, 2002), pp. 65–74.

**Biographies:**

Rafael Prats Rivelles, *Max Aub* (Madrid: Epesa, 1978);

Gérard Malgat, "Max Aub y Francia: Un escritor español sin papeles. Aportación a la biografía del escritor," in *Literatura y cultura del exilio español de 1939 en Francia,* edited by Alicia Alted Vigil and Manuel Aznar Soler (Salamanca: Aemic-Gexel, 1998), pp. 143–160;

Ignacio Soldevila Durante, *El compromiso de la imaginación: Vida y obra de Max Aub* (Segorbe: Fundación Max Aub, 1999).

**References:**

Juan Luis Alborg, "Max Aub," in his *Hora actual de la novela española,* volume 2 (Madrid: Taurus, 1962), pp. 75–136;

Cecilio Alonso, ed., *Actas del Congreso Internacional "Max Aub y el Laberinto Español,"* 2 volumes (Valencia: Ayuntamiento de Valencia, 1996);

Sebastiaan Faber, "Max Aub: Exile as *Aporia,"* in his *Exile and Cultural Hegemony: Spanish Intellectuals in Mexico, 1939–1975* (Nashville, Tenn.: Vanderbilt University Press, 2002), pp. 218–266;

Paul Kohler, "The Literary Image of the Spanish Civil War of 1936–39 in Max Aub's *El Laberinto Mágico,"* dissertation, University of Toronto, 1970;

José Ramón Marra-López, "Max Aub, tragicomedia y compromiso," in his *Narrativa española fuera de España* (Madrid: Guadarrama, 1963), pp. 177–215;

Antonio Muñoz Molina, "Destierro y destiempo de Max Aub," in his *Pura alegría* (Madrid: Alfaguara, 1998), pp. 87–118;

Emir Rodríguez Monegal, "Max Aub: El laberinto mágico," in his *Tres testigos españoles de la Guerra Civil* (Caracas: Monte Avila, 1971), pp. 63–82;

Ignacio Soldevila Durante, *La obra narrativa de Max Aub (1929–1969)* (Madrid: Gredos, 1973);

Manuel Tuñón de Lara, *Introducción al "Laberinto Mágico"* (Segorbe: Fundación Max Aub, 2001);

Michael Ugarte, "The Politics of Exile: Max Aub," in his *Shifting Ground: Spanish Civil War Exile Literature* (Durham, N.C.: Duke University Press, 1989), pp. 111–151.

**Papers:**

Max Aub's correspondence, manuscripts, and personal library are in the archives of the Max Aub Foundation in Segorbe, Castellón, Spain: <http://www.maxaub.org>.

# Francisco Ayala

*(16 March 1906 –   )*

Mercedes Juliá
*Villanova University*

BOOKS: *Tragicomedia de un hombre sin espíritu* (Madrid: Industrial Gráfica, 1925);

*Historia de un amanecer* (Madrid: Castilla, 1926; expanded edition, Madrid: CVS, 1975);

*El boxeador y un ángel* (Madrid: Cuadernos Literarios, 1929);

*Indagación del cinema* (Madrid: Mundo Latino, 1929);

*Cazador en el alba* (Madrid: Ulises, 1930);

*El derecho social en la constitución de la República española* (Madrid: M. Minuesa de los Ríos, 1932);

*El problema del liberalismo* (Mexico City: Fondo de Cultura Económica, 1941; expanded edition, Puerto Rico: Universidad, 1963);

*Oppenheimer* (Mexico City: Fondo de Cultura Económica, 1942);

*Historia de la libertad* (Buenos Aires: Atlántida, 1943);

*El hechizado* (Buenos Aires: Emecé, 1944);

*Histrionismo y representación: Ejemplos y pretextos* (Buenos Aires: Sudamericana, 1944);

*Los políticos* (Buenos Aires: Depalma, 1944);

*Una doble experiencia política: España e Italia,* by Ayala and Renato Treves (Mexico City: El Colegio de México Centro de Estudios Sociales, 1944);

*Razón del mundo: Un examen de conciencia intelectual* (Buenos Aires: Losada, 1944);

*Ensayo sobre la libertad* (Mexico City: El Colegio de México, Centro de Estudios Sociales, 1944);

*Jovellanos* (Buenos Aires: Centro Asturiano, 1945);

*Ideas políticas de Juan de Solórzano* (Seville, 1946);

*Tratado de sociología,* 3 volumes (Buenos Aires: Losada, 1947)–comprises *Historia de la sociología, Sistema de la sociología,* and *Nomenclator bio-bibliográfico de la sociología;*

*La cabeza del cordero* (Buenos Aires: Losada, 1949; edited by Keith Davis, Englewood Cliffs, N.J.: Prentice-Hall, 1968);

*Los usurpadores* (Buenos Aires: Sudamericana, 1949); translated by Carolyn Richmond as *Usurpers* (New York: Schocken, 1987);

*El cine, arte y espectáculo* (Buenos Aires: Argos, 1949; expanded edition, Xalapa: Universidad Veracruzana, 1969);

*Francisco Ayala ( from Estelle Irizarry,* Francisco Ayala, *1977; Thomas Cooper Library, University of South Carolina)*

*La invención del Quijote* (Puerto Rico: Universitaria, 1950);

*Ensayos de sociología política: En qué mundo vivimos* (Mexico City: Instituto de Investigaciones Sociales, Universidad Nacional, 1952);

*Introducción a las ciencias sociales* (Madrid: Aguilar, 1952);

*Historia de macacos* (Santander, 1953; Madrid: Revista de Occidente, 1955; expanded edition, Madrid: Alianza, 2001);

*El escritor en la sociedad de masas, y Breve teoría de la traducción* (Mexico City: Obregón, 1956);

*Derechos de la persona individual para una sociedad de masas* (Buenos Aires: Perrot, 1957);

*Muertes de perro* (Buenos Aires: Sudamericana, 1958); translated by Joan MacLean as *Death as a Way of Life* (New York: Macmillan, 1964; London: Joseph, 1965);

*La crisis actual de la enseñanza* (Buenos Aires: Nova, 1958);

*La integración social en América* (Buenos Aires: Perrot, 1958);

*Tecnología y libertad* (Madrid: Taurus, 1959);

*Experiencia e invención: Ensayos sobre el escritor y su mundo* (Madrid: Taurus, 1960);

*El fondo del vaso* (Buenos Aires: Sudamericana, 1962);

*Razón del mundo: La preocupación de España* (Xalapa, 1962);

*El as de Bastos* (Buenos Aires: Sur, 1963);

*De este mundo y el otro* (Barcelona: Edhasa, 1963);

*Realidad y ensueño* (Madrid: Gredos, 1963);

*La evasión de los intelectuales,* by Ayala and H. A. Murena (Mexico City: Centro de Estudios y Documentaciones Sociales, 1963);

*España a la fecha* (Buenos Aires: Sur, 1965; Madrid: Tecnos, 1977);

*Mis páginas mejores* (Madrid: Gredos, 1965);

*El rapto* (Madrid: Alfaguara, 1965);

*Problemas de la traducción* (Madrid: Taurus, 1965);

*De raptos, violaciones y otras inconveniencias* (Madrid: Alfaguara, 1966)–comprises *El rapto (Prólogo), El rapto, El as de Bastos, Violación en California, Una boda sonada,* and *Un pez;* expanded as *De raptos, violaciones, macacos y demás inconveniencias* (Barcelona: Seix Barral, 1982);

*Cuentos* (Madrid: Anaya, 1966); republished as *El inquisidor y otras narraciones españolas* (Salamanca: Anaya, 1970)–comprises "El inquisidor," "San Juan de Dios," "El abrazo," and "El mensaje";

*España en la cultura germánica. España a la fecha* (Mexico City: Finisterre, 1968);

*Obras narrativas completas* (Mexico City: Aguilar, 1969);

*Hacia una semblanza de Quevedo* (Santander: Bedia, 1969);

*Reflexiones sobre la estructura narrativa* (Madrid: Taurus, 1970);

*El Lazarillo: Nuevo exámen de algunos aspectos* (Madrid: Taurus, 1971);

*El jardín de las delicias* (Barcelona: Seix Barral, 1971);

*Cazador en el alba, y otras imaginaciones* (Barcelona: Seix Barral, 1971);

*Los ensayos: Teoría y crítica literaria* (Madrid: Aguilar, 1972);

*Confrontaciones* (Barcelona: Seix Barral, 1972);

*El hechizado y otros cuentos* (Madrid: Magisterio Español, 1972);

*Hoy ya es ayer* (Madrid: Moneda y Crédito, 1972);

*El rapto, Fragancia de jazmines, Diálogo entre el amor y un viejo* (Barcelona: Labor, 1974);

*Cervantes y Quevedo* (Barcelona: Seix Barral, 1974);

*La novela: Galdós y Unamuno* (Barcelona: Seix Barral, 1974);

*El escritor y su imagen: Ortega y Gasset, Azorín, Valle-Inclán, Machado* (Madrid: Guadarrama, 1975);

*El escritor y el cine* (Madrid: Ediciones del Centro, 1975; expanded edition, Madrid: Aguilar, 1988; expanded again, Madrid: Cátedra, 1996);

*El jardín de las delicias; El tiempo y yo* (Madrid: Espasa-Calpe, 1978);

*Galdós en su tiempo* (Santander: Universidad Internacional Menéndez Pelayo, 1978);

*De triunfos y penas* (Barcelona: Seix Barral, 1982);

*Recuerdos y olvidos 1: Del paraíso al destierro* (Madrid: Alianza, 1982);

*Recuerdos y olvidos 2: El exilio* (Madrid: Alianza, 1983);

*Palabras y letras* (Barcelona: Edhasa, 1983);

*La estructura narrativa y otras experiencias literarias* (Barcelona: Crítica, 1984);

*La retórica del periodismo y otras retóricas* (Madrid: Espasa-Calpe, 1985);

*La imagen de España* (Madrid: Alianza, 1986);

*Recuerdos y olvidos 1: Del paraíso al destierro; 2: El exilio; 3: Retornos* (Madrid: Alianza, 1988);

*El jardín de las malicias* (Madrid: Mondadori, 1988);

*Mi cuarto a espadas* (Madrid: El País/Aguilar, 1988);

*Las plumas del fénix: Estudios de literatura española* (Madrid: Alianza, 1989);

*Relatos granadinos* (Granada: Ayuntamiento de Granada, 1990);

*El escritor en su siglo* (Madrid: Alianza, 1990);

*El tiempo y yo, o El mundo a la espalda* (Madrid: Alianza, 1992);

*Contra el poder y otros ensayos* (Madrid: Universidad de Alcalá de Henares/Comisión V Centenario, 1992);

*El regreso* (Barcelona: Juventud, 1992);

*Relatos* (Madrid: Bruño, 1992; expanded edition, Madrid: Castalia, 1997);

*Narrativa completa* (Madrid: Alianza, 1993);

*De mis pasos en la tierra* (Madrid: Alfaguara, 1996);

*En qué mundo vivimos* (Madrid: El País/Aguilar, 1996);

*Cuentos imaginarios,* selected by Juan Casamayor Vizcaino (Madrid: Clan, 1999);

*Cover for Ayala's 1949 collection of short stories (The Lamb's Head) about the Spanish Civil War (Thomas Cooper Library, University of South Carolina)*

*Un caballero granadino y otros relatos* (Valencia: Institució Alfons el Magnànim, Diputació de València, 1999);

*La niña de oro y otros relatos* (Madrid: Alianza, 2001);

*Historia de macacos y otros relatos* (Madrid: Alianza, 2001).

OTHER: Diego de Saavedra Fajardo, *El pensamiento vivo de Saavedra Fajardo*, edited by Ayala (Buenos Aires: Losada, 1941);

Juan Donoso Cortés, marqués de Valdegamas, *Ensayo sobre el catolicismo, el liberalismo y el socialismo*, introduction by Ayala (Buenos Aires: Americalee, 1943);

Emmanuel Joseph Sieyès, *¿Qué es el tercer estado?* introduction and notes by Ayala (Buenos Aires: Americalee, 1943);

Herbert Spencer, *Hombre contra el estado*, translated by Siro García del Mazo, revised, with introduction

and notes, by Ayala (La Plata: Yerba Buena, 1945);

*Diccionario Atlantic*, edited by Ayala (Buenos Aires: Sudamericana, 1977).

TRANSLATIONS: Ernst Manheim, *La opinión pública* (Madrid: Revista de derecho privado, 1936);

Karl Mannheim, *El hombre y la sociedad en la epoca de crisis* (Madrid: Reus, 1936);

Georges Gurvitch, *Formas de la sociabilidad: Ensayos de sociologia* (Buenos Aires: Losada, 1941);

Thomas Mann, *Las cabezas trocadas* (Buenos Aires: Sudamericana, 1942);

Hans Freyer, *La sociología, ciencia de la realidad* (Buenos Aires: Losada, 1944);

Jeremy Bentham, *Tratado de los sofismas políticos* (Buenos Aires: Rosario, 1944).

Francisco Ayala stands out among other writers as an embodiment of modern Spanish literature. His prose is representative of the many literary techniques employed during the twentieth century, while the content of his works encompasses the sociopolitical struggles of Spain and the Western world in this period. As a writer of fiction, Ayala has produced remarkable novels and short stories with complex inner structures and relationships to one another. Ayala has also written several works of literary criticism and sociology as well as journalistic articles that deal with a variety of topics, including his own works, other authors, the cinema, music, paintings, and history. In his writings there is always a fundamental desire to unravel human nature in all its intricate and puzzling designs. The condensation, lucidity, and elegance of his prose reveal his mastery of the language and keen observations.

Francisco Ayala García Duarte was born in Granada on 16 March 1906, during the reign of Alfonso XIII. His parents were highly regarded in the society of the times, as they belonged to the professional and educated elite. His father, Francisco Ayala Arroyo, was a lawyer, and his mother, María de la Luz García-Duarte González, was a well-regarded painter. Ayala was the oldest of four siblings, including a young sister. By the early 1920s the family had moved to Madrid, where Ayala studied law and philosophy. His passion for literature and creative writing, which had begun when he was quite young, also flourished during these years.

Ayala's first novel, *Tragicomedia de un hombre sin espíritu* (1925, Tragicomedy of a Man without Spirit), was written in 1923 while he was a law student at the University of Madrid. This novel, as well as his next two—*Historia de un amanecer* (1926, History of a Dawn) and the unpublished "Medusa artificial" (Artificial Medusa)—were written in a realistic style that critics compare to that of nineteenth-century writers Benito Pérez Galdós and Honoré de Balzac. Ayala later transformed this style in his other works as his narrative became more experimental in nature. This experimental tendency can already be observed in his short stories "El boxeador y un ángel" (The Boxer and an Angel) and "Cazador en el alba" (Hunter at Dawn), works that were published first by *Revista de Occidente* during 1929 and then in book form in 1929 and 1930, respectively.

In the early 1930s Ayala received a grant to study sociology at the University of Berlin. While in Germany, he met Nina Vargas, a student from Chile, whom he married in 1930 and with whom he eventually had a daughter. Upon his return to Spain in 1932, he won the Cátedra (Professorship) of Sociology and Political Sciences at the University of Madrid, where he taught from 1933 to 1936. During this period, Ayala collaborated assiduously on *Revista de Occidente,* founded and directed by José Ortega y Gasset, and on *La Gaceta Literaria,* two of the country's best regarded journals of philosophical and literary writings of the time.

After the Spanish Civil War, in which Ayala's father and one of his brothers were killed by fascist forces, the author went into exile in Buenos Aires, Argentina, and lived there from 1939 to 1950. During this time, he founded the journal *Realidad;* published several of his works, including *Los usurpadores* (1949; translated as *Usurpers,* 1987) and *La cabeza del cordero* (1949, The Lamb's Head); and taught sociology at the Universidad del Litoral.

Ayala's first important novel, according to most of his critics, was *Los usurpadores.* This work constitutes a reflection on tragedies throughout history that were caused by the abuse of power. Ayala considers it a novel even though it consists of seven stories, six of them found in Spanish history books and one invented, each occurring during a different time period. Each story is autonomous but related to the others by the theme of power. There are other links among the seven tales of *Los usurpadores,* which are subtle indications of how power is always a usurpation of the freedom of others.

According to Ayala, power is necessary in society if used responsibly, but it can have tragic consequences if employed in excess or neglected. Ayala condenses the plot of each episode in a short, clear narrative made complex by his use of many techniques. Parodies of well-known historical events and many intertextual as well as intratextual references (or allusions to other of Ayala's stories) function as a continuum of the Spanish literary tradition through the centuries. The use of ekfrasis (art from other art, as descriptions of scenes or characters inspired by paintings or photographs) makes the stories appear more graphic in the imagination of

the reader, sometimes achieving a cinematic quality. The language chosen for the narrations gives the tales a flavor of antiquity. In addition, the author presents the resolution of the story at the beginning, so as to focus on the motivations of the characters before and after they assume a position with regard to power. The book invites reflection on the moral implications of each case presented, as each of them echoes the then-recent tragedy of the Spanish Civil War, where brothers fought against one another.

The first story of *Los usurpadores,* "San Juan de Dios," relates the struggle of two brothers. Their violent competition makes both of them lose the love of the women they both cherished. After much suffering, the brothers are reconciled through the love of San Juan de Dios, a saint well known in Granada. This story is the only one in the book that was invented by Ayala and is based on a painting he saw in his home when he was a child. Ayala writes in *De mis pasos en la tierra* (1996, Of My Steps on This Earth) that this painting by an unknown artist depicting the saint giving alms to the poor had belonged to his ancestors. The last episode of the book, "El abrazo" (The Embrace), is also based on a struggle between brothers for the kingdom of Castile in the fourteenth century. This last story ends in the death of Peter I as he embraces his half brother, Enrique de Trastámara (Henry II, who became king of Castile in 1369 with Peter's murder). Their fear and lack of trust were greater than their love for each other. In both stories the rage between brothers brings about self-destruction and inflicts pain on the people around them.

Two of the stories deal with a character's refusal or inability to assume the power bestowed upon him and its consequences, and two other tales concentrate on the obsession of achieving power. "El hechizado" (The Bewitched) is perhaps the most enigmatic tale of *Los usurpadores.* It was published first as a separate book in 1944 and was incorporated in the middle of the novel in 1949. It takes place in the seventeenth century and tells the story of a Peruvian mestizo fascinated by royalty who longs to meet the king of Spain. He travels to Spain, and after many bureaucratic obstacles he reaches the presence of the monarch, Charles II, who according to history was mentally retarded from a congenital disease. When González Lobo, the protagonist, enters the throne room, he finds the king drooling and playing with a little monkey, which captures his sole attention. The story thus metaphorically speaks of the illusion of power, which ultimately amounts to nothing.

Each tale presents a situation where a character has to take a course of action, and the happy or tragic effect depends on how power is used. In *Los usurpadores* a decision taken by one individual has profound conse-

historical novel as well as a thorough study of how power works in many, and sometimes mysterious, ways.

Another important book from the same period is *La cabeza del cordero,* a collection of short stories also related to the Spanish Civil War. Among these tales, the one that has received the most attention from critics and readers alike is the title story, a narrative that presents one day in the life of a person. The many activities of the day, in a foreign land and with people who are perhaps related to him, distract the protagonist from his real tragedy: a sense of guilt from not having done as much as he perhaps could have to save a relative from being killed. Critics agree that the character's feelings, which the reader comes to know near the end of the plot through a nightmare, are emblematic of the gloom of an entire nation that, having survived the disasters of war, is haunted by the many dead and blames itself for having survived. Ayala's deep understanding of the psychological makeup of human nature can be seen in this story, as well as in others that compose this volume.

In 1950, because of the repressive climate of Argentine president Juan Perón's administration, Ayala moved to Puerto Rico, where he helped organize the Program of General Studies at the University of Puerto Rico, in San Juan, and directed the journal *La Torre,* founded by Federico de Onís. One significant work from this period is his novel *Muertes de perro* (1958, Dog's Deaths; translated as *Death as a Way of Life,* 1964), a political satire written in the style of Latin American *novelas de dictador* (dictatorship novels) such as Ramón del Valle-Inclán's *Tirano Banderas* (1926) and Miguel Ángel Asturias's *El Señor Presidente* (1946). In *Muertes de perro,* a handicapped governor, unable to fight, decides to compile all kinds of documents and proofs to provide for posterity "the truth" of his nation's fate. The continuous play between objective and subjective reality emerges in the story through testimony from various characters, which ultimately reveals their personal and individual ways of seeing the conflicts of their nation. The novel, according to some critics, is an allegory of the violence and cruelty human beings have to endure in the modern world, as it exposes the evils that the excess of power brings about in an imaginary Central American country.

In 1958 Ayala left Puerto Rico and moved to the United States, where he taught Spanish literature at several universities, including Rutgers, Bryn Mawr College, Princeton, the University of Chicago, and New York University. In 1960 he began splitting his time between the United States and Spain; he returned to Madrid permanently in 1975.

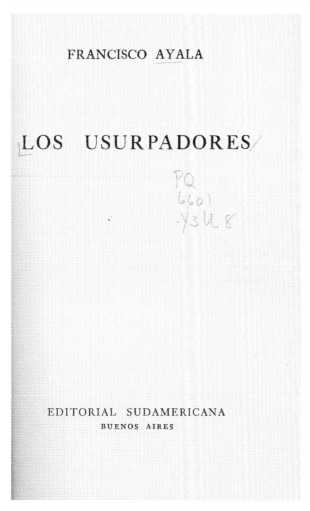

*Title page for Ayala's 1949 novel (translated as* Usurpers, *1987), which consists of seven historical tales connected by the theme of power and its effects (Thomas Cooper Library, University of South Carolina)*

quences on the entire community. Ayala, who knows the classic mentality well, views pride and ambition not only as personal faults but also as sins against society. "Power," says Ayala in an essay titled "Contra el poder" (Against Power), included in *Contra el poder y otros ensayos,* 1992), "is from its most elemental level of animal nature the manifestation of any relationship." Ayala refers to one more mysterious element that plays an important role in the outcome of history. In "El abrazo," fate is an invisible character, suggesting that sometimes even goodwill can do nothing to avoid a tragedy that was imminent from the start. The fragmented structure of this work, the subtle connections among the tales, the relationship between past and recent events in the history of Spain, and the clarity and condensed expositions presented make *Los usurpadores* a sui generis

*El fondo del vaso* (The Bottom of the Glass), written in Puerto Rico but not published until 1962, is a novel that complements *Muertes de perro*. It depicts political evils now under the guise of democracy, in the same imaginary Central American republic. The fact that a different character relates the events under a new government does not change the outcome of things in the novel, which ultimately does not show different political frameworks but underlines the similarities of human behavior over and above any historical contingency.

In 1971 Ayala published *El jardín de las delicias* (The Garden of Delights), the work that perhaps best represents the developmental process of his writings and ideologies, since it is a compendium of the themes and styles he employed throughout his career. The book is divided into two main parts of different lengths, which are reminiscent of Hieronymus Bosch's well-known painting *Garden of Earthly Delights* (circa 1505–1510), a triptych (now at the Prado Museum in Madrid) that exposes the delights and horrors of humankind. Like the painting, in which each figure or group of figures tells a different story or part of the whole, the novel is composed of brief, isolated narratives that expose all kinds of unrelated topics dealing with individuals from different parts of the world. The lack of living space in Japan and its effect on people, a mother killing her own daughter to please her lover, and the feeling of ecstasy in front of a beautiful woman or a work of art are among the topics presented. The volume gives the appearance of a collection of newspaper clippings dealing with everyday events, some highly unusual. The stories are for the most part imaginary, however, though some are taken from experiences of the author. This collection of disparate elements under the umbrella of "novel" is a way of indirectly expressing the complexity of arriving at any glimpse of totality.

"Diablo mundo" (Evil World), the first section of the book, presents an exposition of many types of incongruities and misfortunes. The other section, "Días felices" (Happy Days), narrates situations where beauty and goodness persist. This section is longer, incorporating many of Ayala's own happy memories and revealing his optimistic idealism. The parts are complementary, however, and show that evil and goodness coexist in society. Satire, sarcasm, and irony are employed in the first section to exhibit the malicious capacity of individuals. "Días felices" is written in the preterit; it is a kind of paradise built from happy memories of the past and artistic recollections of places visited. The tone is lighter and more lyrical than in the first section.

As Carolyn Richmond points out in *El universo plural de Francisco Ayala* (1995, The Plural Universe of Francisco Ayala), edited by Manuel Ángel Vázquez Medel, the fragmented structure of the plot reflects the fragmented structure of the modern world, in which there seems to be a lack of ethical solidity. Ayala likes to play with a variety of elements, such as different tones, quotations from well-known writers, and plots found in other classic texts or gathered from his own experiences. He tries to unite them in structures that are related only by aesthetic or moral components. Thus, his best reader is one who, knowing the classic authors and detecting the parodic nature of the texts, can actively participate in making some sense of the values presented.

Emilio Orozco Díaz has studied *El jardín de las delicias* in depth and finds, in the complex structures employed by Ayala, a similitude with those employed by Miguel de Cervantes in *Don Quixote* (1605, 1615). This similitude can be observed in the combination of good and evil, reality and fiction, and subjectivity and objectivity. Not only are the two parts of Ayala's book related by contrasts and differences, but some of the stories seem to have developed out of the same experience. "El ángel de Bernini" (Bernini's Angel), for example, is expanded in a separate story in the same section of the book, "Más sobre ángeles" (More on Angels). For Ayala, the chronology of the stories is unimportant; what matters are the essential aspects of human nature, which can be noticed under different perspectives and situations. His works show an insistence on small, fragmentary moments of everyday life, in which human characteristics can best be observed. *El jardín de las delicias* constitutes in particular an exploration of the reactions of individuals when faced by special circumstances, as when the lack of space in a couple's Japanese apartment forces them to go to a public park to have intimate moments. Nonetheless, Ayala's works focus ultimately on the essential similarities of human instincts and passions. In 1972 he received the Premio de la Crítica (Critics' Prize) for *El jardín de las delicias*.

Of the many essays written by Ayala, two stand out, not only for the clarity and complexity of the expositions but also because they explain comprehensibly and with rigor the works of Cervantes and Francisco Gómez de Quevedo y Villegas, two classic authors from the seventeenth century. These writers are perhaps closer than any other to Ayala's own personality and style. The two essays were published as *Cervantes y Quevedo* in 1974.

What interests Ayala about Cervantes is his ability to structure elements of different natures: "En la composición del *Quijote* se cumple de continuo esa increíble hazaña de conectar, armonizándolas, esferas espirituales al parecer incompatibles, campos literarios que parecen excluirse recíprocamente" (In the composition of *Quixote* one is in continuous awe at seeing how Cervantes connects in harmonious ways spiritual

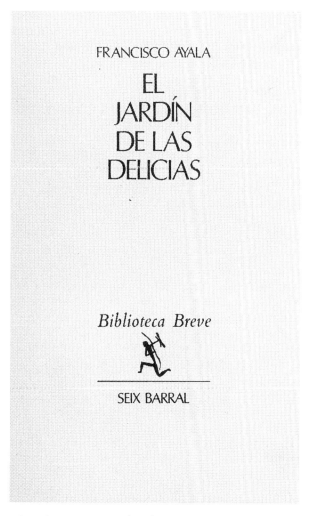

FRANCISCO AYALA

# EL JARDÍN DE LAS DELICIAS

*Biblioteca Breve*

SEIX BARRAL

*Cover for the third edition (1973) of Ayala's 1971 novel, inspired by Hieronymus Bosch's painting* Garden of Earthly Delights, *depicting moments of good and evil in human life (John Willard Brister Library, Memphis State University)*

spheres that appeared to be incompatible, or literary fields that seemed to exclude each other reciprocally). Ayala comments on the multiple combinations of picaresque, pastoral, and Italian styles (from short stories as well as novels) that Cervantes used in complex structures. The clear and eloquent explanations given by Ayala about Cervantes's art not only show his keen analytical capacity but also explain Ayala's own art of composition and writing style.

The author finds equally fascinating Quevedo's radical nihilism. Says Ayala, "Su sátira (de Quevedo) se aplica a la operación, que con tremenda, despiadada genialidad llevará a cabo en sus obras más maduras, de corroer la realidad hasta aniquilarla por completo" (Satire will be employed by Quevedo with great geniality in his mature works to unmask reality, until reality is

destroyed completely). All appearances are implacably dismantled by Quevedo, according to Ayala, until nothingness appears. This explanation applies to Ayala's own work, as his use of satire allows him to expose the absurdities of human behavior.

Upon his return to Madrid after Francisco Franco's death in 1975, Ayala actively participated in the literary world. His works, which until then had for the most part been ignored under Franco's regime, began to be recognized in his country. He began writing in the Spanish newspapers, editing his works in Spain, and establishing a good rapport with well-known Spanish literary critics. One of the first critics to write positively about Ayala's work was Andrés Amorós, in editions of Ayala's books and in interviews with the author. In 1983 Ayala received the Premio Nacional de Narrativa (National Novel and Narrative Prize) for the first volumes of his memoirs, *Recuerdos y olvidos* (1982, 1983; Remembrances and Oversights), and was elected member of Spain's Royal Academy of Letters. In 1992 he was awarded the Premio Cervantes (Cervantes Prize) for his entire career as a writer. He also has been awarded honorary doctorates by several universities, including Madrid's Universidad Complutense, the University of Granada, and the University of Seville.

Ayala has written several autobiographical works. *Recuerdos y olvidos* appeared in three volumes: *Del paraíso al destierro* (1982, From Paradise to Exile), *El exilio* (1983, Exile), and *Retorno* (1988, Return). Ayala thus has divided his life into three parts: in Spain, far away, and back again. The books are written for the most part in an intimate tone.

*De mis pasos en la tierra,* which appeared in 1996, is a collection of remembrances occurring at different moments of the artist's life. It utilizes the metaphor of travel to relive significant isolated episodes. As with many of Ayala's works, this volume is composed of brief descriptions, a few pages long, that speak of memorable experiences. In one of them, for example, Ayala dwells on his infatuation with a girl during a New Year's Eve celebration in Berlin, while he was a student. "Navidades de antaño" (Old-Fashioned Christmas) was written for a friend who asked Ayala to write about old Christmas traditions; the author's sense of humor and mischievous nature are evident, for the story does not go over past traditions but instead recounts the only Christmas of his life that he cannot remember, because he was in Argentina, where it was summer.

Some of the stories narrated in *De mis pasos en la tierra* are related to episodes in *El jardín de las delicias.* Sometimes the autobiographical story adds more details or brings a new perspective to the fictional experience. The elegant and precise prose employed by Ayala in his autobiographical works resembles that used in his fictions. There is also in *De mis pasos en la tierra* a variety of stories told in different tones (lyrical, humorous, sarcastic, ironic), and many accounts of travels around the world. Because the narrator appears lost in so many different places, and the experiences are so rich, disconnected, and fast paced, the prose sometimes evokes an almost nightmarish atmosphere.

In many of Francisco Ayala's works—whether fiction, essay, or autobiography—a set of reasonable possibilities, all of equal value and none capable of becoming the only solution, are exposed. Each narration is part of a puzzle made of many different and complex pieces, which represent Ayala's vision of the world and of himself. As Ayala pointed out in a passage from *De mis pasos en la tierra,* "Descubrí entonces—no ya en cuanto idea teórica, sino en cuanto vivencia propia—la radical incertidumbre de nuestra condición: el mundo se me revelaba ahora de pronto mera apariencia, fluida, inconsistente, evanescente y en último extremo vana" (I discovered very soon in my life the radical uncertainty of our condition: the world seemed to me all of a sudden mere appearance, fickle, inconsistent, evanescent and ultimately trivial). Truth and reality are inapprehensible entities that Ayala tries to capture through the many fragments of his works, in order to arrive at some understanding of the piteous human condition and to offer a glimpse of the writer's own conscience and that of other people in the world.

## Letters:

*Max Aub, Francisco Ayala: Epistolario, 1952–1972,* edited by Ignacio Soldevila Durante (Segorbe: Fundación Max Aub/Biblioteca Valenciana, 2001).

## Interview:

Rosario Hiriart, *Conversaciones con Francisco Ayala* (Madrid: Espasa-Calpe, 1982).

## Bibliographies:

Andrés Amorós, *Bibliografía de Francisco Ayala* (New York: Centro de estudios hispánicos, Syracuse University, 1973);

José Alvarez Calleja, *Bibliografía de Francisco Ayala* (Mieres del Camino: Instituto Bernardo de Quirós, 1983).

## Biographies:

Idelfonso Manuel Gil, *Francisco Ayala* (Madrid: Ministerio de Cultura, 1982);

Enriqueta Antolín, *Ayala sin olvidos* (Madrid: Espasa-Calpe, 1993).

## References:

Alberto Alvarez Sanagustín, *Semiología y narración: El discurso literario de Francisco Ayala* (Oviedo: Universidad de Oviedo, 1981);

*Anthropos,* special Ayala issues, 139 (December 1992) and *Anthropos, Suplementos,* 40 (September 1993);

Maryellen Bieder, *Narrative Perspective in the Post-Civil War Novels of Francisco Ayala: Muertes de perro and El fondo del vaso* (Chapel Hill: Department of Romance Languages, University of North Carolina at Chapel Hill, 1979);

Jovita Bobes-Naves, *Las novelas "Caribes" de Francisco Ayala: Tiempo y espacio* (Oviedo: Universidad de Oviedo, 1988);

Rosalía Cornejo Parriego, *La escritura postmoderna del poder* (Madrid: Fundamentos, 1993);

*Cuadernos Hispanoamericanos,* special Ayala issue, 329–330 (November–December 1977);

Keith Ellis, *El arte narrativo de Francisco Ayala* (Madrid: Gredos, 1964);

Carmen Escudero Martínez, *Cervantes en la narrativa de Francisco Ayala* (Murcia: Universidad de Murcia, 1988);

Rosario Hiriart, *Las alusiones literarias en la obra narrativa de Francisco Ayala* (New York: Eliseo Torres, 1972);

Hiriart, *La cabeza del cordero* (Madrid: Cátedra, 1978);

Hiriart, *Los recursos técnicos en la novelística de Francisco Ayala* (Madrid: Ínsula, 1972);

*Ínsula,* special Ayala issue, 27, no. 302 (January 1972);

Estelle Irizarry, *Francisco Ayala* (Boston: Twayne, 1977);

Irizarry, *Teoría y creación literaria en Francisco Ayala* (Madrid: Gredos, 1971);

Mercedes Juliá, "Entre la modernidad y la postmodernidad: *Los usurpadores* de Francisco Ayala," in her *Historicidad en la novela española contemporánea* (Cádiz: Publicaciones de la Universidad de Cádiz, 1997), pp. 14–26;

*Letras Peninsulares,* special Ayala issue, 3, no. 1 (Spring 1990);

Emilio Orozco Díaz, *Introducción al Jardín de las delicias de Ayala* (Granada: Universidad de Granada, 1986);

Benicia Reyes Camacho, *Expediente escolar de Francisco Ayala* (Granada: Universidad, Servicio de Publicaciones, 1986);

Antonio Sánchez Trigueros and Antonio Chicharro Chamorro, eds., *Francisco Ayala: Teórico y crítico literario* (Granada: Diputación Provincial, 1992);

Manuel Ángel Vázquez Medel, ed., *El universo plural de Francisco Ayala* (Seville: Alfar, 1995);

Agustín Vera Luján, *Análisis semiológico de "Muertes de perro"* (Madrid: Cupsa, 1977).

# Azorín
## (José Martínez Ruiz)
### *(8 June 1873 – 2 March 1967)*

Roberta Johnson
*University of Kansas*

BOOKS: *La crítica literaria en España,* as J. Martínez Ruiz
(Valencia: Ateneo Literario, 1893);

*Moratín Esbozo,* as Cándido (Valencia: Fé, 1893);

*Buscapiés: (Sátiras y críticas),* as Ahrimán (Madrid:
Fernando Fé, 1894);

*Anarquistas literarios: Notas sobre la literatura española,* as
Martínez Ruiz (Madrid: Fernando Fé, 1895);

*Notas sociales,* as Martínez Ruiz (Madrid: Printed by F.
Vives Mora, 1895);

*La literatura,* as Martínez Ruiz (Madrid: Fernando Fé,
1896);

*Charivari: Crítica discordante,* as Martínez Ruiz (Madrid:
Printed by Plaza de Dos de Mayo, 1897);

*Bohemia (cuentos),* as Martínez Ruiz (Madrid: Printed by
V. Vela, 1897);

*Soledades,* as Martínez Ruiz (Madrid: Fernando Fé,
1898);

*Pecuchet, demagogo: Fábula,* as Martínez Ruiz (Madrid:
Printed by Bernardo Rodríguez, 1898);

*La evolución de la crítica,* as Martínez Ruiz (Madrid:
Fernando Fé, 1899);

*La sociología criminal,* as Martínez Ruiz (Madrid:
Fernando Fé, 1899);

*Los hidalgos: (La vida en el siglo XVII),* as Martínez Ruiz
(Madrid: Fernando Fé, 1900);

*El alma castellana: (1600–1800),* as Martínez Ruiz
(Madrid: Librería Internacional Fernández Villegas, 1900);

*Diario de un enfermo,* as Martínez Ruiz (Madrid: Ricardo
Fé, 1901);

*La fuerza del amor, tragicomedia,* as Martínez Ruiz, prologue by Pío Baroja (Madrid: La España, 1901);

*La voluntad,* as Martínez Ruiz (Barcelona: Henrich,
1902);

*Antonio Azorín: Pequeño libro en que se habla de la vida de este
peregrino señor,* as Martínez Ruiz (Madrid: Viuda
de Rodríguez Sierra, 1903);

*Las confesiones de un pequeño filósofo: Novela,* as Martínez
Ruiz (Madrid: Fernando Fé, 1904);

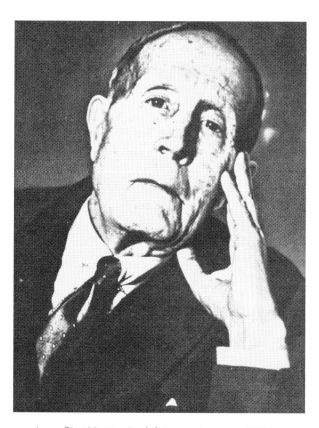

*Azorín (José Martínez Ruiz) (photograph courtesy of Ediciones
Destino; from Kathleen M. Glenn, Azorín [José Martínez
Ruiz], 1981; Thomas Cooper Library,
University of South Carolina)*

*Los pueblos: (Ensayos sobre la vida provinciana)* (Madrid:
Leonardo Williams, 1905);

*La ruta de don Quijote* (Madrid: Leonardo Williams,
1905);

*El político* (Madrid: Librería de los Sucesores de Hernando, 1908);

*España: Hombres y paisajes* (Madrid: Francisco Beltrán,
1909);

*La Cierva* (Madrid: Sucesores de Hernando, 1910);

*Lecturas españolas* (Madrid: Printed by la Revista de Archivos, 1912; Paris & New York: Thomas Nelson, 1912);

*Castilla* (Madrid: Revista de Archivos, 1912); translated by Michael Vande Berg (New York: Peter Lang, 1996);

*Clásicos y modernos* (Madrid: Renacimiento, 1913);

*Los valores literarios* (Madrid: Renacimiento, 1913);

*Un discurso de La Cierva* (Madrid: Renacimiento, 1914);

*Al margen de los clásicos* (Madrid: Residencia de Estudiantes, 1915);

*El licenciado Vidriera: En el Tricentenario de Cervantes* (Madrid: Residencia de Estudiantes, 1915); republished as *Tomás Rueda* (Buenos Aires: Espasa-Calpe, 1941);

*Rivas y Larra: Razón social del romanticismo en España* (Madrid & Buenos Aires: Renacimiento, 1916);

*Un pueblecito: Riofrío de Ávila* (Madrid: Residencia de Estudiantes, 1916);

*Parlamentarismo español: (1904–1906)* (Madrid: Calleja, 1916);

*El paisaje de España visto por los españoles* (Madrid: Renacimiento, 1917);

*Entre España y Francia (páginas de un francófilo)* (Barcelona: Bloud y Gay, 1917);

*Madrid, Guía sentimental,* Biblioteca Estrella, no. 9 (Madrid: Clásica Española, 1918);

*París, bombardeado mayo y junio 1918* (Madrid: Renacimiento, 1919); enlarged as *París, bombardeado, y Madrid, sentimental, mayo y junio 1918* (Madrid: Rafael Caro Raggio, 1921);

*Fantasías y devaneos* (Madrid: Rafael Caro Raggio, 1920);

*Los dos Luises y otros ensayos* (Madrid: Rafael Caro Raggio, 1921);

*Don Juan: Novela* (Madrid: Rafael Caro Raggio, 1922); translated by Catherine Alison Phillips as *Don Juan* (London: Chapman & Dodd, 1923; New York: Knopf, 1924);

*De Granada a Castelar* (Madrid: Rafael Caro Raggio, 1922);

*El chirrión de los políticos, fantasía moral* (Madrid: Rafael Caro Raggio, 1923);

*Una hora de España, entre 1560 y 1590* (Madrid: Rafael Caro Raggio, 1924); translated by Alice Raleigh as *An Hour of Spain between 1560 and 1590* (London: Routledge, 1930);

*Racine y Molière* (Madrid: Cuadernos Literarios de "La Lectura," 1924);

*Los Quinteros y otras páginas* (Madrid: Rafael Caro Raggio, 1925);

*Doña Inés: Historia de amor* (Madrid: Rafael Caro Raggio, 1925); republished as *Doña Inés: Novela* (New York: Las Americas, 1925; edited by Leon Livingstone, New York: Appleton-Century-Crofts, 1969);

*Old Spain, comedia en tres actos y un prólogo* (Madrid: Rafael Caro Raggio, 1926); republished as *Old Spain,* edited by George Baer Fundenburg (New York & London: Century, 1928);

*Brandy, mucho brandy: Sainete sentimental en tres actos* (Madrid: Rafael Caro Raggio, 1927);

*Comedia del arte en tres actos* (Madrid: Prensa Moderna, 1927); *El clamor, farsa in tres actos,* by Azorín and Pedro Muñoz Seca (Madrid: "Artes gráficas," 1928);

*Lo invisible: Trilogía* (Madrid: Prensa Española, 1928);

*Félix Vargas, etopeya* (Madrid: Biblioteca Nueva, 1928); republished as *El caballero inactual* (Madrid: Biblioteca Nueva, 1943);

*El doctor Frégoli o la comedia de la felicidad* (Madrid: Prensa Moderna, 1928);

*Andando y pensando, notas de un transeúnte* (Madrid: Páez, 1929);

*Tiempos y cosas* (Saragossa: Librería General, 1929);

*Leyendo a los poetas* (Saragossa: Librería General, 1929);

*Blanco en azul, cuentos* (Madrid: Biblioteca Nueva, 1929); translated by Warre Bradley Wells as *The Syrens and Other Stories,* Bennington Books, no. 5 (London: E. Partridge at Scholartis Press, 1931);

*Superrealismo: Prenovela* (Madrid: Biblioteca Nueva, 1929);

*Angelita, auto sacramental* (Madrid: Biblioteca Nueva, 1930);

*Pueblo (novela de los que trabajan y sufren)* (Madrid: Biblioteca Nueva, 1930);

*Cervantes o la casa encantado* (Madrid: Compañía Iberoamericana de Publicaciones, 1931);

*Lope en silueta (con una aguja de navegar Lope)* (Madrid: Cruz y Raya, 1935);

*La guerrilla: Comedia en tres actos, el tercero dividido en tres cuadros, original* (Madrid: Rivadeneyra, 1936);

*Trasuntos de España (páginas electas)* (Buenos Aires: Espasa-Calpe Argentina, 1938);

*Españoles en París* (Buenos Aires: Espasa-Calpe Argentina, 1939);

*En torno a José Hernández* (Buenos Aires: Editorial Sudamericana, 1939);

*Pensando en España* (Madrid: Biblioteca Nueva, 1940);

*Valencia* (Madrid: Biblioteca Nueva, 1941);

*Madrid* (Madrid: Biblioteca Nueva, 1941);

*El escritor: (Novela)* (Madrid: Espasa-Calpe Argentina, 1942);

*Cavilar y contar* (Barcelona: Destino, 1942);

*Sintiendo a España* (Barcelona: Tartessos, 1942);

*El enfermo, novela* (Madrid: Adán, 1943);

*Capricho, novela* (Madrid: Espasa-Calpc, 1943);

*Obras selectas,* prologue by Ángel Cruz Rueda (Madrid: Biblioteca Nueva, 1943);

*La isla sin aurora* (Barcelona: Destino, 1944);

*Veraneo sentimental* (Saragossa: Librería General, 1944);

*Palabras al viento* (Saragossa: Librería General, 1944);

*María Fontán (novela rosa)* (Madrid: Espasa-Calpe, 1944);

*Salvadora de Olbena, novela romantica* (Saragossa: Cronos, 1944);

*La farándula* (Saragossa: Librería General, 1945);

*París* (Madrid: Biblioteca Nueva, 1945);

*Los clásicos redivivos. Los clásicos futuros* (Buenos Aires & Mexico City: Espasa-Calpe Argentina, 1945);

*Memorias inmemoriales* (Madrid: Biblioteca Nueva, 1946);

*Ante Baroja* (Saragossa: Librería General, 1946);

*El artista y el estilo,* edited by Cruz Rueda (Madrid: M. Aguilar, 1946);

*Escena y sala* (Saragossa: Librería General, 1947);

*Con Cervantes* (Buenos Aires: Espasa-Calpe Argentina, 1947);

*Ante las candilejas* (Saragossa: Librería General, 1947);

*Obras completas,* 9 volumes, edited by Cruz Rueda (Madrid: Aguilar, 1947–1954);

*Con permiso de los cervantistas* (Madrid: Biblioteca Nueva, 1948);

*Con bandera de Francia* (Madrid: Biblioteca Nueva, 1950);

*La cabeza de Castilla* (Buenos Aires: Espasa-Calpe Argentina, 1950);

*El oasis de los clásicos* (Madrid: Biblioteca Nueva, 1952);

*Verano en Mallorca* (Palma de Mallorca: "Panorama Balear," 1952);

*El cine y el momento* (Madrid: Biblioteca Nueva, 1953);

*El buen Sancho* (Madrid: Editorial Tecnos, 1954);

*Pintar como querer* (Madrid: Biblioteca Nueva, 1954);

*El efímero cine* (Madrid: Afrodisio Aguado, 1955);

*El pasado* (Madrid: Biblioteca Nueva, 1955);

*Cuentos* (Madrid: Afrodisio Aguado, 1956);

*Escritores* (Madrid: Biblioteca Nueva, 1956);

*Dicho y hecho* (Barcelona: Destino, 1957);

*Sin perder los estribos* (Madrid: Taurus, 1958);

*De un transeúnte* (Madrid: Espasa-Calpe, 1958);

*Pasos quedos* (Madrid: Escelicer, 1959);

*Agenda* (Madrid: Biblioteca Nueva, 1959);

*Posdata* (Madrid: Biblioteca Nueva, 1959);

*De Valera a Miró* (Madrid: Afrodisio Aguado, 1959);

*Ejercicios de castellano* (Madrid: Biblioteca Nueva, 1960);

*Historia y vida* (Madrid: Espasa-Calpe, 1962);

*Lo que pasó una vez* (Barcelona: Lumen, 1962);

*Varios hombres y alguna mujer* (Barcelona: Aedos, 1962);

*En lontananza* (Madrid: Bullón, 1963);

*Los recuadros,* edited by Santiago Ríopérez y Milá (Madrid: Biblioteca Nueva, 1963);

*Ni sí, ni no* (Barcelona: Destino, 1965);

*Ultramarinos,* edited by José García Mercadal (Barcelona: EDHA, 1966);

*Los médicos* (Valencia: Prometeo, 1966);

*España clara,* photographs by Nicolás Muller (Madrid: Doncel, 1966);

*La amada España* (Barcelona: Ediciones Destino, 1967);

*Crítica de años cercanos* (Madrid: Taurus, 1967);

*Carta sin nema* (Madrid: "Joyas bibliográficas," 1970);

*Albacete, siempre* (Albacete: Ayuntamiento, 1970).

**Editions and Collections**: *Páginas escogidas* (Madrid: Calleja, 1917);

*Visión de España,* edited by Erly Danieri (Buenos Aires: Espasa-Calpe Argentina, 1941);

*La generación del 98,* edited by Ángel Cruz Rueda (Salamanca: Anaya, 1961);

*Mis mejores páginas* (Barcelona: Mateu, 1961);

*Artículos olvidados de J. Martínez Ruiz,* edited by José María Valverde (Madrid: Narcea S. A. de Ediciones, 1973);

*Rosalía de Castro y otros motivos Gallegos,* edited by Xesús Alonso Montero (Lugo: Celta, 1973);

*Cada cosa en su sitio* (Barcelona: Destino, 1973);

*Las terceras de ABC,* edited by Juan Sampelayo (Madrid: Prensa Española, 1976);

*La hora de la pluma: Periodismo de la Dictadura y de la República,* edited by Victor Ouimette (Valencia: Pre-Textos, 1987);

*Obras escogidas,* 3 volumes, edited by Miguel Ángel Lozano Marco (Madrid: Espasa-Calpe, 1998).

**Edition in English**: *Journeys in Time and Place: Two Works of Azorín,* translated by Walter Borenstein (Rock Hill, S.C.: Spanish Literature Publications, 2002)—comprises "Confessions of a Little Philosopher" and "The Route of Don Quixote."

PLAY PRODUCTIONS: *Old Spain,* San Sebastián, Teatro del Príncipe, 13 September 1926; Madrid, Teatro Reina Victoria, 3 November 1926;

*Brandy, mucho brandy,* Madrid, Teatro del Centro, 17 March 1927;

*Comedia del Arte,* Madrid, Teatro Fuencarral, 25 November 1927;

*Lo invisible,* Madrid, Sala Rex, 24 November 1928—comprises *La arañita en el espejo, El segador,* and *Doctor Death, de 3 a 5;*

*Angelita,* Monóvar, Teatro Principal, 10 May 1930;

*La guerrilla,* Madrid, Teatro Benavente, 11 January 1936;

*Farsa docente,* Burgos, 23 April 1942.

OTHER: Petr Kropotkin, *Las prisiones,* edited and translated by Azorín as J. Martínez Ruiz (Valencia: Printed by Union Tipográfica, 1897);

Vicente Medina, *Aires murcianos,* prologue by Azorín as Martínez Ruiz (Cartagena: Printed by la Gaceta Minera, 1898);

Luis Pérez Bueno, *Artistas Levantinos,* prologue by Azorín as Martínez Ruiz (Madrid: Printed by Cuerpo de Artillería, 1899);

"Génesis del Quijote," by Azorín as Martínez Ruiz, in *Iconografía de las ediciones del Quijote de Miguel de Cervantes Saavedra: Reproducción en facsimile de las portadas de 611 ediciones con notas bibliográficas tomadas directamente de los respectivos ejemplares (del año 1605 al 1905),* 3 volumes, edited by Manuel Henrich (Barcelona: Henrich, 1905);

José Cadalso, *Cartas marueccas,* edited by Azorín (Madrid: Calleja, 1917);

Luis Bello, *Viaje por las Escuelas de España: Extremadura,* prologue by Azorín (Madrid: Espasa-Calpe, 1927);

Simon Gantillon, *Maya: Espectáculo en un prólogo, nueve cuadros y un epílogo,* translated by Azorín (Madrid: La Farsa, 1930);

Miguel de Cervantes Saavedra, *El licenciado Vidriera,* prologue by Azorín (Salamanca: Librería Cervantes, 1960).

Azorín was a major figure in the group of writers he himself labeled, in a series of articles written in 1913, the "Generación del '98" (Generation of '98). This group includes a varying list of names in Spanish literary histories, but those of Pío Baroja, Antonio Machado, Ramiro de Maeztu, Miguel de Unamuno, and Ramón del Valle-Inclán almost always appear along with Azorín's. These intellectuals were concerned with Spain's backwardness vis-à-vis the rest of Europe and sought reforms in Spanish society and intellectual life. Although this interest began in the decade before 1898, the swift defeat of Spain's military forces in the brief war with the United States in that year intensified their efforts. During the first two-thirds of his long life and career Azorín devoted much of his writing to political journalism in which, despite changing political allegiances, he maintained a core of liberal thinking that emphasized the importance of individual freedom. Like other members of his generation, he was interested in philosophy and was influenced by the works of Arthur Schopenhauer, Friedrich Nietzsche, and Jean-Marie Guyau. Azorín was especially concerned with the nature of time and developed theories of history and eternity that underpin many of his fictional narratives. Azorín was also important in creating a more modern and modernist Spanish literary style by ridding its prose of long, ponderous paragraphs and convoluted syntax; even his journalism is highly literary. In addition to some five thousand articles, Azorín wrote short stories, plays, and fourteen novels. Many of his articles were republished in books in which Azorín chronicles the life and landscape of the Spanish countryside and villages. These vignettes created a literary genre–part sketch, part verbal painting, and part lyrical narration–called *estampa.*

Azorín was born José Martínez Ruiz on 8 June 1873 in Monóvar in the interior of Alicante province. He was the first of nine children of Isidro Martínez Soriano, a lawyer, and María Luisa Ruiz Maestre, who came from a family with substantial landholdings in Petrel. Martínez Ruiz was educated at a school in Yecla run by Piarist monks and had access to an impressive library at home. His literary inclinations were encouraged by his mother, but he had a less happy relationship with his politically conservative and autocratic father; Martínez Ruiz also frowned on his father's long relationship with a mistress.

Martínez Ruiz studied law at the University of Valencia from 1888 to 1891; the University of Granada from 1891 to 1896; the University of Salamanca, where he met Unamuno, a professor ten years his senior, in 1896; and, finally, the University of Madrid, also in 1896. He never completed a degree, as his interests had turned to writing early in his university career: by 1891 he had been publishing articles in local Alicante newspapers. To the consternation of his father, he abandoned his studies in 1896 and settled in Madrid. There he spent several years trying to establish himself as a radical young writer out to *épater le bourgeois.* He took a job with the daily newspaper *El País* but soon lost it for writing articles attacking the institution of marriage and advocating free love. He rankled older established writers with barbed criticisms of their style in the pamphlet-like books *Buscapiés: (Sátiras y críticas)* (1894, Squibs: [Satires and Criticisms]) and *Charivari: Crítica discordante* (1897, Charivari: Discordant Criticism). After his dismissal from *El País,* he joined the Federal Party and worked for the republican newspaper *El Progreso.* During these years Martínez Ruiz aligned himself with the anarchist and socialist ideologies that had begun circulating in Spain during the 1870s. In 1897 Leopoldo Alas ("Clarín"), who by the last decade of the nineteenth century was perhaps the most influential Spanish literary critic, took Martínez Ruiz to task for what he considered the younger man's outrageous and imprudent behavior toward his elders. He suggested that Martínez Ruiz read philosophy and turn to more serious writing.

Martínez Ruiz seems to have taken this advice to heart. In 1900 he published *El alma castellana: (1600–1800)* (The Castilian Soul: [1600–1800]), in which he explores Spanish customs of the seventeenth and eighteenth centuries. The book, which José Antonio Maravall calls a "microhistory," introduces the vignette approach to narration that became a hallmark of Azorín's narrative style even in his full-length novels. It also presages what E. Inman Fox has described as

Azorín's bookish approach to writing: his prose is filled with references to other authors and works, particularly Spanish classics such as Fernando de Rojas's *Celestina* (circa 1495; translated as *The Spanish Bawd, Represented in Celestina: Or, The Tragicke-Comedy of Calisto and Melibea,* 1631); the anonymous *La vida de Lazarillo de Tormes y de sus fortunas y adversidades* (1554, The Life of Lazarillo of Tormes and His Fortunes and Misfortunes); the works of the mystical nun and convent founder St. Teresa of Ávila; Miguel de Cervantes Saavedra's *Don Quixote* (1605–1615); the plays of Lope de Vega, Tirso de Molina (pseudonym of Fray Gabriel Téllez), and Pedro Calderón de la Barca; and the prose of Baltasar Gracián and Fray Luis de Granada. His personal copies of these books are heavily annotated from multiple readings. He read French with ease and was a devotee of the works of Michel de Montaigne. His library also contained a large collection of English, German, and Russian books in Spanish translation. An avid literary critic, he often introduced foreign books to the Spanish public, as well as offering his astute opinions about a wide variety of contemporary Spanish works.

Also in 1900 Martínez Ruiz met Baroja, who had garnered fame in Madrid's literary world with the publication that year of *Vidas sombrías* (Somber Lives). The budding writers formed a friendship as they tried to forge names for themselves in what they perceived as the antiquated and hostile intellectual climate of turn-of-the-century Madrid. They traveled to Toledo, where they viewed paintings by El Greco that were later echoed in their prose and witnessed a moving funeral procession for a child. They signed a pact with Maeztu that declared war on Spain's political and literary past, the closest the Generación del '98 ever came to the kind of manifesto usually associated with vanguard literary movements. In 1901 Martínez Ruiz and Baroja organized an homage to José Mariano de Larra, an early-nineteenth-century writer whose acerbic commentaries on the Spain of his time they sought to emulate.

The short *Diario de un enfermo* (1901, Diary of a Sick Man) is Martínez Ruiz's first attempt at a novel; some critics call it a "pre-novel." The main character is a writer who suffers from a modern kind of illness that is more existential angst than physical sickness. His marriage to a young woman promises to alleviate his anguish; but she dies of tuberculosis, and he commits suicide. Here one can see the seeds of Azorín's mature novels: fragmentary, elliptical structures; painterly descriptions; and shadowy character development. During this period Martínez Ruiz, like other writers of his generation, was reading works by German philosophers whose ideas made their way into his novels. Unamuno had just translated Schopenhauer's *Ueber den Willen in der Natur* (1836; revised and enlarged, 1867;

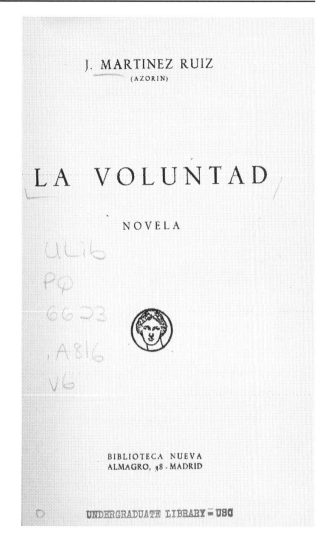

J. MARTINEZ RUIZ
(AZORIN)

## LA VOLUNTAD

NOVELA

BIBLIOTECA NUEVA
ALMAGRO, 38 - MADRID

*Title page for a 1959 edition of Azorín's 1902 novel (The Will), about a successful writer who returns from Madrid to his hometown, marries, and settles into a stultifying provincial existence (Thomas Cooper Library, University of South Carolina)*

translated as *The Will in Nature,* 1877) into Spanish, and *Die Welt als Wille und Vorstellung* (1819; revised and enlarged, 1844; revised and enlarged again, 1854; translated as *The World as Will and Idea,* 1883–1886) was also available in Spanish. Nietzsche was becoming known in Spanish intellectual circles through French translations of his works and books about his philosophy.

In 1902 Martínez Ruiz went to work for the daily *El globo* and published his first full-length novel, *La voluntad* (The Will). The work begins with a long account of the construction of a church in Yecla, which has taken several centuries to complete. The church, situated on the site of several ancient temples, suggests a human permanence that cannot be erased by time. The main character is Antonio Azorín, a young intellectual

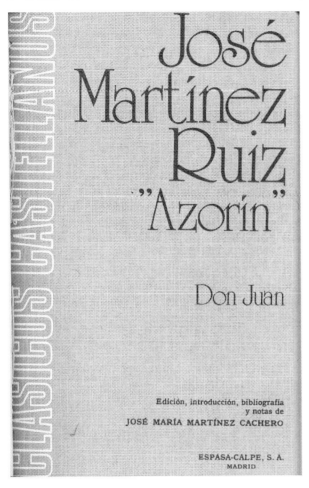

CLÁSICOS CASTELLANOS

JOSÉ
Martínez
Ruiz
"Azorín"

Don Juan

Edición, introducción, bibliografía
y notas de
JOSÉ MARÍA MARTÍNEZ CACHERO

ESPASA-CALPE, S. A.
MADRID

*Paperback cover for a 1977 edition of Azorín's 1922 novel,
in which the legendary lover gives up his philandering
ways for a humble life in a provincial city (Thomas
Cooper Library, University of South Carolina)*

and writer; he engages in philosophical conversations about the nature of time, permanence, and ephemerality with his mentor, Yuste, a devotee of Schopenhauer. Antonio is engaged to Justina, the niece of the priest Puche, a dogmatic conservative who is opposed to Yuste's and Antonio's modern freethinking. Puche forces Justina to break her engagement to Azorín and enter a convent, where she dies trying to conform to a way of life that does not suit her nature. Anticlericalism, especially an aversion to priests' forcing young women into religious life, was a salient topic among members of Azorín's generation.

When Yuste dies, Antonio moves to Madrid and spends ten years developing a career as a writer. Tiring of the hypocrisy and cynicism of the modern city, he returns to his hometown and marries Justina's friend Iluminada. Unlike Justina and Antonio, Iluminada is active and domineering–she proposes to Antonio–and

he sees her as the necessary complement to his lack of will. The epilogue to the novel consists of several letters from "José Martínez Ruiz" to "Pío Baroja," both of whom had known Antonio in Madrid. Martínez Ruiz is visiting Yecla and has looked Antonio up. The onetime intellectual has fallen completely into provincial ways: he apparently no longer reads or writes and spends his days at the local *casino* (men's club). His wife's domestic activities control his life: for example, she has usurped his study for child care and sewing. *La voluntad* poses a situation that the author and many of his contemporaries believed central to Spain's degeneration: it suffered from the national disease of abulia, an exhaustion and lack of decisiveness that prevented it from elevating itself to the level of political and economic development reached by other European countries. The message about modernity in the novel is ambiguous: provincial life can be stultifying, but the more intellectually open city is not ideal, either. Ultimately, the novel questions the whole notion of progress.

*La voluntad* is the first in a trilogy of novels that continues with *Antonio Azorín* (1903); Fox, however, argues that Martínez Ruiz began *Antonio Azorín* before *La voluntad,* and *Antonio Azorín* does have an unfinished quality. As in the former novel, Antonio Azorín has brief interactions with women in his hometown and then goes to Madrid to write. The novel includes much less philosophy than *La voluntad* and more extensive descriptions of Martínez Ruiz's adopted Castile and of the Alicante region where he grew up. The third novel in the trilogy, *Las confesiones de un pequeño filósofo* (1904; translated as "Confessions of a Little Philosopher," 2002), is a series of childhood reminiscences by Antonio Azorín, whose experiences closely parallel those of the author. Each chapter is a vignette centering on school, games, meals, the countryside, or people's appearances and behavior. *Las confesiones de un pequeño filósofo* sets the stage for Azorín's mature style, in which the author's philosophical message is conveyed not in characters' essay-like dialogue but in descriptions of landscape, architecture, and daily routines.

*Confesiones de un pequeño filósofo* was the last work Martínez Ruiz signed with his given name; thereafter, he adopted the name of his character Azorín both for his publications and his correspondence.

In 1904 Azorín moved from *El Globo* to another Madrid newspaper, *España.* After a year there, he joined the prestigious *El Imparcial,* which gave him the opportunity to publish his first book under his new pen name: to mark the tercentenary of the publication of the first part of Cervantes's novel, the newspaper sent him to La Mancha to write a series of articles on the region through which Don Quixote traveled. Azorín collected the articles as *La ruta de don Quijote* (1905; translated as "The Route of Don Quixote," 2002).

In 1907 Azorín began writing for the conservative newspaper *ABC.* That same year he won a seat in congress representing Purchena in Almería province as a member of Antonio Maura's conservative party. In 1908 the former vitriolic critic of the institution of matrimony married Julia Guinda Urzanqui. Political journalism occupied much of his time for the next few years.

Azorín was at the height of his literary art when he published *Castilla* (1912, Castile; translated, 1996) perhaps his best collection of *estampas.* In these vignettes, many of which are modern reworkings of Spanish classics and include a philosophical message about the nature of time, he has perfected his clean, clear Spanish prose. Among the most frequently anthologized pieces is "Las nubes" (The Clouds), in which Azorín uses the characters of Rojas's tragicomedy *Celestina* to convey a bourgeois message about marital felicity. In Rojas's original, Calixto and Melibea fall in love after Calixto sees Melibea while chasing his falcon and seeks the offices of a go-between, Celestina, to arrange a meeting. The two engage in secret trysts in Melibea's garden until Calixto dies in a fall from the ladder he uses to scale the garden wall, and Melibea commits suicide by leaping from the tower of her parents' home. In Azorín's version Calixto and Melibea marry and have a daughter, who, like her mother, will meet a young man chasing a falcon as the clouds constantly change shape overhead, always the same and yet different. In a technique that Leon Livingstone calls "interior duplication," history repeats itself in the parents' and daughter's stories; yet, the cloud metaphor suggests that the daughter's story will be different from that of Calixto and Melibea.

Azorín published several books of criticism that include important interpretations of the Spanish literary tradition: *Lecturas españolas* (1912, Spanish Readings), *Clásicos y modernos* (1913, Classics and Moderns), *Los valores literarios* (1913, Literary Values), and *Al margen de los clásicos* (1915, Alongside the Classics). In 1914 he was elected to congress from Puenteareas in Pontevedra province. In 1915 he published a reworking of Cervantes's novelette "El licenciado Vidriera" (1613, The Glass Licentiate). Azorín interrupted this fertile literary period to devote himself to writing articles for *ABC* in defense of the Allied cause in World War I. Unlike his friend Baroja, who favored the Germans, Azorín was a strong supporter of the Allied cause. In 1916 he was elected to congress from Sorbas in Almería; during that year he regularly sent articles to *La Prensa* in Buenos Aires. In 1917 he was named subsecretary of public instruction in Juan de la Cierva's government, but this

assignment was interrupted by a trip to France in 1918 to write on the American entry into the war. That year he was again elected to congress from Sorbas. He resumed the secretarial post in 1919 but left it later that year to accept election to congress from Sorbas once more.

Azorín continued his updating of Spanish literary classics with *Don Juan* (1922; translated as *Don Juan,* 1923). The novel is based on two dramas: Tirso de Molina's *El burlador de Sevilla; o, El convidado de piedra* (1630, The Trickster of Seville; or, The Stone Guest; translated as *The Love Rogue,* 1924) and José Zorrilla's *Don Juan Tenorio* (1844; translated, 1904). In de Molina's play Don Juan is condemned to hell for his transgressions of God's law and of socially acceptable behavior, while in Zorrilla's version he is saved from damnation by the love of the virtuous Doña Inés. Azorín's novel removes the theological content of both plays and transforms Don Juan into a modern existential hero. His philandering days behind him, he takes up a humble life in an unnamed provincial Spanish city. This setting allows Azorín to describe the various kinds of people typically found in Spanish towns, including priests, nuns, and civil guards, as he chronicles Spain's emerging modernity within an enduring substratum of tradition. In the last chapter Don Juan is at the railroad station seeing off a family that is leaving town when someone shouts from the departing train: "Adiós, España, tierra del amor y de la Caballería" (Good-bye, Spain, land of love and chivalry). Don Juan remains in the traditional town associated with these perennial qualities and becomes a monk, "El hermano Juan" (Brother John). In *Gender and Nation in the Spanish Modernist Novel* (2003) Roberta Johnson argues that *Don Juan* should be read in the context of the feminist movement that arose in Spain after World War I and reached full stride in the 1920s: Don Juan is deprived of his characteristics as a symbol of Spanish masculinity and relegated to an otherworldly ambience.

In 1924 Azorín was named to the Royal Spanish Academy of the Language. The following year he published *Doña Inés: Historia de amor* (Doña Inés: A Love Story). Although the title character's name echoes that of the woman who saves Don Juan from damnation in the Zorrilla play, Azorín's protagonist is quite different from the nineteenth-century Inés. The novel takes place in 1840, four years before Zorrilla's drama was first performed, but reflects 1920s sexual mores: Azorín's Doña Inés is not an innocent young virgin but a financially independent single woman somewhat beyond the bloom of youth who engages in love affairs. The novel opens with Inés walking to an assignation with Don Juan in a Madrid house where they have rented a room. As she waits for him to arrive, she

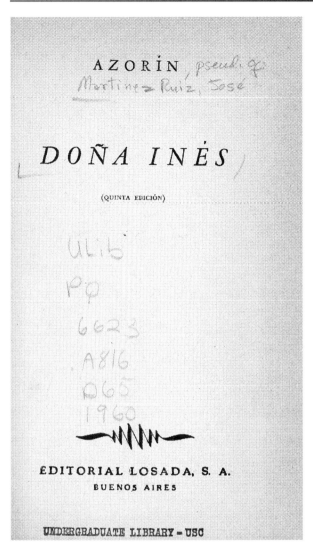

AZORÍN *pseud. of*
*Martinez Ruiz, Jose*

# DOÑA INÉS

(QUINTA EDICIÓN)

ULib
PQ
6623
A816
D65
1960

EDITORIAL LOSADA, S. A.
BUENOS AIRES

*Title page for the fifth edition of Azorín's 1925 novel, in which
Don Juan's former lover returns home to Segovia, causes a
scandal by engaging in an embrace in the cathedral, and
emigrates to Argentina (Thomas Cooper Library,
University of South Carolina)*

examines her aging body in the mirror; always philosophically interested in the passage of time, Azorín became obsessed with aging and illness as he himself grew older. A letter arrives, presumably from Don Juan breaking off their relationship, and Inés moves back to her family home in Segovia. As in his other novels, Azorín uses the settings of capital city and provincial town to contrast Spanish modernity and tradition; he also creates beautifully crafted descriptions of the Segovian countryside and the interiors of Segovian homes.

Inés's Aunt Pompilia and Uncle Pablo live on separate floors of a large home in Segovia and rarely see one another. Pompilia is engaged in contemporary life, holding soirees where young people meet; she is a whirlwind of activity, continually rearranging the furniture in her part of the house. Pablo, on the other hand, is an historian who lives mostly in the past and scarcely participates in the life around him. He is writing the story of Beatriz, an ancestor of his and Inés's in the fourteenth century, who was married to a brutal and fiercely patriarchal nobleman. Discovering that Beatriz was enamored of a handsome poet who had come to their castle, the husband had him killed and placed his blond locks in Beatriz's jewelry box. Beatriz went mad on seeing the shorn hair and lived the remainder of her days at a secluded lodge.

Inés becomes attracted to a younger man, Diego, who sustains himself with a minor bureaucratic post while he writes poetry. One day Diego embraces and kisses Inés in the cathedral; the act causes a scandal in Segovia, where sexual conduct is much more rigidly circumscribed than in Madrid. The bishop visits Pablo and suggests that he urge Inés to marry Diego; but Pablo knows that his independent-minded niece is not like Beatriz, whose parents arranged her marriage. Inés divides her fortune among her friends and relatives and departs for Argentina, where she founds a school for the children of poor Spanish immigrants. María Doménica Pieropán concludes that the work is a feminist novel; but the ending, in which Inés is tending to the children at her school, places the heroine in the motherhood role she has tried to shun.

*Doña Inés* is modern in technique. The plot is developed in an elliptical fashion, without causal explanations or connecting passages between events. Antonio Risco points out that the narration, much in the fashion of the French *nouveau roman* (new novel), is almost entirely in the present tense and restricted to external description. Also reminiscent of the *nouveau roman*, and of the European vanguard novel, is the influence of the cinema: Azorín was a lifelong movie enthusiast, viewing as many as two a day in his later years, and in *Doña Inés* he employs cinematic techniques such as panning a room or landscape, cropping, close-ups, and fade-outs.

Hoping to renovate the Spanish stage, which he believed antiquated compared to those of other European countries, Azorín wrote the plays "Judit" (written in 1926, it was never published or performed), *Old Spain* (1926), *Brandy, mucho brandy* (1927, Brandy, Much Brandy), *Comedia del arte* (1927), and *Angelita* (1930). All of these plays have an avant-garde, experimental quality.

Azorín's innovative novelistic style reaches its zenith in *Félix Vargas, etopeya* (1928, Félix Vargas, Portrait of a Character); it was published at the height of the vanguard-novel movement in Spain, which Gustavo Pérez Firmat dates between 1926 and 1934.

The title character is spending the summer in a northern Spanish village attempting to write about three women who served as companions and muses to Benjamin Constant and whose strong ideas influenced his political writing: Isabel de Charrière, Anne-Louise-Germaine de Staël, and Juliette Récamier. Félix is so immersed in his study of the eighteenth century that he experiences a rapport with the three dead Frenchwomen, which shows how a writer can abandon present reality and acquire a secondary reality based on written texts. Félix's work is interrupted when he receives a letter from the Madrid Fémina-Club inviting him to present a series of lectures on St. Teresa to its members. (The Fémina-Club is based on the Lyceum Club, founded in Madrid in 1926 by women of intellectual interests who were looking for a way to enter Spain's flourishing arts scene. Modeled on clubs in other European countries and in the United States, the Lyceum Club was ridiculed by male intellectuals; Azorín's parody of the Lyceum Club in *Félix Vargas, etopeya* is milder than those of many of his contemporaries.) Félix wrestles with the problem of writing about the sixteenth-century nun, whose remoteness in time makes her an elusive subject. He proposes to transfer the energy St. Teresa manifested during the Spanish Imperial Age to contemporary Spain, and he attempts to unite the past and the present by imagining Teresa in an automobile with a telegram in her hand. These images are not the catalyst he needs to complete his lectures, however, and he finally travels to a French city humming with the sounds of crowds and honking automobile horns. He is able to complete the lectures after an encounter with a Frenchwoman named Andrea.

The comparisons of the six women who occupy Félix's consciousness—Constant's three companions; the Fémina-Club secretary, María Granés; St. Teresa; and Andrea—suggest a comparison between the Spanish women and the more intellectually and sexually advanced French women. Azorín's admiration for Spanish women is reserved for St. Teresa, on whom he wrote several journal articles. In typical vanguard fashion, Azorín reduces Spanish women such as Granés to a series of curves and a honeyed, bird-like voice. Kathleen M. Glenn has pointed out that most of Azorín's portraits of women frame them as art objects.

*Superrealismo: Prenovela* (1929, Superrealism: Prenovel) can also be classified as a vanguard novel: a highly self-conscious work with no real plot, it centers, like *Félix Vargas,* on the act of writing. After a series of relatively disconnected scenes that evoke various aspects of Castile, the narrator announces that it is high time that a protagonist appeared in the novel. Later chapters include dialogues between this protagonist, whose name is Joaquín Albert, and the author. These

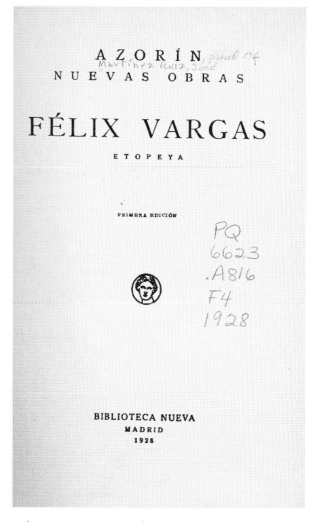

*Title page for Azorín's novel (Félix Vargas: Portrait of a Character) about a writer struggling to compose works on three eighteenth-century Frenchwomen and a sixteenth-century Spanish nun (Thomas Cooper Library, University of South Carolina)*

metafictional elements overlie Azorín's time-honored approach to fiction, in which he is primarily interested in portraying regional types and customs and capturing Spanish landscapes in words that imitate painting in their emphasis on light and color. The work pays homage to his native region, to which he rarely returned after his marriage; Julia, a *madrileña* (native of Madrid), apparently did not care for the area. After the initial ten chapters that focus on Castile, the remaining chapters deal with the women, geography, wines, and two languages—Castilian and Valencian—of Alicante. The "superrealism" of the title refers to the supernatural, rather than to the dream imagery associated with Surrealism. One of the elements that binds the loosely connected scenes together is an angel who acts as a catalyst for the sensations that Albert experiences as he moves through Castile and Alicante.

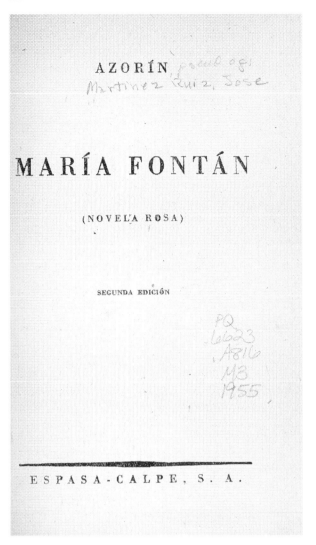

AZORÍN

MARÍA FONTÁN

(NOVELA ROSA)

SEGUNDA EDICIÓN

ESPASA-CALPE, S. A.

*Title page for the second edition of Azorín's 1944 novel (María Fontán [Romantic Novel]), in which a Spanish Jew changes her name, moves to Paris, marries, returns to Spain as a rich widow, and marries an impoverished painter (Thomas Cooper Library, University of South Carolina)*

Although Azorín did not visit his hometown after attending the opening of his play *Angelita* in Monóvar in 1930, he kept in regular contact with his brother Amancio, who continued to live in the family home. The Casa-Museo Azorín (Azorín's Museum-House), which occupies the building today, contains letters in which Azorín asked his brother to send him books from the family library. He also sent many of the books inscribed to him by other writers to be stored there.

In 1930 Azorín, while retaining the stylistic and structural innovations that distinguished his narrative style, turned to more socially and politically committed themes. *Pueblo (novela de los que trabajan y sufren)* (The People [Novel of Those Who Work and Suffer]) deals

with the impoverished masses who also populated novels by such authors as John Steinbeck and John Dos Passos during the Great Depression. Further indicating a shift from the politically conservative position he had adopted around 1907, Azorín supported the Second Spanish Republic when it was founded in 1931 and became a member of the Association of Intellectuals at the Service of the Republic that year. In 1932–1933 he worked for the periodical *Luz;* in 1933 he joined *La Libertad;* in 1934 he began writing for *Ahora.* During this period Azorín showed an interest in the Socialist Party. When the Civil War broke out between Republicans and General Francisco Franco's Nationalist forces in 1936, Azorín went into self-imposed exile in Paris. He returned to Spain after Franco won a definitive victory in 1939 but was not allowed to publish in the Spanish press. He made ends meet by publishing articles in the Buenos Aires daily *La Prensa.* During this period he wrote the short stories that were collected in *Españoles en París* (1939, Spaniards in Paris), *En torno a José Hernández* (1939, About José Hernández), *Pensando en España* (1940, Thinking about Spain), *Cavilar y contar* (1942, To Muse and Tell), and *Sintiendo a España* (1942, Feeling Spain). In 1941 Franco's brother-in-law Ramón Serrano Suñer, a government minister, intervened to allow him to obtain his journalist's credentials. In the 1940s Azorín republished *Félix Vargas* and *Superrealismo* with the titles *El caballero inactual* (1943, The Uncontemporary Gentleman) and "Libro de Levante" (1948, The Book of the Levant), respectively. Franco's regime looked to Spanish tradition for its emblems and the sense of nation it wished to project, and the title *El caballero inactual,* while it emphasizes Félix's "out of timeness," his quality of not being of the present age, also suggests a relationship to Don Quixote, "El Caballero de la Triste Figura" (The Knight of the Woeful Countenance). In changing *Superrealismo* to "Libro de Levante" for volume 5 of his *Obras completas* (1947–1954, Complete Works) Azorín made an official show of distancing himself from his work during the pre-Franco period. The new title emphasizes the interest of the work in Spanish regions, rather than its vanguard aspects.

In the early 1940s Azorín produced six novels in fairly quick succession. In *El escritor* (1942, The Writer) an older novelist, Antonio Quiroga, recounts the life of the younger writer Carlos Dávila. Quiroga has difficulty at first in understanding the younger generation, of which he is envious, but he finally comes to appreciate Dávila's talent. In keeping with Azorín's notion of time as circular, but with significant differences introduced in each repetition, Quiroga's experience of passing through the phases of a writer's career—tension with the older generation, followed by a period of popularity, and finally a time of withdrawal and reflection–is repeated by Dávila.

*El enfermo* (1943, The Sick Man) also focuses on an older writer, Víctor, who is preoccupied with his waning powers of creation. Víctor's requirements for writing are those of the aging Azorín: absolute quiet and tranquility, which necessitate his rising at 2:00 A.M. and working until 8:00 A.M. Víctor is writing a novel about a sick man, for which he conducts research in medical books. (Azorín's library at the Casa-Museo Azorín includes many such books, which he read and underlined–especially in his later years, when he was something of a hypochondriac.) Robert E. Lott points out that *El enfermo* is one of the few novels in which Azorín focuses on the psychology of his main character without excursions into descriptions of people and locales.

Azorín's next two novels are in the fantasy genre. Like most of his novels since the mid 1920s, *Capricho* (1943, Caprice) is metanovelistic: the author announces at the outset that he intends to follow Cervantes's lead in *Don Quixote* and break the narrative illusion whenever he wishes to interject something. A wealthy man leaves a million pesetas in the house of a poor family; then, the author attempts to find an ending to the story through conversations with the characters. In *La isla sin aurora* (1944, The Island without Dawn) a poet dreams of taking a voyage with a novelist and a playwright; in the twilight dream state the artists are poised between the real and the unreal and can cancel the effects of time. Finally, a ship, the *Sin retorno* (Without Return), arrives and ends the illusion of timelessness created in the poet's dreamworld.

Azorín's last two novels feature female protagonists. The heroine of *María Fontán (novela rosa)* (1944, María Fontán [Romance Novel]), the Spanish Jew Edit Maqueda, adopts the name Mary Fontan and marries a wealthy man in Paris. After her husband's death she returns to Spain as the heiress María Fontán and marries an impoverished painter. The themes of time and change are viewed from a less pessimistic perspective in this novel: rather than being weighed down by the progress of her life, María Fontán is able to effect positive transformations in each of the stages through which she passes.

*Salvadora de Olbena, novela romantica* (1944, Salvadora de Olbena, Romantic Novel) returns to Azorín's earlier emphasis on the Spanish spirit and countryside. Olbena is the quintessential provincial Spanish town, and Salvadora feels deeply tied to the locale. As in *El escritor* and *Capricho,* Azorín intervenes in the action with authorial commentaries–here, about the difference between historical and imaginary writing. Salvadora's relationship with Don Juan Pimentel has been broken

off; the novel ends with a series of chapters that offer conflicting versions of what happened between the two, highlighting the impossibility of arriving at a fixed truth through history or fiction.

For most of the rest of his life Azorín wrote short stories, which were published as *Cuentos* (1956, Stories), *Pasos quedos* (1959, Slow Steps), and *Lo que pasó una vez* (1962, What Happened Once), and articles for newspapers, the last of which appeared in 1965. He received many honors and awards, including the Gran Cruz de Alfonso el Sabio in 1956 and the Juan March Foundation Literary Prize in 1958. He died in Madrid on 2 March 1967. When democracy was reestablished in Spain after Franco's death in 1975, and especially during the Socialist government of the 1980s, Azorín fell out of favor, probably because of the widespread perception that he supported the Franco regime–a view that was supported by his favorable comments about Franco in some of his articles. Despite the shifting political winds, Azorín's innovative prose style and novelistic forms are among the great achievements of twentieth-century Spanish literature. In 1990 his remains were disinterred and taken by special train from Madrid to Monóvar, where they were reburied in the local cemetery in an elaborate two-day ceremony.

**Bibliographies:**

E. Inman Fox, *Azorín: Guía de la obra completa* (Madrid: Castalia, 1992);

Roberta Johnson, *Las bibliotecas de Azorín* (Alicante: Caja de Ahorros del Mediterráneo, 1996).

**Biographies:**

Luis S. Granjel, *Retrato de Azorín* (Madrid: Guadarrama, 1958);

José García Mercadal, *Azorín: Biografía ilustrada* (Barcelona: Destino, 1967);

Santiago Riopérez y Milá, *Azorín íntegro: Estudio biográfico, crítico, bibliográfico y antológico. Iconografía azoriniana y epistolarios inéditos* (Madrid: Biblioteca Nueva, 1979).

**References:**

Ángel Cruz Rueda, *Mujeres de Azorín* (Madrid: Biblioteca Nueva, 1953);

Miguel Enguídanos, "Azorín en busca del tiempo divinal," *Papeles de Son Armadans,* 14 (1959): 13–32;

E. Inman Fox, *Azorín as a Literary Critic* (New York: Hispanic Institute of the United States, 1962);

Kathleen M. Glenn, *Azorín (José Martínez Ruiz)* (Boston: Twayne, 1981);

Glenn, *The Novelistic Technique of Azorín (José Martínez Ruiz)* (Madrid: Plaza Mayor, 1973);

Manuel Granell, *Estética de Azorín* (Madrid: Biblioteca Nueva, 1949);

Roberta Johnson, *Gender and Nation in the Spanish Modernist Novel* (Nashville: Vanderbilt University Press, 2003);

Gayana Jurkevich, *In Pursuit of the Natural Sign: Azorín and the Poetics of Ekphrasis* (Lewisburg, Pa.: Bucknell University Press, 1999);

Anna Krause, *Azorín, the Little Philosopher: Inquiry into the Birth of a Literary Personality* (Berkeley: University of California Publications in Modern Philology, 1948);

Leon Livingstone, "Interior Duplication and the Problem of Form in the Modern Spanish Novel," *PMLA,* 73 (1958): 393–406;

Livingstone, "The Pursuit of Form in the Novels of Azorín," *PMLA,* 77 (1962): 116–133;

Livingstone, "Self-Creation and Alienation in the Novels of Azorín," *Journal of Spanish Studies: Twentieth Century,* 1 (1973): 2–43;

Livingstone, *Tema y forma en las novelas de Azorín* (Madrid: Gredos, 1970);

Livingstone, "The Theme of Intelligence and Will in the Novels of Azorín," *Romanic Review,* 58 (1968): 83–94;

Robert E. Lott, "Azorín," in *European Writers: The Twentieth Century,* edited by George Stade (New York: Scribners, 1989), pp. 639–663;

Lott, "Azorín's Experimental Period and Surrealism," *PMLA,* 79 (1964): 305–320;

Lott, "Considerations on Azorín's Literary Techniques and the Other Arts," *Kentucky Romance Quarterly,* 19 (1971): 423–434;

Lott, "Sobre el método narrativo y el estilo en las novelas de Azorín," *Cuadernos Hispanoamericanos,* 76 (1968): 192–219;

José Antonio Maravall, "Azorín, idea y sentido de la microhistoria," *Cuadernos Hispanoamericanos,* 76 (1968): 28–77;

José María Martínez Cachero, *Las novelas de Azorín* (Madrid: Ínsula, 1960);

Carlos Mellizo, ed., *Homenaje a Azorín* (Laramie: University of Wyoming, Department of Modern and Classical Languages, 1973);

José Ortega y Gasset, "Azorín: Primores de lo vulgar," *El Espectador,* 2 (1917): 73–154;

Ramón Pérez de Ayala, *Ante Azorín* (Madrid: Biblioteca Nueva, 1964);

Gustavo Pérez Firmat, *Idle Fictions: The Hispanic Vanguard Novel, 1926–1934* (Durham, N.C.: Duke University Press, 1982);

Manuel M. Pérez López, *Azorín y la literatura española* (Salamanca: Universidad de Salamanca, 1974);

María Doménica Pieropán, "Una re-visión feminista del eterno retorno en *Doña Inés,* de Azorín," *Hispania,* 72 (1989): 233–240;

Humberto Piñera, *Novela y ensayo en Azorín* (Madrid, 1971);

Marguerite C. Rand, *Castilla en Azorín* (Madrid: Revista de Occidente, 1956);

José Rico Verdu, *Un Azorín desconocido: Estudio psicológico de su obra* (Alicante: Instituto de Estudios Alicantinos, 1973);

Antonio Risco, *Azorín y la ruptura con la novela tradicional* (Madrid: Alhambra, 1980);

Mirella d'Ambrosio Servodidio, *Azorín, escritor de cuentos* (New York: Las Américas, 1971);

Robert C. Spires, "1902–1925: Martínez Ruiz (Azorín) and Vanguard Fiction," *Siglo XX/20th Century,* 4 (1986–1987): 55–62;

Spires, *Transparent Simulacra: Spanish Fiction, 1902–1926* (Columbia: University of Missouri Press, 1988).

**Papers:**

Azorín's papers and personal library are in the Casa-Museo Azorín, Monóvar.

# Pío Baroja

*(28 December 1872 – 30 October 1956)*

Nelson R. Orringer
*University of Connecticut*

and

Sebastiaan Faber
*Oberlin College*

BOOKS: *Vidas sombrías* (Madrid: Antonio Marzo, 1900);

*La casa de Aizgorri: Novela en siete jornadas* (Bilbao: Cardenal, 1900);

*Larra (1809–1837): Aniversario de 13 de febrero de 1901*, by Baroja, Azorín (José Martínez Ruiz), and others (Madrid: Imprenta de Felipe Marques, 1901);

*Aventuras, inventos y mixtificaciones de Silvestre Paradox* (Madrid: Rodríguez Serra, 1901);

*Idilios vascos* (Madrid: Rodríguez Serra, 1902);

*Camino de perfección (Pasión mística)* (Madrid: Rodríguez Serra, 1902);

*El mayorazgo de Labraz* (Barcelona: Henrich, 1903); translated by Aubrey F. G. Bell as *The Lord of Labraz* (New York: Knopf, 1926);

*El tablado de Arlequín* (Madrid: Caro Raggio, 1903);

*La busca* (Madrid: Fernando Fé, 1904); translated by Isaac Goldberg as *The Quest* (New York: Knopf, 1922);

*Mala hierba* (Madrid: Fernando Fé, 1904); translated by Goldberg as *Weeds* (New York: Knopf, 1923);

*Aurora roja* (Madrid: Fernando Fé, 1904); translated by Goldberg as *Red Dawn* (New York: Knopf, 1924);

*La feria de los discretos* (Madrid: Fernando Fé, 1905); translated by Jacob S. Fassett Jr. as *The City of the Discreet* (New York: Knopf, 1917);

*Paradox, rey* (Madrid: Hernando, 1906); translated by Nevill Barbour as *Paradox, King* (London: Wishart, 1931);

*Los últimos románticos* (Madrid: Hernando, 1906);

*Las tragedias grotescas* (Madrid: Hernando, 1907);

*La dama errante* (Madrid: R. Rojas, 1908);

*La ciudad de la niebla* (Madrid: Hernando, 1909);

*Zalacaín el aventurero: Historia de las buenas andanzas y fortunas de Martín Zalacaín el aventurero* (Barcelona: Domenech, 1909); translated by James P. Diendl

as *Zalacaín the Adventurer: The History of the Good Fortune and Wanderings of Martín Zalacaín of Urbia* (Fort Bragg, Cal.: Lost Coast Press, 1997);

*César o nada* (Madrid: Renacimiento, 1910); translated by Louis How as *Caesar or Nothing* (New York: Knopf, 1919);

*Las inquietudes de Shanti Andía* (Madrid: Renacimiento, 1911);

*El árbol de la ciencia* (Madrid: Renacimiento, 1911); translated by Bell as *The Tree of Knowledge* (New York: Knopf, 1928);

*El mundo es ansí* (Madrid: Renacimiento, 1912);

*El aprendiz de conspirador* (Madrid: Renacimiento, 1913);

*El escuadrón del brigante* (Madrid: Renacimiento, 1913);

*Los caminos del mundo* (Madrid: Renacimiento, 1914);

*Con la pluma y con el sable: Crónica de 1820 á 1823* (Madrid: Renacimiento, 1915);

*Los recursos de la astucia* (Madrid: Renacimiento, 1915);

*La dama de Urtubi: Novela inédita* (Madrid: La Novela Corta/Tip. Antonio Palomino, 1916);

*La ruta del aventurero* (Madrid: Renacimiento, 1916);

*Nuevo tablado de Arlequín* (Madrid: Caro Raggio, 1917);

*Juventud, egolatría* (Madrid: Caro Raggio, 1917); translated by Fassett and Frances L. Phillips as *Youth and Egolatry* (New York: Knopf, 1920);

*El capitán Mala Sombra* (Madrid: La Novela Corta, 1917);

*La veleta de Gastizar* (Madrid: Caro Raggio, 1918);

*Los caudillos de 1830* (Madrid: Caro Raggio, 1918);

*Idilios y fantasías* (Madrid: Caro Raggio, 1918);

*Las horas solitarias: Notas de un aprendiz de psicólogo* (Madrid: Caro Raggio, 1918);

*El cura Santa Cruz y su partida: Folletos de actualidad* (Madrid: Caro Raggio, 1918);

*Páginas escogidas* (Madrid: Calleja, 1918);

*Momentum catastrophicum* (Madrid: Caro Raggio, 1919);

*Pío Baroja (AP Photo, AP#6760034)*

*La caverna del humorismo* (Madrid: Caro Raggio, 1919);

*La Isabelina* (Madrid: Caro Raggio, 1919);

*Cuentos* (Madrid: Caro Raggio, 1919);

*Divagaciones sobre la cultura* (Madrid: Caro Raggio, 1920);

*Los contrastes de la vida* (Madrid: Caro Raggio, 1920);

*La sensualidad pervertida: Ensayos amorosos de un hombre ingenuo en una época de decadencia* (Madrid: Caro Raggio, 1920);

*El sabor de la venganza* (Madrid: Caro Raggio, 1921);

*Las furias* (Madrid: Caro Raggio, 1921);

*La leyenda de Juan de Alzate* (Madrid: Caro Raggio, 1922);

*El amor, el dandysmo y la intriga* (Madrid: Caro Raggio, 1922);

*El laberinto de las sirenas* (Madrid: Caro Raggio, 1923);

*El nocturno del Hermano Beltrán* (Madrid: Caro Raggio, 1923);

*Crítica arbitraria* (Madrid: Imp. Ciudad Lineal, 1924);

*Divagaciones apasionadas* (Madrid: Caro Raggio, 1924);

*Las figuras de cera* (Madrid: Caro Raggio, 1924);

*La nave de los locos* (Madrid: Caro Raggio, 1925);

*Arlequín, mancebo de botica, o, Los pretendientes de Columbina: Sainete en un cuadro* (Madrid: Editorial Siglo XX, 1926);

*La casa del crimen* (Madrid: Rivadeneyra/La Novela Mundial, 1926);

*El horroroso crimen de Peñaranda del Campo* (Madrid: Rivadeneyra/La Novela Mundial, 1926);

*Las veleidades de la fortuna* (Madrid: Caro Raggio, 1926);

*El gran torbellino del mundo* (Madrid: Caro Raggio, 1926);

*Los amores tardíos* (Madrid: Caro Raggio, 1927);

*Entretenimientos (Dos sainetes y una conferencia)* (Madrid: Caro Raggio, 1927);

*Las mascaradas sangrientas* (Madrid: Caro Raggio, 1927);

*El horroroso crimen de Peñaranda del Campo y otras historias* (Madrid: Caro Raggio, 1928);

*Humano enigma* (Madrid: Caro Raggio, 1928);

*La senda dolorosa* (Madrid: Caro Raggio, 1928);

*Yan-Si-Pao o La esvástica de oro* (Madrid: Prensa Moderna, 1928);

*Los pilotos de altura* (Madrid: Caro Raggio, 1929);

*El poeta y la princesa o El cabaret de la cotorra verde (Novela film)* (Madrid: Atlántida/La Novela de Hoy, 1929);

*La Canóniga* (Madrid: Cosmópolis, 1929);

*La estrella del capitán Chimista* (Madrid: Caro Raggio, 1930);

*Los confidentes audaces* (Madrid: Espasa-Calpe, 1931);

*La venta de Mirambel* (Madrid: Espasa-Calpe, 1931);

*Intermedios* (Madrid: Espasa-Calpe, 1931);

*Aviraneta o la vida de un conspirador* (Madrid: Espasa-Calpe, 1931);

*La familia de Errotacho* (Madrid: Espasa-Calpe, 1932);

*El cabo de las tormentas* (Madrid: Espasa-Calpe, 1932);

*Los visionarios* (Madrid: Espasa-Calpe, 1932);

*Juan Van Halen, el oficial aventurero* (Madrid: Espasa-Calpe, 1933);

*Las noches del Buen Retiro* (Madrid: Espasa-Calpe, 1934);

*Siluetas románticas y otras historias de pillos y extravagantes* (Madrid: Espasa-Calpe, 1934);

*La formación psicológica de un escritor: Discurso leído ante la Academia Española en la recepción pública del Sr. D. Pío Baroja* (Madrid: Espasa-Calpe, 1935);

*Elizabide el vagabundo* (San Sebastián: Navarro y del Teso, 1935);

*Vitrina pintoresca* (Madrid: Espasa-Calpe, 1935);

*Crónica escandalosa* (Madrid: Espasa-Calpe, 1935);

*Desde el principio hasta el fin* (Madrid: Espasa-Calpe, 1935);

*El cura de Monleón* (Madrid: Espasa-Calpe, 1936);

*Rapsodias: Discursos y crónicas* (Madrid: Espasa-Calpe, 1936);

*Locuras de carnaval* (Madrid: Espasa-Calpe, 1937);

*Susana* (San Sebastián: B.I.M.S.A., 1938); republished as *Susana y los cazadores de moscas* (Barcelona: Juventud, 1941);

*Comunistas, judíos, y demás ralea,* edited by Ernesto Giménez Caballero (Valladolid: Reconquista, 1938);

*Ayer y hoy* (Santiago, Chile: Ercilla, 1939);

*Historias lejanas* (Santiago, Chile: Ercilla, 1939);

*Laura; o, La soledad sin remedio* (Buenos Aires: Sudamericana, 1939);

*El tesoro del holandés* (Seville: Editorial Católica-Española, 1939);

*Los espectros del castillo y otras narraciones* (Barcelona: Pallas, 1941);

*Chopin y Jorge Sand, y otros ensayos* (Barcelona: Pallas, 1941);

*Los impostores joviales* (Madrid: Hesperia, 1941);

*Fantasías vascas* (Buenos Aires & Mexico City: Espasa-Calpe Argentina, 1941);

*El diablo a bajo precio* (Barcelona: Pallas, 1942);

*El caballero de Erláiz* (Madrid: La Nave, 1943);

*Pequeños ensayos* (Buenos Aires: Sudamericana, 1943);

*El estanque verde: Novela inédita* (Madrid: La Novela Actual, 1943);

*Canciones del suburbio* (Madrid: Biblioteca Nueva, 1944);

*El escritor según él y según los críticos* (Madrid: Biblioteca Nueva, 1944);

*Familia, infancia y juventud* (Madrid: Biblioteca Nueva, 1944);

*Final del siglo XIX y principios del XX* (Madrid: Biblioteca Nueva, 1945);

*El puente de las ánimas* (Madrid: La Nave, 1945);

*El Hotel del Cisne* (Madrid: Biblioteca Nueva, 1946);

*Obras completas,* 8 volumes (Madrid: Biblioteca Nueva, 1946–1952);

*Galería de tipos de la época* (Madrid: Biblioteca Nueva, 1947);

*La intuición y el estilo* (Madrid: Biblioteca Nueva, 1948);

*Los enigmáticos: Historias* (Madrid: Biblioteca Nueva, 1948);

*Reportajes* (Madrid: Biblioteca Nueva, 1948);

*Bagatelas de otoño* (Madrid: Biblioteca Nueva, 1949);

*El cantor vagabundo* (Madrid: Biblioteca Nueva, 1950);

*Tríptico* (Buenos Aires: Sudamericana, 1950);

*La dama de Urtubi y otras historias* (Madrid: A. Aguado, 1952);

*La obsesión del misterio* (Madrid: Rollán, 1952);

*Los amores de Antonio y Cristina* (Madrid: Tecnos, 1953);

*El país vasco* (Barcelona: Destino, 1953);

*Intermedio sentimental* (Madrid: A. Aguado, 1953);

*Los contrabandistas vascos* (Madrid: Biblioteca Nueva, 1954);

*La obra de Pello Yarza y algunas otras cosas* (Buenos Aires: Espasa-Calpe Argentina, 1954);

*Memorias* (Madrid: Minotauro, 1955);

*Paseos de un solitario: Relatos sin ilación* (Madrid: Biblioteca Nueva, 1955);

*Aquí París* (Madrid: El Grifón, 1955);

*La decadencia de la cortesía, y otros ensayos* (Barcelona: Raid, 1956);

*Allegro final, y otras cosas* (Madrid: A. Aguado, 1957);

*Escritos de juventud (1890–1904),* edited by Manuel Longares (Madrid: Cuadernos para el Diálogo, 1972);

*Hojas sueltas,* 2 volumes, edited by Luis Urrutia Salaverri (Madrid: Caro Raggio, 1973);

*Paisaje y paisanaje: Artículos y ensayos,* edited by Joan Costa (Barcelona: Talleres Gráficos Edigraf, 1973);

*Desde el exilio: Los artículos inéditos publicados en la Nación de Buenos Aires, 1936–1943,* edited by Miguel Ángel García de Juan (Madrid: Caro Raggio, 1999);

*Libertad frente a sumisión: Las colaboraciones periodísticas publicadas en España durante 1938,* edited by García de Juan (Madrid: Caro Raggio, 2001);

*Los inéditos de Hoy: Los artículos inéditos publicados en "Hoy" de México,* edited by García de Juan (Madrid: Caro Raggio, 2003).

**Editions and Collections:** *Mis mejores páginas* (Barcelona: Mateu, 1961);

*Aventuras, inventos y mixtificaciones de Silvestre Paradox,* edited by E. Inman Fox (Madrid: Espasa-Calpe, 1995);

*Zalacaín el aventurero: Historia de las buenas andanzas y fortunas de Martín Zalacaín el aventurero,* edited by Joan Estruch (Barcelona: Vicens Vives, 1995);

*Cuentos de fantasmas,* edited by Domingo Blanco (Madrid: Acento, 1997);

*El árbol de la ciencia,* edited by Julio Caro Baroja and Fox (Madrid: Cátedra, 1998);

*El mayorazgo de Labraz,* edited by Miguel García-Posada (Madrid: Alfaguara, 1998);

*Las inquietudes de Shanti Andía,* edited by Caro Baroja (Madrid: Cátedra, 1999);

*La nave de los locos,* edited by Francisco José Flores Arroyuelo (Madrid: Caro Raggio/Cátedra, 1999);

*Zalacaín el aventurero,* edited by Ricardo Senabre and Óscar Barrero Pérez (Madrid: Espasa-Calpe, 1999);

*Cuentos,* edited by Caro Baroja (Madrid: Alianza, 2000);

*Zalacaín el aventurero,* edited by Juana María Marín (Madrid: Grupo Anaya, 2001);

*Los pilotos de altura,* edited by Marín (Madrid: Grupo Anaya, 2002).

**Edition in English:** *The Restlessness of Shanti Andía, and Selected Stories,* translated by Anthony Kerrigan and Elaine Kerrigan (New York: New American Library of World Literature, 1962).

PLAY PRODUCTIONS: *El mayorazgo de Labraz: Drama trágico en cuatro actos, en prosa,* by Baroja and Eduardo M. del Portillo, Madrid, Teatro Cervantes, 27 April 1923;

*Arlequín, mancebo de botica, o, Los pretendientes de Columbina: Sainete en un cuadro,* Madrid, El Mirlo Blanco, 11 March 1926.

Pío Baroja is one of the most influential Spanish novelists after Miguel de Cervantes and Benito Pérez Galdós. He stands out as twentieth-century Spain's chief contributor to the modernist novel. His first work of prose fiction appeared in 1900, and for the next fifty-six years he published prolifically: sixty-six novels, not to mention short stories, essays, travel pieces, memoirs, plays, and even a poetic anthology. As a modernist, Baroja esteemed newness and change so much that he had no sustained formula for literary creation. As he writes in his autobiographical essay *Juventud, egolatría* (1917, translated as *Youth and Egolatry,* 1920), "No cambiar por temor a los demás es una de las formas más bajas de la esclavitud. Cambiemos todo lo que podamos. Mi ideal sería cambiar constantemente de vida, de casa, de alimentación y hasta de piel" (Not to change for fear of other people is one of the lowest forms of slavery. Let us change all we can. My ideal would be constantly to change our lives, our homes, our favorite foods, even to shed our skin time and again). Thus, Baroja preferred to try his hand at many novelistic forms: philosophical novels and adventure novels, novels in dialogue and novels without it, novels with complicated plots and plotless novels, historical novels and descriptive novels, symbolic novels and social novels.

For Baroja, the novel was a multifaceted, open-ended genre, and correspondingly his work is characterized by constant change and innovation in terms of style, subject matter, and ideology. "En muchos aspectos Baroja es un escritor fundamentalmente experimental," critic and novelist Manuel Vázquez Montalbán writes; "era . . . el primer cronista o periodista . . . que al tratar de expresarse mediante novela abre caminos para un novelar libre, un novelar que respondiera a su propia consigna estética: en la novela cabe todo" (In many respects Baroja is a fundamentally experimental writer. . . . He was . . . the first chronicler or journalist . . . who, trying to express himself in a novel, clears the way for a free way of novel writing, one that responds to his own aesthetic lemma: a novel has space for everything).

The worldview of Baroja and many of his protagonists seems determined, above all, by doubt, uncertainty, and disorientation. This uncertainty also means that their lives are rife with paradox and contradiction, in thought as well as in action. Rejecting authority of all kinds, Baroja lashed out at the Catholic Church in Spain, at the Spanish system of education, and at corrupt Spanish politics both in the capital and the provinces, and both on the Right and on the Left. Yet, with sharp irony, he also criticized the excessive pretenses of natural science, while not wholly losing faith in the progress of modern medicine.

Baroja's literary production was often autobiographical and always intensely personal. "En su forcejeo con los personajes y la realidad," Vázquez Montalbán remarks, "Baroja se ha caído con ellos en el guiso del libro y sorprende encontrar al cocinero en el centro del estofado" (In his struggle with his characters and with reality, Baroja has fallen into the book soup with them, and one is surprised to find the cook himself floating in the stew). For Baroja, in fact, "sincerity" was a sine qua non for all literature. Sincerity was the same word that the modernist poet Rubén Darío had used in the late nineteenth century to denote his aesthetic ideal of spontaneity and originality, particularly in his Parnassianist poetic anthology *Prosas profanas* (1896, Profane Prose). Baroja, however, employs the word in a different sense: for him, sincerity designates a rejection of false rhetoric and embellishment—including Darío's 1896 preciosity—in order to depict truth in all its complexity, but in as plain and direct a language as possible. As he wrote in *Juventud, egolatría,* "Yo no pretendo ser hombre de buen gusto, sino hombre sincero; tampoco quiero ser consecuente; la consecuencia me tiene sin cuidado" (I do not claim to be a man of good taste, but a sincere man; nor do I wish to be consistent; consistency holds no concern for me). The novelist, then, is a servant to truth, not to intellectual or aesthetic abstraction.

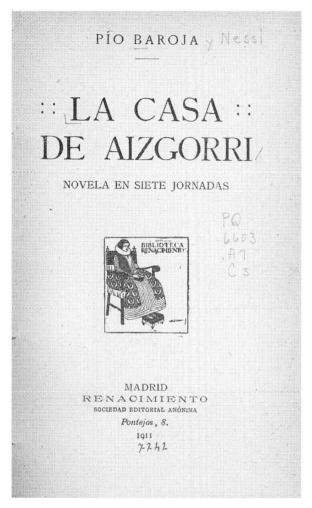

*Title page for a later edition of Baroja's 1900 novel (The House of Aizgorri: A Novel in Seven Acts), written entirely in dialogue, about a fledgling artist with a background of hereditary decadence (Thomas Cooper Library, University of South Carolina)*

Pío Baroja y Nessi was born on 28 December 1872 in the city of San Sebastián in the Spanish Basque country. This seaside birthplace always seemed to him to augur a life and a love of liberty and change. He belonged to a middle-class Basque family with four children, including two older brothers and a younger sister. Their father, Serafín Baroja y Zorzona, a native of San Sebastián, could write both in Castilian and in Basque. A mining engineer, he also taught natural history in the local high school and served as correspondent for the Liberal Madrid newspaper *El Tiempo*. Pío found him benevolent and cheerful, with a reputation for being a rather arbitrary nonconformist. Pío's mother, Carmen Nessi y Goñi, born in Madrid, had married at age seventeen and was nine years younger than her husband. The novelist describes her as fatalistic and resigned,

having been raised in a puritanical atmosphere. Life held few joys for her, many obligations, and an overarching seriousness. The family moved to Madrid when Pío was seven, to Pamplona when he was nine, back to Madrid when he was fourteen, and to Valencia when he was nineteen. This continual exposure to new settings gave Baroja's fiction a national breadth but also a preference for wandering characters.

Baroja's readings as an adolescent were undisciplined. As he writes in *Juventud, egolatría*,

En la época que a mí me parece más trascendental para la formación del espíritu, de los doce a los veinte años, viví alternativamente en seis o siete pueblos; no era posible andar de un lado a otro con libros, y llegué a no guardar ninguno. El no haber tenido libros me ha hecho el no repetir las lecturas, el no haberlos saboreado y el no haberlos anotado.

(In the period which seems to me to be most transcendental for the formation of the spirit, from twelve to twenty years of age, I lived alternatively in six or seven towns; it was not possible to go from place to place taking any books, and I never came to keep any. Not having books made me not read any over again, nor savor any, nor take notes in any).

He perused whatever reading matter came into his possession, especially novels, without regard for the opinions of the critics. He reports having read works by Jules Verne, Daniel Defoe, Alexandre Dumas *père*, Victor Hugo, Eugene Sue, Emile Zola, Alphonse Daudet, Honoré de Balzac, and George Sand, as well as Charles Dickens, Stendhal, Ivan Turgenev, Fyodor Dostoevsky, and Leo Tolstoy. He was an avid reader of the plays of Henrik Ibsen. As far as poetry was concerned, he read the Spaniards Gustavo Adolfo Bécquer and José Espronceda, the American Edgar Allan Poe, and the Frenchmen Charles Baudelaire and Paul Verlaine.

Literature early acquired a special aura for Baroja. As a child in Madrid, he was introduced by his father to Manuel Fernández y González, a serial novelist then in his prime, who deeply impressed the boy with his fearful appearance; his height; his cross, homely face; his raspy voice; and his Andalusian accent. Years later, as a teenager, Baroja attended Fernández y González's funeral. At the wake he found the old man unrecognizable, lacking the ferocity of his earlier years, and endowed in death with "una cara plácida, de cura" (the placid face of a priest).

Baroja's lifelong irony, so essential an ingredient of his literary style, developed during his adolescence. At fifteen he had to choose a professional career and hit upon medicine as the course of study with the least unlikeable professors. His more pretentious teachers at the universities of Madrid and Valencia, such as the once highly acclaimed pathologist José de Letamendi, became the target of his sarcasm in novels and personal memoirs. He wrote of his teacher in *El árbol de la ciencia* (1911; translated as *The Tree of Knowledge,* 1928) that Letamendi was one of those "hombres universales a quienes no se les conocía ni de nombre pasados los Pirineos" (universal men who were not known, not even by name, beyond the Pyrenees). At best a mediocre student, Baroja rebelled against academic authority. At age seventeen he began attending patients at the Madrid General Hospital, a dilapidated building largely governed, he later recalled, by rampant immorality. With his father's transferral to Valencia in 1891, Baroja proceeded with his medical studies at the university of that city, from which he received his master's degree in medicine two years later. Valencia did not arouse his enthusiasm. He recalled once having spotted at the theater the prestigious Valencian novelist Vicente Blasco Ibáñez—a disappointment because, instead of resembling a dashing Italian condottiere, he turned out to have a high-pitched voice, a blondish beard, and a portly frame.

Valencia was also the place where Baroja first became acquainted with philosophy. According to *Juventud, egolatría,* a text on pathology by Letamendi inspired Baroja to purchase Spanish translations of the works of Immanuel Kant, Johann Gottlieb Fichte, and Arthur Schopenhauer. Fichte irritated him against philosophy as a whole because of his incomprehensibility, but Schopenhauer's *Parerga and Paralipomena* (1851) reconciled him with the discipline. Baroja later bought French translations of Kant's *Critique of Pure Reason* (1781) and Schopenhauer's *The World as Will and Representation* (1819). Schopenhauer left a lasting impression on him, as did Schopenhauer's interlocutor Friedrich Nietzsche, whom Baroja read much later. Together, Schopenhauer and Nietzsche had the most direct influence on Baroja's fiction.

Baroja's medical career was brief. In 1893 he moved to Madrid to obtain his doctorate, and in the same year he successfully defended his short doctoral thesis, a psychophysical study of pain. He took a post as physician in Cestona, a town in his native province of Guipúzcoa, where he felt he had returned to his Basque roots. Rural town life, however, including the inevitable rivalry among the local physicians, annoyed him. Abandoning his position in Cestona in 1895, he returned to his birthplace in San Sebastián. Although he had applied for a transfer to the towns of Zar…z or Zumaya, both on the Basque coast, he never obtained one. Aware of his own lackluster medical ability, he decided to leave the profession.

When his older brother Ricardo became tired of running their aunt's bakery in Madrid, Baroja took it over. This business failed, however. He dabbled in the stock market, but with little success: Spain's economy had been hard hit by the country's humiliating defeat by the United States in the Spanish-American War of 1898, which deprived the country of overseas colonial markets and raw material. Having nothing more enticing to do, Baroja decided in 1899 to become a writer. With friends he began frequenting the offices of the newspaper *El País* and the journal *Revista Nueva.* In the same year he made his first trip to Paris. The city did not impress him: "París es un pueblo de *poseurs*" (Paris is a town of poseurs), he wrote in an 1899 newspaper article about his experience in the French capital (quoted in Eduardo Gil Bera's 2001 biography). Moreover, the latest developments in the notorious Dreyfus Affair—in which Alfred Dreyfus, a Jewish officer in the French army, was falsely accused of treason and convicted in 1894, to the alarm of prominent intellectuals such as Zola, who argued his case in the famous newspaper article "J'Accuse" (1898, I Accuse)—convinced Baroja that Western European cultural decadence had begun.

In 1900 Baroja published his first book, *Vidas sombrías* (Shadowed Lives), a collection of short stories. Set in the Basque country, these texts already display the modernist traits, as well as the variety, that characterize most of Baroja's later work. In *Vidas sombrías* he touches a range of moods and themes, including slice-of-life Basque despair at being drafted ("El carbonero"); lyrical sentimentality ("Mari Belcha"); Poe-like Gothic horror ("Medium"); and the depth of Schopenhauerian pessimism ("Marichu"). The Basque setting thus serves as a pretext for assimilating diverse foreign influences. Before the year was over, Baroja published his first novel, *La casa de Aizgorri: Novela en siete jornadas* (1900, The House of Aizgorri: A Novel in Seven Acts). It was the first installment of the trilogy *Tierra vasca* (Basque Country), which continued with *El mayorazgo de Labraz* (1903; translated as *The Lord of Labraz,* 1926) and *Zalacaín el aventurero: Historia de las buenas andanzas y fortunas de Martín Zalacaín el aventurero* (1909; translated as *Zalacaín the Adventurer: The History of the Good Fortune and Wanderings of Martin Zalacaín of Urbia,* 1997). In *La casa de Aizgorri,* the Basque ambience recedes into the background as the novel focuses on the life of a fledgling artist. Written entirely in dialogue form (Baroja first conceived of it as a play), the novel enables Baroja to dramatize in symbolic fashion the notions of hereditary decadence found in the works of Max Nordau and Ibsen.

In the same year that his first two books came out, Baroja came into contact with some of the mem-

# RED DAWN

*(From a painting by JOHN DOS PASSOS)*

# BY PIO BAROJA
Author of *Caesar or Nothing*, etc.

*Dust jacket, with painting by John Dos Passos, for the 1924 English translation of Baroja's 1904 novel* Aurora roja. *It is the third volume in his trilogy* La lucha por la vida *(The Struggle for Life), which examines how modernism arose from the clash between religion and post-Darwinian science (Collection of Richard Layman).*

bers of what was later classified as his literary generation. He met his lifelong friend, the essayist, journalist, and politician José Martínez Ruiz, better known under his pen name, Azorín. Azorín eventually coined the term "Generation of 1898" to denote the disunified bevy of writers galvanized by Spain's colonial defeat of that year, and among those writers Azorín included Baroja as well as himself. Baroja always denied the existence of a unified Generation of 1898, however, notwithstanding the success of the formula among Spanish literary historians. Baroja found in that so-called generation no common points of view, no shared aspirations, no solidarity among its members, and not even the bond produced by a common chronological age. At most, with Azorín and the journalistic essayist Ramiro de Maeztu, Baroja formed the short-lived group calling themselves "Los Tres" (The Threesome), participating together in protests and political and liter-

ary events to criticize the injustices of Spanish society and politics. When introducing Baroja in 1901 to Galdós, the greatest living Spanish novelist, Maeztu said of Baroja that he was the man who spoke ill of everyone, Galdós included.

On 13 February 1901 Azorín and Baroja organized a group of nine Madrid youths in an homage at the tomb of Mariano José de Larra, one of Spain's greatest nineteenth-century writers. Larra had killed himself in 1837 at age thirty-eight after dedicating his short but intense literary and journalistic career to criticizing traditional Spanish society in the sharpest of terms. While Larra's belief in the value and necessity of rational critique was strongly indebted to the Enlightenment, he was also a quintessential Romantic, tormented by his inner contradictions, his failed aspirations, and the painful awareness of his own hypocrisy. At the homage Azorín acclaimed Larra as the teacher of the young people of the times by bringing to art the inner impression of life, together with a moving, artistic personalism. The Larra homage later became an act symbolic of the Generation of 1898, even though only two of its best-known members, Baroja and Azorín, had actually participated. Baroja, Azorín, and the other participants wrote a description of this homage in a pamphlet titled *Larra (1809–1837): Anniversario de 13 de febrero de 1901,* with a trenchant paraphrase of Azorín's speech, characterizing Larra as a great writer and rebel, a restless, tormented spirit full of yearnings, doubts, and ironies.

In 1901 Baroja published his second novel, *Aventuras, inventos y mixtificaciones de Silvestre Paradox* (Adventures, Inventions, and Deceits of Silvestre Paradox), with which he also inaugurated a second trilogy, titled *La vida fantástica* (The Life of Fantasy). Critics agree that in this novel Baroja discovers his distinct way of writing, setting the tone for the rest of his fiction. Open and apparently structureless, the novel breaks with the linear causation dominating nineteenth-century realism. Accidents, gratuitous events, farce, and absurdity prevail. The protagonist, Silvestre Paradox, is an inventor, sage, and author. He read Verne and Defoe in his youth, writes murder mysteries, and eventually co-founds an insurance company that charges its clients a fee for praying to heaven asking for life after death. Equally as extravagant are secondary characters such as Silvestre's friend Don Avelino Diz de la Iglesia–collector of stamps, coins, excess books, and prehistoric relics–or Dr. Labarta, a nonpracticing doctor who owns a declining bakery and who, in both character and appearance, is suspiciously similar to Baroja himself.

In 1902 Baroja started to become more widely known as a writer. He served for some months as editor-in-chief of the newspaper *El Globo,* for which he also wrote theater criticism, and held a position as special envoy to Tangiers to report to the nation about events in Morocco. More important for his literary career, however, was the publication of *Camino de perfección (Pasión mística)* (1902, Way to Perfection [Mystic Passion]), the second installment of *La vida fantástica,* which was immediately recognized as an outstanding novel. Some of the best-known Spanish intellectuals of the day threw a highly publicized banquet in Baroja's honor to celebrate its appearance. His friends Azorín and Maeztu attended, as did the playwright Ramón del Valle-Inclán and the older novelists Galdós and José Ortega Munilla.

The protagonist of *Camino de perfección,* the painter Fernando Ossorio, is one of the first of a series of typical Baroja heroes: disillusioned and disoriented young men who can stand as a symbol of the author's own intellectual generation. They are heroes, moreover, who share some striking similarities with the portrait that Baroja and Azorín had painted of Larra one year earlier. Ossorio, open and flexible in the face of new sensations, rejects medicine conceived as a positivistic science. Since modernism implies innovation and experimentation, Ossorio refutes artistic naturalism and tries out pictorial symbolism, but to no avail. He renounces the imitation of nature and prefers to rely on memory as reservoir of sense perception. Yet, he comes to regard himself as a mental degenerate, so oppressed by his family heritage that he lacks the will to create. To free himself of religious and social prejudices—a modernist aspiration—he devotes himself first to carnal excesses, then to mystical hallucinations. The need for escape impels him to wander, as it did Silvestre Paradox. In a search for lost faith, Ossorio reacts as an artist to the beauty of old Castilian churches while rejecting the Catholic dogma. Finally, with the help of Schultze, a German Hispanophile, Ossorio discovers Nietzsche as his liberator. Baroja, typically, leaves the ending of the novel open. On the one hand, Ossorio has high hopes for his newborn second son, who is either to become a "lion"—the metaphor is Nietzschean—and develop strength, or an "eagle" with high aspirations. On the other hand, while Ossorio prepares the child to fly free of the life-denying past that has ruined his own life project, Ossorio's mother-in-law has quite different plans, guiding her grandson toward the conventional Catholicism that can ruin him.

In *El mayorazgo de Labraz,* the second part of the *Tierra vasca* trilogy, secondary characters give expression to a modernist's critique of progressivism as well as Spanish moral corruption in love, religion, and politics, and an application to contemporary society of Charles Darwin's notion of survival of the fittest. The novel tells the story of a blind nobleman who leaves his village in disgrace, but who is redeemed by the love of a young woman.

Whereas the trilogy *La vida fantástica* features protagonists with overly powerful creative imaginations, in the 1904 trilogy *La lucha por la vida* (The Struggle for Life) Baroja disciplines his own imagination and sets down episodes and characters observed by him in the poorer districts on the outskirts of Madrid. The Darwinian title of the trilogy refers to the fact that modernism has arisen from the clash between established religion and post-Darwinian science. Consisting of the novels *La busca* (translated as *The Quest,* 1922); *Mala hierba* (translated as *Weeds,* 1923), and *Aurora roja* (translated as *Red Dawn,* 1924), *La lucha por la vida* draws on the novels of Dickens, the nineteenth-century Russians, and French writers such as Sue. But it seems to draw its main inspiration from the picaresque novel—although it has a looser, less deductive structure than the Spanish Golden Age models. In Baroja, disconnected episodes of misery follow each other in quick succession, with a cumulative effect of general desolation. Moreover, whereas the picaresque normally uses the first person, in this trilogy the narrator assumes an ironic third-person voice. This voice allows the narrator to maintain a critical distance from the protagonist, the fifteen-year-old Manuel Alcázar, the serving boy who is present in all three novels.

Like the typical antihero of the picaresque novel, Manuel lives on the edge of urban society and moves from one menial job location to another: a boarding-house, a shoe-repair shop, a grocery store, a bakery. Serving as a passive spectator, he comes to conclude that life is sad and senseless and that people behave as egotistical predators toward their fellow human beings. Like Galdós, Baroja likes to compare his characters to animals: "El Bizco" (Cross-Eyes) looks like a chimpanzee; "Besuguito" (Little Sea Bream) resembles a fish; "Conejo" (Rabbit) has a nose that quivers; and Don Alonso is "el Hombre Boa" (Boa Man). However, more than in Galdós, the characters engage in exploitative relationships and are clearly part of a Darwinian struggle for survival. Further, Baroja, in contrast with Galdós, has not sought to portray local color or to paint scenes that make Madrid poverty seem unique. Baroja prided himself on the fact that the scenes and characters of his works were based as much as possible on personal observations and careful note-taking. At the same time, his outlook is cosmopolitan; he remarks in retrospect that the misery of the outskirts of Madrid is virtually identical to that of Paris and London. So direct and hard-hitting are these scenes of human wretchedness that the three novels of *La lucha por la vida*

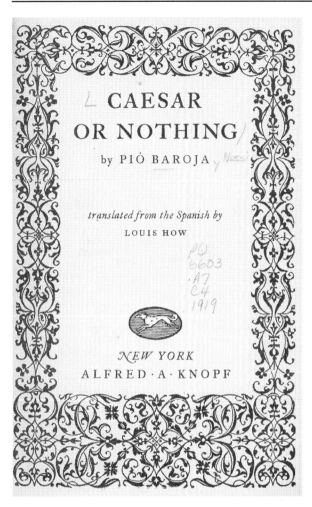

*Title page for the English translation of Baroja's 1910 novel* César
o nada, *in which a protagonist based on Cesare Borgia tries to
implement populist reform in the Castilian city of Castro Duro
(Thomas Cooper Library, University of South Carolina)*

seem to have attracted the most attention outside Spain of any of Baroja's books. They have appeared in translation in English, French, German, Italian, and Russian.

In Azorín's autobiographical novel *La voluntad* (1902, Will), the author included a detailed verbal portrait of Baroja, thinly disguised as the character Enrique Olaiz. Azorín depicts Baroja as prematurely bald, with a blond, pointed beard; an intelligent, penetrating look; and a hint of mystery, of hermeticism, about him. According to Azorín, he loved everything strange and paradoxical, including psychological subtleties or complexities. Azorín found Baroja himself a paradox: so complex in himself, he cultivated simplicity in his personal and literary style. His writing struck Azorín as simple, flowing effortlessly and seemingly without preparation. His limpid transparency appeared to overwhelm his critics to such a degree that, in

Azorín's judgment, he had not received the full critical admiration he deserved. The literary milieu in which he moved mostly admired what it regarded as a "brilliant" style, while Baroja lacked "brilliance" in the conventional sense. But Azorín deemed this preference a passing rhetorical and syntactical fashion; Baroja conveyed deep feeling, originality, picturesqueness, and suggestiveness, so what did it matter that at times his grammar showed faults? Azorín's opinion weighed heavily upon subsequent Baroja criticism, blinding it for a long time to his versatility and to the extreme care with which he elaborated even his apparently most facile prose.

Nevertheless, Baroja undeniably wrote and published quickly. By the end of 1904, only four years after his first book had appeared, he had no fewer than ten works in print. Baroja kept up this high level of production for most of his life. Despite appearances of verbal facility, however, Baroja strove for a precision that he usually achieved. The transparency and swift pace that characterize his style are generally attained through the use of brief sentences in short, clipped paragraphs, expressed in straightforward language rushing toward an open ending. As Baroja confesses in his memoirs, "Ahora escribir con sencillez es muy difícil, y exige mucho tiempo; más de lo que la gente se figura" (Now, to write with simplicity is very difficult, and demands a great deal of time; much more than people imagine).

In 1906 Baroja published *Paradox, rey* (1906; translated as *Paradox, King*, 1931), the third installment of the *La vida fantástica* trilogy. It once more features Silvestre Paradox, but this time in a novel with a striking plot, accidentally elevating him to the rank of king of a utopian state in Africa with a geography not unlike that of the Iberian Peninsula. His companions in this utopia include Diz de la Iglesia, who had already appeared in *Aventuras, inventos y mixtificaciones de Silvestre Paradox,* as well as an odd assortment of other eccentrics, such as the maimed former soldier Hardibrás, the Manchester needle manufacturer Simpson, and the German geologist-naturalist Thonelgeben. Together they resist and dominate the natives before establishing their model state. This state has a fixed governmental system but no army, no police force, and no true constitution, for its founders—disillusioned with established religious and political authority, as well as with imperialism and colonialism—reject all of the major forms of state, including monarchy, totalitarianism, communism, and democracy. The state that emerges is essentially anarchistic and celebrates individual creativity above everything else.

At a climax of the novel, after the main characters have dynamited the land to form a new lake, a mythical cyclops mysteriously appears to eulogize destruction as the equivalent of creation. Just as enigmatically, Baroja inserts into the novel an "Elogio de los viejos caballos del tíovivo" (Praise of Old Merry-Go-Round Horses), in reference to poet Verlaine's use of the animals on the merry-go-round as symbols of life as a desperate circular journey without rest, without purpose, and without end—as if human progress were at base an illusion. The novel ends with the failure of the "paradoxical" state when the imperialistic French usurp the government, bringing disease, demoralization, and devastation along with modern civilization.

*Zalacaín el aventurero* is the masterpiece of the trilogy *Tierra vasca*. It features a romantic, Nietzschean hero by the name of Martín Zalacaín, a Basque smuggler and spy for the Carlists during the Second Carlist War. His tutor, his great-uncle Tellagorri, inculcates in him individualism, restlessness, independence, and the disdain for authority that is characteristic of Baroja's modernism. After a series of adventures—including an escape from prison and love affairs with three different women—this strong and cunning, yet basically noble, protagonist ultimately perishes to treachery.

In 1909 Baroja ran without success for municipal councilman as a Republican for the Partido Radical (Radical Party), which had just been founded by the prominent populist politician Alejandro Lerroux. Reformist politics stood at the forefront of his thinking in 1910, when he published *César o nada* (translated as *Caesar or Nothing*, 1919). The title is inspired by Cesare Borgia's motto, "Aut Caesar, aut nihil," expressing the unbreakable will to be a ruler or not to be anything at all. Baroja had initially planned to go to Rome to write an historical account about Borgia but finally decided to turn the book into a work of fiction. The protagonist of *César o nada,* César Moncada, is endowed with heroic qualities as a man of action who develops an ambitious plan for reform in the reactionary Castilian city of Castro Duro. His aim is "destrozar a los caciques, acabar con el poder de los ricos, sujetar a los burgueses . . . entregar las tierras a los campesinos, mandar delegados a las comarcas para hacer obligatoria la higiene" (destroying the political bosses, doing away with the power of the rich, subduing the bourgeois . . . giving the land over to the peasants, sending delegates to the provincial regions to make hygiene obligatory). Given Moncada's tendency toward self-doubt, melancholy, and moments of inertia, however, his plan fails.

In the first edition of the novel, Moncada seems to have been wooed away from politics by an appreciation for art, similar to Ossorio's in *Camino de perfección.* In subsequent editions, the ending is different: gravely wounded by assassins' bullets, Moncada loses power to the reactionaries, and Castro Duro returns to the old order. The fountains dry up; Moncada's new school closes; the saplings in the park named after him get plucked up; and the city continues to live in its traditional fashion, which envelops it in dust, dirt, and grime. While both a political and an adventure novel, *César o nada* also includes chapters of travel literature on the Rome of the Borgias, among other European sites of interest. The notion of destruction as a form of creation, already suggested in *Paradox, rey,* returns in *César o nada*. In a chapter titled "Elogio de la violencia" (Praise of Violence), Moncada claims to be a partisan of violence, willing to set fire to the jail and to the entire city; for "el primer deber de un hombre es violar la ley—gritó—cuando la ley es mala" (the first duty of a man is to violate the law—he screamed—when the law is evil). And, like the protagonists of *Paradox, rey,* César Moncada is defined more by what he rejects than by what he embraces; he is anticlerical, as well as anti-German, anti-French, anti-English, and antiaristocratic.

Baroja's next novel, *Las inquietudes de Shanti Andía* (1911; translated as "The Restlessness of Shanti Andía," 1959), both marks a departure from the urban fiction of *César o nada* and establishes some important continuities with previous works. Set in the fictitious Basque fishing village of Lúzaro, Baroja's novel constitutes an act of rebellion against well-known realist seaside novels such as *Sotileza* (1884) by José María de Pereda. While Pereda's novel deplored the loss of the old patriarchal tradition, buttressed by an orthodox Catholic way of life, Baroja's narrator, the retired old seafarer Santiago "Shanti" Andía, emphasizes the pointlessness of life. His worldview is similar to that conjured up by the image of the merry-go-round in *Paradox, rey:* "No hay fin en la vida. El fin es un punto en el espacio y en el tiempo, no más transcendental que el punto precedente o el siguiente" (There is no end in life. The end is a point in space and in time, no more transcendental than the preceding or the following point).

Structurally, *Las inquietudes de Shanti Andía* is a frame story, much like *The Arabian Nights,* which Baroja said he admired. The main plot serves as a framework within which a variety of stories unfold, most of them associated with seagoing. On the last page of the novel, Shanti reveals that after wandering beside the sea in his retirement, he spins his yarns by the hearth of his kitchen: "Allí cuento yo mis aventuras, y las adorno con detalles sacados de mi imaginación; pero las he contado tantas veces que mi mujer me reprocha un poco burlonamente que las repito demasiado" (There I tell my adventures, and I adorn them with details taken from my imagination, but I have told them so often that my wife reproaches me a little waggishly that I repeat them too much). Shanti, then, is an unreliable narrator, but one whose skill in impressing his audience matters more than the truth value of the narrative content.

Shanti assumes many of the same postures toward his storytelling as Baroja did toward his writing. Calling himself, at the start, a rough-hewn sailor, unlearned in rhetoric, Shanti claims to hold no literary pretensions, but he writes with a sentiment of sincerity, notwithstanding the clumsiness of his form. Still, just as the unfolding narrative gives the lie to his reputation for indolence, optimism, indiffence, and apathy, it also seems to deny his lack of literary pretensions by showcasing his dexterity as a writer. In chapter 2, titled "El mar antiguo" (The Sea of Yesteryear), Shanti takes on lyric tonalities as he laments the loss of mystique suffered by the sea with the advent of bourgeois, modern times: "Antes, el mar era nuestra divinidad, era la reina endiosada y caprichosa, altiva y cruel; hoy es la mujer a quien hemos hecho nuestra esclava. Nosotros, marinos viejos, marinos galantes, la celebrábamos de reina y no la admiramos de esclava" (In earlier times, the sea was our divinity, it was the deified, whimsical queen, haughty and cruel; today it is the woman we have made our slave. We old mariners, gallant mariners, celebrated her as our queen and do not admire her as our slave).

The novel is composed of seven parts, all seemingly centering on different stages of the narrator's life, yet actually thrusting the interest of the reader beyond Shanti Andía and toward a fascinating gallery of characters in the community of Lúzaro. Part 1, an introduction to the narrator and selected members of his family, especially brings to the fore Shanti's singular aunt Ursula, able to narrate the most insignificant happenings with solemnity, and prone to filling her nephew's head with visions of pirate boats, shipwrecks, and desert isles. Among the bizarre characters occupying the family archives is Lope Aguirre, self-defined "traitor" under Philip II. The lurid account of his life precedes the introduction to Shanti's uncle Juan Aguirre, who, though buried in absentia in part 1, chapter 7, actually reappears on his deathbed in the middle of part 3, and subsequently comes alive in Shanti's adventure stories throughout the novel, especially in part 7, tying together the previous accounts through his handwritten autobiography.

After many blood-spattered adventures, Shanti offers the open ending so compatible with Baroja's aesthetics. Shanti says that the Basques no longer put to sea as previously, and that he rejoices that his own sons follow this new path; yet, the ellipse with which the novel ends indicates a reservation on his part about the abandonment of the sea life by his descendants.

*El árbol de la ciencia* is the third volume of Baroja's *La Raza* (Race) trilogy, following *La dama errante* (1908, The Wandering Lady) and *La ciudad de la niebla* (1909, The City of Confusion). *El árbol de la ciencia* occupies a place of privilege among Baroja's novels. Many critics, including E. Inman Fox and Joaquín Casalduero, have deemed it Baroja's best. He himself has called it his most complete philosophical novel. It recapitulates his biography until his thirty-ninth year, his novelistic production until that point, and his peculiar style of modernism. *El árbol de la ciencia* has a strong autobiographical base—so much so that many paragraphs from the novel reappear, transposed from third-person to a first-person narrative, in *Familia, infancia y juventud* (1944, Family, Infancy, and Youth), the second volume of Baroja's memoirs, collectively titled *Desde la última vuelta del camino* (1944, From the Final Bend in the Road). The protagonist of the novel, Andrés Hurtado—clearly Baroja's alter ego—displays what he calls a "new sensitivity," a yearning for sincerity in all he thinks and does. Andrés, however, finds his surroundings a bastion of the "old sensitivity," a series of false formulas disguising a will to live, to promote the ego in an exploitative, Darwinian world.

The clash between the two sensitivities, the modernist and the traditional, unfolds in the seven parts of the novel. In part 1, which chronicles a student's life in end-of-the-nineteenth-century Madrid, Baroja satirizes through Andrés his own disappointments as a medical student, when his intellectual curiosity was stifled by false, theatrical professors. Andrés, with his native sympathy, feels hostile toward cruel, venal classmates, and his sociopolitical reformism clashes with his father's conservatism. In part 2, Baroja satirizes the hypocritical morality of the old sensitivity, embodied by the petit bourgeois widow Doña Leonarda, who has allegedly told one of Andrés's classmates, "A mis hijas hay que tratarlas como si fueran vírgenes, Julito, como si fueran vírgenes" (My daughters must be treated as if they were virgins, dear Julio, as if they were virgins). Julio, a Darwinian Don Juan, out only for his own animal pleasure, cares little if he obtains the older daughter's favors through false promises of marriage: insincere, he belongs to the old sensitivity, and with him, Niní, the girl he pursues. By contrast, her sister Lulú sees through Julio's falseness and with her sincerity and helplessness in a predatory society wins Andrés's sympathy, friendship, and eventual love: she partakes of the new sensitivity.

Part 3 foreshadows the tragic ending of the novel through the narration of the final days of Andrés's youngest brother, Luis, who is virtually another

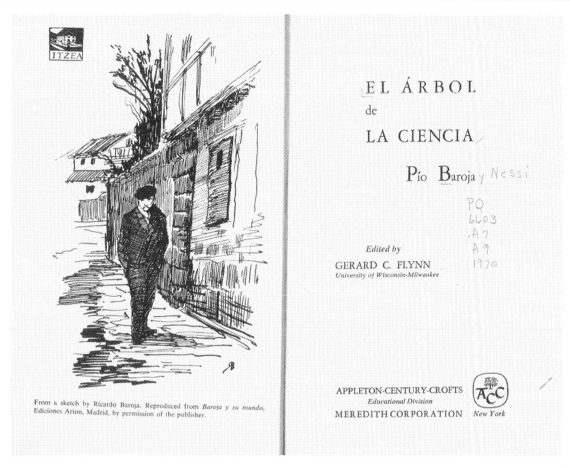

From a sketch by Ricardo Baroja. Reproduced from *Baroja y su mundo*, Ediciones Arion, Madrid, by permission of the publisher.

EL ÁRBOL
de
LA CIENCIA

Pío Baroja y Nessi

*Edited by*
GERARD C. FLYNN
*University of Wisconsin-Milwaukee*

APPLETON-CENTURY-CROFTS
*Educational Division*
MEREDITH CORPORATION   *New York*

*Frontispiece and title page for a later edition of Baroja's 1911 novel (translated as* The Tree of Knowledge, *1928),
in which the autobiographical protagonist is caught between modernist and traditional sensibilities
(Thomas Cooper Library, University of South Carolina)*

Andrés: studious, sedentary, and imaginative. As is clear from Baroja's memoirs, the episode stylizes the death of Baroja's own brother Darío. As long as Andrés's family obeys his own scientific hygiene by exposing the tubercular Luis to fresh air, the child thrives. When his father—representative of the old sensitivity—causes the child to be shut away indoors, however, he dies of tubercular meningitis.

Part 4, at the exact center of the novel, recapitulates the story up to that point and orients the reader toward the conclusion. This part also makes explicit the philosophical dialectic lying at the base of the novel. Having undergone so many disappointments, Andrés seeks guidance in the world and a plan of action for the immediate future. He consults his uncle Iturrioz, a father figure who, contrary to Andrés's real father, is sincere and congenial to the new sensitivity. From their conversations it becomes clear that Andrés is a philosopher, a lover of truth, while Iturrioz is a "biophile," a lover of life. Iturrioz, Darwinian in his outlook, reveres the Tree of Life in the Garden of Eden

at the expense of truth; Andrés, more analytical, chooses the Tree of Knowledge and favors the pursuit of truth even at the cost of life. Baroja's own work was marked by an inability to choose between these two positions. His novelistic heroes up to this point have been contemplative (Paradox, Ossorio) or active (Zalacaín). Andrés, contemplative like Baroja himself, is fated to succumb to the Tree of Life.

Part 5, narrating Andrés's experience as a country physician, draws on Baroja's own experience as a village doctor in Cestona. Baroja stations Andrés not in the Basque country, however, but in a town in La Mancha, a village where Don Quixote might have lived. This choice allows him to present town life as characteristic of Spain as a whole: "Las costumbres de Alcolea eran españolas puras, es decir, de un absurdo completo" (The customs of Alcolea were pure Spanish, that is, completely absurd). According to the narrator, the townspeople lack any kind of solidarity. Moreover, their agriculture belongs to the past, and their politics display traditional corruption without possibility of change. Inevitably, the old, traditional sensitivity dominating the Spanish countryside clashes with Andrés's modern worldview, and he departs the town in disappointment, afflicted with neurasthenia.

Part 6, marking Andrés's return to Madrid, brings him the new disillusionment of discovering the falseness of Spanish patriotism: with the humiliating defeat to the United States in the colonial war of 1898, Spaniards of the old sensitivity, in complete indifference, continue to go to the theater and the bullfights as if nothing had happened. With falseness on all sides, Andrés in part 7 creates an oasis of sincerity with Lulú, whom he marries. Against the advice of Iturrioz the biophile, who warns Andrés not to have children, since they would inherit their parents' congenital sickliness, Andrés succumbs to the Tree of Life, that is, to Lulú's desire for offspring, oblivious to the truth of her physiological incapacity. Lulú and the baby die in childbirth, and Andrés uses his medical training to poison himself swiftly and painlessly. Nonetheless, Baroja gives Andrés's life an open-ended meaning and the whole novel a kind of open ending: a knowledgeable physician at the end of the work says of Andrés that he was ahead of his time, a man of a rare, Northern European, scientific mentality devoted to the disclosure of truth, the Tree of Knowledge.

After writing *El árbol de la ciencia,* Baroja delved for his material with ever greater insistence into his own biography, making the finished product almost predictable. As a bachelor with ample leisure time to write and travel–he never married or had any significant romantic relationships–Baroja allowed his impressions of Italy, England, France, and Switzerland to abound in his novels, as in *César o nada* and in *El mundo es ansí* (1912, The World Is Thus-and-Such), recounting the pan-European disillusionments of Russian medical student Sacha Savarof. Between 1911 and 1935 Baroja also embarked on his most ambitious project: *Memorias de un hombre de acción* (Memoirs of a Man of Action), a twenty-two-volume series of historical novels centering on a single figure, his distant relative Eugenio Aviraneta, who was a guerrilla fighter in the Spanish War of Independence (1808–1812) and a Liberal, Masonic conspirator afterward.

Like all of his work, Baroja's historical series has a modernist inspiration, subordinating tradition to inventiveness. He chooses a Basque hero all but forgotten by history, as if to return to his familial roots. Further, as he asserts at the outset of the first volume in the series, *El aprendiz de conspirador* (1913, The Conspirator's Apprentice), he has endowed his hero with a passion for truth in a nation of empty rhetoric–a passion witnessed as well in Andrés Hurtado of *El árbol de la ciencia.* As in the case of Andrés, however, this passion eventually leads to Aviraneta's downfall.

Baroja's novelistic treatment of his heroic family member also marks a rebellion vis-à-vis Galdós, who set a precedent for historical fiction in his forty-six *Episodios nacionales* (1873–1912, National Episodes). Baroja claims in *La intuición y el estilo* (1948, Intuition and Style) that Galdós sought brilliant events to make history out of them, whereas Baroja has concentrated on his hero– a Nietzschean man of action. Moreover, while Galdós pursued a panoramic spectacle of happenings, Baroja worked in a more impressionistic manner, choosing isolated but intense incidents. In his *Memorias* (1955, Memoirs) he expressed his own preference for French pictorial impressionism as the best cultural product to have emerged from the end of the nineteenth century; and he particularly praised Edgar Degas, Edouard Manet, Alfred Sisley, Vincent Van Gogh, and Henri de Toulouse-Lautrec.

In their appreciation of novelty over tradition and their subversive attitude stemming from the crisis of religion clashing with post-Darwinian science, Baroja's writings display the general characteristics of all world modernism. Within the modernist mindset, Baroja belongs to the so-called *Edad de Plata* or Silver Age of Spanish literature, that is, the second greatest period of cultural creativity in Spain, which started approximately in 1874 with the Bourbon Restoration and ended in about 1936, with the outbreak of the Spanish Civil War. Like Baroja, the intellectuals from this period were generally marked by an acute awareness of living in a period of Spanish decadence and tended to perceive their own era as a break with the country's former greatness. This awareness spurred an aspiration to end the downward spiral and to elevate Spanish culture once more to the level of the rest of Western Europe.

As Baroja wrote in the 24 August 1903 article "Estilo modernista" (included in volume eight of his *Obras completas* [1946–1952, Complete Works]), the overused word "modernism" denoted admiration for "lo fuerte, lo grande y lo anárquico" (what is strong, great, and anarchic) and included in art "todos los rebeldes" (all the rebels), in whose ranks Baroja situated Dickens, Ibsen, Dostoevsky, Nietzsche, and Auguste Rodin. Although the term irritated him, he accepted it for lack of an alternative: "Modernista! Indudablemente, la palabra es fea, es cursi; pero los que abominan de ella son imbéciles" (Modernist! Doubtlessly the word is ugly, is shoddy; but those who abominate it are imbeciles).

While Baroja can be considered part of the general artistic and intellectual movement called modernism, however, it is important to keep in mind that he

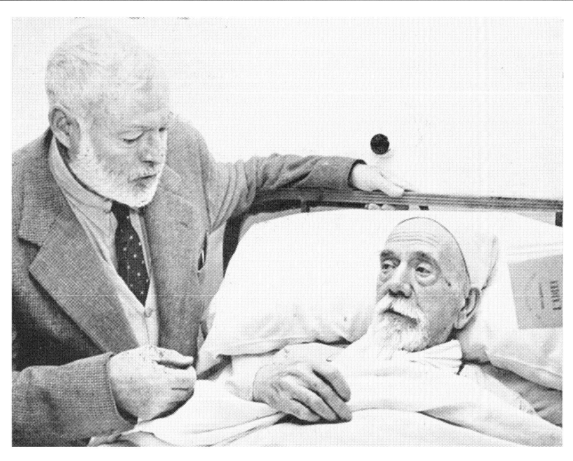

*Ernest Hemingway visiting Baroja shortly before Baroja's death in October 1956 (from Fernando Baeza,*
Baroja y su mundo, *1961; Thomas Cooper Library, University of South Carolina)*

was also a quintessential loner whose attitudes, views, and actions were generally at odds with the tendencies of his intellectual environment: "Yo he sido siempre un liberal radical, individualista y anarquista" (I have always been a radical liberal, individualist and anarchist), he wrote in volume five of his *Obras completas*. Even those of his contemporaries who did not agree with his views sometimes expressed admiration for his steadfast individualism. "Baroja no se contenta con discrepar en más o menos puntos del sistema de lugares comunes y opiniones convencionales," José Ortega y Gasset, the Spanish philosopher, wrote, "sino que hace de la protesta contra el modo de pensar y sentir convencionalmente nervio de su producción" (Baroja is not content to disagree more or less with some points of the system of commonplaces and conventional opinions, but he turns the protest against the conventional way of thinking and feeling into the center of his production).

　　Throughout his life Baroja insisted on marking his disagreement with the prevalent opinion of his times, both in speech and in action. During World War I, in which Spain declared itself strictly neutral, most intellectuals supported the Allied forces; Baroja openly rooted for Germany. In 1915 he argued in the prominent magazine *España:* "Si hay algún país que pueda sustituir los mitos de la religión, de la democracia, de la farsa de la caridad cristiana por la ciencia, por el orden y por la técnica, es Alemania" (If there is any country that can replace the myths of religion, democracy, and the farce of Christian charity with science, order, and technique, it is Germany). When the Spanish Civil War broke out in 1936, Baroja, after a skirmish with a group of right-wing militants and a short detention, went into exile in Paris. After General Francisco Franco's victory, however, when hundreds of Spanish intellectuals chose exile in preference to living under a reactionary dictatorship, Baroja returned to Madrid in 1940.

　　Baroja's publishing continued unabated until his death on 30 October 1956 from cerebral arteriosclerosis. With his solid reputation as a heterodox and a rebel, he received many visitors from Spain and abroad. When asked to serve as one of Baroja's pall-bearers, Ernest Hemingway, who had visited him only weeks before his death, declined on the grounds that he did not deserve so great an honor.

According to Ortega y Gasset, most readers will react to Baroja with indignation. Baroja's work is rife with strong, potentially offensive statements, owing in part to his lifelong tendencies toward anti-Semitism, anticlericalism, and misogyny; his rejection of parliamentary democracy; and his belief in the existence of "weak" and "strong" races. But his offensiveness is also partly caused by the fact that Baroja, his narrators, and his characters tend to be opinionated and express themselves in a straightforward, nonrhetorical style. Like his preferred philosopher, Nietzsche, Baroja's heterodox opinions left him vulnerable to being mobilized by extreme right-wing political movements. Thus, during the Spanish Civil War, a prominent intellectual in the Spanish fascist party, Ernesto Giménez Caballero, published an anthology of passages from Baroja's work under the title *Comunistas, judíos y demás ralea* (1938, Communists, Jews, and Others of the Kind), meant to prove that Baroja was a "Spanish precursor of fascism," preceding even Benito Mussolini. For Vázquez Montalbán, a leftist intellectual who grew up in post–Civil War Spain and who dedicated a great part of his youth to opposing the Franco regime, these Francoist appropriations of Baroja initially made it difficult to appreciate the author's significance.

While Giménez Caballero's image of Baroja as a fascist is clearly slanted, later biographies have also called attention to the misleading nature of the image that Baroja himself liked to present to the world. The most critical of Baroja studies was a biography published in 2001 by Gil Bera, who begins by expressing his surprise that, almost half a century after the author's death, "apenas se conoce un dato de su vida que no proceda de su propia versión" (hardly a fact is known of his life that does not originate in his own version of it). Gil Bera then goes on to expose the many "lies" and "omissions" in Baroja's life story as told by himself.

Pío Baroja's influence on twentieth-century literature was significant and by no means limited to Spain. In the United States, Hemingway and John Dos Passos were among his greatest admirers. Most importantly, Baroja expanded the boundaries of the novel as narrative genre. As Vázquez Montalbán writes, Baroja was always breaking through the frontiers: "destruye el encantamiento novelesco desde dentro . . . no cree en la novela como sacramento" (he destroys the magic of the novel from the inside . . . he doesn't believe in the novel as a sacrament). With his aspiration to rough-hewn rebelliousness and his penchant for plain speaking in prose, Baroja deeply affected the fiction of great novelists who came later—notably, Spanish Nobel laureate Camilo José Cela, but also Ramón Pérez de Ayala, Miguel Delibes, José María Gironella, Ignacio Aldecoa, Luis Martín-Santos, and Juan Benet Goita. Cela affirms, in his *Cuatro figuras del 98* (1961, Four Figures of [18]98), that every Spanish novel published since Baroja in some way derives from his work.

**Letters:**

*Epistolario Pío Baroja–Eduardo Ranch Fuster (1933–1955),* edited by Amparo Ranch and Cecilio Alonso (Valencia: Vicent Llorens, 1998).

**Bibliography:**

Jorge Campos, "Bibliografía," in *Baroja y su mundo,* 3 volumes, edited by Fernando Baeza (Madrid: Arion, 1961), I: 323–389.

**Biographies:**

Ángel Granjel, *Retrato de Pío Baroja* (Barcelona: Barna, 1953);

Miguel Pérez Ferrero, *Vida de Pío Baroja: El hombre y el novelista* (Barcelona: Destino, 1960);

Antonio Manuel Campoy, *Pío Baroja: Un autor en un libro* (Madrid: Compañía Bibliográfica Española, 1963);

Sebastián Juan Arbó, *Pío Baroja y su tiempo* (Barcelona: Planeta, 1963);

Eduardo Gil Bera, *Baroja o el miedo: Biografía no autorizada* (Barcelona: Península, 2001);

Eduardo Mendoza, *Pío Baroja* (Barcelona: Omega, 2001).

**References:**

Azorín (José Martínez Ruiz), *La voluntad,* second edition, edited by E. Inman Fox (Madrid: Clásicos Castalia, 1972);

Mary Lee Bretz, *Encounters across Borders: The Changing Visions of Spanish Modernism, 1890–1930* (Lewisburg, Pa.: Bucknell University Press, 2001);

Camilo José Cela, *Cuatro figuras del 98* (Barcelona: Aedos, 1961);

Eugenio G. de Nora, *La novela española contemporánea (1898–1927),* second edition (Madrid: Gredos, 1963), I: 97–229;

Lawrence B. Gamache, "Toward a Definition of Modernism," in *The Modernists: Studies in a Literary Phenomenon,* edited by Gamache and Ian S. MacNiven (Rutherford, N.J.: Fairleigh Dickinson University Press, 1987);

Ángel Ganivet, *Idearium español y El porvenir de España,* edited by Nelson R. Orringer (Salamanca: Almar, 1999);

Sumner Greenfield, "La estilística de Larra: Anticipaciones del 98 y el estilo moderno," in *Divergencias y unidad: Perspectivas sobre la Generación del 98 y Antonio Machado,* edited by John P. Gabriele (Madrid: Orígenes, 1990), pp. 61–79;

Carmen Iglesias, *El pensamiento de Pío Baroja* (Mexico: Antigua Librería Robredo, 1963);

Roberta Johnson, *Crossfire: Philosophy and the Novel in Spain, 1900–1934* (Lexington: University of Kentucky Press, 1993);

C. A. Longhurst, "*Camino de perfección* and the Modernist Aesthetic," in *Hispanic Studies in Honour of Geoffrey Ribbans* (Liverpool: Liverpool University Press, 1992), pp. 191–203;

Longhurst, *Pío Baroja: El mundo es así* (London: Grant & Cutler, 1977);

Longhurst, "The Turn of the Novel in Spain: From Realism to Modernism in Spanish Fiction," in *A Further Range: Studies in Modern Spanish Literature from Galdós to Unamuno,* edited by Anthony H. Clarke (Exeter, U.K.: University of Exeter Press, 1999), pp. 1–43;

José Antonio Maravall, "Historia y novela," in *Baroja y su mundo,* edited by Fernando Baeza (Madrid: Arion, 1961), I: 162–182;

Nelson R. Orringer, "Introduction to Hispanic Modernisms," *Bulletin of Spanish Studies,* 79, no. 2–3 (March–May 2002): 133–148;

José Ortega y Gasset, "Ideas sobre Pío Baroja" and "Una primera vista sobre Baroja," in his *Obras completas* (Madrid: Alianza, 1983), II: 69–125;

Beatrice P. Patt, *Pío Baroja* (New York: Twayne, 1971);

Gonzalo Sobejano, *Nietzsche en España* (Madrid: Gredos, 1967);

Manuel Vázquez Montalbán, "La pervertida sentimentalidad de Pío Baroja," in his *El escriba sentado* (Barcelona: Crítica, 1997), pp. 65–81.

# Vicente Blasco Ibáñez

*(29 January 1867 – 28 January 1928)*

Richard A. Cardwell
*University of Nottingham*

BOOKS: *Fantasías: Leyendas y tradiciones* (Valencia: El
  Correo de Valencia, 1887);
*El conde Garci-Fernández: Novela histórica del siglo X* (Valen-
  cia: El Correo de Valencia, 1888);
*Por la patria! Romeu el guerrillero* (Valencia: El Correo de
  Valencia, 1888);
*El adiós a Schubert. Mademoiselle Norma. Un idilio nihilista.
  Marinoni. La muerte de Capeto* (Valencia: El Correo
  de Valencia, 1888);
*El conde de Balsega* (Valencia, 1889);
*Historia de la revolución española, desde la guerra de la indepen-
  dencia a la restauración en Sagunto, 1808–1874,* 3 vol-
  umes (Barcelona: La Enciclopedia Democrática,
  1890–1892);
*La araña negra,* 2 volumes (Barcelona: Seix, 1892, 1893);
*París: Impresiones de un emigrado* (Valencia: M. Senent,
  1893);
*¡Viva la República! Novela histórica,* 2 volumes (Valencia:
  La Propaganda Democrática, 1893, 1894);
*El juez: Drama en tres actos y en prosa* (Valencia: Printed by
  Ripollés, 1894);
*Los fanáticos: Novela,* 2 volumes (Barcelona: Seix, 1895);
*Arroz y tartana, novela* (Valencia: Sempere, 1895); trans-
  lated by Stuart Edgar Grummon as *The Three
  Roses* (New York: Dutton, 1932);
*Flor de mayo: Novela* (Valencia: Sempere, 1895); trans-
  lated by Arthur Livingston as *The Mayflower (Flor
  de Mayo): A Tale of the Valencian Seashore* (New
  York: Dutton, 1921);
*Cuentos valencianos* (Valencia: Printed by Manuel Alufre,
  1896);
*En el país del arte: Tres meses en Italia* (Valencia: Printed by
  P. de Pellicers, 1896); translated by Frances Doug-
  las as *In the Land of Art (En el país del arte)* (New
  York: Dutton, 1923);
*Caerse al cielo* (Valencia: Printed by Luis Ortega, 1898);
*La barraca: Novela* (Valencia: Promoteo, 1898); edited by
  Hayward Keniston (New York: Holt, 1910);
  translated by Francis Haffkine-Snow and Beatrice
  M. Mekota as *The Cabin (La barraca)* (New York:
  Knopf, 1919); translated by Lester Clark and Eric

*Vicente Blasco Ibáñez (Hulton/Getty Images)*

Farrington Birchall as *The Holding = La barraca,*
  introduction and notes by Patricia McDermott
  (Warminster, U.K.: Aris & Phillips, 1993);
*Cuentos grises* (Valencia: Aguilar, 1899);
*La condenada* (Madrid: Fernando Fé, 1900);

*Entre naranjos: Novela* (Valencia: Sempere, 1900); translated by Isaac Goldberg and Arthur Livingston as *The Torrent (Entre naranjos)* (New York: Dutton, 1921);

*Sónnica la cortesana* (Valencia: Sempere, 1901); translated by Douglas as *Sónnica* (New York: Duffield, 1912);

*Cañas y barro: Novela* (Valencia: Sempere, 1902); translated by Goldberg as *Reeds and Mud (Cañas y barro)* (New York: Dutton, 1928);

*La catedral: Novela* (Valencia: Sempere, 1903); translated by Mrs. W. A. Gillespie as *The Shadow of the Cathedral,* introduction by William Dean Howells (New York: Dutton, 1919);

*El intruso: Novela* (Valencia: Sempere, 1904); translated by Gillespie as *The Intruder (El intruso)* (New York: Dutton, 1928);

*La voluntad de vivir* (Valencia, 1904);

*La bodega: Novela* (Valencia: Sempere, 1905); translated by Goldberg as *La Bodega (The Fruit of the Vine): A Novel* (New York: Dutton, 1919);

*La horda* (Valencia: Sempere, 1905); translated by Mariano Joaquín Llorente as *The Mob (La horda)* (New York: Dutton, 1929);

*La maja desnuda: Novela* (Valencia & Madrid: Sempere, 1906); translated by Keniston as *Woman Triumphant (La maja desnuda)* (New York: Dutton, 1920); translated by Frances Partridge as *The Naked Lady* (London: Elek, 1959);

*Oriente* (Valencia: Sempere, 1907);

*Sangre y arena* (Valencia: Sempere, 1908); translated by Douglas as *The Blood of the Arena* (Chicago: McClurg, 1911);

*Los muertos mandan: Novela* (Valencia: Sempere, 1909); translated by Douglas as *The Dead Command* (New York: Duffield, 1919); original Spanish version republished as *Los muertos mandan (novela),* edited by Frederick Augustus Grant Cowper and John Thomas Lister (New York & London: Harper, 1934);

*Luna Benamor: Novela* (Valencia: Sempere, 1909); translated by Goldberg as *Luna Benamor* (Boston: J. W. Luce, 1919);

*La Argentina y sus grandezas* (Madrid: Editorial Española Americana, 1910);

*Los argonautas: Novela* (Valencia: Prometeo, 1914);

*Historia de la guerra europea de 1914,* 13 volumes (Valencia: Prometeo, 1914–1919);

*Los cuatro jinetes del Apocalípsis: Novela* (Valencia: Prometeo, 1916); translated by Charlotte Brewster Jordan as *The Four Horsemen of the Apocalypse* (New York: Dutton, 1918);

*Mare Nostrum: Novela* (Valencia: Prometeo, 1918); translated by Jordan as *Mare Nostrum (Our Sea): A Novel* (New York: Dutton, 1919);

*Los enemigos de la mujer: Novela* (Valencia: Prometeo, 1919); translated by Irving Brown as *The Enemies of Women (Los enemigos de la mujer)* (New York: Dutton, 1920);

*Artículos sobre Méjico* (Mexico: "El Hogar," 1920);

*El militarismo mejicano: Estudios publicados en los principales diarios de los Estados Unidos* (Valencia: Prometeo, 1920); translated by Livingston and José Padín as *Mexico in Revolution* (New York: Dutton, 1920);

*Vistas sudamericanas,* edited by Carolina Marcial Dorado (Boston & New York: Ginn, 1920);

*El préstamo de la difunta: Novelas* (Valencia: Prometeo, 1921);

*La tierra de todos: Novela* (Valencia: Prometeo, 1922); translated by Leo Ongley as *The Temptress (La tierra de todos)* (New York: Dutton, 1923);

*El paraíso de las mujeres: Novela* (Valencia: Prometeo, 1922);

*La familia del doctor Pedraza* (Madrid: Sucesores de Rivadeneyra, 1922);

*El sol de los muertos* (Madrid: Sucesores de Rivadeneyra, 1923);

*La reina Calafia: Novela* (Valencia: Prometeo, 1923); translated anonymously as *Queen Calafia* (New York: Dutton, 1924);

*Una nación secuestrada: El terror militarista en España* (Paris: J. Dura, 1924); translated by Ongley as *Alfonso XIII Unmasked: The Military Terror in Spain* (New York: Dutton, 1924; London: Eveleigh Nash & Grayson, 1925);

*Novelas de la costa azul* (Valencia: Prometeo, 1924);

*Lo que será la República española: Al país y al ejército* (Valencia: Gutenberg, 1924);

*Por España y contra el rey,* anonymous (Valencia: Gutenberg, 1924);

*La vuelta al mundo, de un novelista,* 3 volumes (Valencia: Prometeo, 1924–1925); translated by Ongley and Livingston as *A Novelist's Tour of the World* (New York: Dutton, 1926);

*El Papa del mar: Novela* (Valencia: Prometeo, 1925); translated by Livingston as *The Pope of the Sea: An Historical Medley* (New York: Dutton, 1927);

*A los pies de Venus (los Borgia): Novela* (Valencia: Prometeo, 1926); translated by Livingston as *The Borgias; or, At the Feet of Venus* (New York: Dutton, 1930);

*Novelas de amor y de muerte* (Valencia: Prometeo, 1927);

*Adaptación al cinematógrafo* (Barcelona: Establecimiento Bistagna, 1928);

*La explosión: Novela* (Madrid: Cosmópolis, 1928);

*Guerra sin cuartel: Novela* (Madrid: Cosmópolis, 1928);

*En el crater del volcán* (Madrid: Cosmópolis, 1928);

*En París* (Madrid: Cosmópolis, 1928);

*En busca del Gran Kan (Cristóbal Colón)* (Valencia: Prometeo, 1929); translated by Livingston as *Unknown Lands: The Story of Columbus* (New York: Dutton, 1929);

*El caballero de la Virgen (Alonso de Ojeda): Novela* (Valencia: Prometeo, 1929); translated by Livingston as *The Knight of the Virgin* (New York: Dutton, 1930; London: Butterworth, 1933);

*El fantasma de las alas de oro: Novela* (Valencia: Prometeo, 1930); translated by Livingston as *The Phantom with Wings of Gold: A Novel* (New York: Dutton, 1931);

*Biografía de don Hugo de Moncada* (Valencia: Lo Rat-Penat, 1933);

*Estudios literarios* (Valencia: Prometeo, 1934);

*Discursos literarios* (Valencia: Prometeo, 1966).

**Editions and Collections:** *Obras completas,* 40 volumes (Valencia: Prometeo, 1923–1934);

*El préstamo de la difunta y otros cuentos,* edited by George Baer Fundenburg and John F. Klein (New York & London: Century, 1925);

*Siete cuentos,* edited by Sturgis E. Leavitt (New York: Holt, 1926);

*La barraca,* edited by Paul T. Manchester (New York: Macmillan, 1933);

*Obras completas: Con una nota bibliográfica,* 3 volumes (Madrid: Aguilar, 1946);

*La voluntad de vivir: Novela póstuma* (Barcelona: Planeta, 1953);

*Contra la restauración: Periodismo político, 1895–1904,* edited by Paul Smith (Madrid: Nuestra Cultura, 1978);

*Los mejores artículos de Blasco Ibáñez,* edited by Smith (Valencia: Prometeo, 1982).

**Editions in English:** *The Last Lion and Other Tales,* edited by Mariano Joaquín Llorente (Boston: Four Seas, 1919)—comprises "The Last Lion," "The Toad," "Compassion," "The Windfall," "Luxury," and "Rabies";

*Blood and Sand,* translated by Mrs. W. A. Gillespie (New York: Dutton, 1919);

*The Old Woman of the Movies and Other Stories* (New York: Dutton, 1925)—comprises "The Old Woman of the Movies," "The Hero," "The Widow's Loan," "A Shot in the Night," "Sunset," "The Four Sons of Eve," "The Caburé Feather," "The Serenade," "The General's Automobile," "Martínez's Insurrection," "A Life Sentence," "A Serbian Night," "The Monster," "The Sleeping Car Porter," and "The Mad Virgins";

*Blood and Sand,* translated by Frances Partridge (New York: Ungar, 1958).

TRANSLATIONS: Onesimo Reclus and Eliseo Reclus, *Novísíma geografía universal,* 6 volumes (Madrid: Española-Americana, 1907);

Ernesto Lavisse and Alfredo Rambaud, eds., *Novísima historia universal, desde los tiempos prehistóricos hasta nuestros días,* 16 volumes (Madrid: Española-Americana, 1908–1910);

J. C. Mardrus, trans., *El libro de las mil noches y una noche,* 23 volumes, translated into Spanish by Blasco Ibáñez (Valencia: Prometeo, 1915).

Novelist, short-story writer, historian, political essayist, travel writer, playwright, and translator, Vicente Blasco Ibáñez was the most controversial Spanish writer of the early twentieth century and the best-known Spanish novelist internationally after Miguel de Cervantes. While academic scholarship would cite Benito Pérez Galdós, Leopoldo Alas, or Pío Baroja as superior novelists at the end of the nineteenth century, the sales of Blasco Ibáñez's books, both in the original Spanish and in translation (into languages that include English, French, Chinese, German, Italian, Polish, and Russian), suggest that he had a far greater popular appeal. His reputation abroad was enhanced in 1921 by the movie version of his *Los cuatro jinetes del Apocalipsis* (1916; translated as *The Four Horsemen of the Apocalypse,* 1918), one of Hollywood's most successful early motion pictures. The movie versions of *Los enemigos de la mujer* (1919; translated as *The Enemies of Women,* 1920) in 1923 and *Mare Nostrum* (1918; translated as *Mare Nostrum [Our Sea],* 1919) in 1926 created a renewed market for his novels, which sold in the hundreds of thousands, while those of his contemporaries Baroja, Enrique Martínez Ruiz, Ramón Pérez de Ayala, and Miguel de Unamuno were published in limited editions. This popularity was gained in the face of hostility from the conservative political, literary, and critical establishments that continued throughout his career and for nearly fifty years after his death.

Blasco Ibáñez was born in Valencia on 29 January 1867. His Aragonese parents, Gaspar Blasco Teruel and Ramona Ibáñez Martínez, owned a successful grocery in the old quarter of the city and a country house in Burjasot on the *huerta,* the fertile plain that surrounds Valencia and is the setting for many of Blasco Ibáñez's novels. He received a Catholic education in the Escuelas Pías and was sent in 1875 to the Colegio Levantino in Valencia. Despite this privileged childhood, which he shared with a younger sister, Blasco Ibáñez rejected the conservative values of his parents. At fourteen he wrote the first of fifteen stories in the style of the still fashionable historical romance: "La torre de Boatella" (The Boatella Tower) appeared in November 1882 in the almanac *Lo Rat-Penat,* named

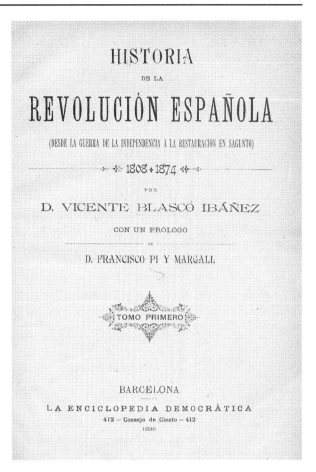

*Decorated title page and title page for the first volume of Blasco Ibáñez's three-volume (1890–1892)*
*history of Spain from its conquest by Napoleon Bonaparte to the end of the First Republic*
*(University of Nebraska Library)*

after the bat that appears on the Valencia city arms. At sixteen he dropped out of the University of Valencia and ran away to Madrid with the manuscript for a lengthy historical novel. Scorned by the Madrid publishers, he took the post of amanuensis to the serial novelist Manuel González y Fernández. While the heyday of the historical romance in serialized form had passed, the genre was still popular, and Blasco Ibáñez published a dozen serials of his own between 1888 and 1892. He frequented the left-wing and revolutionary clubs in Madrid and made his first contact with the police, who constantly harassed political agitators. He also launched two short-lived political journals.

On his return to Valencia in February 1884, Blasco Ibáñez published a poem advocating the execution of the crowned heads of Europe starting with the king of Spain. He was arrested, tried, and sentenced to six months in prison, but the sentence was suspended because of his youth.

The republican experiment had collapsed in 1874 with the restoration of the Bourbon dynasty, but the

death of King Alfonso XII in 1885 offered the opportunity for a revival. Blasco Ibáñez became a disciple of the idealistic republican program enunciated by Francisco Pi y Margall and Manuel Ruiz Zorrilla and was soon engaging in confrontations with the police in the streets of Valencia. In 1889 he received a master's degree in civil and canonical law from the University of Valencia and married Maria Blasco del Cacho; they had five children: a daughter who died three days after being born, three sons, and another daughter. The year of his marriage he founded a radical weekly, *La Bandera federal* (The Federal-Republican Banner). He became so involved in political activity at the university that in 1890 he was forced to flee to Paris to escape prosecution as an antimonarchist conspirator. He returned to Valencia the following year. In Paris, inspired by the radical circles in which he moved and by reading the novels of Eugène Sue, he had written *La araña negra* (1892, 1893, The Black Spider) and *¡Viva la República!* (1893, 1894, Long Live the Republic!), both of which received a hostile critical reception. The first novel is harshly anticlerical and anti-Jesuit; the second relates the struggle and death of a young man for the ideals of the French Revolution. While in Paris he had also written the three-volume *Historia de la revolución española, desde la guerra de la independencia a la restauración en Sagunto, 1808–1874* (1890–1892, History of the Spanish Revolution, from the War of Independence to the Restoration in Sagunto, 1808–1874), which had considerable success in spite of negative reviews by the conservative critical establishment. In 1893 he published a volume of essays, *París: Impresiones de un emigrado* (Paris: Impressions of an Emigrant).

In 1894 Blasco Ibáñez founded the daily newspaper *El Pueblo* (The People) to provide a voice for his own views and those of the Valencian masses. He spent sixteen to eighteen hours a day on the paper, often producing issues single-handedly. In 1895 he was imprisoned for a month; on his release he participated in demonstrations against the war in Cuba and the promulgation of a state of military siege in Valencia, then fled into self-imposed exile in Italy. There he wrote the first of his travel books, *En el país del arte: Tres meses en Italia* (1896, In the Land of Art: Three Months in Italy; translated as *In the Land of Art [En el país del arte]*, 1923). On his return to Valencia he came into renewed conflict with the authorities and was sentenced at a court-martial to two years' imprisonment. The sentence was commuted in March 1897 on the condition that he move to Madrid. Despite being under police supervision and distant from Valencia and thus unable to campaign or mobilize his supporters, he was overwhelmingly elected in March 1898 to represent Valencia in the Cortes (national parliament). His first act in the Cortes was to denounce the war against the United States and the occupation of Cuba, as well as working conditions in Valencia. Although being a member of the Cortes should have afforded him immunity from arrest, he was imprisoned on several occasions, including a detention on 27 October 1899 from which he was released on 1 November after a massive public outcry. He was reelected in 1899, 1901, 1903, 1905, and 1907. From the late 1890s to 1905 he campaigned against corruption and gambling and for greater access to education for the poor. He was constantly harassed by the local authorities and was detained no fewer than thirty times; *El Pueblo* was frequently suppressed or ceased publication while its owner languished in a cell in the San Gregorio prison.

During these years Blasco Ibáñez published his "Valencian cycle" of six novels and two collections of short stories. In the novel *Arroz y tartana* (1895, Rice and a Horse-Carriage; translated as *The Three Roses,* 1932) the twice-widowed Manuela rears her children in luxury but undermines the family silk business through her social climbing and extravagance. Attempting to rescue the family fortunes, her son speculates in the stock market. Manuela is forced to become the mistress of a wealthy man. When her son discovers her secret, he has a mental breakdown. News of the stock-market crash destroys his will to live, and he dies broken-hearted and repenting his follies.

The title of the novel *Flor de mayo* (1895; translated as *The Mayflower [Flor de Mayo]: A Tale of the Valencian Seashore,* 1921) is the name of a boat purchased by two brothers of a Valencia fishing family with the proceeds of a successful tobacco-smuggling expedition to Algeria. Tonet's neglected wife tells El Retor that he has been cuckolded for years by his brother. The novel ends with nature acting in sympathy with the torment of El Retor as a violent storm sends the ship inexorably toward the rocky coastline.

In *La barraca* (1898, The Holding; translated as *The Cabin [La barraca],* 1919) the poor immigrant Batiste is persuaded to take over a plot of land that has been boycotted for ten years by the local peasants because of the unjust treatment of one of their fellows, *Tío* (Uncle) Barret, who was evicted for unpaid debts by a rapacious landlord and, maddened by the loss of his holding, murdered his tormentor and died in prison. The trials of Batiste, which include an attack on his horse and his daughter and the death of his infant son, are set against a brooding portrayal of the *huerta* as an animalistic presence that seems to conspire against human beings. The epic struggle between Batiste and the roguish leader of the peasants, Pimentó, ends with the failure of Batiste's hopes and the death of his antagonist.

In *Entre naranjos* (1900; Among the Orange Trees; translated as *The Torrent [Entre naranjos],* 1921) Rafael Brull, a member of the Cortes and the son of the local political boss, meets his childhood sweetheart, Leonora, after many years of separation. Leonora, who was trained abroad as an opera singer and has been the mistress of many powerful men, has returned to the *huerta* seeking peace among the orange groves. Her hard attitude toward men is gradually softened by the influence of the beauties of nature, especially the profusion of orange blossoms. Rafael and Leonora begin an affair but are soon exposed to gossip and scandal. The lovers flee, but a friend persuades Brull to abandon the relationship. He sends a cowardly letter of separation, and Leonora returns to her cosmopolitan European haunts. They meet again eight years later, when the aging Brull is at the height of his career; he is still infatuated with her, but the moment has passed. Social mores have destroyed love.

The leading Spanish novelist of the day, Pérez Galdós, presided over a banquet in Blasco Ibáñez's honor in 1900. That same year the translation of *La barraca* into French brought him international recognition.

The next novel in the Valencia cycle, *Sónnica la cortesana* (1901, Sónnica the Courtesan; translated as *Sónnica*, 1912), is an historical work about the heroic but unsuccessful resistance of the city of Saguntum (today Sagunto), near present-day Valencia, against Hannibal's Carthaginian army in 219 B.C. The final novel of the Valencian cycle is *Cañas y barro* (1902; translated as *Reeds and Mud [Cañas y barro]*, 1928). *Tío* (Uncle) Paloma is an old fisherman nostalgic for freer times before modern customs, laws, and agricultural methods. His grandson Tonet, who is averse to the hard labor of fishing and growing rice, wins the choicest fishing ground in the annual lottery and enlists the financial assistance of *Tío* Cañamel, a rich debauchee. Tonet is attracted to Cañamel's wife, Neleta, and begins an affair with her after her husband's death. Like Leonora in *Entre naranjos*, Neleta is a powerful and sexual woman with green eyes and golden hair who is, inevitably, destructive to the men who become involved with her. This archetype appeared in many works at the end of the nineteenth century, especially in French decadent novels. Neleta becomes pregnant; when the child is born, she tells Tonet to go to Valencia and leave the baby there as a foundling. Instead, he tosses the infant into the lake. Later, he finds the decaying corpse and, grief stricken, commits suicide.

The short-story collections of the Valencian cycle are *Cuentos valencianos* (1900, Valencian Tales) and *La condenada* (1899, The Condemned Woman). All of the works in the cycle except *Cañas y barro* first appeared in serial form in *El Pueblo*.

Aside from *Sónnica la cortesana*, the novels of the Valencian cycle are set in the near past and present and in the city or on the *huerta* outside Valencia. Valencian critics have attested to the accuracy of names, places, and customs depicted. In *Arroz y tartana*, for example, the pre-Lenten carnival, the *Fallas* (fireworks festival of 19 March), the Corpus Christi procession, and the *Feria de Julio* (July Bull Festival) are described. Portrayals of character types, festivals, and vignettes of provincial life form the basis of the nineteenth-century realist experiment in the novel. Blasco Ibáñez's works also bear the imprint of the parallel Spanish tradition of *costumbrismo*, a sanitized depiction of pastoral life seen through the prism of a conservative ideology that seeks to arrest political and religious progress. Thus, some of the harsh realities of country life are subordinated to an Arcadian or Edenic vision of the *huerta*. At odds with this form of literary representation is naturalism, a feature in Blasco Ibáñez's works that has led to the label "the Spanish Emile Zola" being applied to him. Naturalism is based on a revolutionary outlook and incurred

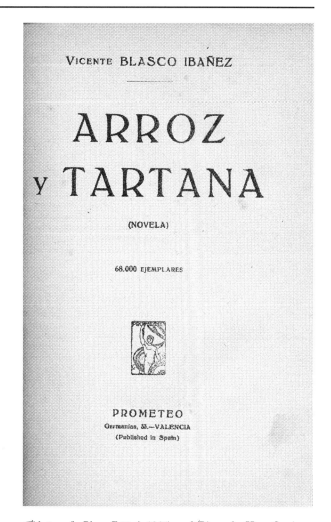

VICENTE BLASCO IBAÑEZ

# ARROZ y TARTANA

(NOVELA)

68.000 EJEMPLARES

PROMETEO
Germanias, 33.—VALENCIA
(Published in Spain)

*Title page for Blasco Ibáñez's 1895 novel (Rice and a Horse-Carriage, translated as* The Three Roses, *1932), about a woman who undermines her family's silk business through her social climbing and extravagance (University of Colorado at Boulder Library)*

the hostility of reactionary circles, especially in Catholic Spain. *Flor de mayo*, *La barraca*, and *Arroz y tartana* portray the hardships endured by the fisherfolk on the beach and the Albufera lagoon and by the peasants on the *huerta*, all of whom are victims of absentee landlords, the law, oppressive rents, and eviction, while *Entre naranjos* is set against the background of local and national politics and provides firsthand insights into political patronage and corruption. Many of the novels of the Valencian cycle end on a note of desolation and failed hopes. The structure is circular: *Arroz y tartana* ends with the old man who had started the silk business contemplating the ruin of his life's efforts as he stands on the spot where he had been found abandoned as a child; *Flor de mayo* begins and ends with a shipwreck; *La barraca* begins with dawn breaking over a ruin that is

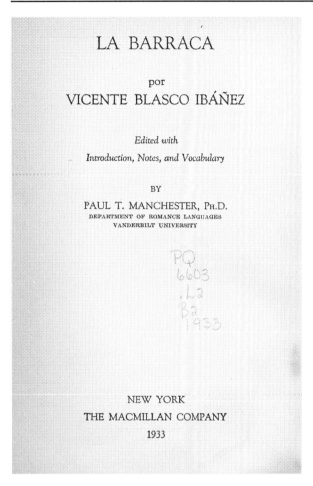

LA BARRACA

por

VICENTE BLASCO IBÁÑEZ

Edited with

Introduction, Notes, and Vocabulary

BY

PAUL T. MANCHESTER, PH.D.
DEPARTMENT OF ROMANCE LANGUAGES
VANDERBILT UNIVERSITY

PQ
6603
.L2
B2
1933

NEW YORK
THE MACMILLAN COMPANY
1933

Title page for a U.S. edition of Blasco Ibáñez's 1898 novel
(The Holding, translated as The Cabin, 1919), about
a poor immigrant who takes over a plot of land that has
been boycotted for ten years by the local peasants because
of an injustice committed by the landlord against
a former tenant (Thomas Cooper Library,
University of South Carolina)

restored over the course of the narrative and ends with dawn breaking over the ashes of the building. Characters are portrayed in deterministic terms as people are reduced to the level of beasts by alcohol, powerful sexual urges, gambling, infirm will, or failure to adapt to their milieu. Nature itself conspires to beguile, to menace, and often to destroy the characters: in *Entre naranjos* the perfume of the orange blossoms precipitates the maddened passions of Rafael and Leonora, and those passions lead to their tragic separation; the menacing aspect of the *huerta* in *La barraca* and of the Albufera in *Arroz y tartana* have been compared by Sherman H. Eoff and Richard A. Cardwell to depictions of nature in Zola's *Germinal* (1885; translated, 1885) and *La Terre* (1887; translated as *The Soil: A Realistic Novel*, 1888). Many of the descriptions of the Spanish landscape echo those of the African jungle evoked in the travel books Blasco Ibáñez was reading at the time.

Blasco Ibáñez's early novels, then, reflect the whole range of literary modes available to the writer of the late nineteenth and early twentieth centuries: realism, naturalism, *costumbrismo,* and romance; Blasco Ibáñez used all of them to create an amalgam that was popular with the reading public. But his firebrand political activism–his constant attacks in the Cortes, in the pages of *El Pueblo,* and in the streets on the ruling elites and on Restoration politics–finds no echo in the pages of these novels. He never mobilizes his fiction to serve his revolutionary vision; nowhere in the Valencia cycle or in his later works is there an indication of a political program. Instead, along with naturalistic pessimism, he offers a nostalgic view of an imaginary former time of rural harmony, a supposed lost past of the early nineteenth century before the disentailment of Church lands and the rise of the bourgeois landlords. In *La barraca* the struggle is not, as the novel seems initially to indicate, between absentee landlords and exploited tenants but between the peasants themselves: the natives and the interloper from Aragón. A blind shepherd, a prophet of the tragedy to come, is the spokesman for a lost preindustrial and prebourgeois period when the Church owned the lands and times were better. The same outlook is evoked in *Cañas y barro* when *Tío* Tomba nostalgically recalls the age of the aristocracy, an era before binding contracts, bailiffs, land laws, and enclosures, when the peasant could roam freely. Such sentiments are hardly radical or even republican; they might reasonably be interpreted as conservative, even Carlist. Carlism–from Don Carlos María Isidro de Borbón, Conde de Molina, who sought the throne on the death of his brother Ferdinand VII in 1832 in place of the legitimate successor, the infant princess Isabella (later Isabella II)–was a profoundly conservative, Catholic, and absolutist political creed that sought to return Spain to a quasi-feudal government of throne, aristocracy, and altar. The province of Valencia, like many rural areas in Spain in the nineteenth century, was home to many Carlists, including Blasco Ibáñez's father.

After completing *Cañas y barro,* Blasco Ibáñez began writing a sequence of four novels that are concerned with social issues but, again, include little that might form the basis for a program of political action. *La catedral* (1903; translated as *The Shadow of the Cathedral,* 1919) depicts the stultifying effects of Catholicism in Spain at the end of the nineteenth century. Gabriel Luna, exhausted by years of anarchist activity, comes home to Toledo to find spiritual peace. The narrative is interrupted by lengthy digressions–the Gothic cathedral of Toledo is portrayed in astonishing detail, down to the sensual sculptures of the medieval craftsmen hidden in dark corners, and a conversation between Luna and the chapel master introduces a long disquisition on church music; and Gabriel's declaration of love for his niece, the reformed prostitute Sagrario, as Ludwig van Beethoven's *Es muss sein* (1826, It Must Be) is played on the cathedral organ smacks of the romances Blasco Ibáñez composed during his Madrid exile. Gabriel shares with the lower classes the anarchist idealism he has gleaned from the writings of Pierre-Joseph Proudhon, Petr Kropotkin, and Mikhail Bakunin, but his vision of social justice and redistribution of wealth goes badly wrong when his disciples take practical action by stealing the treasures of the cathedral. Gabriel attempts to stop the theft and is dealt a fatal blow: he is killed not by the exploiters but by the exploited. The novel drew sharp criticism for the anticlerical views expressed in it.

*La catedral* had been inspired by a visit to Toledo, and Blasco Ibáñez's next novel, *El intruso* (1904; translated as *The Intruder [El intruso]*, 1928), originated in a series of political rallies he attended in the Basque country. The work is set in the environs of the industrial city of Bilbao; the "intruder" is an immigrant worker whose presence is resented by the devout and nationalistic Basques in the same way that the Aragonese Batiste is resented by the men of the *huerta* in *La barraca*. But the locals here are led by the powerful and wealthy Society of Jesus. To Dr. Aresti, the spokesman for the author's views, the influence of the Jesuits is insidious; he suggests that they are the true "intruders." The liberal physician, who serves the poor and the exploited miners, is pitted against the Jesuits, who destroy love relationships and independent thought. The harsh working conditions in the mines, foundries, and shipyards are vividly described. But Blasco Ibáñez romanticizes the Basque peasants, who support the fanatical religious and conservative views of the pretender Carlos. The liberal program is never clearly established; nostalgia for the preindustrial rhythms of the countryside seems more attractive than radical action to remedy social ills.

In *La voluntad de vivir* (1904, The Will to Live) the "will to live" is embodied by Valdivia, an aging scientist who believes that one should live "come what may, for the pleasure of life." He meets the exotic golden-eyed Lucha (the name means "Struggle") at a diplomatic soiree and embarks on a passionate secret relationship with her. Like Leonora in *Entre naranjos* and Neleta in *Cañas y barro*, Lucha is another example of the femme fatale of decadent and semipornographic novels of the period. The affair swings from violent embraces to jealousy. After separating from Lucha, Valdivia returns to spy on her, and they quarrel once more. Faced with permanent separation, he commits suicide. The will to live is destroyed by the very passions that engender it.

Cover for Blasco Ibáñez's 1904 novel (translated as The Intruder, 1928), about the pernicious influence of the Jesuits on exploited Basque miners and foundry workers (University of Oklahoma Library)

(Valdivia was based on a real person whose identity was so recognizable that Blasco Ibáñez decided to destroy the entire print run of the novel. On 27 April 1907 he wrote to his publisher and asked that the novel be pulped. It was republished from a single surviving copy in 1953 with the subtitle *Novela póstuma* [Posthumous Novel].)

In *La bodega* (1905, The Wine Cellar; translated as *La bodega [The Fruit of the Vine]*, 1919) the villain, Luis Dupont, a typical Andalusian *señorito* (young upper-class playboy), is the nephew of the owner of the finest winery in Jerez de la Frontera; he is pitted against Fernando Salvatierra (the surname means "saver of land"), who expresses the author's ideas. The Civil Guard breaks up a strike, resulting in a bloodbath for the workers—including the judicial murder of a farm boy. But the conflict between capital and labor is relegated to a secondary concern by the story of Dupont's seduction of

*Cover for Blasco Ibáñez's 1905 novel (The Wine Cellar, translated as* The Fruit of the Vine, *1919) in which the playboy nephew of a vineyard owner is murdered by the lover of a girl he has seduced (Wesleyan University Library)*

María de la Luz and his murder by her lover, Rafael Montenegro. An interpolated story about Mari-Cruz, a gypsy girl who is trampled to death by a bull freed by Dupont, is a further distraction from the political theme. Blasco Ibáñez restates his naturalist view that the spirit of defiance has been exhausted by alcohol and exploitation and that the old order will remain unchallenged.

The last novel of the second cycle, *La horda* (1905; translated as *The Mob [La horda],* 1929), is set in Madrid. By this time Blasco Ibáñez had settled in the capital and was able to draw on firsthand experience of the slums and workshops on the periphery of the city. The protagonist, Isidro Maltrana, is intelligent and educated but of humble origins. His lover, Feliciana, dies in childbirth, and her corpse is sent to a medical school for dissection; her father, a poacher, is shot by the royal guards. But once more, no program for reform is

offered. José, Isidro's stepfather, points out that priests cannot harm the sensible ordinary man and that the clergy and the military are necessary for a stable society, and Isidro does not dissent from this viewpoint. Any vestige of radicalism Blasco Ibáñez possessed seems to have evaporated.

In Blasco Ibáñez's first two cycles the characters are motivated by basic emotions and react to their circumstances; little exploration is made of their inner lives. Thus, while powerfully evoked, they remain two-dimensional. Blasco Ibáñez had made an attempt to remedy this weakness in *La voluntad de vivir* and strives to do so in the sequence of novels that begins in 1906 with *La maja desnuda* (1906, The Naked Belle; translated as *Woman Triumphant [La maja desnuda],* 1920). Powerful passions, especially love and jealousy, form the central theme of the cycle, which reflects Blasco Ibáñez's experiences of high society in Madrid and in visits to other parts of Spain. *La maja desnuda* was inspired by Francisco Goya's painting of that title (1798–1805), which Blasco Ibáñez had seen in the Prado. The painter Mariano Renovales is obsessed by the similarity between Goya's nude and the body of his own wife. Disgusted by Mariano's portrayal of her, she prudishly destroys the canvas. Mariano then takes her former school friend as a mistress and longs for his wife's death. After a long illness exacerbated by jealousy, she does die; but he is not free, since he experiences recurrent visions of her. He finds a model who might allow him to re-create his wife's image; but when she appears in the deceased woman's dress, he collapses into insanity and ultimately dies.

Blasco Ibáñez was made a member of the French Legion of Honor on 11 December 1906. In August 1907 he set out on a tour that took him to France, Switzerland, Germany, Austria-Hungary, Italy, and Constantinople (modern-day Istanbul, Turkey), where he was entertained by the sultan of the Ottoman Empire. Returning to Spain, he narrowly escaped injury in a railway accident. He described his experiences in the travel book *Oriente,* published at the end of the year.

In 1908 Blasco Ibáñez resigned from the Cortes and began planning a lecture tour of South America. That same year he published the novel *Sangre y arena* (Blood and Sand; translated as *The Blood of the Arena,* 1911). *Sangre y arena* is like a Greek tragedy: once the events are set in motion, the outcome is inevitable; and the hero is the victim of his own gifts. Blasco Ibáñez did research for the novel by making many visits to the corrida and talking to bullfighters. The work is set in Seville, and the author indulges in long descriptions of the city, the Corpus Christi procession, and the bullfight. Juan Gallardo, the son of a poor shoemaker, has risen through determination and courage to the height of fame, fortune, and honor as a matador. Although he is happily married, he enters into an adulterous relationship with Doña Sol ("Sunlight"), the niece of a bull breeder. Another femme fatale, Doña Sol entangles and plays with her lover like a spider with its prey and callously abandons him. In emotional turmoil, Juan performs badly in the arena. Jeered by the crowd who once adored him, he is gored to death as Sol watches.

*Los muertos mandan* (1909; translated as *The Dead Command,* 1919) returns to the naturalist atmosphere of the Valencian cycle. Jaime Ferrer, the last of a once wealthy noble family, is frustrated in his search for fulfillment by the weight of heredity and tradition. When his attempt to marry a wealthy Jewish woman is thwarted, he seeks to escape the legacy of his dead ancestors by living as a peasant. Yet, even here, family connections stand in the path to love. When he is shot by a rival and nursed to health by his beloved, Margarida, he realizes that the dead do not command; rather, life and love do. In a sense, this novel offers a reply to *La voluntad de vivir.* The social problems of marriage across class and race are set against superb descriptions of the Baleeric Islands: Blasco Ibáñez had first visited Majorca in 1902 and, ever the documentary realist, had returned in 1908 to gather material for his novel. But his descriptions are lyrical and at times as symbolic as the prose of his fellow Levantine, Gabriel Miró.

Blasco Ibáñez arrived in South America in 1909. His tour of more than 120 lectures across Argentina, Paraguay, and Chile was a success. He returned to Spain in 1910 and spent the next six months writing an enormous history, *La Argentina y sus grandezas* (1910, Argentina and Its Splendors). His labor on the project was so great that on one occasion he fainted in the street. In return for writing the history, the Argentine government had offered Blasco Ibáñez a land concession in Patagonia. He returned to Argentina on 8 June 1909 with a shipload of would-be settlers hoping to tame the cold, dry terrain. At the same time he undertook a similar venture in the tropical Corrientes province, making the four-day journey between the two sites each week. By 1913, faced with an economic downturn, he put his concessions up for sale and went to Paris to resume his career as a writer. That same year he founded a publishing house, Editorial Prometeo (Prometheus), in Valencia that produced translations of works by Bakunin, Kropotkin, Karl Marx, Friedrich Engels, David Friedrich Strauss, Joseph-Ernest Renan, and Friedrich Nietzsche. When the sale of his South American holdings fell through, he returned to Argentina to salvage what he could. Abandoning the settlers, he embarked on the last German liner to Europe before the outbreak of World War I in the summer of 1914. The journey provided material for his next novel, *Los*

*argonautas* (1914, The Argonauts). His illustrated *Historia de la guerra europea de 1914* (1914–1919, History of the European War of 1914) was published in weekly supplements in Valencia and collected in thirteen volumes, and he toured Spain speaking on behalf of the Allied cause.

In 1915 Blasco Ibáñez returned to Paris and began writing *Los cuatro jinetes del Apocalípsis;* published the following year, it became his best-known novel. Set on the Argentine pampas, the work is the tale of an émigré family, drawn from three nations, that becomes embroiled in the war. In part the novel speaks for the Allied cause, but it deals principally with the ties of family, love, and loyalty at a moment when decisions cannot be clear-cut or easy. The novel offers Blasco Ibáñez's familiar blend of realism—based on firsthand experience of the pampas and a visit to the Marne front in the company of the French prime minister, Raymond Poincaré—and romance, and it is deeply pessimistic in its suggestion that the "four horsemen" of War, Famine, Pestilence, and Death will reappear. The 1918 English translation brought Blasco Ibáñez international acclaim. Within two years more than a million hardback copies of the Spanish and English versions had been sold, a record for the time; the rights for the 1921 movie brought Blasco Ibáñez $200,000—equivalent to $10,000,000 in 2005 dollars. (The novel was filmed again in 1962, with the setting changed to World War II.)

Blasco Ibáñez wrote *Mare Nostrum* between August and December 1917. Published in 1918, it is the story of Ulises Ferragut, an adventurer who supplies the German navy with submarines in the Mediterranean during World War I. Blasco Ibáñez had experimented with symbolism timidly in *La barraca* and more boldly in *Los argonautas,* but in this novel the symbolism is extensive: the plot recalls the voyages of Odysseus (in Latin, Ulysses) in Homer's *Odyssey,* and characters based on Telemachus, Penelope, and Circe also appear. Nordic mythology is represented in the person of yet another femme fatale, Freya Talberg, the German spy who persuades Ferragut to supply her country's navy; her introduction is juxtaposed with a description of predatory sea creatures.

The first relatively balanced assessment of Blasco Ibáñez from a member of the conservative establishment came in 1918 in Julio Cejador y Frauca's *Historia de la lengua y literatura castellana* (1915–1922, History of Castilian Language and Literature). A professor of Spanish at the University of Madrid, the former Jesuit priest was scathing in his criticism of Blasco Ibáñez's portrayal of the clergy and Catholicism in his novels. Nevertheless, Cejador y Frauca allowed that Blasco

VICENTE BLASCO IBAÑEZ

# LA HORDA

— NOVELA —

F. SEMPERE Y COMPAÑÍA, EDITORES

Calle del Palomar, 10 || Olmo, 4 (Sucursal)
VALENCIA || MADRID

192307

*Title page for Blasco Ibáñez's 1905 novel (translated as* The Mob, *1929) about a man of humble origins who accepts the injustices society inflicts on people of his class (William T. Young Library, University of Kentucky)*

Ibáñez was a writer of note, especially for a mass readership.

The final novel of Blasco Ibáñez's World War I cycle, *Los enemigos de la mujer,* appeared in 1919. A group of intelligent and gifted men gather in a neutral country and agree to forswear the company of women for the duration of hostilities out of male solidarity, friendship, and economic concerns. Inevitably, one of them, the exiled Russian prince Miguel, is attracted to the beautiful, strong, and promiscuous Duchess Alicia. A subplot about Alicia's son, Jorge, a prisoner of war in Germany, furnishes the pretext for descriptions of the conflict and an approving mention of the entry of the United States into the war.

*Sangre y arena* had been filmed in Spain in 1916, but the Hollywood version of 1922, *Blood and Sand,* starring Rudolph Valentino, was much more successful and increased Blasco Ibáñez's worldwide fame and his wealth. That year he published the novel *La tierra de todos* (Land for All; translated as *The Temptress [La tierra de todos],* 1923), which is based on his experiences in Argentina. Another femme fatale, the beautiful, seductive, and agile Elena, undermines a new colony by creating jealousy among the male settlers. The symbolic frame—like her namesake, Helen of Troy, Elena begins a war among the men—and Blasco Ibáñez's naturalistic depiction of the characters' unconscious drives are interwoven to create a powerful narrative of human weakness and degradation.

*La reina Calafia* (1923; translated as *Queen Calafia,* 1924) is set in California in the 1920s and in an imagined period in the early 1600s. As Blasco Ibáñez relates in a long disquisition in chapter 3, the title is taken from the Amazon ruler of the island of California in the chivalric romance *Los quatro libros del Virtuoso cauallero Amadís de Gaula* (1508, The Four Books of the Virtuous Cavalier Amadís of Gaul), attributed to Garci Rodríguez de Montalvo. Like her Amazon counterpart and Blasco Ibáñez's earlier femmes fatales, Concha Caballos, a descendant of the early settlers of California, is beautiful and strong: she incites jealousy that provokes duels, and she knocks a suitor to the ground and places her stiletto-heeled shoe on his face. But by the end of the novel she has been forced to come to terms with the aging process and her maternal feelings.

After Alfonso XIII acquiesced in the establishment of the military dictatorship of Miguel Primo de Rivera in 1923, Blasco Ibáñez went into self-imposed exile in Menton on the French Riviera and joined other intellectuals (including Unamuno, who was in exile in Paris) in condemning the king's action. His clandestinely circulated pamphlets *Lo que será la República española: Al país y al ejército* (1924, What the Spanish Republic Should Be: To the Country and to the Army) and *Por España y contra el rey* (1924, For Spain and against the King) resulted in an orchestrated campaign by the Spanish conservative press to defame him and his work. The titles of two pamphlets published in response indicate the conservative outrage: *El novelista que vendió a su patria ó Tartarín, revolucionario: Una triste historia de actualidad* (1924, The Novelist Who Sold His Homeland; or, Tartarín, Revolutionary: A Sad True Story) and *Blasco Ibáñez la vuelta al mundo en 80.000 dóllars* (1924, Blasco Ibáñez: Around the World for 80,000 Dollars). The attacks provoked Blasco Ibáñez to have this essay republished commercially in Paris, to avoid the Spanish censors, in 1925.

Blasco Ibáñez's wife died on 21 January 1925. In October of the same year he married Elena Ortuzar, who had been a close friend of Blasco Ibáñez and his first wife.

After extensive research, Blasco Ibáñez wrote *El Papa del mar* (1925; translated as *The Pope of the Sea: An*

*Historical Medley,* 1927). The story of the Borgia family and the struggles in the papal courts after Clement V in the early fourteenth century is related through a series of lectures given by a modern historian, Claudio Borja (his name is the Spanish version of Borgia), who is romantically attached to a wealthy widow, Rosaura Salcedo de Pineda. Places visited by the couple provoke symbolic references to Richard Wagner's opera *Tannhäuser* (1845). The story of Pedro de Luna, who became the schismatic Pope Benedict XIII of Avignon, is related at appropriate intervals to underline the main theme. In *A los pies de Venus (los Borgia)* (1926; translated as *The Borgias; or, At the Feet of Venus,* 1930) the history of the Borgia court is set alongside the cooling love affair of Claudio and Rosaura. The novel concludes with a reference to the part played by Pope Alexander VI (Rodrigo Borgia) in the division of the New World between Portugal and Spain.

Blasco Ibáñez died in Menton on 28 January 1928 of extreme fatigue and heart failure. Three more novels were published posthumously. In *En busca del Gran Kan (Cristóbal Colón)* (1929, In Search of the Great Khan [Christopher Columbus]; translated as *Unknown Lands: The Story of Columbus,* 1929) the discovery of the New World serves as the background for the love story of the Christian Fernando and the Jew Lucero. Medieval attitudes to the ethnic and religious divide are explored, as are the characters of Christopher Columbus and Martín Alonso Pinzón, the captain of Columbus's caravel the *Pinta.* The main focus is on Columbus, on whom Fortune smiles before abandoning him to a lonely exile and death, unaware of the significance of his discovery. *El caballero de la Virgen (Alonso de Ojeda)* (1929; translated as *The Knight of the Virgin,* 1930) relates the adventures of Alonso de Ojeda, a captain on Columbus's second voyage, as he searches for gold and fame. Fernando and Lucero are now the founders of the first successful settlement in the New World and are happy and fulfilled. The novel makes clear that in Blasco Ibáñez's view the natives and the creole offspring of the conquistadors have more right to the New World than do the European interlopers. *El fantasma de las alas de oro* (1930; translated as *The Phantom with Wings of Gold,* 1931) is set in the Monte Carlo casino and weaves a tangled web of intrigue around a love that is ultimately unfulfilled. The heroine, a woman of strong will and powerful sexuality, is the last in the line of femmes fatales who appear in Blasco Ibáñez's novels from 1903 onward.

The Spanish press continued its campaign of vilification after Blasco Ibáñez's death; but with the founding of the Second Republic in 1931, a commemorative tablet was dedicated in Valencia, and Blasco Ibáñez's image appeared, along with those of other republican

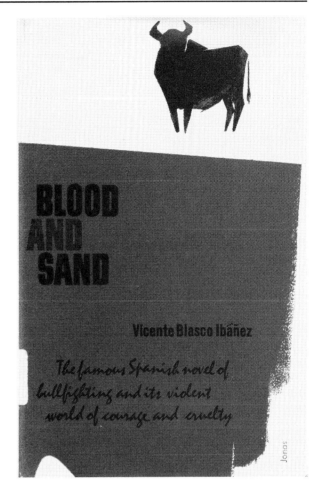

Dust jacket for a 1966 edition of the 1958 English translation of Blasco Ibáñez's 1908 novel, Sangre y arena, *about a poor shoemaker's son who becomes a renowned matador and is gored to death after being abandoned by the woman with whom he has had an adulterous affair (Richland County Public Library)*

intellectuals, on a series of commemorative postage stamps. In 1933 his body was returned from France to Valencia; a large crowd greeted the ship and accompanied the coffin to the city cemetery, where he was reinterred with full military honors. A commemorative booklet was published by the Republican city authorities.

During the Civil War of 1936 to 1939 the offices of *Prometeo* were sacked by the Nationalists. The Nationalist victory inaugurated a renewal of the anti-Blasco Ibáñez campaign: *El Pueblo* was closed, his grave was desecrated, and his house in Malvarrosa, near the beach in Valencia where he had lived on his frequent returns from Madrid, Menton, and foreign travels, was burned down. A campaign was orchestrated during the dictatorship of Francisco Franco to relegate Blasco Ibáñez to the second rank as a writer, to declare him a

*Cover for Blasco Ibáñez's 1916 novel (translated as* The Four Horsemen of the Apocalypse, *1918), about a multinational family that has fled Europe and settled on the Argentine pampas but nevertheless becomes embroiled in World War I (Thomas Cooper Library, University of South Carolina)*

poor grammarian and a plagiarist, and to impugn his work as immoral. In the second edition of *Panorama de la literatura española contemporánea* (1961, Panorama of Contemporary Spanish Literature) the Francoist Gonzalo Torrente Ballester said that he "lacked any spiritual or intellectual virtues. Blasco Ibáñez's spirit is enormously vulgar. His extraordinary vitality–his only authentic virtue–rejected every norm from the wearing of a tie to religious faith." Torrente Ballester accused Blasco Ibáñez of "sexual and passionate themes," "cheap ideology," and "lack of taste." The conservative camp, applying moral and social rather than aesthetic judgments, was able to ban Blasco Ibáñez from the canon. Only outside Spain was he taken seriously by academic critics.

Studies by British and American scholars in the 1970s, followed by a more positive Spanish response in the late 1990s, have finally ensured Blasco Ibáñez's place among his contemporaries. The house in Malvarrosa has been restored as a museum, and the avenue on which the University of Valencia is located bears his name. Major studies have begun to appear, and publishing houses have brought out new editions of his works with scholarly apparatus. More than a hundred pages of Juan Luis Alborg's *Historia de la literatura española* (1966–1999, History of Spanish Literature) are devoted to Blasco Ibáñez and his work. In 1998, which the Valencia city council proclaimed the year of Blasco Ibáñez, an international congress on the author was held in the city; the proceedings appeared in 2000 in two large volumes comprising sixty-six essays on his life and works.

Judgment of Blasco Ibáñez's status as a writer is, inevitably, clouded by the many campaigns of vilification in Spain's official critical press and by the uncritical acclaim of his supporters. To date no independent or unbiased assessment of his multitudinous and multifaceted works has appeared. The majority of studies dwell on his early writings, although, as the 1998 Valencia symposium demonstrates, critics have begun to assess a wider range of his oeuvre, including his travel books. Despite the opprobrium heaped upon him he became, by far, the most successful Spanish novelist of the twentieth century. He had an instinctive sense of his public and little trust in the critical establishment. In a letter to Cejador y Frauca of 6 March 1918 he wrote:

If the critic is blind and lazy, the public, the great public, with its crowd instinct, will know how to "sense" (even though it does not see it) what exists within the work. In the same way that religions will always count on the gratitude of the faithful, who have received from them consolation and hope, the novels that *are* novels, which vibrate a chord of life and bestow hours of illusion, will be loved by thousands and thousands of readers, even though the critics insist on showing that they are worthless. Criticism appeals to reason, and the work of art appeals to sentiment, to everything in us that forms the world of the unconscious, the world of sensibility, the broadest and the most mysterious world we carry within us, since no one knows its limits even remotely, whereas reason is limited.

Against the grain of the vogue for "intellectual" novels, for the modernist self-regarding and self-obsessed worlds evoked in the works of Baroja, Azorín, Unamuno, and Pérez de Ayala–novels that reflect the existential condition of the author and the intellectual zeitgeist of the early twentieth century–Blasco Ibáñez invokes the ancient Greek view of artistic creation:

The true and unique constructor is instinct, the subconscious, the mysterious and invisible force that the ordinary masses label "inspiration." A true artist does things the right way because, being himself, he cannot do them in any other way. . . . The artist who creates beauty is the most unconscious of all producers. This is nothing new. It is a truth as old as the earth. Plato, speaking of poets, said that they utter the most beautiful things without being aware why they say them. . . . To achieve this, the participation of the subconscious is necessary as the principal factor: the mysterious divination, presentiments, the affective elements, which are, most often, diametrically opposed to the intellectual elements.

Blasco Ibáñez admits that he is an instinctive, even compulsive writer: he calls writing "a nervous agitation" and "a real illness" and says, "My hand and breast ache, my eyes ache, my stomach, but, nevertheless, I cannot stop writing." His enormous output of novels, short stories, travel books, histories, and political pamphlets bears witness to his compulsions. He also stresses the effect of the environment on the writer, which accounts for the naturalistic elements in his work. But he never mentions the symbolism that is a prominent feature of his later work. Far from unconscious, it is a feature that he shares with his fellow modernists as much as their concern with mirroring and the story within the story. Thus, he bridges the late nineteenth century and the revolutionary aspects of the twentieth. If his prolific output suffers from a major flaw, it is his inability to resist the interpolation, to omit or prune the experience or the research; he cannot exercise the role of what he calls the "grim critic" who must cut.

Vicente Blasco Ibáñez lived his novels; they were the mirror of his life and his obsessions. From the *huerta* of Valencia to South America, from the beau monde of Monte Carlo and the impact of the Great War on Europe, he acted as the chronicler of his class and his age, an acute observer of the many and varied societies in which he moved.

## Bibliography:

Paul C. Smith, *Vicente Blasco Ibáñez: An Annotated Bibliography,* Research Bibliographies and Checklists, no. 14 (London: Grant & Cutler, 1976).

## Biographies:

Camille Pitollet, *V. Blasco Ibáñez, sus novelas y la novela de su vida* (Valencia: Prometeo, 1921);

Ramón Martínez de la Riva, *Blasco Ibáñez, su vida, su obra, su muerte, sus mejores páginas* (Madrid: Mundo Latino, 1929);

Juli Just Gimeno, *Blasco Ibáñez i València* (Valencia: Prometeo, 1931);

Emilio Gascó Contell, *Genio y figura de Vicente Blasco Ibáñez* (Madrid: Afrodisio Aguado, 1957).

## References:

Juan Luis Alborg, *Historia de la literatura española,* volume 5, part 3 (Madrid: Gredos, 1999), pp. 949–1059;

C. L. Anderson, *Vicente Blasco Ibáñez: The Evolution of a Novelist in His Imagery* (Ann Arbor, Mich.: University Microfilms International, 1982);

César Barja, *Libros y autores modernos,* second edition (New York: Las Américas, 1964), pp. 391–414;

Eduardo Betoret Paris, *El costumbrismo en la obra de Blasco Ibáñez* (Valencia: Prometeo, 1958);

Carlos Blanco Aguinaga, *Juventud del 98* (Barcelona: Crítica, 1978), pp. 189–228;

El Caballero Audaz (pseudonym of José María Carretero), *El novelista que vendió a su patria ó Tartarín, revolucionario: Una triste historia de actualidad* (Madrid: Renacimiento, 1924);

Richard A. Cardwell, *Blasco Ibáñez:* La barraca (London: Tamesis/Grant & Cutler, 1973; revised, 1994);

Cardwell, "Vicente Blasco Ibáñez, la protesta social y la generación del '98: Una contribución al debate," in *Modernismo y 98,* edited by José-Carlos Mainer, volume 6/1 of *Historia crítica de la literatura española,* edited by Victor García de la Concha (Barcelona: Grijalbo-Mondadori, 1994), pp. 207–213;

Julio Cejador y Frauca, *Historia de la lengua y literatura castellana,* 14 volumes (Madrid: Revista de Archivos, Bibliotecas y Museos, 1915–1922), IX: 467–480;

Alfonso Cucó Giner, *Sobre la ideología blasquista: Un assaig d'aproximació* (Valencia: Eliseu Climent, 1979);

José Manuel Cuenca Toribio, ed., *Siete temas sobre historia contemporánea del País Valenciano* (Valencia: Universidad de Valencia, 1974);

A. Grove Day and Edgar Knowlton Jr., *V. Blasco Ibáñez* (New York: Twayne, 1972);

Thomas J. di Salvo, *El arte cuentístico de Vicente Blasco Ibáñez* (Madrid: Pliegos, 1988);

Sherman H. Eoff, *The Modern Spanish Novel* (New York, 1961), pp. 115–119;

José Luis León Roca, *Cómo escribió Blasco Ibáñez* La barraca (Valencia: Printed by Masí Montaña, 1978);

León Roca, *Vicente Blasco Ibáñez,* fourth edition (Valencia: Prometeo, 1990);

León Roca and Jean-Noel Loubés, *Vicente Blasco Ibáñez: Diputado y novelista. Estudio e ilustración de su vida política* (Toulouse: Université de Toulouse-Le Mirail, 1972);

Yvan Lissourges, *Realismo y Naturalismo en España en la segunda mitad del siglo XIX* (Barcelona: Anthropos, 1988);

Manuel Lloris, "Vicente Blasco Ibáñez o la formación de un escritor de masas," *Ínsula*, 407 (1980): 1, 12;

Jeremy T. Medina, "The Artistry of Blasco Ibáñez's *Cañas y barro*," *Hispania*, 60 (1977): 275–284;

Medina, "The Artistry of Blasco Ibáñez's *Flor de mayo*," *Hispania*, 65 (1982): 197–208;

Medina, "Blasco Ibáñez: *Arroz y tartana*," *Hispanic Journal*, 5 (1984): 151–168;

Medina, *The Valencian Novels of Vicente Blasco Ibáñez* (Valencia & Chapel Hill, N.C.: Albatros-Hispanófila, 1984);

Janine Modave, "Blasco Ibáñez et le naturalisme français," *Lettres romanes*, 12 (1958): 300–301;

Maria José Navarro Mateo, "Blasco Ibáñez y las novelas de la guerra europea. (Entretejiéndose a sí mismo en el cañamazo de la Historia)," dissertation, University of Valencia, 1991;

Joan Oleza and Javier Lluch, eds., *Vicente Blasco Ibáñez 1898–1998: La vuelta al siglo de un novelista. Actas del Congreso Internacional celebrado en Valencia del 23 al 27 de noviembre de 1998,* 2 volumes (Valencia: Biblioteca Valenciana, Generalitat Valenciana/Consellería de Cultura i Educació, 2000);

Ramiro Reig, *Blasquistas y clericales: La lucha por la ciudad en la Valencia de 1900* (Valencia: Institución Alfonso el Magnánimo, 1986);

Reig, *Vicente Blasco Ibáñez* (Madrid: Espasa bibliografías, 2002);

Vicente Ribelles Pérez, *Vicente Blasco Ibáñez* (Madrid: Planeta, 1967);

Walter Rubin, "Vicente Blasco Ibáñez y el honor malentendido: *La catedral*," *Revista de literatura*, 49 (1987): 187–196;

Enric Sebastià, *València en les novel·les de Blasco Ibáñez: Proletariat y burgesia* (Valencia: L'Estel, 1966);

Bernardo Suárez, "La creación artística en *La barraca*," *Cuadernos hispanoamericanos*, 371 (1981): 371–385;

Gonzalo Torrente Ballester, *Panorama de la literatura española comtemporánea*, second edition, 2 volumes (Madrid: Guadarrama, 1961), I: 129–131;

Federico Vergara Vicuña, *Blasco Ibáñez la vuelta al mundo en 80.000 dóllars* (Paris: Tancrède, 1924);

*Vicente Blasco Ibáñez, la aventura del triunfo, 1867–1928* (Valencia: Institución Alfonso el Magnánimo, 1986).

**Papers:**

Vicente Blasco Ibáñez's papers are mostly dispersed in private hands. Some are in the Casa-Museo Blasco Ibáñez in Malvarrosa.

# Camilo José Cela

*(11 May 1916 – 17 January 2002)*

Lucile C. Charlebois
*University of South Carolina*

See also the Cela entry in *DLB Yearbook: 1989*.

BOOKS: *La familia de Pascual Duarte* (Madrid & Burgos: Aldecoa, 1942); translated by John Marks as *Pascual Duarte's Family* (London: Eyre & Spottiswoode, 1946); translated by Anthony Kerrigan as *The Family of Pascual Duarte* (Boston: Little, Brown, 1964);

*Nuevas andanzas y desventuras de Lazarillo de Tormes* (Madrid: La Nave, 1944); revised as *Nuevas andanzas y desventuras de Lazarillo de Tormes, y siete apuntes carpetovetónicos* (Madrid: Airon, 1952);

*Pabellón de reposo* (Madrid: Afrodisio Aguado, 1944); bilingual edition, with English translation by Herma Briffault as *Rest Home* (New York: Las Américas, 1961);

*Pisando la dudosa luz del día: Poemas de una adolescencia cruel* (Barcelona: Zodíaco, 1945; revised and enlarged edition, Palma de Mallorca: Ediciones de los Papeles de Son Armadans, 1963);

*Esas nubes que pasan* (Madrid: Afrodisio Aguado, 1945);

*Mesa revuelta* (Madrid: Ediciones de los Estudiantes Españoles, 1945; enlarged edition, Madrid: Taurus, 1957);

*El bonito crimen del carabinero, y otras invenciones* (Barcelona: José Janés, 1947); excerpts republished as *El bonito crimen del carabinero* (Barcelona: Picazo, 1972);

*Las botas de siete leguas: Viaje a la Alcarria, con los versos de su cancionero, cada uno en su debido lugar* (Madrid: Revista de Occidente, 1948); translated by Frances M. López-Morillas as *Journey to the Alcarria* (Madison: University of Wisconsin Press, 1964); revised as *Nuevo viaje a la Alcarria* (Barcelona: Plaza y Janés, 1986);

*San Juan de la Cruz,* as Matilde Verdú (Madrid: Hernando, 1948);

*El gallego y su cuadrilla y otros apuntes carpetovetónicos* (Madrid: Ricardo Aguilera, 1949; revised and enlarged edition, Barcelona: Destino, 1967);

*La colmena* (Buenos Aires: Emecé, 1951; Barcelona: Noguer, 1955); translated by J. M. Cohen and

Camilo José Cela *(photo by Francisco García Marquina; from the cover for* Cristo versus Arizona, *1988; Thomas Cooper Library, University of South Carolina)*

Arturo Barea as *The Hive* (London: Gollancz, 1953; New York: Farrar, Straus & Young, 1953);

*Avila* (Barcelona: Noguer, 1952); translated by John Forrester as *Avila* (Barcelona: Noguer, 1952);

*Santa Balbina, 37, gas en cada piso* (Melilla: Mirto y Laurel, 1952);

*Del Miño al Bidasoa: Notas de un vagabundaje* (Barcelona: Noguer, 1952);

*Timoteo el incomprendido* (Madrid: Rollán, 1952);

*Baraja de invenciones* (Valencia: Castalia, 1953);

*Café de artistas* (Madrid: Tecnos, 1953);

*Mrs. Caldwell habla con su hijo* (Barcelona: Destino, 1953); translated by J. S. Bernstein as *Mrs. Caldwell Speaks to Her Son* (Ithaca, N.Y.: Cornell University Press, 1968);

*Ensueños y figuraciones* (Barcelona: G. P., 1954);

*Historias de Venezuela: La catira* (Barcelona: Noguer, 1955);

*Vagabundo por Castilla* (Barcelona: Seix Barral, 1955);

*Judíos, moros y cristianos: Notas de un vagabundaje por Avila, Segovia y sus tierras* (Barcelona: Destino, 1956);

*El molino de viento y otras novelas cortas* (Barcelona: Noguer, 1956);

*Mis páginas preferidas* (Madrid: Gredos, 1956);

*Cajón de sastre* (Madrid: Cid, 1957);

*Nuevo retablo de don Cristobita; invenciones, figuraciones y alucinaciones* (Barcelona: Destino, 1957);

*La rueda de los ocios* (Barcelona: Mateu, 1957);

*Historias de España: Los ciegos, los tontos* (Madrid: Arión, 1957); enlarged as volume 1 of *A la pata de palo* (Barcelona: Noguer, 1965);

*La obra literaria del pintor Solana* (Madrid: Papeles de Son Armadans, 1957);

*Recuerdo de don Pío Baroja* (Mexico City: De Andrea, 1958);

*La cucaña: Memorias* (Barcelona: Destino, 1959); republished as *La rosa* (Barcelona: Destino, 1979; revised edition, Madrid: Espasa-Calpe, 2001);

*Primer viaje andaluz: Notas de un vagabundaje por Jaén, Córdoba, Sevilla, Segovia, Huelva y sus tierras* (Barcelona: Noguer, 1959);

*Cuadernos del Guadarrama* (Madrid: Arión, 1960);

*Los viejos amigos,* 2 volumes (Barcelona: Noguer, 1960, 1961);

*Cuatro figuras del 98: Unamuno, Valle-Inclán, Baroja, Azorín, y otros retratos y ensayos españoles* (Barcelona: Aedos, 1961);

*Tobogán de hambrientos* (Barcelona: Noguer, 1962);

*Gavilla de fábulas sin amor* (Palma de Mallorca: Papeles de Son Armadans, 1962);

*Obra completa,* 25 volumes (Barcelona: Destino, 1962–1990);

*Garito de hospicianos; o, Guirigay de imposturas y bambollas* (Barcelona: Noguer, 1963);

*El solitario,* published with Rafael Zabaleta, *Los sueños de Quesada* (Palma de Mallorca: Papeles de Son Armadans, 1963);

*Toreo de salón: Farsa con acompañamiento de clamor y murga* (Barcelona: Lumen, 1963);

*Once cuentos de fútbol* (Madrid: Nacional, 1963);

*Las compañías convenientes y otros fingimientos y cegueras* (Barcelona: Destino, 1963);

*Izas, rabizas y colipoterras: Drama con acompañamiento de cachondeo y dolor de corazón,* text by Cela, photographs by Juan Colom (Barcelona: Lumen, 1964);

*Páginas de geografía errabunda* (Madrid: Alfaguara, 1965);

*Viaje al Pirineo de Lérida: Notas de un paseo a pie por el Pallars, Sobirá, el Valle de Arán y el Condado de Ribagorza* (Madrid: Alfaguara, 1965);

*A la pata de palo,* 4 volumes (Madrid: Alfaguara, 1965–1967)–comprises volume 1, *Historias de España;* volume 2, *La familia del héroe; o, Discurso histórico de los últimos restos (ejercicios para una sola mano);* volume 3, *El ciudadano Iscariote Reclús;* and volume 4, *Viaje a U.S.A.; o, El que la sigue la mata;* republished in one volume as *El tacatá oxidado: Florilegio de carpetovetonismos y otras lindezas* (Barcelona: Noguer, 1973);

*Nuevas escenas matritenses,* 7 volumes (Madrid: Alfaguara, 1965–1966); republished in one volume as *Fotografías al minuto* (Madrid: Sala, 1972);

*Madrid* (Madrid: Alfaguara, 1966);

*Calidoscopio callejero, marítimo y campestre* (Madrid: Alfaguara, 1966);

*María Sabina* (Madrid: Papeles de Son Armadans, 1967); republished with *El carro de heno; o, El inventor de la guillotina* (Madrid: Alfaguara, 1970);

*Diccionario secreto,* 2 volumes (Madrid: Alfaguara, 1968, 1972);

*La bandada de palomas* (Barcelona: Labor, 1969);

*Víspera, festividad y octava de San Camilo del año 1936 en Madrid* (Madrid: Alfaguara, 1969); translated by John H. R. Polt as *San Camilo, 1936* (Durham, N.C.: Duke University Press, 1991);

*Homenaje al Bosco, I: El carro de heno; o, El inventor de la guillotina* (Madrid: Papeles de Son Armadans, 1969);

*Al servicio de algo* (Madrid: Alfaguara, 1969);

*Barcelona* (Barcelona: Alfaguara, 1970);

*La Mancha en el corazón y en los ojos* (Barcelona: EDISVEN, 1971);

*Obras selectas* (Madrid: Alfaguara, 1971);

*La bola del mundo: Escenas cotidianas* (Madrid: Sala, 1972);

*oficio de tinieblas 5; o, novela de tesis escrita para ser cantada por un coro de enfermos* (Barcelona: Noguer, 1973);

*A vueltas con España* (Madrid: Semanarios y Ediciones, 1973);

*Balada del vagabundo sin suerte y otros papeles volanderos* (Madrid: Espasa-Calpe, 1973);

*Cuentos para leer después del baño* (Barcelona: La Gaya Ciencia, 1974);

*Prosa,* edited by Jacinto Luis Guereña (Madrid: Narcea, 1974);

*Rol de cornudos* (Barcelona: Noguer, 1976);

*La insólita y gloriosa hazaña del cipote de Archidona* (Barcelona: Tusquets, 1977);

*Enciclopedia del erotismo* (Madrid: Sedmay, 1977); enlarged as *Diccionario del erotismo,* 2 volumes (Barcelona: Grijalbo, 1988);

*Los sueños vanos, los ángeles curiosos* (Barcelona: Argos Vergara, 1979);

*Album de taller* (Barcelona: Ambit, 1981);

*El espejo y otros cuentos* (Madrid: Espasa-Calpe, 1981);

*Los vasos comunicantes* (Barcelona: Bruguera, 1981);

*Vuelta de hoja* (Barcelona: Destino, 1981);

*Mazurca para dos muertos* (Barcelona: Seix Barral, 1983); translated by Patricia Haugaard as *Mazurka for Two Dead Men* (New York: New Directions, 1992);

*El juego de los tres madroños* (Barcelona: Destino, 1983);

*El asno de Buridán* (Madrid: El País, 1986);

*Las orejas del niño Raul* (Madrid: Debate Literatura Infantil, 1986);

*Dedicatorias* (Madrid: Observatorio, 1986);

*Conversaciones españolas* (Barcelona: Plaza y Janés, 1987);

*Cristo versus Arizona* (Barcelona: Seix Barral, 1988);

*Los caprichos de Francisco de Goya y Lucientes* (Madrid: Silex, 1989);

*El hombre y el mar* (Barcelona: Plaza y Janés, 1990);

*Galicia,* text by Cela, illustrations by Laxeiro, photographs by Víctor Vaqueiro (Vigo: Ir Indo, 1990);

*Discurso para unha xove dama amante dos libros* (Vigo: Ir Indo, 1991);

*Cachondeos, escarceos y otros meneos* (Madrid: Ediciones Temas de Hoy, 1991);

*Desde el palomar de Hita* (Barcelona: Plaza y Janés, 1991);

*Páginas escogidas,* edited by Darío Villanueva (Madrid: Espasa-Calpe, 1991);

*Torerías: El gallego y su cuadrilla, Madrid, Toreo de salón y otras páginas taurinas,* edited by Andrés Amorós (Madrid: Espasa-Calpe, 1991);

*El camaleón soltero* (Madrid: Grupo Libro 88, 1992);

*El huevo del juicio* (Barcelona: Seix Barral, 1993);

*Memorias, entendimientos y voluntades* (Barcelona: Plaza y Janés/Cambio 16, 1993);

*El asesinato del perdedor* (Barcelona: Seix Barral, 1994);

*La cruz de San Andrés* (Barcelona: Planeta, 1994);

*La dama pájara y otros cuentos* (Madrid: Espasa-Calpe, 1994);

*A bote pronto* (Barcelona: Seix Barral, 1994);

*El color de la mañana* (Madrid: Espasa-Calpe, 1996);

*Poesía completa* (Spain: Galaxia Gutenberg / Barcelona: Círculo de lectores, 1996);

*Diccionario geográfico popular de España* (Madrid: Comunidad de Madrid/Fundación de Camilo José Cela, Marqués de Iria Flavia/Noésis, 1998);

*Historias familiares* (Barcelona: Macia & Nubiola, 1998);

*Madera de boj* (Madrid: Espasa-Calpe, 1999); translated by Haugaard as *Boxwood* (New York: New Directions, 2002);

*Homenaje al Bosco, II: La extracción de la piedra de la locura; o, El inventor del garrote* (Barcelona: Seix Barral, 1999).

PLAY PRODUCTION: *María Sabina,* libretto by Cela, translated by Luz Castaños and Theodore S. Beardsley, score by Leonardo Balada, New York, Carnegie Hall, 17 April 1970.

OTHER: *Homaneje y recuerdo a Gregorio Marañón (1887–1960),* edited by Cela (Madrid: Papeles de Son Armadans, 1961);

Fernando de Rojas, *La Celestina puesta respetuosamente en castellano moderno por Camilo José Cela quien añadió muy poco y quitó aun menos,* adapted by Cela (Barcelona: Destino, 1979);

Miguel de Cervantes Saavedra, *El Quijote,* edited by Cela (Alicante: Rembrandt, 1981).

TRANSLATION: Bertolt Brecht, *La resistible ascensión de Arturo Ui* (Madrid: Júcar, 1975).

In 1942 Camilo José Cela published his first major work of narrative fiction, the novel *La familia de Pascual Duarte* (translated as *Pascual Duarte's Family,* 1946), which signaled the reemergence of Spain's tradition of excellence relative to the modern European novel. This book secured for him a place alongside other young Spanish novelists whose works were indicators of Spain's gradual recovery from the Civil War their country had endured from 18 July 1936 through 1 April 1939. Cela's reputation grew rapidly, and because he remained in Spain instead of going into exile, his works give testimony to his country's struggle through the thirty-six years of Francisco Franco's rule and the eventual emergence in 1975 of Spain as a democracy. Despite the controversies that have always surrounded his chosen themes and stylistic devices and his opinions about such matters as democracy, homosexuality, prostitution, technology, and younger Spanish writers, Cela's unwavering dedication to the profession of writing was recognized toward the end of his career when he was awarded important Spanish literary prizes, such as the Premio Nacional (1984), the Príncipe de Asturias (1987), the Planeta Prize (1994), and the Cervantes Prize (1995). In 1989 he was awarded the Nobel Prize in literature. He received the Pluma de Oro (Golden Pen) in 1995 and the Premio Gallegos del Mundo de las Letras (Galicians of the World of Arts Prize) in 2001 for his lifetime literary achievements.

*Dust jacket for the 1964 English translation of Cela's controversial first
novel,* La familia de Pascual Duarte *(1942), in which a prisoner
explains that his family background caused him to become
a murderer (Richland County Public Library)*

Cela wrote short stories, essays, poetry, drama,
travel books, and newspaper columns, but his novels in
particular pay tribute to the strength of the Spanish
spirit. They also attest to Cela's self-imposed goal of
renewed experimentation with narrative style. Cela's
works confirm his dissatisfaction with conformity.
Decades of repression and censorship, which had
become a way of life for Spaniards since 1936, were cat-
alysts for Cela's literary audacity, his penchant for scandal, and a purposeful disregard for historical accuracy,
as well as a rejection of in-depth psychological character
portrayals. In light of the public scrutiny to which he
had been subjected when censors deemed *La familia de
Pascual Duarte* the product of a depraved mind, Cela
intentionally fashioned the offensive public persona to
which his only son, Camilo José Cela Conde, attests in
*Cela, mi padre* (1989, Cela, My Father). Such acrimony
culminated in Cela's chosen epitaph: "El que resiste,
gana" (He who withstands, wins).

Cela was born Camilo José Manuel Juan Ramón
Cela y Trulock in Iria Flavia (O Coruña), Spain, on 11
May 1916, of Italian, British, Welsh, and Spanish ancestry. His parents were Camila Emmanuela Trulock y
Bertorini and Camilo Cela y Fernández. He had four
siblings: Jorge, Rafael, Juan-Carlos, and Teresa María.
Cela often boasted of his lineage, believing that it gave
him a special objectivity with which to understand his
country, its history, and its traditions. His father
worked as a customs official, and in 1933 the family
established permanent residence in Madrid. In his autobiographical volume *La cucaña: Memorias* (1959, The
Greasy Pole: Memoirs; republished as *La rosa* [1979],
The Rose), Cela depicts himself as a difficult child, and
his eccentricities began to take root in his university
years (1934–1935 and 1939), during which he began
and abandoned studies of medicine and law at the Central University of Madrid. In 1934 the first of two bouts
with tuberculosis changed his life: his convalescence
afforded him the opportunity to read the seventy-one-
volume collection of the Biblioteca de Autores
Españoles (Library of Spanish Authors), thereby fostering his budding literary aspirations. Cela did not take a
university degree. Instead, his friendship with Pedro
Salinas, a leading Spanish poet and critic, inspired him
to start writing poetry.

Cela's first work was *Pisando la dudosa luz del día:
Poemas de una adolescencia cruel* (Treading the Dubious
Light of Day: Poems of a Cruel Adolescence), written
in 1936 but not published until 1945 because of his feelings of insecurity as an inexperienced writer and
because of wartime hardships that limited publication
of works by unknown authors. It is a collection of viru-
lently expressive poems written at the height of the
aerial bombings of Madrid in the first phase of the civil
war. From 1940 on, when Cela began to frequent the
prestigious Café Gijón *tertulia* (literary discussion
group) in Madrid, the way was paved for the unflag-
ging literary output of the six decades of his life as a
writer.

In 1937 he was drafted into the Nationalist army
and was discharged two years later for wounds received
in the line of duty. Those of his critics who have been
less than favorable have made a practice of emphasizing
the fact that Cela fought on the side of the insurgents in
addition to having worked for a brief period as a censor
for various publications in the early days of the Francoist regime.

Cela's first novel, *La familia de Pascual Duarte,* is
about a disadvantaged man who was born to a violent,
alcoholic father and an unschooled, promiscuous, and
loveless mother in the early part of the twentieth century in Extremadura, one of the poorest regions of
Spain. Pascual is a criminal who, while imprisoned,

writes a first-person account of the events of his life. He continually assures the anonymous *señor* (sir) to whom his discourse is directed of his repentance, but ultimately the reader must make the final judgment concerning Pascual's sincerity and the cause of his murderous acts and the matricide with which his narration ends. Playing right into the predetermined innocence of his symbolic name (the Paschal lamb sacrificed at the first Passover), he casts himself in the role of victim, all the while narrating his crimes in distorted chronological fashion. His inherited bad blood is underscored by the first lines of his written confession: "Yo, señor, no soy malo aunque no me faltarían motivos para serlo. Los mismos cueros tenemos todos los mortales al nacer y sin embargo, cuando vamos creciendo, el destino se complace en variarnos como si fuésemos de cera" (I am not, sir, a bad person, though in all truth I am not lacking in reasons for being one. We are all born naked, and yet, as we begin to grow up, it pleases Destiny to vary us, as if we were made of wax [translated by Anthony Kerrigan]). As he begins to recount the events of his life (and the lives of his parents, sister Rosario, retarded brother Mario, and wives Lola and Esperanza), contradictions, gaps, and enigmas surface. His recollection is spotty and replete with an accompanying rationale that is meant to condone his repeated acts of violence.

As John Kronik has pointed out, Pascual re-creates himself through his memoirs and thus permits his narrative to vacillate between the points of view of one who is sentenced to death and of the young man from Extremadura whose manhood was constantly brought into question. Five of his chapters are self-proclaimed moments of poetic and existential insight more befitting a poet than a murderer. On the other hand, his memory is tainted with colloquialisms, folk sayings, and a crudely scatological depiction of those events he selected to include in the episodic plotting of his story. In the same breath with which he excuses his bad memory, he nevertheless provides ample descriptions that can only be credited to fabrication and/or outright self-contradiction. In sum, his retrospection is lucid and graphic, as are his well-phrased jailhouse meditations on life and its meaning.

Cela frames Pascual's words in a context of subversion, beginning with a "Preliminary Note by the Transcriber," who claims to have "found the pages here transcribed in the middle of 1939 in a pharmacy at Almendralejo (God knows who put them there in the first place!). And from that day to this I have . . . brought some order into them, transcribed them, and made them make sense." The note is followed by other quasi-official documents: "Duarte's letter to the First Recipient of His Manuscript" (don Joaquín Barrera

López, who was a good friend of the Count of Torremejía, don Jesús González de la Riva, whom Pascual murdered); an "Extract from the Last Will and [Handwritten] Testament of don Joaquín Barrera López"; and lastly, Pascual's own tongue-in-cheek dedication to his victim, "don Jesús . . . who, at the moment when the author of this chronicle came to kill him, called him Pascualillo, and smiled." As Pascual ends his confession with the words he uttered after having killed his mother ("I could breathe"), more documents are appended by the Transcriber, including a further explanation about the perplexing chronology of Pascual's life after the matricide and the murder of don Jesús, the lack of information concerning the crime for which Pascual received the death sentence, and the fate of the manuscript of his confession. Included are also two letters, dated 9 and 12 January 1942, from eyewitnesses, both of which are at odds regarding Pascual's demeanor at the time of his death by garrotte. These materials further confound Pascual's veracity while purposefully exacerbating the ambiguities that plague the discourse.

The shocking and sordid details in *La familia de Pascual Duarte* were condemned by censors and critics alike on the first publication of the novel. The second edition was seized by government censors in 1943 and held for two years until it could be published again in Spain. Since then, however, *La familia de Pascual Duarte* has gone through more than 250 editions, second only to Miguel de Cervantes's *Don Quixote*. It has been translated into thirty-three languages and continues to generate much debate, particularly concerning the pathology of criminality. The novel launched a series of works, such as *Nada* (1944, Nothing) by Carmen Laforet, that shared in Pascual's graphic depiction of the conditions of life in Spain in the time preceding and following 1939. Studies in historiography have made it possible to view Cela's Paschal lamb as the first of many disavowals of the Francoist regime's sanitization of Spanish history.

In "Algunas palabras al que leyere" (A Few Words to Whoever Might Read This), his prologue to *Mrs. Caldwell habla con su hijo* (1953; translated as *Mrs. Caldwell Speaks to Her Son*, 1968), Cela classifies his second novel, *Pabellón de reposo* (1944; translated as *Rest Home*, 1961), as the antithesis of *La familia de Pascual Duarte*. Even those harsh critics of Cela's first novel praised *Pabellón de reposo* for its lyrically sensitive treatment of seven patients who are dying of tuberculosis as well as for its use of their narrating voices in what constitutes a new beginning for them in the face of death. The work is admittedly tied to Cela's firsthand experience with the same illness, itself the invisible protagonist to whom reverence is paid by way of the diary entries, letters, and other modes of narrative discourse

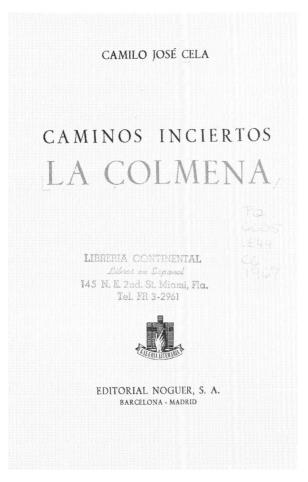

CAMILO JOSÉ CELA

CAMINOS INCIERTOS

LA COLMENA

LIBRERIA CONTINENTAL
*Libros en Español*
145 N. E. 2nd. St. Miami, Fla.
Tel. FR 3-2951

EDITORIAL NOGUER, S. A.
BARCELONA - MADRID

*Title page for a later edition of Cela's 1951 novel (translated as* The
Hive, *1953), which uses snippets of overheard conversations, shifting
cinematic scenes, and more than 350 characters to depict two days
in the bustling street life of 1940 Madrid (Thomas
Cooper Library, University of South Carolina)*

in which these ailing men and women express their innermost fears and longings.

Except for one character named Felisa, all of the patients are identified by numbers (52, 37, 14, 40, 11, 73, and 103 [Felisa]). An authorial voice is heard sparingly over the course of the otherwise fragmented narrative discourse, breaking forth only to inform readers of a letter received from a "well-known physician and specialist in tuberculosis, Dr. A. M. S.," who begged its recipient to stop publishing the novel in weekly newspaper installments. Overall, the commentaries of the sanatorium residents are what provide the details of their profiles: for example, number 37 says that her "friend in 52" is "a dreamer and a romantic"; and number 40 says of number 14 that "His eyes are more burning than ever, his smile more bitter, his nose more pinched in his face that is whiter. He looks like an amorous romantic poet, triumphant and suicidal, and scarcely

twenty-five years old." Their lives give poignancy to their illness as they attempt to find happiness, plan for the future, attend to business, and mend broken family relationships from within their confinement. A masterpiece of structural symmetry, the novel is divided into two equal parts, each one subdivided into seven chapters that in turn correspond to their respective patient-narrators. The refrain-like appearance of a redheaded gardener, pulling his rusted green wheelbarrow, marks the end of each chapter in the second part of the novel, thereby signaling the objective correlative of death carting away its victims one by one with unrelenting predictability.

This symmetry substantiates Cela's preference for aesthetics over stylistics in dealing with the topic of tuberculosis. William David Foster comments that *Pabellón de reposo* represents "the first . . . of Cela's many attempts to order the chaos of the universe into a meaningful pattern." Other critics, such as J. M. Castellet, point to the determinism and sustained *tremendista* modality as indicative of Cela's commitment to technical innovation. This work, which appears milder than *La familia de Pascual Duarte,* is in reality shockingly intimate, however lyrical, regarding the insidious power of death over the characters, whose blood-spattered bedclothes are a constant reminder of their impending fate.

Interspersed with the publication of Cela's first two novels are the picaresque adventures he created for Spain's archetypal rogue, Lazarillo de Tormes (*Nuevas andanzas y desventuras de Lazarillo de Tormes* [1944, New Adventures and Misfortunes of Lazarillo de Tormes]), and the first of many short stories that are an important segment of his work. Among these collections of short works of prose fiction are *Esas nubes que pasan* (1945, Those Clouds that Go Past and Disappear), *El bonito crimen del carabinero, y otras invenciones* (1947, The Tidy Crime of the Armed Policeman and Other Tales), and *Las botas de siete leguas: Viaje a la Alcarria, con los versos de su cancionero, cada uno en su debido lugar* (1948, The Boots of Seven Leagues: Journey to the Alcarria, with Verses from Its Songbook of Poems, Each One in Its Due Place; translated as *Journey to the Alcarria,* 1964). The latter was one of the products of Cela's ardent desire to fathom the essence of Iberian Spain through a series of walking tours. In 1949 he published more short prose works under the heading of *El gallego y su cuadrilla y otros apuntes carpetovetónicos* (The Galician and His Troupe and Other Thoroughly Spanish Notes). These tales led to the creation of a subgenre known as the *apunte carpetovetónico,* which, in a fashion similar to the hybrid prose works of his literary forebears of the "Generation of 1898" and José Ortega y Gasset (in his "walking and seeing" essays), is likened by Cela to a slice-of-life sketch, in either narration or drawing, of a character type or way of life that is specific to a certain time and place in Spain and whose particular pathos is derived from its own bittersweet quality.

Cela's *apuntes* flourished throughout the 1950s and 1960s, as evidenced in *Del Miño al Bidasoa* (1952, From The Miño to the Bidassoa Rivers), *Judíos, moros y cristianos* (1956, Jews, Moors and Christians), *Cuadernos del Guadarrama* (1960, Guadarrama Notebooks), and *Páginas de geografía errabunda* (1965, Pages about Wandering). Within this same time frame he also published the novellas *Timoteo el incomprendido* (1952, Timoko the Misunderstood), *Santa Balbina, 37, gas en cada piso* (1952, Santa Balbina Street, or Gas in Every Apartment), *El molino de viento y otras novelas cortas* (1956, The Windmill and Other Short Novels), and *Café de artistas* (1953, Artists' Café), as well as more collections of short stories: *Baraja de invenciones* (1953, Pack of Tales), *Nuevo retablo de don Cristobita* (1957, Don Cristobita's New Tableau), *La rueda de los ocios* (1957, The Chorus of Those who Possess Leisure Time), *Cajón de sastre* (1957, Hodgepodge), and *Historias de España: Los ciegos, las tontos* (1957, Stories about Spain: The Blind Ones, the Foolish Ones). His literary fecundity of the 1950s was enhanced by three new novels: *La colmena* (1951; translated as *The Hive*, 1953), *Mrs. Caldwell habla con su hijo*, and *Historias de Venezuela: La catira* (1955, Stories of Venezuela: The Blonde).

*La colmena* was first published in Buenos Aires, because the Spanish censors objected to its themes of hunger, depravity, promiscuity, violence, and repression. The novel takes up the desperation and sense of hopelessness felt by the sickly characters in *Pabellón de reposo*. This time, the emotions are seen through the quasi-objective style of a roving journalist who injects his narration with slice-of-life conversations among more than 350 characters who live in Madrid in early 1940, during a time of severe shortages as the Spanish capital struggled through the aftermath of its civil war. Characterized technically by qualities of simultaneity, cinematography, fragmentation, and deconstruction, *La colmena* is one of its author's most accomplished works. In writing about the novel as literary genre in "Algunas palabras al que leyere," Cela refers to *La colmena* as a "clock novel . . . made of multiple wheels and tiny pieces which work together in harmony so that it [the clock] works." The novel moves around the actions of a two-day period. Of the six parts of the novel, chapters 1, 2, and 4 constitute the first day, with the second day being spread out over chapters 3, 5, and 6. Everything occurs from afternoon through late night, with only the "Finale" taking place in the morning three or four days later.

Readers are plunged midstream into the mundane conversations of Madrid's teeming masses, with particular emphasis on Doña Rosa's café "La Delicia," Don Celestino's bar "Aurora," brothels, and the apartments of married couples, as well as the open space of streets and the empty lot outside Madrid's bullring. The novel opens with a timely reminder from Doña Rosa: "Don't let's lose our sense of proportion," an admonition that is immediately muted by the swell of the buzzing voices of the "hive." Against the backdrop of incessant coughing (implying tuberculosis) and music, one soon gets the impression of overhearing private matters (clandestine sexual encounters, financial problems, and illicit propositions of various kinds) amid the nervousness of a society just getting used to a regime in which suspicious behavior or criticism of the new government warranted prosecution. Little of what is presented makes sense (in any true narrative fashion) until the dead body of Doña Margot is found in the early evening hours of the first day (chapter 2). From that point on, various individuals' names begin to provide direction, as characters such as her son, his homosexual partner, and the itinerant Martín Marco subtly are connected with other characters, incidents, and bits of information, thus forming story lines that hold the promise of solving the murder.

The descriptions of people and places are pointedly realistic, and all-encompassing abject poverty is depicted with genuine pathos evoked for children and young women such as Elvira, who is lucky to have a stale orange and a fistful of roasted chestnuts for supper. Much of the action involves liaisons between relatively affluent married men and less-fortunate women, such as Merceditas (sold into bondage at the age of thirteen), Purita (in charge of five younger siblings), or Victorita (who will go to any lengths to get money for the medicine that her boyfriend needs if he is to survive the tuberculosis from which he suffers). Among the more helpless is a six-year-old gypsy boy who lives under a bridge and eats sporadically, depending upon how many coins he collects from people who like to hear him sing. Just when tensions converge concerning Doña Margot's murder (and other illicit activities), the action is brought to an irregularly open-ended conclusion, as friends and family of Martín Marco read in the morning newspaper that he is being sought for questioning, at the same time that he, happier than ever before, is on his way to the cemetery to pay his respects at his mother's grave.

*La colmena* received resounding praise from such respected critics as Ricardo Gullón, Gonzalo Torrente Ballester, Dámaso Alonso, Gregorio Marañón, and González Ruano; yet, many of the more conservative literary critics of the time condemned its radical departure from the prevailing literary realism of the 1950s. Eugenio de Nora, for example, whose seminal *La novela*

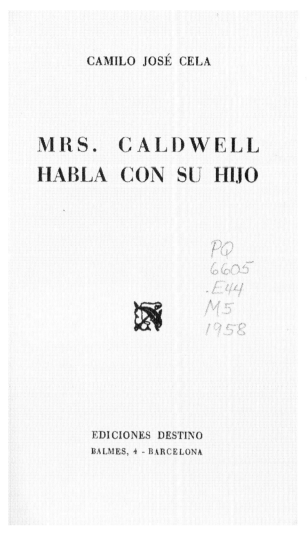

CAMILO JOSÉ CELA

# MRS. CALDWELL HABLA CON SU HIJO

EDICIONES DESTINO

BALMES, 4 - BARCELONA

*Title page for a later edition of Cela's 1953 novel (translated as* Mrs. Caldwell Speaks to Her Son, *1968), which shocked the Spanish reading public by introducing taboo themes such as the incestuous relationship of the title characters (Thomas Cooper Library, University of South Carolina)*

*contemporánea* (1968, The Contemporary [Spanish] Novel) assured his place as a voice of authority, branded Cela a rebellious author whose works, like *La familia de Pascual Duarte,* were hyperrealistic, crudely offensive, and unacceptable for the literary and moral sensibilities of Franco's conservative Catholic Spain. Even present-day Hispanists, such as biographer Ian Gibson, persist in denigrating Cela's achievement in *La colmena* by underscoring the precedent set by John Dos Passos's novel *Manhattan Transfer* (1925) and hence casting aspersions on the originality of *La colmena* and the revolutionary point of departure it heralded for the Spanish novel.

*Mrs. Caldwell habla con su hijo* shocked the Spanish reading public of its day by way of its taboo-driven

theme of incest. The implied dialogue of the title is embedded in a narrative discourse of bawdy double entendres and heightened fragmentation. In a foreword to the novel, Mrs. Caldwell is identified by a friend and the editor of her papers as someone who has "died in the Royal Insane Asylum" of London; the 213 segments of her written tribute to her son, Eliacim (who died a sailor while on a training mission in the Aegean Sea), are irregular in length and coherence, matching perfectly the grieving mother's self-centered, schizophrenic discourse. Because this mother-son relationship could only have been handled indirectly by way of the surrealistic images that break forth from Mrs. Caldwell's writings, their conversation had to be equally as evasive. Her narrative consciousness aside, Eliacim's mother is fully aware that she is treading new ground and provides a cleverly veiled rationale for her statements: "It's a long and strange story, Eliacim darling, that I don't think ought to be told entirely." In addition, a chapter titled "The Devil's Presence" proffers strong evidence that Mrs. Caldwell was probably sexually abused as a child by her father, hence transferring her sexual deviance to her only child.

Mrs. Caldwell follows Pascual Duarte's need to bare her soul in writing, while at the same time sharing with the reporter-narrator of *La colmena* an understanding of the tragedy of the human condition: "The people who pass in the street, my son, are . . . boring, resigned, monotonous . . . With their debts, their stomach ulcers, their family problems, their insane, miraculous plans, etc., walk with their spirits cowed, in no particular direction, with the secret hope that death will catch them by surprise, like the ax murderer who waits in ambush at the doors of schools." She also resembles her predecessors in *Pabellón de reposo,* for she too awakes with increasing regularity to a blood-stained pillow. Her fragmentary messages are encoded in contradiction and ambiguity, at times sworn to her son to be truthful yet at the same time outrightly "lying." Mrs. Caldwell creates her own and her son's characters, together with episodes related to their friends, habits, and lives, all of which are based solely on her distorted perception of reality. What makes good sense to her comes across as absurd, as in the titles of her scribbles ("In the Swimming Pool" [chapter 13], "Lord Macaulay" [chapter 42], and "China and Crystal" [chapter 114]). Contrary to Cela's previous novels, *Mrs. Caldwell habla con su hijo* offers no sustained editorial interference except the "Letters from the Royal Insane Asylum" and a concluding "Editor's Note" that provides a keen tongue-in-cheek exegesis of her final statement: "In Mrs. Caldwell's original, there follow two blurred, and completely undecipherable pages with obvious signs of moisture, showing unmistakable signs of having spent hours and hours under water, like a drowned sailor."

By allowing a mentally and physically ill character such freedom of expression, Cela introduced the way for a repertoire of subjects that had, for the most part, been off-limits for Spanish readers. Mrs. Caldwell attests to marital infidelity, suicide, vice, fetishism, sexual abuse, violence, and hatred. In keeping with the prudence that was still required of Spanish writers in the early 1950s, Cela purposefully conferred upon his female narrator a name that was obviously not Spanish, bestowing her with autonomy but at the same time offering pointed, stylized commentary about Spanish mothers: "In far-off Spain, mothers bite their sons on the neck, drawing blood, to demonstrate their tenacious, unchanging love." Such public national self-scrutiny, in turn, facilitated more criticism relative to such sacred institutions as "Family Life" (chapter 110) and marriage (in chapter 199, "The Well-Matched Married Couple"), all of which served as metaphors for the hypocrisy of the rules of etiquette and social decorum. It is not surprising that overall the novel has generated scant critical attention.

Similar outrage among critics was expressed when Cela was promised a sizable amount of money in 1953 by the Venezuelan government to spend time in that country in order to write a novel *(La catira)* that would accurately depict the nation's spirit. Like *Nuevas andanzas y desventuras de Lazarillo de Tormes* of 1944, *La catira* has never been considered one of Cela's major works; yet, it earned him the Critics' Prize and the Andrés Bello Medal of Honor, which was conferred upon him by Venezuelan president Ramón José Velásquez. Also at this juncture in his career, Cela was inducted into the Royal Spanish Academy of the Language (1957); since then, he has been looked on as a leading literary figure and pioneer in post–Spanish Civil War prose fiction.

Cela moved to Majorca in 1956. He named the journal he founded that same year *Papeles de Son Armadans* (Papers from Son Armadans), after the neighborhood in Palma where he lived with his wife, María del Rosario Conde Picavea, whom he had married in 1944, and their son, born in 1946. *Papeles de Son Armadans* grew to be one of the only viable publishing outlets available to international writers and artists whose works would be otherwise banned by the regime on the Iberian Peninsula. With his brother Jorge, Cela also established the Alfaguara publishing house, which became one of the leading presses in Spain for the contemporary Spanish novel. Until 1989, when he returned to Spain to live (outside of Madrid in Guadalajara), he spent what were perhaps the most productive years of his career in his beloved Balearic house in La

Bonanova. There he was instrumental in starting the *Conversaciones Poéticas de Formentor,* a colloquium for artists and writers such as Joan Miró and Robert Graves. There he also became friends with Pablo Picasso, who contributed various drawings to illustrate *Papeles de Son Armadans* that were later incorporated into Cela's *Gavilla de fábulas sin amor* (1962, Bundle of Loveless Fables). In his pictorial essay (1964) *Izas, rabizas y colipoterras: Drama con acompañamiento de cachondeo y dolor de corazón* (the title words are neologisms without a suitable translation; the subtitle is Drama Accompanied by Joking and Heartache), Cela collaborated with the photographer Juan Colom, whose striking images of streetwalkers and other destitute Spanish women of the time boldly raised public consciousness about prostitution.

Cela continued to write such varied works as *La cucaña,* the first part of his autobiography; *La obra literaria del pintor Solana* (1957, The Literary Works of the Painter [José Gutiérrez] Solana), which originated as his acceptance speech for membership in the Royal Spanish Academy of the Language; tributes to Spanish intellectuals such as Pío Baroja and Gregorio Marañón; and more travel journals, such as *Primer viaje andaluz: Notas de un vagabundaje por Jaén, Córdoba, Sevilla, Segovia, Huelva y sus tierras* (1959, First Andalusian Trip: Notes of a Traveler through Jaén, Córdoba, Sevilla, Segovia, Huelva and Their Lands), *Viaje al Pirineo de Lérida: Notas de un paseo a pie por el Pallars, Sobirá, el Valle de Arán y el Condado de Ribagorza* (1965, Journey to the Pyrenees of Lérida: Notes of a Passage on Foot through Pallars, Sobirá, the Valle de Arán and the Condado de Ribagorza), *Madrid* (1966), and *Barcelona* (1970). His repertoire of short stories also expanded with *Garito de hospicianos* (1963, Gambling Den of Hospiced People), *El solitario* (1963, The Recluse), *Toreo de salón* (1963, Armchair Bullfighting), and *La bandada de palomas* (1969, The Flock of Pigeons).

During the 1960s Cela's propensity for innovation resulted in increasing diversity and critical acclaim. In 1961 he wrote *Cuatro figuras del 98* (Four Important People of the Generation of 1898) in tribute to his literary and spiritual mentors. This volume was followed by short works including *Nuevas escenas matritenses* (1965–1966, New Scenes from Madrid) and *Tobogán de hambrientos* (1962, Toboggan of Starving People), which critics such as Jorge A. Marbán consider to mark the apex of his excellence as an *apuntes* writer. Cela's iconoclasm advanced his radical departure from literary conventions, as evidenced in such titles as *Cuentos para leer después del baño* (1974, Stories to Read after One's Bath) and *Enciclopedia del erotismo* (1977, Encyclopedia of Eroticism). His works became markedly layered with scatology and sexual innuendos, as, for example, in *Diccionario secreto* (1968, 1972; Secret Dictionary) and *Rol*

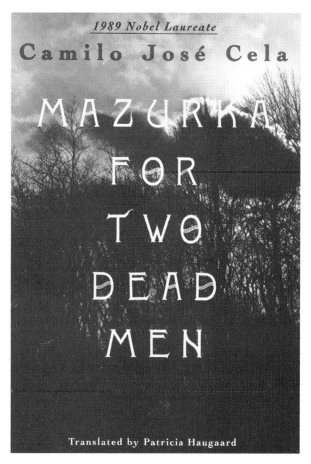

*Dust jacket for the 1992 English translation of Cela's 1983 novel,* Mazurca para dos muertos, *about a family obsessed with avenging the deaths of two of their kinsmen during the Spanish Civil War (Richland County Public Library)*

*de cornudos* (1976, Catalogue of Cuckolds). This period of experimentation also yielded Cela's debut as a playwright with *María Sabina* (1967) and *Homenaje al Bosco, I: El carro de heno; o, El inventor de la guillotina* (1969, Homage to Bosch, I: The Haywain; or, The Inventor of the Guillotine).

Spanish readers became familiar with Cela's thoughtful yet unflinchingly provocative side when his essays about the state of affairs in Spain as the Franco dictatorship waned began appearing in Spanish dailies such as *El País, El Independiente,* and *ABC.* These essays were later republished in such collections as *Al servicio de algo* (1969, In the Service of Something), *A vueltas con España* (1973, Again Talking about Spain), *Vuelta de hoja* (1981, Next Page), *Los vasos comunicantes* (1981, Communicating Vessels), *El camaleón soltero* (1992, The Unmarried Chameleon), *El huevo del juicio* (1993, The Egg of Judgment), and *El color de la mañana* (1996, The Color of the Morning).

In Cela's widely misunderstood Spanish Civil War novel, *Víspera, festividad y octava de San Camilo del año 1936 en Madrid* (1969, Eve, Feast and Octave of St. Camillus's Day 1936 in Madrid; translated and commonly referred to as *San Camilo, 1936,* 1991), an anonymous narrator attempts to appease his guilt and sense of cowardice for not having participated in the events of the outbreak of the civil war and in particular in the siege of the Montaña Barracks in Madrid, which took the lives of many of his friends. He feels obliged to keep a written account of the events, and his most useful writing tool is a looking glass that fuels his introspection and serves as a metaphor for the stream-of-consciousness mode of storytelling in the novel. Maryse Bertrand de Muñoz speaks of the "river-paragraphs" that overtake a fluctuating second- and third-person narration of fact and fiction surrounding 18 July 1936, as the narrator "write[s] and write[s] telling God what's happening on earth" while also pleading for an explanation concerning why "in Spain only the dead are important." Cela's concern for symmetry is again manifested in the subtitles and pertinent epigraphs that emphasize the upheavals of a country on the brink of civil war. *San Camilo, 1936* is divided into three parts: structured around "The Eve of St. Camillus's Day," "St. Camillus's Day," and "The Octave of St. Camillus." Also included is a somewhat dissonant epilogue in which the young narrator and his mentor-uncle, Jerónimo, discuss how to survive the impending catastrophe. The narrator's hallucinatory verbal odyssey is meticulously punctuated by a numerical ordering of things in twos and threes and a carefully orchestrated progression of events in harmony with precise clock time, radio news bulletins, and conversations in bars throughout Madrid. The urban landscape is similar to that of *La colmena,* but the sustained focus on the city brothels gives the impression that the Spanish capital has nothing else with which to provide refuge for its politicians and ordinary citizens.

*San Camilo, 1936* is also propelled by the constant movement set in motion in part 1 as a result of the deaths of the prostitute Magdalena and two important political figures from opposing sides, Lieutenant Colonel José Castillo and Joaquín Calvo Sotelo. As the syncopated narration of their funeral corteges fuels the action, other characters emerge and posit a future of further destruction, such as the young woman Virtudes, who dies in childbirth, and the frightened homosexual Matiítas, who commits suicide in a spectacularly grotesque manner once the war begins. The horror of the war notwithstanding, the narrator finds solace in his uncle Jerónimo's words of wisdom: "don't squander your twenty years in the service of anybody. . . . look out for the Spaniard you carry inside you . . . even though you think this is the end of the world it's not . . . it's only a purgation of the world, a preventive and bloody purgation but not an apocalyptic one."

As with much of Cela's work after *La colmena*, criticism of *San Camilo, 1936* has been varied. Those who view it positively, such as David Herzberger, Pierre Ullman, and Bertrand de Muñoz, share a postmodern orientation. Paul Ilie, on the other hand, exemplifies less-favorable commentaries in his assessment of "the politics of obscenity" that underscore the novel. Still others fail to discern that the kernels of Cela's life that are integrated into the novel disparage Cela by attributing to him the narrator's cowardice. The stridency of this response, however, culminated with the publication in 1973 of Cela's outlandish novel *oficio de tinieblas 5* (office of darkness 5), which is written entirely in lowercase letters, with minimal punctuation. It borrows from Gottfried Wilhelm Leibniz in its division of the narration into 1,194 "monads" (short text fragments) that confirm the first of three epigraphs to the work: "naturally, this is not a novel but rather the purge of my heart."

The irregular structure of *oficio de tinieblas 5* is clarified by a long subtitle: *novela de tesis escrita para ser cantada por un coro de enfermos* (thesis novel written to be sung by a choir of sickly people). It is intended to take place on the first of April, when ecclesiastical homage is rendered to those people who have successfully passed through the process of canonization on their way to official sainthood. Sarcasm and parody of church rituals and belief aside, the date is significant because it marks the official proclamation in 1939 of the end of the Spanish Civil War and the beginning of Franco's rule. In addition, the thematics of the novel and the criticism it levels on modern society signal the pinnacle of Cela's career in terms of breaking with tradition. Taboos are unleashed in an unceasing litany of sexual freedom and deviance. The characters (more than 120 of them), whether real (Napoleon Bonaparte, the Roman emperor Trajan, Picasso) or fictitious, are spared no mercy as the stylized sketches of their lives are converted into deconstructed stories that are grouped together as fiction, sometimes in sequenced monads, for example, numbers 939–941 (El Cid and Charlemagne). As with Cela's use of the titular number 5 to indicate an absence of logic, a poetics of deceit governs every absurdity coming from the narrator-author as he is reminded that people love to be entertained with lies (monad 372). He understands that his existence, like that of the narrator of *San Camilo, 1936,* is one of negation and self-destruction facing emotional and spiritual bankruptcy (monad 449). For him, his "office of darkness" facilitates searching for what holds humankind

hostage: "it is magic in the service of evil struggling against mankind" (monad 1097).

The narration, in the first and second persons, flows from introspection about "defeat . . . at twenty-five years of age" to the certainty of death. The narrator's anonymity is carried over to those family members whose antics and bizarre relationships become an integral part of his written testimony: they are referred to as "yourcousin" (written as one word), "your father don't mention his name," "your little grandmother," and "your mother." Because "yourcousin" bears on his forehead a signature wrinkle in the shape of an inverted question mark (unique to Spanish orthography), it is clear that the family is of Spanish-speaking lineage. Such nonsensical practices as the grandfather's obsession with making tape recordings of chirping dead birds confound every aspect of the narration and any semblance of a story. In contrast to the anonymity within the narrator's family, however, is a panoply of invented and real names, such as "monseñor metrófanes david peloponesiano" (monad 1186), "sir joshua nehemit" (monad 1189), James Meredith, Fred Hampton, and Martin Luther King, all of which lift the narrative from its Spanish origins and catapult it into a universal realm where it is not uncommon to hear references to the Holocaust, Vietnam, or Bosnia.

In sum, the story in *oficio de tinieblas 5* is about the life and death of humankind as it is refracted in characters such as Napoleon, El Cid, "yourcousin," or "your father don't mention his name," whose endeavors respond to a dynamics of negation and annihilation. For that reason the narrative axis (beginning with monad 794) follows along the lines of fourteen death notices (of some of the more cohesively sustained characters) and ends with the minute-by-minute account of the narrator's own demise at "23h, 59' 59" yes, it would have been more convenient to be defeated on time 0h 0' 0"" (monad 1194).

The broadened scope and increasingly uninhibited tenor of Cela's literary undertakings during the 1970s prompted even critics and enthusiasts who had praised *La familia de Pascual Duarte* and *La colmena* as premier examples of post–Spanish Civil War fiction to proclaim that his career as a novelist had come to an end. Cela continued nonetheless to write short fiction (collected in *Balada del vagabundo sin suerte y otros papeles volanderos* [1973, The Luckless Vagabond's Ballad and Other Loose Papers], *El espejo y otros cuentos* [1981, The Mirror and Other Short Stories], and *Las orejas del niño Raúl* [1986, Young Raul's Ears]), essays, and *Nuevo viaje a la Alcarria* (1986, New Journey to Alcarria), a revised version of his acclaimed 1948 travel book. Two years after Franco's death in 1975, Cela was named by King Juan Carlos I as a senator to the Spanish parliament, a ser-

Camilo José Cela
Cristo versus Arizona

Novela

Seix Barral ⅄ Biblioteca Breve

*Cover for Cela's 1988 novel (Christ versus Arizona), a history from 1895 to 1988 of the "Sodom and Gomorrah" of Tombstone, Arizona, where "law and order are worthless," as narrated by an eyewitness (Thomas Cooper Library, University of South Carolina)*

vice that prompted him to write a series of essays about Spain's transition to democratic rule. In 1980 he was inducted into the Galician Academy, and, much to his critics' surprise, in 1984 he was awarded the country's Premio Nacional (National Prize) for his novel *Mazurca para dos muertos* (1983, translated as *Mazurka for Two Dead Men,* 1992), which was a resounding success, selling more than 180,000 copies in 1984 and another 235,000 in 1990.

*Mazurca para dos muertos* hails a return to more traditional storytelling while also implementing a new discursive model. With perhaps the exception of *La colmena* and *oficio de tinieblas 5,* the fictive truths around which Cela's novels revolve are disclosed at the outset: Pascual is a criminal; the patients in *Pabellón de reposo* know

they are going to die; Mrs. Caldwell's son has already died; and the Spanish Civil War is an historical fact. The same unveiling applies in *Mazurca para dos muertos* despite its protracted account of the full details of the story. Someone with obvious narrative omniscience begins by explaining that "In that whorehouse where he earned his living, Gaudencio would play a fairly wide repertoire of tunes but there is one mazurka, *Ma Petite Marianne,* that he played only twice: in November 1936 when Lionheart [Afouto] was killed, and in January 1940 when Moucho was killed. He never would play it again." Because nobody understands much about what is taking the lives of so many of their men, the narration is dismissive of the significance of the war, and it is overshadowed by what remains foremost in the minds of the Gamuzo family: avenging the untimely deaths of two of their kinsmen, Afouto and Lázaro Codesal. Afouto was murdered by Fabián Minguela Abrogán (Moucho), while Lázaro Codesal died on military assignment "at the Tizzi-Azza post in Morocco," where he "was treacherously killed by a Moor [from the Tafersit tribe]." The events pertaining to both are told to don Camilo on a visit to his family after years of having been away, with narrative and chronological time blending into "the prudent onward march of the world spinning and turning as the drizzle falls with neither beginning nor end."

The typically lush landscape and bountiful legends and superstitions of Galicia support an atmosphere in which death and annihilation, vengeance, murder, violence, and family honor are the principle coordinates of a narrative grid of incidents that have made widows of most of the women. The voices of matriarchs such as Ramona and Adega are crucial to the discourse that expands with each retelling of basically the same events. Everything don Camilo hears centers around what happened before and after either the Spanish Civil War or Afouto's murder.

The oscillating rhythm of past memory and present narration emphasizes the oral transmission of information, while references to the mazurka mark the musical substructure of circularity, repetition, and refrain in the novel: "I play whatever I like. . . . That piece of music isn't for any Tom, Dick, or Harry and I'm the only one that knows when to play it and what it means." The alternating voices that carry on the oral tradition offer brief conversational vignettes that clarify previous utterances, introduce new characters, or explain linguistic peculiarities that are a part of the Galician lexicon that is intrinsic to the novel (Cela included in the Spanish edition a map of the area and a vocabulary of Galician terms). The discourse unfolds in ritualistic fashion as pieces of information are disseminated relative to the family's plans for avenging Afouto's murder. Moucho is eventually killed by Tanis Gamuzo's two dogs, Sultan and Moor, and poetic justice is inversely conferred upon Lázaro Codesal, whose life was ended by a Moorish assassin.

The move away from Madrid as chosen fictive space for Cela's later novels is most evident in *Cristo versus Arizona* (1988, Christ versus Arizona), which takes place in Tombstone, Arizona, and covers the years from 1895 through 1988 amid the desert flora and fauna of the southwestern United States, where Spain left an indelible mark on the diverse indigenous cultures. The narrator, Wendell Espana, offers what he repeatedly states to be a true report of the events he witnessed during his life in the "Sodom and Gomorrah" of Tombstone, where "law and order are worthless." In contrast to his sworn truthfulness, his testimony is dotted with tongue-in-cheek insistence on the inaccuracies of the episodes included in his chronicle, primarily because he writes down what has been told him by word of mouth, thus following *Mazurca para dos muertos* in preferring oral over written transmission. Aware of the licentious and graphic quality of the stories, Wendell is insistent upon not publishing his chronicle until all of his sources are dead, a narrative strategy that calls to mind the confusing paratextual documents that frame Pascual's confession-driven manuscript.

Unlike Pascual, however, Wendell is merely the chronicler of the hybridized time and place into which he was born and of which his identity bears all the signs (including the mark his father made on him with a branding iron to commemorate the beginning of the twentieth century). Wendell, at twenty-two years of age, haphazardly made his mother's acquaintance in the brothel where she worked, after he had paid for her services. Whereas matricide forever seals Pascual's fate, Wendell (like Eliacim in *Mrs. Caldwell habla con su hijo*) is plagued with the consequences of his implied incest. Perhaps for that reason he insists upon clarifying repeatedly that his name is "Wendell Espana, Wendell Liverpool Espana, maybe it is Span or Aspen instead of Espana, I never really found out," despite the fact that "many people keep thinking that my name is Wendell Liverpool Lochiel, that was before knowing who my parents had been."

He never reveals the real motive for keeping his written record, but at the same time he fills it with information, dates of events, and names of characters, such as the well-known prostitutes Big Nose Kate, Pumice Stone, Big Minnie, and Betty Pink Casey; the Earp and Clanton families; Sheriff Sam W. Lindo; Sitting Bull; and Cochise. His account models "the litany to Our Lady who is the armor that preserves us from sin," which echoes rhythmically throughout the narration. In addition, the litany to the Mother of God also parallels a registry that the prostitute Cyndy keeps of her regular clients. Interspersed with the sordid background of barroom and brothel scenes, lynchings, and gunfights are legends (about snakes, desert plants, and elixirs) and indigenous mythologies (including the invocation of a litany to St. Joseph in order to stave off poisonous vipers). Once again, a chain of character-driven incidents holds the narration together.

Wendell's story is made up of one hyperbolically long sentence. His is the prose of an unschooled individual, but it is, nevertheless, pointedly critical of the malevolence visited upon native America by the colonizing Spaniards (and, by extension, Europeans), and also remindful of certain themes that are in the forefront of Cela's later novels, among them the depiction of twentieth-century life as a division between "winners and losers" whose actions square them off with a legal system in which poorly trained judges and executioners purportedly strive to achieve justice. Most visible in *Cristo versus Arizona* are the criminals and foreigners who make their way to Tombstone, where "more than half of the hanged were foreigners"; equally striking are the large numbers of Chinese and African Americans. The same applies to the Native American population: "the Sioux were defeated by the White Man at Wounded Knee, the heroic adventures of Chief Little Big Man had nothing to do with the movie." For all of the incriminatory words about how "everything Yankee is bad," no one bears the brunt of Cela's chastisement more than the Spaniards themselves, as Wendell calls to mind his own ethnic background by naively explaining his use of Spanish: "one has to perpetrate the savage act in the same language and with the same tongue as the one with which one curses and blesses." In full recognition and public admission of the many sins covering a "heart-shaped stone" that is a symbolic gathering point in the nearby Arizona desert as well as a metaphor for Europe's expansion into the Americas by way of Tombstone, a serious "examination of conscience" precedes Wendell's parting plea for mercy in the Agnus Dei litany with which he ends his chronicle. Luis Blanco Vila is correct in his assertion that *Cristo versus Arizona* enjoyed little popularity in Spain because its readers were unable to grasp the meaning of the Wild West and were therefore unwilling to accept Wendell's invitation for self-scrutiny.

Cela received the Nobel Prize in literature in 1989. That same year his divorce from his wife of forty-four years fueled a wave of public criticism, which intensified in 1991 when he wed Marina Castaño, a journalist several decades his junior. Despite his waning career, he composed the second part of his long-awaited autobiography: *Memorias, entendimientos y voluntades* (1993, Memories, Understandings and Wishes). In

*Dust jacket for the 2002 English translation of Cela's 1999 novel,*
Madera de boj, *in which the narrator's uncle attempts to build
a house out of decorative shrubbery in an allegory about the
struggle to attain what is beyond reach (Richland
County Public Library)*

addition, he developed more *apuntes*-type works, such as
*Cachondeos, escarceos y otros meneos* (1991, Jokes, Dabblings
and Other Fidgeting), *La sima de las penúltimas inocencias*
(1993, The Sinkhole of Penultimate Innocence), *La
dama pájara y otros cuentos* (1994, Lady Bird and Other
Tales), and *Historias familiares* (1998, Familiar Stories).
Also among these works is a return (as with prior
works devoted to Solana and Picasso) to the world of
art: *Los caprichos de Francisco de Goya y Lucientes* (1989,
Francisco de Goya's Caprices). In 1999 *Homenaje al
Bosco, II: La extracción de la piedra de la locura; o, El inventor
del garrote* (Homage to Bosch, II: The Origins of the
Source of Insanity; or, The Inventor of the Garrote),
the second part of his 1969 play *El carro de heno*, was
published but, despite having been commissioned for
the celebration of the quincentennial discovery of the
Americas, never staged because of its projected length
(almost six hours) and proposed budget (millions of
pesetas). He also wrote three novels of considerable

length: *El asesinato del perdedor* (1994, The Murder of the
Loser), *La cruz de San Andrés* (1994, St. Andrew's Cross),
and *Madera de boj* (1999; translated as *Boxwood*, 2002),
which all share the same themes as Cela's fiction over
the years: social deviance and rejection of authority and
fanaticism.

In *El asesinato del perdedor*, Mateo Ruecas is jailed
for having shown public affection to his girlfriend
Soledad in a Spanish town called N.N. His case is
emblematic of the many others in the novel whose
"errors" form the mismatched episodic vignettes that
destabilize an already dizzying, fragmented text for
which several narrator-authors claim responsibility. It is
made clear at the onset that any "concession to the collective good taste, to cunning and uneducated public
good taste" is out of order. The novel opens with a solil-
oquy of sorts by Michael Percival, "el Agachadizo" (the
Stooped-Over), who lived some two hundred years
ago. He mumbles about how to deal with enemies,
addressing some invisible listeners: "make every effort
to infect them with some humiliating illness . . . AIDS
or leprosy or nostalgia." Even though Percival's enigmatic figure resurfaces rarely over the course of the
novel, he functions as a marker in an otherwise aimless
narration of disconnected characters and events. He
also becomes loosely associated with Mateo, a metaphor for those whom society has labeled as "losers."
Unlike Pascual, Mateo feels an overwhelming sense of
shame for having spent time in jail, which causes him to
take his own life. His "error" is juxtaposed with lascivi-
ous and scatological stories that mirror and at the same
time minimize greatly his own. An array of silly characters (including Mrs. Belushi, Juan Grujidora, Estefanía
Yellowbild, Zaqueo Nicomediano, Professor Maurus
Waldawj, M.D., and Pamela Pleshette of Restricted
Beach, Florida) underscores the ridiculousness of
Mateo's faux pas, again attesting to Cela's use of parody and sarcasm as a means of cutting down to size all
societally sanctioned pretensions of greatness. In this
way, Cela undermines even his own narratorial authority and, therefore, favors literary invention over historical accuracy. The masses, however, continue to be
entertained by the misfortunes of such "losers" (prostitutes, beggars, people with physical impediments and
little formal education), who end up in public executions for which people clamor to get tickets.

The discourse amounts to a catalogue of utterances and antics replete with gymnastics, pantomime,
and Chaplinesque mimicry. The gossip that spreads in
everyday life about people's misfortunes runs current
with the spontaneity of the text; short snippets of conversations parody the narration and allow the discourse
to proceed along the same chatty lines. Periodic references are made to a "choir of beggars" who provide the

music for the public executions. Also distinguishable is a constrained theatrical subtext that transforms *El asesinato del perdedor* into a linguistic, narrative, thematic, philosophical, and fictive spectacle, not the least of which is the metamorphosis of Pascual Duarte into Esteban Ojeda, who confirms the transformation by claiming that he "was pretty famous years ago, when I wrote a few pages which began like this: I am not, sir, a bad person, though in all truth I am not lacking in reasons for being one, etc." Later, Ojeda says that he "would like to write in the first person, it is always easier. It's as if I were Mateo Ruecas, I close my eyes and I feel like I am Mateo Ruecas, the loser about whom they speak in this true story. My girlfriend is called Soledad." Continuing Cela's fondness for accompanying documents, readers are also presented with a letter written by Juana Olmedo, Coordinator of the Mateo Ruecas Effort, to Mr. Sebastián Cardeñosa López of O Coruña (Galicia), reminding him of the harm that was done to Mateo because of his modest social status and the "errors" of the Spanish judicial system; she cites a need to change "article 431 of the Penal Code, referring to public scandals" and asks that he write a formal condemnation of the matter so that, as petitioned her by Mateo's mother, no other poor Spanish family ever again has to suffer the abuses of a legal system that is rife with poorly trained judges.

*El asesinato del perdedor* provoked ire, frustration, and disillusionment among readers accustomed to the more traditional storytelling format to which Spanish novels had returned in the 1980s, and it has been given little critical attention. Nevertheless, Pascual Duarte's late-twentieth-century reincarnation is evidence of Cela's lifelong commitment to artistic invention. The same can be said of *La cruz de San Andrés,* which intertwines elements of theater and narrative in keeping with its author's goal of constant renewal. This novel deals with multiple themes ranging from metafiction to philosophy, feminism, religious fanaticism, historiography, literary invention, and life at the end of the millennium. It chronicles the collapse of the López Santana family, which is celebrated as a "black Mass of confusion" and is unabashedly thrown, like "rotten entrails," to its readers as transcribed from the original "manuscript" of sorts, which was boastfully written by narrator Matilde Verdú (under whose name Cela published the book) on rolls of toilet paper.

The structure of the novel, like that of *Mazurca para dos muertos,* echoes a more traditional manner of writing; yet, the chapters are given subtitles that are befitting of plays: "Dramatis personae," "Plot," "Exposition," "Complication," and "Denouement/Ending, Final Coda, and Internment of the Last Puppets." The dramatic vicissitudes of the López Santana family are highlighted by myriad references to icons of pop culture (Betty Boop, Ava Gardner, Marilyn Monroe, Robert Taylor, and L. Ron Hubbard). There is one prevailing third-person voice that comments on the other narrators. Additionally, recognition is given to the source document that was written by the character Pilar Seixón, but Matilde Verdú, who sometimes also refers to herself as Matilde Lens and Matilde Meizoso, remains the primary chronicler.

Matilde tells her story based on cues from her own conversational interludes with an unnamed interrogating voice who occasionally says things such as "Take a short break and continue," or "Do you believe that history has to be told in detail and stopping for minutia and nuisances?" Matilde also embellishes her tale with parts of her own life, principally claiming that she and her husband, because of their political affiliation with the Republican faction of the Spanish Civil War, were crucified on St. Andrew's crosses. When, however, it is revealed that Matilde is simply satisfying the editorial demands of her literary agent, Paula Fields, in order to earn the $600,000 she has been promised for her manuscript, the noble undertaking of her chronicle turns as farcical as the toilet paper on which it is written. As Fran, the last of the López Santana family members, slits his writs in obedience to the leader of the secret cult of the "Community of the Daybreak of Jesus Christ," so too disintegrates the family and, by extension, the ignoble chronicle.

*Madera de boj* is both a tribute to those who drowned in the waters off the coast of Spain's northwestern promontory and a narrative elegy to that portion of the Atlantic Ocean that bathes Galicia's "Coast of Death" and *finisterre* (land's end). The litany-like narration is intentionally mired in sentences that go on for pages, interrupted by casual conversational exchanges, a Galician register of terms and expressions, recipes, legends and superstitions, aphorisms, punctilious references to the area's maritime topography, flora and fauna, and a blend of foreign names (Knut Skien, Juanito Jorick, James and Hans E. Allen, and Marco Polo). The endless tossing of the discourse is a metaphor for a sea that is an "open book in which everything was written and could be read with ease" and also the source of a "never-ending list of shipwrecks" that populate a virtual world of dead people. Both narrator and reader assume the role of "sailors" and, as such, have scant assurance that the compass that the narrating voice inherited will be of use because of the disquieting, yet alluring, submerged gold from the teeth of all the sailors who drowned there—which, seafarers say, throws reliable navigational instruments wildly off course.

The anonymous narrator shows extensive knowledge of the maritime and the English-speaking worlds.

Having developed a successful whaling industry (which ended up dividing them), his ancestors were also tied to water: his Norwegian uncle, Knut Skien, hunted whales and the mythical Marco Polo ram; his cousin, Vitiño Leis Agulleiro, was the captain of the shipwrecked *Arada;* and his grandfather founded the Royal Regatta Club of Galicia in 1902. Their favorite pastimes included playing rugby, tennis, and cricket, and reciting Edgar Allan Poe's poetry in Galician while facing the sea. The most wealthy among them, Uncle Dick, spent an entire lifetime aimlessly pursuing his dream of building a house out of boxwood, a shrub that is used decoratively in gardens but unsuitable for the construction of large structures. Given the clearly enunciated premise that legend and fantasy are "more powerful than the truth," *Madera de boj* constitutes an allegorical superstructure about struggling to attain what is beyond reach.

In 2000 Camilo José Cela University was founded on the outskirts of Madrid. It is a small, private institution that uses computer-based instruction with an emphasis on research and critical inquiry.

Cela died on 17 January 2002. He bequeathed his small forest resort along the coast of Sant Elm in Majorca to the Grup d'Ornitologia Balear (Balearic Ornithology Group). He also left several unfinished projects, among them a novel to be called "Dry sicuta" (Dry Hemlock). In November 2002 his widow appeared at the Reina Sofía Museum in Madrid to unveil *Cuadernos de El Espinar* (Notebooks from The Espinar Residence), facsimiles of twelve etchings by Cela. Public scrutiny of his work continued, focusing on an accusation of plagiarism in *La cruz de San Andrés,* of which he was posthumously found not guilty, and a prior agreement with the Planeta publishing house to present the novel for consideration in its yearly awarding of the prize by the same name, which Cela won. Gaspar Sánchez Salas, Cela's last assistant and secretary, has asserted that the Nobel laureate is innocent of these charges, as well as of using ghostwriters toward the end of his career. Cela's death also drew attention because of questions of inheritance, the legal rights to his literary legacy, and the future direction of the Cela Foundation, which he had established some years before in Iria Flavia, Galicia, as the repository for his manuscripts and relevant papers. The degree to which Cela's life and works have generated both praise and criticism is brought home by several biographical accounts of his life: *Cela: Un cadáver exquisito* (2002, Cela: An Exquisite Corpse) by his friend and fellow writer Francisco Umbral; *Desmontando a Cela* (2002, Dismantling Cela) by journalist Tomás García Yebra; *Cela, el hombre que quiso ganar* (2003, Cela, the Man Who Wanted to Win) by Gibson; and the two published

works of Sánchez Salas, *Cela: El hombre a quien vi llorar* (2002, Cela: The Man I Saw Cry) and *Cela: Mi derecho a contar la verdad* (2004, Cela: My Right to Tell the Truth).

As has often been stated, Camilo José Cela's works of prose fiction do not placate the painful soul-searching of the human condition. To quote the Nobel committee, his is a "rich and intensive prose, which with restrained compassion forms a challenging vision of man's vulnerability." Cela's novels far surpass capturing the spirit of Spain in the twentieth century; they lay bare the workings of the human species over the course of time. Cela's disjointed language parallels the truncated bond between people of all places and walks of life. The shocking imperfections and personal failings of his characters are exponentially equivalent to Cela's disdain for the entrapment of politically constrained social and literary correctness. In the words of the anonymous narrator of *Madera al boj,* "the model is Emile Zola or doña Emilia Pardo Bazán, now it's not anymore like before, now people have discovered that the novel is a reflection of life and life has no ending other than death, that pirouette that is never the same."

**Interview:**

Valerie Miles, "Camilo José Cela: The Art of Fiction CXLV," *Paris Review,* 139 (Summer 1996): 124–163.

**Biographies:**

Camilo José Cela Conde, *Cela, mi padre* (Madrid: Ediciones Temas de Hoy, 1989);

Francisco Umbral, *Cela: Un cadáver exquisito* (Barcelona: Planeta, 2002);

Gaspar Sánchez Salas, *Cela: El hombre a quien ví llorar* (Barcelona: Ediciones Carena, 2002);

Tomás García Yebra, *Desmontando a Cela* (Madrid: Libertarias, 2002);

Ian Gibson, *Cela, el hombre que quiso ganar* (Madrid: Aguilar, 2003);

Sánchez Salas, *Cela: Mi derecho a contar la verdad* (Barcelona: Belacqva, 2004).

**References:**

Maryse Bertrand de Muñoz, "El estatuto del narrador en *San Camilo, 1936,*" in *Crítica semiológica de textos literarios hispánicos,* edited by Miguel Angel Garrido Gallardo (Madrid: Consejo Superior de Investigaciones Científicas, 1986), pp. 579–589;

Luis Blanco Vila, *Para leer a Camilo José Cela* (Madrid: Palas Atenea, 1991);

Silvia Burunat, "El monólogo interior en Camilo José Cela," in her *El monólogo como forma narrativa en la novela española* (Madrid: José Porrúa Turanzas, 1980), pp. 57–82;

J. M. Castellet, "Iniciación a la obra narrativa de Camilo José Cela," *Revista Hispánica Moderna,* 28 (1962): 107–150;

Lucile C. Charlebois, *Understanding Camilo José Cela* (Columbia: University of South Carolina Press, 1998);

William David Foster, *Forms of the Novel in the Work of Camilo José Cela* (Columbia: University of Missouri Press, 1967);

Paul Ilie, *La novelística de Camilo José Cela* (Madrid: Gredos, 1961);

Ilie, "The Politics of Obscenity in *San Camilo, 1936,*" *Anales de la Novela de Posguerra,* 1 (1976): 25–63;

*Ínsula,* special Cela/Nobel Prize in literature issue, 518–519 (February–March 1990);

Robert Kirsner, *The Novels and Travels of Camilo José Cela* (Chapel Hill: University of North Carolina Press, 1964);

John Kronik, "Pascual's Parole," *Review of Contemporary Fiction,* 4, no. 3 (1984): 111–118;

Jorge A. Marbán, "Fases y alcance del humorism en los apuntes carpetovetónicos de Cela," *Hispanic Journal,* 2 (Spring 1981): 71–79;

Eloy E. Merino, *El nuevo* Lazarillo *de Camilo J. Cela: Política y cultura en su palimpsesto* (Lewiston, N.Y.: Edwin Mellen Press, 2000);

Janet Pérez, *Camilo José Cela Revisited* (New York: Twayne, 2000);

José Luis S. Ponce de León, *La novela española de la Guerra Civil* (Madrid: Ínsula, 1971);

Olga Prjevalinsky, *El sistema estético de Camilo José Cela* (Valencia: Castalia, 1960);

*Review of Contemporary Fiction,* special Cela issue, 4, no. 3 (1984);

Darío Villanueva, "La intencionalidad de lo sexual en Cela," *Los Cuadernos del Norte,* 51 (October–November 1988): 54–57.

**Papers:**

Camilo José Cela's papers are at the Cela Foundation in Iria Flavia, Galicia, Spain.

# Rosa Chacel

## (3 June 1898 – 7 July 1994)

## Elizabeth Scarlett
### State University of New York at Buffalo

See also the Chacel entry in *DLB 134: Twentieth-Century Spanish Poets, Second Series.*

BOOKS: *Estación: Ida y vuelta* (Madrid: Ulises, 1930; revised edition, Madrid: CVS, 1974);

*A la orilla de un pozo* (Madrid: Héroe, 1936; revised edition, Valencia: Pre-Textos, 1985);

*Teresa* (Buenos Aires: Nuevo Romance, 1941; revised edition, Madrid: Aguilar, 1963);

*Memorias de Leticia Valle* (Buenos Aires: Emecé, 1945; revised edition, Barcelona: Lumen, 1971); translated by Carol Maier as *Memoirs of Leticia Valle* (Lincoln: University of Nebraska Press, 1994);

*Sobre el piélago* (Buenos Aires: Imán, 1952);

*Poesía de la circunstancia: Cómo y por qué de la novela* (Bahía Blanca, Argentina: Universidad Nacional del Sur, 1958);

*La sinrazón* (Buenos Aires: Losada, 1960; revised edition, Bilbao: Albia, 1977; Barcelona: Bruguera, 1981);

*Ofrenda a una virgen loca* (Jalapa, Mexico: Universidad Veracruzana, 1961);

*Icada, Nevda, Diada* (Barcelona: Seix Barral, 1971);

*La confesión* (Barcelona: EDHASA, 1971);

*Saturnal* (Barcelona: Seix Barral, 1972);

*Desde el amanecer: Autobiografía de mis primeros diez años* (Madrid: Revista de Occidente, 1972; revised edition, Barcelona: Bruguera, 1981);

*Barrio de Maravillas* (Barcelona: Seix Barral, 1976; revised edition, Barcelona: Bruguera, 1980); translated by D. A. Démers as *The Maravillas District* (Lincoln: University of Nebraska Press, 1992);

*Versos prohibidos* (Madrid: Caballo Griego para la Poesía, 1978);

*Timoteo Pérez y sus retratos del jardín* (Madrid: Cátedra, 1980);

*Novelas antes de tiempo* (Barcelona: Bruguera, 1981);

*Los títulos* (Barcelona: EDHASA, 1981);

*Alcancía: Ida; Vuelta,* 2 volumes (Barcelona: Seix Barral, 1982);

*Rosa Chacel (portrait by her husband, Timoteo Pérez Rubio; from the cover for* Barrio de Maravillas, *1976; Thomas Cooper Library, University of South Carolina)*

*Acrópolis* (Barcelona: Seix Barral, 1984);

*Rebañaduras: Colección de artículos* (Salamanca: Junta de Castilla y León, Consejería de Educación y Cultura, 1986);

*Ciencias naturales* (Barcelona: Seix Barral, 1988);

*La lectura es secreto* (Madrid: Júcar, 1989);

*Balaam y otros cuentos* (Madrid: Montena, 1989);

*Obra completa,* 6 volumes, edited by Ana Rodríguez Fischer and Félix Pardo (Valladolid: Diputación Provincial de Valladolid/Centro de Creación y Estudios Jorge Guillén, 1989);

*Poesía (1931–1991),* edited by Antoni Marí (Barcelona: Tusquets, 1992);

*Alcancía: Estación termini,* edited by Carlos Pérez Chacel and Antonio Piedra (Valladolid: Consejería de Educación y Cultura, 1998).

**Editions:** *Estación: Ida y vuelta,* edited by Shirley Mangini (Madrid: Cátedra, 1989);

*Barrio de Maravillas,* edited by Ana Rodríguez Fischer (Madrid: Castalia, 1993).

OTHER: T. S. Eliot, *Reunión de familia,* translated by Chacel (Buenos Aires: Emecé, 1953);

Nikos Kazantzakis, *Libertad o muerte,* translated by Chacel (Buenos Aires: Carlos Lohlé, 1963);

Renato Poggioli, *Teoría del arte de vanguardia,* translated by Chacel (Madrid: Revista de Occidente, 1964);

Albert Camus, *La peste,* translated by Chacel (Barcelona: EDHASA, 1977);

Sor Juana Inés de la Cruz, *Sonetos y endechas,* preface by Chacel (Barcelona: Labor, 1980);

Jean Racine, *Seis tragedias,* translated by Chacel (Madrid: Alfaguara, 1983);

Walmir Ayala, *Museo de cámara,* translated by Chacel (Madrid: Xanela, 1986).

Rosa Chacel is a fiction writer and intellectual for whom art, history, and self-reflection are inextricably interwoven. Her early work is primarily known as a fictionalization of the philosopher José Ortega y Gasset's central principles, as well as of Miguel de Unamuno's notions of *intrahistoria* (inner history) and writing as meditation; as a representative of Spanish prose of the historic avant-gardes; and despite her protest, as an example of a woman writing against the current in a discourse often defined by men. Her later career registers the restlessness and nostalgia of the writers and intellectuals who lived in exile after the Republicans were defeated by General Francisco Franco's Nationalist forces in 1939. A third phase of her career is her gradual return to Spain and to the attention of Spanish readers after the end of the dictatorship, when she was able to influence a generation of writers who had grown up in her absence.

Along with María Teresa de León and Ernestina Champourcín, Chacel can be seen as a female contemporary to the Generation of 1927, a group of writers and artists that coalesced in Madrid around the tricentennial commemoration of Luis de Góngora's death. Chacel was something of a social outsider in terms of the group's inner circle, which included the internationally renowned Federico García Lorca, Jorge Guillén, Luis Cernuda, Pedro Salinas, Vicente Aleixandre, Luis Buñuel, and Salvador Dalí: she was not enrolled at the Residencia de Estudiantes (Residence of Students), as the majority of these writers were (her option would have been the female counterpart, the Residencia de Mujeres [Residence of Women]). She was away from Spain during the group's formative years, from 1922 until 1927. Like the male authors associated with this group, however, Chacel displays an openness to experimentation, invigorated particularly by the theories of Sigmund Freud, while maintaining a certain classicism of style. She adopts the baroque mode (rather than the automatic writing of the Surrealists) as a language of excess that affords freedom to plumb the depths of consciousness in writing.

Rosa Chacel Arimón was born in Valladolid, capital of the province of the same name in Old Castile (known today as the autonomy of Castilla-León). Her father, Francisco Chacel Barhero, had prepared briefly for a military career but left it behind at the age of sixteen upon the death of his father, a military officer. Her mother, Rosa-Cruz Arimón y Pacheco, was born in Caracas to a Spanish family who had moved there for political reasons; when her father died, the family moved back and settled in Valladolid. The Romantic dramatist José Zorrilla y Moral, author of *Don Juan Tenorio* (1844), was part of Chacel's ancestry through marriage, and she felt an affinity with him despite his questionable versification, which she criticizes through Leticia Valle, the protagonist of her *Memorias de Leticia Valle* (1945; translated as *Memoirs of Leticia Valle,* 1994). She also felt close to several of the figures of the Generation of 1898, the year of her birth: Ramón del Valle-Inclán became her teacher in Madrid, and her insistence upon the inner life as the essential one echoes Unamuno's stance. Chacel grew up as an only child: her sister, Blanca, was not born until 1914, and her six-month-old brother died when she was three. She was a child prodigy who learned to impress adults by reciting long poems from memory.

Chacel was educated at home by her mother, who had earned a degree in teaching. She soon became interested in the visual arts and studied drawing and sculpture while still in Valladolid. Later, she moved to Madrid in 1908 with her parents, where they lived with her mother's relatives in the Maravillas district, a setting for one of her later novels. Chacel continued to blossom as an artist. In 1915 she entered the Escuela Superior de Bellas Artes de San Fernando, where she studied sculpture for three years, enjoying the mentorship of Valle-Inclán in his capacity as professor of aesthetics and meeting her future husband, the painter Timoteo Pérez Rubio. Chronic ill health forced her to leave the academy, where she had been obliged to work in drafty basement studios that worsened her condition. She turned to the literary and

Memoirs
of
Leticia Valle

Rosa Chacel

TRANSLATED AND WITH AN
AFTERWORD BY CAROL MAIER

*Front cover for the English translation (1994) of Chacel's 1945
novel,* Memorias de Leticia Valle, *about a girl who
seduces her tutor and drives him to commit suicide
(Richland County Public Library)*

intellectual life of Madrid, which was beginning to hum with the first vanguard movements, such as *ultraísmo* (ultraism), with which she became associated. In addition to reading extensively, she shared dialogues with other thinkers and artists at the Ateneo and the many *tertulias* (literary circles) that enlivened Madrid after World War I.

Chacel and Pérez Rubio married in 1921. He had been awarded a scholarship to continue his work at the Spanish Academy of the Roman School of Art, and the two left for Italy in 1922. Chacel took with her the Spanish translations of Freud's complete works and James Joyce's *Portrait of the Artist as a Young*

*Man* (1916), both of which were instrumental in the formulation of her first novel. In June of the same year, Chacel's first publication appeared, a short prose work titled "El amigo de voz oportuna" (The Friend with the Opportune Voice) in the review *La Esfera*. The couple traveled throughout Italy, Germany, Austria, and France, with an extended stay in Paris in the winter of 1924–1925, where André Breton's *Manifeste du surréalisme* (1924, Surrealist Manifesto) was under debate, and they were frequent guests in the home of Max Ernst. Back in Rome, Chacel continued to read Marcel Proust as well as Ortega y Gasset's latest material (the academy subscribed to the *Revista de Occidente* and *El Sol*). She worked on her first story, "Chinina Migone," and her first novel, *Estación: Ida y vuelta* (Station/Season: Round-Trip), publishing a chapter of the latter in *Revista de Occidente* in May 1927. The following year, the couple returned to Spain to live in Pérez Rubio's studio, and in 1930 Julio Gómez de la Serna (the brother of Ramón) published Chacel's first novel in his printing house Ulises under the series "Valores Actuales."

*Estación: Ida y vuelta* is a meditation on the genesis of love, of the literary text, and of new life. It seeks to illustrate the workings of artistic creation in the way that it is written, and in turn links artistic creation with other forms of creativity (romantic love, pregnancy), showing them all to be guided by the erotic drive. The plot is glimpsed rather than followed: the narrator conducts a courtship with his young neighbor. The building that gives them shelter is also viewed poetically as the structure that unites them in love. Once they have been together for some time, the protagonist's attention turns to his fledgling literary career, and to a provocative dancer who ignites his interest, forming a love triangle. Brooding upon his possibilities as a writer, he expresses self-doubt and even thoughts of suicide, while feeling guilty about his infidelity as well. When he learns that his first, true love is pregnant, however, he races to be by her side. The embryo grows and takes shape alongside the protagonist's first text. Chacel's son, Carlos Pérez Chacel, was born in 1930, not long after she finished work on the manuscript.

While trying different genres to find the one that fits his creative impulse, the narrator considers writing a movie script. Cinema was a passion for Chacel as for many of her contemporaries; she had joined the Madrid Cinema Club, so she was well informed about the incipient art form. In *Estación,* however, the narrator appears to discard the motion picture as a possible mode of expression on account of the limited roles it assigned to women. In her writing, iconoclasm is a driving force for many of the author's meditations on existing art forms, much as Ortega y Gasset advocated in *La deshumanización del arte* (1925, The Dehumanization of Art), but in this case it is practiced with a feminist consciousness that is absent from Ortega y Gasset's writings. Furthermore, in consonance with his *Ideas sobre la novela* (1925, Ideas on the Novel), the inner portraiture of the soul, rather than the material reality of conventional realism, is the main object. Ortega y Gasset's insistence on "new art" as a privileging of metaphor is brought to life by Chacel in many vivid figures of speech that recall Ramón Gómez de la Serna's ingenious *greguerías,* a form of brief, witty aphorism that Gómez de la Serna defined as "humor plus metaphor":

> ¿Qué es eso del sentimentalismo? ¿Qué microbio es ése? No es microbio; es un bicho, una araña casera, de esas arañas conservadoras, que están siempre, como en la orilla del puerto, dispuestas a echarle un cable a todo lo que llega. ¡Todo lo atan, todo lo dejan lleno de amarras! Yo creo que en esas casas donde los ladrones abren el armario y no se llevan lo más importante, no es porque no lo han visto; es que la araña tutelar lo tenía tan bien atado que no hubo fuerza capaz de arrancarlo.

> (What is sentimentality? What kind of germ is it? It's not a germ; it's a creature, a house spider, one of those conservative spiders, who are always, as if waiting beside the harbor, ready to throw a line around anything that comes along. They attach everything and leave it all full of ties! I believe that in houses where burglars open the closet but leave behind what is most important, it's not because they did not see it; it's because the tutelary spider of the house had it so well secured that no power was great enough to pull it out.)

Chacel's text also plays upon the Freudian notion of the female psyche as permeable: the male narrator complains of his lack of a fixed and stable identity and at several points speaks as though fused with one of his female counterparts. The pregnancy is seen as a doubling of the heroine; her sense of identity expands to include another, just as the text crystallizes within the narrator's mind. When both processes reach their end point, something new, with a life of its own, has been produced. Thus, the rejoicing finale of the novel: "Algo ha terminado; ahora puedo decir: ¡principio!" (Something has ended; now I can say: Beginning!)

*Estación: Ida y vuelta* has become one of the chief examples of Spanish avant-garde fiction of the 1920s and 1930s, along with novels by Benjamín Jarnés, Pedro Salinas, and Antonio Espina. The freshness of structural and linguistic innovations inspired by Joyce, Proust, and Freud, along with the creative vitality of

the Spanish "Silver Age," combine to make this moment distinct for the experimental Spanish novel, despite the predominance of poetry and drama in this period. Shirley Magnini, Eunice Myers, and Carol Maier have underlined the feminine perspective of Chacel as a pioneering writer who aspired to being taken as seriously as her male peers, a role similar to that of Virginia Woolf in English letters. Although never one to make explicitly feminist pronouncements, she interacted with the persistent misogyny of European literary, philosophical, and psychoanalytic discourses as she came to terms with herself as a young artist.

The flow of consciousness into writing exemplified in *Estación: Ida y vuelta,* anticipating the *nouveau roman,* was modified and made more coherent in Chacel's subsequent works. The novel serves, nonetheless, as a showcase for the themes that continued to surface throughout her career: the relationship between personal guilt and artistic self-doubt; the erotic origin of all creativity, with a strong underlying current of homoeroticism; the need for confession as a prime motivation in narrative; and the struggle of the woman artist, who must break the mold of woman-as-object to become a bona fide female subject in discourse. Furthermore, the practice of leaving at least part of the central plot in ellipsis, which she called *intríngulis* (ulterior motive or snag), continued to lend ambiguity and secrecy to her subsequent works.

Chacel spent six months in Berlin in 1933, in part to escape from the sadness that she experienced upon the death of her mother. In 1936 she published *A la orilla de un pozo* (At the Edge of a Well), a sonnet collection with echoes of Góngora and Juan Ramón Jiménez's "pure poetry." During the Second Spanish Republic, from 1931 until 1936, she and her husband were aligned with the Left. Pérez Rubio was an assistant director of the Museum of Modern Art, and Chacel signed many petitions on behalf of human rights in conjunction with causes of the Popular Front government. When civil war broke out, it was necessary for her to flee with her son to Barcelona, then to Valencia, and finally into exile abroad.

By this time Chacel had completed work on her second novel, *Teresa,* but it was not published in full until 1941 in Buenos Aires. A fictional biography of Teresa Mancha, the lover of Spanish poet José de Espronceda y Delgado who prompted him to write "Canto a Teresa" (1840–1842, Song to Teresa), *Teresa* was meant to be part of a series envisioned by Ortega y Gasset called "Vidas extraordinarias del siglo XIX" (Extraordinary Nineteenth-Century Lives). Such biographies were in vogue in other European nations, and Ortega y Gasset saw an opportunity for Spanish writ-

*Paperback cover for Chacel's 1976 novel (translated as* The
Maravillas District, *1992), about the coming-of-age of
young people in a Madrid neighborhood in the early
twentieth century (Thomas Cooper Library,
University of South Carolina)*

and Athens before moving to Rio de Janeiro with her
husband. She spent much time in Buenos Aires, where
she had many contacts that included other exiled writers and Jorge Luis Borges's sister Norah. As her exile
began, she also started what eventually became four
volumes of memoirs. *Alcancía: Ida* (Safe Box: Departure) includes diary entries starting in June 1940, as
she prepares to set sail from Bordeaux, and continuing
until June 1966. *Alcancía: Vuelta* (Safe Box: Return)
takes up from the beginning of 1967 through May
1981. Both volumes were published in 1982; from this
time until her death she worked on a another volume,
*Alcancía: Estación termini* (Safe Box: Final Station), published posthumously, as she had intended, in 1998.
Her son, who grew up to be an architect, served as co-
editor of this last volume. In addition, she produced a
dream-like memoir of her childhood, *Desde el amanecer:
Autobiografía de mis primeros diez años* (Since Dawn: Autobiography of My First Ten Years), published in 1972.

Chacel's third novel was mainly written in the
1930s but was published in Argentina in 1945. *Memorias de Leticia Valle* is an ingenious reworking and subversion of the figure of woman as temptress. At liberty
this time to create her own protagonist, Chacel develops a precocious, vivacious, and somewhat perverse
girl about to become a woman. Not content with
learning everything her tutors, a married couple, can
teach her, eleven-year-old Leticia falls in love with
both of them. Toward Daniel she feels envy and a
desire for revenge for his many slights; toward his
wife she feels nothing but a pure longing for closeness.
She maneuvers herself into a position where she is
able to dishonor the man by seducing him. Thus
reversing the mechanism by which women were traditionally dishonored, she forces her tutor to take his
own life in order to cleanse his family's honor. *Memorias de Leticia Valle* is written compellingly from the perspective of a girl who perceives that knowledge is
power and who is uninhibited about displaying and
exercising both. It is a major example of the existentialist novel, which came to characterize postwar European fiction, although it precedes the heyday of that
genre. It compares well to other Spanish entries in this
category, also known as "novelas de protagonista"
(protagonist novels), such as Camilo José Cela's *La
familia de Pascual Duarte* (1942, The Family of Pascual
Duarte) and Carmen Laforet's *Nada* (1944, Nothing).
There is an ellipsis surrounding the seduction scene
and the tutor's suicide; one must read between the
lines to get the truth from the narrator's suddenly
spare words regarding the outcome of her plot. The
ellipsis makes sense, however, as part of an account
from an unreliable narrator who barely understands
the chaos she has caused.

ers to re-create and perhaps revise their own history,
educating readers in the process. He assigned to
Chacel the task of reconstructing a lost Romantic
female subject, since Mancha was known only as
Espronceda's forsaken lover. The result is an uneven
work that nonetheless succeeds in giving voice to a figure that had been subsumed under the archetype of
the temptress, showing her to be more a victim of the
selfishness of the male poet and of social opprobrium
directed against the "fallen woman." While in general
Chacel disliked identifying with victims, she portrayed
Mancha as engrossed in escaping from the cage in
which her illicit relationship had confined her.

As the Spanish Civil War escalated, Chacel left
Spain and passed through Paris, Geneva, Alexandria,

For the first decade of her life in exile Chacel refrained from starting another novel. She translated several important European works into Spanish, published poetry and prose in Argentine periodicals such as *Sur* and *La Nación,* and wrote the short stories published in 1952 as *Sobre el piélago* (Over the Ocean). In the 1950s, Chacel worked on her most extensive text, *La sinrazón* (1960, Unreason), which she considered her masterpiece. She returns to the inner life of the intellectual, whose self-doubt and guilt leave him desperate and suicidal. The contemplative novel provides her with a vehicle for exploring Unamuno's notion of "unreason," associated with faith and madness. Conventional faith is not an option for the skeptical and restless protagonist, Santiago Hernández, who is drawn into marriage and then an affair with a dancer. In the heartbreak and chaos that result from his straying, he is at least comforted by a seemingly supernatural power to move objects at will. When this power also deserts him, he finds no further escape beside suicide. The pessimism of *La sinrazón* results from the conflict between living in accordance with one's "vital reason" (Ortega y Gasset's notion of a personal logic shaped by the circumstances of the individual) and enduring the self-reflection enforced by the possession of memory and conscience, without the possibility of relief in the form of the sacrament of confession.

Chacel received a grant from the Guggenheim Foundation in 1959, and she spent the next two years in New York City, where she gave lectures and worked on her book-length essay *Saturnal* (1972). In the summer of 1960 she was in Mexico, with her sister, Blanca, and friends Cernuda and Concha de Albornoz. Her second volume of stories, *Ofrenda a una virgen loca* (Offering to a Mad Virgin), published in 1961. Following her New York sojourn, Chacel traveled to Madrid and Paris, renewing ties with the philosopher Julián Marías and meeting a new generation of writers and Hispanists. In 1963 she returned to Rio, and *Teresa* was reprinted in Spain, ensuring the continued resurgence of interest in her work in her homeland. She began a correspondence with the younger writer Ana María Moix and wrote the book-length essay *La confesión* (1971, The Confession). In the early 1970s she made two more trips to Spain, and many of her earlier works were reprinted there along with editions of new ones, such as the short-story collection *Icada, Nevda, Diada* (1971). She returned to Spain definitively in 1974, supported at first by a grant from the March Foundation. She lectured extensively in her native country and traveled throughout Europe with her sister. In 1976 she published *Barrio de Maravillas* (translated as *The Maravillas District,* 1992), which won the Premio de la Crítica (Critics' Prize).

The first volume in an eventual trilogy she referred to as the "Escuela de Platón" (School of Plato), *Barrio de Maravillas* portrays the coming-of-age of a group of young people in this residential neighborhood of Madrid in the early twentieth century. The girls in the group in particular must come to terms with themselves as sexual beings and objects of desire in most forms of artistic expression, while they struggle to develop identities as artists in their own right. A departure from the first-person sole narrators of most of her other novels (with the exception of *Teresa*), *Barrio de Maravillas* is presented as something approaching a symphony in which the voices of characters converge and enter into dialogue with each other. It re-creates the heady cultural atmosphere of the Spanish capital in the early decades of the twentieth century, when innovation fed upon rich traditions.

A second volume of poetry, *Versos prohibidos* (Forbidden Poems), was published in 1978, and *Memorias de Leticia Valle* was made into an undistinguished movie directed by Miguel Angel Rivas in 1979. In 1980 Chacel finished the artistic biography of her husband, who had died in 1977, *Timoteo Pérez y sus retratos del jardín* (Timoteo Pérez and His Garden Portraits). The following year her volume of stories *Novelas antes de tiempo* (Novels before Their Time) and another with articles and essays called *Los títulos* (The Titles) were published.

In 1984 the second novel of her trilogy, *Acrópolis,* appeared in print. This novel and the subsequent third installment of the trilogy, *Ciencias naturales* (1988, Natural Sciences), were considered disappointing and needlessly obscure by many critics, including the author herself, who expressed regret at having published *Acrópolis.* This series charts the lives of the neighbors of *Barrio de Maravillas,* who have become uprooted and lost in the labyrinth of social turbulence, war, and exile. In 1986 Chacel bequeathed her papers to the Jorge Guillén Study Center in Valladolid, where the local government awarded her a lifetime pension. In 1987 she was awarded the Premio Nacional de las Letras Españolas (National Prize in Spanish Literature) for her life's work in literature. The University of Valladolid conferred an honorary doctorate on the author in 1989.

In the early 1990s, Rosa Chacel continued to write in her diary and grant interviews. Her son and daughter-in-law looked after her as her health declined. Chacel, along with Rafael Alberti and Francisco Ayala, came to be regarded as a living national treasure, one of the few survivors of the flowering of Spanish arts and letters in the first third of the twentieth century, known as the "Edad de Plata" (Silver Age), rivaled only by the Golden Age of the sixteenth and seventeenth centuries. She died in Madrid on 7 July 1994.

**Letters:**

*Cartas a Rosa Chacel,* edited by Ana Rodríguez Fischer (Madrid: Cátedra, 1992);

*De mar a mar: Epistolario Rosa Chacel–Ana María Moix,* edited by Rodríguez Fischer (Barcelona: Península, 1994).

**References:**

Teresa Bordons and Susan Kirkpatrick, "Chacel's *Teresa* and Ortega's Canon," *Anales de la Literatura Española Contemporánea,* 19 (1992): 283–299;

Kathleen M. Glenn, "Fiction and Autobiography in Rosa Chacel's *Memorias de Leticia Valle,*" *Letras Peninsulares,* 4, nos. 2–3 (1991): 285–294;

Roberta Johnson, "*Estación. Ida y vuelta:* Un nuevo tiempo en la novela," in *Prosa hispánica de vanguardia,* edited by Fernando Burgos (Madrid: Orígenes, 1986), pp. 201–208;

Carol Maier, "Siting *Leticia Valle:* Questions of Gender and Generation," *Monographic Review/Revista Monográfica,* 8 (1992): 79–98;

Shirley Mangini, "Women and Spanish Modernism: The Case of Rosa Chacel," *Anales de la Literatura Española,* 12, nos. 1–2 (1987): 17–28;

Eunice Myers, "*Estación. Ida y vuelta:* Rosa Chacel's Apprenticeship Novel," *Hispanic Journal,* 4, no. 2 (1983): 77–84;

Wilma Newberry, "Rosa Chacel's *Barrio de Maravillas:* The Role of the Arts and the Problem of Spain," *Hispanic Journal,* 9 (Spring 1988): 37–44;

Alberto Porlan, *La sinrazón de Rosa Chacel* (Madrid: Anjana, 1984);

Ana Rodríguez Fischer, "El tiempo abarcado," in *Rosa Chacel: Premio Nacional de las Letras Españolas,* edited by Luis Revenga (Madrid: Biblioteca Nacional/Ministerio de Cultura, 1988), pp. 9–23;

Elizabeth Scarlett, "Rosa Chacel," in her *Under Construction: The Body in Spanish Novels* (Charlottesville: University Press of Virginia, 1994), pp. 46–98;

Luis Antonio de Villena, "*Memorias de Leticia Valle:* La seducción inversa," in *Rosa Chacel: Premio Nacional de las Letras Españolas,* edited by Revenga, pp. 41–44.

**Papers:**

Rosa Chacel's papers are at the Jorge Guillén Study Center in Valladolid.

# Miguel Delibes
## (17 October 1920 –    )

### Yaw Agawu-Kakraba
*Pennsylvania State University–Altoona College*

BOOKS: *La sombra del ciprés es alargada* (Barcelona: Destino, 1948);

*Aún es de día* (Barcelona: Destino, 1949);

*El camino* (Barcelona: Destino, 1950); translated by John and Brita Haycraft as *The Path* (New York: John Day, 1961; London: Hamilton, 1961);

*Mi idolatrado hijo Sisí* (Barcelona: Destino, 1953);

*La partida* (Barcelona: Luis de Caralt, 1954);

*Diario de un cazador* (Barcelona: Destino, 1955);

*Un novelista descubre América: Chile en el ojo ajeno* (Madrid: Editora Nacional, 1956); enlarged as *Por esos mundos* (Barcelona: Destino, 1961);

*Siestas con viento sur* (Barcelona: Destino, 1957)—comprises "La mortaja," "El loco," "Los nogales," and "Los raíles";

*La barbería* (Barcelona: Editorial G.P., 1957);

*Diario de un emigrante* (Barcelona: Destino, 1958);

*La hoja roja* (Barcelona: Destino, 1959);

*Las ratas* (Barcelona: Destino, 1962); translated by Alfred Johnson as *Smoke on the Ground* (Garden City, N.Y.: Doubleday, 1972);

*Europa, parada y fonda* (Madrid: Cid, 1963);

*La caza de la perdiz roja* (Barcelona: Lumen, 1963);

*Viejas historias de Castilla la Vieja* (Barcelona: Lumen, 1964);

*El libro de la caza menor* (Barcelona: Destino, 1964);

*Cinco horas con Mario* (Barcelona: Destino, 1966); translated by Frances M. López-Morillas as *Five Hours with Mario* (New York: Columbia University Press, 1988);

*USA y yo* (Barcelona: Destino, 1966);

*La primavera de Praga* (Madrid: Alianza, 1968);

*Vivir al día* (Barcelona: Destino, 1968);

*Parábola del náufrago* (Barcelona: Destino, 1969); translated by López-Morillas as *The Hedge* (New York: Columbia University Press, 1983);

*Mi mundo y el mundo* (Valladolid: Miñón, 1970);

*Con la escopeta al hombro* (Barcelona: Destino, 1970);

*La mortaja* (Madrid: Alianza, 1970);

*La caza en España* (Barcelona: Destino, 1972);

*Un año de mi vida* (Barcelona: Destino, 1972);

*Miguel Delibes ( from the dust jacket for* The Stuff of Heroes, *1990; Richland County Public Library)*

*El príncipe destronado* (Barcelona: Destino, 1973); translated by Thomas Molloy as *The Dethroned Prince* (Madrid: Iberia, 1986);

*Las guerras de nuestros antepasados* (Barcelona: Destino, 1975); translated by Agnes Moncy as *The Wars of Our Ancestors* (Athens: University of Georgia Press, 1992);

*S.O.S. (El sentido del progreso desde mi obra)* (Barcelona: Destino, 1975);

*Aventuras, venturas y desventuras de un cazador a rabo* (Barcelona: Destino, 1977);

*Mis amigas las truchas* (Barcelona: Destino, 1977);

*El disputado voto del señor Cayo* (Barcelona: Destino, 1978);

*Castilla, lo castellano y los castellanos* (Barcelona: Planeta, 1979);

*Un mundo que agoniza* (Barcelona: Plaza & Janes, 1979);

*Dos días de caza* (Barcelona: Destino, 1980);

*Las perdices de domingo* (Barcelona: Destino, 1981);

*Los santos inocentes* (Barcelona: Planeta, 1981);

*Cinco horas con Mario: Versión teatral* (Madrid: Espasa-Calpe, 1981);

*Dos viajes en automóvil: Suecia y Países Bajos* (Barcelona: Plaza & Janes, 1982);

*Tres pájaros de cuenta* (Valladolid: Miñon, 1982);

*El otro fútbol* (Barcelona: Destino, 1982);

*Cartas de amor de un sexagenario voluptuoso* (Barcelona: Destino, 1983);

*El tesoro* (Barcelona: Destino, 1985);

*La censura de prensa en los años 40: Y otros ensayos* (Valladolid: Ambito, 1985);

*Castilla habla* (Barcelona: Destino, 1986);

*337A, madera de héroe* (Barcelona: Destino, 1987); translated by López-Morillas as *The Stuff of Heroes* (New York: Pantheon, 1990);

*La hoja roja: Versión teatral* (Madrid: Espasa-Calpe, 1987);

*Mi vida al aire libre: Memorias deportivas de un hombre sedentario* (Barcelona: Destino, 1989);

*Pegar la hebra* (Barcelona: Destino, 1990);

*La guerras de nuestros antepasados en teatro,* by Delibes and Ramón García (Barcelona: Destino, 1990);

*Señora de rojo sobre fondo gris* (Barcelona: Destino, 1991);

*El último coto* (Barcelona: Destino, 1992);

*Los niños* (Barcelona: Planeta, 1994);

*Diario de un jubilado* (Barcelona: Destino, 1995);

*He dicho* (Barcelona: Destino, 1996);

*El hereje* (Barcelona: Destino, 1998);

*España, 1936–1950: Muerte y resurrección de la novela* (Barcelona: Destino, 2004);

*La tierra herida: Qué mundo heredarán nuestros hijos?* by Delibes and Miguel Delibes de Castro (Barcelona: Destino, 2005).

**Collections:** *Obra completa,* 5 volumes (Barcelona: Destino, 1964–1968);

*Los estragos del tiempo,* Mis libros preferidos, no. 1 (Barcelona: Destino, 1999)–comprises *El camino, La mortaja,* and *La hoja roja;*

*Dos mujeres,* Mis libros preferidos, no. 2 (Barcelona: Destino, 2000)–comprises *Cinco horas con Mario* and *Señora de rojo sobre fondo gris;*

*Castilla como problema,* Mis libros preferidos, no. 3 (Barcelona: Destino, 2001)–comprises *Las ratas, El tesoro,* and *El disputado voto del señor Cayo;*

*Los diarios de Lorenzo,* Mis libros preferidos, no. 4 (Barcelona: Destino, 2002);

*Nuevas formas narrativas,* Mis libros preferidos, no. 5 (Barcelona: Destino, 2003)–comprises *Parábola del náufrago* and *Las guerras de nuestros antepasados.*

PRODUCED SCRIPT: *El camino,* television, Radio-televisión Española, 1978.

OTHER: "Breve reflexión sobre mi obra literaria," in *Aspekte der Hispania im 19 un 20 Jahrhundert,* edited by Kremer Dieter (Hamburg: Buske, 1983), pp. 165–174.

SELECTED PERIODICAL PUBLICATIONS–UNCOLLECTED: "El recuerdo," *Mundo hispánico,* 2, no. 21 (December 1949): 58–59;

"Nuestra senil novela joven," *Ateneo: Revista de ateneos de España* (6 June 1953): 6;

"Medio siglo de novela española," *Compadre: Revue de Politique de la Culture,* 17–18 (1957): 242–247;

"Notas sobre la novela española contemporánea," *Cuadernos,* 63 (August 1962): 34–38;

"La Milana," *Mundo hispánico anico,* 16, no. 182 (May 1963): 73–76;

"La experimentación narrativa en España," *Boletín de la Academia Hondureña de la lengua,* 24, no. 26 (June 1982): 267–269.

Miguel Delibes has emerged not only as one of the most prominent and prolific Spanish writers but also as one of the most widely read authors of the twentieth century. The fact that most of Delibes's novels, novelettes, and short stories have been translated into more than ten languages suggests that his importance as a novelist, essayist, and humanist has transcended his native Spain. Delibes has earned wide recognition for his descriptions of provincial and rural life in *El camino* (1950; translated as *The Path,* 1961), *Las ratas* (1962; translated as *Smoke on the Ground,* 1972), and *Los santos inocentes* (1981, The Innocent Saints) and for his psychological analyses of middle- and lower-class characters in *Cinco horas con Mario* (1966; translated as *Five Hours with Mario,* 1988) and *Cartas de amor de un sexagenario voluptuoso* (1983, Love Letters of a Voluptuous Sexagenarian).

Born in the provincial city of Valladolid on 17 October 1920, the third of eight children, Miguel Delibes Setién grew up in a conservative middle-class milieu. His parents, Alonso Delibes Cortés and María Setién, emphasized morality, religion, and domestic life. He was first educated by Carmelite nuns and later by the Brothers of La Salle.

The summers Delibes spent with his paternal grandmother, Saturnia Cortés, in Molledo-Portolín, a mountainous village in Santander, instilled in him a love for the countryside and an acute awareness of the negative influence of the city. For Delibes, the city represented "progress" and civilization in its most detestable form, while nature was the ultimate sanctuary for the individual caught in the cogs of mass society. Despite his idealization of the countryside, Delibes was aware of the violence and primitivism of life in the Castilian landscape, with its poverty, misery, desolation, and barren fields. Rural settings are featured in the novels *El camino*, *Las ratas*, *Viejas historias de Castilla la Vieja* (1964, Old Tales of Old Castile), and *Los santos inocentes*. Delibes's lifelong love of hunting manifests itself in *La caza de la perdiz roja* (1963, Hunting the Red Partridge), *El libro de la caza menor* (1964, The Book of Small-Game Hunting), *La caza en España* (1972, Hunting in Spain), *Las perdices de domingo* (1981, Quail on Sunday), and *El último coto* (1992, The Last Hunting Ground).

Delibes had just finished high school when the Spanish Civil War broke out in 1936. Too young to enlist in the military and unable to enter the university because it had been closed, he took classes at the School of Commerce in Valladolid. When he was of age, Delibes enlisted in Francisco Franco's Nationalist navy; he served briefly on the cruiser *Canarias*, patrolling the coast and enforcing blockades. Although Delibes hardly came into contact with the enemy, seeing victims of war and participating in the rescue of a torpedoed tourist boat produced a loathing for war. His 1987 novel, *337A, Madera de héroe* (translated as *The Stuff of Heroes*, 1990), highlights the horrors of war and questions what really constitutes heroism.

From 1939 to 1941 Delibes took intensive courses to complete the equivalent of university degrees in law and commerce. He then took a job at the Banco Castellano (Bank of Castile) and began preparing to take the degree examinations for a position as professor at the business school at the University of Valladolid. Among the texts he studied, Joaquín Garrigues's two-volume *Curso de Derecho Mercantil* (1936, 1940, Course on Mercantile Law) had a profound influence on him. The clarity of Garrigues's text, Delibes asserts in Ramón García Domínguez's *Miguel Delibes: La imagen escrita* (1993, Miguel Delibes: The Written Image), made him aware of the importance of the precision of language and the necessity of resolving the difficulties of expression. During this period he also worked as a caricaturist for the newspaper *El norte de Castilla* (The North of Castile). While preparing for his degree examinations, he continued studying toward a doctorate in law, spent three months doing an intensive course in journalism in Madrid, and also prepared for the notorious *oposiciones* (competitive examinations to select personnel for posts in the public sector). In 1944 he began writing editorials and movie reviews for *El norte de*

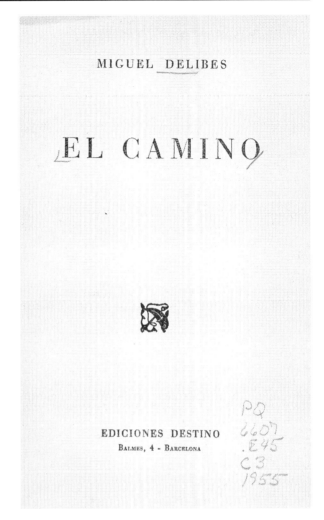

MIGUEL DELIBES

EL CAMINO

EDICIONES DESTINO
BALMES, 4 - BARCELONA

*Title page for an early edition of Delibes's 1950 novel (translated as* The Path, *1961), in which a child reminisces about his native village the night before he is to leave for boarding school (Thomas Cooper Library, University of South Carolina)*

*Castilla*. In 1945 Delibes became professor of mercantile law in the business school of the University of Valladolid; soon thereafter he moved to the chair of the history of culture in the business school.

Delibes married Angeles de Castro in 1946. In 1947 they had a son, Miguel, and shortly afterward Delibes started working on his first novel, *La sombra del ciprés es alargada* (1948, Long Is the Cypress's Shadow), to give vent to the obsession with death that had plagued him since childhood. Notwithstanding Delibes's admitted artistic shortcomings—the novel was deficient not for what it lacked but for its excesses—*La sombra del ciprés es alargada* won the prestigious and highly endowed Nadal Prize, beating out such well-established writers as Manuel Pombo Angulo. Delibes later admitted that had he not won the prize, his writing career would have ended. In an interview with García Domínguez he said, "Quizá si mi clasificación hubiese sido segundo o tercero las cosas hubieran seguido el mismo rumbo que ganando, pero, puedo asegurarte que de haber quedado en la zona templada, hubiera colgado la pluma. Mi temor al ridículo era y sigue siendo muy elevado" (Perhaps if I had won second or third instead of first prize, things would have turned out the same for me as a writer, but let me assure you that if I had been eliminated from the competition for the Nadal Prize, I would have put away my pen for good. My fear of being ridiculed was and is still a major concern to me).

The competition for the prize provoked an acrimonious attitude toward Delibes by those who supported Pombo Angulo, whose *Hospital general* (1948, General Hospital) was runner-up to *La sombra del ciprés es alargada*. Personal attacks in the magazine *Destino* hurt Delibes so much that rather than moving to a more-prestigious artistic center such as Madrid or Barcelona, he decided to remain in Valladolid, eschewing not only the cliques but also the stylistic vogues that emerged in those capitals.

Delibes took seriously the constructive criticisms of his first novel, which included objections to the prevalence of pessimism and melancholy. In 1949 he published *Aún es de día* (Still It Is Day), a complete antithesis to his novel. It depicts aspects of Spanish society and the national economy and reveals what the author believes are injustices in Spain at that time. In spite of the squalid, seminaturalistic, and bleak conditions that circumscribe the main characters of the novel, there is an overarching exaggerated optimism. Critics were quick to pick up the contrast between the two novels by referring to them in terms of pessimism and optimism.

Considered by critics one of Delibes's best works, *El camino* eschews the cumbersome style that was a hallmark of his earlier two novels. As he explained in an interview with César Alonso de los Ríos:

> Cuando escribí *La sombra del ciprés* . . . lo hice en tal estado de virginidad literaria que entendía que la literatura debía ser engolada, grandilocuente. . . . A raíz del Nadal empiezo a leer un poco obras de ficción y entonces llego al conocimiento de que, abandonando la retórica y escribiendo como hablo, tal vez pueda mejorar la cosa.
>
> Así fue como entré en ese cambio de lenguaje, o de técnica, o de las dos cosas, a que te refieres. En *El camino* me despojé por vez primera de lo postizo y salí a cuerpo limpio.
>
> (I wrote *La sombra del ciprés* . . . when I was in such a state of literary virginity that I believed at the time that

literature should be complex and grandiloquent. . . . After receiving the Nadal Prize I began to read some fiction and I came to understand that, by abandoning rhetoric and writing as I speak, I could perhaps improve my work product.

> In this way I began to change the language I used, or my technique, or both, as you have mentioned. In *El camino* I shed affectations and continued on unburdened by such things.)

*El camino* revolves around the recollections of the protagonist the night before he is to leave the village in which he has lived since birth to attend school in a nearby provincial city.

In 1952 Delibes became a subdirector of *El norte de Castilla*. Although in his fourth novel, *Mi idolatrado hijo Sisí* (1953, My Adored Son Sisí), he still experiments with narrative style, he also returns to the moralizing, the traditional values, and the somberness of his first two novels. The narcissistic and impetuous protagonist fathers a child in order to continue his egotistical lifestyle and maintains strict control over his only offspring. The success of the novel with critics and its wide readership sealed Delibes's prominence as a literary figure.

Delibes taught in the mornings, wrote his newspaper columns in the afternoons and evenings, and wrote fiction and hunting books during university vacations. In 1954 he published *La partida* (The Departure), a collection of short stories. The following year he published the novel *Diario de un cazador* (Diary of a Hunter), which won the Miguel de Cervantes National Literary Prize. The protagonist, Lorenzo, is concerned about the well-being of wildlife and opposes making hunting a tourist attraction in Spain. Delibes published *Un novelista descubre América: Chile en el ojo ajeno* (1956, A Novelist Discovers America: Chile in the Eyes of Others), following his trip to Chile at the invitation of the Círculo de Periodistas (Circle of Journalists) in Santiago. He spent nearly three months lecturing in Chile and also traveled to Argentina, Brazil, and Uruguay. Another travel book, *Por esos mundos* (1961, Round about the World), incorporates *Un novelista descubre América* and gives Delibes's impressions of the Canary Islands. Yet another product of Delibes's travels is the novel *Diario de un emigrante* (1958, Diary of an Emigrant), which relates the emigration to Chile of Lorenzo, the protagonist of *Diario de un cazador*. What characterizes both books is the obsession that the same protagonist has for hunting and the inclination toward exploring street language and the jargon of the various environments in which he finds himself.

Delibes's *Siestas con viento sur* (1957, Siestas with the Summer Breeze), a collection of four novellas, won the Fastenrath Prize of the Royal Spanish Academy. Two of the stories take place in the countryside, two in cities. Each of them is narrated by one of the characters in the story. What makes these novellas remarkable is the absence of the philosophizing nature that characterizes Delibes's earlier novels. The novelist's international importance among scholars was manifested by an invitation to visit Italy and Portugal in 1957. On both trips he became aware of the profound interest that professional Hispanists had in the literature of the Iberian Peninsula.

Delibes was nominated to head *El norte de Castilla* on several occasions, but his promotion to director was blocked by Franco's Ministry of Information until 1958. After Delibes ascended to the directorship, the paper began advocating agrarian reforms for victims of drought and of Franco's agricultural and immigration policies. Delibes urged his staff to write about the pathetic economic conditions of rural Castile produced by the neglect and misguided policies of the central government. He also called for free compulsory education in primary, secondary, and postsecondary schools. He employed young and determined journalists willing to broach subjects previously considered untouchable and published bold articles in *El caballo de Troya* (The Trojan Horse), the Sunday supplement of *El norte de Castilla*. These articles, the most audacious in the Spanish press since the Civil War, led Delibes to confrontations with the ministers of information and agriculture. After being summoned several times to Madrid and receiving many visits from the ministers he was forced to resign his directorship in May 1963.

Delibes's forced resignation from *El norte de Castilla* showed him that novels were a much more potent means than journalism of highlighting the social inequalities in Spain. In a 1991 interview with Marie-Lise Gazarian Gautier, Delibes noted that "If you study my books, you will see that from *La sombra del ciprés es alargada* to *The Path*, *La hoja roja*, *Las ratas*, and *Five Hours with Mario*, there was increasing room for me to move. On this front, I struggled with censorship continuously and this fight bore its fruits. I think the majority of Spanish writers also did this, and that is why today, with forty years of censorship behind us, we can be proud of our work. We wrote more or less good literature, but we never rolled over and played dead for those in power."

During his years as director of *El norte de Castilla* Delibes published two important novels, *La hoja roja* (1959, The Red Leaf) and *Las ratas,* that subtly critique the underdeveloped conditions of Spain. With little plot and limited action, *La hoja roja* recounts the experiences of a newly retired municipal worker and his single young maid, who is nostalgic for her rural village. The plot of *Las ratas* concerns the protagonist's cave-dwelling,

*Dust jacket for the 1988 English translation of Delibes's 1966 novel,* Cinco horas con Mario, *a complex and virtually plotless work in monologue form (Richland County Public Library)*

rat-hunting lifestyle and the government's demand that he give up his cave home. Awarded the Critics' Prize, *Las ratas* deals with the issue of agrarian reform that Delibes had explored in his newspaper. The Critics' Prize was the ultimate recognition a Spanish author could hope for; by coming just after Delibes's resignation from *El norte de Castilla,* it signaled the implicit support of the Spanish critical establishment for his stance on agrarian reform in Castile. Delibes's experiences at *El norte de Castilla* and his disgust with the censorship of the Franco government are the subjects of his 1985 collection *La censura de prensa en los años 40: Y otros ensayos* (Censorship of the Press in the 1940s: And Other Essays).

In 1963 Delibes published *Europa, parada y fonda* (Europe, Stop and Inn), a collection of travel impressions of Portugal, France, and Italy. In 1964 he spent a semester as visiting professor at the University of Maryland. The Delibes family's stay in Maryland, along with visits to other American universities, forms the basis of another travel book, *USA y yo* (1966, USA and I).

*Delibes and his wife, Angeles de Castro, in Prague, 1968
(from César Alonso de los Ríos,* Conversaciones con
Miguel Delibes, *1971; Thomas Cooper Library,
University of South Carolina)*

In 1966 Delibes published *Cinco horas con Mario,* a marked departure from his earlier novels that focused on the Castilian landscape, villages, and people. Mario's widow, Carmen, evokes her memories of marital strife in a monologue; the time frame of the novel is compressed to one night. The disappearance of almost all plot structure and the subjective reflections of Carmen make *Cinco horas con Mario* one of Delibes's most complex and most studied novels.

Delibes wrote a testimonial book, *La primavera de Praga* (1968, Prague Spring), following the few weeks he spent as a guest of universities in Czechoslovakia in the spring of 1968. Delibes was pleasantly surprised to notice the flourishing attempts at democracy and freedom within the Communist political structure. *La primavera de Praga* was in press when the Russian invasion

of Czechoslovakia crushed those reforms, but Delibes was able to add a short foreword in which he expressed his sadness about the Soviet response. He dedicated the book to the heroic people of Czechoslovakia, expressing the hope that the freedoms they enjoyed prior to the invasion would not be lost.

While *Cinco horas con Mario* appeared to signal a narrative shift, Delibes's 1969 novel, *Parábola del náufrago* (Parabola of the Shipwrecked One; translated as *The Hedge,* 1983), surprised critics and readers even more. This work represents a fundamental departure from Delibes's earlier writings, in which neorealism is the dominant technique, in favor of intense subjectivism. In spite of this narrative shift, perhaps made in response to the newest literary trend in Spain, one still encounters the themes of the urban-rural dichotomy and criticism of society. Much of the novel is written in stream-of-consciousness style, and includes arbitrary punctuation, artificial language, and long and complicated sentences, all designed to highlight the dehumanized condition in which the protagonist finds himself. The novel harks back to Delibes's concern with unbridled technological development and its adverse effects on the environment and on human beings.

*Mi mundo y el mundo* (1970, My World and the World) is an anthology of selections from Delibes's fiction and nonfiction works for readers from eleven to fourteen. The "Mi mundo" section comprises selections from *El camino, Diario de un cazador, Las ratas,* and *La sombra del ciprés es alargada.* The second part of the book, "El mundo," is made up of excerpts from his travel writings. Delibes's next novel, *El príncipe destronado* (1973; translated as *The Dethroned Prince,* 1986), uses a child's fantasies and perceptions to expose some of the social problems of Spain. Characters such as the protagonist's parents, siblings, and the family servants characterize middle-class values and mores.

Delibes's wife died in 1974, and he went almost three years without writing because he was unable to concentrate. He was inducted into the Spanish Academy in 1975; his inaugural speech was published that year as *S.O.S. (El sentido del progreso desde mi obra)* (S.O.S. [The Question of Progress from the Perspective of My Work]). When he finally returned to writing in 1977, it was, as he put it to García Dominguez, "para evadirme de mi propia historia, para escapar de mi mismo" (in order to close myself off from my own history, to escape from myself).

Delibes's novel *El disputado voto del señor Cayo* (1978, The Disputed Vote of Mr. Cayo) reiterates the urban-rural dichotomy of such works as *Las ratas* and *El camino.* Campaigning in rural Castile, a city politician attempts to win over señor Cayo, a farmer. While the politician's rhetoric is characterized by ambiguity, falsehood, and aggression, the farmer's language is sincere, innocent, articulate, and economical.

The 1981 novel *Los santos inocentes* takes the city-country dyad to a more intense level as a wealthy city bachelor uses rural peasants to satisfy his passions for women and hunting. Delibes contrasts the harsh reality of peasant life with the elegance and willful neglect of the rich landowner. At the end of the novel the peasants rebel against the "señorito" (master) who dies violently.

*Cartas de amor de un sexagenario voluptuoso*, published in 1983, is a parody of the epistolary genre that subverts the convention whereby the woman passively awaits for the letters of her lover. In this novel the inexperienced and aging male lover adopts the expectant role.

Delibes returns to the dichotomy of urban and rural Spain in his 1985 novel, *El tesoro* (The Treasure). The discovery of an archaeological treasure in a Castilian village transforms the dormant community into a center for academicians and bureaucrats from Madrid. Misunderstanding and intolerance between sophisticated city dwellers and peasants eventually leads to violence.

The 1987 novel *337A, madera de héroe* (337A, the Stuff of Heroes) is Delibes's definitive statement about the Spanish Civil War and violence in general. He indicates that the atrocities of war can occur in any society when intolerance becomes the order of the day. Delibes focuses on the effect of the conflict on each character's life, with a message of tolerance toward all.

Delibes deals with the loss of his wife in his 1991 novel, *Señora de rojo sobre fondo gris* (Lady in Red against a Gray Background). In a meditative monologue Delibes's alter ego, a well-known painter, recounts the lives and deaths of his wife and their daughter, Ana. Driven to alcoholism and creative sterility, he uses the color red to evoke his wife's passion and vitality. The gray background signifies the absence, death, and passivity that have become the narrator's lot after his wife's and daughter's deaths.

Delibes satirizes Spanish consumerism in *Diario de un jubilado* (1995, Diary of a Retired Person). In this sequel to *Diario de un cazador* and *Diario de un emigrante*, an older Lorenzo is still a vital and colorful character but undergoes a fundamental change when he is seduced by the materialistic world that surrounds him.

In 1998 Delibes published a voluminous historical novel, *El hereje* (The Heretic). In Valladolid, Bernardo Salcedo, baptized Cipriano, an orphan since birth, is raised by a wet nurse and becomes a prosperous trader influenced by the Protestant doctrines that are clandestinely being introduced into the peninsula. The novel paints a vivid picture of Valladolid during Charles V's rule.

In 1999 Delibes's main Spanish publisher, Ediciones Destino, began a series of collections of his work under the title "Mis libros preferidos" (My Favorite Books). Each volume is introduced by a well-known literary critic and comprises works related by theme. For example, *Los estragos del tiempo* (1999, The Ravages of Time), the first volume in the "Mis libros preferidos" series, consists of *El camino, La mortaja,* and *La hoja roja.*

With most of his novels translated into English, Portuguese, German, Italian, Swedish, and French, among other languages, it is fair to say that the primarily Castilian regional content of Miguel Delibes's literary world does not prevent a broad international audience from enjoying his works. He is a masterful novelist and an equally accomplished journalist who fearlessly critiques government social, economic, and agricultural policies. Although a reclusive individual, Delibes has, nevertheless, been a public figure through his teaching, lectures, interviews, and environmental concerns. He is a social novelist with a concern for correcting injustices and promoting changes that will allow his countrymen to enjoy fundamental human rights.

**Letters:**

Delibes and Josep Vergés, *Correspondencia, 1948–1986* (Barcelona: Destino, 2002).

**Interviews:**

José Ramón Chicote, "Miguel Delibes: 'Lo que más admiro: la tolerancia y la lealtad,'" *Arriba,* 5 April 1964, p. 19;

Juby F. Bustamante, "El autor enjuicia su obra," *Estafeta literaria,* 318 (22 May 1965): 22;

José Luis Castillo-Puche, "La base de la clase media se va ampliando (Declaraciones de Miguel Delibes)," *Ya,* 16 July 1965, pp. 5–6;

Chicote, "España es la cenicienta de Europa, dice Miguel Delibes," *Ya,* 5 September 1965;

César Alonso de los Ríos, *Conversaciones con Miguel Delibes* (Madrid: EMESA, 1971);

María A. Salgado, "Miguel Delibes, Nuevo miembro de la Academia," *Hispania,* 56, no. 3 (September 1973): 729–730;

Manuel Leguineche, "De caza con Delibes," *El País Semanal,* 10 September 1978, pp. 10–15;

Pilar Concejo Alvarez, "Entrevista con Miguel Delibes," *Anales de la Narrativa Española Contemporánea,* 5 (1980): 165–170;

Soledad Alameda, "Miguel Delibes, entre el alba y el crepúsculo: 'Es que soy triste,'" *El País Semanal,* 6 January 1980, pp. 10–13;

Luis Miguel de Dios, "Delibes: 'Intento decirlo todo en el menor número de páginas,'" *El País,* 27 September 1981, p. 5;

Norma Sturniolo, "Miguel Delibes y la función de la literatura," *Nueva Estafeta,* 48–49 (November–December 1982): 55–63;

Javier Goñi, *Cinco horas con Miguel Delibes* (Madrid: Anjana, 1985);

Marie-Lise Gazarian Gautier, *Interviews with Spanish Writers* (Elmwood Park, Ill.: Dalkey Archive Press, 1991), pp. 112–125;

Ramón García Domínguez, "De mis encuentros con Delibes," in *Miguel Delibes: Premio letras españolas, 1991* (Madrid: Ministerio de Cultura, Dirección General del Libro y Bibliotecas, Centro de las Letras Españolas, 1994), pp. 11–27.

**Bibliography:**

Glenn G. Meyers, *Miguel Delibes: An Annotated Critical Bibliography* (Lanham, Md.: Scarecrow Press, 1999).

**References:**

Yaw Agawu-Kakraba, *Demythification in the Fiction of Miguel Delibes* (New York: Peter Lang, 1996);

Manuel Alvar, *El mundo novelesco de Miguel Delibes* (Madrid: Gredos, 1987);

Teresa Boucher, *Existential Authenticity in Three Novels of Spanish Author Miguel Delibes* (Lewiston, N.Y.: Edwin Mellen Press, 2004);

María Luisa Bustos-Deuso, *La mujer en la narrativa de Delibes* (Valladolid: Secretariado de Publicaciones, Universidad de Valladolid / Salamanca: Caja Salamanca, 1991);

Janet Díaz, *Miguel Delibes* (New York: Twayne, 1971);

Ramón García Domínguez, *Miguel Delibes: La imagen escrita* (Valladolid: 38 Semana Internacional de Cine, 1993);

Agnes Gullón, *La novela experimental de Miguel Delibes* (Madrid: Taurus, 1980);

Domingo Gutiérrez, *Claves de Los santos inocentes* (Madrid: Ciclo, 1989);

David Herzberger, "Automatization and Defamiliarization in Delibes' *Parábola del náufrago,*" *Modern Language Notes,* 95 (1980): 357–375;

Leo Hickey, *Cinco horas con Miguel Delibes, el hombre y el novelista* (Madrid: Prensa Española, 1968);

Mercedes Jiménez González, "*337A, madera de héroe:* La Guerra Civil española según Miguel Delibes," *Cuadernos de Aldeeu,* 46 (1990): 29–36;

John W. Kronik, "Language and Communication in Delibes' *Parábola del náufrago,*" *American Hispanist,* 1, no. 1 (1975): 7–10;

Edgar Pauk, *Miguel Delibes: Desarrollo de un escritor (1947–1974)* (Madrid: Gredos, 1975);

Alfonso Rey, *La originalidad novelística de Delibes* (Santiago de Compostela: Universidad de Santiago de Compostela, 1975);

Javier F. Sánchez Pérez, *El hombre amenazado: Hombre, sociedad y educación en la novelística de Miguel Delibes* (Salamanca: Universidad Pontífica de Salamanca, Biblioteca de la Caja de Ahorros y M. de P. de Salamanca, 1985);

Francisco Umbral, *Miguel Delibes* (Madrid: ESPESA, 1970);

Ramona del Valle Spinka, *La conciencia social de Miguel Delibes* (New York: Torres, 1975).

# Luis Mateo Díez

*(21 September 1942 –    )*

Antonio Candau
*Case Western Reserve University*

BOOKS: *Equipo Claraboya: Teoría y poemas,* by Díez, Agustín Delgado, Angel Fierro, and José Antonio Llamas (León: Everest, 1971);

*Señales de humo* (León: Institución Fray Bernardino de Sahagún, 1972);

*Memorial de hierbas* (Madrid: Magisterio Español, 1973);

*Parnasillo provincial de poetas apócrifos,* by Díez, Delgado, and José María Merino (Madrid: Endymion, 1975);

*Apócrifo del clavel y la espina. Blasón de muérdago* (Madrid: Magisterio Español, 1977);

*Ja Díez,* by Díez, Delgado, and Merino (Madrid: Servicio de Publicaciones del Ministerio de Educación y Ciencia, 1977);

*Relato de Babia* (Valencia: Nácher, 1981; revised edition, Madrid: Espasa-Calpe, 1991);

*Las estaciones provinciales* (Madrid: Alfaguara, 1982);

*León, traza y memoria,* by Díez, Antonio Gamoneda, Merino, and Félix de Cárdenas (León: Antonio Machón, 1984);

*Las cenizas del fénix,* by Díez, Merino, and Juan Pedro Aparicio, as [collectively] Sabino Ordás (León: Diputación Provincial, 1985);

*La fuente de la edad* (Madrid: Alfaguara, 1986);

*El sueño y la herida* (Madrid: Almarabú, 1987);

*Brasas de agosto* (Madrid: Alfaguara, 1989);

*Cuentos de la Calle de la Rúa,* by Díez, Merino, and Aparicio (Madrid: Editorial Popular, 1989);

*Las horas completas* (Madrid: Alfaguara, 1990);

*El expediente del náufrago* (Madrid: Alfaguara, 1992);

*El porvenir de la ficción* (Madrid: Caballo Griego para la Poesía, 1992);

*Los males menores* (Madrid: Alfaguara, 1993);

*Valles de leyenda,* by Díez, Florentino-Agustín Díez González, and Antón Díez (León: Edilesa, 1994);

*Camino de perdición* (Madrid: Alfaguara, 1995);

*Tres cuentos* (Holme Olstrup: Sangill Bogtryk, 1995);

*El espíritu del Páramo* (Madrid: Ollero & Ramos, 1996);

*La mirada del alma* (Madrid: Alfaguara, 1997);

*Días del desván* (León: Edilesa, 1997);

*Luis Mateo Díez (from <http://ccma.ntu.edu.tw/~luisa/picture/diez.JPG>)*

*León fascinante,* by Díez and others (León: Leonesas, 1997);

*El paraíso de los mortales* (Madrid: Alfaguara, 1998);

*La ruina del cielo: Un obituario* (Madrid: Ollero & Ramos, 1999);

*Las estaciones de la memoria,* by Díez and Miguel Díez Rodríguez (León: Edilesa, 1999);

*Lunas del Caribe* (Madrid: Anaya, 2000);

*El pasado legendario* (Madrid: Alfaguara, 2000)–includes "El árbol de los cuentos";

*Las palabras de la vida* (Madrid: Temas de Hoy, 2000);

*Laciana: Suelo y sueño,* text by Díez, photographs by Manuel Rodríguez (León: Edilesa, 2000);

*Balcón de piedra: Visiones de la Plaza Mayor,* text by Díez, photographs by Amaia de Diego (Madrid: Ollero & Ramos, 2001);

*El diablo meridiano* (Madrid: Alfaguara, 2001)–includes *El diablo meridiano, La sombra de Anubis,* and *Pensión Lucerna;*

*El oscurecer: Un encuentro* (Madrid: Ollero & Ramos, 2002);

*El reino de Celama* (Barcelona: Plaza & Janés, 2003)–includes *El espíritu del Páramo, La ruina del cielo,* and *El oscurecer;*

*El eco de las bodas* (Madrid: Alfaguara, 2003)–includes *El eco de las bodas, El limbo de los amantes,* and *La viuda feliz;*

*Voces del espejo (Una aproximación)* (Málaga: Diputación Provincial, 2004);

*Las lecciones de las cosas* (León: Edilesa, 2004);

*Fantasmas del invierno* (Madrid: Alfaguara, 2004);

*El fulgor de la pobreza* (Madrid: Alfaguara, 2005).

SELECTED PERIODICAL PUBLICATION– UNCOLLECTED: "La mano del sueño," *Tierras de León,* no. 13 (2001).

"Estar en Babia" (roughly, to be in the moon or to have one's head in the clouds) describes the state of absentmindedness or daydreaming in Spanish. Luis Mateo Díez's *Relato de Babia* (Babia's Story), a collection of vignettes published in 1981, brought that expression back to its real geographical referent–a remote, rural area of beautiful landscapes in northwestern Spain. The book depicts a fragile and dying world, precariously kept alive by the strength of a few ghostly words and old stories. Besides Babia, there are other spaces–all connected to the author's life and his family's history– that have occupied Díez. These territories include the rural area of Laciana, where he was born; the city of León, especially during Spain's dark postwar period of the 1950s; the "Valle de Luna," an area transformed by the construction of a reservoir; and the barren plateau known as "El Páramo," an area of proverbial poverty, emigration, and depopulation also transformed by a reservoir. Díez, a literary writer with a great interest in oral narratives and the traditions of his ancestors, creates an original mixture of fiction and reality, rooted in a deep sense of loss and a profound need to fight against, to complement, and also, to give back to those grim territories.

The fourth of five children, all boys, Díez was born on 21 September 1942 to Florentino Agustín and Milagros Díez in Villablino, a small town in the province of León, in northwestern Spain, that is part of Laciana. When Díez was twelve, his father, a lawyer working for the civil administration, was transferred to the provincial capital, the city of León. The father was a poet and writer of books on the rural areas of León, with a good library, and he transmitted his passion for reading and his interest in literature to his sons. One of many Spanish provincial cities that endured the harsh realities of postwar Spain under General Francisco

Franco's regime, León dates back to pre-Roman times. Established definitively by the Roman invaders as a military post (Legio VII) because of its economic and strategic importance, it became the capital of the northern Christians' push against the Arabs and, during the Middle Ages, was one of the centers of the emerging kingdom of Castile and León. The palaces, churches, and magnificent Gothic cathedral are signs of that glorious past in an otherwise relatively modest urban center. Díez grew up surrounded by those buildings, by that past, and he was increasingly affected by the oppressive atmosphere endured by its inhabitants during a period of significant religious and political intolerance.

After completing high school, Díez studied law at the Universidad Autónoma de Madrid. An admittedly poor student, more interested in writing and reading than in law, he eventually finished his degree at the University of Oviedo–another northern, provincial capital. In the early 1970s he became director of judicial documentation for the city of Madrid, where he has lived ever since. He and his wife, the former Margarita Álvarez, have two sons: Gonzalo and Jaime.

Over the years Díez has maintained strong relationships with several authors from León. His collaborations and his biographical similarities with two of them, José María Merino and Juan Pedro Aparicio, gave rise to the term "Grupo leonés" to refer to these three writers. This label initially produced some interesting critical discussions but seems to have lost validity, in part because of clear stylistic and thematic differences among the authors. The move from León to Madrid did not lead Díez to abandon references to his hometown and its surrounding areas in his fiction. Moreover, while his two friends have written works set outside of these "original territories," Díez has only occasionally dealt with other areas or localities in his writing. The 2001 collection of thirty vignettes about Madrid's Plaza Mayor, titled *Balcón de piedra* (Stone Balcony), is his first volume devoted entirely to a location outside of León and the Spanish northwest. Except for that work, Díez's production deals with three major groups of spaces: first, Laciana, Luna, and Babia, the small towns and the country of his childhood; second, the city of León; and, lastly, the region of El Páramo.

León and northwestern provincial cities such as Oviedo are Levitic gray towns, heirs to those of Gustave Flaubert and Clarín (Leopoldo Alas) in the nineteenth century, but with an almost expressionist appearance that recalls Ramón del Valle-Inclán's *esperpentos.* The main characters are unknown poets, salesmen, librarians, and employees in dead-end positions at bureaucratic institutions. Laciana, Luna, and Babia are all spaces marked by the mythical values created in, and associated with, childhood. Díez has expressed his admiration for Cesare Pavese and other Italian writers of his generation–such as Vasco Pratolini and Giorgio Bassani–who succeeded in creating universal spaces rooted in careful portraits of their small towns. The tiniest provincial town, used as the setting of a well-told story, becomes a microcosm, a universal space.

Díez's memory of his childhood includes episodes of oral readings and communal storytelling. Besides his father's influence on his development as a young reader, Díez has talked about the role of his grade-school teachers, who read the Spanish classics aloud in the classroom, and the traditions of the *calecho* or *filandón*–gatherings of neighbors for communal storytelling during the long and snowy winter nights. One of the stories from Díez's first published collection was included by the director José María Martín Sarmiento in the 1984 motion picture *El filandón*, together with the stories of other narrators from León.

Díez has produced several works in collaboration with other writers and artists. Many of these projects reflect his anthropological interests and include books that combine travel narratives, photography, art, and history. All of them have a strong connection with his biography through his family or friends and are proof that Díez shares the interest of many of his fictional characters in creating stories and books to complement and to memorialize experience.

His first collaborative project, and his first published work, was in poetry. Between 1963 and 1968 he worked with several poets from León on the journal *Claraboya*. The journal is a prime example of the power that a group of motivated writers can muster to overcome adverse circumstances and a closed, intolerant environment, topics that later were included in Díez's urban novels. *Claraboya* published original poems, translations, and critical essays, and was a worthy enterprise in the culturally deprived provincial Spain of the 1960s. The volume *Equipo Claraboya: Teoría y poemas* (Claraboya Group: Theory and Poems), appearing in 1971, is an anthology and poetic manifesto of its authors, who dismiss two of the main poetic schools of the period: "social poetry" and that of the "novísimos" (truly new ones). They find the first one too simplistic and too rooted in traditional topics, and the second one frivolous and immature. In 1972 Díez published his next collection of original poems, *Señales de humo* (Smoke Signals).

In 1973 he published the short-story collection *Memorial de hierbas* (Herbal Brief) and won the Café Gijón Prize for his novella "Apócrifo del clavel y la espina" (Apocryphal with Carnation and Thorn). The latter work was not published until 1977, in a volume that also included another novella, "Blasón de muérdago" (Mistletoe's Coat of Arms). In "Apócrifo del

Cover for Díez's 1986 novel (The Fountain of Youth), about a group of free-spirited poets who play elaborate hoaxes on members of the upper classes in León in the 1950s (Thomas Cooper Library, University of South Carolina)

clavel y la espina" Díez connects his love for oral narration with his readings in Spanish literature, as the narrator, Ovidio el Cojo, speaks from his retirement home in 1881 about the losses he has witnessed in his life and in the country where he has lived. These texts incorporate the rural worlds of Laciana and Luna, which are closely connected with the author's family history. "Blasón de muérdago" narrates the vanishing way of life of an old noble family and of a way of looking at the whole world, from humans and their institutions to the flowers, herbs, rivers, mountains, and fauna.

The irreverent *Parnasillo provincial de poetas apócrifos* (Little Provincial Parnassus of Apocryphal Poets) appeared in 1975 and was written with Agustín Delgado and Merino. It presents the fictional biographies of several poets and an anthology of their poems. The volume satirizes the limited cultural life and some of the banal habits and motifs of provincial Spain.

*Relato de Babia* was published by the author in 1981 but appeared in a definitive edition in 1991. It represents a notable step forward in Díez's career. There is still a re-creation of a concrete space in a mythical way, but anthropological and linguistic elements are incorporated as documentation to provide a more complete picture of the customs and dialect of the area.

*Las estaciones provinciales* (1982, The Provincial Seasons) presents a detective-like story involving a journalist and an illegal sausage-producing and distributing operation. The only season of the yearly cycle absent is spring, the time of rebirth and hope. The novel is set in León during the 1950s, and the lack of expectations and of real possibilities for action and change (a lack that immobilizes the long list of characters) clearly represents the situation of all of Spain during the second decade of Franco's regime. The circular inquiries of the protagonist, Marcos Parra, contrast with the lack of a solution to his personal problems and those of the city and the country. This novel incorporates for the first time the theme of the search–in this case, a fruitless search–as a key element in the topics and structure of the work. The author repeats such a theme and structural model in several of his subsequent novels.

In *León, traza y memoria* (León, Design and Memory) from 1984, Díez works with three artists from León–Merino, the poet Antonio Gamoneda, and the illustrator Félix de Cárdenas. They create a series of texts and illustrations that tell the stories of and offer personal reflections on different buildings, corners, and areas of the city.

With Merino and Aparicio, Díez created the fictitious Sabino Ordás, an intellectual who had been exiled in America during Franco's dictatorship and who returns to Spain with the arrival of democracy and encounters the many economic, social, and cultural changes of the time. Under Ordás's name the three authors published articles in the daily press of León, and later they produced a volume titled *Las cenizas del fénix* (1985, The Phoenix's Ashes). Ordás gives voice to some of the most immediate and specific concerns of the three writers, often related to what they perceive as Spain's neglect of the history, the culture, and the people of the city of Léon and its surrounding areas in favor of Castile, Madrid, and other regions. Ordás also defines a "northwestern" territory that incorporates cities and areas belonging to different provinces and regions of that corner of Spain. He sees the northwest as a community with a particular way of looking at the world that is reflected in similar myths and customs.

*La fuente de la edad* (1986, The Fountain of Youth) is an irreverent and ultimately bleak portrait of what life during the 1950s was like in provincial cities such as León. At times carnivalesque, or *esperpéntica,* with good doses of gross humor, it has a long list of characters–mainly from the ranks of underachievers, losers, and "has-beens"–who interact and explore the streets and the establishments in the city. Everything is presented as behind the times, second-rate, and handed down, under the shadow of better places, better times, and better dreams. *La fuente de la edad* catapulted its author to the best-seller list and wide critical acclaim, receiving both the Critics Prize and the National Literature Prize, and it was made into a television miniseries in 1991 with a script by the director, Julio Sánchez Valdés, and the writer Julio Llamazares. In this work an irreverent group of poets clashes with the city establishment because of several elaborate hoaxes, including the search for the mythical fountain of youth. Exposed by their enemies, who belong to the social upper ranks, the poets plot their revenge to coincide with the main event of the social season, the election of the beauty queen and the awards of the literary contest. *La fuente de la edad* follows in its first part the thematic and structural elements of the search: the journey of several characters seeking a mythical place and object.

After the collection of short stories *Brasas de agosto* (1989, August's Embers), the novel *Las horas completas* (1990, The Complete Hours) presents the short but eventful car trip of a group of old priests. They encounter car trouble and meet their match in a strange character who has undertaken the tradition of the pilgrimage to the city of Santiago de Compostela. This choice of subject was an original one during a period when the trend was for Spanish novelists to set their stories in foreign, mostly European countries. The misfortunes of the group of priests, especially while dealing with machines and new technology, represent the contrasts between the old, traditional Spain and a new, more secular country that sees those traditions as a relic of the past.

*El expediente del náufrago* (1992, The Shipwreck Dossier) further develops the role of literary imagination in the grim environment of the city of León during Franco's regime. It depicts the adventures of Fermín Bustarga, a librarian and aspiring writer in search of Saelices, a reclusive local poet of almost mythical reputation among a small group of followers. It also incorporates the structure of the search, with plot twists, recognitions, and surprises. The novel does vindicate the powers of fantasy to survive in bleak 1950s Spain, and it includes vivid descriptions of different neighborhoods, streets, restaurants, and bars, as well as an underground lair inhabited by a demented character and his mural paintings. The itinerary of search for the writer and his story through the different spaces of the city is also an itinerary of self-discovery for Fermín Bustarga, a journey that at times parallels that of his hero the poet. It is, however, a journey that ends, for both, with unequivocal disillusionment.

*El porvenir de la ficción* (1992, The Future of Fiction) is a miscellaneous volume. It includes some new stories, stories already published, brief essays, and poems dealing with different aspects of the production and reception of literature in Spain. With *Los males menores* (1993, The Lesser Evils) Díez tries his hand again at the short story, in this case the "micro-story," since many of these tales are only a few hundred words in length.

*Valles de leyenda* (Legendary Valleys) from 1994 is a collaborative work that includes photographs, art, and texts on the history of several rural landscapes connected with Díez's life. It shows the writer's commitment to the real stories of the territory and the people who helped him shape his fictional work.

With *Camino de perdición* (1995, Road to Perdition), Díez returned to the novelistic genre with an extended "road novel" set in postwar provincial Spain. The adventures and characters encountered by the salesman Sebastián Odollo have an air of disenchantment, of lost dreams and opportunities, a lack of will or a will defeated by circumstances or other people. The novel has again the search or quest structure, this time involving a mysterious debt to a woman who holds captive the protagonist's will and sends him in his never-ending travels through ghostly small towns and establishments. Spain's northwest region is the geographical referent of the novel, but Díez makes an effort to present these spaces and his characters in a new way. He connects people and animals with mythological figures; chronology and history are blurred with dreamlike sequences and references to legends and myths. The constant movement of the protagonist reflects not so much a liberating process as a labyrinthine course, as expressed also in the title of the book.

*El espíritu del Páramo* (1996, The Spirit of El Páramo), *La ruina del cielo* (1999, Heaven's Ruin), and *El oscurecer: Un encuentro* (2002, Darkness Falls: An Encounter) form the "Celama trilogy," inspired by a traditionally poor and barren plain between the Esla and Órbigo Rivers, in the south central part of León. The construction of a reservoir transformed the lives of its inhabitants. Díez collected all three novels in the volume *El reino de Celama* (2003, The Kingdom of Celama). The word *páramo*–a barren, inhospitable plain–is of pre-Roman origins; it is one of the oldest documented words in the Spanish language and is a fitting symbol of the legendary tones of these works, an extraordinary lit-

erary document on the disappearance of rural ways of life. *El espíritu del Páramo* also was awarded the Critics Prize and the National Literature Prize. The introductory section includes information on the history and geography of the area, which on Díez's fictional map includes the five different spaces of Las Hectáreas, La Hemina, La Llanura, Valma, and Armenta. Following the almost cartographic description, several voices tell ghostly stories, apparently independent but connected through certain symbolic and poetic elements and the frequent recurrence to an obsession with water. All of them present Celama as a territory and a population on the brink of disappearance.

In *La ruina del cielo,* the doctor Ismael Cuende, a character from *El espíritu del Páramo,* starts a census of dead people, using the documentation of his predecessor. The novel incorporates not only geological and anthropological information but also some four hundred characters whose stories and voices intersect with the narrator's, creating a polyphonic discourse. This novel about ways of dying succeeds in keeping alive the ghostly territory introduced in the first volume of the trilogy. Over the hypnotic narrative hangs the premonition of history, about to explode in cruel, inevitable conflicts such as the Spanish Civil War and the two world wars.

The last novel of the "Celama trilogy," *El oscurecer,* tells of the failed attempt of an old shepherd to return to his home, the area of Armenta, after he has been moved out of Celama because of his memory disorder. The novel has the subtitle *Un encuentro* because the old man meets, in a lonely train stop, a boy who follows an opposite trajectory: he is willing to try anything to escape from the area where the old man wants to return. Although there are some references that place the events of this novel in contemporary times, the text still has an air of chronological and historical vagueness, as legends and old ways of living and telling blur the references to news items from Spain's recent past.

*La mirada del alma* (1997, The Soul's Glance) is a short novel set in an urban environment and deals with the recollections of an old patient in a hospital. *Días del desván* (Days in the Attic), also from 1997, deals directly with Díez's and his brother's childhood experiences in Laciana. This autobiographical text explores how the space of the attic and the company of his brother helped the author develop his imagination and some of his storytelling skills.

*El paraíso de los mortales* (1998, Mortals' Paradise) chronicles the adventures of Mino Mera, a teenager left alone in an unidentified city to study for his failed classes over the summer. The quiet city streets are the setting for a tale of adolescent encounters with fear, mystery, and sexuality, in a narrative structured around

*Luis Mateo Díez*

LA RUINA
DEL CIELO

OLLERO & RAMOS

*Cover for Díez's 1999 novel (The Ruin of Heaven: An Obituary),
the second volume of a trilogy about life on the bleak Celama
plain in León (Thomas Cooper Library,
University of South Carolina)*

Mino's search for his uncle Fabio. The two key spaces in the quest–the boardinghouse "La Eternidad" and the riverbank–are presented to the surprised eyes of Mino with magical qualities. His uncle's life and his own escapes offer Mino a door to possible escapes from the gray and closed environment of his city.

The space of the childhood attic and the powerful weapon of the imagination reappear in the novella *Lunas del Caribe* (2000, Caribbean Moons), in which the memories of an attic are the common thread for different stories set around the adventures of a group of children in the 1940s in Spain. Oral storytelling and literary readings accompany the experiences of the group, one of whose members, the bookish Opal, meets a tragic end.

*Laciana: Suelo y sueño* (2001, Laciana: Ground and Dream) is another collaborative work, featuring photo-

graphs by Manuel Rodríguez and designs by Antón Díez. The volume explores the geography and history of the territory of the author's childhood. He provides the texts to accompany the landscapes, portraits, and sculptures that are reproduced in full color.

*El eco de las bodas* (2003, The Echo of Weddings) includes three novellas in which the author presents a lighter, ironic approach to the aspirations and limitations of his characters. Doña Dega, the protagonist of *La viuda feliz* (The Happy Widow), travels the barren spaces of El Páramo by train following the deaths of three husbands and accompanied by her healthy daydreaming, her generosity, and her acceptance of her strange fate. *El limbo de los amantes* (The Limbo of Lovers) offers the sarcastic point of view of a character witnessing a wedding in a provincial town. *El eco de las bodas* focuses on a major component also present in the other two novellas: the role that chance plays in human lives, especially in matters of the heart.

*Las lecciones de las cosas* (2004, The Lessons of Things) won the Miguel Delibes Prize for Narrative. It is divided in three parts and includes the title novella and several short stories, some of them already published in other collections. All the stories are set in the Laciana valley. The first part, "Lecciones," depicts a fictitious trip undertaken by three major historical figures to the valley to open new schools. The three characters–Gumersindo de Azcárate, Manuel Bartolomé Cossío, and Francisco Giner de los Ríos–were connected to reformist efforts for Spanish education and society at the beginning of the twentieth century; inspired by the ideas of the nineteenth-century German philosopher Karl Christian Friedrich Krause, they created the influential Institución Libre de Enseñanza (Free Institute of Teaching). The story "Cielo de la distancia" (Distance's Sky) deals with the Spanish-American War and the loss of Cuba, Puerto Rico, and the Philippines. The second part, "Revelaciones" (Revelations), and the final section, "Recuerdos" (Recollections), include microstories connected with characters and events relevant to Laciana. In all of the stories, childhood is presented not only as an age but also as a state of mind where humans are capable of creating and getting inspired by new worlds, both real and fictitious.

In 2001 Díez received the Castile and León Letters Award, recognizing the "relevant imaginative and stylistic value of his long and intense work, which has focused on the storytelling tradition of Castile and León and has achieved universal resonance." Díez's success is evident in this award and the many others he has received and in the translations of his texts into other languages. Díez has seen the need to reorganize and publish old materials in new editions. He has reedited, anthologized, and rearranged many of his stories, short novels, and articles in different volumes. His most popular novels have also been published in scholarly editions. He frequently writes prologues for these new editions, reflecting on the texts included in them and on his literary trajectory up to that point. His most prominent statement on the place of his work in the larger literary context, however, is his induction speech to the Spanish Royal Academy, the most prestigious cultural institution in Spain, to which he was elected in 2000. Titled "La mano del sueño" (Dream's Hand), it reviews his literary production and his life marked by the paradoxical interaction of the imagination–a tool to transcend one's circumstances–and of memory, a way to try to recapture the circumstances from which one wants to escape.

One of Díez's volumes of essays and recollections, *Las palabras de la vida* (2000, Life's Words), closes with a figure similar to many of the characters in his fiction. After discussing Aristotle's and the Sophists' ideas about language, Díez turns to his memories from León and speaks of a modest high-school teacher nicknamed Cesidio Aristóteles:

> "We are house and city," one of my dearest professors from the provincial high school used to say, "and there is a word that connects us with that small world of our home and our survival, the daily word of the domestic interior, where food and feelings go together. But there is another communal, civic, social word, a word that joins speech and action together; this word is the root of our true creativity, is the word that creates the reality itself that we inhabit and that sustains us." This professor who was never able to show his students a clean chin in spite of shaving up to three times a day used to say: "what we are we are together with everybody, and whatever happens has an effect in the word that marks our destiny, the word that illuminates our life together."

When the professor falls seriously ill, Díez and some of his friends go to the hospital to visit him. The picture of the emaciated professor mumbling the students' names with equal degrees of difficulty and gratitude is the moving emblem of Díez's love of and focus on those left behind–the unsuccessful, losers, and outsiders. The most insignificant person, if a character in a well-told story, becomes a universal hero.

Luis Mateo Díez's works embody the changes undergone by Spain since the end of the Franco dictatorship. His texts bridge the gap between "high" literary and popular oral narratives, offering a demanding writing style and entertaining stories. His accounts of rural Spain and of the entire country during the difficult decades of the 1940s and 1950s are invaluable cultural documents of conditions that are disappearing or already forgotten in the twenty-first century.

**References:**

Santos Alonso, *Literatura leonesa actual* (Valladolid: Junta de Castilla y León, 1986);

Samuel Amell, "Tradición y renovación, un difícil balance en la novela española actual," *Crítica Hispánica,* 14, nos. 1–2 (1986): 363–383;

Antonio Candau, "Luces de provincia: Luis Mateo Díez," in his *Las provincias de la literatura* (Valladolid: Universitas Castellae, 2002), pp. 211–239;

Carlos Javier García, *La invención del grupo leonés: Estudio y entrevistas* (Madrid: Júcar, 1995);

Domingo Luis Hernández Álvarez and Asunción Castro Díez, eds., *Luis Mateo Díez: Los laberintos de la imaginación* (Santa Cruz de Tenerife: La Página, 2003);

Vance Holloway, *El postmodernismo y otras tendencias de la novela española (1967–1995)* (Madrid: Fundamentos, 1999);

Dieter Ingenschay and Hans-Jörg Neuschäfer, eds., *Abriendo caminos: La literatura española desde 1975* (Barceloma: Lumen, 1994);

Manuel Longares, "El 'Bloomsbury leonés,'" *Cambio 16* (23 November 1987): 174–176;

José María Merino, "Luis Mateo Díez, en la provincia del mundo," *Página,* 1 (1989): 13;

Randolph Pope, "La oscura orilla de la fuente de la edad: Visión de América de José María Merino y Luis Mateo Díez," in *España y América en sus literaturas,* edited by Ángeles Encinar (Madrid: Instituto de Cooperación Iberoamericana/Saint Louis University, 1993), pp. 103–126;

Santos Sanz Villanueva, "Generación del 68," *El Urogallo,* 26 (June 1988): 28–31;

Sanz Villanueva, "Luis Mateo Díez, entre la crítica y la invención," *Página,* 1 (1989): 1–11;

Darío Villanueva, "La novela," *Letras españolas 1978–1986* (Madrid: Castalia, 1987), pp. 19–64.

# Belén Gopegui
*(19 October 1963 – )*

## Eva Legido-Quigley
*Letra Hispánica, Salamanca*

BOOKS: *La escala de los mapas* (Barcelona: Anagrama, 1993);

*Cualladó, puntos de vista,* by Gopegui and Tomás Llorens (Madrid: Fundación Colleción Thyssen-Bornemisza, 1995);

*Tocarnos la cara* (Barcelona: Anagrama, 1995);

*La conquista del aire* (Barcelona: Anagrama, 1998);

*Michael Andrews. Luces: Contextos de la colección permanente nº 9,* by Gopegui and William Feaver (Madrid: Fundación Colleción Thyssen-Bornemisza, 2000);

*Lo real* (Barcelona: Anagrama, 2001);

*El lado frío de la almohada* (Barcelona: Anagrama, 2004).

PRODUCED SCRIPT: *El principio de Arquímedes,* motion picture, Alta Films, 2004.

OTHER: "En desierta playa," in *Cuentos de este siglo: 30 narradoras españolas contemporáneas,* edited by Angeles Encinar (Barcelona: Lumen, 1995), pp. 311–320.

SELECTED PERIODICAL PUBLICATIONS–
UNCOLLECTED: "Los cepos de la realidad," *Diario 16,* 27 February 1993, p. 12;

"Contribucion acerca del sentido de *La conquista del aire,*" *Ojáncano: Revista de Literatura Española,* 16 (April 1999): 86–89;

"El sí de cado no," *El País,* 24 July 2000;

"El padre de Blancanieves," *El País,* 3 November 2001, p. 10;

"Un libro que no miente," *El País,* 11 January 2003, p. 7;

"El lado frío de la almohada," *El Cultural,* 26 January 2003, p. 12.

*Belén Gopegui (photograph © Alberto Fernández de Agirre; from the cover for* Tocarnos la cara, *1995; Jean and Alexander Heard Library, Vanderbilt University)*

Belén Gopegui's work deals with contemporary socio-economic conflicts in the context of the last two decades of the twentieth century in Spain. What she describes, however, can be applied to any part of the world, since her themes have deep philosophical implications. Each novel represents an ethical examination of society, economics, politics, and the ways in which these forces influence the lives of individuals. As Encinar, an emblematic character in her novel *Tocarnos la cara* (1995, Touching Our Faces), states (quoting Aristotle): "Yo soy contigo y las instituciones" (I exist together with you and our institutions). Her protagonists are worried about projects that fail and about people who are not true to their dreams. She explores the difference between facts and words (what one actually does and what one says), the precariousness of feelings (solitude, love, suffering, making others suffer), and the transformation of principles through time.

Her creative endeavors have developed rapidly, gaining the recognition of critics and readers, even though she is not on best-seller lists. Literary critics agree that she is one of the most original voices among the younger Spanish writers, and her works have been translated into French, Italian, German, Finnish, Portuguese, and Serbian. Gopegui's literary style has developed in a variety of directions since her first novel, *La escala de los mapas* (The Scale of Maps), appeared in 1993 from the renowned publishing house Anagrama. In the beginning she used a poetic prose; in later novels she has favored a more realistic expression. In a similar way, she has veered from philosophical and abstract deliberations to more pragmatic and prosaic topics affecting contemporary Spain. She is considered to be a demanding intellectual who does not accept flowery language, clichés, or uncritical commonplaces. She does not want to blur reality through discourse leading to imposture. Gopegui has been praised often for her clarity, her capacity for analysis, and the piercing intelligence with which she unravels some of the darkest aspects of reality and human nature.

Belén Ruiz de Gopegui was born in Madrid on 19 October 1963. Her father, Luis Ruiz de Gopegui, a notable astronomer and writer, served as the director of the National Aeronautics and Space Administration in Madrid. Her mother, Margarita Durán, is a volunteer worker with Amnesty International.

Gopegui earned a degree in law from the Universidad Autónoma de Madrid in 1986; but she never practiced law, as from an early stage in her studies she was drawn to literature. She began her writing career with book reviews and interview contributions to the literary supplement in the magazine *El Sol.* She was also an editor for publishing houses until the publication of *La escala de los mapas,* when she took to writing as her main profession. Her literary career also involves giving lectures at such universities as the Universidad Autónoma de Madrid; Emory University in Atlanta, Georgia; and the University of Massachusetts, Amherst. She contributes an occasional column to *Babelia,* the prestigious literary magazine supplement of *El País.* Apart from novels, Gopegui has written short stories (such as "En desierta playa" [On a Deserted Beach], 1995) and texts for art books published by the Thyssen-Bornemisza Art Museum in Madrid. She has also served as a member of juries for literary prizes, such as that of La Casa de las Américas in Cuba.

*La escala de los mapas* was an instant success that won her the prestigious Tigre Juan literary prize in 1993 and the Iberoamerican Santiago del Nuevo Extremo Prize for first novel in 1994. The novel also was republished by RBA Editores in 1994 as part of the "Narrativa Actual: Autores de Lengua Española" (Recent Narrative: Authors in Spanish) series, which includes famous writers such as Juan Goytisolo and Ana María Matute. The protagonist of *La escala de los mapas,* Sergio Prim, is a solitary man who wants to find "un hueco" (a hollow) that will provide him with warmth and comfort. He is shy and often panics before a reality that overwhelms him. He resolves to remain on his own, instead of sharing his life with Brezo, the woman he loves. The meticulous description of the psychological complexity and understanding of this autistic character is one of the most notable accomplishments of the novel. The author's lyrical expression stands out for its provocative tropes and metaphors related to the cosmos.

Carmen Martín Gaite, one of the most renowned figures in twentieth-century Spanish literature and a mentor to the young writer, described Gopegui's first novel as both a love story for all times and a contemporary drama accessible to any reader. She praised Gopegui's original techniques and distinctive rhythm. Gopegui paid homage to Martín Gaite, who died in 2000, in a roundtable of the Salamanca author's *Cuadernos de todo* (2002, Notebooks of Everything) and in an article for *El País,* "El sí de cada no" (2000, The Yes of Every No).

Gopegui's second novel, *Tocarnos la cara,* is the story of an idealist group of friends who want to contribute to the good of the community through theater. Their goal is to design an unusual type of playhouse where actors play roles that their customers create. The actors want people to take the first step toward real actions by putting their wishes into practice and by making them watch the possibilities of changing their lives. This project, however, does not last long since conflicts such as lack of unity and divergent interests and needs arise among the members of the company.

Ethics and politics are the basis of this allegorical novel that investigates the Aristotelian principle of the necessity for human beings to have a social or political imperative grounded in a sound ethical sense. Gopegui explores, through notions such as reciprocity and "lo común" (the common good), the ways in which one can develop social awareness in contemporary society. The title of the novel suggests this idea of mutual influence but also, in a more metaphorical sense, the notion of caring and doing good for each other.

*La conquista del aire* (1998, The Conquest of the Air), Gopegui's third novel, had a major impact beyond

BELÉN GOPEGUI

*Tocarnos la cara*

**ANAGRAMA**
Narrativas hispánicas

*Cover for Gopegui's second novel (Touching Our Faces), published
in 1995, in which a theater group tries to inspire audiences
to pursue their goals by showing them the potential results
of taking action (Jean and Alexander Heard
Library, Vanderbilt University)*

the reading public when director Gerardo Herrero made it into the motion picture *Las razones de mis amigos* (The Reasons of My Friends) in 2000, with a script by Angeles González Sinde. The story centers around Carlos Maceda, a young entrepreneur who has a financial crisis with his small electronics business, bringing it to the brink of bankruptcy. He asks three close friends to lend him three million pesetas (approximately $17,500), which they offer after some deliberations. As Carlos postpones the repayment, their friendship suffers a test, and the pressures of the respective partners fill the relationships with mistrust. These characters, no longer in their twenties, had grown up with the stories of the generation of progressive students who in the 1960s and 1970s had ideals, fought against Francisco Franco's dictatorship, and were members of revolutionary political organizations. Through this plot, Gopegui examines in

depth how the capitalist values of the 1980s and 1990s have eroded the progressive thought of these students, who started their professional lives under the administration of Socialist prime minister Felipe González Márquez and profited from an improved financial situation as members of a wealthy bourgeoisie.

In the style of the committed social novelists of the nineteenth century, Gopegui gives readers a prologue in which she provides some clues for the interpretation of her novel. She explains that writing should be a search for knowledge ("El narrador quiere saber y por eso narra" [The narrator wants to know and for that reason narrates]) that should encompass both emotion and consciousness, feeling and reason. The characters represent a contemporary society completely socialized by money, in the sense that money actually creates people's ethical consciousness, to the detriment of values such as friendship, love, solidarity, sympathy, and justice. This lesson is not to be disregarded in an historical period that ended in many scandals of corruption. *La conquista del aire* was a finalist for the 1999 Premio Nacional de Narrativa (National Prize for Novels), which was won by the well-established novelist Miguel Delibes.

In her novel *Lo real* (2001, The Real), Gopegui shows a growing interest in topics of society and public life. In a 2002 interview with Winston Manrique Sabogal, she stated that in the beginning she thought that "Literature" with a capital "L" only could protect one from exterior pressures, the pain inflicted by others and the pain one is driven to cause others. Now, however, she considers that outside pressure is an inexorable influence, and she wants to fight against it and show its lack of legitimacy. *Lo real* does not have a pamphleteering tone, but the ideological and political frame stands out in the references to the class struggle, the importance of money, and the disadvantages of capitalism. In the Sabogal interview Gopegui reflected: "¿Qué acciones puede un hombre o una mujer llevar a cabo, en compañía de quién, a las órdenes de quién, con el capital de quién?" (What actions can a man or a woman take, in the company of whom, under whose orders, with whose capital?).

The narrator of this novel, Irene Arce, is unhappy with her job as a television producer. Trying to become more motivated, she decides to write the story of one of her colleagues who has recently joined the workplace. In her account, Edmundo Gómez Risco leads the intricate, secretive way of life he has imposed on himself in order to change some of his ideas about society and injustice. He is the son of a businessman who participated in one of the great financial scandals during Franco's dictatorship and was later sentenced to prison, while his bosses remained free of charges. Although

Edmundo wants to find a secure position in life, he feels a kind of vengeful satisfaction in destroying the lives and reputations of corrupted upper-class professionals. His main wish is not to be a servant ("no ser criado"); that is, not to be exploited, humiliated, or deceived. But he will do so clandestinely, in a Machiavellian way, blackmailing his targets. As in her previous novels, Gopegui examines whether there is a way to counteract social injustice and also questions contemporary definitions of human beings as mere wealth or merchandise according to their market value.

Gopegui has become more daring in her experimentation with narrative techniques. In *Lo real,* as in the old Greek theater, there is choral commentary, in this case by "Coro de asalariados y asalariadas de renta media reticentes" (A chorus of reticent salaried middle-class men and women) who pass judgment about the protagonist's actions. "Lo real," an abstract and philosophical term, refers to what Gopegui has described as the collective unconscious or the acceptance of unfair and untruthful reality as it is: what really happens and what people really do versus what one thinks happens and what one says one wants to happen.

Gopegui wrote the screenplay for the movie *El principio de Arquímedes* (2004, Archimedes' Principle), directed by Herrero. Her next novel, *El lado frío de la almohada* (2004, The Cold Side of the Pillow), describes the relationship between Philip Hull, a U.S. diplomat stationed in Madrid in 2003, and Laura Bahia, a young Spanish agent of Cuban origin. It is a story of love, spying, and the Cuban revolution. This piece of social literature, with strong political content and a provocative antagonist discourse, has received both negative criticism and a warm welcome. In an interview for the Cuban magazine *La Jiribilla,* Gopegui stated her political view: "Cuba es real, es un proyecto revolucionario real" (Cuba is real, it is a real revolutionary project).

There is a critical consensus that Gopegui is an exceptional analyst of contemporary Spanish society because of her knowledge of economic and political issues and their ethical and philosophical implications, and because of her thorough descriptions of the professional microworlds of her generation, such as the computer industry, the media, image consultancy, psychiatry, and theater enterprises. In times of commercial writing, Gopegui stands out as a committed writer with a genuine subversive side. She is a daring researcher who breaks through the surface of things and shows their most sinister aspects. As she stated in a 1999 interview with Eva Legido-Quigley: "De actuar hay que actuar con la idea de que va a cambiar algo. Creo que la única vía es una vía política. Debemos intentar cambiar las reglas que ordenan los actos" (If one does something, one has to do it believing that something will be

**BELÉN GOPEGUI**

*La conquista del aire*

**ANAGRAMA**
Narrativas hispánicas

Cover for Gopegui's 1998 novel (The Conquest of the Air), about a man whose relationships with three close friends suffer after he borrows a large sum of money from them (William T. Young Library, University of Kentucky)

changed. I think that the only way is a political way. We have to try to change the rules that order actions). Literature, for her, in an art that should make the invisible visible.

As a public figure, Gopegui has been active in the call for social justice. In 2001 she signed the manifesto "Con la guerra y el terror no se construye la paz" (With War and Terror You Do Not Construct Peace), along with other Spanish intellectuals against the war in Afghanistan; she has contributed several articles to the on-line *Diario Mundo Obrero* (Workers' World) magazine; and she has given lectures to groups of alternative thinkers, such as Ateneo XXI in Madrid. "Los nuevos valores de nuestra literatura" (New Values in Our Literature) and "¿Por qué escribir una novela hoy?" (Why

Should One Write Novels?) are just two examples of lectures in which she explores the relationship between literature and sociopolitical issues.

Gopegui's rigorous work and linguistic accuracy go hand in hand with her lucidity and her strong stance against the imposture and hypocrisy of contemporary Spanish society. Her authenticity and idealism bring a force of renewal in Spanish letters, giving a new voice to the old concerns and the greater challenges her generation faces when questioning whether peace can exist without justice, whether it is possible to work without being submissive, or whether people can still make a difference in the well-being of their communities. These questions remain open, but she addresses them determined not just to expose uninformed, misleading, and false interpretations of reality but to react to them.

**Interviews:**

Marta Rivera de la Cruz, "Belén Gopegui: Cada vez hay menos gente que quiere asumir la responsibilidad de saber más que otro," *Espéculo: Revista de Estudios Literarios,* no. 7 (November 1997–February 1998) <http://www.ucm.es/info/especulo/numero7/gopegui.htm>;

Eva Legido-Quigley, "Conversación con Belén Gopegui: La necesidad de una vía política," *Ojáncano: Revista de Literatura Española,* 16 (April 1999): 90–104;

María del Mar López-Cabrales, "Belén Gopegui: La cartografía urbana se traza con palabras," in her *Palabras de mujeres* (Madrid: Narcea, 2000), pp. 73–83;

Santiago Fernández, "Belén Gopegui: 'Me preocupa el precio que tenga que pagar para poder vivir de escribir,'" *Babab,* no. 6 (January 2001) <http://www.babab.com/no06/belen_gopegui.htm>;

Winston Manrique Sabogal, "Me interesa saber si es posible escribir contra los temas de siempre," *El País,* 7 September 2002, p. 2.

**Reference:**

Eva Legido-Quigley, "La superación de una *episteme* posmoderna saturada: El caso de Belén Gopegui en *Tocarnos la cara,*" *Monographic Review/Revista Monográfica,* 17 (2001): 146–164.

# Juan Goytisolo

*(5 January 1931 –   )*

Randolph D. Pope
*University of Virginia*

BOOKS: *Juegos de manos* (Barcelona: Destino, 1954); translated by John Rust as *The Young Assassins* (New York: Knopf, 1959; London: MacGibbon & Kee, 1960);

*Duelo en el paraíso* (Barcelona: Destino, 1955); translated by Christine Brooke-Rose as *Children of Chaos* (London: MacGibbon & Kee, 1958);

*El circo* (Barcelona: Destino, 1957);

*Fiestas* (Barcelona: Destino, 1958); translated by Herbert Weinstock (New York: Knopf, 1960; London: MacGibbon & Kee, 1961);

*La resaca* (Paris: Club del Libro Español, 1958);

*Problemas de la novela* (Barcelona: Seix Barral, 1959);

*Campos de Níjar* (Barcelona: Seix Barral, 1960); translated by Luigi Luccarelli as *The Countryside of Níjar*, in *The Countryside of Níjar; and, La Chanca* (Plainfield, Ind.: Alembic, 1987), pp. 81–151;

*Para vivir aquí* (Buenos Aires: Sur, 1960);

*La isla* (Barcelona: Seix Barral, 1961); translated by José Yglesias as *Island of Women* (New York: Knopf, 1962); translation republished as *Sands of Torremolinos* (London: Panther, 1964);

*La Chanca* (Paris: Librairie Espagnole, 1962); translated by Luccarelli in *The Countryside of Najar; and, La Chanca* (Plainfield, Ind.: Alembic, 1987);

*Fin de fiesta: Tentativas de interpretación de una historia amorosa* (Barcelona: Seix Barral, 1962); translated by Yglesias as *The Party's Over: Four Attempts to Define a Love Story* (London: Weidenfeld & Nicolson, 1966; New York: Grove, 1967);

*Pueblo en marcha: Instantáneas de un viaje a Cuba* (Paris: Librairie Espagnole, 1963);

*Examen de conciencia* (Ebenhausen, Germany: Langewiesch-Brandt, 1966);

*Señas de identidad* (Mexico City: Mortiz, 1966; revised, 1969); translated by Gregory Rabassa as *Marks of Identity* (New York: Grove, 1969; London: Serpent's Tail, 1988);

*El furgón de cola* (Paris: Ruedo Ibérico, 1967);

*Reivindicación del conde don Julián* (Mexico City: Mortiz, 1970); translated by Helen Lane as *Count Julián*

*Juan Goytisolo (photograph by Lufti Ozkok; from the dust jacket for Kessel Schwartz,* Juan Goytisolo, *1970; Richland County Public Library)*

(New York: Viking, 1974); revised as *Don Julián*, edited by Linda Gould Levine (Madrid: Catédra, 2004);

*Juan sin tierra* (Barcelona: Seix Barral, 1975); translated by Lane as *Juan the Landless* (New York: Viking, 1977);

*Disidencias* (Barcelona: Seix Barral, 1977);

*Libertad, libertad, libertad* (Barcelona: Anagrama, 1978);

*España y los españoles* (Barcelona: Lumen, 1979);

*El problema del Sáhara* (Barcelona: Anagrama, 1979);

*Makbara* (Barcelona: Seix Barral, 1980); translated by Lane (New York: Seaver, 1981);

*Paisajes después de la batalla* (Barcelona: Montesinos, 1982); translated by Lane as *Landscapes after the Battle* (New York: Seaver, 1987);

*Crónicas sarracinas* (Paris: Ruedo Ibérico / Barcelona: Ibérica de Ediciones y Publicaciones, 1982); translated in part by Lane as *Space in Motion* (New York: Lumen, 1987);

*Contracorrientes* (Barcelona: Montesinos, 1985);

*Coto vedado* (Barcelona: Seix Barral, 1985); translated by Peter Bush as *Forbidden Territory: The Memoirs of Juan Goytisolo, 1931–1956* (San Francisco: North Point, 1989; London: Quartet, 1989);

*En los reinos de taifa* (Barcelona: Seix Barral, 1986); translated by Bush as *Realms of Strife: The Memoirs of Juan Goytisolo, 1957–1982* (San Francisco: North Point, 1990; London: Quartet, 1990);

*Las virtudes del pájaro solitario* (Barcelona: Seix Barral, 1988); translated by Lane as *The Virtues of the Solitary Bird* (London: Serpent's Tail, 1991);

*Estambul otomano* (Barcelona: Planeta, 1989);

*Aproximaciones a Gaudí en Capadocia* (Madrid: Mondadori, 1990);

*La cuarentena* (Madrid: Mondadori, 1991); translated by Bush as *Quarantine* (Normal, Ill.: Dalkey Archive Press, 1994);

*Cuaderno de Sarajevo: Anotaciones de un viaje a la barbarie* (Madrid: El País/Aguilar, 1993);

*La saga de los Marx* (Madrid: Mondadori, 1993); translated by Bush as *The Marx Family Saga* (London: Faber & Faber, 1996);

*Argelia en el vendaval* (Madrid: El País/Aguilar, 1993);

*El bosque de las letras* (Madrid: Alfaguara, 1995);

*El sitio de los sitios* (Madrid: Alfaguara, 1995); translated by Lane as *State of Siege* (San Francisco: City Lights Books, 2002);

*Paisajes de la guerra con Chechenia al fondo* (Madrid: El País/ Aguilar, 1996); translated by Bush as *Landscapes of War: From Sarajevo to Chechnya* (San Francisco: City Lights Books, 2000);

*Las semanas del jardín: Un círculo de lectores* (Madrid: Alfaguara, 1997); translated by Bush as *The Garden of Secrets* (London: Serpent's Tail, 2000);

*De la Ceca a la Meca* (Madrid: Alfaguara, 1997);

*El universo imaginario* (Madrid: Espasa, 1997);

*Fuerte como un turco* (Barcelona: Galaxia Gutenberg, 1998);

*Cogitus interruptus* (Barcelona: Seix Barral, 1999);

*Carajïcomedia: de Fray Bugeo Montesino y otros pájaros de vario plumaje y pluma* (Barcelona: Seix Barral, 2000); translated by Bush as *A Cock-Eyed Comedy: Starring Friar Bugeo Montesino and Other Faeries of Motley Feather and Fortune* (London: Serpent's Tail, 2002);

*El peaje de la vida: Integración o rechazo de la emigración en España,* by Goytisolo and Sami Naïr (Madrid: Aguilar, 2000);

*Pájaro que ensucia su propio nido* (Barcelona: Galaxia Gútenberg/Círculo de Lectores, 2001);

*Paisajes de guerra: Sarajevo, Argelia, Palestina, Chechenia* (Madrid: Aguilar, 2001);

*Tradición y disidencia* (Mexico City: TEC de Monterrey, 2001);

*Telón de boca* (Barcelona: El Aleph, 2003);

*España y sus ejidos* (Madrid: HMR, 2003).

**Collection:** *Obras completas,* 2 volumes, edited by Pere Gimferrer (Madrid: Aguilar, 1977).

**Editions in English:** *Saracen Chronicles: A Selection of Literary Essays,* translated by Helen Lane (London: Quartet, 1992);

*Cinema Eden: Essays from the Muslim Mediterranean,* translated by Peter Bush (London: Eland, 2003).

PRODUCED SCRIPT: *Alquibla,* television, TVE and Eclipse Films SA, 1990, 1992.

OTHER: José María Blanco White, *Obra inglesa,* translated, with a prologue, by Goytisolo (Buenos Aires: Formentor, 1972).

Juan Goytisolo is arguably the most controversial writer of his generation. He has questioned critically not only the repressive regime that governed Spain after the Spanish Civil War, as many other writers also did, but also the totality of Spanish culture that took shape in the late fifteenth century by defining as essentially Spanish only Castilian language and Catholic religion, while excluding the Jews and Moors who had for centuries been an integral, and in many ways the most creative, part of Spanish society. Goytisolo found in the writings of Américo Castro, which he started to read in the early 1960s, the scholarly underpinning for this position; yet, it grew from a deep and compassionate concern for the excluded and downtrodden. His novels challenge the reader with frequent experimentation and essayistic or satirical passages that rail aggressively against common ideas. Uncharacteristically for a Spanish writer, he has made his own examined life not only the subject matter of many of his novels and of two books of memoirs, but also an example of consistency between his ideas and life. His topics have ranged from an early rebellion against bourgeois society–he embraced a bohemian existentialism tinged with Marxism–to gender and ethnic issues, especially regarding North African immigration into Europe. Goytisolo has published twenty novels, several travel narratives, and many books of essays and collections of journalistic reports and has worked in the documentary form, as well. He is a frequent contributor to the most important newspaper in Spain, *El País,* and a well-known and respected public intellectual.

Juan Goytisolo Gay was born in Barcelona on 5 January 1931, the third son of five children born to José María Goytisolo and Julia Gay. The elder Goytisolo was reasonably well-off financially, thanks to his grandfather's exploitation of a sugar plantation in Cuba during the nineteenth century. The discovery by the fledgling writer of the origin of his family's fortune when he was at the university in Barcelona profoundly affected him, precipitating a break with his personal, familial, and national past. This experience of rejecting his roots has been inscribed in his novels and memoirs repeatedly, most often as the instant of reading a letter from a Cuban slave to his owner. Of Goytisolo's three brothers and one sister, José Agustín became an accomplished poet, and Luis also became a novelist; yet, the house in which they were reared was not characterized by exceptional learning. Goytisolo's mother was an avid reader, but her influence on her children was cut short when she was killed in 1938 during an air raid over Barcelona by Francisco Franco's forces. His father, who was the manager of a small company that made fertilizer and glue, tried as a sideline to implement what turned out to be disastrous agricultural innovations in a country house he owned, which both Juan and Luis Goytisolo frequently and fondly remember in their books. His father became ill in 1937, and his perceived weakness increased the growing distance from his son. Nevertheless, Goytisolo has noted that his father was proud of his early literary success; to avoid upsetting his father, he concealed from him some of his opinions and especially his sexual orientation. This conflicted relationship of disdain and affection is also seen in Goytisolo's reiterated announcements that he is leaving behind his family history, national tradition, language, and other marks of identity that he proceeds then to revisit in his following text. While such an attachment to what is in theory rejected could appear inconsistent, in the context of his whole work it is more rewardingly understood as a relentless exploration of human memory and its colonized condition. For Goytisolo, the creation of a self with which one can identify must contend with the illusory nature of private existence: language and culture, the economy and history, sex and trauma, all involve a never-ending interplay with others, not only in the present but also in a past that keeps recurring, many times uninvited, in the mind.

Goytisolo studied in religious schools, first with the Jesuits and then with the Brothers of the Christian Doctrine, and he recalls as a child during the Civil War a sortie with a maid who wanted both of them to

*Dust jacket for the U.S. edition (1960) of the English translation of Goytisolo's 1958 novel, which interweaves stories of people living in a Barcelona apartment building (Richland County Public Library)*

become martyrs by defying the Republican soldiers. This early period of his life, when he was a model student in school and in the first year of law at the university, has been denounced repeatedly by Goytisolo as inauthentic. In the prologue of *Cogitus Interruptus* (1999, Interrupted Thinking), he describes his education as a process of indoctrination by his teachers, countereducation by haphazard encounters with books and people outside of school, and a long period of learning on his own. Nevertheless, the notable ethical ideals that power his work, his abhorrence of hypocrisy and his commitment to the poor and marginalized, may well have become ingrained by the rhetoric he heard in these schools, which he recalls, not unlike James Joyce, often with scorn in his novels. Also, his later interest in the work of Sufi mystics as well as in San Juan de la Cruz reveals that his quest for a sincere rhetoric of transcendence has never been quite abandoned.

Goytisolo's first published novel is *Juegos de manos* (1954, A Sleight of Hand; translated as *The Young Assassins,* 1959), a finalist for the Nadal Prize, the most important competition at that time. Written in 1953, when he was just twenty-two years old and his readings were still limited to what Spain could offer within the limitations of censorship, the novel creates a credible world in the tradition of existentialist fiction. The main themes are boredom and engagement. A group of university students, tired of a gray and repressive society and unable to become interested in the goals their parents offer them, attempt to go beyond their social class in bohemian excursions and ardent conversations. They decide to assassinate Francisco Guarner, a politician who to them represents the establishment. Whoever gets the lowest hand in a poker game must perform the deed; the choice falls on David, a hesitant member of their group, who is unable to kill Guarner when he has the opportunity. Goytisolo's aversion to dogmatism is already present, since the reader is led to suspect that these revolutionaries are driven by badly digested theory and are blind to the complexities of reality. David is at the same time a hero—since he decides to follow his own belief that a single act of violence will not alter an unjust society—and a traitor who fails to keep his word and help transform history.

In the early 1950s the merits of armed revolt were frequently discussed in Spain. At the end of the decade, Fidel Castro led an uprising that Goytisolo long supported, even visiting Cuba in 1961 during the Bay of Pigs invasion. At the same time, however, *Juegos de manos* shows the corruption of the supporters of the "good" cause, since David's poker hand is the result not of chance but of sleight of hand designed to put him to a test. Since he does recoil from murder, he in turn must be executed, and this imperative is carried out by Agustín, one of the leaders of the group. That this character bears the name of Goytisolo's great-grandfather, a leader of sorts of the family destiny, may be more than a coincidence. Agustín murders David and then calmly waits for the police to arrive. *Juegos de manos* is a flawed novel: characters are thinly characterized, the conflict is overblown, and the students' discussions bookish. Yet, there are in the novel already many of the preoccupations typical of the author's mature work, including a concern for ethical issues, a rebellion against all forms of authority, and the importance of role-playing in the process of defining the true self.

*Duelo en el paraíso* (translated as *Children of Chaos,* 1958) appeared in 1955 after it was delayed by censors who demanded Goytisolo remove the profanity from the dialogue of the Nationalist soldiers. He complied with this request but cleaned up the language of the Republican army, as well. This incident convinced him that he could not express his full view of the world under a censorious government and confirmed his decision to leave the country. He had been in Paris briefly in 1953; while there in 1955 he met Monique Lange, an editor for Editions du Seuil who became his lifelong companion (the two married in 1978), and by 1957 he had already settled permanently in France. Since 1967 he has also lived in Marrakesh.

*Duelo en el paraíso* tells the story of the murder of a child, Abel, at the hands of a group of children who are briefly left alone at a camp without any supervision as the war front changes sides. Abel is an outsider, since he comes from a higher social class, lives in a manor called Paraíso (Paradise), and shows preternatural insight. As his namesake in the Bible, Abel is an innocent victim of other people's envy. The children have learned from the military conflict going on around them that violence is an appropriate solution for eliminating a person who is different and therefore apparently threatening. By showing the pervasive indoctrination to which all children are subjected, Goytisolo touches on one of his central concerns, the threat that comes from within, from a set of pernicious values that have been interiorized. In *Duelo en el paraíso,* as in *Juegos de manos,* the complexity comes from the fact that the victims, Abel and David, are both willing to be sacrificed, since they also despise the weaknesses and privileges singled out for punishment by their killers. The novel represents the beginning of Goytisolo's rejection of a comfortable bourgeois condition and his search for an alternative self. Ultimately, though, *Duelo en el paraíso* is more interesting as a project than an accomplished work, as Goytisolo himself has acknowledged.

In this early period in Goytisolo's career he was apparently driven by a restless quest for expression and self. On the one hand, during the late 1950s he established himself in Paris and there met Jean Genet, who offered him a role model in several aspects: in life, Genet was openly homosexual and apparently classless; as a writer, he offered the example of a luminous, elegant, and lyrical style that knew no boundaries of propriety. On the other hand, Goytisolo wrote a series of novels in which he applied the social realism prevalent at the time, a theory he defends in a book of essays he has subsequently disavowed, *Problemas de la novela* (1959, Problems of the Novel). These novels, *El circo* (1957, The Circus), *Fiestas* (1958; translated, 1960), and *La resaca* (1958, The Undertow), were grouped by Goytisolo as a trilogy under the title of *El mañana efímero* (The Fleeting Tomorrow), taken from a poem by Antonio Machado in which he claims the past has engendered only an empty and fortunately fleeting future. There is in fact a deep, even if unacknowledged, relation between Goytisolo and the writers of the Generation of '98, such as Pío Baroja, Machado, and Miguel de Unamuno, who also were critical of the decadence of the nation and wrote scathingly about the complacency of traditional ideology. The main difference is that Goytisolo does not accept their celebration of a mythical and essential Spain, Castilian and austere.

*El circo* was not included by Goytisolo in his edition of *Obras completas* (1977, Complete Works), probably because this entertaining novel, while touching on some of his main topics—homosexuality, sadism, masochism, rebellion, and alternate personalities—does so mostly with veiled allusions and in a relatively negative tone so as to make it past the censors. In a sense, the publication of the novel itself is proof of the author's acquiescence, though he was fast moving away from presenting himself as a respectable upholder of common values. As in his previous novels, there is also here a murder, in this case of a man whose main fault, in the eyes of the lower-class immigrant who kills him, is to be rich. Responsibility for the crime is assumed by the main character of the novel, Utah, a bohemian painter who is in a wild search for authenticity. Though innocent of the murder, he sees in the act the realization of a deeply felt need to get rid of his own father. Claiming responsibility for the murder, however, is portrayed as a fraudulent solution to Utah's problems, an unsatisfactory simulacrum of the action he is incapable of taking. A lucid, if muffled, denunciation of the games intellectuals play, the novel merits further critical attention.

*Fiestas* focuses on life in Barcelona during the World Faith Congress, specifically in an apartment building that the authorities use in their attempt to present a sanitized version of the city to the visitors. The many interwoven stories in the novel revisit topics characteristic of Goytisolo: for example, the fascination of a young man for a strong sailor of a lower class—an as-yet-unacknowledged homosexual fascination. Another plot strand involves the death of another innocent victim, in this case a young woman who, disappointed because she did not win a raffle, elopes with a Frenchman. Instead of taking her to Rome as promised, he murders her. This novel is shrill, revealing an exasperated frustration with life in Barcelona, but it includes memorable moments of evocative writing. In chapter 4, a young man goes to a park to meet a contact from an underground political group. Another man, Sebastián, is waiting there for a homosexual encounter, and the two men each mistake the other as the one whom they are expecting. The confusion is dispelled only when Sebastián attempts to kiss the young revolutionary, who runs to the police to denounce him. Goytisolo has

*Dust jacket for the U.S. edition (1969) of the English translation of Goytisolo's autobiographical novel* Señas de identidad *(1966), in which the protagonist, Álvaro Mendioza, is attacked for turning against his class and for bringing Spain into disrepute by exposing the poverty there (Richland County Public Library)*

described in his books of memoirs how his awakening to his own homosexuality was slow and painful, since he at first rejected his feelings and denounced as calumnious any comment about his possible orientation. In France he could begin to explore his sexuality more openly; in 1965, in a letter, he acknowledged to Lange his homosexuality, but he has been distrustful of embracing gay causes. Some of his best critics, such as Paul Julian Smith or Bradley Epps, have noted that his portrayal of homoeroticism remains guarded and somewhat stereotypical. Nevertheless, scenes such as Sebastián's painful encounter with the reality of repression even by the supposedly progressive Left are testimonies of a more repressive time.

*La resaca* is Goytisolo's final attempt to portray the life of the poor in Barcelona; it was published in France, since its raw portrayal of slum dwellers, prostitutes, and political activists would not have made it through censorship in Spain. But by the end of the decade Goytisolo was entering into the stage of his writing that established his fame: inspired by his readings in France, especially of structuralism, he staked as his territory of action not political activism—a field he has never quite entered nor abandoned altogether—but language itself. His next three novels are by far his most important accomplishment and are frequently known as a trilogy of destruction or liberation.

Before beginning his second trilogy, however, Goytisolo published two fictionalized travel books, participating in a tradition that had been reinvigorated, if not established, by Camilo José Cela with his *Viaje a la Alcarría* (1948, Journey to the Alcarría). *Campos de Níjar* (1960; translated as *The Countryside of Níjar,* 1987) includes a map and photographs to aver for the reality of the trip to this impoverished region of Spain. In *La Chanca* (1962; translated, 1987) a traveler, like the author an intellectual in self-exile in France, visits Almería and searches for a worker whom he discovers has disappeared, probably at the hands of the secret police. Both of these narratives have the immediacy of a testimony and convey in a series of memorable vignettes the efforts of the poor to survive harsh geographic, political, and economic conditions. There is no stridency, only a contemplative and thoughtful presentation of the poor enduring a life in which the only hope seems to come from immigration to France or Germany. The book occasioned in Spain a spirited denunciation from some Almerían locals against what they considered its partial and distorted presentation of the region, and especially Goytisolo's failure to appreciate its picturesque quality.

The first novel in Goytisolo's second trilogy is *Señas de identidad* (1966; translated as *Marks of Identity,* 1969). The title refers to the many data that identify an individual in society, from one's place, date of birth, and physical features to profession, marital status, and all the many elements that represent a person's history. Goytisolo sees this identity as a conglomerate of images, documents, memories, public monuments, and archives, through which an individual has to fight his way to self-creation.

The novel opens with a barrage of invectives from the Spanish media and critics against the protagonist, Álvaro Mendiola, a Spanish photographer living in Paris, accusing him of not upholding the memory of his father, executed by the Republicans during the war; of turning against his class and reneging on the promise of his privileged education; and of desecrating his country with a documentary he has directed exposing poverty in Spain. These accusations are taken almost verbatim from actual attacks on Goytisolo in the Spanish press, clippings of which are archived in a special collection at Boston University. Álvaro cannot escape these voices or a continued sense of kinship with the country that he tried to exorcise through exile and immersion in another culture:

Así hablaban de ti, al divulgarse el incidente del documental, en cafés y tertulias, . . . los hombres y mujeres satisfechos que un decreto irrisorio del destino te había otorgado al nacer, como paisanos, borrosos amigos de infancia, inocuos compañeros de estudio, parientes de mirada frígida y torva, familiares virtuosos y tristes, encastillados todos en sus inexpugnables privilegios de clase, miembros conspicuos y bien pensantes de un mundo otoñal y caduco que te habían dado, sin solicitar tu permiso, religión, moral y leyes hechas a su medida: orden promiscuo y huero del que habías intentado escapar, confiando, como tantos otros, en un cambio regenerador y catártico que, por misterios imponderables, no se había producido y, al cabo de largos años de destierro, estabas de nuevo allí, en el doliente y entrañable paisaje de tu juventud . . .

(That was how they were talking about you when the incident of the documentary became known, in cafés and gatherings, meetings and parties, the self-satisfied men and women whom a laughable decree of fate had awarded you at birth as fellow countrymen: dim childhood friends, innocuous schoolmates, female relatives with cold and severe looks, virtuous and sad acquaintances, all entrenched in their impregnable class privileges, conspicuous and right-thinking members of an autumnal and doddering world that had given you, without asking your permission, religion, morals, and laws made to its own measure: a promiscuous and hollow order from which you tried to escape, confident, like so many others, of a regenerating and cathartic change and cathartic that, because of mysterious imponderables, had not come about and, after long years in exile, there you were again, in the painful and affectionate landscape of your childhood. . . . )

Álvaro's plan becomes focused and clear to him: only a systematic destruction of that order based in the myth of a Spanish essence and only the recovery of a dissident country, silenced and ignored, can bring about liberation. For Álvaro (and by implication for Goytisolo himself), such a change must occur in the mind, in the realm of language, where he feels "envuelto una vez más en las mallas de un diálogo que te oprimía y asfixiaba, prisionero de un personaje que no eras tú, confundido con él y por él suplantado" (once more caught up in the web of dialogue that oppressed and asphyxiated you, trapped by a character that was not you, yet people thought he was you and he replaced you). The novel has a strong autobiographical component: Álvaro's affluent upbringing is based on the exploitation of slaves in Cuba, for example, and as a child he seeks martyrdom attempting to approach a burning church. Yet, *Señas de identidad* is far from being the usual loose skein of much autobiographical writing. It is composed with precision and symphonic complexity. Most chapters counterpoint diverse points of view, contrasting experiences. In the first, Álvaro remembers his childhood; in the second, his university years; and in the third, he describes his father's death. In the next chapters he speaks about his exile, and finally he offers several paths to liberation, through emigration, political activism, and the disassembling of language. The novel closes with Álvaro's contemplating Barcelona through a telescope from a promontory high above the city, as if he had taken wing and therefore could also leave behind the prosaic language in which he has conducted his investigation and move on to poetry and the rhythms of chant. The freedom from capital letters at the start of sentences, the abandonment of regular punctuation, and the mix of languages all give testimony of a newfound freedom:

> aléjate de tu grey tu desvío te honra
> cuanto te separa de ellos cultívalo
> lo que les molesta en ti glorifícalo
> negación estricta absoluta de su orden esto eres tú

> (get away from your flock your detour honors you
> cultivate everything that separates you from them
> glorify whatever in you bothers them
> the strict and absolute negation of their order that is what
>     you are.)

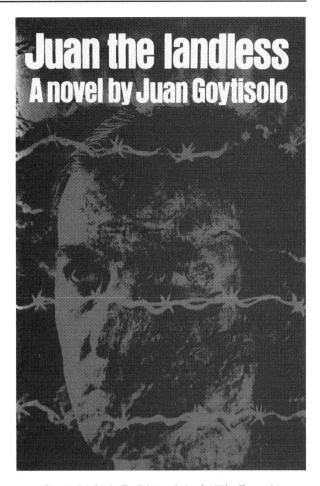

*Dust jacket for the English translation (1977) of* Juan sin tierra *(1975), the final novel in Goytisolo's Álvaro Mendioza trilogy, in which the protagonist explores his memories, emotions, desires, and fantasies (Richland County Public Library)*

Goytisolo by now had found his voice, and his next novel, *Reivindicación del conde don Julián* (1970; translated as *Count Julian*, 1974), is probably his best known and most studied. The nameless narrator, a Spanish exile in Tangiers, goes through his day engaged in a battle with his past, daydreaming about a Moorish invasion of Spain and observing life around him. Goytisolo has frequently remarked that his novels gain in richness when read aloud—he sees himself as a modern version of the marketplace storyteller—and from this novel on, his texts justify this assertion. *Reivindicación del conde don Julián* requires the reader to slow down to take in the many layers and allusions, the satirical debunking of Spanish myths, and the parodies of literary tradition; yet, for the patient reader the novel offers an alternative version of Spanish history and culture.

Count Julian was a Christian Moor and the governor of Ceuta, a port in northern Africa, who was one of the reputed leaders of the invasion of Spain in 711 that brought Arab culture into the peninsula for close to eight centuries, until the final defeat of the Moorish kingdom of Granada in 1492. The novel rails against the repressive society created by the triumphant Castile and wishes it overthrown. It is divided into four chapters. The first tells a recognizable story, following the narrator as he wakes up, contemplates Spain from afar, collects flies in his kitchen, breakfasts in a café, has a penicillin shot for his syphilis, visits a library, and goes to the movies, where he drowsily sees the James Bond movie *Thunderball* (1965), finally visiting a public bath.

Most memorable is his visit to the public library, where he crushes flies between the pages of Spanish Golden Age classics. This act of rage could be seen as a response to what Harold Bloom has called the anxiety of influence, the need writers have to come out from under the shadow of their famous predecessors;

but this conclusion would be to simplify Goytisolo's more complex claim. These writers of Golden Age Spain, according to him, have been used to celebrate and sustain a culture based on racial and religious exclusion, gender stratification and gender-based abuse, and linguistic arrogance. Many actual texts incorporated into *Reivindicación del conde don Julián*, taken from canonical Spanish authors, show their exaltation of bloody revenge in the case of a woman's infidelity, loving descriptions of arid landscapes, and an arrogant conception of the ideal Christian warrior. In the usual counterpoint to which Goytisolo submits his material, the Baroque poet Luis de Góngora emerges as the model writer, perhaps in part because he saw language not as constrained by local tradition but open to experimentation, offering an example of creative freedom.

In the second chapter the narrator watches Spanish television programs, which he contemplates dreamily after having smoked marijuana, interspersing memories of his childhood, especially related to his sexual initiation. In a freewheeling and daredevil mood, the narrator pokes fun at Spanish rhetoric, sexual mores, and school education while starting his extended encomium of the manly beauty of the seductive Moorish warrior. Some of these scenes may prove disturbing for many readers, since they would appear to condone and even celebrate the molesting of young children; yet, they must be read in the context of the novel and of Goytisolo's life. An important part of his memoirs is devoted to the sexual molestation he suffered at the hands of his maternal grandfather and the consequences of this event: the expulsion of the relative from the family's house and a lingering sense of guilt and shame for the child. By transposing such an event into an encounter that not only brings negative consequences, but also offers in this case a fascinating joy to its victim, Goytisolo—in the tradition of the Marquis de Sade, Jean-Jacques Rousseau, and Genet—presents an unflinching and disturbing insight into human nature.

In chapter 3 the narrator imagines the destruction of his homeland; a particularly outrageous scene involves a visit to a circus-like attraction that houses the vagina of Queen Isabella the Catholic. The point here, again, is an examination of myth, of the silences surrounding the mores and heroes of any culture, which protects them from reconsideration by making them sexless, distant, and untouchable. As an iconoclast, Goytisolo invites readers to realize that these characters are not the actual people but images that have become frozen in a repetitive, myopic, and lazy language. Among the best and funniest pages written by Goytisolo are some found in this chapter, in which

on the one hand he celebrates the rich language of Latin American writers and, on the other, progressively subtracts words with an Arabic origin from Spanish. He imagines the public watching a bullfight, where they see the philosopher José Ortega y Gasset, a representative of the Spanish intellectuals who ignored the Arab tradition, get gored; the audience is uncharacteristically silent because they are unable to respond with the traditional "olé," a word with Arabic roots. The last chapter imagines the rape and suicide of the narrator's alter ego as a child in Barcelona twenty-five years earlier. Clearly, the narrator has survived, however, since he probably lived in his imagination then, as well. He finishes the day having accomplished only an imaginary invasion of Spain that fades away with the coming of the night. The novel ends with "lo sabes, lo sabes: mañana será otro día, la invasión recomenzará" (you know, you know: tomorrow will be another day, the invasion will begin again), meaning not only that the exile will continue to dream his second African invasion of Spain, but also that Spain, through memories, books, and media, will continue to invade the exile's mind.

*Juan sin tierra* (1975; translated as *Juan the Landless,* 1977) is in a sense the most difficult of the novels in the trilogy, but at the same time, if read appropriately, the most playful and enjoyable. Gone is the pretext of a developed argument, the return of the exile or his day abroad, and the reader encounters only a dazzling array of snippets from a writer at work. This thin character appears to be remarkably similar to the author: he lives in Paris at the same address as Goytisolo and shares his by now well-known themes. Yet, the novel is not autobiographical in a traditional sense; it is the imagined exploration of the memories, emotions, desires, and fantasies that obsess the narrator, in a sort of literary fireworks display. The novel opens with the narrator's addressing himself as he contemplates postcards, a record jacket, and photographs, weaving in a meditation about the denial of bodily functions in Western culture, which he defines as puritan occultation. One voice—more representative of a form of rhetoric than of a well-rounded character—preaches about how black slaves on a Cuban plantation must adopt and admire European modesty, while another (or the same, it little matters) celebrates the fact that angels and saints do not appear to have ever defecated, since such an occurrence is not recorded.

The satire is blunt; yet, it accomplishes its purpose of making evident the fact that society relegates certain parts of the body and their functions to the invisible space of the obscene. The body is thus the locus of a vast archive of secretive and marginalized information, and those who have not the privilege of privacy (such as the slaves in the plantation), or those who chose to commit the unspeakable sin of anal penetration, are branded negatively. The narrator's plan to oppose the ideological system that colonizes his mind is triggered again by the encounter with the slave's humble letter addressed to the narrator's ancestor:

> Interrumpirás la lectura de documentos: frases extraídas de los libros y fotocopias se superponen en tu memoria a la carta de la esclava al bisabuelo resucitando indemne tu odio hacia la estirpe que dio el ser; pecado original que tenazmente te acosa con su indeleble estigma a pesar de tus viejos, denodados esfuerzos por liberarte de él: la página virgen te brinda posibilidades de redención exquisitas junto al gozo de profanar su blancura: basta un simple trazo de pluma: volverás a tentar la suerte.

> (You will break off your reading of the documents: passages copied from books and photocopies are superimposed in your memory on the letter of the slave woman to your great-grandfather, reviving intact your hatred toward the race that gave birth to you; the original sin that relentlessly pursues you with its indelible stigma despite your long-standing, intrepid efforts to free yourself of it: the virgin page offers you matchless possibilities of redemption, together with the pleasure of profaning its whiteness: a simple stroke of the pen is enough: you will try your luck once more.)

The text, then, is more a transcript of a ritual ceremony of purification than simply an entertaining narrative, even if readers can certainly be amused along the way. Yet, unless one understands Goytisolo's quest for liberation and sympathizes with it, the text will not be fully understood. The novel is in a sense similar to later forms of jazz, where the melody is only intermittently heard and freedom from the strictures of tradition allows almost a contemplative exploration of the voices of each instrument.

The second chapter of *Juan sin tierra* looks at the limits of sex, establishing a core of the permissible in the form of the heterosexual sexual union of a married couple, which the narrator despises. Goytisolo's animus against heterosexuality is based on its exclusion of any other form of sexual activity, relegating the other forms to the designations of sin, deviance, or even crime. The third chapter introduces T. E. Lawrence, one of the many "heroes" that Goytisolo invokes in his work to create a circle of men with whom he can identify. They are all characterized for being in some way outsiders by choice. Lawrence started out working to defend the interests of the British Empire in the Middle East, with the considerable knowledge about the Arabic culture he had obtained at Oxford; yet, the experi-

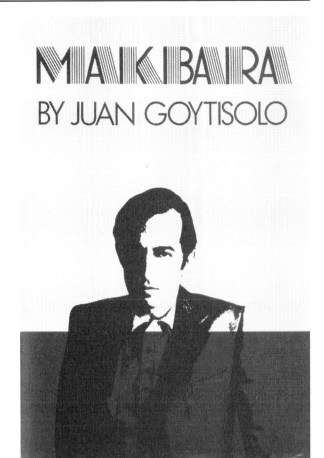

*Dust jacket for the English translation (1981) of Goytisolo's 1980 novel, in which a love-struck angel follows an African man through the streets of Paris and an American city similar to Pittsburgh (Richland County Public Library)*

ence of fighting side by side with the Arabs in their revolt against the Turkish Empire shifted his allegiance against the colonial efforts of the British. Unable to stand his reputation as a hero, which he found unmerited, and the betrayal by his country of his Arab friends, he spent his life after he returned to England living under an assumed name in the Royal Air Force and in the Tank Corps.

Another supporter of the Arab world and dissenter from the ideology of European superiority also appears in *Juan sin tierra*, Charles Eugène Vicompte de Foucauld, a member of an aristocratic French family, an unruly soldier and bon vivant who, in contact with the desert and its people in Algeria, had a deep religious experience that led him first to become a Trappist monk in France and then a monk in an even more austere order in Morocco and Algeria. The third chosen ancestor who appears as a character in *Juan sin tierra* is

Anselm Turmeda, who was born in Majorca in 1352 and died approximately between 1425 and 1430. Lawrence, Foucauld, Turmeda, and Goytisolo share being well connected and well educated yet rejecting the contention of European superiority and embracing instead the Arab world. Turmeda, a Franciscan who studied in Bologna and Paris, converted to Islam in 1387, married, and lived in Tunis until the end of his life. Later on Goytisolo adds other names to his chosen ancestry: the Spaniard José María Blanco White, a Catholic priest who converted in England to several other denominations and lived the latter part of his life in exile; and San Juan de la Cruz, persecuted by his fellow Catholics for his advocacy of a strict rule that threatened the comfortable life of some monasteries, a poet whose verse has many connections with Islam, as would have been natural in sixteenth-century Spain. In his essays Goytisolo also points to a literary tradition that includes, among other works, Juan Ruiz's *Libro de Buen Amor* (1330, The Book of Good Love), a poem that reveals the complexity of the Spanish Middle Ages; Francisco de Rojas's *La Celestina* (1499), the author of which has been identified as a converted Jew; and Francisco Delicado's *Retrato de la Loçana andaluza* (1528, Portrait of the Lusty Andalusian Woman), the ribald story of a prostitute in Rome and a book, like *La Celestina,* of unbridled expression and sensuality. Among the contemporary writers his allegiance has been mostly with Genet and some Latin American writers, such as the Mexican Carlos Fuentes.

*Juan sin tierra* concludes with the disintegration of Spanish into phonetic spelling and with the intromission of Arabic words, ending in an Arabic text of which the first six lines correspond to Surah 109 of the Qur'an, "The Disbelievers." This text is supposed to act as a door that closes behind the narrator as he passes over into Muslim culture, remaining therefore incomprehensible to readers who do not know Arabic:

> You who do not understand,
> Stop following me.
> Our communication has ended.
> I am definitely on the other side,
> With the poor,
> Who sharpen their knives.

The trilogy includes many creative and even outrageous passages, such as the discussion between the "author" and a defender of realism in *Juan sin tierra* or the mesmerizing invitation to the reader to become disoriented in Fez—a call to let go in a different space and culture—titled "Variaciones sobre un tema fesí" (Variations on a Fez Theme). The trilogy is a series of daring texts that start as traditional novels but end in a dispersion of genres—poetic prose, essay, and drama.

Together with Goytisolo's two volumes of memoirs, they constitute a masterful and altogether distinctive exploration of being a reticent Spaniard during the Franco years. The many editions of these novels and memoirs indicate that they continue to enjoy the favor of critics and the general public in spite of their challenging difficulty.

Of course, Goytisolo did not abandon the Spanish language nor did he interrupt his communication with his readers. Since the abrupt ending of *Juan sin tierra,* he has published nine new novels. *Makbara* (1980; translated, 1981), the title of which is the Arabic word for cemetery, can be slightly confusing until one realizes it is patterned after an oral narration and supposedly the speaker is telling his story in the historic market of Marrakesh. Like Goytisolo's other novels, it is meant to be heard more than read. Having as pretext the adventures of an African who wanders through Paris and an American city similar to Pittsburgh, accompanied at times by an angel who has fallen in love with him, the novel is an imaginative romp through two markets, the capitalist market of postindustrial and global society, where everything becomes merchandise, and the still human-sized African market. Goytisolo's concern with authenticity and freedom is turned here against the barrage of inane messages that pursue all consumers daily. The novel ends with an extended and notable description of the Marrakesh market itself.

*Paisajes después de la batalla* (1982; translated as *Landscapes after the Battle,* 1987) presents a writer again much like Goytisolo himself, living in Paris and imagining that all street signs, as well as all newspapers, are suddenly changed to Arabic. Confusion ensues when the natives must navigate their own city with the uncertainty that is common to the Arab migrant worker. The seventy-seven segments of the novel, each with its own bemusing title, are loosely held together by being related to the reclusive writer, but they range widely from descriptions of the urban chaos to encounters with terrorist groups or meditations about the end of ideologies. As usual, Goytisolo includes his own description of what he is doing:

> Un repaso a las ciento sesenta páginas de su manuscrito descubre la existencia de un ser fragmentado: ideas, sentimientos, libido tiran por diferentes caminos, el desdichado cronista de su vida ha sido incapaz de aglutinarlos. Hojear su relato acuciado por la premura del tiempo es lancinante ejercicio de irrealidad: al final, ya no sabe si es el remoto individuo que usurpa su nombre o ese goytisolo lo está creando a él.
>
> (A rereading of the 170 pages of his manuscript reveals the existence of a fragmented being: ideas, feelings,

libido pull in different directions, and the wretched chronicler of his life has been unable to put them together again. Leafing through his story under the pressure of time passing is an acutely painful exercise in unreality: in the end, he no longer knows if he is the distant individual who usurps his name or if that Goytisolo is creating him.)

The search for an authentic individual that runs through many of his earlier novels and still reveals the aspirations of high modernism, existentialism, and Marxism, has melted here into postmodern air. The alter ego or chosen predecessor is no longer a war hero or religious convert but has become Charles Lutwidge Dodgson, the author of *Alice's Adventures in Wonderland* (1865) under the pseudonym of Lewis Carroll. *Paisajes después de la batalla* does share some of the whimsy of Carroll's *Through the Looking-Glass* (1871) and its irreverent humor. What principally brings him into Goytisolo's novel, however, is his many-faceted personality: a lecturer of mathematics at Oxford, a deacon, and a photographer with a penchant for young girls. The variegated nature of this eccentric writer, his suspect respectability, seductive imagination, and literary accomplishments, serve as an emblem of a personality that is now accepted as fragmented, conflictive, and even contradictory. The unfortunate writer who is the main character of the novel confesses he has been unable to bring himself together, but this condition, as the multiethnic and multicultural streets of Paris, is now embraced as the reality of life.

Goytisolo has often written about death, and his preoccupation with mortality has only become more insistent with time, especially since AIDS started to decimate the gay community in the 1980s. In 1988 he published *Las virtudes del pájaro solitario* (translated as *The Virtues of the Solitary Bird,* 1991), a novel that combines the mystical experience across ages and cultures with the suffering brought about by homosexual love. This novel is extremely complex and cannot be easily summarized, especially because its greatest accomplishment comes from the seamless and complete blending into one text of many voices—no indication is given when a text from another author is integrated into the narrative—a textual equivalent of the AIDS memorial quilt begun in San Francisco in June 1987. The novel begins with a re-creation of a famous gay bathhouse that existed in Paris and the presentation of a voice of unstable gender that enjoys promiscuous sex until the threat of AIDS closes the place down, and Death, as the Grim Reaper, makes his appearance. The novel then shifts to a conference on San Juan de la Cruz that takes place in an oppressive Kafkaesque location, where one of the participants, delirious because of an accident,

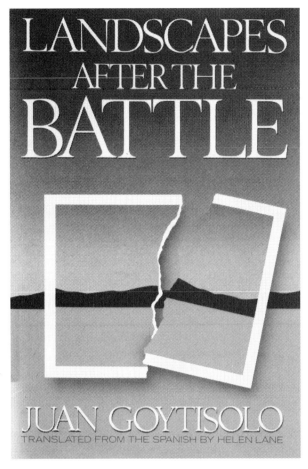

*Dust jacket for the English translation (1987) of Goytisolo's novel* Paisajes después de la batalla *(1982), in which a Spanish writer living in Paris imagines that the letters in newspapers and on street signs have suddenly been replaced by Arabic (Richland County Public Library)*

identifies himself with San Juan. He draws an analogy to the Spain of San Juan's lifetime, where innovative thought was suffocated through the threat of the Inquisition—recalled here by a visit to a library of forbidden books—and so-called blood purity (not being of Jewish or Moorish origin) was made a condition for advancement. The identification of gay men with birds allows Goytisolo a link with *Manteq el-teyr* (The Conference of the Birds), a mystical poem of the thirteenth-century Persian poet Farid od-Din 'Attar, in which a large number of birds goes off in the search for the King of Birds, of whom they know only that his name, Simurg, means *thirty*. Only thirty of them make it to the end of the quest and find a mirror in which they contemplate themselves. The narrator of this novel sees himself at the end surrounded by fellow marginal "birds," the pariahs with whom he likes to identify himself, in a search to overcome sickness, repression, and even death. This novel has many autobiographical elements in it, including Goytisolo's revelation of his homosexuality to Lange in 1965, an incident also movingly recalled at the end of *En los reinos de taifa* (1986; translated as *Realms of Strife: The Memoirs of Juan Goytisolo, 1957–1982,* 1990). Its significance goes far beyond a private experience, however, to encompass not just the period in which a new threat and motive for repression came into gay life, but also all occasions in which love, sex, and independent thought must fight for their freedom.

Another real event, this time not sickness but war, is the deeper subject of *La cuarentena* (1991; translated as *Quarantine,* 1994): the Persian Gulf War of 1991. The novel consists of forty brief chapters in which the narrator follows a recently deceased friend on her journey into the netherworld, imagined as a combination of Dante's vision, modern amenities, and Muslim faith where Goytisolo's friends and foes receive their reward or punishment. The narrator, again an autobiographical voice, imagines also his own private judgment after death and meditates about the value of his work. Most moving is the horror of war and loss of life that the novelist suggests by representing his own mother among the dead in the Gulf War, transposing her from the fallen in Barcelona in 1936. If people can truly see each victim as their own mother, the text suggests, they may be able to understand its real desolation and pain. The text reads somewhat as a Kaddish or a medieval *ubi sunt* ("where are"; a poem on the transitory nature of things), more an inspired prose poem than a traditional novel. It is not surprising that in awarding him the Octavio Paz Prize for Poetry and Essay in 2002 the jury mentioned "the poetry that inhabits his novels."

Goytisolo has been a keen observer of life in the cities, especially Paris and New York, where he has been several times as a visiting professor at New York University, and in the late 1980s he started to reread the works of Karl Marx for their descriptions of the situation of the urban underclass created and needed by industrial development. The fundamental conceit of *La saga de los Marx* (1993; translated as *The Marx Family Saga,* 1996), that Marx has lived to see how his prognosis of the triumph of the proletariat did not come true, also allows Goytisolo to show the continuity of the anguish of the poor. The novel opens with an episode based on an actual event: a ship of Eastern Europeans, fleeing Marx's failed utopia for Texas, the new paradise of consumerism as seen on television, lands on a fashionable Italian beach. The novelist narrator attempts to tell Marx's story through several dif-

ferent approaches, one of them being a corny television script. Marx is shown as authoritarian within his own family, revealing in his life–Goytisolo seeks always this connection between theory and practice–the despotic personality that later becomes an integral part of the regimes he inspired. As the novel opens up to show his family, however, a different story emerges, of a loving wife, talented daughters, a struggling domestic economy, and a lover. Ultimately, the novel concludes that Marx was right in his diagnosis even if he erred in the solution. The masses of impoverished immigrants, drug addicts, homeless people, criminals, and exploited workers living in large cities next to a minority of extremely wealthy people indicate that the problem is still with humanity. Goytisolo has been active in the defense of immigrants and in denouncing European racism, as evidenced by several of his books, including *El peaje de la vida: Integración o rechazo de la emigración en España* (2000, The Toll of Life: Integration or Rejection of Immigration in Spain).

While Goytisolo has cultivated in his work the image of a recluse and would appear to some to be narcissistic, it has become more evident in time that the core of his work is compassion and truth, creativity and freedom. During the siege of Sarajevo, which killed more than twelve thousand people and lasted four years beginning in 1992, Goytisolo, naturally sympathetic with the suffering of a city where 44 percent of the population was Muslim, twice visited there. He wrote a journalistic report, *Cuaderno de Sarajevo: Anotaciones de un viaje a la barbarie* (1993, Notebook of Sarajevo: Annotations of a Journey to Barbarism), which was awarded the Mediterraneo Prize in 1994, and a novel, *El sitio de los sitios* (1995; translated as *State of Siege,* 2002). This latter text is a complex web of documents and narrators, a whodunit with a disappearing corpse, that eventually makes all truth, especially the "official truth," suspect. The novel closes with a "Nota del autor" (Note of the Author; not included in the English translation) that perfectly illustrates Goytisolo's approach to literature, in its possibilities and limitations:

Con mediano valor y algunos puntos de civismo, el escritor estuvo dos veces en Sarajevo durante los peores días del cerco: el horror e indignación de cuanto vio le consumen aún y tuvo que recurrir a la ficción para huir y curarse de las imágenes que a su vez le asediaban. Tal es el poder de la literatura.

Pero el sitio continúa y trescientas mil personas siguen atrapadas en la otrora hermosa ciudad sin ninguna posibilidad de huida ni curación a la vista. Tal es el límite final de la literatura.

(With relative courage and some inklings of a good citizen, the writer visited Sarajevo twice during the worse days of the siege: the horror and the indignation he felt from what he saw still pursue him, and he had to resort to fiction to escape and be cured from the images that haunted him. Such is the power of literature.

But the siege continues, and three hundred thousand persons are still trapped in that city that was once so beautiful; they have no possibility of escape or hope of being healed. That is the ultimate limit of literature.)

Goytisolo's subsequent novels revisit central topics of his work, but in fresh and highly innovative ways. *Las semanas del jardín: Un círculo de lectores* (1997; translated as *The Garden of Secrets,* 2000) is composed of twenty-eight brief chapters, one for each letter of the Arabic alphabet, each narrated by a different persona. The novel is attributed by these narrators to a fictionalized version of Juan Goytisolo. Each chapter uses a different style, and the novel becomes a virtuoso performance in which the author shows his dexterity. The plot attempts to reconstruct the story of a poet, Eusebio, who was arrested in Melilla in the first days of the Spanish Civil War and sent to a psychiatric hospital, from where he either escaped or was let go after being reeducated into conformity. Especially noteworthy is a chapter on men who become stalks and fly between Africa and Europe, a story based on a local tradition of Marrakesh and one with which Goytisolo, having bridged the two continents for decades, can easily identify.

*Carajicomedia: De Fray Bugeo Montesino y otros pájaros de vario plumaje y pluma* (2000; translated as *A Cock-Eyed Comedy: Starring Friar Bugeo Montesino and Other Faeries of Motley Feather and Fortune,* 2002) is based on a collection of ribald poetry published in Valencia in 1519. The poems are used as the springboard to describe different gay lovers and sexual encounters. A second important text is also woven into the novel: *Camino* (1934, The Way), an inspirational book by the founder of the conservative Catholic organization Opus Dei, Josemaría Escrivá de Balaguer. The sixteenth-century *Carajicomedia* uses religious language and mixes it with vulgar words to describe in detail bodies and sex. Goytisolo follows the same strategy and has fun hijacking Escrivá's rather hyperventilating expressions of piety and applying them to homoerotic life. The novel also intersperses fragments of an apocryphal diary of Roland Barthes's adventures in a cinema famous for its gay encounters. The parody would be sophomoric—the reduction of the language of mysticism to sex—if the novel did not, as it progresses, fall under its own spell and ultimately transmute the bodies of occasional lovers into radiant incarnations of eternal beauty and

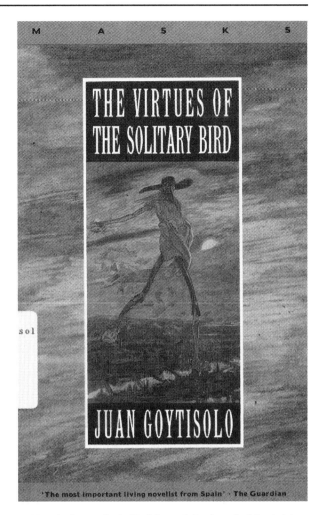

*Paperback cover for the English translation (1991) of Goytisolo's novel* Las virtudes del pájaro solitario *(1988), about homosexuality, AIDS, and a mystical quest (Richland County Public Library)*

transcending love. What the language of religion would condemn and exclude, through the fire of this acerbic parody becomes embraced and celebrated.

Goytisolo's novel *Telón de boca* (2003, Front Curtain) is a surprisingly accessible story that starts with the narrator's missing his recently deceased wife. The autobiographical elements are evident here, since Lange died in October 1996 at age seventy, after four decades of sharing her life with Goytisolo, and the novel was written between 1996 and 2002. This melancholic occasion serves for recalling past events, this time in the aura of Leo Tolstoy, with whom the author compares himself, especially for the Russian master's rejection of his privileged status and his embracing of a simple life and the poor. The novel concludes with the narrator's affirming that he is still around, in his orchestra seat, awaiting for the curtain of the theater to rise and show what is beyond this life.

Juan Goytisolo has not just been one of the most important novelists of his generation and a superb essayist who has brought to the attention of a wide audience a lively, creative, heterodox tradition that Spain had mostly repressed. In his sustained, unforgiving, courageous, erudite, and lucid exploration of the self, distinctive in Spanish literature, he can be compared to Michel Eyquem de Montaigne; in his unflinching search for sincerity, his demand to put literature to the test of life, his openness to others, and his concern for the suffering of the marginalized and downtrodden he has indeed risen to a stature similar to Genet or Rousseau. In spite of Goytisolo's disdain for personal heroics, few other Spanish authors–Mariano José de Larra and Unamuno come to mind–have so profoundly combined life and literature to leave readers with admirable, if controversial, images of themselves.

## Letters:

*El epistolario: Cartas de Américo Castro a Juan Goytisolo (1968–1972),* edited by Javier Escudero Rodríguez (Valencia: Pre-Textos, 1997).

## References:

*Anthropos,* special Goytisolo issue, nos. 60–61 (1986);

Stanley Black, *Juan Goytisolo and the Poetics of Contagion: The Evolution of a Radical Aesthetic in the Later Novels* (Liverpool: Liverpool University Press, 2001);

Annie Bussière-Perrin, *Le théâtre de l'expiation: Regards sur l'oeuvre de rupture de Juan Goytisolo* (Montpellier: Université Paul-Valéry, Centre d'études et de recherches sociocritiques, 1998);

Bussière-Perrin, ed., *Encuentro con Juan Goytisolo* (Montpellier: Editions du Cers, 2001);

Juan Carlos Curutchet, "Juan Goytisolo y la destruccíon de la España sagrada," in his *A partir de Luis Martín Santos: Cuatro ensayos sobre la nueva novela española* (Montevideo: Alfa, 1973), pp. 87–129;

Miguel Dalmau, *Los Goytisolo* (Barcelona: Anagrama, 1999);

Inger Enkvist and Angel Sahuquillo, *Los múltiples yos de Juan Goytisolo: Un estudio interdisciplinar* (Almería: Instituto de Estudios Almerienses, Diputación de Almería, 2001);

Enkvist, ed., *Un círculo de relectores: Jornadas sobre Juan Goytisolo, Lund, 1998* (Almería: Instituto de Estudios Almerienses, 1999);

Bradley Epps, *Significant Violence: Oppression and Resistance in the Narratives of Juan Goytisolo, 1970–1990* (Oxford: Clarendon Press / New York: Oxford University Press, 1996);

Javier Escudero Rodríguez, *Eros, mística y muerte en Juan Goytisolo (1982–1992)* (Almería: Instituto de Estudios Almerienses, Departamento de Arte y Literatura, 1994);

Myriam Gallego Fernández de Aránguiz, *La narrativa simbólica de Juan Goytisolo* (Salamanca: Almar, 2001);

Pere Gimferrer, ed., *Voces: Juan Goytisolo* (Barcelona: Montesinos, 1981);

Instituto de Estudios Almerienses, *Escritos sobre Juan Goytisolo: Actas del II Seminario Internacional sobre la obra de Juan Goytisolo: Las Virtudes del pájaro solitario, Almería, 7, 8 y 9 de septiembre, 1989* (Almería: Instituto de Estudios Almerienses, 1990);

Instituto de Estudios Almerienses, *Escritos sobre Juan Goytisolo: Coloquio en torno a la obra de Juan Goytisolo, Almería, 1987* (Almería: Instituto de Estudios Almerienses, 1988);

Marco Kunz, *La saga de los Marx, de Juan Goytisolo: Notas al texto* (Basel: Universität Basel, Romanisches Seminar, 1997);

Jesús Lázaro, *La novelística de Juan Goytisolo* (Madrid: Alhambra, 1984);

Emmanuel Le Vagueresse, *Juan Goytisolo, écriture et marginalité* (Paris: L'Harmattan, 2000);

Linda Gould Levine, *Juan Goytisolo, la destrucción creadora* (Mexico City: Mortiz, 1976);

Yannick Llored, *Aproximación al lenguaje nómada de Juan Goytisolo en* Las virtudes del pájaro solitario (Almería: Instituto de Estudios Almerienses, Diputación de Almería, 2001);

José Manuel Martín Morán, *Semiótica de una traición recuperada: Génesis poética de* Reivindicación del conde don Julián (Barcelona: Anthropos, 1992);

Jaime Martínez Tolentino, *La cronología de* Señas de identidad *de Juan Goytisolo* (Kassel: Reichenberger, 1992);

Christian Meerts, *Technique et vision dans* Señas de identidad *de J. Goytisolo* (Frankfurt am Main: Klostermann, 1972);

Gonzalo Navajas, *La novela de Juan Goytisolo* (Madrid: Sociedad General Española de Librería, 1979);

José Ortega, *Juan Goytisolo; Alienación y agresión en* Señas de identidad *y* Reivindicación del Conde don Julián (New York: Torres, 1972);

Genaro J. Pérez, *Formalist Elements in the Novels of Juan Goytisolo* (Potomac, Md.: Porrúa Turanzas, 1979);

José-Carlos Pérez, *La trayectoria novelística de Juan Goytisolo: El autor y sus obsesiones* (Saragossa: Oroel, 1984);

Randolph D. Pope, *Understanding Juan Goytisolo* (Columbia: University of South Carolina Press, 1995);

Ryan Prout, *Fear and Gendering: Pedophobia, Effeminophobia, and Hypermasculine Desire in the Work of Juan Goytisolo* (New York: Peter Lang, 2001);

Alberto M. Ruiz Campos, *Estructuras literarias en la nueva narrativa de Juan Goytisolo* (Almería: Instituto de Estudios Almerienses, 1996);

Manuel Ruiz Lagos, *La atracción del Sur: La configuración de un centro ideológico. Estudios literarios sobre Juan Goytisolo* (Seville: Instituto de Desarrollo Regional Universidad de Sevilla, 1988);

Ruiz Lagos, *Juan Goytisolo: El centro y el método* (Seville: Guadalmena, 1995);

Ruiz Lagos, *Lector apud Goytisolo: Las paradojas del texto hermético. Sobre* El sitio de los sitios (Seville: Guadalmena, 1996);

Ruiz Lagos, *Retrato de Juan Goytisolo* (Barcelona: Galaxia Gutenberg, 1993);

Ruiz Lagos, *Sobre el discurso del método: La saga de los Marx de Juan Goytisolo* (Seville: Universidad de Sevilla, 1994);

Ruiz Lagos, *Sur y modernidad: Estudios literarios sobre Juan Goytisolo:* Las virtudes del pájaro solitario, Los libros de Altisidora, no. 11 (Seville: Don Quijote, 1992);

Ruiz Lagos, ed., *Juan Goytisolo* (Madrid: Instituto de Cooperación Iberamericana, Ediciones de Cultura Hispánica, 1991);

Santos Sanz Villanueva, *Lectura de Juan Goytisolo* (Barcelona: Pozanco, 1977);

Claudia Schaefer-Rodríguez, *Juan Goytisolo, del "realismo crítico" a la utopía* (Madrid: Porrúa Turanzas, 1984);

Kessel Schwartz, *Juan Goytisolo* (New York: Twayne, 1970);

Abigail Lee Six, *Goytisolo:* Campos de Níjar (London: Grant & Cutler, 1996);

Six, *Juan Goytisolo: The Case for Chaos* (New Haven & London: Yale University Press, 1990);

Gonzalo Sobejano and others, *Juan Goytisolo* (Madrid: Editorial Fundamentos, 1975);

Carmen Sotomayor, *Una lectura orientalista de Juan Goytisolo* (Madrid: Editorial Fundamentos, 1990);

Michael Ugarte, *Trilogy of Treason: An Intertextual Study of Juan Goytisolo* (Columbia: University of Missouri Press, 1982).

# Luis Goytisolo

## (17 March 1935 –   )

**Pamela DeWeese**
*Sweet Briar College*

BOOKS: *Las afueras* (Barcelona: Seix Barral, 1958);
*Las mismas palabras* (Barcelona: Seix Barral, 1962);
*Sátiro y sátira* (Barcelona: Esplugas II, 1968);
*Ojos, círculos, buhos,* text by Goytisolo, illustrations by Joan Ponç (Barcelona: Anagrama, 1970);
*Recuento* (Mexico City: Avándano, 1973; New York: Torres, 1975; Barcelona: Seix Barral, 1976);
*Los verdes de mayo hasta el mar* (Barcelona: Seix Barral, 1976);
*Devoraciones,* by Goytisolo and Ponç (Barcelona: Anagrama, 1976);
*La cólera de Aquiles* (Barcelona: Seix Barral, 1979);
*Teoría del conocimiento* (Barcelona: Seix Barral, 1981);
*Fábulas* (Barcelona: Bruguera, 1981);
*Estela del fuego que se aleja* (Barcelona: Anagrama, 1984);
*Investigaciones y conjeturas de Claudio Mendoza* (Barcelona: Anagrama, 1985);
*La paradoja del ave migratoria* (Madrid: Alfaguara, 1987);
*Estatua con palomas* (Madrid: Destino, 1992);
*Indico,* edited by Luis Rubio Gil (Barcelona: Serbal, 1992);
*Mzungo* (Barcelona: Mondadori, 1996);
*Placer licuante* (Madrid: Alfaguara, 1997);
*Escalera hacia el cielo* (Madrid: Espasa, 1999);
*Diario de 360°* (Barcelona: Seix Barral, 2000);
*El porvenir de la palabra* (Madrid: Taurus, 2002);
*Liberación* (Madrid: Alfaguara, 2003);
*Oído atento a los pájaros* (Madrid: Alfaguara, forthcoming 2006).
**Edition:** *Antagonía,* 4 volumes (Barcelona: Seix Barral, 1976–1981).

OTHER: "Gestación de *Antagonía,*" in *El Cosmos de Antagonía,* edited by Ricardo Gullón (Barcelona: Anagrama, 1983), pp. 15–19.

SELECTED PERIODICAL PUBLICATIONS–
UNCOLLECTED: "Memoria y ceniza," *Quimera,* 26 (December 1982): 62;
"Cuatro retratos catalanes. Vida light," *El País semanal,* 20 April 1986;

*Luis Goytisolo (photograph by Leopoldo Pomés; from the cover for the 1979 edition of* Las afueras; *Thomas Cooper Library, University of South Carolina)*

"Geografía, historia y mito," *El País,* 12 August 1986;
"El futuro de lo improbable," *El País,* 8 February 1987;
"Final del milenio," *El País,* 17 January 1988;
"Recuento de una narrativa," *Ojáncano,* 1, no. 1 (October 1988): 81–89;
"La novela del siglo XX y el porvenir del género," *Letra internacional,* 20 (Winter 1990–1991): 19–20;
"La historia de las dos orillas," *ABC,* 21 February 1992;
"Barcelona. Una ciudad que se desvanece y reaparece," *Diario 16. Gente,* 19 July 1992, pp. 10–16;

"El enigma de mi tía Consuelo Gay," *Diario 16,* 24 October 1992;

"Dos textos," *La página,* 11–12, nos. 1–2 (1993): 117–122;

"Tiempo de escarolas," *La Vanguardia,* January 1997;

"La novela que no fue," *ABC Cultural,* 17 February 2001;

"El declive de la cultura verbal," *El País,* 3 March 2001;

"Sexualidad y creación literaria," *El País,* 12 May 2001.

Luis Goytisolo is an indefatigable traveler. His fictional trips have taken him to the far reaches of human imagination and experience. His real-life travels have carried him throughout North America, South America, Africa, Europe, and Asia. Goytisolo has won the Premio Nacional de Narrativa (National Prize for Narrative) in Spain (1993); he is a member of the prestigious Real Academia Española de la Lengua (Royal Spanish Academy of Language); his best-known novel, *Antagonía,* originally published in four installments between 1973 and 1981, has been judged to be one of the most important of the twentieth century; yet, this writer is still restless, constantly searching through his art and his life to understand the paradoxes of human existence, limited in space and time and yet unlimited in potential. The details of his own life, marked by the Spanish Civil War and several family tragedies, have become well known to his readers, particularly since he has used them as elements that provide points of entry into his work.

Luis Goytisolo was born on 17 March 1935 in Barcelona to Julia Gay Vives and José María Goytisolo Taltavull. He was the couple's fifth and last child. His oldest brother, Antonio, died of tubercular meningitis in 1927. His other siblings are a sister, Marta, ten years his senior, and brothers José Agustín, a poet, and Juan, also a novelist, seven and four years older, respectively. Before the Civil War, which lasted from 1936 until 1939, the family formed part of the prosperous Catalan bourgeoisie in Barcelona.

On his father's side, the Goytisolo family fortune can be traced back to Luis's great-grandfather, Don Agustín Goytisolo Lizarazaburu, who left his Basque homeland in the hope of finding a better life in Cuba. He amassed a fortune as the owner of a sugar plantation in Cienfuegos and married Doña Estanisláa Digat in 1844. Later in life he invested in property in Barcelona. He built a palatial residence on the Plaza de Cataluña in 1873 and lived there with his wife, his son Antonio, and his daughters, Trina and Fermina, until his death in 1886. Don Agustín's oldest son, Agustín Fabián, returned to Cuba after receiving his education to administer the family plantation; and his other son, Antonio, the grandfather of the author, remained in Barcelona, where he married Catalina Taltavull Victory.

The family lived in Barcelona during most of the year and then spent the summers at their country estate, Torrentbó, where the author's father, José María, was born. The house, the Masía Gualba, was surrounded by fruit orchards, vineyards, and forests. The farm later offered a view of life to young Luis that contrasted sharply with that in the city. In Torrentbó he came to appreciate the cycles of nature and the need for humans to be connected to them. Torrentbó and the Masía Gualba both significantly influenced Luis Goytisolo's values and found many echoes in his work.

José María Goytisolo Taltavull, one of ten siblings in a staunchly conservative and Catholic family, was a scientist by vocation but not a good businessman. He married Julia Gay Vives, who came from a well-established, artistic, and eccentric family in the city. Luis's mother was killed in the infamous Coliseum bombing raid in Barcelona on 17 March 1938 while in the city shopping for her family. Her death occurred on Luis's third birthday. Afterward, her husband was unable to bear even the sound of her name, and so her side of the family played much less of a part in the lives of the Goytisolo children. In general, their mother's family's heritage was communicated to them through muted whispers and innuendo.

The rapidly changing political events in Spain during the 1940s and 1950s marked Goytisolo and his generation of artists profoundly. He was an infant when the Civil War began. Because of the war his family eventually abandoned their Barcelona residence and fled to the relative tranquillity of the country, first to Torrentbó and subsequently to the small town of Caldetas. They returned to Barcelona in 1937, and there Don José María contracted pneumonia in a damp jail cell when he was detained briefly by the Republican forces. He was operated on to remove one of his lungs and faced a long convalescence. The family retired that same year to the country village of Viladrau, in part to help the senior Goytisolo recuperate but also to escape the mounting violence and the bombing raids by the Francoist Nationalists on civilian populations. Luis did not return to Barcelona until after the war. The family's fortunes changed in many ways during the war years, but its members gradually adjusted to their postwar circumstances. Like many others throughout Spain, they had lost not only loved ones, but also financial security because of the precarious state of the Spanish economy, the infrastructure of which had been decimated by the war. Matters were complicated by the father's propensity to invest in financial schemes that ended disastrously.

*Cover for the 1979 paperback edition of Goytisolo's first novel (The Outskirts), originally published in 1958, a collection of seven stories set in the aftermath of the Spanish Civil War (Thomas Cooper Library, University of South Carolina)*

Given Goytisolo's father's conservative background, he and his brothers inevitably attended strict parochial schools. Education in Francoist Spain was based on a strong foundation of the Catholic faith and fervent nationalism. The state fostered religious, political, and linguistic homogeneity. The use of regional languages, such as Catalan, Euskera, and Gallician, was prohibited in public media, and several layers of censorship assured the absence of any criticism. Spanish was the exclusive language used in the Goytisolo home, even though Catalan was sometimes spoken in his mother's family.

Goytisolo began writing poetry as a young adolescent but quickly turned to narrative as his preferred genre. By the mid to late 1950s his life was full of activity: he had established a continuing relationship with María Antonia Gil Moreno de Mora, later his wife and

the mother of his two sons, Gonzalo and Fermín; he was studying law at the University of Barcelona (although he did not finish the degree); he was writing continuously; he was involved in clandestine political activities aimed at undermining the government of Francisco Franco; and he was attending literary seminars at the university and *tertulias* (get-togethers of people with similar interests), where literature was the main topic of discussion.

The aspiring author began to submit his work for literary prizes, and in 1956 he won the Premio Sésamo (Sésamo Prize) for the short story "Niño malo" (Bad Boy). This story was later incorporated into Goytisolo's first published novel, *Las afueras* (The Outskirts), for which he received the Biblioteca Breve literary prize from the publishing house Seix Barral in 1958. His first published story, however, was "Claudia," which appeared in the magazine *Destino* in 1957.

Goytisolo's first works have in common several themes that reflect his interest in the social and political issues of the time. Opposition to the Franco government was strictly prohibited. University students and other opponents of the dictator's regime had few options if they wished to protest the lack of justice and human rights. In 1956 Goytisolo joined the underground Communist Party in Spain because it offered one of the few organized political alternatives for dissidents. For three years he participated in party activities, traveling often to Paris on party business and even attending a conference in Prague; but then, disillusioned with the hypocrisy of its politics and rhetoric, he left the party.

In "Claudia" and in *Las afueras,* the theme of class and ethnic prejudices is reflected in situations that deal with the unjust treatment of the country workers and poor immigrants who were flooding Catalonia at the time in search of work. The upper classes tend to be depicted as decadent, egocentric, and apathetic toward the laborers. "Claudia" relates the story of an unhappy young woman, sequestered by her mother in an isolated existence. When she develops a relationship with the gardener, a man with gypsy-like physical traits, the mother fires him. The story ends dramatically in a matricide that frees Claudia to join what she perceives to be the freer life of the working poor.

*Las afueras* was a somewhat confusing work to the readers and critics of the late 1950s, who were used to a realistic and objective approach to narrative. The predominant literary style of the time in Spain was social realism. This approach sought to demonstrate social injustices by presenting obvious examples, such as the problems of miners or farmworkers, in a work free from direct comment by the narrator. The exposition of the situations was such that it led the reader to draw conclusions that inevitably cast blame on a rigid and unjust social and political system for the plight of the poor and working classes. Although Goytisolo's first two novels, *Las afueras* and *Las mismas palabras* (1962, The Same Words), both criticize the upper-class apathy and disregard for the problems of the working class, neither strictly conforms to the style of social realism.

*Las afueras* is a collection of seven stories, each of which focuses on individuals of various ages and social and economic levels who are dealing with the many changes in their lives in the aftermath of the Civil War. The stories are held together by themes of social injustice, disillusionment, and the emptiness of the characters' lives. The work represents a departure from social realism in its subjective tone and in its structure, to the point that some critics do not classify it as a novel. The characters do not repeat from one story to the next, but, taken as a group, they reflect multiple perspectives on the reality of Spain in the mid 1950s. The novel lays the groundwork for Goytisolo's future novels in its use of a subjective tone; its structural complexity; its use of characters who are trying to understand their changing world and their place in it; and its use of urban and country locations, with a definite preference for the natural world.

Although Goytisolo abandoned any connection with the Communist Party in 1959, he was arrested and accused of clandestine political activity against the Franco regime the following year and sent to the Carabanchel Prison in Madrid. His brother Juan organized a petition-signing campaign in Paris; the petition was sent in the form of a letter of protest to the Paris newspaper *Le Monde* over the signatures of Pablo Picasso and members of the French intellectual elite such as Jean-Paul Sartre, Marguerite Duras, and Alain Robbe-Grillet. In Spain, protests over the arrest were made by such scholars as Ramón Menéndez Pidal and the future Nobel Prize winner Camilo José Cela. Goytisolo was kept in isolation and had no idea of the efforts being made to free him. As difficult as his circumstances were–he contracted a form of tuberculosis in prison that threatened his life–the experience was crucial to the crystallization of ideas for an ambitious new novel. While in prison he began work on *Antagonía,* writing on toilet paper slipped to him by a guard. When he was released after four months, he was forced by ill health to retreat to Viladrau to recuperate.

Although *Antagonía* had begun to occupy the author's thoughts, on his release he returned to the writing of *Las mismas palabras*. In his prologue to the second edition of the novel (1987), Goytisolo describes the time period and his frustrations regarding his second novel, which he had begun in 1959. *Las mismas palabras* focuses on a group of middle-class friends as their rela-tionships slowly disintegrate. It is composed of a series of interrelated stories, each with its own protagonist and point of view. The basic theme is the emptiness of the lives of these young Spaniards. Their dialogue is a continuous repetition of inane and superficial chatter, as the title of the work reflects. No one does anything in this novel; the characters feel powerless to change their future, and their lives are built on empty words.

Goytisolo returned to the writing of *Antagonía* in 1963. In early 1966 he married María Antonia Gil Moreno de Mora. They had two sons: Gonzalo, born in 1966, and Fermín, born in 1968.

As Goytisolo notes in his prologue, *Las mismas palabras* did not excite the critics or even cause the confusion seen in the case of *Las afueras*. There were problems as well with the official censors of the Franco regime, and the author's own self-censoring limited the work. Still, the novel allowed him to experiment and to develop confidence in his own literary style.

*Antagonía* is a novel of epic themes and proportions written over a period of nearly twenty years. It is composed of four parts: *Recuento* (1973, The Recounting); *Los verdes de mayo hasta el mar* (1976, The Greening of May Down to the Sea); *La cólera de Aquiles* (1979, The Wrath of Achilles); and *Teoría del conocimiento* (1981, Theory of Knowledge). It was originally published in four separate parts mainly because of time and editorial considerations, one being its length of more than 1,500 pages. *Recuento* was published first in Mexico to avoid censorship in Spain. All of the volumes were published in Spain after Franco's death in 1975, when the country became a constitutional monarchy.

*Antagonía* is an ambitious project in multiple ways. The overarching theme of the work is an exploration of the ways in which human beings form a vital and active part of the universe through their creative power. The title of the work comes from a Greek word that the author defines as the eternal struggle between what exists and what does not. The fact that something does not exist in material form does not mean that it does not have its own force and power. Through its plots and subplots, *Antagonía* focuses on the tension that arises from these forces and its effects on the lives of the characters and civilization in general.

The first part of the cycle, *Recuento,* begins as the biography of the main character, Raúl Ferrer Gaminde, whose life includes many autobiographical details of Goytisolo's life. From a child's perspective, he witnesses the Civil War and its aftermath. His mother dies in a bombing raid during the war, and his father has financial difficulties and a defeatist attitude toward life. The young Raúl must adapt to the harsh demands of a rigid Catholic school that inculcates guilt and fear in its stu-

Luis Goytisolo

# LOS VERDES DE MAYO HASTA EL MAR

**SEIX BARRAL**
Biblioteca Breve

*Paperback cover for the second part (The Greening of May Down to the Sea, 1976) of Goytisolo's four-part epic novel* Antagonía *(1973–1981), begun in 1959 while he was a political prisoner in Madrid (Thomas Cooper Library, University of South Carolina)*

dents in order to assure conformity to the values of church and state.

Neither the church nor the state manages to convince Raúl that their values are anything more than hypocritical and self-serving, and as a young university student he and his friends join the Communist Party, hoping to change Spain for the better. Over time, this illusion cannot be sustained, and Raúl gradually separates himself from the party. The police have been following the group's activities, however, and they finally arrest Raúl and several of his friends. He is sent to jail, where, in spite of brutal treatment and isolation, he experiences an epiphany about his life: he comes to understand that he has been living a lie by trying to conform to everyone else's expectations of him. The only one to whom he has not been true is himself.

While in prison he begins work on the novel that becomes *Recuento*. At the end of the novel, when Raúl accepts his need to write as his means to understanding his own identity and place in the universe, the narrative changes from a third-person biographical point of view to a first-person autobiography that signals his maturation as a person and a writer/creator.

Plot is never the most important aspect of Goytisolo's narrative. The style of *Recuento* is baroque, featuring many structural complexities and an emphasis on important symbols and metaphors that run throughout *Antagonía*. Each of its nine chapters centers on a key episode in the protagonist's life and then both flashes back and looks ahead to other incidents that relate to it. These incidents relate to broader themes, such as the role of the church, the family, and other political and social institutions in society. The author uses satire and parody to expose the hypocrisy of the rhetoric used by these institutions as they attempt to convince the public to adopt and conform to their point of view. In the end, for Raúl, the only truth is his own creativity. He must trust it to lead him to an understanding of life.

The second book of *Antagonía, Los verdes de mayo hasta el mar,* continues using the first-person narrator from the end of *Recuento*. Now Raúl is in Las Rosas, a small coastal town, with his wife as they try to patch up their floundering marriage. They interact with an unusual and decadent group of friends, mostly from an upper-class background. Raúl is keeping a series of notes and short passages that represent the work he is doing on a novel in progress. The various levels of the story revolve around Raúl's perceptions of his relationship with his wife and their friends and the fictions he is creating that spring from those perceptions. The lines between the "real" story of Raúl and his fictional double, Ricardo, occasionally become blurred in sections, and it becomes difficult to identify the narrative voice.

The final chapter is a fantastic, dream-like sea voyage in which characters from the past and future, fictional and real, from literature, history, and movies, go to the center of the earth, where they see, paradoxically, the whole expanse of the firmament. They then travel through space and finally return to the boat in which they began their journey, which capsizes. All aboard perish except for a lone survivor, who, after being swallowed by a whale, is coughed up and is able to drag himself to shore. Raúl imagines this story as a parable about the necessity of taking a perilous inner voyage to determine one's true nature.

The third part of *Antagonía* is *La cólera de Aquiles*. In this book, Raúl Ferrer Gaminde is a secondary character, and the narrator is his cousin, Matilde Moret. As a character, Raúl is not well defined or realistic. He exists mostly as an intellectual entity. Matilde, on the other hand, has a strong personality. She lives in the coastal town of Cadaqués, is a member of the Spanish upper class, and is married; she has left her husband, however, and now has a lesbian lover, Camila, who, in turn, is involved in a relationship with a man. Matilde's thoughts and reflections in this book revolve around her campaign to recover her lover. At the same time, she makes clear to the reader, whom she addresses constantly in the work, her opinions about everything from literature to how to treat servants. She attempts to dominate everyone into agreeing with her point of view. Matilde is overbearing, boastful, and unreliable as a narrator, despite the occasional validity of her attitudes and observations.

This book focuses on the role of the reader as a collaborator with the author in the actualization of a text. Matilde reads and comments on Raúl's work and on her own short novel, "El Edicto de Milán" (The Edict of Milan), which forms chapters 4, 5, and 6 of this nine-chapter book. Matilde's understanding of her own work—represented in part by her rationalizations in response to critics, including Raúl—is flawed by her inability to see past the mask that she has created for herself. Matilde cannot see herself truly because she has not faced her weaknesses and fears. She feigns superiority to hide her vulnerability, but that posture only makes her weaknesses clearer to others.

The final book of *Antagonía* is *Teoría del conocimiento*. This book represents the completed product of the notes that constitute *Los verdes de mayo hasta el mar*. The book bears two title pages, one indicating that Luis Goytisolo is the author and the other giving credit to Raúl Ferrer Gaminde. It is divided into three parts, each with its own narrator. The narrator of the first section is an adolescent male, Carlos, who is writing a narrative in the form of a diary. The central episode in the diary is Carlos's attraction to an older woman, Aurea, who lives in the apartment building across the street from him. They watch each other voyeuristically until, finally, they agree to meet. When Carlos arrives at the building, there is no one home, and the doorman says that Aurea is in Manila. Carlos is sure that he must be wrong; but when he returns home to listen to the message he had taped of their conversation, only his voice has been recorded.

The second narrator is a middle-aged man, Ricardo, who is experiencing a midlife crisis. He questions his career choice as an architect and has retreated to a small hotel away from Barcelona to reflect on his life and to write his own narrative. The center of his reflections is his relationship with Margarita, a distant cousin with whom he had an affair in his youth. Her sister (who shares many characteristics with Matilde Moret) and brother also played important roles in his

past. Margarita died suddenly in a car accident and left a picture of her room in the family's country home in an envelope with Ricardo's name on it. This picture becomes a mystery that Ricardo feels he needs to solve in order to reclaim power over his own life.

In the third section the narrator is El Viejo (The Old Man), who is about to die. He is, in fact, the great-grandfather of Carlos, and he is a kind of local chieftain. His family all think that he is leaving them a large inheritance and so are hovering about him, waiting for his death. He records his thoughts on a tape recorder, but he is leaving it to his grandson-in-law, Carlos (the father of the first narrator), to transcribe them.

El Viejo says that the only treasure he has to leave is his experience and his thoughts. He decries the decadence of modern society and stresses that he values the things that matter—a close tie with nature and the natural cycles of life, good music, and most importantly, power. He does have a nemesis, however, a man he calls "El moro," with whom he has fought his whole life as they each sought to control the village. Once again, Goytisolo uses irony to help the reader see the weaknesses in the old man's arguments. Like Matilde, he makes some good points, but then he undermines his own narrative by being too controlling and overbearing.

The old man reflects at length on the question of knowledge and the kinds of knowledge that are important to understanding one's life and the greater cosmos. He points to Aesop as the ultimate thinker, wise and yet practical, and he hopes his descendants will learn to appreciate that kind of knowledge, because he considers it to be the ultimate treasure, far greater than financial riches.

*Teoría del conocimiento,* as the culminating part of *Antagonía,* combines many details concerning plot, characters, and setting that are repeated throughout the entire novel. Their repetition, in a sense, renders them less significant in their details, freeing the reader to focus on the meaning behind them: that one must be bold in the search for identity, no matter what the stage of life, and that creativity is of great importance in connecting humans to the greater universe of which they are a part.

The writing of *Antagonía* dominated Goytisolo's activities from 1963 until 1980, although in 1970 he published *Ojos, círculos, buhos* (Eyes, Circles, Owls), a short book in collaboration with illustrator Joan Ponç. The text is a series of brief fables, reflections, and ironic passages that comment on ideas and the absurdities of life. Another collaboration with Ponç, *Devoraciones* (Devourings), was published in 1976. These two books were revised and collected with an additional story,

LUIS
GOYTISOLO

*Estela del fuego
que se aleja*

Narrativas hispánicas
Editorial Anagrama

*Paperback cover for Goytisolo's 1984 novel (The Path of the Fire in
the Distance), in which the narrator descends into madness while
writing about a man he believes to be his opposite in every way
(Thomas Cooper Library, University of South Carolina)*

"Una sonrisa a través de una lágrima" (A Smile through a Tear), as *Fábulas* (Fables) in 1981.

By the time all the parts of *Antagonía* had been published, the death of Franco and the subsequent changes in Spanish society made publishing much easier. Goytisolo's work as a writer was beginning to be appreciated by readers and critics. *Antagonía* became the subject of essays and dissertations. Some of his work was translated into other languages, such as French, Italian, Russian, German, and Polish. He was able to travel more widely and by the late 1980s had visited Cuba, the United States, India, and the Pacific Rim countries.

In 1984 Goytisolo published *Estela del fuego que se aleja* (The Path of the Fire in the Distance). The author has stated that it was inspired by a nightmare. There are two main characters: "A" and "B." "A" is the protagonist of the first chapters and is somewhat similar to the character of Ricardo in *Antagonía*. He is a successful architect who is dissatisfied with his life because he has never attempted to follow his creative instincts. He begins to review his life and write his impressions, which then leads him to question many of his assumptions and the thin line that exists between sanity and madness. About halfway through the novel, his reflections have solidified into a project in which his main character, "B," would be his opposite in every way. "B" has made his lifework the study of shame as a concept. He has likewise decided that he needs to change the focus of his life and, in his turn, begins to write a novel about a born winner in life, whom he calls "A." The themes of sanity and madness, reality and fiction, and the instability of human identity are woven into the complex layers of the characters' reflections on life. The novel begins with an ironic tone but ends as a disquieting essay on the fragility of human identity. The novel received the Critics' Award in Spain.

Goytisolo published *Investigaciones y conjeturas de Claudio Mendoza* (The Research and Speculations of Claudio Mendoza) in 1985. A collection of stories and an autobiographical text, this short work has a comic tone. Claudio Mendoza (Matilde Moret's pseudonym in *La cólera de Aquiles*) is an academic whose research has gone offtrack. He makes ludicrous assumptions about such diverse topics as conversations between Karl Marx and Vladimir Ilyich Lenin and the failure of a Don Juan character to successfully seduce a woman; and he even includes a reference to a certain Luis Goytisolo, a presumptuous young man whom he knew before he was a famous author. The section of the book titled "Acotaciones" (Stage Directions) is autobiographical and discusses many details of the author's life, with his interpretations of their significance.

*La paradoja del ave migratoria* (The Paradox of Migratory Birds), published in 1987, is basically a detective novel. The main character, Gaspar López, has written a screenplay that is in the process of being produced as a movie. His wife, Virginia, keeps a diary from which Gaspar takes ideas for his movie, in which an attempted matricide goes wrong and the intended assassin instead becomes the victim. The plot is a kind of labyrinth, with many disorienting twists and turns. There are multiple levels of the text (movie, reality, diary), and the characters assume diverse masks in those different levels.

Since the late 1980s Goytisolo has worked for Spanish television in the capacity of scriptwriter for a series of travel programs. He travels with the production crews and provides the narration for the programs. In 1992 he published a book of these travel accounts, *Indico* (The Indian Ocean). These trips have helped him fulfill his childhood dreams of traversing the globe and have added unusual details to some of his novels. In addition he has contributed editorials on a continuing basis to most of the important national newspapers in Spain, notably *El País. El porvenir de la palabra* (2002, The Future of the Word) is a collection of some of his more salient articles about the future of the written word in a world that is increasingly dominated by visual and electronic media.

Goytisolo's first novel in the 1990s, *Estatua con palomas* (1992, Statue with Doves), combines his fascination with the classical history of the Greeks and the Romans with his interest in autobiographical fiction. The text alternates between chapters in which the main character is the Roman historian Tacitus and others that focus on Goytisolo's own life. Although much of the narration about Goytisolo's life is based on verifiable events, the story becomes increasingly fictionalized at the end and is not a true autobiography. The author uses his own life, by now familiar to his readers, to engage them in the text. The points in common between the chapters that focus on Tacitus and those that focus on Goytisolo have to do with the priorities of writers as they decide what to write and how to attract readers to the text, which the readers, in turn, ultimately help to create. This novel returns to an important theme in *Antagonía:* that all great narrative inspires a collaboration of the author and the reader. The writer learns from his or her creation, but the reader learns as well—an important result of the literary process. It is also evident from this novel that Goytisolo sees many points of coincidence upon which he wishes to comment between the rise and fall of the Roman Empire and contemporary civilization. In 1993 *Estatua con palomas* received the Premio Nacional de Narrativa from the Spanish Ministry of Culture.

In 1993 Goytisolo and his wife established the Fundación Luis Goytisolo (Luis Goytisolo Foundation) in Cádiz to house a library and an archive for Goytisolo's manuscripts and for those of his older brother, José Agustín. The foundation also holds an annual symposium on contemporary Hispanic narrative. Goytisolo's wife died of lung cancer in August 1992, and the first symposium, held in November 1993, was dedicated to her memory. In 1995 Goytisolo was inducted into the Real Academia Española, which is responsible for compiling the words and phrases collected in the official dictionary of the Spanish language.

By the late 1990s Goytisolo had relocated to Madrid. He married Elvira Huelbes, a journalist and freelance writer, in 1998. They reside in Madrid with her daughter, Marta. Goytisolo's son Gonzalo is a painter, and his son Fermín is a scientist.

In 1996 Goytisolo published *Mzungo* (Swahili for *red;* the term is used to refer to Caucasians). Part of the

Paperback cover for Goytisolo's 1992 novel (Statue with Doves), in which autobiographical chapters alternate with episodes set in ancient Rome (Thomas Cooper Library, University of South Carolina)

novel describes the travels of a group of Europeans as they cruise along the coast of Africa, visiting various ports. There are other stories of European tourists who claim that they want to know the "real" Africa. Unable to understand the native cultures that the Europeans once sought to subjugate, they are caught in circumstances that, at the least, are embarrassing, and in some cases are fatal. The book was released with a CD-ROM that includes games offering alternative endings for the mysteries presented in the text with regard to the fate of the cruise.

*Placer licuante* (1997, Liquid Pleasure) is an erotic novel based on the problems of a woman who leaves her obsessive author husband for a dynamic architect (Goytisolo's two favorite professions for his characters). This book also incorporates the computer as the means by which the wife is able to monitor her husband's thoughts after she leaves him and eventually to learn that he plans to kill her and her lover as revenge. She is able to turn the tables on him with this knowledge, however, and kills him first, making it appear to be a suicide.

*Diario de 360⁰* (A 360⁰ Diary), published in 2000, marks a return to many of the themes on the meaning of life and the role of creativity that Goytisolo explores in *Antagonía*. The book is in the form of a diary written over the course of a year. There are themes that are associated with the entries for each day of the week. Wednesdays, for example, tend to be reflections on the nature of God; Thursdays are autobiographical in nature; Fridays explore topics related to sexuality; and Sundays are entries that seem to be drafts for a future novel. As a totality, the work creates a mosaic of references, reflections, opinions, and story lines that when juxtaposed and connected by language, style, and theme become a novel that examines the way in which each individual human being comes to understand life and the universe.

Goytisolo's career has extended into the twenty-first century with the publication of his novel *Liberación* (2003, Liberation). According to the author, it is the book that came to him most quickly and completely, taking only four months to write. *Liberación* deals with the search for knowledge that can liberate the individual from the constraints of time and space and the absurdities and violence of human existence. Once again Goytisolo mixes historical characters–in this case, the Stoic philosopher and Roman emperor Marcus Aurelius–and contemporary ones to demonstrate that although times change, the human situation does not, and that perhaps the only hope of overcoming that situation is to create new realities through the imagination. Another novel, *Oído atento a los pájaros*, is scheduled to be published in February 2006. According to Goytisolo, it touches on similar themes as *Diario de 360⁰* and *Liberación* and returns to some of their characters.

For Luis Goytisolo, life is still full of mystery, surprise, and wonder. These elements permeate his work, and he seeks to communicate them to readers who join him in his creative journey.

**Interviews:**

Ludovico Nolens, "Haciendo recuento: Entrevista con Luis Goytisolo," *Quimera,* 2 (December 1980): 26–30;

Julio Ortega, "Entrevista con Luis Goytisolo," in *El Cosmos de* Antagonía, edited by Ricardo Gullón (Barcelona: Anagrama, 1983), pp. 141–152;

Fernando Valls, "Sobre la trayectoria narrativa de Luis Goytisolo: Una conversación," *Nuevas letras,* 6 (1987): 81–90.

**Bibliography:**

Fernando Valls, "Para una bibliografía completa de Luis Goytisolo," *Antagonía,* 1 (1996): 47–71.

**References:**

Danny J. Anderson, "Creativity and Convention: The Antagonism of *Los verdes de mayo hasta el mar,*" *Revista de Estudios Hispánicos,* 21, no. 1 (January 1987): 101–116;

Lisa Bonee Arbués, "*Teoría del conocimiento:* Raúl's *Antagonía,*" *Revista Hispánica Moderna,* 47, no. 2 (December 1994): 493–504;

Terri M. Carney, "Good Intentions Aren't Enough: Intellectuals and Violence in Luis Goytisolo's *Mzungo,*" *Ojáncano: Revista de literature española,* 24 (October 2003): 69–78;

Carney, "Luis Goytisolo beyond *Antagonía:* The Search for Agency in Democratic Spain," *Letras Peninsulares,* 14 (Winter 2001–2002): 487–501;

Miguel Dalmau, *Los Goytisolo* (Barcelona: Anagrama, 1999);

Pamela DeWeese, "*Antagonía* y la trascendencia," *Página,* 11–12, nos. 1–2 (1993): 41–60;

DeWeese, *Approximations to Luis Goytisolo's* Antagonía (New York: Peter Lang, 2000);

DeWeese, "Aspectos de lo femenino en *Antagonía* de Luis Goytisolo," in *Luis Goytisolo: El espacio de la creación,* edited by Manuel Angel Vázquez Medel (Barcelona: Lumen, 1995), pp. 34–55;

DeWeese, "La memoria y sus diálogos en *Recuento* de Luis Goytisolo," *Ojáncano: Revista de literatura española,* 4 (October 1990): 59–69;

DeWeese, "The Structural Dynamics of Creativity: *Antagonía* by Luis Goytisolo," dissertation, University of North Carolina at Chapel Hill, 1988;

Carlos Javier García, "Rectificaciones: La escritura como falsificación en *La cólera de Aquiles,*" *Revista Hispánica Moderna,* 67, no. 1 (June 1994): 157–166;

Beckie Sue Gardiner de Arias, "Cosmogonic Myth in *Antagonía* by Luis Goytisolo: A Creation of Creations," 2 volumes, dissertation, University of Kansas, 1989;

Ricardo Gullón, ed., *El Cosmos de* Antagonía (Barcelona: Anagrama, 1983);

David K. Herzberger, "Luis Goytisolo's *Recuento:* Towards a Reconciliation of the Word/World Dialectic," *Anales de la novela de posguerra,* 3: 39–55;

Herzberger and M. Carmen Rodriguez-Margenot, "Luis Goytisolo's *Antagonía:* A Portrait of the Artist as a Young Man," *Revista Canadiense de Estudios Hispánicos,* 13, no. 1 (1988): 79–92;

José Ortega, "Asedio a *Recuento* de Luis Goytisolo," *Cuadernos Hispanoamericanos,* 385 (July 1982): 208–216;

Margarita A. Pillado-Miller, "El elemento autobiográfico en *Antagonía* de Luis Goytisolo," dissertation, Washington University, 1990;

Randolph Pope, "Una brecha sobrenatural en *Teoría del conocimiento,*" *Revista Monográfica,* 3, nos. 1–2 (1987): 129–136;

Pope, "The Different Architectures of Metafiction in Juan and Luis Goytisolo," *España contemporánea,* 1 (Winter 1988): 145–150;

Mario Santana, "*La cólera de Aquiles* como metanovela: Discurso autorial e insubordinación textual," *La Página,* 11–12, nos. 1–2 (1993): 61–71;

Gonzalo Sobejano, "La proyección satírica de *Antagonía,*" *Ojáncano: Revista de la literatura española,* 2 (April 1989): 17–28;

Sobejano, "Sobre la comparación en la prosa narrativa de Luis Goytisolo," *La página,* 11–12, nos. 1–2 (1993): 7–18;

Antonio Sobejano-Morán, "Ironía y parodia en *Recuento* de Luis Goytisolo: Crítica y destrucción de la España de posguerra," *Hispania,* 72 (September 1989): 510–515;

Sobejano-Morán, *La metaficción creadora en* Antagonía *de Luis Goytisolo* (Lewiston, N.Y.: Edwin Mellen Press, 1993);

Andrew W. Sobiesuo, *Luis Goytisolo's Narrative and the Quest for Literary Autonomy* (York, S.C.: Spanish Literature Publications, 1997);

Robert C. Spires, *Beyond the Metafictional Mode: Directions in the Modern Spanish Novel* (Lexington: University Press of Kentucky, 1984);

Spires, "Discursive Constructs and Spanish Fiction of the 1980s," *Journal of Narrative Technique,* 27, no. 1 (Winter 1997): 128–146;

Kevin Eugene Teegarden, "The Reader in Luis Goytisolo's *Antagonía* Tetralogy: A Study in Narrative Communication," dissertation, Indiana University, 1994;

José Angel Valente, "*Recuento,*" *Ínsula,* 341 (April 1975): 1, 12–13;

Kathleen Vernon, "The Masks of Eros: Luis Goytisolo's *Antagonía,*" *Río Piedras: Universidad de Puerto Rico, Facultad de Humanidades,* 21, no. 1 (January 1987): 85–116;

Vernon, "*Mise en Abyme* and the Making of Meaning in Luis Goytisolo's *Antagonía,*" in *A Ricardo Gullón: Sus discípulos* (Erie, Pa.: Publicaciones de la Asociación de Licenciados y Doctores Españoles en Estados Unidos, 1995), pp. 229–241.

**Papers:**
Luis Goytisolo's manuscripts will be at the Fundación Luis Goytisolo in the Palacio del Marqués de Villarreal in El Puerto de Santa María, across the bay from Cádiz, when renovations to the building are complete.

# Carmen Laforet

*(6 September 1921 – 28 February 2004)*

Jeffrey Oxford
*University of Wisconsin–Milwaukee*

BOOKS: *Nada* (Barcelona: Destino, 1945); translated by Inez Muñoz as *Nada, a Novel . . .* (London: Weidenfeld & Nicolson, 1958); translated by Charles Payne as *Andrea* (New York: Vantage, 1964);

*El piano* (Madrid: Rollan, 1952);

*La isla y los demonios* (Barcelona: Destino, 1952);

*La muerta* (Madrid: Rumbos, 1952);

*El viaje divertido* (Madrid: Cid, 1953);

*Un noviazgo* (Madrid: Tecnos, 1953);

*Los emplazados* (Madrid: Cid, 1954);

*La niña* (Madrid: Cid, 1954);

*La llamada* (Barcelona: Destino, 1954);

*La mujer nueva* (Barcelona: Destino, 1955);

*Mis páginas mejores* (Madrid: Gredos, 1956);

*Un matrimonio. Portada de del Barrio* (Madrid: Mon, 1956);

*Gran Canaria* (Barcelona: Noguer, 1961); translated by John Forrester as *Grand Canary* (Barcelona: Noguer, 1961);

*La insolación* (Barcelona: Planeta, 1963);

*Paralelo 35* (Barcelona: Planeta, 1967);

*La niña y otros relatos* (Madrid: EMESA, 1970);

*Artículos literarios de Carmen Laforet,* edited by Heather Leigh (Eastbourne, U.K.: Stuart-Spence, 1977);

*Mi primer viaje a U.S.A.* (Madrid: PPP, 1985);

*Al volver la esquina,* edited by Cristina Cerezales, Agustín Cerezales, and Israel Rolón Barada (Barcelona: Destino, 2004).

**Collection:** *Novelas* (Barcelona: Planeta, 1957).

*Carmen Laforet (frontispiece for* Novelas, *seventh edition, 1969; Thomas Cooper Library, University of South Carolina)*

Carmen Laforet suddenly appeared on the Spanish literary scene in 1944 with the awarding of the first Premio Nadal. The novel for which she won the prize, *Nada* (1945, Nothingness), is widely considered one of the most important works of post–Civil War Spain. The author's penchant for perfectionism, however, and an admitted tendency to become easily distracted from writing led to few book-length publications. Only four novels appeared between 1945 and 1963. Her last collection of short stories was published in 1970, and *Al volver la esquina* (2004, On Turning the Corner), the second of the "Tres pasos fuera del tiempo" (Three Steps out of Time) trilogy, begun in 1963 with *La insolación* (Sunstroke), was published only posthumously owing to the efforts of her son, Agustín Cerezales. The third volume of the trilogy, "Jaque mate" (Checkmate), exists only in manuscript.

Laforet's literary corpus comprises novels, short stories, travel notes, and literary commentary. In all of her novels, with the exception of *La insolación,* as well as in the majority of her short stories, the protagonist and many of the main characters are female. Roberta Johnson, who wrote the first extensive biography of Laforet in 1981, contends that although each novel "has very different characters and life situations," "The theme of all four of Laforet's novels is the rite of passage, a growing awareness on the part of the protagonist of his or her identity and how he or she fits into society. The family, its members, its setting, and the interaction of these elements form the microcosm in which the rite takes place."

Carmen Laforet Díaz was born on 6 September 1921 in Barcelona but grew up in Las Palmas in the Canary Islands. The family name comes from her French great-grandfather, whose son, Eduardo Laforêt, Carmen's grandfather, was a painter and an art instructor in Barcelona. Her family's interest in art spilled over into her own life—Carmen's grandfather had given her parents, as a wedding present, an original painting by the seventeenth-century Spanish painter Bartolomé Esteban Murillo—to such an extent that she was later invited by an art professor at the university to attend his classes. When Laforet was two years old, her father, Eduardo Laforet (who had dropped the use of the circumflex), and mother, Teodora Díaz, moved to the Canary Islands, where her father was employed until his death as arquitecto provincial (provincial architect) and director of the Escuela Industrial de Las Palmas. Carmen's growing up away from the mainland, isolated from direct involvement in the military conflicts of the Spanish Civil War, led to her acquiring an objectivity concerning the war and time period not common in other writers of the day. Her writings similarly reflect a society impacted by the legacy of war, instead of a society in the throes of war—the common point of view of narratives by her contemporaries.

Laforet's mother started a family custom of leading Laforet and her two younger brothers, Eduardo and Juan José, in reading aloud passages of literature after lunch. About the same time, Laforet began to tell to her siblings her own stories, which she disguised by claiming that they were dreams. When Laforet was thirteen, her mother died from a surgical infection, and her father remarried. Laforet and her brothers did not get along with their stepmother, and she used her discovery of her father's love letters to her stepmother-to-be—written before her mother's death—as a means of obtaining even more freedom than that she had already been enjoying. Because of that liberty, she spent considerable time outdoors, participating, as did her brothers, in many sports and escaping from school in order to go swimming on the beach, openly flaunting the rules of the Francisco Franco regime concerning proper beach attire. Consuelo Burell—who was Laforet's language

teacher and later became a lifelong friend—tired of the truancy and sent her word that she would fail even if she could write "better than angels," at which point Laforet's scholastic endeavors took a more serious turn.

In 1939 Laforet went to study at the Universidad de Barcelona a week after her close friend Ricardo Lezcano had left Las Palmas to continue his studies in the same city. While there, she lived with her relatives and was under the watchful eyes of her grandmother, aunts, and uncles. One of her classmates, Linka Babecka, whose family had immigrated to Spain from Poland seeking asylum from the German and Russian invaders, became a lifelong friend. In 1942, Laforet followed Babecka to Madrid and enrolled in law school, living with her and her family. Although Laforet never completed a university degree, many of the experiences she underwent during the time are related in her novels, novelettes, and short stories, and many critics have noted various elements of her life that have inspired her writing. The period in Barcelona proved productive in the development of her literary career, as well, providing her with opportunities to expand her creative talents and to realize the publication of some of her short stories in the journal *Mujer* (Woman).

From January to September 1944, Laforet wrote *Nada* (Nothingness). Babecka introduced her to a friend, the journalist and literary critic Manuel Cerezales, who convinced her to submit the manuscript to the newly announced Nadal Prize competition, sponsored by the publishing house Ediciones Destino. Cerezales promised that his publishing company would publish the work should it not win the award. Laforet entered the competition, without taking the time to alter or clean up the manuscript, and the novel was awarded the 1944 prize; the next year, *Nada* was also awarded the Fastenrath Prize by the Real Academia Española, and the novel has since served as the basis for multiple movies by both Spanish and foreign directors.

*Nada* is Laforet's most recognized work and links her forever to *tremendismo,* the literary movement introduced and popularized by her contemporary Camilo José Cela that emphasizes the repulsive, the grotesque, and the violent. In *Nada,* which uses as its epigraph a poem with the same title by Juan Ramón Jiménez, the young protagonist, Andrea, describes her experiences in the pessimistic atmosphere of Barcelona immediately after the Civil War. She has come to the big city from the Canary Islands in order to study at the university; her sojourn in Barcelona is somewhat facilitated by her taking up residence with her grandmother, aunts, and uncles. Her uncle Román, a libertine, had served as a double agent in the Civil War, and her other uncle, Juan, is a painter supported by his wife's gambling. Representative of the society of the day, the various

*Paperback cover for the U.S. edition (1958) of the English translation of Laforet's first novel (1945), in which a young woman from the Canary Islands moves in with her dysfunctional family in Barcelona (Thomas Cooper Library, University of South Carolina)*

bled by their political or religious differences and never overtly denigrated opposing views in her writings, but tension in their marriage resulted from Cerezales, along with the reading public, pressuring her to write more works of the caliber of *Nada*. Finally, Laforet and Cerezales separated in 1970–never officially divorcing– after having had five children: Marta (born in 1946), Cristina (born in 1948), Silvia (born in 1950), Manuel (born in 1952), and Agustín (born in 1957). Cristina and Agustín Cerezales have become somewhat famous writers in their own right.

Laforet had a religious experience in 1951 and became an active Catholic; her newfound faith in human nature is most notable in "El aguinaldo" (The Christmas Gift), a short story included in the 1952 collection *La muerta* (The Dead Woman). Over the next several years, however, she was unable to come to terms with the fundamentalism of the church, and she finally concluded, seven years later, that her attempts at reconciling the militant (Spanish) church dogma with her own independent nature was an exercise in futility. She took up the position that a rational understanding of religion is not necessary. In 1954 *La llamada* (The Calling), a collection of short stories, several of a religious nature, was published. Laforet expanded upon her religious experience, along with her theological philosophizing and misgivings, in her 1955 *La mujer nueva* (The New Woman)–a novel originally written using a first-person narrator and then rewritten in the third person. Although the novel received the Premio Menorca in 1955 and the Premio Nacional de Literatura in 1956, academic literary circles have by and large ignored the work. The majority of the critical attention bestowed upon *La mujer nueva* has been from the theological perspective. Unlike the young adolescents of Laforet's earlier narratives, the main character of *La mujer nueva*, Paulina, is an adult, married woman from León, and the time frame is a chronological span of many years. Paulina's life, including her estrangement from her parents, her university studies, and her marriage to her unfaithful husband, Eulogio, is the primary subject of analysis, although, in the end, Paulina's decision to return to Eulogio and live with him demonstrates an embracing of religious morality dictated by imposed cultural norms. Johnson notes that "Of all Laforet's works, *The New Woman* contains the most explicit social criticism. It is a plea for a humanized Catholic Church, one that allows the consolation of faith without the attendant, destructive hypocrisy. *The New Woman* is in many ways a period piece, documenting the second decade of Franco's regime in Spain."

*La isla y los demonios* (The Island and the Demons) was also published in 1952 and has many similarities to Laforet's first novel, *Nada*. The main character, Marta,

family members are not amicable and are continually feuding. Likewise, neither the grandmother nor her aunt Angustias, a spinster, are positive role models, so Andrea must fend for herself the best she can during the year she is in Barcelona. At the end of the novel, her close friend Ena has moved to Madrid, and Andrea accepts a job in the office of Ena's father. While Laforet has consistently denied that the novel is truly autobiographical, many of the events and emotions that Andrea experiences are undeniably reflections of the author's memories of her time in Barcelona.

In 1946 Laforet married Manuel Cerezales, who was twelve years her senior. He was a practicing Catholic, a Nationalist (pro-Franco), and more conservative than the agnostic and liberal Laforet. She was not trou-

is a young girl from the Canary Islands. The setting, however, is during the Civil War and on the island, and the novel is related by a third-person narrator. Marta, whose closeted-away mother is traumatized by the death of Marta's father in an automobile accident, lives on the family's estate with her mother, her stepbrother José, and his wife, Pino. The central conflicts of the novel are Marta's troubles with José–who attempts to control all the actions of both his wife and Marta– and her coming to terms with the incompatibilities of her own dreams and the reality of the world in which she lives. Eventually, her mother dies, and José permits Marta to go to Madrid to study.

Laforet borrowed the title of an 1888 novel written by the Spanish naturalist writer Emilia Pardo Bazán for the name of her fourth novel, *La insolación,* the first of a trilogy titled *Tres pasos fuera del tiempo.* This series was to be an examination of the fictional Martín Soto and his friends during the three summers of 1940–1942 *(La insolación),* the years leading up to 1950 *(Al volver la esquina),* and from 1950 to 1960 ("Jaque mate"). Although revisions were made to the galleys of the second volume, Laforet never submitted those changes to the press, both because her idea of how the trilogy should take shape had changed and because her personal life had become complicated by illness. Only during the last three years of her life were the corrected galleys found in a box, and her children Agustín and Cristina had the novel published posthumously in May 2004.

*La insolación* has been called Laforet's answer to the criticism of her as a writer of stories about females and portrays, as does *Nada,* a young Spaniard's existentialist search for identity in the hedonistic society of post–Civil War Spain. In *La insolación* the main character, Martín, is a teenage boy who lives with his maternal grandparents because his mother is deceased. During each of three consecutive summers he goes to visit his father, Eugenio, whose present wife, Adela, takes offense at the boy's presence. Thus, Martín spends quite a bit of time with a neighboring friend, Carlos, and his sister Anita. Each summer brings more maturity to the youths; during the third and final summer, Adela manipulates circumstances to convince Eugenio that Carlos and Martín are engaged in a homosexual relationship. Bruised from the ensuing beating, Martín departs for Alicante, where he is welcomed by his grandmother.

At the invitation of the State Department, Laforet traveled to the United States in 1963; her experiences became the subject of her 1967 *Paralelo 35* (The Thirty-fifth Parallel), a title that Marie-Lise Gazarian-Gautier, in her *Interviews with Spanish Writers* (1992), quotes Laforet as saying was imposed by the publisher. In

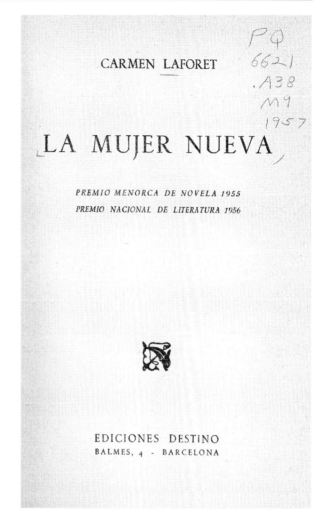

CARMEN LAFORET

LA MUJER NUEVA

PREMIO MENORCA DE NOVELA 1955
PREMIO NACIONAL DE LITERATURA 1956

EDICIONES DESTINO
BALMES, 4 - BARCELONA

*Title page for Laforet's 1955 novel (The New Woman), about a woman's estrangement from her parents, her university studies, and her unfaithful husband (Thomas Cooper Library, University of South Carolina)*

1967 she undertook, for the journal *Actualidad,* a trip to Poland and was accompanied by friend and translator Babecka. During the 1960s and 1970s she traveled to various parts of the world, living in Rome from 1975 until 1979, and all but retired from the literary scene, writing practically nothing, maintaining little correspondence, and denying almost all interviews. Two important interview exceptions were made–the first in June 1976 with Johnson, the second in 1989 with Gazarian-Gautier–both of which aided in the production of critical analyses of the author. In the 1980s Laforet returned to Spain, living with her children, or alone, until, suffering from Alzheimer's disease, she moved into a geriatric facility in Madrid.

In spite of Carmen Laforet's retirement and illness, interest in her works surged on the publication of

*Puedo contar contigo: Correspondencia* (2003, I Can Count On You: Correspondence), a collection of her correspondence with the Spanish novelist Ramón Sender between 1965 and 1975 in which she addresses her literary and social inactivity, her literary work, her family, and religion in general; the republication of *La mujer nueva;* and prepublication announcements of *Al volver la esquina.* Laforet, who had been an occasional columnist for the Barcelona weekly *Destino* in the 1950s, the Madrid daily *ABC* in the 1970s, and *El País* in the 1980s, was recognized by many critics as one of the most important writers of twentieth-century Spain as well as a vivid narrator of the conflict between human aspirations and the obstacles imposed by reality. She died on 28 February 2004.

**Letters:**

*Puedo contar contigo: Correspondencia,* edited by Israel Rolón Barada (Barcelona: Destino, 2003).

**Interview:**

Marie-Lise Gazarian-Gautier, "Carmen Laforet," in her *Interviews with Spanish Writers* (Elmwood Park, Ill.: Dalkey Archive, 1992), pp. 151–164.

**Biographies:**

Roberta Johnson, *Carmen Laforet* (Boston: Twayne, 1981);

Agustín Cerezales, *Carmen Laforet* (Madrid: Ministerio de Cultura, Dirección General de Promoción del Libro y la Cinematografía, 1982);

Immaculada de la Fuente, *Mujeres de la posguerra* (Barcelona: Planeta, 2002).

**References:**

Rafael Aguayo Q., "Carmen Laforet en la nueva novela española," *Stylo,* no. 11 (1971): 9–23;

Fernando Barroso, "La mujer nueva en Carmen Laforet," *Monographic Review/Revista Monográfica,* 13 (1997): 252–261;

Stacey Dolgin Casado, "Structure as Meaning in Carmen Laforet's *Nada:* A Case of Self-Censorship," in *Studies in Honor of Gilberto Paolini,* edited by Mer-

cedes Vidal Tibbits (Newark, Del.: Juan de la Cuesta, 1996), pp. 351–358;

Mark P. del Mastro, "Cheating Fate: Female Adolescent Development and the Social Web in Laforet's *Nada,*" *Hispanic Journal,* 18 (Spring 1997): 55–66;

Charles Fite, *A Study of Carmen Laforet and Her Criticism of the Post-War Spanish Society after the Civil War of 1936* (Hickory, N.C.: Privately printed, 1991);

Carolyn L. Galerstein, "Carmen Laforet and the Spanish Spinster," *Revista de Estudios Hispánicos,* 11 (1977): 303–315;

Kathleen M. Glenn, "Animal Imagery in *Nada,*" *Revista de Estudios Hispánicos,* 11 (1977): 381–394;

Antonio de Hoyos, "El arte literario de Carmen Laforet," in his *Ocho escritores actuales* (Murcia, Spain: Aula de Cultura, 1954);

Graciela Illanes Adaro, *La novelística de Carmen Laforet* (Madrid: Gredos, 1971);

Roberta Johnson, "Light and Morality in Carmen Laforet's *La insolación,*" *Letras Femeninas,* 12 (Spring–Autumn 1986): 94–102;

Barry Jordan, *Laforet: Nada* (London: Grant & Cutler, 1993);

José Luna Borge, "Carmen Laforet: Entre la inocencia y el desencanto," *Quimera,* 123 (1994): 30–31;

Donna Janine McGiboney, "Paternal Absence and Maternal Repression: The Search for Narrative Authority in Carmen Laforet's *Nada,*" *Romance Languages Annual,* 6 (1994): 519–524;

Elizabeth Ordóñez, *Nada: Initiation into Bourgeois Patriarchy* (Jamaica, N.Y.: Bilingual Press, 1976);

Sara E. Schyfter, "The Fragmented Family in the Novels of Contemporary Spanish Women," *Perspectives on Contemporary Literature,* 3, no. 1 (1977): 23–29;

Michael Thomas, "Symbolic Portals in Laforet's *Nada,*" *Anales de la Novela de Posguerra,* 3 (1978): 57–74;

Phyllis Zatlin, "Passivity and Immobility: Patterns of Inner Exile in Postwar Spanish Novels Written by Women," *Letras Femeninas,* 14 (Spring–Fall 1988): 3–9.

# Julio Llamazares

*(28 March 1955 –     )*

Caridad R. Kenna
*Stanford University*

BOOKS: *La lentitud de los bueyes,* as Julio Alonso Llamazares (Madrid: Hiperión, 1979);

*El entierro de Genarín: Evangelio apócrifo del último heterodoxo español,* as Alonso Llamazares (Madrid: Endymion, 1981; revised and enlarged edition without photographs, as Llamazares, Madrid: Ayuso, 1984; revised edition, introduction by Llamazares, Barcelona: B, Ediciones–Grupo Z, 1996);

*Memoria de la nieve* (Madrid: Consejo General de Castilla y León, Servicio de Publicaciones, 1982);

*Luna de lobos* (Barcelona: Seix Barral, 1985);

*La lluvia amarilla* (Barcelona: Seix Barral, 1988); translated by Margaret Jull Costa as *The Yellow Rain* (London: Harvill, 2003; Orlando, Fla.: Harcourt, 2003);

*El río del olvido: Viaje* (Barcelona: Seix Barral, 1990);

*En Babia* (Barcelona: Seix Barral, 1991);

*Escenas de cine mudo* (Barcelona: Seix Barral, 1994);

*En mitad de ninguna parte* (Barcelona: Ollero & Ramos, 1995);

*Nadie escucha* (Madrid: Santillana, 1995);

*Retrato de bañista* (Badajoz: Del Oeste, 1995);

*Tres historias verdaderas,* Textos tímidos, no. 3 (Madrid: Ollero & Ramos, 1998);

*Los viajeros de Madrid* (Madrid: Ollero & Ramos, 1998);

*Trás-os-montes: Un viaje portugués* (Madrid: Alfaguara, 1998);

*Cuaderno del Duero* (León: Edilesa, 1999);

*Cine y literatura: Reflexiones a partir de* Flores de otro mundo, by Llamazares and Icíar Bollain, edited by Joaquín Rodríguez (Madrid: Páginas de Espuma, 2000);

*El cielo de Madrid* (Madrid: Alfaguara, 2005).

**Collections:** *La lentitud de los bueyes; Memoria de la nieve* (Madrid: Hiperión, 1985);

*Sobre la nieve: La poesía y la prosa de Julio Llamazares,* edited by José Carlón (Madrid: Espasa, 1996).

PRODUCED SCRIPTS: *El techo del mundo,* motion picture, screenplay by Llamazares and Felipe Varga, Canal + España/Cocodrile Productions/Fama

*Julio Llamazares ( photograph by Cecilia Orueta; from the dust jacket for* The Yellow Rain, *2003; Richland County Public Library)*

Film/Marea Films/Roehrich y Asociados/Televisión Española, 1995;

*Luna de lobos,* motion picture, screenplay by Llamazares and Julio Sánchez Valdes, Brezal P.C., 1997;

*Flores de otro mundo,* motion picture, screenplay by Llamazares and Icíar Bollaín, Alta Films/La Iguana, 1999.

OTHER: "Mi tío Mario," in *Cuentos de la isla del tesoro* (Madrid: Santillana, 1994), pp. 11–56;

Biblioteca de Fotógrafos Españoles, *Navia,* introduction by Llamazares (Madrid: Photo Bolsillo, 2000).

Julio Llamazares is a protean innovator within the traditional narrative modes that have defined contemporary Spanish fiction. His work defies traditional genre expectations and challenges critics to classify him within the conventions of literary history as a novelist, poet, essayist, journalist, movie scriptwriter, literary philosopher, or a combination of all of these endeavors. His narratives present a myriad of linguistic codes and registers while offering a highly original worldview that, on the surface, appears to be expressed in conventional prose forms. The mixture of literary genres in his work stems from a desire to present various facets of the same reality. His observation of Spanish society's desire to forget its traumatic past under the Francisco Franco dictatorship and its emphasis on living for the present at the expense of obliterating history led him to make memory a cornerstone of his work. Photographs, myths, oral tales, fantasy, and childhood remembrances are intertwined in his writing. Llamazares's concern with time and memory is an effort to recover and to "rewrite" the collective memory of the Spanish people at a time when they face an historical crossroads.

Llamazares is a private man, and not much information is available about his personal life or family. Julio Alonso Llamazares was born on 28 March 1955 in the village of Vegamián in the region of León; today the village is covered by the Porma Reservoir. His father, Nemesio Alonso, a schoolteacher, was one of the few people in Vegamián who owned books. At eleven Alonso Llamazares fell ill and spent nearly a year in bed; he invented stories to get through the ordeal. At twelve he left Vegamián to attend boarding school in Madrid. He studied law, although he knew that his true calling was to be a writer. He soon abandoned the practice of law to become a journalist for the Madrid newspaper *El país.*

Julio Alonso Llamazares began his literary career with *La lentitud de los bueyes* (1979, The Slowness of the Oxen). The twenty poems in the collection were written in the spring of 1978 in the seaport of Gijón on the Bay of Biscay. The themes of time and nature that characterize Llamazares's work first appear here. The book received the Antonio González de Lama Prize.

The nonfiction work *El entierro de Genarín* (1981, The Burial of Genarín) is a pandemonium riddled with characters driven mad by alcohol and a bohemian and dissolute existence. It describes the "drinking" liturgy—a carnival-like procession from bar to bar in a parody of the Stations of the Cross—celebrated in León every Holy Thursday in honor of Jenaro (nicknamed Genarín) Blanco y Blanco, the town drunk and a womanizer, who was killed at dawn by a street-cleaning truck while urinating on a wall after a night of debauchery. Although the organizers of the 1981 León Book Fair tried to persuade the author not to attend the event, since *El entierro de Genarín* was considered in poor taste; the five thousand copies of the first edition sold out in three days during the fair.

After moving to Madrid in 1981, Julio Alonso Llamazares dropped his father's surname and adopted his mother's maiden name, Llamazares (which means "swampy terrain"), as his professional name. In the fall of 1981 he wrote *Memoria de la nieve* (1982, Remembering the Snow), a collection of thirty poems about his home region. In the poems, snow is symbolic of oblivion. The book won the Jorge Guillén Poetry Prize, awarded by the General Council of Castile.

Llamazares wrote the script for and appeared in "Retrato de bañista" (Portrait of a Bather), a segment of a documentary on León writers titled *El Filandón* (The Talking Circle) that was directed by José María Martín Sarmiento and released in 1984. Coincidentally, at the time of the filming in 1983 the Porma Reservoir was emptied, and Vegamián briefly resurfaced. Llamazares seized the opportunity to visit his hometown and stroll through the muddy streets for the movie.

In 1985 Llamazares published his first novel, *Luna de lobos* (Wolf Moon), the saga of four Loyalist *maquis* (guerrilla fighters) who hide in the mountains from the Francoist authorities after their defeat in the Civil War of 1936 to 1939. Based on stories Llamazares had heard from former *maquis* as a child, *Luna de lobos* was well received by both critics and the reading public and was made into a movie directed by Julio Sánchez Valdés in 1987.

Llamazares's second novel, *La lluvia amarilla* (1988; translated as *The Yellow Rain,* 2003), is the story of a crumbling village and its last inhabitant; it was inspired by the author's visit to the abandoned town of Sarnago in Soria in the mid 1980s. *La lluvia amarilla* is set in Ainielle in the Pyrenees; like many other small towns in contemporary Spain, it has been abandoned as its inhabitants sought better opportunities elsewhere. Andrés refuses to forsake the dying village and thus condemns himself to a life of loneliness and hopelessness. His wife, unable to tolerate the isolation, commits suicide, leaving Andrés alone with his dog and the ever-present snow. For ten years Andrés sustains himself by clinging to his memories of his son's and friends' departure from Ainielle, the death of his four-year-old daughter, and his wife's suicide and by visiting with imaginary ghosts from the past. Finally, knowing that his own death is near, Andrés mercifully kills his faithful dog to spare him loneliness. *La lluvia amarilla* was an instant best-seller; it went through fifteen editions in two years and has been translated into English, French, and Korean.

In 1981 Llamazares had traveled by foot along the Curueño River in León to the old town of Llamazares. The notes he made on the trip became the travel memoir *El río del olvido* (1990, The River of Oblivion). The book is the story of the author's pilgrimage in search of his roots as he follows his childhood "upstream," describing the scenery and recording the legends, traditions, and important names of the area. His dog, Bruna, is included in the dedication of *El río del olvido,* along with his four traveling companions.

*En Babia* (1991, In Babia) is a collection of journalistic articles, chronicles, and essays. (Babia is an area in the León region; "to be in Babia" is a colloquial expression meaning to be out of touch with reality.) *Escenas de cine mudo* (1994, Shots from a Silent Movie) is dedicated "A mi madre, que ya es nieve" (To my mother, who is already snow). The novel is based on Llamazares's memories of growing up in Vegamián, and the protagonist's name is Julio, but Llamazares insists in the introduction that the work is not an autobiography. Remembrances come alive by means of a family album that contains twelve photographs—one for each of Julio's twelve years in Vegamián. A picture evokes the smell of powdered milk, of coal burning in the school stove and of wood burning in the fireplace, and of the ink used by the schoolteacher. The text relates the trials and tribulations of growing up in a poor mining town in the León mountains, the protagonist's childhood awareness of the Franco dictatorship, the arrival of television, the assassination of American president John F. Kennedy, the first moon landing, the awakening of his sexuality, and the discovery of a wider world available through the open window of the movies. Llamazares concludes that each person's own memory is the best novel. Also in 1994 Llamazares wrote the script for *El techo del mundo* (1995, The Roof of the World) in collaboration with the director of the movie, Felipe Vega.

In 1995 *Retrato de bañista* was published as a book; it incorporates the 1983 script and includes photographs, with Llamazares's handwritten annotations, of Vegamián's resurfacing when the Porma Reservoir was emptied. *En mitad de ninguna parte* (1995, In the Middle of Nowhere) is a collection of short stories about defeated people, surreal situations, myths, and authenticity. A second collection of journalistic pieces, *Nadie escucha* (1995, Nobody Listens), is dedicated to his dog, who died in 1994: "To Bruna, who did listen."

*Los viajeros de Madrid* (1998, The Travelers of Madrid) is based on a series of articles Llamazares wrote in the mid 1980s for a Madrid newspaper. He selected thirty articles from two well-known travel journals, *Viajes*

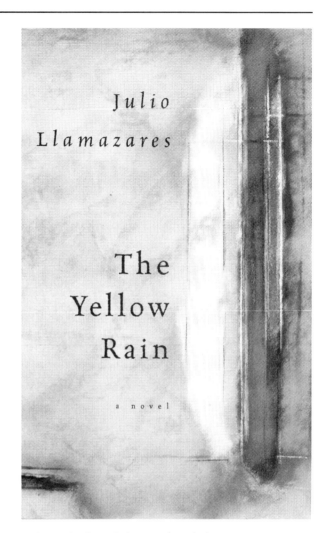

*Dust jacket for the U.S. edition (2003) of the English translation of Llamazares's 1988 novel,* La lluvia amarilla, *about the last inhabitant of an abandoned town in the Pyrenees (Richland County Public Library)*

*por España* (1972, Travels through Spain), edited by José García Marcadal, and *Los curiosos impertinentes: Viajeros ingleses por España* (1976, The Impertinent Snoops: English Travelers through Spain), edited by Ian Robertson, in which foreign travelers, from the Roman Camilo Borghese at the end of the sixteenth century to Ernest Hemingway in the twentieth century, relate their impressions of Madrid, creating a composite view of the city. The travelers include geographers, diplomats, spies, writers, adventurers, and a Bible salesman.

The travel book *Trás-os-montes: Un viaje portugués* (1998, Trás-os-montes: A Portuguese Journey) describes an automobile trip through northeastern Portugal, a region whose name, which means "Behind-the-Mountains," suggests a rugged, little-known land. The "viajero" (traveler), as Llamazares refers to himself in the third person, is an educated, compulsive

Julio Llamazares
Escenas de cine mudo

Novela

Por el autor de «La lluvia amarilla»

Seix Barral ⅄ Biblioteca Breve

*Cover for Llamazares's 1994 novel (Shots from a Silent Movie), based on his memories of his childhood in the mining town Vegamián (James Branch Cabell Library, Virginia Commonwealth University)*

wanderer who dislikes museums, armies, and modern commerce. He is also a passionate observer of people and an engaging visitor who makes friends readily, despite varying degrees of ability to communicate with the natives. *Trás-os-montes* recounts Portugal's history from King Don Dinis in the fourteenth century to the static present of churches, abandoned castles, and a seemingly deserted town in which an old man, a dog, and a beautiful girl appear out of nowhere. The traveler visits villages known for native sons such as the explorer Ferdinand Magellan and the writers Camilo Castelo Branco and Miguel Torga, but the residents are unimpressed by local celebrities of the past or by the sites of historic significance in their midst.

In 1984 the council of Castille and León had commissioned Llamazares to travel the length of the Duero and write a book about the areas along the river. He never completed the trip or the book, but in 1999 he published his unedited journal notes from the fourteen-day journey. *Cuaderno del Duero* (Duero Notebook) follows the river through the provinces of Soria, Burgos, and Valladolid and presents a panoramic view of their capital cities and of the peoples' lives, the ever-present rain, and the cold weather. Discussions of Spanish history from El Cid and the Reconquest to the Civil War and of Spanish literature from don Juan Manuel in the fourteenth century to Antonio Machado in the twentieth enrich the journey through lands that are now dominated by abandonment, misfortune, the remains of old mansions and palaces, and aged residents resigned to loneliness and boredom.

Also in 1999 *Flores de otro mundo* (Flowers from Another World), for which Llamazares and the director, Icíar Bollaín, wrote the script, won the Best Film at the International Critics' Week at the 1999 Cannes International Film Festival. The movie is based on a true story: a village with no women and no future organizes a bachelor party and invites single women from across Spain to attend. The three main characters meet on the "bus of hope" chartered by the village. Patricia, an illegal immigrant from the Dominican Republic, is looking for the home and financial security she cannot find in Madrid. Marirrosi, from Bilbao, has a job and a house but is lonely. Twenty-year-old Milady, born in Havana, is dying to see the world.

*El cielo de Madrid* (2005, The Sky of Madrid) is set in the 1980s, a time of the transition from the vestiges of the Franco dictatorship to democracy and modernity. It is divided into four chapters. In "Limbo" the protagonist, Carlos, and his artist and writer friends arrive in the Spanish capital in search of happiness and success. The sky of Madrid, represented in a painting on the ceiling of a bar where the friends meet every day, becomes a metaphor for the barrier between dreams and reality, two worlds that are impossible to unite. The friendships collapse, and a romance fails. In "Infierno" (Hell) Carlos's success as an artist brings personal emptiness. In "Purgatorio" (Purgatory) he retreats to a small town outside Madrid, where he meets young, happy people. A new love chases away his fears and brings back hope for the future in spite of his apathy. The three-page final chapter, "Cielo" (Heaven), is a happy ending. In *El cielo de Madrid,* as in Llamazares's previous novels, memory provides the backbone of the narrative structure.

Julio's Llamazares's fiction leads readers to reflect on a world that is about to disappear and allows them to meet marginal people whom he elevates to the stature of primary characters. His narratives create a space where there are no frontiers between past, present, and future. For Llamazares, writing is an attempt to make memories immortal.

**Interviews:**

José Manuel Fajardo, "La llama de la memoria," *Cambio 16* (Madrid), 7 March 1988, p. 8;

María José Obiol, "En memoria del olvido," *El País* (Madrid), 28 January 1990, pp. 24–25;

Almudena Solana, "La vida en Babia," *El País Estilo* (Madrid), 22 July 1990, pp. 24–26;

Alejandro López Andrada, "La memoria rural en Julio Llamazares," *Córdoba*, 21 January 1993, pp. 5–8;

Obiol, "Agujeros negros en la memoria," *El País* (Madrid), 12 March 1994, pp. 14–15;

Emma Rodríguez, "Julio Llamazares: Las novelas son para hacer más soportable la vida, no para pasar el rato," *El Mundo* (Madrid), 14 March 1994, p. 79;

Santos Alonso, "Julio Llamazares: La memoria recuerda en blanco y negro," *Leer* (Madrid), 71 (Spring 1994): 30–32;

Pilar Castro, "Nadie escucha," *ABC Cultural*, 190 (23 June 1995): 10.

**References:**

Santos Alonso, "La poesia de Julio Llamazares: El canto epico de la memoria," *Cuadernos de narrativa*, 3 (December 1998): 73–86;

Inge Beisel, "La memoria colectiva en las obras de Julio Llamazares," in *La novela española actual: Autores y tendencias*, edited by Alfonso de Toro and Dieter Ingenschay (Kassel: Reichenberger, 1995), pp. 193–229;

Miguel Casado, "La poesía de Julio Llamazares: Los bueyes y los bardos," in his *Esto era y no era: Lectura de poetas de Castillos y León* (Valladolid: Ambito, 1995), pp. 233–262;

Carmen Cubero, "Julio Llamazares: *La lluvia amarilla*," in *Narradores y espacios narrativos en la España de los ochenta*, edited by Julio Peñate, Rumbos, no. 11 (Neuchâtel: Institut d'Espagnol de l'Université de Neuchâtel, 1993), pp. 51–68;

Concepción Grande-González, "La Guerra Civil en la novela de la Democracia: En busca de una identidad perdida (Julio Llamazares, Eduardo Alonso, Leopoldo Azancot, Manuel Villar Raso)," dissertation, University of Massachusetts, 1993;

José María Guelbenzu, "Las tres generaciones y el lobo feroz," *El País* (Madrid), 29 November 1987, p. 13;

Sonja Herpoel, "Entre la memoria y la historia: La narrativa de Julio Llamazares," in *La memoria histórica en las letras hispánicas contemporáneas: Simposio internacional, Amberes 18–19 de noviembre de 1994*, edited by Patrick Collard (Geneva: Droz, 1977), pp. 99–110;

José María Izquierdo, "Julio Llamazares: Un discurso neorromántico en la narrativa española de los ochenta," *Iberromania*, 41 (1995): 55–67;

Caridad R. Kenna, "Cómo filmar recuerdos por escrito. Director: Julio Llamazares," in *Del rascacielos a la*

*Catedral: Un regreso a las raíces, Actas de la XVI Asamblea General de ALDEEU Encuentro Internacional en la Universidad de León 8–12 de julio de 1996*, edited by Santiago Tejerina Canal (León: Universidad de León, 2001), pp. 60–64;

Kenna, "Con la cámara en la novela, o el enfoque de Julio Llamazares," *Revista Hispánica Moderna*, 1 (June 1997): 190–204;

Kenna, "El entierro de Genarín: Carnaval y espíritu ensayístico," *Cuadernos de narrativa*, 3 (December 1998): 73–86;

Kenna, "La falsa inocencia: Julio Llamazares, Luis Landero y Gustavo Martín Garzo," in *Los nuevos nombres 1975–2000: Primer suplemento*, edited by Francisco Rico, Historia y crítica de la literatura española, volume 9/1 (Barcelona: Crítica, 2000), pp. 391–394;

Kenna, "Tiempo y memoria en la narrativa de Julio Llamazares," dissertation, Stanford University, 1997;

Jo Labnanyi, "Espacio y horror en *Luna de lobos* de Julio Llamazares," in *Référence et autoréférence dans le roman espagnol contemporain: Actes du Colloque international de Talence, 1992*, edited by Geneviève Champeau (Bordeaux: Maison des Pays Ibériques, 1994), pp. 149–155;

John Macklin, "Memory and Oblivion: Personal and Rural Identities in the Narrative Writings of Julio Llamazares," in *The Scripted Self: Textual Identities in Contemporary Spanish Narrative*, edited by Ruth Christie, Judith Drinkwater, and John Macklin (Warminster, U.K.: Aris & Phillips, 1995), pp. 31–47;

Susan Martín-Márquez, "Vision, Power and Narrative in *Luna de lobos*: Julio Llamazares' Spanish Panopticon," *Revista Canadiense de Estudios Hispánicos*, 19 (Winter 1995): 379–387;

Beatriz Monreal, "Presencia machadiana en *La lluvia amarilla* de Llamazares," in *Antonio Machado hoy: Actas del congreso internacional conmemorativo del cincuentenario de la muerte de Antonio Machado*, volume 3: *Relaciones e influencias: Teoría poética machadiana* (Seville: Alfar, 1990), pp. 149–160;

Francisco Reus Boyd-Swan, "El cronotopo idílico en *La lluvia amarilla*," in *Bajtín y la literatura: Actas del IV Seminario internacional del Instituto de semiótica literaria y teatral. Madrid, UNED, 4–6 de julio, 1994*, edited by José Romera Castillo (Madrid: Visor, 1995), pp. 373–381;

Maricarmen Rodríguez Margenot, "Modes of Characterization in the Postmodern Spanish Novel: Luis Martín Santos, Juan Goytisolo, Juan Benet, Luis Goytisolo, Julio Llamazares, Carmen Martín Gaite," dissertation, University of Connecticut, 1991.

# José Ángel Mañas

*(22 October 1971 –   )*

### Germán Gullón
*University of Amsterdam*

and

### Cristina Martínez-Carazo
*University of California Davis*

BOOKS: *Historias del Kronen* (Barcelona: Destino, 1994);

*Mensaka* (Barcelona: Destino, 1995);

*Soy un escritor frustrado* (Madrid: Espasa, 1996);

*Ciudad rayada* (Madrid: Espasa, 1998);

*Sonko95: Autorretrato con negro de fondo* (Barcelona: Destino, 1999);

*Mundo burbuja* (Madrid: Espasa, 2001);

*El caso Karen* (Barcelona: Destino, 2005).

PRODUCED SCRIPT: *Historias del Kronen,* by Mañas and Montxo Armendáriz, motion picture, Alta Films SA, 1995.

SELECTED PERIODICAL PUBLICATION–UNCOLLECTED: "Literatura y punk," *Ajoblanco,* 108 (1998): 38–43.

José Ángel Mañas is one of the most well-received writers of the Spanish "Generación X," a term coined by the press following the publication of Douglas Coupland's novel *Generation X: Tales for an Accelerated Culture* (1991). That generational label is used to identify a group of writers born between 1961 and 1981 who are considered the last literary generation to come of age before the new century. The use of colloquial language and profanity, an emphasis on orality versus the literary, and a penchant for the banal define the fiction of these writers in Europe as well as in the United States. Ever since his first novel, *Historias del Kronen* (Stories from the Kronen), appeared in 1994, Mañas has attracted more attention than any other Spanish writer of his generation. Although the success of each novel has been uneven, *Historias del Kronen* sold more than one hundred thousand copies. This number is unheard-of in a country such as Spain, in which most print runs for first novels hardly ever surpass three thou-

*José Ángel Mañas (photograph by Dominique Houyet; from <www.houyet-foto.be>)*

sand copies. With this novel, Mañas achieved an outstanding status within contemporary Spanish narrative.

Mañas's literary career, as well as those of his generational companions (including Ray Lóriga, Daniel Múgica, Gabriela Bustelo, and Martín Cassariego), has been deeply influenced by the social and political events of the 1990s. Spain's economic prosperity, its full integration into Europe, the enormous freedom enjoyed in contrast to the long repression during General Francisco Franco's dictatorship (1939–1975), and the willingness to forget the past are all factors shaping the writing of the Spanish Generación X. Within that frame of mind the cultural movement labeled *la movida* (literally, the move) was born in Madrid. This movement was led by the youth of the growing middle class, whose interests were structured around popular culture, media (cinema and television above all), design, fashion, rock music, and photography. From the vantage point of that readily accepted reality one can best understand the postmodern culture that Mañas and his cohorts seek to portray. Their fictional world is articulated in terms of pleasure, instant gratification, an estrangement from history, and above all, a desire to transgress the values of the previous generation. The attitude of these young people has been blamed, in part, on their parents' emphasis on overachievement, since the members of that generation were more concerned with becoming established in their own careers and consolidating their finances than with caring for their children.

José Ángel Mañas was born on 22 October 1971 in Madrid, into a professional upper-middle-class family. His father, José Mañas Martínez, a civil engineer, is also known as a great book collector and as the author of an erudite monograph about a nineteenth-century engineer: *Eduardo Saavedra, ingeniero y humanista* (1983; Eduardo Saavedra, Engineer and Humanist).

Literature and languages have always played an important role in the Mañas household. From his father Mañas learned to love books, and from his mother he inherited a liking for foreign cultures, as well as a cosmopolitan outlook on life. Along with his sister, Mañas attended an English private elementary school. Thus, from an early age he was fluent in English and Spanish. In 1988 Mañas enrolled at the Universidad Autónoma of Madrid, graduating with a degree in contemporary history in 1993. He spent two out of these five college years living and studying abroad: one year at the University of Sussex in England and another in Grenoble, France.

Mañas began his writing career while in college. He achieved his first success with "La pena del fraile" (The Friar's Sorrow), a short story that won the Premio Nacional Miguel Hernández (Miguel Hernández National Prize) in 1989 but was never published. In 1994 his first novel, *Historias del Kronen,* made the rounds of several publishing houses before it was submitted for the prestigious Nadal Prize. The novel came in second in the contest.

*Historias del Kronen* is set in Madrid and has a deceitfully simple plot. It tells of the comings and goings of a group of college-age friends in the city during the first days of summer vacation, before they disperse to go with their families to the coastal towns. Every night, they hang out in the most popular discotheques, where they engage in bouts of drinking, smoking, and consumption of mari-

juana and cocaine while deafening rock music blasts all around them. Casual sex is also frequent. A good part of their time is spent in their favorite hangout, the Kronen bar (named after the French beer Kronenburg). The novel ends with the unexpected death of Fierro, a diabetic boy who is forced to drink more than he can tolerate during a birthday celebration. This event is reported in first person by an impassive narrator; the effect is that of filming a documentary with the camera focusing on a long shot.

The characters' experiences are meant to symbolize the coming of age of a generation of Spaniards born in a time of affluence and social optimism in sharp contrast with the political realities lived by their parents. Mañas has said that he wrote *Historias del Kronen* in fifteen days, and that he had read Bret Easton Ellis's *American Psycho* (1991) before writing it. The impact of this American thriller, as well as the stories of Raymond Carver, Dennis Cooper, and Coupland, on Mañas's works was, however, overstated by many reviewers. They treated the book with disdain, alleging that Mañas tried to emulate the Anglo-American "dirty-realist" novel. Traditional critics described Mañas's book as poorly conceived, with a language full of trite expressions, and a referent limited by its reliance on a youth subculture of drugs, music videos, rock, and television. Even though *Historias del Kronen* was dismissed on conventional literary grounds, readers responded favorably to its authenticity and soon turned it into a best-seller. The novel was translated into German and Dutch and achieved similar success. Part of the popularity of the book was a result of its good timing, since it appeared just when young Spaniards were seeking to be recognized by the international European scene.

Part of the success of *Historias del Kronen* derived from the movie adaptation by Spanish director Montxo Armendáriz, who wrote the script in collaboration with Mañas in 1995. The movie emphasized the sociological content rather than the psychological behavior of the group. Armendáriz eliminated much of the psychological violence and many sexually explicit components of the original, thereby creating a more superficial and moralistic version. The movie was shown at the Cannes festival in 1995, and in 1996 it won a prestigious Goya Award in Spain for best screenplay adapted from a novel.

Mañas's second novel, *Mensaka* (1995; Motorbike Messenger), was also viewed with disdain by the critical establishment, although readers bought it in great numbers. The plot of *Mensaka* is better developed than that of *Historias del Kronen,* but it never achieved the emblematic status of its predecessor. Javi, Fran, and David belong to a second-rate rock band and are trying to sign a contract with a multinational record company. In the meantime, they survive by doing menial jobs and by receiving occasional parental help. David's occupation as a *mensaka,* a messenger in the jargon of this underworld, gives the

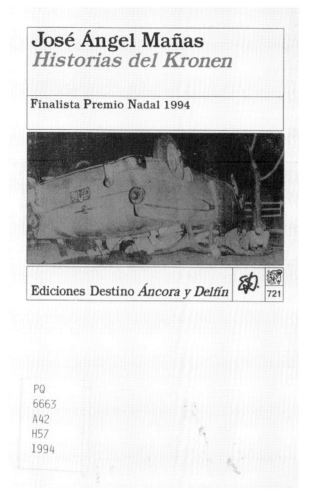

José Ángel Mañas
*Historias del Kronen*

Finalista Premio Nadal 1994

Ediciones Destino *Áncora y Delfín*    721

*Cover for Mañas's first novel (Stories from the Kronen), about the sex-and drug-filled life of a group of college-age friends at their favorite Madrid bar, named for a beer (Joyner Library, East Carolina University)*

novel its name. During his daring motorcycle forays through Madrid's traffic jams and urban chaos, David's thoughts blend with those of the other characters in a collective stream of consciousness, in which failure, violence, frustration, and love or the lack of it make up the emotional scaffolding. The atmosphere of alcohol and cocaine consumption, sporadic sexual encounters, and jarring noise is also present in this novel.

There is an autobiographical element in this story, since Mañas himself also belonged to a rock band whose members tried to model themselves after the Ramones, an American punk group. In 1998 Mañas published an apologetic article about punk music, "Literatura y punk" (Literature and Punk), in the magazine *Ajoblanco*. The article condenses some of the poetics of his own writing, since he states that in order to understand contemporary music or literature, one must not focus on the precision of the exe-

cution but instead try to comprehend the level of expressiveness reached in the performance. He cites as an example that when one congratulates a kindergartner for a picture he or she has drawn, one does not praise the quality of the artistic technique but rather the expressiveness achieved by the child.

In 1996 Mañas published the novel *Soy un escritor frustrado* (I am a Frustrated Writer), an academic satire he had written at twenty-two, while a student at the Universidad Autónoma of Madrid. *Soy un escritor frustrado* is a straightforward story narrated in a conventional manner. A middle-aged alcoholic university professor, "J," longs for social prominence and success as a writer. J aims to be a famous author in order to acquire the notoriety he cannot achieve with his scholarly work, but he has never been able to fulfill this dream. The opportunity arises when a student, Marian, asks him to review her fiction manuscript before sending it to the publisher. Impressed by the young woman's writing, he decides to appropriate her book and publish it under his own name. The fear of getting caught becomes obsessive to the point of his kidnapping Marian. While he holds her captive, he discovers that she had a copy of the manuscript in her mother's apartment. A new wave of panic leads the professor to set fire to the apartment, with Marian's mother inside. During the year that he keeps Marian prisoner, J publishes her novel, divorces his wife, and starts a relationship with the wife of his best friend, Mozart, also a professor at the same university and a relatively successful writer. Finally, J realizes that he is in love with Marian. By that time, however, she has refused to eat for several days, and she dies. All these plots come to a resolution when the police appear shortly after the girl's death and arrest J. Only after Marian's demise and after being caught by the police does J find the inspiration to write his own novel–the one the reader now holds. *Soy un escritor frustrado* sent the message to the academic milieu that critics are frustrated writers ready to obliterate young authors with their censorship while in fact they thirst for the spontaneity and success of those authors.

In 1998 *Mensaka* was made into a movie directed by Salvador García Ruíz. The script, by Luis Marías, received a Goya Award for best adapted screenplay in 1999. Unlike the cinema adaptation of *Historias del Kronen,* that of *Mensaka* is faithful to the crudeness of its literary source.

*Ciudad rayada* (1998, Scratched City) is Mañas's fourth novel. It is another generational chronicle set in Madrid's nightlife. The senior citizens' ritual of *salir de copas* (going out for an evening drink) has been replaced in the juvenile world of Mañas by the contemporary practice of *ir de marcha* (going on the move). *Ir de marcha* refers mainly to the nocturnal activity of wandering from one bar to another, "nightclubbing," or just checking out the action on the street. *Ciudad rayada* opens on an ironic note of explicit self-criticism. Mañas himself appears as a secondary character in the night scene and is presented as having shady connections to the underworld of drug dealing and violence, "puesto hasta la muelas y queriendo pillar una pipa" (high as a kite and wanting to find a gun). Furthermore, Kaiser, the protagonist and narrator, dismisses Mañas's writing style as minimalist and uninventive: "para escribir como él, casi cualquiera" (almost anyone can write like him). Kaiser adds that "casi todo lo de su última novela es verdad" (almost everything in his last novel is true). The underworld of drugs is an ever-present reality. Seventeen-year-old Kaiser earns a living by dealing drugs and lacks any other goals. He is a high-school dropout ignored by his parents, and his only emotional support comes from his teenage girlfriend, Tula. Kaiser's modus vivendi is altered when Gonzalo, the son of a prominent businessman, enters the drug circuit Kaiser monopolizes. Violence soon erupts and reaches a climax when Kaiser shoots and kills Gonzalo. The accelerating pace of the novel, marked by chase scenes, betrayals, and fear, is only tempered by the presence of the police. Spain's ineffectual attempts to control a drug world that has become a part of society makes the nightlife in Madrid a realistic setting for such psycho-thriller situations.

The atmosphere is similar to the one found in Mañas's previous novels, but here the innovation lies in the writing style. The novel is written in a peculiar way: neologisms flow in a stream of verbal invention. The words are inspired by rock lyrics and the slang of motorcyclists, youth, the alcohol and drug culture, gypsies, and the police. The sum of these complex elements is simple: the life of young people is a spiral of banality, a meaningless existence with crime always lurking beyond the edge. The parents remain in the background, noticeably absent, too busy to listen and to care for their children. They feel that the houses and the vacations they provide their offspring should be enough, but they are not. The novel points a finger at contemporary Spanish society, with its accepted ways of behavior seen as the culprit.

A striking characteristic of the novel is Mañas's innovative use of spelling. Hundreds of words are deliberately misspelled; for example, *novela* is spelled *nobela* to differentiate it from the usual word and to shock the reader. The text reminds the audience of the quick cuts and cryptic messages of graffiti. Mañas challenges the conventions of good writing, but he does it so skillfully that readers have no difficulty understanding what is meant. *Ciudad rayada* can also be described as almost a graphic novel, similar to a comic book. Sometimes the page seems a conjunction of image and text, as in comics, and readers are forced to follow the text in an unconventional way. They must read it to themselves and also view the text as placed on a surface, as an image, an advertisement, or gratuitous scratches on a wall.

The title of the novel is difficult to translate. On the one hand, it evokes the unsettling noises of the night that sometimes recall the sound of a scratched record. On the other hand, it refers to the lines *(rayas)* of cocaine consumed in discotheques by this generation of young people. The characters always make the wrong choices, and the reader feels a sense of unease represented by the sound of a broken record. The record goes on and on: money, drugs, sex, alcohol, more money, more drugs, more sex, more alcohol. Humanity, love, and common sense have all dissipated in the night of the city, and the next day brings not the song of birds but the same record playing over again and again.

The attention given to the superficial in the last two decades by Spanish young people in particular, evident in the interest in fashion trends and bodily appearance, is also visible in *Ciudad rayada*. The way these young people speak, their repetition of words, and the way they pronounce and write them reveal an interest in the unconventional. It seems that the language they have inherited is insufficient to express their experiences. The characters in the novel are disdainful of common sense and of thinking in general. Their lives are dominated by sensory experiences, ranging from the look of clothes seen in advertisements to the mind-clogging effects of alcohol and drugs. Thus, the reading of this ultimately graphic novel forces the audience to experience the superficiality of the text, the sensory otherness expressed on the page.

*Ciudad rayada* was intended to join *Historias del Kronen* and *Mensaka* as a trilogy about the life of young people in Madrid. To the readers' surprise, another novel soon appeared, *Sonko95: Autorretrato con negro de fondo* (1999; Sonko95: Self-Portrait with Dark Background). The blurb on the back cover stated that this novel was the last part of a tetralogy. Thus, the trilogy was expanded, probably for marketing reasons. Critics again reacted with indifference, and the usual or general readers were even less enthusiastic because the theme was yet another variation on the ones that had made the author renowned. Mañas considers *Sonko95* his most autobiographical novel. Like the protagonist, Mañas himself also opened a bar with some friends and closed it later. This fact explains the subtitle of the novel.

The novel, narrated in the first person, has a double plot. In the odd-numbered chapters a successful writer—the literary version of Mañas himself—lends money to his friends to help them solve the financial problems at Sonko, a disco bar in a central Madrid neighborhood known as Alonso Martínez. The bar is the protagonist, since the characters base their existence on their relationship with this establishment. The even-numbered chapters are a crime novel written by the narrator of the odd-num-

José Angel
Mañas:
Mensaka

PQ
6663
.A42
M46
1997.

destinolibro
406

*Cover for Mañas's 1995 novel (Motorcycle Messenger), in which three friends survive on menial day jobs while trying to get their rock band a contract with a record company (Z. Smith Reynolds Library, Wake Forest University)*

bered chapters and centered on two police detectives, Julián Pacheco and Nacho Duarte, who are investigating the death of a movie producer. The novel has a visual style, full of dialogue and limited descriptions. Mañas announced on the back cover of *Sonko 95* that the novel closes a cycle in his literary career and opens a new one devoted to the crime novel, a genre to which he has always been attracted as a writer.

In 1999 Mañas moved to Toulouse, France, to devote himself to writing far away from the distractions of popularity and from the setting that gave him his start and was the source of his themes. Most biographical notes reveal that he does not enjoy publicity; rather, he defends his privacy and writing space. He is reportedly searching for a new style and other themes. In the meantime, he married and had a son.

Contrary to Mañas's previous affirmations, his next novel, *Mundo burbuja* (2001, Bubble World), does not fit into the crime-novel genre. Instead, the plot revolves around the experiences of a young Erasmus student at the Universities of Sussex and Grenoble. Besides returning to some of his basic themes, Mañas tries to find new formulas by resorting to conventional literary procedures, among them references to the nineteenth-century novel (including those by Gustave Flaubert, Stendhal, and Marcel Proust) and digressions about literature. This seemingly paradoxical turn seems aimed at showing that, despite having based the plots of his early novels on trivial topics such as sex, drugs, and alcohol, the author also can handle cultured literary registers. However, this shift adds little to the novel. The narrator, the characters, and even the author himself appear to have similar opinions and the same voice; thus, the world of fiction is diluted. Although this novel seems to have been intended as an attempt to open up a new fictional territory, it has failed to attract many readers and has not received any critical attention so far.

In March 2005 Mañas, who had recently moved back to Spain from France, published *El caso Karen,* a crime novel in which Pacheco and Duarte investigate the death of a famous female writer. The detectives interview a wide array of the victim's friends and acquaintances, including an editor, a graduate student, a movie director, and a fellow writer, and travel through marginal areas of Madrid inhabited by alcoholics, drug addicts, and prostitutes.

The general conduct exhibited by the characters in Mañas's novels—the Spanish youth of the 1990s—began as a rebellion against their parents, the baby-boom generation. Ultimately, this behavior is turning out to be a search for the sources of authority, a search for values that can guide one's life. The radical pursuit portrayed in Mañas's tetralogy leads to a wasteland, because the characters find no answers to their questions. In any case, the Spanish middle-class youth of the 1990s have had a mirror set in front of them and a chance to see if the image fits. Meanwhile, their parents and the critics look on disapprovingly. In the final analysis, the success of the early novels of José Ángel Mañas can be understood within the context of the need new generations have of finding their own identity, of relating to a set of cultural referents more attuned to their times, and of discovering a worldview closer to their daily lives. One of Mañas's undisputed achievements has been his ability to bring literature to younger generations whose cultural diet has been based almost exclusively on new media, including fan magazines and other forms that are quite foreign to the world of traditional writing. Because of the enormous success of Mañas's first works, *Historias del Kronen* is now one of the texts employed for the teaching of literature at the high-school level. Mañas accurately reflects the nihilism and disenchantment of the Spain of the 1990s, which is the mind-set that settled into the country after the Madrid euphoria of *la movida*. No matter what direction Mañas takes as a writer, his literary production already constitutes a milestone in the Spanish narrative of the end of the twentieth century.

## References:

Athena Alchazidu, "Generación X: Una modalidad finisecular de tremendismo," *Etudes Romanes de Brno,* 32, no. 23 (2002): 99–108;

Isolina Ballesteros, "Juventudes problemáticas en el cine de los 80 y de los 90: Comportamientos generales y globales en la era de la indiferencia," in her *Cine (Ins)urgente* (Madrid: Fundamentos, 2001), pp. 233–269;

Tomás Calvo Buezas, *Valores en los jóvenes españoles, portugueses, latinoamericanos* (Madrid: Libertarias, 1997);

Pilar Capanaga, "La creación léxica en *Historias del Kronen*," in *Lo Spagnolo d' Oggi: Forme della Comunicazione* (Rome: Bulzoni, 1995), pp. 49–59;

Miguel Ángel del Arco, "Generación del Kronen," *Tiempo,* 15 May 1995, pp. 10–17;

Toni Dorca, "Joven narrativa en la España de los 90: La generación X," *Revista de Estudios Hispánicos,* 31 (1997): 309–324;

Sally Faulkner, "*Historias del Kronen:* Violence in Abstract Space," in her *Literary Adaptations in Spanish Cinema* (Rochester, N.Y.: Tamesis, 2004), pp. 67–72;

Ángel Fernández-Santos, "*Historias del Kronen:* Una película exemplar," *El País,* 30 April 1995;

Santiago Fouz-Hernández, "Generation X? Spanish Urban Youth Culture at the End of the Century in Mañas's/Amendáriz's *Historias del Kronen,*" *Romance Studies,* 18, no. 1 (2000): 83–98;

Germán Gullón, "¿Cómo se lee una novela de la última generación (apartado x)?" *Ínsula,* 605 (1997): 13–15;

Gullón, "El miedo al presente como materia novelable," *Ínsula,* 634 (1999): 15–17;

Gullón, "La novela multimediática: *Ciudad rayada,* de José Ángel Mañas," *Ínsula,* 625–626 (1999): 33–34;

Dieter Ingenschay, "José Ángel Mañas, 'Historias del Kronen': La novela, la película y la estética desesperada de la posmovida," in *La dulce mentira de la ficción,* volume 2: *Ensayos sobre la literatura española actual,* edited by Hans Felten, Agustín Valcárcel, and David Nelting, Abhandlungen zur Sprache und Literatur, no. 114 (Bonn: Romanistischer Verlag, 1998), pp. 151–166;

Alberto Madroña Fernández, "Narradores españoles de la última década: Maestre y Mañas. Diferentes caminos, conclusiones semejantes," *Moderna Sprak,* 97, no. 1 (2003): 84–89;

Cristina Moreiras Menor, "Realismo y origen de la violencia en *Historias del Kronen,*" in her *Cultura herida* (Madrid: Libertarias, 2002), pp. 214–230;

Guillermo Ortiz, "José Ángel Mañas: Un juguete roto," *Babab,* no. 21 (September 2003) <http://www.babab.com/no21/manas.php>;

Jesús Palacios, "*Historias del Kronen:* Una especie de película filogay de los 70," *Fotogramas,* no. 1819 (May 1995);

Maria T. Pao, "Sex, Drugs, and Rock & Roll: *Historias del Kronen* as Blank Fiction," *Anales de la Literatura Española Contemporánea,* 27, no. 2 (2002): 245–260;

José Ribas, "José Ángel Mañas," *Ajoblanco* (March 1994): 31–35;

Anthony Robb, "La problemática de la generación X en *Historias del Kronen* de Mañas: La nueva narrativa española llevada a la pantalla," *Annual of Foreign Films and Literature,* 5 (1999): 113–121;

María Pilar Rodríguez, "Nihilism and Simulacrum: The Two *Historias del Kronen,*" in *Cinematic and Literary Representations of Spanish and Latin American Themes,* edited by Nora Glickman and Alejandro Varderi (forthcoming);

E. Rodríguez Marchante, "*Historias del Kronen* o el viaje precipitado a ninguna parte," *ABC* (28 April 1995);

Santos Sanz Villanueva, "Cambio de rumbo en el Nadal," *Suplemento Semanal de Diario 16,* 19 February 1994, p. 2;

Carmen de Urioste, "Cultura punk: La 'Tetralogía Kronen' de José Ángel Mañas o el arte de hacer ruido," *Ciberletras* (October 2004) <http://www.lehman.cuny.edu/faculty/guinazu/ciberletras/v11/urioste.html>;

Urioste, "La narrativa española de los noventa: ¿Existe una generación X?" *Letras Peninsulares,* 10.2–10.3 (1997–1998): 455–476;

Manuel Vázquez Montalbán, "La generación x, y, z," *El País,* 2 September 1995, p. 30;

Roger Wolfe, "Descenso a los infiernos de las envidias literarias," *El Mundo,* 12 October 1996, p. 32.

# Javier Marías

*(20 September 1951 –    )*

Alexis Grohmann
*University of Edinburgh*

BOOKS: *Los dominios del lobo* (Barcelona: Edhasa, 1971; revised and enlarged edition, Barcelona: Anagrama, 1987; enlarged edition, Madrid: Alfaguara, 1999);

*Travesía del horizonte* (Barcelona: La Gaya Ciencia, 1972 [i.e., 1973]);

*Tres cuentos didácticos,* by Marías, Félix de Azúa, and Vicente Molina-Foix (Barcelona: La Gaya Ciencia, 1975);

*El monarca del tiempo* (Madrid: Alfaguara, 1978; enlarged edition, Barcelona: Reino de Redonda, 2003);

*El siglo* (Barcelona: Seix Barral, 1983; revised and enlarged edition, Barcelona: Anagrama, 1995; enlarged edition, Madrid: Alfaguara, 2000);

*El hombre sentimental* (Barcelona: Anagrama, 1986; enlarged edition, Madrid: Alfaguara, 1999); translated by Margaret Jull Costa as *The Man of Feeling* (London: Harvill, 2003; New York: New Directions, 2003);

*Todas las almas* (Barcelona: Anagrama, 1989); translated by Costa as *All Souls* (London: Harvill, 1992; New York: New Directions, 2000);

*Mientras ellas duermen* (Barcelona: Anagrama, 1990; enlarged edition, Madrid: Alfaguara, 2000);

*Pasiones pasadas* (Barcelona: Anagrama, 1991);

*Corazón tan blanco* (Barcelona: Anagrama, 1992); translated by Costa as *A Heart So White* (London: Harvill, 1995; New York: New Directions, 2000);

*Vidas escritas* (Madrid: Siruela, 1992; enlarged edition, Madrid: Alfaguara, 2000); translated by Costa as *Written Lives* (New York: New Directions, 2006);

*Literatura y fantasma* (Madrid: Siruela, 1993; enlarged edition, Madrid: Alfaguara, 2001);

*Mañana en la batalla piensa en mí* (Barcelona: Anagrama, 1994); translated by Costa as *Tomorrow in the Battle Think on Me* (London: Harvill, 1996; New York: Harcourt Brace, 1997);

*Vida del fantasma: Entusiasmos, bromas, reminiscencias y cañones recortados* (Madrid: El País/Aguilar, 1995);

*Cuando fui mortal* (Madrid: Alfaguara, 1996); translated by Costa as *When I Was Mortal: Short Stories* (Lon-

*Javier Marías (photograph by Jerry Bauer; from the dust jacket for* Tomorrow in the Battle Think on Me, *1997; Richland County Public Library)*

don: Harvill, 1999; New York: New Directions, 2000);

*El hombre que parecía no querer nada,* edited by Elide Pittarello (Madrid: Espasa-Calpe, 1996);

*Mano de sombra* (Madrid: Alfaguara, 1997);

*Si yo amaneciera otra vez,* by Marías and Manuel Rodríguez Rivero (Madrid: Alfaguara, 1997)–includes Marías's translation of William Faulkner, *A Green Bough;*

*Miramientos* (Madrid: Alfaguara, 1997);

*Negra espalda del tiempo* (Madrid: Alfaguara, 1998); translated by Esther Allen as *Dark Back of Time* (New

York: New Directions, 2001; London: Chatto & Windus, 2003);

*Mala índole* (Barcelona: Plaza & Janés, 1998);

*Seré amado cuando falte* (Madrid: Alfaguara, 1999);

*Desde que te vi morir: Vladimir Nabokov, una superstición* (Madrid: Alfaguara, 1999);

*Salvajes y sentimentales: Letras de fútbol* (Madrid: Aguilar, 2000);

*A veces un caballero* (Madrid: Alfaguara, 2001);

*Vida del fantasma: Cinco años más tenue* (Madrid: Alfaguara, 2001);

*Tu rostro mañana,* 2 volumes (Madrid: Alfaguara, 2002, 2004)–comprises volume 1, *Fiebre y lanza;* and volume 2, *Bailo y sueño;* volume 1 translated by Costa as *Your Face Tomorrow: Fever and Spear* (London: Chatto & Windus, 2005; New York: New Directions, 2005);

*Harán de mí un criminal* (Madrid: Alfaguara, 2003).

RECORDING: *No más amores,* read by Marías, Madrid, Alfaguara Audio, 1997.

OTHER: *Cuentos únicos,* edited by Marías, translated by Marías and Alejandro García Reyes (Madrid: Siruela, 1989; enlarged edition, edited by Marías, translated by Marías, García Reyes, and Antonio Iriarte, Barcelona: Reino de Redonda, 2004).

TRANSLATIONS: Thomas Hardy, *El brazo marchito y otros relatos* (Madrid: Alianza, 1974);

Laurence Sterne, *La vida y las opiniónes del caballero Tristram Shandy; Los sermónes de Mr. Yorick* (Madrid: Alfaguara, 1978);

Edith Holden, *La felicidad de vivir con la naturaleza: El diario de Edith Holden* (Barcelona: Blume, 1979);

Robert Louis Stevenson, *De vuelta del mar* (Madrid: Hiperión, 1980);

Joseph Conrad, *El espejo del mar: Recuerdos e impresiones* (Madrid: Hiperión, 1981);

Isak Dinesen, *Ehrengard* (Barcelona: Bruguera, 1984);

William Butler Yeats, *El crepúsculo celta* (Madrid: Alfaguara, 1985);

Sir Thomas Browne, *Religio Medici; Hydriotaphia; De los sueños* (Madrid: Alfaguara, 1986);

John Ashbery, *Autorretrato en espejo convexo* (Madrid: Visor, 1990);

W. H. Auden, *Un poema no escrito* (Madrid: Pre-Textos, 1996);

Wallace Stevens, *Notas para un ficción suprema* (Madrid: Pre-Textos, 1996).

Few Spanish writers of the twentieth and twenty-first centuries can rival the national and international critical recognition that has distinguished Javier Marías.

A man of letters, Marías is a translator, newspaper columnist, essayist, and publisher, although, first and foremost, he is a novelist and, to a lesser extent, a short-story writer. He has made a considerable contribution to Spanish and European literature and has become one of Spain's most original and eloquent voices. His narrative work has undergone a singular evolution, and he has forged a distinct style of his own.

Javier Marías Franco was born on 20 September 1951 in Madrid, in the district of Chamberí, where he grew up and resided on and off until 1995. He is the fourth of five sons of Dolores Franco Manera and Julián Marías Aguilera. His father, a well-known philosopher, was imprisoned during General Francisco Franco's dictatorship because of his Republican affiliations during the Spanish Civil War, and he suffered further reprisals, as he was not permitted to teach at Spanish universities for a long time. As a result, he regularly traveled to the United States to undertake teaching at various universities, sometimes accompanied by his family. Thus, Javier spent the first year of his life in Massachusetts, where his father was teaching at Wellesley College, and at the age of four he spent another five months in New Haven when his father worked at Yale.

Marías was educated in Madrid at the Colegio Estudio and at home, a house abounding in books and frequented by many intellectuals as well as by foreign students to whom his parents gave private tuition. In 1968 he enrolled for an arts degree at the Universidad de Complutense in Madrid. During that period he began translating and co-authoring scripts for his uncle and his cousin, the moviemakers Jesús and Ricardo Franco, as well as working as a production assistant and appearing as an extra in some of their pictures. Marías has always demonstrated a predilection for the cinema, on which subject he has written extensively. His first novel, *Los dominios del lobo* (1971; The Domains of the Wolf), bears witness to this interest.

Marías explains in the preface to the 1987 revised edition of *Los dominios del lobo* that after completing his first year at the university he decided to write a novel set in the United States–but not the real United States: his setting and primary subject matter was to be the country as reflected in American movies of the 1930s, 1940s, and 1950s. Having already written the initial pages, Marías went in July 1969 to Paris, where Henri Langlois's Cinémathèque française and several others were screening American movies of that era. The Cinémathèque française educated an entire generation of motion-picture directors and theorists, such as François Truffaut, Jean-Luc Godard, and Eric Rohmer, who became the main representatives of French New Wave cinema after 1959. Marías immersed himself in this cinematic culture, and, during the month and a half he

*Dust jacket for the English translation (2003) of Marías's 1986 novel,*
El hombre sentimental, *in which an opera star dreams
about the affair he had with a banker's wife
(Richland County Public Library)*

spent at Jesús Franco's apartment, he watched no fewer than eighty-five movies and wrote the bulk of his first novel.

*Los dominios del lobo* both parodies and pays homage to Hollywood comedies, melodramas, and particularly gangster and film noir movies of the three decades. The action of the novel is made up of wittily recounted and entertaining tales of gangster rivalry, femmes fatales, racketeering, corruption, double-crossing, blackmail and murder, prisoners and hidden treasures, greed and sex, and friendship and love. The story lines are set from 1861 to 1962, and, although time unfolds chronologically within each of the eleven episodes that make up the novel, the sequence of episodes follows no chronological or other order. Each episode is characterized by an internal temporal and spatial unity and can be read as a self-contained short story independent of the others. The episodes are loosely and subtly interrelated through the reappearance of mostly secondary characters, and these casual connections emphasize the relatively fragmentary nature of the novel as well as the role of chance in shaping the various story lines, pointing to a latent interconnectedness underlying the lives of the characters.

The third-person, semiomniscient narration of the stories incorporates the points of view of the various protagonists. The novel is replete with dialogue and devoid of any moral assessment of the relative violence and cruelty of the action and the crimes committed, which go unpunished; the effects are playful and comic rather than serious or moralizing. The settings of the adventures span the entire United States of America–from New York to San Francisco and Los Angeles, from Minnesota and Illinois to Louisiana, Mississippi, and Alabama–and the characters are exclusively North American.

After his return from Paris and during his second academic year (1969–1970), Marías, who did not have any intention of publishing *Los dominios del lobo,* let friends read it and undertook revisions as a result of their comments. Eventually the manuscript was passed on to Juan Benet, the writer and engineer who had become an important literary figure at that time, offering young writers a way out of a seeming impasse in Spanish literature through the publication of *Volverás a Región* (1967, You Will Return to Región) and his rejection of the social realism that had dominated much Spanish literature after the Spanish Civil War. Marías joined Benet's circle of friends, which included Juan García Hortelano, Eduardo Chamorro, Antonio Martínez Sarrión, Félix de Azúa, and Vicente Molina-Foix. Benet had a profound impact on Marías on both a literary and personal level, becoming a mentor and a close friend; largely through his efforts, *Los dominios del lobo* was published in 1971, with a dedication to Benet and Molina-Foix, who had suggested the title.

In July 1971 Marías began writing his second novel, *Travesía del horizonte* (Crossing of the Horizon), which was published in 1973, although the year of publication that is given is 1972. It included a text in English in Benet's handwriting reproduced on the endpaper. Like his first novel, Marías's second is a narrative exclusively set abroad, wholly populated by non-Spanish characters, and imitative of non-Spanish narratives. Unlike his first novel, however, the models are entirely literary: Henry James, Joseph Conrad, and, to a lesser extent, Arthur Conan Doyle. Given that Conrad and James in particular were two of the most significant innovators of the modern novel, had an acute awareness of formal aspects of writing, and were highly accomplished stylists, *Travesía del horizonte* has a much more elaborate narrative structure than *Los dominios del lobo.* It is stylistically far more intricate (for example, the use of adjectives is now extensive, and the sentences are substantially longer and include expanding subordinate clauses, elements that became permanent features of Marías's style) and has a significantly richer language. It echoes the Edwardian novelists' work to the extent that one can speak of not only the foreignness of Marías's subject matter but also that of his prose, as Pere Gimferrer argued in a review in *Destino* (24 February 1973). The imitative quality of *Travesía del horizonte* is more pronounced than that of his first work, as the parody becomes more self-conscious. As a result, his second novel is more self-reflective than the first, including a commentary on its own status as fiction and on the process of writing and reception of fiction in general.

*Travesía del horizonte* is the story of the reading of a manuscript, "La travesía del horizonte," the title of which is identical to that of Marías's novel but for the definite article, and the events surrounding the reading, including a secret enveloping the author of the text. The manuscript tells of a novelist who embarks on a voyage to the South Pole because he is intrigued by, and gradually becomes obsessed with, a mysterious incident involving another passenger. This story includes further smaller-scale narratives. The adventure that the passengers seek eludes them, as their journey is cut short after only a cruise around the Mediterranean Sea. So, on the one hand, Marías's second novel is an adventure novel, as well as a parodic unmasking of the fallacy of adventure stories. On the other hand, as the secrets of both main narratives, although discovered by the protagonists, are not revealed to the reader, the narratives remain ambiguous. The importance of the creation of uncertainty and its value for storytelling, as well as the impossibility of knowing things or truth for certain, are formal and thematic elements that became permanent features of Marías's narratives.

As Marías has acknowledged in the preface to the 1987 edition of *Los dominios del lobo* and in an essay, "Desde una novela no necesariamente castiza" (From a Novel Not Necessarily Spanish), included in *Literatura y fantasma* (1993, Literature and Ghost), his literary beginnings are characterized by a conscious attempt at a literary formation through imitation; like many Spanish writers of his generation, such as the *novísimos* poets (so called because of the inclusion of their work in José María Castellet's 1970 anthology, *Nueve novísimos poetas españoles* [Nine Original Spanish Poets]), a group that included some of the writers of Benet's circle, Marías opted for imitative writing as a first step in his artistic development. Both of his first two novels also constitute his rejection of the realism that had dominated Spanish literature up to that point. Through imitation of foreign models and their concomitant non-Spanishness or cosmopolitanism, Marías and many of the *novísimos*

intended to break with Spanish literary tradition more generally and renounce Spain as a theme and the presence of any form of Spanishness whatsoever in literature.

This break was a conscious one, because, as Marías has explained on more than one occasion, he and many of his contemporaries felt (somewhat unjustly, as he has since recognized) that virtually the entire Spanish novelistic tradition was uninteresting because it was dominated by what they saw as a singularly unattractive realism; they were also satiated by Spain as a theme in literature. Furthermore, they considered many of their literary elders to be politically and ideologically unsympathetic figures. Having been born after the end of the Spanish Civil War in 1939, Marías and his contemporaries had had no direct contact with a war that had influenced previous generations of writers, nor had they known a Spain other than Franco's Spain. They thus equated Spain and Spanishness with Francoism, so that their rebellion against Franco entailed an indissociable repudiation of Spain and any element of Spanishness through a turn to its opposite in the form of extreme cosmopolitanism and foreignness—elements that characterize Marías's first two novels.

Marías quickly became aware, however, that he could not continue along this path; as he explains in "Desde una novela no necesariamente castiza":

> Pero era evidente que aquella actitud "extranjerizante a ultranza" no podía durar eternamente. Yo deseaba que en España fuera posible—y no una extravagancia—escribir una novela no necesariamente castiza, pero tampoco tenía particular empeño en cultivar una novela obligadamente extraterritorial. Después de la publicación de mi segundo libro, de estructura y estilo más complejos que el primero, vi con claridad que si seguía única y exclusivamente por ese camino paródico, corría el riesgo de convertirme en una especie de falso cosmopolita a lo Paul Morand. . . . Sin embargo, me había alejado tanto de mi propia carne, como aquel insigne crítico había venido a llamar a mi realidad, que no podía salvar las distancias rápidamente y de un salto. Por lo demás debo confesar . . . que a mis veintitrés años, aún en pleno período de formación, no tenía especial urgencia por decir ni contar nada en particular.

> (But it was evident that this "extreme foreign-tending" attitude could not last forever. I wanted it to be possible—and not extravagant—to write a not necessarily Spanish novel in Spain, but, equally, I was not intent on cultivating a compulsorily extraterritorial novel. After the publication of my second book, which was of a more complex style and structure than the first, it became very clear to me that if I followed this parodic course exclusively, I was running the risk of becoming a type of false cosmopolitan *à la* Paul Morand. . . . But I

Cover for the English translation (1992) of Marías's autobiographical novel, Todas las almas (1989), about a teacher of Spanish language and literature at Oxford (Richland County Public Library)

had distanced myself to such an extent from my own flesh, as that distinguished critic had called my reality, that I could not bridge the gap quickly and in one attempt. Moreover, I have to admit . . . that at the age of twenty-three and still in the process of becoming a writer I felt no great urgency to say or narrate anything in particular.)

Marías completed his university degree in 1973 with a specialization in English studies. In 1974 he moved to Barcelona, where he began working as a literary consultant for the Alfaguara publishing house, and in 1977 he began writing for newspapers and other periodicals. During the years between the publication of his second and third novels, he dedicated much of his time to the translation of mainly English literature into Spanish, a practice he saw as an intrinsic and significant part of his literary apprenticeship. The authors whose work he has translated have been writers from whom he wanted to learn. In 1974 he published a volume of translations of short stories by the English poet and novelist Thomas Hardy, and in October 1978 his translation of Laurence Sterne's novel *The Life and Opinions of Tristram Shandy, Gentleman* (1760–1767) appeared; Marías won the Spanish National Prize for Translation for the Sterne work a year later. His next original novel, *El monarca del tiempo* (The Monarch of Time), was also published in October 1978. By that time he had returned to Madrid and moved in with his father, following the death of his mother on 24 December 1977.

*El monarca del tiempo* is not a novel in a strict sense: it consists of five sections, three of which are short stories, one an essay, and one a short play dominated by extensive and subjective stage directions. The jacket flap of the first edition of *El monarca del tiempo* refers to it simply as a book rather than attaching a genre label. Even though in the preface to the 2003 enlarged edition he says he is indifferent to what the work is perceived to be, Marías has been referring to it as a novel for two reasons: first, because the novel is a genre that has come to absorb many other genres; and second, because the various parts of *El monarca del tiempo* are united in their exploration of truth and its relationship to the present. The essay section, "Fragmento y enigma y espantoso azar" (Fragment and Enigma and Frightening Chance), explicitly analyzes this relationship through a detailed examination of the end of act 3 of William Shakespeare's play *Julius Caesar* (1599) and the conventional nature of truth. The other four pieces enact this theme and also, as Elide Pittarello points out, introduce several passive and irresolute characters with febrile imaginations, who reappear in subsequent novels. In *El monarca del tiempo* one can also recognize a conjectural and nihilistic voice that contemplates known, possible, and unknown worlds. As Pittarello has argued, this voice, already present to some extent in *Travesía del horizonte* but graver and more accentuated here, became a hallmark of Marías's later narratives. *El monarca del tiempo* is a first step toward bridging the gap between the writer and his reality, because it is not as foreign a work as his previous ones: it is set nowhere in particular, neither abroad nor in Spain; its characters are of no specific nationality; and it is not overtly parodic, imitative, or frivolous, although it is still playful, albeit in a much more solemn tone.

In 1979 Marías began his collaboration with the newspaper *El País*, and he published translations of poems by Robert Louis Stevenson in 1980 and of Joseph Conrad's 1906 autobiographical narrative, *The Mirror of the Sea*, in 1981. As Marías has acknowledged, the translation of the latter and also of three of Sir Thomas

Browne's texts had a significant bearing on the style of his next novel, *El siglo* (1983, The Century). *El siglo* consists of nine chapters alternating between the first and third person and reintroduces the reader to many of the characters of *El monarca del tiempo*. The four even-numbered chapters, in third-person omniscient narration, tell the story of Casaldáliga from his birth in 1900 up to the age of thirty-nine. He is a spineless and irresolute individual who, having been inculcated by his father with the need to find a clear and unmistakably individual destiny, unsuccessfully tries to become a martyr through marriage and then as a war hero, before succeeding in becoming an informer in 1939. The five odd-numbered chapters are narrated in the first person by the moribund Casaldáliga himself, who, as a wealthy retired judge, focuses mostly on his present circumstances and his encroaching death.

With this novel Marías advances further toward Spain as a subject: although the names of the characters are again ambiguous enough to be non-Spanish and there is no explicit mention of any Spanish place-names, there is little doubt that the setting of the novel is Spain and that the civil war referred to is the Spanish one. Casaldáliga becomes an informer in 1939, the year the Spanish Civil War ended. Marías thus approaches Spain and its history, albeit obliquely. Marías also moves closer to his biography, since it is a family matter that provides the source of inspiration for the novel: his father's denouncement to the authorities in 1939 and his imprisonment for his Republican affiliations. Nevertheless, *El siglo* is not simply the story of an informer, as the initial subject matter is transformed through the baroque style of the novel: the narrative voices, the diction, the choice of rhetorical figures and devices, and the form of the sentences become prominent.

In 1983 Marías was appointed to a three-year post as lecturer at the University of Oxford, where he gave classes on Spanish literature and translation. He took unpaid leave in the autumn term of 1984 to spend a semester lecturing on Miguel de Cervantes's *Don Quijote de la Mancha* (1605–1615) at Wellesley College, where his father had taught, and resigned from the post at Oxford on 30 September 1985. He continued to publish Spanish translations of English literature throughout the 1980s. For two years after leaving Oxford he spent considerable periods of time in Venice, where he completed a novel he had begun in Oxford, *El hombre sentimental* (1986; translated as *The Man of Feeling,* 2003). It earned the Premio Herralde de Novela and, after being translated into Italian, the Premio Internazionale Ennio Flaiano.

This novel is Marías's first to be set explicitly in Spain, although not all its characters are Spanish, and none of them is a resident of Madrid, where the action of the narrative unfolds. It is narrated by a tenor, El León de Nápoles (The Lion of Naples), who also appeared in the previous two works. The narration consists of the story of the tenor's dream, which is a precise replication of events he has lived: the initial stages and ill-fated consequences of a relationship that comes to an end when the woman in question, Natalia Manur, leaves the narrator the night he has his dream. Reality becomes indistinguishable from, and is conflated with, the dream and also contaminated by it, since it can no longer be an independent reference point, a pure and certain basis of narration, as the narrator cannot tell the two apart.

Furthermore, the narrator does not know how the story he is recounting will end. His act of narrating is as errant as the author's act of writing, thus reflecting Marías's creative process, as Alexis Grohmann has argued in *Coming into One's Own: The Novelistic Development of Javier Marías* (2002). As Marías has explained in an essay titled "Errar con brújula" (Erring with a Compass), included in *Literatura y fantasma,* he is not interested in knowing in advance what his narratives will be about nor how they will end when he sets out to write them:

> No sé lo que quiero escribir, ni adónde quiero llegar, ni tengo un proyecto narrativo que yo pueda enunciar antes ni después de que mis novelas existan, sino que ni siquiera sé, cuando empiezo una, de qué va a tratar, o lo que va a ocurrir en ella, o quiénes y cuántos serán sus personajes, no digamos cómo terminará. . . . Lo cierto es que todavía hoy sigo escribiendo sin mucho propósito y sin ningún objetivo del que pueda hablarse.
>
> (I do not know what I want to write, or what destination I would like to reach, nor do I have a narrative plan that I can articulate before or after my novels come into being, and I do not even know, when I begin a novel, what it is going to be about, or what will happen in it, or who and how many its characters will be, not to mention how it will end. . . . The fact is that today I still write rather aimlessly and without an objective worth talking about.)

This lack of interest in mapping his novels in advance extends to story line, form, and structure and constitutes Marías's decision, as he says in this essay, to position himself in a sphere of uncertainty while writing, which, in turn, permits him to digress and let his inventions take shape without premeditation. This cultivated uncertainty is reflected in virtually all of his narrators' preference for speculation, hypothesis, and conjecture.

In the second half of 1987 Marías returned to Madrid. In October of that year he began teaching the theory of translation at the Universidad de Complutense, continuing to do so until 1992. And in 1989

*Dust jacket for the British edition (1995) of the English translation of Marías's novel* Corazón tan blanco *(1992), in which the narrator tries to learn why his maternal aunt, who was his father's first wife, shot herself shortly after returning from her honeymoon (Richland County Public Library)*

Anagrama published *Todas las almas* (translated as *All Souls,* 1992), for which he was awarded the Premio Ciudad de Barcelona a year later.

The protagonist of *Todas las almas* is a nameless first-person narrator who, two and a half years after his return to Madrid, recounts the story of his sojourn of two academic years at the University of Oxford teaching Spanish language and literature. The narrator compares the elements making up his storytelling to a state of temporary disturbance, from which he recovers after his return to Madrid. Coupled with the narrator's superstitiousness, this disturbance is responsible for the digressive elements of the storytelling, and the narration is also the story of this disturbance. So, as in the previous novel, the creative process is enacted in the narrative.

There is, however, a difference between this novel and Marías's preceding ones: much of this novel is based on empirical reality. The author consciously incorporates experiences from his own time in Oxford. The narrator of the novel and Marías share other parallels, including an exacerbated associative capacity that determines their narratives. There are also several correspondences between characters in the novel and persons who exist or existed in reality, such as various members of the Sub-Faculty of Spanish of the University of Oxford. In addition, Marías introduces as a character the little-known English writer John Gawsworth.

Marías decided to lend this narrator his own voice—the one Marías uses in his nonfiction articles, essays, and letters to friends—rather than create a fictional one as he had done for all of his previous narrators. This voice becomes one of the distinguishing features of Marías's style: all of his narratives after *Todas las almas* are recounted by the same clearly recognizable voice and from the point of view of a male first-person protagonist who always approximates the figure of the author to some extent, making each of these narrators, in the words of Marías, "quien yo pude ser pero no fui" (he whom I could have been but was not).

The relationship between author and narrator in *Todas las almas* and between the narrative and reality is therefore shrouded in ambiguity. Various reviewers, including Juan Antonio Masoliver Ródenas in *La Vanguardia* (28 April 1989) and Jens Jessen in the *Frankfurter allgemeine Zeitung* (17 November 1992), read this novel as an autobiographical narrative; but although several elements are borrowed from empirical reality, they are imaginatively associated with purely fictional ones, creating a narrative of another nature. As Pittarello has argued: "El desafío de su escritura consiste justamente en someter cualquier material al mismo proceso de indeterminación que no permite reconocer la diferencia entre lo que podría ser ficticio y es verdadero o lo que podría ser verdadero y es ficticio" (Precisely the challenge his writing presents is to subject any material to the same process of uncertainty that does not allow one to identify the difference between what could be fictional but is real or what could be real but is fictional).

From this period onward Marías's interest in narrating his own and other people's lives, especially those of foreign writers, gradually increased. This interest is reflected in the biographical and autobiographical elements in his fiction and in his essays, articles, and weekly newspaper columns (since 1996), which have been collected in a series of volumes with titles that often are suggestive of the process of indetermination to which literature subjects reality: *Pasiones pasadas* (1991, Past Passions), *Vidas escritas* (1992; translated as *Written Lives,* 2006), *Vida del fantasma* (1995, Life of the Ghost),

*Mano de sombra* (1997, Hand of a Ghost), *Miramientos* (1997, Courtesies), *Seré amado cuando falte* (1999, I'll Be Loved When I'm Gone), *Salvajes y sentimentales* (2000, Savages and Sentimentals), *A veces un caballero* (2001, Sometimes a Gentleman), and *Harán de mí un criminal* (2003, They Will Make a Criminal of Me).

In 1990 Anagrama published Marías's first collection of short stories. Many of the tales in *Mientras ellas duermen* (1990, While They Sleep) are ghost stories, such as "La dimisión de Santiesteban" (The Resignation of Santiesteban), about a specter in the library of the British Council in Madrid. This story had first appeared in 1975 in a volume Marías had co-authored with Azúa and Molina-Foix, titled *Tres cuentos didácticos* (1975, Three Didactic Tales). The 2000 enlarged edition of *Mientras ellas duermen* also includes Marías's first published narrative, "La vida y la muerte de Marcelino Iturriaga" (The Life and the Death of Marcelino Iturriaga), which was written when the author was fourteen and which first appeared in a Barcelona daily in 1968. Ghosts also figure prominently in Marías's second collection of short fiction, *Cuando fui mortal* (1996; translated as *When I Was Mortal*, 1999), which also includes a story–"En el viaje de novios" (On Honeymoon)–that coincides to a great extent with a scene in *Corazón tan blanco* (1992; translated as *A Heart So White*, 1995), the novel that followed *Todas las almas*.

*Corazón tan blanco* established Marías as one of Spain's most noteworthy living authors. Not only did it earn him considerable critical recognition both in Spain and abroad, but it also became a popular success, most notably in Germany where, as in Spain, it remained among the leading best-selling works of fiction for almost a year. The novel also garnered three more literary prizes: the Spanish Premio de la Crítica, the French Prix l'Oeil et la Lettre, and the IMPAC International Dublin Literary Award.

*Corazón tan blanco* is set in Madrid, and all its main characters are Spanish. Nevertheless, the first-person narrator, Juan, who is an interpreter, travels frequently, and the novel is not set exclusively in Spain but also in Havana, New York, and Geneva. The first sentence plunges the reader into the key scene:

No he querido saber, pero he sabido que una de las niñas, cuando ya no era niña y no hacía mucho que había regresado de su viaje de bodas, entró en el cuarto de baño, se puso frente al espejo, se abrió la blusa, se quitó el sostén y se buscó el corazón con la punta de la pistola de su propio padre, que estaba en el comedor con parte de la familia y tres invitados.

(I did not want to know, but I have come to know that one of the girls, when she was no longer a girl and shortly after having returned from her honeymoon, went into the bathroom, stood in front of the mirror, unbuttoned her blouse, took off her bra and pointed her own father's gun at her heart, while her father was in the dining room with members of the family and three guests.)

The shot that was then fired unleashed the chain of events that affect Juan and make up the narrative. The woman who committed suicide, Teresa, was the first wife of Juan's father, and one of the questions this beginning introduces is the reason for this suicide, a question that remains unanswered until the penultimate chapter, when another death is revealed. The two deaths frame the narrative, and the mystery and secrecy surrounding the initial suicide and the father's past create an air of suspense and uncertainty that permeates the novel. The suicide also introduces the importance of chance in determining life and death (a recurrent theme in subsequent novels), as Juan's father only became his father when, after the suicide, he went on to marry Teresa's sister, Juan's mother.

Juan is a passive observer of life who is unwilling to delve into the past because he is apprehensive of the effects of knowledge and the power of words once uttered, which is a main theme of the novel; another main theme is the interconnectedness of past and present. Juan's apprehensiveness and his resistance to knowledge are linked to his premonitions and his malaise, which surface on his wedding day. He thus superstitiously–he, like all of Marías's narrators since *El hombre sentimental*, is superstitious–associates marriage with illness and death, and a sense of foreboding pervades the entire novel. This premonitory atmosphere is further accentuated by various patterns of repetitions and explicit and implicit references to Shakespeare's play *Macbeth* (circa 1606), which help to shape the themes of guilt, innocence, instigation, secrets, and the effects of knowledge. The title of the novel also comes from *Macbeth:* "My hands are of your colour; but I shame / To wear a heart so white."

Another Shakespeare play, *Richard III* (circa 1591–1592), and its 1955 cinematic adaptation starring Laurence Olivier are echoed in Marías's next novel and furnish its title: *Mañana en la batalla piensa en mí* (1994; translated as *Tomorrow in the Battle Think on Me,* 1996). It appeared the year after the death of Marías's friend Benet, a profound loss for him. *Mañana en la batalla piensa en mí* earned the Premio Fastenrath de la Real Academia Española, the Premio Internacional de Novela Rómulo Gallegos, the Premio Arzobispo Juan de San Clemente, the Prix Femina du Roman Etranger, and the Premio Mondello Città di Palermo.

The structure of *Mañana en la batalla piensa en mí* is, like that of *Corazón tan blanco,* circular: it opens with the

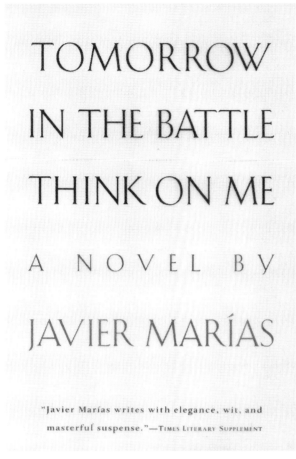

TOMORROW
IN THE BATTLE
THINK ON ME

A NOVEL BY

JAVIER MARÍAS

"Javier Marías writes with elegance, wit, and
masterful suspense."—TIMES LITERARY SUPPLEMENT

*Dust jacket for the U.S. edition (1997) of the English translation of
Marías's 1994 novel,* Mañana en la batalla piensa en mí, *which opens with a married woman suddenly dying in the
narrator's arms (Richland County Public Library)*

relation of one death and ends with another. As in the previous novel, the opening scene depicts a woman's mysterious death, and the circumstances surrounding the death have repercussions and create a web of unanswered questions that comes to constitute a secret interwoven into the life of the protagonist and revealed at the end of the narrative. Indeed, Marías's novels from *El hombre sentimental* to *Mañana en la batalla piensa en mí* all begin or end or both begin and end with the relation of one or more deaths, so death not only is explored thematically in Marías's narratives but also helps structure them and serves as a driving force, setting off events and posing questions. Moreover, the final scene of *Mañana en la batalla piensa en mí* is identical in its form to the penultimate scene of the previous novel, as the narrator, Víctor, listens to the revelation of a secret while he interpolates (in brackets) his own parenthetical, digressive thoughts, which are repetitions and syntheses of ones introduced earlier in the narrative. Víctor is, once again, a superstitious first-person narrator with a

conjectural and associative mind and a distinctive and recognizable voice. As a script- and ghostwriter he is a professional whose tools are words and who thus has an acute awareness of language and the effects of words.

Unlike the narrator of *Corazón tan blanco,* however, Víctor is not passive; he becomes implicated in, and haunted by, the sudden death of a woman, and he obsessively, yet errantly, pursues a series of unanswered questions raised by this death, while not revealing what he knows. Another difference between the two narratives is that *Mañana en la batalla piensa en mí* is the first of Marías's novels in which a Spanish city has a significant presence and role. Madrid not only provides the specific setting by way of all the particular streets and locations through which Víctor wanders, but it also appears as an insular, enchanted, and spectral place, and it is explored in detail, particularly as a city with a past. There are frequent references to Madrid's history, including the city under siege by Nationalist forces during the Spanish Civil War, and the past of the city becomes interrelated with Víctor's own past. The city becomes the spatial representation of a continuum linking past and present through urban spaces that contain traces of both collective (historical) and personal memory.

These interconnected urban and personal pasts come to form a web of ties with the present time of the narration. *Mañana en la batalla piensa en mí* highlights the interconnectedness of the past and present, as well as of the dead and the living, and it also shows how potential realities or unrealities are related to the actual world. As all of Marías's novels from *El siglo* onward, this novel includes abundant conjectural passages and scenes in which the narrator contemplates what could be and what could have been and how these potential realities and unrealities have effects and determine the world by constituting a latent reality, like the past, which forms an intricate part of life. Paraphrasing part of a verse from another of Shakespeare's plays, *The Tempest* (1611), Víctor in *Mañana en la batalla piensa en mí* repeatedly refers to these latent realities as "la negra espalda del tiempo" (the dark back of time), which became the title of Marías's next full-length narrative.

*Negra espalda del tiempo* (1998; translated as *Dark Back of Time,* 2001) can be seen as the culmination of a particular feature of Marías's work. Marías's literature bears witness to the belief that narratives cannot faithfully and realistically represent existing reality. In his works this freedom of literature is allegorized in particular through the recurrent equation of narrative, storytelling, and writing with the temporary states of obsession, dream, disturbance, malaise, and haunting that befall his narrators and protagonists. As Grohmann has argued in *Coming into One's Own,* these states result in irregular or deviant apprehensions of the realities surrounding them, further fueled by the narrators' superstitiousness and their exacerbated imaginative, errant, and associative minds; their narratives thus reveal a profound distrust of certainty and an extreme skepticism regarding the possibility of representing the world truthfully.

*Negra espalda del tiempo* makes this distrust explicit, and it becomes one of the major themes of the narrative, as is made evident in the opening chapter:

> En realidad la vieja aspiración de cualquier cronista o superviviente, relatar lo ocurrido, dar cuenta de lo acaecido, dejar constancia de los hechos y delitos y hazañas, es una mera ilusión o quimera, o mejor dicho, la propia frase, ese propio concepto, son ya metafóricos y forman parte de la ficción. "Relatar lo ocurrido" es inconcebible y vano, o bien es sólo posible como invención.

> (In reality the age-old ambition of any chronicler or survivor, to relate what occurred, to give an account of what happened, to record the facts and crimes and exploits, is but an illusion or chimera, or rather, the phrase or concept itself is already metaphorical and forms part of fiction. "To relate what occurred" is inconceivable and vain, or it is only possible as an invention.)

Despite this belief, Marías does attempt in this work to recount the ways in which a fiction, his novel *Todas las almas,* invaded his life. Since the publication of that novel in 1989 he had begun to detect bizarre coincidences or parallels between fiction and reality, and *Negra espalda del tiempo* revolves around the curious impact his Oxford novel had on his life. Unlike his previous narratives, this work has no internal structure or plot, and the narrator bears the name of, and appears to be, Javier Marías. So, *Negra espalda del tiempo* is not a novel in a strict sense: it is a mosaic of biographical, autobiographical, and fictional passages, a narration of episodes that, in the main, originate in existing reality, although they are all inevitably filtered by the author's imagination and therefore undergo the process of invention of which Marías speaks. This process is why he has called it a false novel.

Among the many ways in which the fiction of *Todas las almas* invaded Marías's life, as recounted in *Negra espalda del tiempo,* is through the character of Gawsworth. Terence Ian Fytton Armstrong, who used the pseudonym John Gawsworth, was a poet and bibliophile. In 1947 Gawsworth became the second "king" of the mythical kingdom of Redonda, a Caribbean island to which the father of Gawsworth's friend M. P. Shiel had laid claim and which Shiel had bequeathed to

*Dust jacket for the U.S. edition (2001) of the English translation of* Negra espalda del tiempo (1998), *in which Marías ,discusses the ways that his novel* Todas las almas *both paralleled and affected his life (Richland County Public Library)*

Gawsworth, who freely bestowed dukedoms on his friends. In 1997 Gawsworth's anointed successor, the publisher Jon Wynne-Tyson, abdicated in favor of Marías, who, crowned King Xavier I, became a successor of one of his characters. In 2000 Marías founded the publishing house Reino de Redonda (Kingdom of Redonda) with the aim of publishing, among others, some of the works of the former kings, having also become their literary executor. And he instituted a literary prize of the same name awarded on an annual basis since 2001 to men of letters and movie directors.

In 2002 and 2004 Marías published the first two volumes of *Tu rostro mañana* (Your Face Tomorrow), a novel that is to consist of at least three parts. In *Fiebre y lanza* (translated as *Your Face Tomorrow: Fever and Spear,* 2005) and *Baile y sueño* (Dance and Dream) the narrator, Jacques Deza, leaves Madrid to work in Great Britain: first for BBC Radio and then in the employment of an unidentified British secret agent as an "intérperete de vidas" (interpreter of lives), someone who has the ability not only to detect the true character of a person but to forecast his or her future behavior. The narrative develops some of Marías's recurring themes and ideas and explores new ones, such as denunciation and treason; the effects of talking, of keeping quiet, and of secrets; the relationship between the dead and the living; what constitutes a person's identity; and the interrelationship of past and present. The novel delves extensively into the pasts of Britain and Spain, particularly the Spanish Civil War and World War II, as refracted through the biographies and memories of Jacques's father and Sir Peter Wheeler.

Jacques is the same person as the unnamed narrator of *Todas las almas*, who now returns to Britain after having left Oxford to live in Madrid. He had previously occupied the post of lector of Spanish at the University of Oxford, and a great part of the first volume of the novel takes place in Oxford and in the home of the brother of one of the main characters of *Todas las almas*. This novel is also suffused with a substantial autobiographical strand, but not to the extent of creating the generic indeterminacy of *Negra espalda del tiempo*. Although somewhat more meditative and digressive, Jacques's is the same uncertain, imaginative, conjectural voice of all of Marías's narrators since *Todas las almas*.

Maarten Steenmeijer has affirmed that Javier Marías's work is the most adventurous, idiosyncratic, concentrated, and consistent in quality of any post-1975 Spanish writer. Marías's writing is characterized by a distinctive style and a singular voice, and his development as a writer is a particular one. In addition, the nature of his work has contributed to his growing international success and stature (something attested, not least, by the number of literary prizes he has been awarded for his work as a whole, including the German Nelly Sachs Preis, the Premio Comunidad de Madrid, and the Italian Premio Grinzane Cavour and Premio Alberto Moravia). This international attention has meant that he has made a significant contribution to breaking the cultural isolation of Spain. Marías is one of the few truly cosmopolitan, original, and extraordinary writers to come out of Spain since the end of the Spanish Civil War in 1939.

**References:**

Inés Blanca, "Ficción autobiográfica en la narrativa española actual: *Todas las almas* (1989) de Javier Marías," in *Actas del congreso en homenaje a Rosa Chacel,* edited by M. P. Martínez Latre (Logroño: Universidad de La Rioja, 1994), pp. 215–222;

Geneviève Champeau, "L'Auteur dans le texte: A propos de *Negra espalda del tiempo* de Javier Marías," in *Théories du texte et pratiques méthodologiques,* edited by

Milagros Ezquerro (Caen: Presses Universitaires de Caen, 1998), pp. 79–90;

Ruth Christie, "*Corazón tan blanco:* The Evolution of a Success Story," *Modern Language Review,* 93 (January 1998): 83–93;

Christie, Judith Drinkwater, and John Macklin, *The Scripted Self: Textual Identities in Contemporary Spanish Narrative* (Warminster, U.K.: Aris & Phillips, 1995);

Sylvie Coreen, "Un aspect des 'novísimos': *El hombre sentimental* de Javier Marías," in *Formes et imaginaire du roman: Perspectives sur le roman antique, médiéval, classique, moderne et contemporain,* edited by Jean Bessière and Daniel-Henri Pageaux (Paris: Honoré Champion, 1998), pp. 213–224;

Isabel Cuñado, *El espectro de la herencia: La narrativa de Javier Marías* (Amsterdam & New York: Rodopi, 2004);

María Dolores de Asís, "Javier Marías," in her *Última hora de la novela en España* (Madrid: Eudema, 1989), pp. 351–353, 396–399;

Rita de Maeseneer, "Sobre la traducción en *Corazón tan blanco* de Javier Marías," *Espéculo: Revista de Estudios Literarios,* no. 14 (March–June 2000) <http://www.ucm.es/info/especulo/numero14/jmarias.html>;

Alfonso de Toro, "Javier Marías: *Todas las almas:* Autobiografía ficcional como tematización de lo turbador del eterno extraño," in *Abriendo caminos: La literatura española desde 1975,* edited by Dieter Ingenschay and Hans-Jörg Neuschäfer (Barcelona: Lumen, 1994), pp. 189–201;

Carlos Javier García, "Imágenes como palabras y *Corazón tan blanco,* de Javier Marías," *Revista Hispánica Moderna,* 54 (June 2001): 191–202;

García, "La resistencia a saber y *Corazón tan blanco,* de Javier Marías," *Anales de Literatura Española Contemporánea,* 24 (1999): 103–120;

Manuel González de Ávila, "La Faute et la parole: J. Marías, *Corazón tan blanco,*" *Bulletin Hispanique,* 101 (1999): 199–217;

Alexis Grohmann, *Coming into One's Own: The Novelistic Development of Javier Marías* (Amsterdam & New York: Rodopi, 2002);

Grohmann, "*Los dominios del lobo* by Javier Marías: Hollywood and *anticasticismo novísimo,*" in *Crossing Fields in Modern Spanish Culture,* edited by Federico Bonaddio and Xon de Ros (Oxford: Legenda, 2003), pp. 165–176;

Grohmann, "Javier Marías' *El siglo:* A Question of Style," *Modern Language Review,* 97 (January 2002): 94–107;

Grohmann, "Madrid and the Interconnectedness of the World in Javier Marías' *Mañana en la batalla piensa en mí,*" *Donaire,* 16 (November 2001): 12–20;

Grohmann, "La nobleza literaria de Javier Marías," *Quimera: Revista de literatura,* 252 (January 2005): 61–66;

Grohmann, "Reading the Exergue: *Todas las almas* by Javier Marías—Autobiographical Writing or Fiction?" *Bulletin of Spanish Studies,* 80 (January 2003): 55–79;

Luis Izquierdo, "Una aproximación a los relatos de Javier Marías," *Ínsula,* 568 (1994): 19–21;

Javier Marías website <http://www.javiermarias.es/main.html>;

Ilse Logie, "Aspectos performativos en dos novelas de Javier Marías: *Corazón tan blanco* y *Mañana en la batalla piensa en mí,*" in *Estudios en honor del Profesor Josse De Kock,* edited by Nicole Delbecque and Chris de Paepe (Louvain: Leuven University Press, 1998), pp. 889–897;

Miguel Martinón, "Narración reflexiva: *Corazón tan blanco,* de Javier Marías," *Letras Peninsulares,* 9 (1997): 355–369;

Juan Antonio Masoliver Ródenas, "El pensamiento incesante," *Vuelta,* 216 (1994): 60–63;

Sara Molpeceres Arnaiz, "*Macbeth* de William Shakespeare en *Corazón tan blanco* de Javier Marías," *Estudios Humanísticos, Filología,* 22 (2000): 161–173;

Juan Antonio Rivera, "La negra espalda de Javier Marías," *Claves de razón práctica,* 111 (April 2001): 68–76;

Isidro Rojo, "Javier Marías: Un escritor singular," in *Seis calas en la narrativa española contemporánea* (Alcalá de Henares: Fundación Colegio del Rey, 1989), pp. 85–90;

César Romero, "Del azar y sus nombres: Sobre Javier Marías y su última novela," *Generació,* 7 (1995): 99–116;

Romero, "La voz prestada," *El ojo de la aguja,* 7 (1996): 83–87;

Karen Margrethe Simonsen, "*Corazón tan blanco*—A Postpostmodern Novel by Javier Marías," *Revista Hispánica Moderna,* 52 (June 1999): 193–212;

Robert C. Spires, "Discursive Constructs and Spanish Fiction of the 1980s," *Journal of Narrative Technique,* 27 (1997): 128–146;

Spires, "Perturbation/Information: *Todas las almas,*" in his *Post-Totalitarian Spanish Fiction* (Columbia & London: University of Missouri Press, 1996), pp. 223–234;

Maarten Steenmeijer, "El tabú del franquismo vivido en la narrativa de Mendoza, Marías y Muñoz Molina," in *Disremembering the Dictatorship: The Politics of Memory in the Spanish Transition to Democracy,* edited by Joan Ramón Resina (Amsterdam & Atlanta: Rodopi, 2000), pp. 139–155;

Steenmeijer, ed., *El pensamiento literario de Javier Marías* (Amsterdam & New York: Rodopi, 2001);

Enrique Turpin, "La sutil omnisciencia del fantasma: *Cuando fui mortal,* de Javier Marías," *La nueva literatura hispánica,* 2 (1998): 127–142;

Fernando Valls, "Un estado de crueldad o el opio del tiempo: Los fantasmas de Javier Marías," in *Brujas, demonios y fantasmas en la literatura fantástica hispánica,* edited by Jaume Pont (Lérida: Universitat de Lleida, 1999), pp. 361–367;

Valls, "'Lo que dijo el mayordomo,' de Javier Marías, o la disolución de los géneros literarios narrativos," in *Mestizaje y disolución de géneros en la literatura hispánica contemporánea,* edited by Irene Andrés-Suárcz (Madrid: Verbum, 1998), pp. 168–173.

# Juan Marsé

*(8 January 1933 – )*

Rosemary Clark
*University of Cambridge*

BOOKS: *Encerrados con un solo juguete* (Barcelona: Seix Barral, 1960);

*Esta cara de la luna* (Barcelona: Seix Barral, 1962);

*Ultimas tardes con Teresa* (Barcelona: Seix Barral, 1966; revised, 1975);

*La oscura historia de la prima Montse* (Barcelona: Seix Barral, 1970);

*Si te dicen que caí* (Mexico City: Novaro, 1973; Barcelona: Seix Barral, 1976; revised, 1989); translated by Helen R. Lane as *The Fallen* (Boston: Little, Brown, 1976; London: Quartet, 1994);

*Señoras y señores* (Barcelona: Punch, 1975; enlarged edition, Barcelona: Planeta, 1977);

*Libertad provisional* (Madrid: Ediciones Sedmay, 1976);

*Confidencias de un chorizo* (Barcelona: Planeta, 1977);

*La muchacha de las bragas de oro* (Barcelona: Planeta, 1978); translated by Lane as *Golden Girl* (Boston: Little, Brown, 1978);

*Un día volveré* (Esplugues de Llobregat [i.e., Barcelona]: Plaza y Janés, 1982);

*Ronda del Guinardó* (Barcelona: Seix Barral, 1984); translated anonymously as *The Guinardó Beat* (Madrid: Iberia, 1989);

*El fantasma del Cine Roxy* (Madrid: Almarabú, 1985);

*La fuga del río Lobo* (Madrid: Debate, 1985);

*Teniente Bravo* (Barcelona: Seix Barral, 1987);

*El amante bilingüe* (Barcelona: Planeta, 1990);

*El embrujo de Shanghai* (Barcelona: Plaza y Janés, 1993);

*Rabos de lagartija* (Barcelona: Lumen, 2000); translated by Nick Caistor as *Lizard Tails* (London: Harvill, 2003);

*Un paseo por las estrellas* (Barcelona: RBA, 2001);

*Cuentos completos,* edited by Enrique Turpín (Madrid: Espasa-Calpe, 2003);

*Momentos inolvidables del cine* (Barcelona: Carroggio/Scrinium, 2004);

*Canciones de amor en Lolita's Club* (Barcelona: Areté, 2005).

**Editions and Collections:** *Los misterios de Colores* (Córdoba: Diario Córdoba, 1977);

*Juan Marsé (© Palomares; from the cover for* El embrujo de Shanghai, *1997; Thomas Cooper Library, University of South Carolina)*

*El Pijoaparte y otras historias* (Barcelona: Bruguera, 1981);

*Las mujeres de Juanito Marés,* edited by José Méndez (Madrid: Espasa-Calpe, 1997);

*La gran desilusión* (Barcelona: Seix Barral, 2004).

OTHER: *Imágenes y recuerdos 1929–1940: La gran desilusión,* edited by Marsé (Barcelona: Difusora Internacional, 1971);

*Imágenes y recuerdos 1939–1950: Años de penitencia,* edited by Marsé (Barcelona: Difusora Internacional, 1971);

*Historia de España, vista con buenos ojos,* edited by Marsé (Barcelona: Punch, 1975);

*Imágenes y recuerdos 1949–1960: Tiempo de satélites,* texts by José María Carandell, prologue by Marsé (Barcelona: Difusora Internacional, 1976);

Olegario Sotelo Blanco, *La emigración gallega en Catalunya,* prologue by Marsé (Barcelona: Sotelo Blanco, 1991);

Sotelo Blanco, *Perfiles del Guinardó,* prologue by Marsé (Barcelona: Ronsel, 2002).

TRANSLATIONS: Yukio Mishima, *El pabellón de oro* (Barcelona: Seix Barral, 1963);

Eugenio Calfari, *El poder económico en la URSS* (Barcelona: Seix Barral, 1965);

Cesare Zavattini, *Straparole* (Barcelona: Llibres de Sinera, 1968).

The first novel Juan Marsé submitted for publication, *Encerrados con un solo juguete* (1960, Shut in with Just One Toy), was greeted by the Barcelona publishing house Seix Barral as a potential weapon in its opposition to the dictatorship of Francisco Franco, who had ruled Spain for twenty-one years. The editorial board believed that it had found not only a Barcelona-born Catalan who was writing about his own city and culture—though necessarily in the Castilian Spanish imposed by the regime—but also an *escritor-obrero* (writer-worker) with communist sympathies whose narratives would depict the postwar "years of penance" in images that would contrast starkly with the triumphalistic rhetoric of Franco's National Catholic regime. His subsequent novels, short stories, children's book, satirical writings, and articles, including movie criticism, showed the limitations of their initial concept. Marsé's playful approach to writing, while never losing the sharp critical edge that characterizes his observations of his society, claims for literature a play space in which the imagination can push the boundaries of creativity and engage the reader in games of make-believe that challenge the changing narratives of politics, religion, and history.

Marsé's works move across social, political, and religious divides, exploring the tensions within a society fragmented beneath the superficial unity imposed by the Franco regime. He maps the Barcelona of his youth: the bombed sites, the parish church of Las Ánimas del Purgatorio (The Souls in Purgatory), streets and bars, rich and poor districts, and rich and poor beaches. He also explores literary means of representing issues of dictatorship and democracy, power and exploitation,

stagnation and creativity, and fear and daring. He mimics traditional genres such as the *novela rosa* (romantic novel) and detective fiction, and the political rhetoric and religious discourses of the time. He also plays with scriptwriting, multiple narrators, and poetry. His child narrators and his humor often disarm opposition—only one of his novels was banned by the Francoist censors—but since the transition to democracy, his open criticism of the language policies of his native Catalonia and his continued use of Castilian in his writing have aroused hostility. He has won such major prizes as the Biblioteca Breve for *Ultimas tardes con Teresa* (1966, Last Evenings with Teresa) and the Premio Internacional de Novela México (Mexico International Prize for the Novel) for *Si te dicen que caí* (1973, If They Tell You That I Fell; translated as *The Fallen,* 1976), but not until *Ronda del Guinardó* (1984; translated as *The Guinardó Beat,* 1989) did he win the Ciudad de Barcelona (City of Barcelona) Prize. In 2002 he was at last given the Catalan Gold Medal for Cultural Merit.

Marsé was born Juan Faneca Roca in the Barcelona suburb of Sarriá on 8 January 1933. His mother, Rosa Roca, died giving birth to him, and his father, Domingo Faneca, gave him up for adoption and only saw him again at his first Communion and at a family wedding. He was adopted by Josep Marsé and Berta Carbó; his novel *Un día volveré* (1982, One Day I Shall Return) is dedicated to his adoptive father. Except for military service in Africa and a stay in Paris, he has lived in Barcelona all his life and has set all but two of his novels in the city. The novels offer detailed images of the aftermath of the 1936–1939 Civil War, when he roamed among the ruins of the last major city to yield to Franco's Nationalist troops. During his childhood he visited grandparents in the traditional Catalonian towns of L'Arboç and Calafell, the latter a fishing village. His novel *La muchacha de las bragas de oro* (1978, The Girl with the Golden Panties; translated as *Golden Girl,* 1978) is set in Calafell, while *El embrujo de Shanghai* (1993, Shanghai Enchantment) is dedicated to "la Rosa de Calafell" and "la Berta de L'Arboç."

After the Civil War, Marsé's adoptive mother worked at the Barcelona Telephone Exchange; his father worked on a municipal pest-control team but was repeatedly arrested for having Catalan separatist sympathies and being a Communist: Josep Marsé had been a member of the Communist PSUC (Partit Socialista Unificat de Catalunya [United Socialist Party of Catalonia]) during the Civil War. Marsé attended the Colegio del Divino Maestro (College of the Divine Master) and frequented the parish center, the only place that offered recreational activities to children of poor families in the postwar years; he depicts it in *Si te dicen que caí* and *La oscura historia de la prima Montse* (1970,

# Juan Marsé
# SI TE DICEN QUE CAÍ

**SEIX BARRAL**
Biblioteca Breve

*Cover for the Spanish edition (1976) of Marsé's novel (translated as*
The Fallen, *1976) about children scarred by the Civil War
and its aftermath of repression in 1940s Barcelona.
The work was first published in Mexico City in
1973 to evade censorship by the Franco regime
in Spain (Thomas Cooper Library,
University of South Carolina).*

Cousin Montse's Dark Story). Though he has spoken warmly of the faith of his mother, his hostility to the Church as an institution is everywhere evident in his writings.

Leaving school at thirteen, Marsé went to work in a jewelry workshop. During this time he read European classics in translation, including works by Guy de Maupassant, Stendhal, Charles Dickens, and Sir Arthur Conan Doyle. He also enjoyed comic books, whose characters he cites in his works: the aviator Bill Barnes is evoked by the Royal Air Force pilot Bryen O'Flynne in *Rabos de lagartija* (2000; translated as *Lizard Tails,* 2003); the adventurous *guerrero del antifaz* (masked war-

rior) is mimicked by the child Joan Marés in *El amante bilingüe* (1990, The Bilingual Lover); and the heroic Juan Centella exemplifies for Marsé the penetration of political propaganda into the lives of children in the post–Civil War period. The character was modeled on José Antonio Primo de Rivera, who founded the right-wing Spanish paramilitary organization Falange in 1933; executed under the Republic in 1936, Primo de Rivera was used by Francoist propaganda to epitomize the martyr to the Nationalist cause. Marsé's reading, like his schooling, was in Castilian; at home and with friends he spoke Catalan. His novels reflect the linguistic mix in which he grew up. From 1955 to 1957 he edited the short-lived journal *Arcinema,* for which he wrote movie and theater criticism.

During his eighteen months of military service in Ceuta, a Spanish enclave in northern Morocco, in 1956–1957 Marsé sent poems and short stories in letters to a girlfriend in Barcelona. On his return from Africa he retrieved the letters and made them the basis for his first novel, *Encerrados con un solo juguete.* Andrés Ferrán's father disappeared in the war, and his mother exhausts herself to support her unemployed son. He despises his hardworking sister; her equally "cuadrado" (square) fiancé; and even his childhood friend Martín, whose father died in prison, leaving Martín to support his blind mother. Andrés spends his time with the prostitute Julita or his girlfriend, Tina Climent, of whom his sister disapproves. Defiantly, he drinks, smokes, and invents stories. Tina dreams of a future with her father, who is working in Brazil, until he stops sending home money and contact is cut. Martín's rape of Tina, her mother's collusion in that rape, and the mother's sudden death leave Andrés as Tina's only refuge. The absence of fathers and the frailty of mothers intensifies the uncertainty facing the young on the brink of adulthood. *Encerrados con un solo juguete* was the runner-up for the 1961 Biblioteca Breve Prize. The critic Gonzalo Sobejano views the novel as social criticism detailing the dullness of life in post–Civil War Spain, where sex is the "only toy," while Rosemary Clark considers it a playful exploration of the imagination and the processes of storytelling.

The group of writers and intellectuals associated with the Seix Barral publishing house—Carlos Barral, José María Castellet, Jaime Gil de Biedma, José Agustín Goytisolo, Helena Valentí, and Gabriel Ferrater—exposed the young novelist to a culture that his home background had not offered. Barral and Castellet obtained a grant from the Congreso Cultural de Europa (Cultural Congress of Europe) that enabled Marsé to go to Paris in 1961. After spending all of his grant money in a fortnight, he took a job as a laboratory assistant at the Pasteur Institute. He also made contact with the Spanish Communist Party in exile; he attended the training sessions offered by Jorge Semprún but found them unrelated to the reality of Spain as he knew it. Censured for his relationship with the wife of a Communist who was fighting in Algeria, he broke with the party but retained his membership. Later, he allowed Communist groups to use the family apartment in Barcelona for meetings when he, his parents, and his sister were not at home.

In Paris, Marsé wrote the novel *Esta cara de la luna* (1962, This Face of the Moon), which he considers sketchy and unfinished. Family wealth relieves Miguel Dot of the need to work, and he conceives romantic fantasies about working-class resistance. When he outlines his plans to start "una publicación con conciencia de clase" (a class-conscious publication) to workers in a bar, they drunkenly dismiss the idea as "una idiotez y una mierda" (stupid shit). Miguel abandons the project.

Returning to Barcelona in 1962, Marsé wrote summaries for book covers for Seix Barral. He also produced the first translation into Spanish of a work by the Japanese author Yukio Mishima, using the 1961 French version of *Kinkakuji* (1956; translated as *The Temple of the Golden Pavilion*, 1959) as the basis for his *El pabellón de oro* (1963). In 1963 he married Joaquina Hoyas. They had two children: Sacha, born in 1968, and Berta, born in 1969.

Marsé's third novel, *Ultimas tardes con Teresa*, appeared in 1966. Manuel Reyes gate-crashes a party in a wealthy Barcelona suburb in search of a rich girl-friend to be his ticket to a better life. But in a comedy of errors, the *charnego* (southern immigrant) motorcycle thief mistakes the maid, Maruja, for her mistress, Teresa Serrat, and embarks on an affair with a girl of the "wrong" class. Teresa imagines the life of Communist dissidents in the poor districts of Barcelona as a series of colorful encounters that are more interesting than the bourgeois morality of her family. Bored with her impotent if "heroic" student-militant boyfriend, Luis Trias de Giralt, she wants to defy conventional morality by losing her virginity; she is attracted to Manuel sexually and because of what she believes to be his status as a worker. Manuel, not the struggling worker Teresa imagines him to be but a manipulator eager to join the middle class by marrying a rich girl, misunderstands her use of the term "*pecé*"–the initials *PC,* for *Partido Comunista* (Communist Party)–and thinks that she is referring to *peces* (fish). Parental intervention frustrates a relationship that has been built on misconceptions. Marsé's delicate treatment of the dreams and myths that motivate his characters gained him international accolades; the Peruvian novelist Mario Vargas Llosa noted the "explosive sarcasm" of Marsé's social critique in *Ultimas tardes con Teresa.*

The roguish Manuel Reyes reappears four years later in *La oscura historia de la prima Montse.* Inspired by the Catholic Church's social gospel, Montse attempts to find work for the former convict Manuel; but her efforts are thwarted by her bourgeois parents' disapproval of him. She leaves home, moves in with him, becomes pregnant, and kills herself after being betrayed by an affair between Manuel and her sister, Nuria. The novel is narrated by Montse's cousin, Paco Bodegas, a half-Andalusian atheist and heavy drinker (his surname means "wine cellars") who feels that he is as much an outsider in this Catholic Catalan family as Manuel. Paco lays the blame for Montse's suicide and the death of her unborn child on the Catalan bourgeoisie and the Catholic Church, whose unrealistic teachings she had tried to follow. Nuria's marriage to Salvador Viella (the first name means "Savior") a Catalan businessman who is active in the Church, is approved by her parents but makes her profoundly unhappy. Paco's love for Nuria, pity for Montse, and jealousy of Salvador make him a biased commentator, whose arguments with Salvador on the Second Vatican Council of 1962 to 1965 are motivated by sexual jealousy as much as by intellectual disagreement.

Marsé managed to elude censorship until *Si te dicen que caí* was banned from publication in Spain; the novel was published in Mexico City in 1973. In *La oscura historia de la prima Montse* Paco's pity, love, and humor soften the tragic events; in contrast, the violence and corruption depicted in *Si te dicen que caí* are intensified by the voices of narrators who are barely out of a childhood scarred by the Civil War and its aftermath of repression. Those voices are mediated to the reader by the vengeful mind of the now-adult Sarnita, whose flawed memory adds a further layer of uncertainty as to the reliability of these images of 1940s Barcelona and of the repression organized by the victorious Nationalist regime and implemented by the Falange. The crippled and perverted former Nationalist soldier Conrado Galán conflates his experiences of war and torture with biblical stories of the Archangel Michael's war against the serpent-dragon Lucifer both when directing a religious play performed by street children who have come to the parish center of Las Animas del Purgatorio for recreational activities and at his home, where he uses child prostitutes in sadomasochistic dramas. Contaminated by these perverse pleasures, the children, who witnessed the terrors of the Communist secret police during the Civil War and saw the Falange take over the Communist torture chambers after the war, reenact these experiences in the church crypt. The title of the novel, a line from the Falange anthem, *Cara al sol* (Facing the Sun), acquires a double meaning: "If they tell you that I fell" might refer to falling in battle or to fall-

Juan Marsé

## Ronda del Guinardó

Novela

Seix Barral ⅄ Biblioteca Breve

*Cover for Marsé's 1984 novel (translated as* The Guinardó
Beat, *1989), about a policeman patrolling a poor district of
Barcelona in 1945 (Thomas Cooper Library,
University of South Carolina)*

ing from grace like Lucifer and Adam and Eve. These
images, mingling in the narrators' childish imaginations
with Hollywood movie villains such as Fu Manchu,
constitute a storytelling game of *"aventis"* (adventures).
Interviewed by the critic Jack Sinnigen, Marsé
explained:

> Los muchachos, a esa edad, jugábamos a contar "aventis"
> en la calle, y siempre nos llegaban "noticias" de familiares
> muertos, desaparecidos, exiliados, etc. Por eso esos juegos
> constituían con frecuencia historias de violencia; en nues-
> tros relatos mezclábamos películas que habíamos visto con
> tebeos, novelas de aventuras y hechos reales. Lo original
> del juego consistía en que los protagonistas éramos
> nosotros. . . . Tenías que inventar e imaginar.

> (At that age, we boys used to play at telling "aventis"
> out in the street, and we were always hearing "news" of

deaths in our families, people disappearing and going
into exile, etc. So our games were often about violence;
in our stories we would mix together films we had seen
and comics, adventures from novels and real events.
What was special about the game was that we were the
heroes. . . . You had to be inventive and imaginative.)

*Si te dicen que caí* is a parody of detective fiction,
one in which the crime is not solved but covered up.
Sarnita, working in a hospital mortuary in the 1960s,
recognizes the corpse of the ragpicker Java, who had
been one of Galán's boy prostitutes in the 1940s. Sarnita's investigation into Java's death brings back memories of Java's own childhood investigation into the death
of a prostitute, the "puta roja" (Red Whore), which laid
the blame equally on Francoist repression of "Reds"
and on the Church, whose moral and political align-
ment with the regime made it a partner in the repression. In the past and the present, the storytelling game
offers contradictory reports and rumors that mimic the
confusion engendered by censorship in the Franco
years.

Critics described Marsé's first four novels as
works of social realism, but he dismissed that characterization in a 1977 interview with Angelo Morino:

> En realidad, yo creo que ni siquiera mi primera novela
> tiene mucho que ver con la vertiente del realismo y del
> objetivismo. Es una novela que va ya un poco a con-
> trapelo de lo que se estaba haciendo. Me parece más
> bien decadente, intimista, con una atmósfera
> enrarecida. . . . Pero como salió en un momento en que
> el realismo social y la novela objetivista estaban en
> auge, fue automáticamente clasificada con esa etiqueta.

> (In fact, I don't think that even my first novel had much
> to do with social realism or objectivity. Rather, it's a
> novel that went against the grain of what others were
> doing at the time. I think of it more as decadent, inti-
> mate, with a strange atmosphere. . . . But because it was
> published at a time when social realism and objectivity
> were becoming popular, it was automatically labeled
> that way.)

While producing novels of increasing structural
complexity and literary quality, Marsé edited *Imágenes y
recuerdos* (1971–1976, Images and Memories), three volumes of personal memories, songs, and other ephemera
that evoke the mood of the decades from 1929 to 1960.
In 1974 the satirical magazine *Por Favor* appeared, with
Marsé as editor in chief; his column "Señoras y
señores" (Ladies and Gentlemen), which ran from 1974
to 1976, was taken up by *El País* from March to December 1977 and was published in book form in 1975 and
1977.

After Franco's death in 1975, many writers attempted exposés of the dictatorship. Pointing to the impossibility of objectivity, Marsé mocked these efforts in his 1978 novel, *La muchacha de las bragas de oro,* in which the former Falangist historian Luys Forest tries to rewrite the history of the dictatorship while being obsessed with the question of whether his niece Mariana's golden panties are, in fact, bare skin. Forest's attempts to piece together the past are likened to the Tangram, a geometrical puzzle with which he is playing, in which components can be put together to form more than two hundred figures. Forest suspects that his dog, Mao—the name suggests Forest's shifting political sympathies—is moving the pieces of the puzzle. He is alarmed to see them forming a threatening dagger but continues to play Russian roulette with his pistol and reinvent the past. His narrative, too, is constantly shifting, like the sand in his garden on the beach at Calafell and like Mariana's identity, which changes from niece to lover to daughter. Realization that he has committed incest with his daughter comes shortly before he is found shot to death with his own gun—a warning of the dangers of "husmeando corrupciones" (sniffing corruption), as the dog sniffs rubbish on the beach and as the historian has done in his own past and that of the dictatorship.

Marsé's popularity led to the republishing of extracts from his novels featuring Manuel Reyes. Manuel's experiences on a *cursillo de cristiandad* (religious retreat), recounted in *La oscura historia de la prima Montse,* appeared in 1977 as *Los misterios de Colores* (The Mysteries of Colors). Other excerpts from the Reyes novels were published in *El Pijoaparte y otras historias* (1981, Pijoaparte and Other Stories).

Marsé's 1982 novel, *Un día volveré,* begins with a familiar cinematic cliché. A Humphrey Bogart figure in hat and trench coat emerges from the darkness into the light of a street lamp to scold a group of boys who are urinating on the Falangist symbol of a yoke and arrows painted on a wall. The man is Jan Julivert Mon, and he is the uncle of Néstor, one of the boys. Mon has just been released from prison after serving a sentence for fighting in the anti-Franco resistance. The boys assume that he will now kill Klein, the judge who put him behind bars. Instead, Mon takes a job as bodyguard to the alcoholic judge. At the Klein home the Falangist yoke and arrows and an icon of the Catalan patron saint, St. George, recall wartime tensions, while the contrasts of wealth and poverty and order and crime and the presence of Mon's former colleagues in the resistance show the fragility of the peace for which Mon longs. When the judge is shot and killed, Mon deliberately brings about his own death by appearing to reach for his gun; after he, too, is shot, he pulls out a neatly folded handkerchief. The novel is narrated in retrospect by a now-adult friend of Néstor's.

The lengthy *Un día volveré* was followed in 1984 by the short and shocking *Ronda del Guinardó,* a starkly violent depiction of poverty and repression set in 1945. Orphans, crippled children, and criminals pass before the reader in a parade of joyless sex and death, as a dyspeptic policeman uncovers crime on his beat in a poor district of Barcelona. This somber work is dedicated to Marsé's children, Berta and Sacha. In 1985 Marsé published his only children's book, *La fuga del río Lobo* (The Flight of Wolf River), with illustrations by Berta.

*Teniente Bravo* (1987, Lieutenant Bravo) consists of four short stories. "Historia de detectives" (Detective Story), set amid the ruins of post–Civil War Barcelona, features an unexplained suicide and a beautiful and enigmatic woman whom the boy detectives and inventors of *aventis* Juanito Marés and David Bartra track while weaving erotic fantasies about her. Susana's stationery store and Catalan bookshop and the Roxy Cinema from "Historia de detectives" return in the second story, "El fantasma del Cine Roxy" (The Ghost of the Roxy Cinema), written in the form of a movie screenplay, in which Falangist thugs repeatedly threaten Susana's business with escalating brutality. The title story is set in Africa and describes the boredom of army recruits forced to watch their lieutenant attempt to vault a pommel horse until his injuries from falls are so severe that he is carried off on a stretcher. "Noches de Bocaccio" (Nights in the Bocaccio Bar) satirizes real and fictional members of Barcelona's intellectual "gauche divine" (divine left)—humorously written *goxdivín* to mimic Catalan pronunciation—including Barral, Castellet, and Marsé himself, whose opposition never effectively challenged the power of the Francoist state.

The first parliament of the newly autonomous Generalitat de Catalunya (Community of Catalonia) had been elected in 1980, and in 1983 it had passed the Linguistic Normalization Act to make Catalan the official language of the region. Marsé's 1990 novel, *El amante bilingüe,* sets the language debate in a context of adultery, betrayal, and the mental and linguistic breakdown of the protagonist, Juanito Marés, one of the child detectives of "Historia de detectives." Like the author, Marés is Catalan but bilingual; like Marsé, Manuel Reyes, and Paco Bodegas, he looks Andalusian. Marés crosses social boundaries to marry the middle-class Norma Valentí, who works in the linguistic normalization bureau, but he cannot satisfy her insatiable appetite for the *charnego* lovers who are as essential to her as non-Catalan speakers are to those promoting normalization of the language. To win her back, Marés masquerades as a *charnego* until, like the overly ambitious people in the biblical story of the Tower of Babel, his

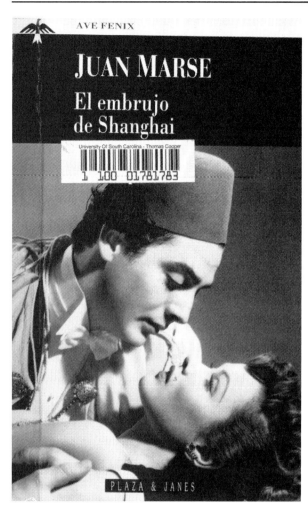

AVE FENIX

# JUAN MARSE
## El embrujo de Shanghai

University Of South Carolina - Thomas Cooper

1 100 01781783

PLAZA & JANES

*Cover for a 1997 edition of Marsé's 1993 novel (Shanghai Enchantment), in which parallel stories are set in post–Civil War Barcelona and in a fictional Shanghai inspired by movies of the 1940s and 1950s (Thomas Cooper Library, University of South Carolina)*

languages are confounded. The novel ends in a virtually nonsensical babble of phonetically transcribed southern-accented intermingled Catalan and Castilian that is far removed from the linguistic purity that the 1983 act aimed to achieve.

In Marsé's 1993 novel, *El embrujo de Shanghai,* two stories run parallel to each other: one is about Daniel and Susana in Barcelona; the other is about Susana's father's adventures in a fictional Shanghai inspired by Hollywood movies of the 1940s and 1950s. Susana desires to escape from the poverty of the war-torn Barcelona from which her former resistance-fighter father has fled, and from the glassed-in gallery to which she is confined by tuberculosis. The aspiring artist Daniel is obsessed with Susana and wants to paint her. Marsé inverts the story from the Book of Susanna in the Apoc-

rypha, in which the prophet Daniel defended the virtuous Susana who was accused of immorality by two lustful elders: here the elders are replaced by the *charnego* Chacón brothers, who are thieves but guard Susana faithfully, while Daniel is consumed with lust for her.

In 1997 the debating group Foro Babel (Babel Forum) issued a statement demanding that Catalonia's bilingualism be maintained; it was signed by ninety intellectuals and writers, including Marsé. That same year, popular demand led to the publication of a selection of chapters about women from Marsé's novels as *Las mujeres de Juanito Marés* (Johnny Marés's Women).

Marsés's 2000 novel, *Rabos de lagartija,* comprises three interlinked narratives woven around the beautiful, pregnant Rosa Bartra: one is told by her son, David, the character from "Historia de detectives," who is now a photographer; the second is told by the policeman from *Ronda del Guinardó,* who is pursuing Rosa's husband, Víctor, a former anti-Nationalist resistance fighter; and the third appears to be told by her unborn child. Quotations from William Blake's poem "The Sick Rose," from *Songs of Innocence and of Experience* (1794), warn that Rosa will die: the "Invisible Worm" in Blake's poem that will kill Rose is identified with a Royal Air Force pilot sheltered by the Bartras during World War II, whose plane bears that name in a magazine photograph on David's wall, and with the fetus, which may be the pilot's love child. David's attempts to capture on film the atmosphere of the 1951 Barcelona tram strike are halted when he is hit by a tram; the fetus, once born, cannot speak, revealing that its apparent "narrative from the womb" has actually been an imaginary reconstruction of the past.

Marsé's idea for a novel about the Spanish sex trade in women from poor countries attracted the interest of the director Fernando Trueba, who had brought *El embrujo de Shanghai* to the screen in 2002. Marsé wrote a script for a movie version but, pressured by his publisher, adapted it into the novel *Canciones de amor en Lolita's Club* (2005, Songs of Love at Lolita's Club); the movie has not been produced. Betraying its origin as a screenplay, the narrative is told largely in the present tense and with a predominance of dialogue. The twins Raúl and Valentín are identical in appearance but opposite in character: Raúl is a brutal policeman in Galicia; in Catalonia, the mentally retarded Valentín gently waits on the women in a brothel, doing their shopping and bringing them food. Raúl beats a young motorcyclist who is taunting an immigrant woman and her child; he is suspended pending an inquiry and, since the boy comes from a wealthy family with criminal connections, is sent home to Catalonia for his own safety. There he learns that Valentín is romantically involved with a prostitute, Milena. Accustomed to protecting the vulnerable Valentín, Raúl tries to disillusion him about Milena while using threats to make her leave his brother. Milena's passivity shows the powerlessness of women controlled by gangland interests. Finally, Raúl persuades the girl to have sex with him; Valentín, who is not supposed to drive because of his retardation, becomes distraught and leaves in a car. He is mistaken for his brother and shot dead in reprisal for Raúl's having injured the motorcyclist.

Juan Marsé's novels and other writings provide detailed information about, and insights into, more than seven turbulent decades of Barcelona history. The main merits of his work, however, are his unashamedly personal slant on the times he depicts and his ceaselessly questioning critical approach, which counters conflict with humor and challenges the reader to take nothing at face value.

**Interviews:**

Angelo Morino, "Una conversación con Juan Marsé," *El Viejo Topo* (4 January 1977): 41–44;

Mercedes Beneto, "Con el último Premio Planeta a lo largo de la obra de Juan Marsé," *Destino* (26 October–1 November 1978): 32–33;

Jack Sinnigen, *Narrativa e ideología* (Madrid: Nuestra Cultura, 1982), pp. 111–122;

Montse Casals, "Entrevista con Juan Marsé," *El País,* Sunday supplement, 8 April 1984, p. 71.

**References:**

Ramón Buckley, "Del Realismo Social al Realismo Dialéctico," *Ínsula,* 326 (1974): 1, 4;

Geneviève Champeau, "A propos de *Si te dicen que caí,*" *Bulletin Hispanique,* 85 (1983): 359–378;

Rosemary Clark, *Catholic Iconography in the Novels of Juan Marsé* (London: Boydell & Brewer, 2003);

Colectivo Lantaba, "Yo no milito," *Cuadernos para el diálogo* (21 January 1978): 44–45;

José Domingo, "Del realismo proscrito a la nueva novela," *Ínsula,* 290 (January 1971): 5;

Gene S. Forrest, "From Masquerade to Reminiscence: Modes of Parody in Juan Marsé's *El amante bilingüe,*" *Hispanófila,* 113 (January 1995): 45–53;

Diane I. Garvey, "Juan Marsé's *Si te dicen que caí:* The Self-Reflexive Text and the Question of Referentiality," *Modern Language Notes,* 95 (1980): 376–387;

Linda Gould Levine, "*Si te dicen que caí:* Un kaleidoscopio verbal," *Journal of Spanish Studies: Twentieth Century,* 7, no. 3 (1979): 309–327;

Shirley Mangini González, "Ultimas tardes con Teresa: Culminación y destrucción del realismo social en la novelística española," *Anales de la Narrativa Española Contemporánea,* 5 (1980): 13–20;

Carolyn Morrow, "Breaking the rules: Transgression and Carnival in *Ultimas tardes con Teresa,*" *Hispania,* 74 (1991): 834–840;

Geraldine C. Nichols, "Dialectical Realism and Beyond: *Ultimas tardes con Teresa,*" *Journal of Spanish Studies: Twentieth Century,* 3 (1975): 163–174;

Joan Lluís Pérez Francesch, ed., *Torras i Bages L'Església i el Regionalisme i altres textos (1887–1899)* (Barcelona: La Magrana, 1985);

Josep E. Piñol, *El Nacionalcatolicisme a Catalunya i la Resistència, 1926–1966* (Barcelona: Edicions 62, 1993);

Hilari Raguer, "El día de los tranvías o la huelga que fue una fiesta," in *Cataluña durante el franquismo,* edited by Josep Solé i Sabaté (Barcelona: Biblioteca de La Vanguardia, 1985), pp. 114–116;

Joan Ramon Resina, "Juan Marsé's *El amante bilingüe* and Sociolinguistic Fiction," *Journal of Catalan Studies,* 3 (1999–2000) <http://www.fitz.cam.ac.uk/jocs/3/articles/resina5/>;

Jack Sinnigen, *Narrativa e ideología* (Madrid: Nuestra Cultura, 1982), pp. 81–122;

Abigail Lee Six, "Blind Woman's Buff: Optical Illusions of Feminist Progress in Juan Marsé's *El amante bilingüe,*" *Journal of Iberian and Latin American Studies,* 6, no. 1 (2000): 29–41;

Six, "La oscura historia del primo Paco/Francesc: Code-switching in Juan Marsé's *La oscura historia de la prima Montse,*" *Bulletin of Hispanic Studies,* 76 (1999): 359–366;

Gonzalo Sobejano, *Novela española de nuestro tiempo (en busca del pueblo perdido)* (Madrid: Prensa Española, 1975), pp. 446–459.

# Carmen Martín Gaite

### (8 December 1925 – 23 July 2000)

Catherine Jaffe
*Texas State University–San Marcos*

BOOKS: *El balneario* (Madrid: Alianza, 1954);

*Entre visillos* (Barcelona: Destino, 1957); translated by Frances M. López-Morillas as *Behind the Curtains* (New York: Columbia University Press, 1990);

*Las ataduras: Relatos* (Barcelona: Destino, 1960);

*Ritmo lento* (Barcelona: Seix Barral, 1963);

*El proceso de Macanaz: Historia de un empapelamiento* (Madrid: Moneda & Crédito, 1970); republished as *Macanaz, otro paciente de la Inquisición* (Madrid: Taurus, 1975);

*Usos amorosos del dieciocho en España* (Madrid: Siglo Veintiuno, 1972); translated by Maria G. Tomsich as *Love Customs in Eighteenth-Century Spain* (Berkeley: University of California Press, 1991);

*La búsqueda de interlocutor y otras búsquedas* (Madrid: Nostromo, 1973);

*Retahílas* (Barcelona: Destino, 1974);

*Fragmentos de interior* (Barcelona: Destino, 1976);

*A rachas: Poesía,* edited by Jesús Muñárriz (Madrid: Peralta/Ayuso, 1976); revised and enlarged as *Después de todo: Poesía a rachas,* edited by Muñárriz (Madrid: Hiperión, 1993);

*El conde de Guadalhorce, su época y su labor* (Madrid: Colegio de Ingenieros de Caminos, Canales y Puertos, 1977);

*El cuarto de atrás* (Barcelona: Destino, 1978); translated by Helen R. Lane as *The Back Room* (New York: Columbia University Press, 1983);

*Cuentos completos* (Madrid: Alianza, 1978); enlarged as *Cuentos completos y un monólogo* (Barcelona: Anagrama, 1994);

*El castillo de las tres murallas* (Barcelona: Lumen, 1981);

*El cuento de nunca acabar: Apuntes sobre la narración, el amor, y la mentira* (Madrid: Trieste, 1983);

*El pastel del diablo* (Barcelona: Lumen, 1985);

*Usos amorosos de la postguerra española* (Barcelona: Anagrama, 1987); translated by Margaret E. W. Jones as *Courtship Customs in Postwar Spain* (Lewisburg, Pa.: Bucknell University Press / London: Associated University Presses, 2004);

*Carmen Martín Gaite (photograph © G. Giovannetti/Effige; from the cover for* Lo raro es vivir, *1996; Thomas Cooper Library, University of South Carolina)*

*Desde la ventana: Enfoque femenino de la literatura española* (Madrid: Espasa-Calpe, 1987);

*Caperucita en Manhattan* (Madrid: Siruela, 1990);

*Nubosidad variable* (Barcelona: Anagrama, 1992); translated by Margaret Jull Costa as *Variable Cloud* (London: Harvill, 1997);

*Agua pasada: Artículos, prólogos y discursos* (Barcelona: Anagrama, 1993);

*La reina de las nieves* (Barcelona: Anagrama, 1994); translated by Costa as *The Farewell Angel* (London: Harvill, 1999);

*Esperando el porvenir: Homenaje a Ignacio Aldecoa* (Madrid: Siruela, 1995);

*Hilo a la Cometa: La visión, la memoria y el sueño,* edited by Emma Martinell (Madrid: Espasa-Calpe, 1995);

*Lo raro es vivir* (Barcelona: Anagrama, 1996); translated by Anne McLean as *Living's the Strange Thing* (London: Harvill, 2004);

*Irse de casa* (Barcelona: Anagrama, 1998);

*La hermana pequeña* (Barcelona: Anagrama, 1999);

*Los parentescos* (Barcelona: Anagrama, 2001);

*Poemas* (Barcelona: Plaza & Janés, 2001);

*Pido la palabra* (Barcelona: Anagrama, 2002);

*Cuadernos de todo,* edited by María Vittoria Calvi, prologue by Rafael Chirbes (Barcelona: Arctć, 2002);

*Visión de Nueva York,* edited by Ignacio Álvarez Vara and A. B. Márquez (Madrid: Siruela, 2005).


PLAY PRODUCTION: *La hermana pequeña,* Madrid, El Centro Cultural de la Villa, 19 January 1999.


PRODUCED SCRIPT: *Teresa de Jesús,* Televisión Española, 1984.


OTHER: *Ocho siglos de poesía gallega: Antología bilingüe,* edited by Martín Gaite and Andrés Ruiz Tarazona (Madrid: Alianza, 1972).


TRANSLATIONS: Ignazio Silone, *Vino y pan* (Madrid: Alianza, 1968);

Eva Figes, *Actitudes patriarcales: Las mujeres en la sociedad* (Madrid: Alianza, 1972);

Eça de Quierós and Ramalho Ortigâo, *El misterio de la carretera de Sintra* (Madrid: Nostromo, 1974);

Bruno Bettelheim, ed., *Los Cuentos de Perrault: Seguidos de los cuentos de Madame d'Aulnoye y de Madame Le Prince de Beaumont* (Barcelona: Crítica, 1980);

William Carlos Williams, *Viaje hacia el Amor y otros poemas (1954–1962)* (Madrid: Trieste, 1981);

Virginia Woolf, *Al faro* (Barcelona: EDHASA, 1982);

Gustave Flaubert, *Madame Bovary* (Barcelona: Bruguera, 1982);

Italo Svevo, *Senectud* (Barcelona: Bruguera, 1982);

Emily Brontë, *Cumbres borrascosas* (Barcelona: Bruguera, 1984);

Rainer Maria Rilke, *Cartas francesas a Merline, 1919–1922* (Madrid: Alianza, 1987);

Primo Levi, *El sistema periódico* (Madrid: Alianza, 1987);

Levi, *Historias naturales* (Madrid: Alianza, 1988);

C. S. Lewis, *Una pena observada* (Madrid: Trieste, 1988);

Natalia Ginzburg, *Querido Miguel* (Barcelona: Lumen, 1989);

Fernando Pessoa, *El marinero* (Alcalá de Henares: Fundación Colegio del Rey, 1990);

Felipe Alfau, *Cuentos españoles de antaño* (Madrid: Siruela, 1991);

George MacDonald, *La princesa y los trasgos* (Madrid: Siruela, 1995);

Ginzburg, *Nuestros ayeres* (Madrid: Debate, 1996);

Charlotte Brontë, *Jane Eyre* (Barcelona: Alba, 1999);

Mariana Alcoforado, *Cartas de amor de la monja portuguesa Mariana Alcoforado* (Barcelona: Círculo de Lectores, 2000).


SELECTED PERIODICAL PUBLICATION–UNCOLLECTED: "The Virtue of Reading," translated by Marcia Welles, *PMLA,* 104 (May 1989): 348–353.


A fierce dedication to the profession of writing and an unfailing belief in the communicative and redemptive power of storytelling characterize the prolific literary career of Carmen Martín Gaite. Her works chronicle the lives of ordinary Spaniards, especially those of women, during the passage of the nation from the repression of the 1940s, 1950s, and 1960s to the heady and confusing freedoms of the post-Franco years. While many of her novels are set in Madrid, where she lived her entire adult life, Martín Gaite often turned to her memories of a provincial childhood and adolescence in Salamanca and happy summers in Galicia to explore the role of imagination and creativity in personal development. She subtly portrayed the stifling atmosphere following the Spanish Civil War by creating characters who struggle for happiness and fulfillment against stultifying social strictures and conventions. After Francisco Franco's death, Martín Gaite continued to explore the effects their parents' experience of the postwar years had on Spain's younger generation, as well as the function of memory and dreams and the uncertain limits of reality. Throughout all her work, Martín Gaite asserts the value of creative human expression, whether through the living communication of conversation or through the written word that creates its own interlocutor. As Marie-Lise Gazarian Gautier observed in her "Conversación con Carmen Martín Gaite en Nueva York" (1983, Conversation with Carmen Martín Gaite in New York), because of Martín Gaite's ability to create life-like dialogue, reading her books seems much like paying her a visit.

Carmen Martín Gaite was born in the university town of Salamanca on 8 December 1925; her father, José Martín López, was a cultured and intellectual attorney from Madrid who had frequented writers' gatherings there while studying law; her mother, María Gaite Veloso, the daughter of a geography professor, was from Orense, Galicia, where the family later spent summer vacations. Martín Gaite describes a happy childhood playing with her older sister, Ana María, on the quiet, provincial plaza where they lived, although she

Cover for Martín Gaite's semi-autobiographical 1978 novel
(translated as The Back Room, 1983), in which a
writer recalls her childhood during the Civil War
in a midnight conversation with a mysterious
visitor (Thomas Cooper Library,
University of South Carolina)

also notes in "Bosquejo autobiográfico" (Autobiographical Sketch), written in 1980, first published in Spanish with English translation in Joan Lipman Brown's *Beyond the Back Room: The Fiction of Carmen Martín Gaite* (1987) and collected in Martín Gaite's *Agua pasada: Artículos, prólogos y discursos* (1993, Water under the Bridge: Articles, Prologues, and Discourses), that Salamanca was a "ciudad de costumbres rígidas y de muchos prejuicios" (city of rigid customs and many prejudices). Her father's office was in their house, and since he did not wish to send his children to church-run schools, Carmen and Ana María were taught at home by tutors and by their father himself, who nurtured his daughters' love of art, history, and literature. This intimate and harmonious relationship with loving parents who shared with their children a love of learning was an important aspect of their childhood. Later, Martín Gaite completed high school at the Feminine Institute of Salamanca, which was attended by girls of various social classes and where she had several excellent professors who later became members of the Spanish Royal Academy. Martín Gaite credits her years at this institute with fostering in her an acceptance of friends from different social backgrounds and the beginnings of her literary vocation.

Another notable aspect of Martín Gaite's childhood was her experience of the Civil War, characterized, as it was for so many people, by distrust, privation, and the reality of violence. As a young child, she had to learn that what was spoken of in private, among friends and relatives, could never be mentioned outside the house. In particular, in her "Los encartados de Ciudad Rodrigo" (The Accused of the City of Rodrigo) from *Agua pasada* she recounts the arrest of a favorite uncle, Joaquín Gaite, who was executed in August 1936 for being a member of the Socialist Party, despite a plea from her uncle's former teacher, Miguel de Unamuno. (This incident was also narrated in her autobiographical novel *El cuarto de atrás* [1978; translated as *The Back Room,* 1983].) Although her father held liberal views, he was never imprisoned because he had never joined any political party. Martín Gaite's proud independence as a writer who developed a distinctive personal style and never became affiliated with any literary school or philosophy can be traced to her early experience with her independent-minded parents, who, although not untraditional in their own lifestyle, nevertheless fully supported their daughter's uncommon ambitions. During the 1950s, when he was working in Madrid, José Martín even delivered a lecture in the Academy of Jurisprudence asserting women's right to work and to economic independence, an unusually progressive stance for that time. María Gaite, although a traditional wife and mother herself, staunchly defended her daughter's right to pursue an education and a career. In *El cuarto de atrás,* for example, the protagonist, C, recalls her mother's swiftly contradicting a woman who has just rebuked C's studiousness by quoting the old refrain, "Mujer que sabe latín no puede tener buen fin" (A woman who knows Latin will come to a bad end). Her mother tartly replies, "Hasta a coser un botón aprende mejor una persona lista que una tonta" (Even to sew on a button, a smart person learns better than a stupid one).

Martín Gaite began working toward a degree in Romance philology in 1943 at the University of Salamanca, where she formed friendships with future writers such as Ignacio Aldecoa. Although also tempted during those years by her keen interest and talent for the theater, Martín Gaite continued to devote herself to literature and spent a summer studying in Coimbra, Portugal, where she determined to write a doctoral thesis on the Galician-Portuguese songbooks of the thirteenth century. After finishing her degree in 1948, she went on a summer scholarship to Cannes, a trip that proved decisive to her career. The freedom and independence she experienced in France, and the new authors she read, such as Jean-Paul Sartre, Albert Camus, Antoine de Saint-Exupéry, André Gide, and Marcel Proust, all made her realize that she would not continue living in Salamanca upon her return to Spain. She moved to Madrid that autumn to begin work on her doctorate, but when her old friend Aldecoa brought her into his circle of young writers, which included Alfonso Sastre, Medardo Fraile, Jesús Fernández Santos, and Rafael Sánchez Ferlosio, her scholarly pursuits gradually lost their interest for her. She met other artists, actors, and journalists and enjoyed the cultural life of Madrid until she fell seriously ill with typhus. She returned to Salamanca to recuperate, and soon her father requested a transfer to Madrid. The whole family moved to live in the capital in early 1950. After attempting to teach in a girls' school (with disastrous results, apparently), Martín Gaite worked as a clerk in her father's office and became engaged to Sánchez Ferlosio, whom she married in 1953.

After their marriage, the young couple spent some time with Sánchez Ferlosio's family in Rome and traveled throughout Italy. During this visit, Martín Gaite read the works of contemporary Italian writers, such as Cesare Pavese and Italo Svevo, whom she claimed influenced her greatly. Upon their return to Madrid, the couple moved into an apartment, given to them by Martín Gaite's father, on Dr. Esquerdo Street in the affluent Salamanca district. Martín Gaite lived in this apartment for the rest of her life. The young writers settled down, determined to earn a living from their writing. As Martín Gaite recalls in "Bosquejo autobiográfico," "Nunca tuvimos criada, nos repartíamos las tareas domésticas y trabajábamos con total independencia uno de otro. La misma independencia que manteníamos en todo, sin interferir nunca uno en las amistades ni en las manías del otro, y recibiendo continuamente a los buenos amigos. Él escribía sobre todo de noche, y yo también me volví bastante nocturna y muy poco esclava de los horarios" (We never had a servant. We divided the domestic chores and we worked with complete independence from one another; the same independence that we maintained in everything, without one of us ever interfering in the friendships or in the manias of the other, all the while continually wel-

coming good friends. He wrote mainly at night, and I also became quite nocturnal and was not bound to any schedule).

The couple began to collaborate in a literary review, *Revista española* (Spanish Review), which Sánchez Ferlosio had founded with Sastre and Aldecoa. Martín Gaite's earliest stories, such as her tale of a girl's experience of class prejudice, "La chica Downstairs," reveal the influence of her association with this midcentury generation of prose writers. They combined an interest in Italian neorealist fiction, American writers such as William Faulkner and John Dos Passos, and the French *nouveau roman* with a defense of the social concerns of their generation, which had experienced the Civil War as children and had come of age during the years of postwar monotony.

In 1954 Martín Gaite was awarded the Gijón Prize by a prestigious writers' group for her first novella, *El balneario* (1954, The Spa). As was her custom, she did not show this book to her husband until after it had been published, because she did not want to be influenced or discouraged by his criticism. *El balneario* tells the story of a woman's boredom with her lonely, routine existence. Her desires and anxieties erupt when she arrives at the orderly, monotonous world of a spa. Combining realistic narration with an increasingly fantastic account of the woman's dream—or nightmare—of escape, Martín Gaite leads her readers on a puzzling journey, using skillful narrative techniques to obscure the boundaries of the real and the dreamed. This novella, although recognized by her fellow writers, did not garner Martín Gaite wider, popular acclaim. It was published together with several short stories, and more short stories were added in later editions. Eventually, *El balneario,* the stories, and a later novella, *Las ataduras: Relatos* (1960, Binding Ties: Stories), were published together in a collection, *Cuentos completos* (1978, Complete Stories).

The late 1950s were years of both success and sorrow for Martín Gaite. After receiving the Gijón Prize in the spring of 1954, her first child, Miguel, was born in October, only to die of meningitis in May 1955. Her second and last child, Marta, was born in May 1956. *Entre visillos* (1957; translated as *Behind the Curtains,* 1990), Martín Gaite's first long novel, earned her the Nadal Prize in 1958. She had submitted it under a pseudonym to the prize committee to avoid any connection between her and her husband, who had won the same prize two years earlier. The publicity surrounding the Nadal Prize helped Martín Gaite win both fame and a measure of economic relief. The novel, set in a provincial town in the 1950s, is loosely based on her experiences at the Feminine Institute of Salamanca. Through a combination of first- and third-

CARMEN MARTÍN GAITE

CAPERUCITA EN MANHATTAN

SIRUELA

*Paperback cover for the 1996 edition of Martín Gaite's 1990 novel (Little Red Riding Hood in Manhattan), a modern-day retelling of Charles Perrault's classic fairy tale (Thomas Cooper Library, University of South Carolina)*

provincial world of Salamanca she left behind when she moved to Madrid.

Her second novel, *Ritmo lento* (A Slower Rhythm), was published in 1963. It also deals with a character who resists assimilation to social norms. On a wider scale, the story of David Fuente, an unusual young man who takes every action of his own and of others extremely seriously, scrutinizes conventional, bourgeois morality and criticizes its tendency to repress its compromises with the truth. Through the long, first-person, chronologically disjointed monologue of David, who has ended up in a sanatorium because he cannot accept hypocrisy, and the more objective initial and final chapters, the author shows the impossibility of David's uncompromising attitude. In its psychological complexity, *Ritmo lento* moves beyond the social realism of *El balneario* to embrace existential themes. Perhaps because of the complexity of the novel, or the advent of the novels of the Latin American boom, Martín Gaite's second novel did not receive much recognition when it was published.

During the following years Martín Gaite moved away from novel writing and undertook research in the literature and history of the eighteenth century. Seeking at first, she claimed, merely to fill a gap in her knowledge, she became so interested in her subject that, in an almost ten-year break from fiction, she produced several important scholarly works: *El proceso de Macanaz: Historia de un empapelamiento* (1970, The Macanaz Case: History of a Lawsuit), about a forgotten figure of the early Spanish Enlightenment; and *Usos amorosos del dieciocho en España* (1972; translated as *Love Customs in Eighteenth-Century Spain*, 1991), a groundbreaking study of women's cultural history that has become a classic in its field. The latter work also served as the dissertation for her doctorate, awarded the same year.

In *Usos amorosos del dieciocho en España* Martín Gaite studies the scandalous late-eighteenth-century custom of the *cortejo,* the male companion who attended a married woman, showering her with the attention not provided by her husband. She analyzes the daily lives of women as seen in commentary in the new periodical press and other literature and discusses the deficiencies of women's education. She gives attention to linguistic detail, such as the shades of meaning implied by words such as *bachillera,* which in its masculine form had referred to a male student but evolved in its feminine form to mean a woman who talks too much. Because of new social arrangements, such as mixed-gender social gatherings, and Enlightenment ideals of education, she concludes, Spanish women first began to question their ability to achieve happiness in their traditional roles and to feel the contradictions between their expectations

person narration, *Entre visillos* captures the life of the provincial town mainly through the eyes of Natalia, an adolescent schoolgirl with aspirations to a career, and the outsider Pablo Klein, a German instructor at her school, whose one-semester stay sets the chronological boundaries of the novel. Pablo encourages Natalia's vague ambitions, which are discouraged by her family's traditional views on women's proper roles as wife and mother. At the core of the novel is the conflict between stifling convention and more liberal-minded views espousing independence, untraditional lifestyles, less social snobbery, and, in short, an end to the barriers to authentic personal fulfillment for both men and women. The problematic relation of the individual to the social structures he or she must live in is Martín Gaite's central theme, and she acknowledged that she wrote the novel as a rejection of the closed,

and abilities and the possibilities available to them in society.

Martín Gaite returned to these themes repeatedly in her later works, both in essay and fiction. She acknowledged the curious fascination her archival work held for her, and in "En el centenario de don Melchor de Macanaz (1670–1760)" (In the Centenary of Don Melchior de Macanaz [1670–1760]), collected in her *La búsqueda de interlocutor y otras búsquedas* (1973, The Search for an Interlocutor and Other Searches), she explains how becoming acquainted with Don Melchor de Macanaz helped see her through some personal difficulties: "Su trato me sacó de la prisa, y de muchas melancolías y agobios personales." (Dealing with him removed me from haste and helped me out of many personal melancholies and oppressions). Her long effort to breathe life into the random facts and dates of history nourished her later fiction and essays, in which both the idea of the individual in history, and the genesis and possibilities of narration, are major themes. She sensed a connection between eighteenth-century social practices, for example, and the problems faced by twentieth-century women, and she tried to relate "los vicios del *cortejo* con las falacias y tergiversaciones que anidan en la raíz de muchas relaciones extramatrimoniales padecidas por mujeres de hoy" (the vices of the *cortejo* with the fallacies and distortions that are at the root of many extramarital relations suffered by women today).

Martín Gaite separated from her husband in 1970–amicably, by her own account–and continued living with her daughter in their apartment on Dr. Esquerdo Street. In 1974 she published *Retahílas* (Yarns), a narrative tour de force of alternating chapters of monologues exchanged as a conversation between a young man, Germán, and his aunt, Eulalia, who have met at the family's ancestral home in Galicia to keep vigil at the deathbed of Eulalia's grandmother, who is also Germán's great-grandmother. Their unusual dialogue takes them back into the family's past, spinning tales and making connections between their long-felt needs and desires. Germán's mother, Eulalia's former school friend and later sister-in-law, had died when he was young, and the boy and his sister suffered when his father married their prosaic, materialistic nanny. Eulalia defends her absence from her nephew during these years, during which she dedicated herself to a deliberately untraditional lifestyle that she now realizes has led to certain failures, especially her separation from her husband. Eulalia's and Germán's healing communion holds off the imminent arrival of death, at least until the dawn, while they intertwine their memories with the historical events and movements–the Civil War, the monotony of the postwar period, the later generation's

preoccupation with material values, and the youngest generation's sense of loss and moral emptiness–that have so affected them.

While the influence of her historical investigations were evident in *Retahílas,* Martín Gaite changes her lyrical tone in her next novel. Focusing on immediate, fast-paced action rather than on introspection and memory, *Fragmentos de interior* (1976, Interior Fragments) was written in only three months to satisfy a bet with a friend that she could not write a novel that quickly. It tells the story of the well-to-do Alvar family and its servants in Madrid during three days in 1975 and reflects modern city life with all its attractions, distractions, and problems, especially those caused by the rapid change in social standards and relations between the sexes experienced in Spain during the 1970s. Diego Alvar is separated from his wife, who drinks too much and cannot get over her husband. Diego lives with a much younger mistress, who is casually unfaithful to him. Diego's daughter has many relationships, and his son is deciding on his sexual preference. The novel also shows the family's interactions with their servants, whose own struggles with changing social roles and dislocation from country to city set off their employers' self-centered behavior. After an unsuccessful attempt to produce a movie based on the novel, it was later produced as a miniseries for Spanish television.

As further proof of her literary versatility, in 1976 Martín Gaite published a volume of her poetry, *A rachas: Poesía* (In a Gust of Wind: Verse), collecting poems written in her youth and through the 1970s. She considered these works as spontaneous and less serious than her prose compositions, but they are nevertheless interesting to admirers of her prose, who can appreciate how "in both genres she excels at capturing the rhythm of everyday speech," as Brown puts it in *Secrets from the Back Room.* Between 1976 and 1980 Martín Gaite also wrote weekly book reviews for the newspaper *Diario-16,* an exercise that brought her into contact with the work and ideas of many Spanish and foreign authors.

With Franco's death in 1975 came a relaxing of the decades-long censorship that had prevented authors from writing openly and critically about the Civil War, and so a spate of memoirs recounting the war years was published. Martín Gaite herself began writing a novel the day Franco was buried, combining her project to write a fantastic novel in homage to Tzvetan Todorov with her memories of the war and its aftermath. *El cuarto de atrás* won the National Prize in literature in 1978. In this partly autobiographical, partly fantastic fiction, a writer named C receives a midnight visit from a mysterious man in black, although she does not remember having made an appointment with him for an interview. In the course of a stormy night, their conversation ranges widely over her memories of the war and the years after. They discuss politics, childhood games, and her early friendship with the daughter of imprisoned schoolteachers with whom she invented a magical world of escape, "La isla de Bergai" (The Isle of Bergai). She recalls spending nights in bomb shelters and learning about wartime realities such as contraband and rationing. Her memories, drawn forth by the subtle questions of her interlocutor, are linked topically rather than chronologically, and part of the plot of the novel involves how she recalls and unravels the twisted threads of her memories, following back through time the "piedrecitas blancas" (little white stones) of concrete facts that can be ordered and disordered magically. C recounts how, on Franco's death, she felt even more keenly how he had "paralizado el tiempo" (paralyzed time), and that an accounting had to be made of this stilled block of experience. She stresses above all the effect of popular literature, music, and motion pictures on young women's formation and desires for escape, and how she had rebelled against the "conducta sobria" (sober conduct) inculcated during the social service all girls had to perform for the Sección femenina (Feminine Section) founded by the Nationalist group the Falange in 1934 and continued as a government body after the Civil War. Musing on her development as a writer, C describes the back playroom she could retreat to as a child, where she had complete freedom from external rules and order. It has served ever since in her memory as a site of creativity and inspiration, for writing to her never loses its sense of play and adventure. The topsy-turvy state of the back room, both of her memory and of her imagination, reflects Martín Gaite's dedication of the novel to Lewis Carroll, "que todavía nos consuela de tanta cordura y nos acoge en su mundo al revés" (who still consoles us for so much sanity and who welcomes us in his upside-down world). As she talks to her mysterious interlocutor throughout the night, the stack of papers on her desk—her new novel—magically grows. Martín Gaite's ingenious blending of personal anecdote with speculation on the relation between the act of writing and the ordering and disordering of memory make the self-referential *El cuarto de atrás* a masterpiece of contemporary Spanish literature. This novel brought its author recognition among a much wider audience than before and has continued to generate more critical interest than any of her other works.

The same year *El cuarto de atrás* was published, though, Martín Gaite lost both her parents, who had steadfastly supported and encouraged her vocation. In "Bosquejo autobiográfico" she writes movingly of their loss and of "el hueco que me dejaron" (the empty place that they left me) and recalls the influence they had on her career. Because of her early academic successes, her father had wanted her to be a university professor. Later, he suggested that she join the Madrid Ateneo when she was a young mother feeling the need for more intellectual stimulation. José Martín was also a member, and his daughter felt a close connection with him as she spent hours in the library there, sheltered from the hustle and bustle of downtown Madrid. As a young man, her father had attended lectures and talked with many of the turn-of-the-century literary and intellectual figures whose portraits line the walls of that important Madrid cultural institution. If she attributes her academic inclinations to her father, though, she connects her mother most closely with her writing. In a prologue dedicated to María Gaite, while looking at her picture on the wall above her desk, Martín Gaite writes of the difficulty of writing and how her mother always knew when she was working on a new story. Her mother would quietly encourage her, reassuringly reminding her daughter that she always felt doubtful when beginning a project, but that, with time, she would be able to bring it to completion. In "Retahíla con nieve en Nueva York (Para mi madre, *in memoriam*)" (Yarn with Snow in New York [For My Mother, in Memoriam]), published in *From Fiction to Metafiction: Essays in Honor of Carmen Martín Gaite* (1983), she imagines her mother smiling at her as she writes in her rented room in New York, with the snow starting to fall.

Martín Gaite's books of essays, *La búsqueda de interlocutor y otros búsquedas* and *El cuento de nunca acabar: Apuntes sobre la narración, el amor, y la mentira* (1983, The Never-Ending Story: Notes on Narration, Love, and Lies), expand on her idea, vividly portrayed in *El cuarto de atrás,* that creating or finding an interlocutor is necessary to any human expression and that oral storytelling is an innate human enterprise. *La búsqueda de interlocutor y otros búsquedas* unites articles published during a ten-year period, loosely organized around the problem of how people tend to use literature or the popular media, such as television or advertising, as a mirror, a habit that usually produces great dissatisfaction with the image reflected back to them. The author points out the inauthenticity of such mirroring of desire, especially for women, in articles such as "La influencia de la publicidad en las mujeres" (The Influence of Advertising on Women) and "De madame Bovary a Marilyn Monroe" (From Madame Bovary to Marilyn Monroe) and asserts the necessity of finding a true interlocutor to whom one can tell one's own story.

*El cuento de nunca acabar* is a sustained philosophical meditation, in the form of stories, essays, and anecdotes, on the act of narration and writing. Rejecting scholarly works on the subject and traditional organization, Martín Gaite gives an intensely personal and original interpretation of the origin of narrative in childhood. In a distinctive overlapping structure, complemented by whimsical pen-and-ink drawings of "La gentileza y soledad de Miss Mady" (The Kindness and Solitude of Miss Mady) by Paco Nieva, she deliberately blurs generic divisions to express her ideas about the importance of narration to a child's development and to an adult's sense of self—in short, narration as the fundamental mechanism by which an individual relates to the world about him or her.

Drawing on her research into the conflicts women faced in the eighteenth century to find happiness within accepted social roles, and her determination to write a history that drew on her personal experience, Martín Gaite published a new study of the connection between popular culture and women's lives during the post–Civil War period. *Usos amorosos de la postguerra española* (1987; translated as *Courtship Customs in Postwar Spain,* 2004), which won the Anagrama Essay Prize that same year, is a completely original study of women's history. In the introduction, the author explains that she wanted to answer the type of questions that had always been in the back of her mind when she read official, political "histories": What were these people really like? How did they dress, what was their social life like, and how were they brought up? Her book examines many of the cultural factors influencing women's behavior that had been mentioned in *El cuarto de atrás: la novela rosa* (women's sentimental fiction); movies, especially those made in Hollywood; and gender relations, such as courtship customs and marriage arrangements. She shows how the terms *restricción* (restriction) and *racionamiento* (rationing), connected with material hardship and scarcity immediately after the war, eventually shifted semantic fields to encompass ideological control of people's lives and behavior.

In *Desde la ventana: Enfoque femenino de la literatura española* (From the Window: A Feminine Focus on Spanish Literature), also published in 1987, Martín Gaite continues to study women's experience of everyday life, of literature, and of culture. She responds to the question of the existence of a specifically feminine language with a reconsideration of Spanish literary tradition from a woman's viewpoint. Rejecting the scholarly feminism of literary criticism written in English as dry and uninteresting, Martín Gaite writes that she prefers Virginia Woolf's *A Room of One's Own* (1929) and imagines the English writer talking directly to her about their shared profession.

Martín Gaite elaborates an original thesis about women's perspective in literature as that of a *ventanera,* a pejorative name for women more interested in what or who might be passing in the street than in their work in the house. Martín Gaite reevaluates the term to refer to the imagined transcendence of physical reality. She uses *ventanera* to refer to a woman who looks out a window—real or imagined—to observe without being seen, and yet is conditioned by the interior spaces in which she is confined. This concept implies both the possibility of fantasy and escape, often through reading, and the reality of enclosure. Martín Gaite examines many classical and modern works of Spanish literature from this perspective, including those of St. Teresa of Ávila, María de Zayas, and Carmen Laforet, and analyzes how women accepted as their own the models of conduct held out to them in the Spanish sixteenth- and seventeenth-century *comedia* (three-act play) and in literature of the Romantics in the nineteenth century. In this book, and always, Martín Gaite firmly rejects being identified as feminist, whether from a deep-rooted mistrust of being labeled as part of any school or group, or because of the negative image of feminism held in Spanish society even during the 1970s and 1980s, or perhaps for both reasons. In her novels and essays, however, there is no doubt that she develops a distinctive personal style rooted in her own experience as a woman, nor that "she has gradually come to place her subjectivity as a Spanish female at the center of both forms of writing," as Constance A. Sullivan puts it in her "The Boundary-Crossing Essays of Carmen Martín Gaite" (1993).

Buoyed by the success of *El cuarto de atrás,* during the 1980s Martín Gaite became a sought-after speaker at universities in the United States, visiting, among others, Columbia University, the University of Virginia, Vassar College, and the University of Chicago. She pursued her interest in the roots of storytelling in childhood and began to publish children's books that rework traditional fairy-tale themes and plots. Her heroines are strong, clever girls who surmount great odds with valor and win great success. In *El castillo de las tres murallas* (1981, The Three-Walled Castle), *El pastel del diablo* (1985, The Devil's Cake), and *Caperucita en Manhattan* (1990, Little Red Riding Hood in Manhattan), Martín Gaite "created a group of female characters unwilling to remain trapped by their previous fictions and bold enough to rewrite their own texts," as María Elena Soliño observes in her *Women and Children First: Spanish Women Writers and the Fairy Tale Tradition* (2002). *El castillo de las tres murallas* is the story of the evil Lucandro, who keeps his wife, Serena, locked up and separates her from her daughter, Altalé. The young girl becomes the champion of her father's

*Cover for Martín Gaite's 1994 novel (The Snow Queen; translated as* The Farewell Angel, *1999), inspired by a Hans Christian Andersen tale (Thomas Cooper Library, University of South Carolina)*

who longs to escape from both Brooklyn and her traditional mother to explore the exciting world of Manhattan. When given a chance, she runs away to Central Park, which her mother had insisted was a fearful place by night. There she meets Edgar Woolf, a kindly, rich old man with whom she strikes up an immediate friendship, eventually leading to his romance with her grandmother, a former cabaret singer. These stories, while accessible to children, are not merely for young readers. They are fascinating revisions of fairy-tale themes and structures by an author ever attuned to the effects literature has on women.

Martín Gaite's daughter, Marta, died in 1985. Martín Gaite struggled to continue her writing career, although several years passed before she published another novel. As she herself put it, she was unable to work on the novel she thought she would finish just before her daughter's death because "solamente de pensar en *La reina de las nieves* se me helaba el corazón" (even thinking about *The Snow Queen* froze my heart). In 1988 she was honored with the Prince of Asturias Prize for Letters. The sorrow she felt was difficult to overcome, however, as she points out in a footnote to the 1993 republication of "Bosquejo autobiográfico." She says that the sketch was written more than a decade earlier for readers of English unfamiliar with her Spanish context and adds, "En otro orden de cosas, para un lector que no conozca mi biografía reciente, donde lea 'soledad' y 'muerte,' puede estar seguro de que mi vivencia de esas dos nociones era aún bien incompleta" (In another order of things, for a reader who is unfamiliar with my recent biography, where he or she reads *solitude* and *death,* they can be sure that my lived experience of those two notions was as yet quite incomplete).

During the 1990s Martín Gaite returned to novel writing with a series of successful books that became best-sellers in Spain and attracted a flurry of media attention upon their release. *Nubosidad variable* (1992; translated as *Variable Cloud,* 1997) recounts the reunion of two women in their fifties, Mariana León, a successful psychiatrist trying to understand her penchant for dead-end relationships, and Sofía Montalvo, a wife and mother whose creativity has been subservient to her domestic duties for many years. As the two former school friends face the breakup of their relationships and escape from their homes, they find salvation in their letters to each other, finally reuniting at the end of the novel at the beach in Cádiz to collaborate on their mutual story. Martín Gaite was awarded the National Prize for Spanish Letters by the Ministry of Culture in 1994, the same year her next novel, *La reina de las nieves* (translated as *The Farewell Angel,*

repressed subjects, and Serena escapes with her daughter's music teacher. She returns to help her daughter escape also, turning Lucandro into a fish as they leave. Plans to publish this novel in the United States failed, however, because American publishers objected to celebrating an unfaithful wife in a children's book. In *El pastel del diablo,* an elderly couple conceives a daughter, Sorpresa, after years of longing for a child. Sorpresa, however, is destined to be different, predicts a fairy, and as the child grows up she is so bright and asks so many questions that she is put out of school. She causes her parents to disagree and finally begins to write her own stories, since she realizes that she fits into none of the traditional ones. Sorpresa scorns a traditional woman's life and finds salvation in writing stories. *Caperucita en Manhattan,* accompanied by the author's own drawings, tells the story of Sara Allen,

1999), appeared. She had conceived this novel years earlier and had worked on it during a semester in residence at the University of Chicago, but after her daughter's death she put it away for almost a decade. This novel reworks Hans Christian Andersen's "Snedronningen: Et eventyr i syv historier (1844, The Snow Queen: An Adventure in Seven Stories) in the context of 1970s Spain and of the problems of lack of communication and shared values in families. It is a complex narrative, dense with literary references. Drawing on Henrik Ibsen's *Fruen fra havet* (1888, The Lady from the Sea) and on elements of the nineteenth-century novel such as an old house by the sea, a lighthouse, and the son's search to uncover his lost and obscured origins, Martín Gaite tells the story of the recently orphaned Leonardo Villalba, who, on his release from jail, returns to his parents' luxurious house to rummage through his father's papers. He wants to discover the key to his emotional problems and to his icy relationship with the woman he had believed was his mother, a blonde heiress from Chicago. His search, which he records as a journal, leads him to the old house by the sea and the woman who lives there: Casilda, the mother he never knew existed, whose letters he read in his father's study.

A mother-child relationship also underlies Martín Gaite's next novel. *Lo raro es vivir* (1996; translated as *Living's the Strange Thing*, 2004) takes the whirlwind life of youth culture in contemporary Madrid as its background. Its protagonist is a woman in her thirties, Águeda Soler, who must overcome her own self-destructive impulses to pass the final hurdle to maturity. The novel shows her undergoing a crisis as she moves restlessly between different parts of her life, including her work as an archivist, her past as a rock musician, and her strained relationship with her father and his new wife, toward a posthumous reconciliation with her mother, whose self-sufficiency and success as an artist had always intimidated her daughter. In 1997, Martín Gaite received the Gold Medal from the Círculo de Bellas Artes.

*Irse de casa* (1998, Leaving Home) is the final novel Martín Gaite published during her lifetime. It is an ambitious work, told from many intersecting viewpoints, that recounts the return of a successful New York fashion designer, Amparo Miranda, to her hometown, a provincial Spanish city where she had suffered the stigma of being a fatherless child. She passes unrecognized through the town, recalling old acquaintances and noting the changes in the city, musing on her life in New York, her mother, her deceased husband, her current lover, her children, and the person she has become. While the novel deals with the social issues familiar from Martín Gaite's earlier work,

it also reflects newer concerns for the novelist, such as the disastrous effects of drug abuse and AIDS among young people, homosexuality, and incestuous desire. Amparo is finally recognized by a man she used to love, a man who could make her happy, but she nevertheless acts on her determination to return to the life she has made for herself in New York. She plans to collaborate with her son on a screenplay about life in the provincial city. As in all her novels, Martín Gaite weaves a dense web of relationships between individuals trying to break free from their upbringing: the driven, ambitious Amparo, who has used her wealth and plastic surgery to defy the ravages of time; an eccentric aristocrat who defies convention and grows old alone; an almost saintly doctor desperately working to protect young people from their demons. She sets her characters, who struggle to escape outmoded social conventions, against the changing face of the provincial town, with its crumbling buildings and sporadic renovations, and amid the interplay of classic literature such as the *comedia* and popular culture.

*Los parentescos* (2001, Family Ties), left unfinished at Martín Gaite's death, shows again her concern for the feelings of dislocation and malaise resulting from broken families and changing social standards, and the contrast between Madrid and provincial cities. The story is recounted by a child narrator, Baltazar, who tries to make sense of the confusing relationships in his family. His older brothers and sister, he learns, have a different father, and his own father does not live in the house with them. In addition, he discovers there is a hidden tie to the old *marquesa* (marchioness) who sometimes passes his house in the center of Segovia. The haughty aristocrat will not speak to him or his mother, but upon her death she leaves her crumbling mansion to Baltazar, her only grandson. When the family moves to Madrid, they leave the provincial city behind, but not the apparent confusion of their relationships. Baltazar's sensitive reaction to the betrayals and silences of those around him shows his coming-of-age in a family where every member has built him- or herself a protective shell to guard against the upsets of their chaotic household, a microcosm, perhaps, of Spanish society.

Although most famous for her novels, essays, and historical studies, Martín Gaite cultivated other areas of letters, as well. Her collected poetry has been published in several different forms. She wrote a script for a television series on St. Teresa in 1983. She wrote short essays for newspapers, book reviews, and prologues and introductions for the works of other novelists, many of which are collected in *Agua pasada*. In 1999 she published a play, *La hermana pequeña* (The Little Sister), about two half sisters, one of whom goes

CARMEN MARTÍN GAITE

## Lo raro es vivir

**ANAGRAMA**
Narrativas hispánicas

*Paperback cover for Martín Gaite's 1996 novel (translated as* Living's the Strange Thing, *2004), about a woman in her thirties who must overcome her self-destructive impulses if she is to pass the final hurdle to maturity (Thomas Cooper Library, University of South Carolina)*

to be an actress in Madrid, leaving her younger sister behind in her provincial town. Martín Gaite had tried for years to have the play performed before it was finally staged by Ángel García Moreno in 1999. Also significant are the translations published over a thirty-year period that spanned most of her literary career. They include novels and poetry from French, Italian, Portuguese, and English, and her choices are revealing for their influence on the style and themes of her own fiction. Her translations of the works of writers such as Svevo, Natalia Ginzburg, and Primo Levi show an interest in Italian literature that dated back to the early years of her marriage. The Portuguese translations

reflect her Galician background, while writers such as Gustave Flaubert, Woolf, and the Brontës clearly interested her for their insight on the major themes of her fiction: women's struggles for happiness against social pressures and conventions. Martín Gaite produced more than twenty translations during the years when she also published more than twenty-five creative and scholarly books.

In "Bosquejo autobiográfico" Carmen Martín Gaite summarizes her career as she saw it:

> Pero siempre he evitado, aun a costa de vivir más modestamente, los empleos que pudieran esclavizarme y quitarme tiempo para dedicarlo a la lectura, a la escritura y a otra de mis pasiones favoritas: el cultivo de las amistad. Los amigos son para mí la cosa más importante del mundo, la más gratificante y consoladora, y se requieren una delicadeza y un tino especiales para no perderlos. . . . Yo no le temo a la soledad, me he acostumbrado a ella y la aguanto bastante mejor que la mayoría de la gente que conozco, pero siempre estoy dispuesta a quebrarla cuando un amigo viene a perfumarla con su conversación y compañía.

> (I have always avoided, even at the cost of living more modestly, any employment which might make me a slave, and take away time dedicated to reading, writing, and my other favorite passion: the cultivation of friendship. For me friends are the most important thing in the world; the most gratifying and consoling, and they require delicacy and dexterity of a special kind so as not to lose them. . . . I am not afraid of being alone, I have become accustomed to it, and I tolerate it better than most of the people I know. But I am always ready to break my solitude when a friend comes to perfume it with his conversation and company).

Martín Gaite's ear for dialogue, colloquial expression, and new slang and English expressions that have filtered into everyday Spanish draws her readers repeatedly back to her works. Martín Gaite's stories create within her interlocutor, the reader, a feeling of personal connection to a writer in many ways circumspect about her private life. Martín Gaite's work, especially her intimate chronicle of women's lives during the Civil War and the decades that followed it, is an important contribution to Spanish letters in the second half of the twentieth century.

**Interview:**

Marie-Lise Gazarian Gautier, "Conversación con Carmen Martín Gaite en Nueva York," in *From Fiction to Metafiction: Essays in Honor of Carmen Martín Gaite,* edited by Mirella Servodidio and Marcia L. Welles (Lincoln, Nebr.: Society of Spanish and Spanish-American Studies, 1983), pp. 25–33.

## References:

Emilie L. Bergmann, "Narrative Theory in the Mother Tongue: Carmen Martín Gaite's *Desde la ventana* and *El cuento de nunca acabar*," in *Spanish Women Writers and the Essay: Gender, Politics, and the Self*, edited by Kathleen M. Glenn and Mercedes Mazquiarán de Rodríguez (Columbia & London: University of Missouri Press, 1998), pp. 172–197;

Joan Lipman Brown, *Secrets from the Back Room: The Fiction of Carmen Martín Gaite* (University, Miss.: Romance Monographs, 1987);

Debra Castillo, "Never-Ending Story: Carmen Martín Gaite's *The Back Room*," *PMLA*, 102 (October 1987): 814–828;

Ruth El Saffar, "Redeeming Loss: Reflections on Carmen Martín Gaite's *The Back Room*," *Revista de Estudios Hispánicos*, 20 (January 1986): 1–14;

Kathleen M. Glenn and Lissette Rolón-Collazo, eds., *Carmen Martín Gaite: Cuento de nunca acabar/Never-Ending Story* (Boulder, Colo.: Society of Spanish and Spanish-American Studies, 2002);

David K. Herzberger, "Narrating the Past: History and the Novel of Memory in Postwar Spain," *PMLA*, 106 (January 1991): 34–45;

Mirella Servodidio and Marcia L. Welles, eds., *From Fiction to Metafiction: Essays in Honor of Carmen Martín Gaite* (Lincoln, Nebr.: Society of Spanish and Spanish-American Studies, 1983);

Stephanie Sieburth, "Memory, Metafiction and Mass Culture: The Popular Text in *El cuarto de atrás*," *Revista Hispánica Moderna*, 43 (1990): 78–92;

María Elena Soliño, *Women and Children First: Spanish Women Writers and the Fairy Tale Tradition* (Potomac, Md.: Scripta Humanistica, 2002), pp. 77–159, 282–286;

Constance A. Sullivan, "The Boundary-Crossing Essays of Carmen Martín Gaite," in *The Politics of the Essay: Feminist Perspectives*, edited by Ruth-Ellen Boetcher Joeres and Elizabeth Mittman (Bloomington & Indianapolis: Indiana University Press, 1993), pp. 41–56.

## Papers:

Carmen Martín Gaite's papers are privately held by her family.

# Luis Martín-Santos

*(11 November 1924 – 21 January 1964)*

Alison Ribeiro de Menezes
*University College Dublin*

BOOKS: *Grana gris* (Madrid: Afrodisio Aguado, 1945);

*Dilthey, Jaspers y la comprensión del enfermo mental* (Madrid: Paz Montalvo, 1955);

*Tiempo de silencio* (Barcelona: Seix Barral, 1961); translated by George Leeson as *Time of Silence* (New York: Harcourt, Brace & World, 1964; London: Calder, 1965);

*Libertad, temporalidad y transferencia en el psicoanálisis existencial: Para una fenomenología de la cura psicoanalítica* (Barcelona: Seix Barral, 1964);

*Apólogos y otras prosas inéditas,* edited by Salvador Clotas (Barcelona: Seix Barral, 1970);

*Tiempo de destrucción,* edited by José Carlos Mainer (Barcelona: Seix Barral, 1975);

*El análisis existencial: Ensayos,* edited by José Lázaro (Madrid: Triacastela, 2004);

*Condenada belleza del mundo,* edited by Luis Martín-Santos Laffón (Barcelona: Seix Barral, 2004).

OTHER: "Baroja–Unamuno," in *Sobre la generación del 98: Homenaje a Don Pepe Villar* (San Sebastián: Auñamendi, 1963), pp. 103–116;

"Realismo y realidad en la literatura contemporánea," in Juan Luis Suárez Granda, *Tiempo de silencio, Luis Martín-Santos* (Madrid: Alhambra, 1986), pp. 141–142.

SELECTED PERIODICAL PUBLICATIONS–
UNCOLLECTED: "El psicoanálisis existencial de Jean-Paul Sartre," *Actas Lusoespañolas de Neurología y Psiquiatría,* 9 (1950): 164–178;

"Ideas delirantes primarias, esquizofrenia y psicosis alcohólica aguda," *Actas Lusoespañolas de Neurología y Psiquiatría,* 12 (1952): 222–233;

"La paranoia alcohólica," *Actas Lusoespañolas de Neurología y Psiquiatría,* 13 (1954): 263–280;

"Jaspers y Freud," *Revista de Psiquiatría y Psicología Médica de Europa y América Latina,* 2 (1956): 694–699;

"Estudios sobre el delirio alcohólico agudo," *Actas Lusoespañolas de Neurología y Psiquiatría,* 16 (1957): 283–295;

*Luis Martín-Santos ( from the cover for* Tiempo de silencio, *1982; Thomas Cooper Library, University of South Carolina)*

"Descripción fenomenológica y análisis existencial de algunas psicosis epilépticas agudas," *Revista de Psiquiatría y Psicología Médica,* 5 (1961): 26–49;

"Un inédito de Martín-Santos," in José Romera Castillo, "Luis Martín-Santos: Entre la auscultación de la realidad y el análisis dialéctico," *Ínsula,* 358 (1976): 5;

"Luis Martín-Santos: Prosas desconocidas," *ABC Literario,* 11 November 1989, pp. 8–9.

A psychiatrist by training, Luis Martín-Santos only turned to writing fiction in his thirties. He had published one complete novel, *Tiempo de silencio* (1961; translated as *Time of Silence,* 1964), and begun a second, *Tiempo de destrucción* (1975, Time of Destruction), before his death in an automobile accident in 1964. Nevertheless, his literary legacy is significant: *Tiempo de silencio,* with its stylistic innovations, Joycean echoes, and ironic treatment of the foundational myths of Francoist Spain, is generally regarded as a turning point in the development of the contemporary Spanish novel.

Luis Martín-Santos Ribera was born on 11 November 1924 to Leandro Martín Santos, an army surgeon stationed at the time in Larache, Morocco, and Mercedes Ribera Egea. He had a younger brother, Leandro, and a sister, Encarnación, who died when she was about a year old. In 1929, when the boy was five, the family settled in San Sebastián, where Luis spent much of the rest of his life. He attended the Colegio de los Hermanos Marianistas de Aldapeta and was apparently a serious-minded boy, timid but with a passion for reading. He spent several years living with his maternal grandmother, probably as a result of the postpartum depression his mother experienced after the birth of his brother. After completing his secondary education in 1940, Martín-Santos opted to study medicine at the University of Salamanca. In 1946 he earned his degree with distinction.

Martín-Santos moved to Madrid, gaining a doctorate in 1947. Following in the footsteps of his father, he began practicing surgery at the Consejo Superior de Investigaciones Científicas (CSIC). In 1948, through the system of *oposiciones* (state examinations), he won a surgical post at Madrid General Hospital; but he soon gave up surgery for psychiatry. He remained at CSIC under the joint mentorship of Juan José López Ibor and Pedro Laín Entralgo. He published a volume of poetry, *Grana gris* (1945, Gray Grains), and found himself part of the emerging group of writers known as the Generación de medio siglo (Mid-Century Generation). One of his close friends at CSIC was Carlos Castilla del Pino, a future psychiatrist. At *tertulias* (literary gatherings) at the Café Gambrinus, Martín-Santos became acquainted with the scientist and writer Miguel Sánchez Mazas and his brother, Rafael Sánchez Ferlosio, as well as Ignacio Aldecoa, Juan Benet, and Alfonso Sastre. These latter four became key figures in the revitalization of Madrid cultural life in the 1950s. A generation born in or around the Spanish Civil War, but who had played no part in it, they also marked the beginning of a new political opposition to General Francisco Franco's regime–a generation not afraid to speak out and face possible imprisonment as a consequence.

In 1949 Martín-Santos won, again through *oposiciones,* the job of director of the mental hospital in Ciudad Real, but he left soon afterward to pursue his psychiatric studies in Heidelberg, Germany. There he met Carlos Barral, the future publisher of *Tiempo de silencio.* In 1951 Martín-Santos returned to Spain as director of the psychiatric hospital in San Sebastián, and in 1953 he married Rocío Laffón. Now settled in the Donostian capital, he combined clinical practice with research. However, the practice of psychiatry in Franco's Spain, unlike that of general medicine, was far from apolitical. Indeed, the discipline was gravely affected by the ideology of the regime and was harnessed in its project of cultural nationalism. Despite the fact that the complete works of Sigmund Freud had been translated into Spanish in 1923 (at the suggestion of essayist and philosopher José Ortega y Gasset), the writings of this influential European thinker were proscribed by the regime until 1949. Nascent prewar interest in psychoanalysis was thus stunted by the Nationalist victory in 1939, which resulted in a diaspora of opposition thinkers and their replacement by traditionalists in academic posts. In the initial postwar years, support for the right-wing, Catholic ideology of the regime–which depended upon the division of the nation into winners and losers, and which categorized the latter in psychopathological terms–included energetic defenses of the notion of racial purity offered by Antonio Vallejo Nájera, the first professor of psychiatry at Madrid University, and, less vituperatively, in certain writings by López Ibor, his successor in the post. Although partly under López Ibor's tutelage while he prepared his doctoral thesis, Martín-Santos strenuously rejected such racism as an interpretation of Spanish history and an explanation of Spanish identity; instead, he defended the views of his other doctoral supervisor, the liberal Catholic Laín Entralgo, who argued that Spain's problems were not racial but cultural. The future novelist was also greatly influenced by existentialism, a philosophy toward which López Ibor also moved.

Martín-Santos came late to Freud's works, only discovering them in the 1950s, and his prior familiarity with existentialism is fundamental to an understanding of his approach to psychiatry. He was well versed in the German phenomenological tradition, the influence of which is evident in his doctoral thesis, published in 1955 as *Dilthey, Jaspers y la comprensión del enfermo mental* (Dilthey, Jaspers, and the Understanding of the Mentally Ill). An eclectic reader, Martín-Santos spoke fluent French and was especially familiar with the work of Jean-Paul Sartre. The breadth of his learning is evident in his second major essay on psychiatry, *Libertad, tempo-*

*ralidad y transferencia en el psicoanálisis existencial: Para una fenomenología de la cura psicoanalítica* (Freedom, Temporality, and Transference: Toward a Phenomenology of the Psychoanalytic Cure), published posthumously in 1964. Martín-Santos apparently discovered Freud through his reading of Sartre and developed his own form of existential psychoanalysis, which he outlined in *Libertad, temporalidad y transferencia en el psicoanálisis existencial.* Rejecting Freud's emphasis on biological factors and the role of infancy in determining neuroses, Martín-Santos emphasized the importance of the individual's exercise of free will in concrete circumstances. For Martín-Santos, mental illness represented "bad faith" in the existentialist sense of a failure to confront personal problems and to recognize the need for change. The aim of psychoanalysis was, therefore, to enable the patient, through a dialectical exchange with the analyst, to take full and conscious control of his or her life. Martín-Santos insisted, however, that nations could be the subject of psychoanalysis in the same way that individuals could. His rejection of biologism is, then, all the more understandable given the racist element of Francoist ideology, to which he was opposed. Martín-Santos developed this attitude in fictional terms in *Tiempo de silencio.*

While the late 1950s were a busy time for Martín-Santos professionally, they were also an active time politically. A member of the Socialist Party, and representative on its executive committee from 1961 until his death, he was arrested on four occasions. The first time, he was incarcerated for six months in 1957, following the upheavals in the Franco administration that led to the appointment of the so-called Technocrats and the formulation of the first Development Plan for the country. Martín-Santos was arrested a second time in November 1958 at a time of unrest, strikes, and student protest; on this occasion he spent four months in Carabanchel prison in Madrid. Between May and September 1959 he was in prison again and, during this period, took *oposiciones* for the chair of psychiatry at Salamanca University. Although he did not win the chair, as Castilla del Pino recalls, Martín-Santos was taken to the examinations in a police car. He spent a further period in Carabanchel in 1962 because of his socialist beliefs. In comments to Rodolfo Llopis in the French newspaper *Le Socialiste* Martín-Santos noted that his political activities in no way damaged his private practice—quite the reverse, in fact, and he took this approval as an indication of the level of resentment against the regime in San Sebastián at the time. Martín-Santos's opposition to the regime and his experience of detention are both reflected in *Tiempo de silencio,* in which the protagonist, Pedro, spends some time in prison. The prison jargon that the author had picked up is also documented in the stylistic innovations of this groundbreaking novel.

*Tiempo de silencio* is set in Madrid in 1949. Pedro, a promising young scientist who dreams of winning the Nobel Prize for his research into a hereditary form of cancer, lives in a boardinghouse run by three generations of women from the same family—the robust grandmother whose womanizing husband is now dead, her rather masculine and ineffectual daughter, and her pretty illegitimate granddaughter, Dorita. All three seek to arrange the seduction of Pedro by Dorita in the hope that it will lead to marriage and social acceptability for the girl. Funding for scientific research in late 1940s Spain is, however, scant, and Pedro runs out of the strain of genetically modified mice necessary to his experiments. Nevertheless, his lab technician, Amador, has been stealing some of the mice. These purloined mice are bred incestuously, as is required for Pedro's cancer research, by Muecas, who lives in one of the shantytowns in the city. A visit by Pedro and Amador to buy back the mice reveals the deplorable conditions in which Muecas's family live, having constructed a home on top of what is little more than a garbage dump. Yet, they are not the worst off: nearby, Cartucho and his mother live in a cave and have no more than a stone to sit on. This survey of social classes in the Madrid of the immediate postwar period is completed by Pedro's friend Matías, a well-off young man who associates with the scientist simply because of Pedro's intellectual promise.

After a night of drinking and a visit to a brothel in the company of Matías and his fickle friends, Pedro returns home and allows himself to be seduced by Dorita. Following intercourse with the girl, he is awakened by Amador and summoned to the shantytown where Muecas's daughter, Florita, is dying as the result of a botched back-street abortion performed by her father. Although only too aware that he should call for an ambulance and report the incident, Pedro lets himself be talked into attempting to save the girl and, when she dies, in colluding in a cover-up. On the run from the police, he hides in the brothel but is soon arrested and finds himself in prison, having put up little defense against the charge of murdering Florita. Only the intervention of the girl's illiterate mother saves him, for she reveals that not only did her husband kill Florita but also that he was guilty of incest and was the father of the baby. Pedro is thus released without charge. Nevertheless, Cartucho, who loved Florita, blames Pedro for her death and exacts revenge by killing Dorita, who has in the meantime become Pedro's fiancée. The novel closes with Pedro leaving Madrid by train, his scientific career in ruins, and his personal life devoid of meaning.

A social exile, he is condemned to the role of provincial doctor with little prospect of career advancement.

Tiempo de silencio, published in 1961 (not 1962, as is often claimed), is generally taken to be a reaction against the wave of social-realist novels that dominated Spanish fiction in the 1950s. In a letter to the critic Ricardo Domenech, Martín-Santos commented on the novel:

> Temo no haberme ajustado del todo a los preceptos del realismo social, pero verás un poco en que sentido quisiera llegar a un realismo dialéctico. Creo que hay que pasar de la simple descripción estática de las enajenaciones para plantear la real dinámica de las contradicciones *in actu*.

> (I fear that I have not entirely followed the precepts of social realism, but you will see to some extent how I have tried to achieve a dialectical realism. I believe that we must move from the simple, static description of alienation in order to confront the true dynamics of contradictions *in actu*.)

Critics' initial reaction to the novel was to regard it as social commentary, though of a new type that offered a rounded view of Spanish reality. Denouncing social conditions in Francoist Spain, Martín-Santos sought, through the metaphors of cancer and incest, to offer a concrete picture of the moral corruption prevalent at a specific moment in the history of the nation. Despite the pessimism in the novel, however, he also wanted to offer the nation the possibility of cure through an analysis of the myths that underpinned Francoist society. His novel ranges over the wide spectrum of social classes in 1940s Spain but holds in particular contempt the bourgeoisie—epitomized in a satirical scene in which the celebrated philosopher Ortega y Gasset delivers a facile lecture on perspectivism—for their lack of real engagement with the nation's endemic problem, namely an inferiority complex and failure to address adequately the question of modernization.

Nevertheless, Martín-Santos's interest in existentialism and his stated desire to create a dialectical realism (as opposed to a deterministic social realism) suggest that Tiempo de silencio should be read as more than simply a novel of social protest. Emphasis has shifted from the initial picture of Pedro as the sacrificial victim of a repressive and mediocre society toward the suggestion that he is, in fact, a shallow character who is complicit in his own downfall and, by extension, in the moral corruption of his society. This view takes account of the fact that, for Martín-Santos, society does not condition an individual's responses, but that the relationship between social pressures and personal responsibility is a complex, two-way process of negotiation. In this belief there is an echo of the author's approach to psychiatry as set down in Liber-

*Cover for a 1982 paperback edition of Martín-Santos's 1961 novel (translated as* Time of Silence, *1964), about a young physician whose promising career as a cancer researcher is destroyed by his involvement in a botched abortion (Thomas Cooper Library, University of South Carolina)*

tad, temporalidad y transferencia en el psicoanálisis existencial, though it would be an oversimplification to see the novel as a fictional version of that work. Pedro acts in "bad faith," in existentialist terms, since he allows society to constrain him and seeks refuge from decision making by hiding behind the social pressures he feels are upon him. Hence, Pedro—in full awareness of the traps into which he falls—allows himself to be seduced by Dorita, acquiesces in the attempted cover-up of Florita's murder, and fails to speak out when he is wrongly accused. As he leaves Madrid at the close of the novel, his attitude is one of passive acceptance of his fate. The title of the novel thus highlights both the repressive atmosphere of Francoist Spain and Pedro's tacit acquiescence in the silencing of any opposition to the status quo. From a wider perspective, Martín-Santos presents Pedro not as a hero or exemplar but as an antihero who symbolizes the failure of a society to speak out against its subjection. If existentialist psychoanalysis can, as the author believes, be extended to include the analysis and cure of a nation, then Spain itself is the ultimate subject of this novel.

Martín-Santos's treatment of Spanish history in *Tiempo de silencio,* although noted by critics since its publication, has been an intense area of research in later studies. Early criticism explored the use of mythical references to reveal the faults of contemporary society, though it approached the subject from a universal rather than a particularly Spanish perspective and emphasized the manner in which Pedro's experience–akin to the Homeric quest myth–can be seen as an initiation ritual in which he is the victim of divine forces. In an important 1973 essay, Juan Carlos Curutchet explored more specifically Spanish resonances of the mythical references in the novel, stressing the linguistic foundations of the worldview that the author presents. This connection between national myth, language, and cultural circumstance has been most comprehensively analyzed by Jo Labanyi, whose work stands out as the most penetrating study of the novelist to date.

Offering a new perspective on contemporary Spanish fiction as a whole in *Myth and History in the Contemporary Spanish Novel* (1989), Labanyi reads *Tiempo de silencio* as a deconstruction of the foundational myths of Francoist Spain. She argues that Martín-Santos tackles what has become known as the "Spanish problem" with the weapon of irony in order to expose the culturally constructed nature of national myths of both imperial greatness and subsequent degeneration. Linking Martín-Santos's existentialist psychiatry, his critical reading of Freud, and his familiarity with Erich Fromm's Freudian analysis of Nazism, *The Fear of Freedom* (1942), Labanyi suggests that *Tiempo de silencio* identifies Spain's "problem" as being its failure to recognize the existence of a problem. The novel, she contends, offers an interpretation of Spain's silent acquiescence with the Francoist regime: Pedro's existential "bad faith" parallels the nation's complicity in its own repression.

The stylistic innovations of *Tiempo de silencio* are testament to Martín-Santos's general debt to James Joyce. However, while there are Homeric references in the novel that suggest a parallel with Joyce's *Ulysses* (1922), the intentions behind each novelist's use of myth are decidedly different. For Joyce, myth offers a means to comment ironically on modern culture; for Martín-Santos, it is a dangerous cultural construct that must be debunked through irony. Nevertheless, Martín-Santos is indebted to the Irish novelist for the polysemic use of language and variety of narrative perspectives that underpin his ironic demythification of Francoist Spain. *Tiempo de silencio,* in contrast to its social-realist predecessors, is a novel that stresses its own status as

cultural artifact. A plethora of linguistic styles and registers–including the baroque, the scientific, the medical, the legal, the religious, the philosophical, and the mock epic–pervade the work, and there are significant allusions to literary predecessors such as Ortega y Gasset, Pío Baroja, Miguel de Unamuno, and Miguel de Cervantes. This focus on the literary qualities of the text is intended to draw the reader's attention toward the multiple perspectives that language necessarily involves and yet often conceals. The novel, therefore, encourages the reader to engage critically with the issues that it explores. Rather than offering a single, overriding perspective, Martín-Santos seeks out dialogue and intellectual engagement. In formal terms, he borrows from Joyce the use of the interior monologue, which he combines with more conventional third-person narration to underline this multiplicity of perspectives. Such use of interior monologue allows an author to convey characters' thought processes directly, and Pedro is given monologues at crucial points in the novel to expose the motivation behind his actions. Each monologue ultimately reveals his inability to take control of events, thus reinforcing the existentialist theme of the novel.

*Tiempo de silencio* was subject to the standard censoring process of the regime and was passed with minor cuts, mainly relating to religious allusions and irreverent comments on the Catholic Church. The form and style in which the work is written were, however, intended to go some way toward evading the censor by creating a text that, through the use of ellipsis, irony, and metaphor, would convey more than it stated openly. This "possibilist" stance–that is, the acceptance of some censorship in order to be published, as opposed to those writers who refused all censorship and either remained silent or went into exile–was defended by Martín-Santos in the Llopis interview in *Le Socialiste:* "En la actualidad, la única arma con que el español cuenta para la modificación de una realidad insoportable es precisamente la de escribir una novela suficientemente hábil para que pase la censura" (Nowadays, the only weapon on which the Spaniard can count to change an intolerable reality is precisely that of writing a novel which is sufficiently cunning to get past the censor).

Two years after *Tiempo de silencio* was published to great critical acclaim, Martín-Santos's wife died as the result of an accidental gas leak. On 21 January 1964 the novelist himself died in a car crash near Vitoria in the Basque country. He left unfinished the manuscript for his second novel, *Tiempo de destrucción,* which was later edited by José Carlos Mainer. Many aspects of *Tiempo de silencio* are developed in this work–the frustration of living in Francoist Spain, the ironic debunking of myths of Spanish history and national identity, and stylistic innovations and playing with multiple narrative perspectives. Mainer's edition offers two reasonably complete parts of the projected work, which, he believes, was to extend to four sections in all. For parts 3 and 4 little material exists, and Mainer groups together what there is under the heading of part 3.

Although *Tiempo de destrucción* is incomplete, an outline plan of the novel provided by Martín-Santos's brother, Leandro, suggests that it was to have recounted the story of Agustín, a well-educated young man with a lively mind and a gift for sparkling conversation. This protagonist, like Pedro in *Tiempo de silencio,* is immersed in a personal crisis that leaves him exasperated with the world in which he lives. Agustín, however, apparently was intended to be a more complex figure than Pedro, more fully aware of the choices he faces and the responsibility he must take for directing his own life. In this regard, *Tiempo de destrucción* seeks to offer a more nuanced exploration of the notion of dialectical realism, for, as Mainer suggests in his introduction to the novel, it proceeds along two distinct but parallel lines: the frustrations of postwar Spain and their effect on the development of an individual, already evident in *Tiempo de silencio;* and the more-subtle responses of that individual to these pressures upon him. In contrast to Pedro's resigned passivity, Agustín comes willingly to accept his own sexual inadequacies, impotence, and fear of both women and homosexuals, and his tragic destiny thus subverts the values of traditional religion, its myth of maternity, and the guilt complex that it creates.

The early chapters of the novel are characterized by temporal dislocations, fusing a narrative present (Agustín deciding, after his success in gaining a post as a provincial judge, to lose his virginity) with childhood memories of the protagonist's authoritarian mother and his first rebellion against authority at school, for which he is savagely punished. The theme of authority is thus presented in the parallel between Agustín in infancy and as a mature man. In the second part of *Tiempo de destrucción,* the same theme is addressed through Agustín's investigation of the murder of a night watchman, in which certain members of the local oligarchy may be implicated. Although these chapters offer a fairly conventional, straightforward narration of plot, the use of interior monologue does recall the innovations of Martín-Santos's earlier novel. The remaining passages of *Tiempo de destrucción* represent an inward psychological turn with an increased use of interior monologue through which the protagonist explores his sense of identity in allusions to the enslaving myths of the "España eterna" (Eternal Spain) of Francoist rhetoric. The projected ending of the novel remains unclear, but Mainer postulates that it may have involved Agustín's death, which was to be interpreted symbolically as an indictment of the Nationalist *madre patria* (mother country) that suffocates her offspring.

Despite the fact that–as Constance Sullivan cautioned in her review of Mainer's edition of the novel in the *Journal of Spanish Studies: Twentieth Century* (1976)– the existing text of *Tiempo de destrucción* is little more than a provisional draft, the work clearly furthers Martín-Santos's aim of creating a dialectical realism with a strongly existentialist background. As José Ortega suggests in a 1975 article, the form in which the novel is written dramatizes the protagonist's dilemmas without seeking to synthesize this conflict into a harmonious picture. As in *Tiempo de silencio,* the use of irony facilitates the creation of multiple perspectives that undermine any pretense to a single point of view and thus represent a resounding rejection of literary objectivism. The more polished sections of *Tiempo de destrucción* are just as engaging and stylistically experimental as the earlier novel, and a notably effective contrast is established between an objective, almost cynically satirical narrative voice and the subjectivity of Agustín's interior monologues. The fusion of sexual and religious imagery also anticipates one of the great contemporary Spanish novels, Juan Goytisolo's *Reivindicación del conde don Julián* (1970, Recovery of don Julián; translated as *Count Julian,* 1974), suggesting that Martín-Santos's death deprived Spanish literature of a voice that was ahead of its time.

Luis Martín-Santos is a pivotal figure in the development of contemporary Spanish fiction. While critics have begun to question the formerly widely accepted idea of a radical division between works of Spanish fiction that predate and those that postdate *Tiempo de silencio*–suggesting that the former are more complex and stylistically innovative than the simple documentary texts they were initially taken to be, and that the latter owe some of their innovative stance to a putative move toward experimentalism evident in texts of the 1950s–the works of this psychiatrist-turned-novelist represent a bridging point between two different but complementary approaches to the literature of commitment. Martín-Santos lived by his principles, accepting the threat and reality of arrest by the Franco regime for his political activities. He expressed in both his psychiatric and his literary works his opposition to a repressive government and his frustration at Spain's inability–even unwillingness–to face up to and overcome its cultural introversion. His attempt to practice an existentialist psychoanalysis of the nation anticipated the attack on myth that later novelists waged with a vengeance, and his dialectical approach, employing irony rather than direct and vicious satire, offered a subtle and effective tool for the destruction of the shibboleths of Francoist Spain.

**Interview:**

Rodolfo Llopis, "Luis Martín-Santos: Era más que una promesa," *Socialiste,* 6 February 1964, pp. 1–2.

**References:**

Reed Anderson, "Luis Martín-Santos and Juan Goytisolo: Irony and Satire in the Contemporary Spanish Novel," *Orbis Litterarum,* 33 (1978): 359–374;

Jacques Beyrie, ed., *"Tiempo de silencio" de Luis Martín-Santos, "Señas de identidad" de Juan Goytisolo: Deux romans de rupture?* (Toulouse: Le Mirail, 1980);

Carlos Castilla del Pino, "Evocación de Luis Martín-Santos," *Olvidos de Granada,* 13 (1986): 159–162;

Juan Carlos Curutchet, *A partir de Luis Martín-Santos: Cuatro ensayos sobre la nueva novela espanola* (Montevideo: Alfa, 1973);

Emilio Díaz Valcárcel, *La visión del mundo en la novela "Tiempo de silencio" de Luis Martín-Santos* (Río Piedras: Universidad de Puerto Rico, 1982);

Ricardo Domenech, "Luis Martín-Santos," *Ínsula,* 208 (1964): 4;

Carlos Feal, "En torno al casticismo de Pedro: el principio y el fin de *Tiempo de silencio,*" *Revista Iberoamericana,* 116–117 (1981): 203–212;

Ricardo Gullón, "Mitos órficos y cáncer social," *El Urogallo,* 17 (1972): 80–89;

Walter Holzinger, "*Tiempo de silencio:* An Analysis," *Revista Hispánica Moderna,* 37 (1972–1973): 73–90;

Carlos Jérez-Farrán, "'Ansiedad de influencia' versus intertextualidad autoconsciente en *Tiempo de silencio* de Martín-Santos," *Symposium,* 42 (1988): 119–132;

Roberta Johnson, "*El árbol de la ciencia* and *Tiempo de silencio* in Light of Ortega's Ideas on Science," in *La Chispa: Selected Proceedings of the Fourth Louisiana Conference on Hispanic Languages and Literatures,* edited by Gilbert Paolini (New Orleans: Tulane University Press, 1983), pp. 135–141;

Dale F. Knickerbocker, "*Tiempo de silencio* and the Narration of the Abject," *Anales de la Literatura Española Contemporánea,* 19 (1994): 11–31;

Jo Labanyi, *Ironía e historia en "Tiempo de silencio"* (Madrid: Taurus, 1983);

Labanyi, *Myth and History in the Contemporary Spanish Novel* (Cambridge: Cambridge University Press, 1989);

John Lyon, "Don Pedro's Complicity: An Existential Dimension of *Tiempo de silencio,*" *Modern Language Review,* 74 (1979): 69–78;

José Ortega, "Aproximación al realismo dialéctico de *Tiempo de destrucción,*" *Cuadernos Hispanoamericanos,* 303 (1975): 692–703;

Ortega, "*Luces de bohemia* y *Tiempo de silencio:* Dos concepciones del absurdo español," *Cuadernos Hispanoamericanos,* 317 (1976): 303–321;

Ortega, "Realismo dialéctico de Martín-Santos en *Tiempo de silencio,*" *Revista de Estudios Hispánicos,* 3 (1969): 33–42;

Ortega, "La sociedad española contemporánea en *Tiempo de silencio* de Luis Martín-Santos," *Symposium,* 22 (1968): 256–260;

Julian Palley, "The Periplus of Don Pedro: *Tiempo de silencio,*" *Bulletin of Hispanic Studies,* 48 (1971): 239–254;

Gustavo Pérez Firmat, "Repetition and Excess in *Tiempo de silencio,*" *Publications of the Modern Language Association of America,* 96 (1981): 194–209;

Jesús Pérez Magallón, "El proyecto acosado: El fracaso en *Tiempo de silencio* de Luis Martín-Santos," *Revista Hispánica Moderna,* 47 (1994): 134–145;

Ronald F. Rapin, "The Phantom Pages of Luis Martín-Santos' *Tiempo de silencio,*" *Neophilologus,* 7 (1987): 235–243;

Alfonso Rey, *Construcción y sentido de "Tiempo de silencio"* (Madrid: Porrúa Turanzas, 1977);

Alison Ribeiro de Menezes, "Irony, the Grotesque, and the Dialectics of Reading in Luis Martín-Santos's *Tiempo de silencio,*" *Hispanic Research Journal,* 3 (2002): 123–137;

Gemma Roberts, "Conflicto entre razón y vida en *Tiempo de destrucción,*" *Ínsula,* 396–397 (1979): 10;

Roberts, *Temas existenciales en la novela española de postguerra* (Madrid: Gredos, 1973);

Esperanza G. Saludes, *La narrativa de Luis Martín-Santos a la luz de la psicología* (Miami: Universal, 1981);

Saludes, "Presencia de Ortega y Gasset en la novela *Tiempo de silencio* de Luis Martín-Santos," *Hispanic Journal,* 3 (1982): 91–103;

José Schraibman, "*Tiempo de destrucción:* ¿Novela estructural?" *Revista Iberoamericana,* 116–117 (1981): 213–220;

Manuel Sol T, "Don Quijote en *Tiempo de silencio,*" *Cuadernos Hispanoamericanos,* 430 (1986): 73–83;

José Luis Suarez, *Tiempo de silencio: Guía de Lectura* (Madrid: Alhambra, 1986);

June H. Townsend, *William Faulkner y Luis Martín-Santos* (Madrid: Pliegos, 2000);

Michael Ugarte, "*Tiempo de silencio* and the Language of Displacement," *Modern Language Notes,* 96 (1981): 340–357;

Juan Villegas, *La estructura mítica del héroe en la novela del siglo XX* (Barcelona: Planeta, 1973);

Carmen de Zuleta, "El monólogo interior de Pedro en *Tiempo de silencio,*" *Hispanic Review,* 45 (1977): 297–309.

# Ana María Matute

*(26 July 1926 –    )*

Janet Pérez
*Texas Tech University*

BOOKS: *Los Abel* (Barcelona: Destino, 1948);

*Fiesta al noroeste; La ronda; Los niños buenos* (Madrid: Aguado, 1953); "Fiesta al noroeste" translated by Phoebe Ann Porter as *Celebration in the Northwest* (Lincoln: University of Nebraska Press, 1997);

*La pequeña vida* (Madrid: La novela del sábado, 1953);

*Pequeño teatro: Novela* (Barcelona: Planeta, 1954);

*En esta tierra* (Barcelona: Exito, 1955); unexpurgated version revised and enlarged as *Luciérnagas* (Barcelona: Destino, 1993); translated by Glafyra Ennis as *Fireflies* (New York: Peter Lang, 1998);

*Los niños tontos* (Madrid: Arión, 1956);

*El tiempo* (Barcelona: Mateu, 1957);

*El país de la pizarra* (Barcelona: Molino Carville, 1957);

*Los hijos muertos: Novela* (Barcelona: Planeta, 1958); translated by Joan MacLean as *The Lost Children* (New York: Macmillan, 1965);

*El saltamontes verde; El aprendiz* (Barcelona: Lumen, 1960);

*Paulina, el mundo y las estrellas* (Barcelona: Garbo, 1960);

*Primera memoria* (Barcelona: Destino, 1960); translated by Elaine Kerrigan as *School of the Sun* (New York: Pantheon, 1963; London: Quartet, 1991); translated by James Holman Mason as *Awakening* (London: Hutchinson, 1963);

*A la mitad del camino* (Barcelona: Rocas, 1961);

*El arrepentido* (Barcelona: Rocas, 1961);

*Historias de la Artámila* (Barcelona: Destino, 1961); edited by Manuel Durán and Gloria Durán as *Doce historias de la artámila* (New York: Harcourt, Brace & World, 1965);

*Libro de juegos para los niños de los otros* (Barcelona: Lumen, 1961);

*Tres y un sueño* (Barcelona: Destino, 1961);

*Caballito loco; Carnavalito* (Barcelona: Lumen, 1962);

*El río* (Barcelona: Argos, 1963);

*Los soldados lloran de noche* (Barcelona: Destino, 1964); translated by Robert Nugent and María José de la Cámara as *Soldiers Cry by Night* (Pittsburgh, Pa.: Latin American Literary Review Press, 1995);

*El polizón del "Ulises"* (Barcelona: Lumen, 1965);

*Ana María Matute (Archivos de Ana María Matute, Agencia Literaria Carmen Balcells, Barcelona; from Marie-Lise Gazarian-Gautier,* Ana María Matute: La voz del silencio, *1997; Thomas Cooper Library, University of South Carolina)*

*Algunos muchachos* (Barcelona: Destino, 1968); translated by Michael Scott Doyle as *The Heliotrope Wall and Other Stories* (New York: Columbia University Press, 1989);

*La trampa* (Barcelona: Destino, 1969); translated by Nugent and Cámara as *The Trap* (Pittsburgh,

Pa.: Latin American Literary Review Press, 1996);

*La torre vigía* (Barcelona: Lumen, 1971);

*Obra completa,* 5 volumes (Barcelona: Destino, 1971–1976);

*Cuentos completos* (Barcelona: Destino, 1978);

*Sólo un pie descalzo* (Barcelona: Lumen, 1984);

*La virgen de Antioquía y otros relatos* (Madrid: Mondadori, 1990);

*El verdadero final de la Bella Durmiente* (Barcelona: Lumen, 1995);

*Olvidado rey Gudú* (Madrid: Espasa-Calpe, 1996);

*En el bosque: Discurso leído el día de enero de 1998, en su recepción pública,* by Matute and Francisco Rico (Madrid: Real Academia Española, 1998);

*Aranmanoth* (Madrid: Espasa-Calpe, 2000);

*Cuentos de infancia* (Barcelona: Martínez Roca, 2002);

*Suiza y la migración: Una mirada desde España,* by Matute and others (Madrid: Imaginepress, 2004).

**Editions and Collections:** *Fiesta al noroeste,* edited by Luís Alpera (Englewood Cliffs, N.J.: Prentice-Hall, 1971);

*Selecciones de Ana María Matute,* edited by Juana Amelia Hernández and Edenia Guillermo (Princeton, N.J.: FFH, 1982);

*Obra escogida,* edited by José L. Martí and Angel Rubio-Maroto (New York: Longman, 1982);

*Todos mis cuentos* (Barcelona: Lumen, 2000).

**Edition in English:** "Three Children's Stories and The Book of Games for Those Other People's Children," translated by Barbara M. Cohen, M.A. thesis, University of Puerto Rico, 1983.

OTHER: Leo Lionni, *Frederick,* translated by Matute (Barcelona: Lumen, 1969);

Ignacio Aldecoa, *La tierra de nadie y otros relatos,* prologue by Matute (Estella: Salvat, 1972);

Hans Christian Andersen, *La sombra y otros cuentos,* edited and translated by Alberto Adell, prologue by Matute (Madrid: Alianza, 1973);

Lionni, *Nadarín,* translated by Matute (Barcelona: Lumen, 1988);

Antonio Gala, *El corazón tardío,* prologue by Matute (Madrid: Planeta/Espasa, 1998);

Concha López Narváez, *Andanzas de don Quijote y Sancho,* prologue by Matute (Madrid: Bruño, 2005).

SELECTED PERIODICAL PUBLICATION–
UNCOLLECTED: "Notas de una escritora," *Instituto de Estudios Norteamericanos Boletín,* 11 (Spring 1965): 5.

Ana María Matute is one of the two or three most important Spanish women writers of the post–Civil War period; she is also the only major Spanish woman novel-ist of the last six decades of the twentieth century who is still writing in the new millennium. She has received most of Spain's important literary prizes and has been mentioned repeatedly as a candidate for the Nobel Prize in literature. In 1997 she became the third woman in history elected to the Royal Academy of the Spanish Language. Her works have been translated into English, French, Italian, Portuguese, German, Czech, Polish, Russian, and Esperanto. Elected a corresponding member of the Hispanic Society of America in 1960, she is the only Spanish woman writer whose works are required reading for the Advanced Placement Examination in Spanish administered by Educational Testing Service for high-school students seeking college credit.

Matute began publishing during the first decade after the Spanish Civil War of 1936 to 1939, along with considerably older writers such as Camilo José Cela, Gonzalo Torrente Ballester, Elena Quiroga, and Carmen Laforet. She thereby anticipated by more than a decade the debuts of the Spanish writers with whom she is grouped: the "midcentury generation," which also includes Ignacio Aldecoa, Jesús Fernández Santos, Juan Goytisolo, and Carmen Martín Gaite. Practitioners of "social literature"–a euphemism for veiled political protest–these writers targeted socio-economic injustice with their fiction, poetry, and drama, risking official reprisals and persecution for defending the poor and oppressed.

The third of five children, Ana María Matute Ausejo was born in Barcelona on 26 July 1926 to Facundo Matute and Maria Matute, née Ausejo. During her first ten years the family residence alternated between Barcelona and Madrid because of her father's umbrella-manufacturing business. Matute's upper-middle-class mother, educated exclusively for matrimony, gave her children a traditional religious upbringing and was an inflexible disciplinarian. Matute was so terrified of her mother that she began to stutter and eventually ranked last in her class. She seldom portrays mothers in her works; most of her unhappy children characters are orphans.

Matute's mother came from the landed gentry of Old Castile, and the family spent summers at Matute's maternal grandparents' country estate in the mountain village Mansilla de la Sierra near the border of La Rioja and Navarre. Matute and her two sisters and two brothers never learned Catalan, which exacerbated their outsider status in Barcelona. Matute frequently tells interviewers that in Madrid she was *la catalana* (the Catalan girl), in Barcelona *la castellana* (the Castilian girl). The many lonely, isolated, solitary, and alienated children and adolescents in Matute's fiction echo her feeling of not belonging.

Matute suffered life-threatening illnesses at ages four and eight from which she convalesced at her grandparents' home. Contacts with servants and share-croppers' families and attending the one-room village school with underprivileged local children made a lasting impression on her. In Spanish villages in the 1930s grain was still threshed, as in biblical times, by donkeys' hooves; peasants lived in quasi serfdom, washed their clothes in the river from which they also drew their drinking water, used the ancient Roman bridges, and lacked all modern conveniences. With no machinery and often no oxen, many pulled the plows themselves; pregnant women worked in the fields until giving birth, then resumed their tasks. Only the poorest people sent their children to the impoverished public schools, which usually consisted of a room in the schoolmaster's home, without books or heat; schoolteachers' poverty was proverbial, and haggard village schoolmasters abound in Matute's 1961 collections, *Historias de la Artámila* (Stories of la Artámila) and *El arrepentido* (The Repentant One). Such inequities distressed her even before the traumatic events of the Civil War spurred her to seek its causes in the traditional social structure, and the impact of the village echoes through many of her works.

Barcelona and Mansilla are the primary locales for Matute's fiction; while Castile may be the "land of steppes" depicted in her chivalric novels *La torre vigía* (1971, The Watchtower) and *Olvidado Rey Gudú* (1996, Forgotten King Gudú), Madrid is never mentioned in her works. Asked in an unpublished 1964 interview why Madrid never figures in her fiction, she contrasted the aridity, sterility, and blinding sun of the plateau on which the Spanish capital is located with the milder coast that she loves and where Barcelona and Sitges, the seaside village of her summer home, are situated. Settings are not neutral backgrounds for Matute but are coordinated with mood and sometimes shape her characters. The environs of her grandparents' estate in Mansilla de la Sierra are fictionally portrayed as the nameless village in *Los Abel* (1948, The Abel Family); as "la Artámila" in "Fiesta al noroeste" (1953; translated as *Celebration in the Northwest,* 1997) and in the collection *Historias de la Artámila;* and as "Hegroz" in *Los hijos muertos* (1958; translated as *The Lost Children,* 1965).

Political events exacerbated Matute's sense of alienation during the Second Republic of 1931 to 1936. Catalonia's rejection of the central government in Madrid and its establishment in 1932 of an autonomous state, "La Generalitat," with its capital in Barcelona, resulted in the harsh repression after the Civil War that led Matute to denounce the "horrors of peace."

During the Civil War Matute's family was trapped in Barcelona, where the conflict was especially

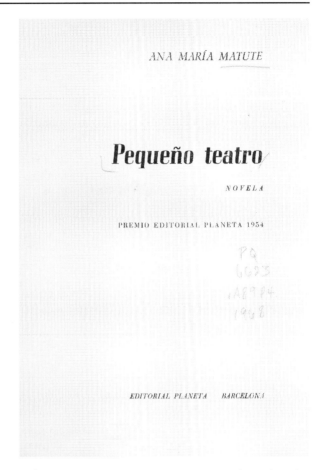

ANA MARÍA MATUTE

# Pequeño teatro

NOVELA

PREMIO EDITORIAL PLANETA 1954

PQ
6623
.A89 P4
1968

EDITORIAL PLANETA    BARCELONA

*Title page for a later edition of Matute's first novel (Little Theater), completed in 1943 but first published in 1954, in which a mysterious confidence man deceives everyone in a Basque fishing village except the promiscuous daughter of the only wealthy man in the town (Thomas Cooper Library, University of South Carolina)*

intense. The Catalan capital suffered not only war but also violent social revolution, terrorism, and political assassinations. In interviews Matute has described how she, her siblings, and her cousins crouched behind closed shutters listening to the fighting and later found dead bodies in the streets; the children wondered why the priests and nuns who had been their teachers and counselors had become targets for terrorists, obliged to flee or to assume lay disguises. These events and their socio-economic causes dominate Matute's writing during her "social realist" first period, from the mid 1940s through the end of the 1960s. In the unpublished 1964 interview Matute recalls her first classrooms, with "their fascinating prints of Cain and Abel"; the biblical conflict between brothers became her metaphor for the Civil War in all of her fiction except *Pequeño teatro* (1954, Little Theater). In her "pacifist" second period, beginning in 1971, she transfers her examination of injustice and war from the twentieth century to the tenth in *La torre vigía* and *Olvidado rey Gudú*.

A precocious, solitary child, often forced to be inactive because of illness, Matute loved museums and the theater. Her father gave her a puppet theater—another recurring motif in her works—and she improvised performances for her siblings and cousins during the war. She says in "Notas de una escritora" (1965, Notes of a Female Writer) that she cannot remember when she began writing, "because I always wrote. . . . Always, from my most remote recollection . . . I wanted to be a writer; I couldn't imagine being anything else." Throughout her childhood she wrote tales of imaginary worlds, animals, warriors and princesses, and gnomes and elves. She also drew and painted. Her mother encouraged her literary interests and preserved her early creative efforts: the Fundación Ana María Matute (Ana María Matute Foundation) in Boston University's Mugar Library includes several "issues"—365 pages—of "La revista de Shybil" (Sybil's Review), the children's magazine Matute produced, probably in 1938, with her stories, poems, news items, and drawings.

The Falange, modeled on Italian dictator Benito Mussolini's brand of fascism, became Spain's sole legal political party after the Civil War; the only organized opposition consisted of clandestine Communist cells. Schools, which had been closed during the war, reopened in 1939 on accelerated schedules. Matute completed only two years of the six-year *bachillerato* (high-school equivalency), abandoning formal education in 1941 to devote herself to writing, art, and music; she studied painting with Nùria Llimona and violin with Juan Masia, both of whom were well-known masters in their fields. She read voraciously; her favorites were the fairy tales of Hans Christian Andersen and the Brothers Grimm, Lewis Carroll's *Alice's Adventures in Wonderland* (1865), and J. M. Barrie's *Peter Pan in Kensington Gardens* (1906). Traces of all of these works abound in her children's fiction. Andersen's dichotomous worldview, contrasting material and spiritual riches, reappears in Matute's juvenilia, her children's stories, and many of her works for adults. She began frequenting literary circles and groups of aspiring writers, and in 1942 her first published story, "El chico de al lado" (The Boy Next Door), appeared in the Barcelona magazine *Destino*. In 1943 she abandoned her study of painting and music to concentrate on literature. She completed her first novel, *Pequeño teatro,* that year, but it remained unpublished until 1954.

In 1945 Matute submitted the manuscript for *Los Abel* for the newly established Nadal Prize; it finished as runner-up to Miguel Delibes's *La sombra del ciprés es alargada* (1948, Long Is the Cypress's Shadow). *Los Abel* launched her career as a novelist when it was published in 1948.

Everything printed in Spain under the fascist regime—even maps, magazine covers, and matchbooks—underwent stringent censorship for morality, religious orthodoxy, and political conformity. Writings could be cut, prohibited, or confiscated; the author's home could be searched and additional works seized; and writers could be jailed. In *Los Abel,* and later in "Fiesta al noroeste" and *Los hijos muertos,* Matute employed a framing device to confuse the censors. Bureaucrats rather than literary critics, censors generally assumed the original narrator of a work to be the protagonist; anticipating this character's return distracted their attention from subversive elements in the plot. In all three works the introductory narrators vanish without explanation, leaving readers—including the censors—to wonder about their fates.

A cousin who spent childhood summers with the Abel family narrates the first eight chapters of *Los Abel;* seeking to solve their wartime disappearance, he finds Valba's diary, which constitutes the remainder of the novel. Updating the biblical myth of fratricidal conflict, Matute describes the two eldest Abel brothers' competition for the family lands and for the same woman. Her characteristic pairing of opposites—fair/dark, good/evil, materialist/idealist—appears in the rival brothers: Aldo is ascetic, rigid, hardworking, and potentially violent, while Tito is hedonistic, charming, and irresponsible. Diary-writer Valba, the elder daughter, is dark, androgynous, tomboyish, and alienated, while Jacqueline, her erstwhile friend, future sister-in-law, and cause of the brothers' murderous conflict, is blond, voluptuous, conventional, and hypocritical. *Los Abel* resembles a nineteenth-century rural novel as it chronicles the decadence, disintegration, and disappearance of this paradigmatic family of landed gentry; subplots concern Valba's psychological maturation and other family members' conflicts. Matute's concern for social injustice appears in economic tensions between landowners and peasants.

Approximately the first third of Matute's 1953 novella "Fiesta al noroeste" is narrated by Dingo, a boyhood friend of the main narrator, Juan Medinao. Dingo absconded with the pair's childhood savings; returning to their home village years later, he accidentally kills a shepherd's child and is arrested. From the jail he calls his former friend, prompting an extended retrospective confession by Juan that makes up the rest of the work. "Fiesta al noroeste" depicts the conflict between landowners and semifeudal sharecroppers and between love for the land and the desperate desire to escape it. The Cain/Abel dichotomy appears in the deformed, fanatically religious Juan Medinao, the elder and legitimate son of a landowning aristocrat, and his handsome half brother Pablo, the landowner's disinherited illegitimate son by a servant. As the local cacique, Juan represents the system that allowed powerful individuals to name representatives to the national assemblies. Juan's confession inadvertently reveals his latent homosexual attraction to Pablo. He attempts to lure Pablo to his house by purchasing Pablo's sweetheart from her destitute parents; but Pablo disappears, leaving Juan with a wife who despises him. He proceeds to rape Pablo's mother, echoing crimes by generations of landowners against peasants and sharecroppers. Matute received her first literary award, the Café Gijón Prize, for "Fiesta al noroeste"; conferred by a literary club, it carried more intellectual prestige than many commercial prizes.

The romantic, sentimental novelette *La pequeña vida* (1953, Small Life) recalls Andersen's doomed orphans. Two mistreated adolescents run away from home; the girl's foot becomes wedged in the railroad track as a speeding train approaches, but rather than escape, the boy embraces her as the train runs over them. The work was renamed "El tiempo" (Time) when it was republished as the title piece of a collection of her stories in 1957.

*Pequeño teatro* competed successfully for the Planeta Prize, which included publication by the Planeta firm, in 1954. Most of the characters and the deliberately trite plot derive from commedia dell'arte antecedents. Zazu, the daughter of the only wealthy man in a Basque fishing village, scandalizes the village by visiting the fishermen's quarter to indulge her erotic urges. When Marco, an attractive stranger, exploits the greed and hypocrisy of the townspeople in an elaborate confidence game, only Zazu perceives his falseness. Fearful of being conquered by him, she walks off the breakwater into a storm-whipped sea. Since suicide was prohibited in literature by the censors, her fate remains undetermined.

Although she had resolved to remain single and devote herself to literature, in November 1952 Matute married another aspiring—but unsuccessful—writer, Juan Eugenio de Goicoechea. In 1954 her only child, Juan Pablo, was born. She began writing children's stories for him, raising the age level of her audience as he grew up. Attempting to repay debts accrued by her husband, she published a book a year from 1954 to 1958, three in 1960, six in 1961, and one a year from 1962 to 1965.

As the family's primary financial support, Matute was forced to "mutilate" her most daring novel when the original version was prohibited by the censors. "Las luciérnagas" (The Fireflies) portrayed Republican supporters and pacifists sympathetically while depicting the

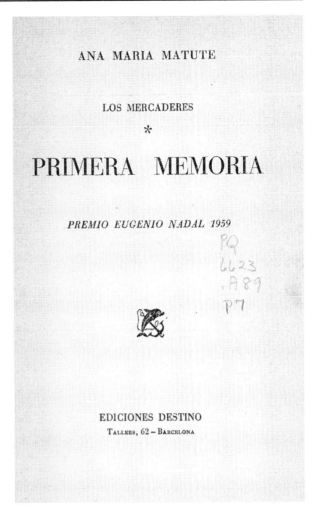

ANA MARIA MATUTE

LOS MERCADERES

*

PRIMERA MEMORIA

*PREMIO EUGENIO NADAL 1959*

EDICIONES DESTINO
TALLERS, 62 – BARCELONA

Title page for Matute's 1960 novel (First Memoir; translated as School of the Sun, 1963), in which she represents the Spanish Civil War in miniature as a conflict between juvenile gangs on the island of Majorca. The work is the first volume in her "Los mercaderes" (The Merchants) trilogy (Thomas Cooper Library, University of South Carolina).

dictatorship's economic failures during the first fifteen postwar years. The clearly pacifistic original version included such statements as "War is a macabre farce that achieves nothing, betters nothing." Matute deleted the final third of the novel, leaving an open-ended, enigmatic tale of young love doomed by war that was published in 1955 as *En esta tierra* (In This Land). She never liked the abridgment and has always considered it her worst artistic error.

*En esta tierra* is narrated by Soledad, the daughter of a bourgeois Barcelona family whose world is destroyed by the Civil War. Although Soledad is a young woman, rather than the ten-year-old that the author was at the time of the events depicted, the novel is Matute's most autobiographical full-length work. Soledad's family's holdings are nationalized by Communist militants, and their home is occupied by militia members. During a bombardment, Soledad and Cristián, a pacifist and draft dodger, take refuge in an abandoned house and become lovers. When General Francisco Franco's Insurgent forces enter Barcelona, Cristián runs toward them, shouting, and is gunned down. The ending leaves undetermined whether his shout signified welcome, defiance, or despair.

Matute's 1958 novel, *Los hijos muertos,* is a family chronicle spanning three generations of an aristocratic rural dynasty, the Corvos, that acquired wealth in the nineteenth century only to lose it in the twentieth; the true protagonist of the work is not introduced until the third generation. In 1929 bank failures in Argentina precipitate family ruin, provoking the suicide of Elías Corvo and the attempted suicide of his brother, Gerardo. Gerardo's daughters—the vigorous, domineering Isabel and the beautiful, dreamy, rebellious Verónica—compete for the affections of Daniel, Elías's illegitimate son. Daniel, whose mother is alleged to have been a mulatto Cuban servant, has been relegated to quasi-servant status, resulting in his hatred for the upper class. Isabel attempts to restore the family fortune by arranging a marriage between fourteen-year-old Verónica and a wealthy old man; Verónica's refusal leads Isabel to plan a marriage of convenience between her father and Beatriz, a moderately prosperous spinster of forty. In 1932, a year after the wedding, Beatriz dies giving birth to a daughter, Mónica.

Jealous of Daniel's preference for Verónica, Isabel expels him from the estate. He and Verónica elope to Barcelona, where she and their unborn child die in an air raid. Daniel serves in the Loyalist (Republican) army during the Civil War; captured by the Francoist forces, he is sentenced to forced labor in the mines. He is released in 1948, broken in body and spirit, and becomes a woodsman on the family estate. Mónica, a younger version of Verónica, falls in love with Miguel Fernández, an urban delinquent who is among the few nonpolitical prisoners in the nearby penal colony. Miguel attempts to escape and is hunted down and killed, like an animal during the annual wolf hunt. (Janet Pérez notes in "The Fictional World of Ana María Matute: Solitude, Injustice and Dreams" [1991] that wolves symbolize the poor, who are forced to violence by necessity: wolves kill only when hungry.) Daniel and Diego Herrera, the director of the penal colony, strive to transcend the war's hurts and rancor. Combatants on both sides lose children and now seek reconciliation. While the primary theme of the novel is the destruction caused by the war, background characters—dispossessed peasants and the Barcelona proletar-

iat—communicate Matute's concern with social justice; but despite her implied critiques of the wealthy, Matute never idealizes the lower classes. *Los hijos muertos* won the Critics' Prize as the best novel of the year in 1958 and the Miguel de Cervantes National Literary Prize in 1959.

In 1960 Matute published *Primera memoria* (First Memoir; translated as *School of the Sun,* 1963), the first volume of her trilogy, "Los mercaderes" (The Merchants). The novel employs the Cain-and-Abel structure to portray Spain's fratricidal conflict symbolically and in miniature. The adolescent Matia, whose father is serving in the Loyalist army, is sent to the supposedly peaceful haven of Majorca to live with her grandmother, a wealthy aristocrat. The grandmother is a Franco supporter, as is Matia's cousin Borja, whose father—Matia's father's brother-in-law—joined the Insurgent army. Violence by juvenile gangs and island terrorists mirrors the war on the mainland on a smaller scale as Matia discovers sordid adult sexuality, treachery, betrayal, death, and her own cowardice. Manuel, a neighbor whose family is scorned as *chuecas* (crypto-Jews), is framed by the jealous Borja for a crime Borja committed; Matia, symbolizing those in Spain who did not protest the postwar imprisonment and executions of thousands who had been loyal to the Republican government, dares not speak in his defense.

Matute received a Fundación March (March Foundation) grant to complete the trilogy, and the second volume, *Los soldados lloran de noche* (translated as *Soldiers Cry by Night,* 1995), appeared in 1964. Two years after the conclusion of the previous novel, Manuel is legitimized by his biological father, the "lord of the island," in a deathbed testament. Suddenly wealthy and revealed to be related to Matia's grandmother, he is released from jail by a fawning establishment but renounces the inheritance in disgust. He gives most of the money to his mother and the man he believed to be his father, keeping only enough to buy a yacht for a secret mission to the mainland to carry out the last wishes of Jeza, a condemned Communist organizer he met in prison. Manuel visits Jeza's widow, Marta, and obtains documents to smuggle to Jeza's comrades in Barcelona. Marta had been raised in a dissolute environment by a promiscuous mother and lived a sordid existence before meeting Jeza, who taught her idealism and commitment. She accompanies Manuel on what both recognize as a suicide mission, but the smuggled documents are no longer needed: they reach Barcelona as Franco's troops are capturing the city. Manuel and Marta man a machine-gun post abandoned by fleeing Republicans and are killed by the advancing Insurgent army. This part of the trilogy clarifies the overall title, "Los mercaderes": according to Matute, humanity comprises "heroes"—the few, the idealists—and "merchants," the materialist majority. Their decision to die for a cause, even one that is not their own, makes Manuel and Marta "heroes."

Matute's marriage was unhappy, but divorce, which had been legalized by the Republic, was abolished by the Franco regime. In 1963 Matute became one of the first women under the dictatorship to seek a legal separation, which required approval from the Catholic Curia in Rome. A Spanish wife was the ward of her husband, unable legally to rent an apartment or have a bank account of her own; Matute lost custody of her son during the separation proceedings. Disinherited by her conservative mother, Matute lived with one of her sisters while awaiting the documents she needed to regain some degree of autonomy (a married woman was not allowed to live alone until she had obtained a legal separation). Literary prizes and popular success brought her some financial security, and in 1965 she obtained her legal separation and won custody of her son. In France, where civil remarriage is permitted after a legal separation, Matute married a Catalan businessman; the marriage lasted until his death twenty-eight years later.

Matute served as visiting professor at the University of Virginia in 1965 and at Indiana University in 1965–1966. In the fall of 1969, the year she published the final volume of the "Los mercaderes" trilogy, *La trampa* (translated as *The Trap,* 1996), she was a visiting professor at the University of Oklahoma.

*La trampa* is set twenty-five years after *Primera memoria.* Matia, fortyish and discontented after a life of futile searching for love, returns to Majorca in response to a summons to attend her hated grandmother's ninety-ninth birthday celebration. The war has changed nothing essential: the grandmother still controls the island; Borja, now a jaded playboy, still waits to inherit her estate; and the family's sordid past, which Matia suspected as a child, persists in the grandfather's sealed secret apartments decorated with pornographic murals. After the war, Matia had joined her exiled father, a Spanish professor, in the United States and had married the son of one of his colleagues; her husband had soon become hopelessly alcoholic. Their college-age son, "Bear," is already on the island; he has been recruited by Mario, supposedly an idealistic revolutionary, to assist in the assassination of a politician. Bear hides Mario in his mother's room, correctly counting on their becoming lovers. Growing fond of Matia, Mario rejects using her son for personal vengeance: his intended victim is not a key politician, as Bear believes, but the man who killed Mario's father years earlier. Arriving outside his mother's room, Bear overhears Mario say that there will be no assassination; but he leaves before learning

Cover for the English translation (1995) of the second volume of Matute's "Los mercaderes" trilogy, Los soldados lloran de noche (1964), in which the protagonist travels from Majorca to the mainland on a suicide mission for the anti-Franco forces during the Civil War (Richland County Public Library)

the reason and carries out the deed himself. Seeking to ruin his grandmother and Borja and all they represent, he makes no effort to conceal his identity. Bear escapes in Borja's yacht, but his capture seems inevitable.

The trilogy, ranked by critics with *Los hijos muertos* as Matute's greatest achievements, brought her further recognition, including the first books devoted to the novelist: Margaret E. W. Jones's *The Literary World of Ana María Matute* (1970) and Janet Díaz's *Ana María Matute* (1971). U.S. student editions appeared of *Doce historias de la Artámila* (1965) and *Fiesta al noroeste* (1971). Anthologists began including Matute's stories, and a collection with a critical introduction, *Selecciones de Ana María Matute* (1982, Selections from Ana María Matute), edited by Juana Amelia Hernández and Edenia Guillermo, followed Matute's inclusion by the Col-

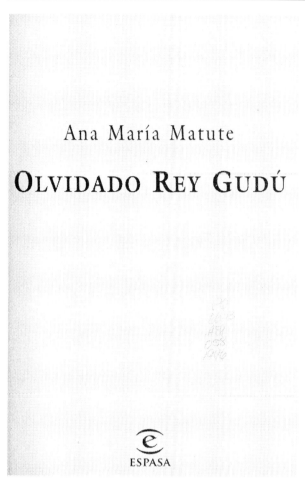

Ana María Matute

OLVIDADO REY GUDÚ

ESPASA

*Title page for Matute's popular 1996 novel (Forgotten King Gudú),
a complex work of nearly nine hundred pages that criticizes social
injustice in the modern world while debunking romantic
notions of chivalry (Thomas Cooper Library,
University of South Carolina)*

lege Board among required authors for the Advanced Placement program in Spanish literature. She also attracted attention from Hispanists in France, Germany, and the Soviet Union.

Matute's health began to deteriorate in the late 1960s; in the 1970s she suffered a serious depression and could write almost nothing for twenty years. The last work she published before lapsing into silence was *La torre vigía* in 1971.

An apocalyptic allegory of good and evil with social realist undertones, *La torre vigía* is set in the tenth century in an unnamed "country of steppes" beset by enemies and extremes of climate and portrays the seamy underside of romanticized courts and chivalric heroes: the work abounds in cruel and violent warlords, sordid affairs, miserable conditions, ignorance, and barbaric behavior; knightly honor is shown to be a

myth. A minor nobleman suspects that the youngest of his four sons, a beautiful boy, is not his; he prefers the others, who are rough and coarse like himself. They become squires for the father's liege, while the youngest is left to sleep under the stairs with the dogs. The fourth son eventually reaches the baron's castle, where, to his brothers' disgust, he distinguishes himself militarily and becomes a favorite. As he progresses in warrior's skills, however, he observes breaches of the chivalric code; the promiscuous and predatory nature of the baron and baroness, who prey on young people of both sexes; and the false glory of war. He begins to spend his time atop the watchtower with the *atalaya* (watchman), a visionary who describes battles of the armies of good and evil that recall the Book of Revelation. While keeping vigil over his weapons in the chapel, the boy realizes that he does not want to become a warlord. He lays down his sword and walks unarmed into the night, where his jealous brothers fall upon him and kill him. (Matute remarked in an unpublished December 1978 interview that she thought that she was avoiding Cain and Abel in this novel but finally realized that, instead, she had created three Cains.) The problem of social injustice is the same in the tenth century as in the twentieth, with humanity divided into victims and victimizers. *La torre vigía* was relatively unnoticed by critics and is one of Matute's least-known works. Matute was writer in residence at the University of Virginia in 1978.

Franco had died in 1975, and Spain had become a constitutional monarchy under King Juan Carlos in 1978. In 1993 an unexpurgated, revised, and enlarged version of *En esta tierra* was published as *Luciérnagas* (translated as *Fireflies,* 1998). In this version Cristián is not killed but is captured near the end of the Civil War and "mobilized" into the Insurgent forces (captive draft-age males could "choose" between joining Franco or execution). Soledad is jailed and discovers that she is pregnant. She and Cristián marry after her release and struggle futilely to make a life for themselves and their child amid economic stagnation and totalitarianism. Cristián attempts to steal medicine for their sick baby and is sent to a penal colony resembling the one in *Los hijos muertos;* both are based on the concentration camp for political prisoners near Matute's grandparents' estate. Soledad moves nearby with their son, and they suffer hunger and hardship. Sociopolitical conditions have destroyed all of their lives.

Between 1971 and 1996 Matute mainly published new editions and collections of her previous works. Except for the children's tale *Sólo un pie descalzo* (1984, Just One Bare Foot), she brought out only one new title: *El verdadero final de la Bella Durmiente* (1995, The True Ending of Sleeping Beauty), an extended, violent version of the traditional fairy tale that does not end happily when the prince and princess are united. Their seemingly endless journey back to his kingdom traverses deep, dark forests for months, perhaps years, before they reach his castle. The Queen Mother, the most evil of mothers-in-law, is an ogress who devours children; she immediately begins planning to cook her two grandchildren. While her husband remains at home, the princess astutely fends off the grandmother's trickery; but when he goes off to war, the ogress becomes more aggressive. Beauty and her children are concealed by a kindly servant but are eventually discovered. In peril of their lives, they are saved by the prince's last-minute return. The work illustrates Matute's conviction that love and family relationships are especially difficult.

Even before *La torre vigía* appeared, Matute's publisher had announced the impending release of *Olvidado rey Gudú;* but the work was delayed for twenty-five years. In interviews in 1993 Matute mentioned a manuscript exceeding two thousand pages; the published version, which appeared three years later, is nearly nine hundred pages long and enormously complex, featuring multiple dynasties, realities, plots, and subplots. It is another exercise in social criticism disguised as an anti-chivalric novel: with rare exceptions the knightly state is completely demythologized, and kings are merely the biggest barbarians. Comparable only to J. R. R. Tolkien's *The Lord of the Rings* trilogy (1954–1955) in its combination of fantasy and reality, magic and misery, and allegory and aspiration to transcendence, *Olvidado rey Gudú* has no precedent in Spanish literature. Glittering tournaments, noble knights and lovely ladies, courtly manners and high ideals seldom appear; instead, everywhere there is murder, rape, pillage, degradation, pain, misery, starvation, filth, disease, cruelty, and disillusionment. Covering nine generations and many kingdoms, the novel blends pseudohistory, myth, and fairy-tale elements: fairies, elves, wizards, witches, nymphs, minor deities, journeys through the air and underground, spells and potions, and seductions and betrayals. Gudú, the consummate warlord, is incapable of loving; old, defeated, and utterly alone, he dies at the hands of two of his sons. His mother, Queen Ardid, is Matute's most complex and only fully empowered female character. Abounding in gore from beginning to end, the novel implicitly constitutes a pacifist statement in its display of the horrors of war.

In 2000 Matute published *Aranmanoth,* a short novel with chivalric and fairy-tale elements; a tale of doomed love, it recalls the legend of Tristan and Isolde. Aranmanoth, born of an encounter between a water sprite and a nobleman of "the North" (a mythical land), is sent at puberty to his father, Orso, who relegates him to servitude. Forced by the king to marry for political reasons, Orso appoints Aranmanoth guardian of his nine-year-old bride, Windumanoth, who is from "the South." The two grow up together as quasi siblings. The similarity in the endings of the names of the unrelated adolescents indicates a transcendent relationship between them, and there are many suggestions of their sacramental character (for example, Aranmanoth's blond hair is repeatedly compared to stalks of wheat, the raw material for the bread of the Eucharist). Windumanoth is homesick for the South; she and Aranmanoth try to journey there but wander for years in endless forests without finding Windumanoth's beloved homeland. They interrupt their journey back to Orso's gloomy castle to consummate their love and almost immediately are slain by Orso's men. Aranmanoth's severed head vanishes, and miracles are later attributed to it; among them is the salvation of Orso, who repents their slaughter and becomes a hermit. *Aranmanoth* is a transparent allegory of redemption through untrammeled love.

While Ana María Matute is better known to critics for the neorealistic social-protest works of her first quarter century, *Olvidado rey Gudú* was her greatest popular success and won her a cult following. Disconcerting to scholars because of their radically changed settings and plots, the works of Matute's later period differ less than it seems from those of her early period: sympathy for the poor and the denunciation of oppression, injustice, violence, and egocentrism are constants throughout her oeuvre.

**Interviews:**

Alicia Redondo de Goicoechea, "Entrevista," *Compás de letras* (1993): 2–13;

Marie-Lise Gazarian-Gautier, *Ana María Matute: La voz del silencio* (Madrid: Espasa-Calpe, 1997).

**References:**

Juan Luis Alborg, *Hora actual de la novela española,* volume 1 (Madrid: Taurus, 1958), pp. 181–190;

Celia Barretini, "Ana María Matute, la novelista pintora," *Cuadernos Hispanoamericanos,* 48 (December 1963): 405–412;

Constance Nock Brown, "Rhetorical Elements in Two Novels by Ana María Matute, *Primera memoria* and *Los soldados lloran de noche,*" M.A. thesis, University of North Carolina, 1970;

Anita Coffey, "Archetypal Figures in Selected Works of Ana María Matute," dissertation, Texas Tech University, 2001;

Claude Couffon, "Una joven novelista, Ana María Matute," *Cuadernos Hispanoamericanos,* 44 (November 1961): 52–55;

Janet Díaz, *Ana María Matute* (Boston: Twayne, 1971);

Díaz, "The Autobiographical Element in the Works of Ana María Matute," *Kentucky Foreign Language Quarterly,* 15, no. 2 (1968): 139–148;

Díaz, "La *commedia dell'arte* en una novela de Ana María Matute," *Hispanófila,* 40 (1970): 15–28;

Olga P. Ferrer, "Las novelistas españolas de hoy," *Cuadernos americanos,* 118 (September–October 1961): 211–223;

Marie-Lise Gazarian, Janet Pérez, and others, *The Literary World of Ana María Matute* (Coral Gables, Fla.: University of Miami, Iberian Studies Institute, 1993);

*Ideas 92,* special Matute issue, edited by Joaquín Roy (1993–1994);

Margaret E. W. Jones, "Antipathetic Fallacy: The Hostile World of Ana María Matute's Novels," *Kentucky Foreign Language Quarterly,* 13, supplement (1967): 5–16;

Jones, *The Literary World of Ana María Matute* (Lexington: University Press of Kentucky, 1970);

Jones, "Religious Motifs and Biblical Allusions in the Works of Ana María Matute," *Hispania,* 51 (September 1968): 416–423;

Eugenio de Nora, *La novela española contemporánea (1927–1960),* volume 2 (Madrid: Gredos, 1962), pp. 288–299, 432–433;

Janet Pérez, "Apocalipsis y milenio, cuentos de hadas y caballerías en las últimas obras de Ana María Matute," *Monographic Review / Revista monográfica,* 14 (1998): 39–58;

Pérez, "Contemporary Spanish Women Writers and the Feminized Quest-Romance," *Intertexts,* 2, no. 1 (1998): 83–96;

Pérez, "The Fictional World of Ana María Matute: Solitude, Injustice and Dreams," in *Women Writers of Contemporary Spain: Exiles in the Homeland,* edited by

Joan Lipman Brown (Newark: University of Delaware Press, 1991), pp. 93–115;

Pérez, "More than a Fairy Tale: *Aranmanoth, Gudú* and *La torre vigía.* Matute and the 'nueva novela caballeresca,'" *Letras Peninsulares,* 15 (Winter 2002–2003): 107–122;

Pérez, "Once Upon a Time: Spanish Women Writers and the Fairy Tale," in *Hers Ancient and Modern: Women's Writing in Spain and Brazil,* edited by Catherine Davies and Jane Whetnall (Manchester, U.K.: Department of Spanish and Portuguese, University of Manchester, 1997), pp. 57–71;

Pérez, "Portraits of the *femme seule* by Laforet, Matute, Soriano, Martín Gaite, Quiroga and Medio," in *Feminine Concerns in Contemporary Spanish Fiction by Women,* edited by Roberto Manteiga, Carolyn Galerstein, and Kathleen McNerney (Potomac, Md.: Scripta Humanistica, 1988), pp. 54–77;

Pérez, "A Subjective Stylist with a Social Conscience," in her *Contemporary Women Writers of Spain* (Boston: G. K. Hall, 1988), pp. 131–137;

Pérez, "Variantes del arquetipo femenino en la narrativa de Ana María Matute," *Letras femeninas,* 10, no. 2 (1984): 28–39;

José María de Quinto, "El mundo de Ana María Matute," *Revista española,* 1 (September–October 1953): 337–341;

Alicia Redondo de Goicoechea, "Un dolorido vivir," *Compás de letras* (1993): 14–23;

Janet Winecoff, "Style and Solitude in Ana María Matute," *Hispania,* 49 (March 1966): 61–68.

**Papers:**

Unpublished juvenilia of Ana María Matute is in the Fundación Ana María Matute, Mugar Library, Boston University.

# Eduardo Mendoza

*(11 January 1943 –   )*

Patricia Hart
*Purdue University*

BOOKS: *La verdad sobre el caso Savolta* (Barcelona: Seix Barral, 1975); translated by Alfred J. Mac Adam as *The Truth about the Savolta Case* (New York: Pantheon, 1992);

*El misterio de la cripta embrujada* (Barcelona: Seix Barral, 1979);

*El laberinto de las aceitunas* (Barcelona: Seix Barral, 1982);

*La ciudad de los prodigios* (Barcelona: Seix Barral, 1986); translated by Bernard Molloy as *The City of Marvels* (San Diego: Harcourt Brace Jovanovich, 1988; London: Collins Harvill, 1988);

*Nueva York* (Barcelona: Destino, 1986);

*La isla inaudita* (Barcelona: Seix Barral, 1989);

*Barcelona modernista,* by Mendoza and Cristina Mendoza (Barcelona: Planeta, 1989);

*Restauraciò* (Barcelona: Seix Barral, 1990); Spanish version published as *Restauración* (Barcelona: Seix Barral, 1991);

*Sin noticias de Gurb* (Barcelona: Seix Barral, 1991);

*El año del diluvio* (Barcelona: Seix Barral, 1992); translated by Nick Caistor as *The Year of the Flood* (London: Harvill, 1995);

*Una comedia ligera* (Barcelona: Seix Barral, 1996); translated by Caistor as *A Light Comedy* (London: Harvill, 2001);

*La aventura del tocador de señoras* (Barcelona: Seix Barral, 2001);

*Pío Baroja* (Barcelona: Omega, 2001);

*El último trayecto de Horacio Dos* (Barcelona: Seix Barral, 2002).

PLAY PRODUCTION: *Restauraciò,* Barcelona, Teatro Romea, 1990; Spanish version produced as *Restauración,* Madrid, 1990.

PRODUCED SCRIPT: *El año del diluvio,* by Mendoza and Jaime Chávarri, Kairos/Gonafilm, 2004.

TRANSLATION: Arthur Miller, *Panorama desde el puente* (Barcelona: Tusquets, 2003).

*Eduardo Mendoza (photograph by Jerry Bauer; from the dust jacket for* The Truth about the Savolta Case, *1992; Richland County Public Library)*

SELECTED PERIODICAL PUBLICATIONS–UNCOLLECTED: "Mayo del 68 posmoderno," *La Nación* (Buenos Aires), 8 August 1993;

"Mi primera lectura del Quijote," *El País,* 18 April 1998;

"La novela se queda sin épica," *El País,* 16 August 1998;

"La muerte de la novela," Seix Barral catalogue (January–March 1999);

"Ingenuidad," *El País,* 21 July 1999;

"¡Basta ya!" *El País,* 23 September 2000.

When the name of Barcelona-born novelist Eduardo Mendoza is mentioned, some of the qualities that come to mind include urbanity, sophistication, and intricate multilingual wordplay. Producing insights into Catalan history, he wrote about the crises of conscience of well-meaning but weak men who cannot act or choose morality over privileges and the rise of ruthless financiers who act without regard to the havoc they wreak. Son of a well-to-do Spanish father and a mother from the cultured Catalan haute bourgeoisie, Mendoza is an uncommon blend of insights into these parallel languages and cultures, equally informed and satirical regarding both. With the publication in 1975 of *La verdad sobre el caso Savolta* (translated as *The Truth about the Savolta Case,* 1992), Mendoza, then a thirty-two-year-old lawyer, sprang to prominence as a writer who owed little apparent debt to the earnest social novel that had dominated Spanish narrative at the end of General Francisco Franco's regime. The release of the book, just months before Franco's death, marked an explosion of social change as the Iberian nation was transformed from a conservative religio-military dictatorship with strict censorship into a diverse, modern European state.

Eduardo Mendoza Garriga was born on 11 January 1943; his father was a lawyer. He had a younger sister, Cristina. At home he spoke Spanish; in the streets with his playmates he learned and spoke Catalan. Though the family was well off, they avoided ostentation. At home and at school, the rules of external comportment were rigid, while the morality and ethics of the Catalan bourgeoisie were often harder to fathom. As a child, Mendoza fantasized about growing up to be a bullfighter, explorer, or seafaring captain, but as there was little professional demand for these activities in the Barcelona of the 1950s and 1960s, he followed a more conventional path.

From seven to seventeen Mendoza received an exacting education with the Hermanos Maristas (Marist Brothers), and from 1960 to 1965 he studied law at the University of Barcelona with a scholarship from the Fundación Juan March, thus fulfilling his family's expectation that he enter a bourgeois profession. Having relieved some of the familial pressure on him to conform by graduating, Mendoza was able to persuade his father to finance an entire year of traveling through Europe. On his return to Barcelona, family connections helped him obtain a generous scholarship to study sociology for a year in London. Although less than successful as a student in London, he took advantage of the time there to begin writing parts of what eventually became *La verdad sobre el caso Savolta* and to learn all the English he could. Already adept in French and Catalan, the young Mendoza developed into a brilliant linguist. Back home in Barcelona in 1968, fresh from London

with its multiple freedoms and politically active youth, Mendoza reluctantly began to work for a Barcelona law firm. Thanks to his social position and quick wit, he had been able to get outside of Spain to experience the vanguard and youth movements in France and England firsthand; still, like most of his contemporaries, he felt that Franco's regime had robbed him of a large component of his youth. Like many of his generation, he was embarrassed at having to cross the border to Perpignan or Biarritz to see movies that were banned in Spain. The resulting cultural inferiority complex is something that recurs relentlessly in his works.

From 1968 to 1972 Mendoza practiced at a law firm involved in the "Barcelona Traction" case. The Barcelona Traction Light and Power Company was incorporated in Canada in 1911 to buy up interest in projects to build and manage tramways and generate electricity in and around Barcelona. Both trams and electrification fascinate Mendoza, and odd details regarding both are discussed often in his work. The Barcelona Traction Company soon owned outright a subsidiary, the Ebro Irrigation and Power Company, which had a permanent concession for hydroelectric power on the Ebro River and two tributaries to supply the power to Barcelona, Terrassa, and Sabadell. Mismanagement and the Spanish Civil War brought the company to the brink of disaster, creating an opportunity for shady Majorcan financier Juan March. The wealthy industrialist had given generously to the Nationalist cause for arms and espionage (through the Servicio de Información del Noroeste de España, or SINFE) during the Civil War and later bribed the Franco government with huge amounts to protect his business interests. The most daring bribe purportedly took place when March apparently paid off judges and others to declare Barcelona Traction bankrupt in the Court of Reus on 12 February 1948. The swift bankruptcy let March repurchase the assets, valued conservatively at $250 million, for about a thousandth of their worth, without properly notifying the major shareholders of Barcelona Traction. Before the shareholders (many of whom were Belgian nationals by this time) knew what had happened, March had taken over all the assets exclusively for his own Fuerzas Eléctricas de Cataluña, S.A. (FECSA), thus consolidating his fortune. In 1955 March, like the Rockefellers, Carnegies, and Fords before him, established a charitable foundation in his name that has generously supported the arts and scientific and social research ever since. The ordinary holders of stock in Barcelona Traction lost everything, while March became the richest man in Spain. Litigation followed. Mendoza worked on the case every day from 8:00 A.M. to 3:00 P.M., searching the archives of the companies involved, reading the documentation

in English, French, and German, and putting his dis-
coveries in order. A note on his website (http://
www.clubcultura.com/clubliteratura/clubescritores/
mendoza) reveals the influence of this work on his subsequent literary endeavors:

> La historia del caso venía dada por un contrato, una
> carta, la minuta de un encuentro, un telegrama. . . .
> Nada de eso tenía ningún sentido por sí solo, pero visto
> todo en perspectiva, formaba una magna operación de
> compraventa. Aunque Mendoza nunca descubrió la
> conspiración que buscaba, sí encontró un recurso lite-
> rario: la forma de ir datando un suceso a base de míni-
> mos detalles marginales.

> (The history of the case was told by a contract here, a
> letter there, the minutes of a meeting, a telegram. . . .
> None of this made any sense by itself, but seen all
> together in perspective, it formed an immense stock
> operation. Although Mendoza never uncovered proof
> of the conspiracy he was seeking, he did find a literary
> device: a way of documenting an event through mini-
> mal, marginal details.)

Early in 1973 Mendoza passed the examinations
given to select trainees for the translation corps at the
United Nations (UN). On 1 December he left for New
York City. In 1974, after eight years of pleadings before
the International Court of Justice in The Hague, where
Belgium demanded expropriation of the FECSA assets
from the Spanish government, the remaining Traction
shares and bonds were canceled, and the case was dismissed.

March became a model for many of Mendoza's
protagonists, whose grade of guilt varies. Recognizing
Mendoza's particular mixture of repulsion and admiration for Catalan business acumen and *seny* (roughly,
"common sense") is key to understanding all of his protagonists, even those least endowed with wealth and
power, or maybe even particularly them. His characters
are able to describe Spanish society from top to bottom
with a privileged, though debased, objectivity. Mendoza's years of frustrated participation on the Traction
case, with its Hollywoodesque proportions, gave him
historical insights into cutthroat business practices in his
part of the country. It also provided useful experience
with the arrogance of Catalan bourgeois men and the
legalese that Mendoza both explains and parodies often
in his novels. The loss of the Traction case tinges virtually everything Mendoza has written with a tincture of
defeatism and impotence.

Mendoza's first novel, *La verdad sobre el caso
Savolta,* narrates the murder in Catalonia of an industrialist followed by that of an even worse arriviste whose
money came from arms trafficking during World War

*Dust jacket for the English translation (1992) of Mendoza's
first novel,* La verdad sobre el caso Savolta *(1975),
in which the murders of an industrialist and an arms
dealer expose ruthless business practices in Catalonia
(Richland County Public Library)*

I. The book has four major characters—Savolta, the rob-
ber baron; Paul-André Lepprince, the glamorous nouveau riche businessman who weds the boss's daughter
while marrying off his mistress to a plodding underling;
Pajarito de Soto, the anarchist newspaper reporter bent
on exposing Savolta's criminal business practices and
seemingly unaware of the danger to himself, particularly when he tries blackmail; and the only character
left standing at the end, Javier Miranda, the clumsy
social climber from the provinces. These main characters embody the four possible ideological outlooks on
success in Catalonia that most interest Mendoza.
Although Miranda recognizes the moral truth of
Pajarito's social theories, he deliberately chooses to ally
himself with Lepprince in the hopes of rising socially
and economically. In a 1976 interview Mendoza told
Amparo Tuñón:

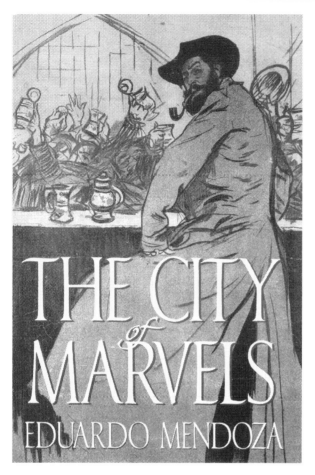

*Dust jacket for the U.S. edition (1988) of the English translation of Mendoza's novel* La ciudad de los prodigios (1986), in *which an impoverished peasant becomes a ruthless tycoon between the Barcelona World's Fairs of 1888 and 1929 (Richland County Public Library)*

Javier Miranda no entiende nada . . . y por eso tiene la ventaja de contar la historia objetivamente. . . . El hombre menos preparado para sobrevivir es el único que sobrevive, el más torpe, el más cobarde, el que tiene menos temple. . . . Eso suele suceder en la vida real.

(Javier Miranda doesn't understand anything . . . and that's why he has the advantage of being able to tell the story objectively. . . . The man least prepared to survive is the only one who survives, the clumsiest, most cowardly, and the one least tempered by experience. . . . That tends to happen in real life.)

With these comments Mendoza articulates the most important theme of his novels: a kind of existential despair at any attempt to act decisively, combined with the novelist's acute insight into the consequences of accepting the self-serving, relativist doctrine of pragmatic greed over a strong ideological stance. In the Tuñón interview he continued:

La literatura al uso presenta una imagen agresiva y virulenta de los regímenes opresivos, pero la realidad no siempre es así. Una vez se imponen por la violencia, los regímenes opresivos, institucionales o de hecho, suelen crear condiciones de vida confortables e incluso gratas para quien no se mete en camisa de once varas.

(The literature in use now presents an aggressive, virulent image of oppressive regimes, but the reality is not always like that. Once they have come to power through violence, oppressive regimes, whether de jure or de facto, tend to create comfortable and even pleasant conditions of life for people who keep their noses clean.)

*La verdad sobre el caso Savolta* includes a mixture of styles and influences, all organized into what early readers took as a sort of historical thriller with moments of farce. The Barcelona literary establishment was not yet prepared to embrace such a postmodern enterprise. Undaunted, Mendoza gave the manuscript to his friend Pere Gimferrer for comments. Gimferrer was an acclaimed poet who worked as an editor at the prestigious publishing house Seix Barral and had the ear of the editorial world and Barcelona's arty, leftish intellectuals, the so-called *gauche divine*. Gimferrer worked with Mendoza on the rewrites of *La verdad sobre el caso Savolta*. Mendoza has sometimes called this assistance the closest he ever came to attending a writing workshop. The book was accepted by Seix Barral. It also scored him the representation of Carmen Balcells, the Catalan agent to the stars of the Latin American Boom and the cream of the Spanish literary crop. One year later the novel was awarded the prestigious Premio de la Crítica (Critics' Prize), and Mendoza's reputation as a prodigy was set.

Mendoza's fascination with Catalan anarchy recurs throughout his work and is not always restricted to the political reality of workers in Catalonia. He also delights in the odd juxtapositions and anomalous stances Spanish anarchism produced. The mixture of tragedy, comedy, and farce used to describe Catalonia's anarchist traditions caught critics of the book by surprise. The reviews became an avalanche of praise, many going so far as to say that *La verdad sobre el caso Savolta* was the first post-Franco novel to be published in Spain.

Mendoza rapidly advanced from translator to simultaneous interpreter at the UN, a position that relied on his quick mind as well as his linguistic ability. As a result, he was able to travel the world first class, gain extensive knowledge of global politics, and learn to speak English and Spanish on a variety of quite specific linguistic, social, and intellectual levels. Moreover, because of the exhausting nature of simultaneous interpretation, a typical day at the UN consisted of a four-hour shift. This schedule left Mendoza large blocks of free time to continue writing, which he did by hand on yellow legal pads in his various New York apartments, going through many revisions.

In 1979 Mendoza surprised the Spanish public with his parodic work *El misterio de la cripta embrujada* (The Mystery of the Haunted Crypt). This novel tells the story of an unnamed resident in a mental hospital who is released by an unscrupulous policeman in the hopes that the patient will serve as an informant on a murder case. Like a Golden Age picaro, the addlepated sleuth describes Barcelona society from top to bottom as he searches for the murderer. Mendoza readily admits that he missed the Spanish transition to democracy completely because he lived abroad during the accession of Juan Carlos de Borbón as king after Franco's death in 1975, the passage of the new constitution in 1978, the unsuccessful military coup attempt by Colonel Antonio Tejero (broadcast live on television) in 1981, and the elections of 1982 that ensured a socialist government. Although *El misterio de la cripta embrujada* was published just before a miniboom of Spanish incursions into the *roman noir* and other genre fiction and movies, some reviewers in Spain deplored what they considered the frivolity of this novel. Coming on the heels of his prizewinning story of ruthless business practices in Barcelona, *El misterio de la cripta embrujada* struck many critics as more *divertimento* (casual entertainment) than novel, though the author himself dismisses this distinction.

In 1982 Mendoza published a sequel to *El misterio de la cripta embrujada,* titled *El laberinto de las aceitunas* (The Labyrinth of Olives), again starring his picaresque protagonist, who gradually comes to be known by one of his aliases, Ceferino. The character is still a police informant and escapee from a mental health institution. Mendoza likes to say that Seix Barral imposed a title change on the book. Originally, he insists, it was to be called "El algorritmo de las aceitunas," but his publishers felt that mentioning algorithms might be off-putting for a postwar-educated Spanish reading public with math anxiety.

The two earlier satirical novels mark a return in Spanish letters to the *esperpento,* Ramón María del Valle-Inclán's term for a style that he described as viewing Spain and its reality through a distorting mirror like those in the Callejón de Eduardo Gato in Madrid. Mendoza recognized a shabby artificiality in the "subversive" Spanish neorealism produced under Franco. By returning to the brilliant wordplay of Valle-Inclán or the rough-hewn observations of Pío Baroja, Mendoza and friends such as Juan Benet and Juan Marsé helped bring Spanish fiction into the latter half of the twentieth

century. Within a few years, with the consolidation of the Spanish democracy, many other writers relaxed and experimented with genre fiction, children's and youth literature, and screenplays.

In 1979 *La verdad sobre el caso Savolta* was made into a movie directed by Antonio Drove, with José Luis López Vázquez as Pajarito de Soto, and in 1981 Cayetano del Real adapted and directed *La cripta,* a low-budget version of *El misterio de la cripta embrujada,* in which José Sacristán played Ceferino. These cinematic adventures resulted in long-term friendships for Mendoza with López Vázquez and Sacristán.

At the end of 1982 Mendoza returned to Barcelona, enthusiastic over the election of Felipe González Márquez as prime minister and convinced that he could no longer write in Spanish while living in the United States. In 1983 Mendoza and Sacristán collaborated on the story for the movie *Soldados de plomo* (1983, Soldiers of Lead); Sacristán wrote the screenplay and acted in and directed the picture. Although he spent dedicated stretches writing fiction, he also reserved six months of the year to do simultaneous interpretation for various international organizations. One of his greatest moments was interpreting during a summit between Ronald Reagan and González Márquez. His website states that because "los intérpretes no tienen memoria" (interpreters have no memory), he cannot remember what was said, but he recalls the American actor-president as communicative and pleasant.

In 1986 Mendoza's most ambitious and acclaimed novel, *La ciudad de los prodigios* (translated as *The City of Marvels,* 1988), was published. The book narrates the rise to prominence of Onofre Bouvila, an impoverished peasant who comes in 1887 to a Barcelona that has not yet invented itself. Bouvila's first job is handing out anarchist leaflets to workers at the 1888 World's Fair, but he soon loses any sense of solidarity and instead sheds his scruples and eventually becomes one of the richest and most powerful men in the country. In many ways, he is a character who combines Lepprince, Miranda, and Pajarito. In the first issue of *SABER/leer,* published by the Fundación Juan March starting in 1987, novelist and engineer Benet wrote a review, "La novela de los prodigios" (The Novel of Marvels), in which he stated that "mientras la mayoría de las novelas españolas aparecidas en estos tiempos pasarán sin pena ni gloria, *La ciudad de los prodigios . . .* quedará como una de las piezas más conseguidas de la narrativa hispánica actual" (while most of the Spanish novels that have appeared lately will pass away without pain or glory, *The City of Marvels . . .* will remain as one of the most successful pieces in contemporary Hispanic narrative). The novel won the Premio Ciudad de Barcelona (City of Barcelona Prize) in 1987 and was cho-

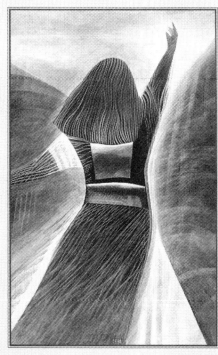

THE YEAR
OF THE FLOOD

EDUARDO MENDOZA

*Dust jacket for the English translation (1995) of Mendoza's novel*
El año del diluvio *(1992), about a nun seduced by a*
*Falangist landowner in a 1950s Catalan village*
*(Richland County Public Library)*

sen best book of the year by the French magazine *Lire* in 1988. It was a finalist in the foreign-novel category for the Italian Grinzane Cavour Prize and a finalist for the French Médicis et Femina Prize, both in 1988.

In 1989 *La isla inaudita* (The Unheard-of Island), based in part on Mendoza's frequent professional stays in Venice, appeared. Fábregas, a Barcelona businessman undergoing a midlife crisis, travels to Venice to escape his family and other responsibilities. Unlike Paul Gaugin in Tahiti, however, Fábregas has no artistic passion to replace his bourgeois routine. Instead, he creates a sort of nihilistic anti-art by sitting in his hotel, inert, slowly discovering his own suffocating identity. The French translation of *La ciudad de los prodigios* also won a prize from *Lire* magazine that year as best book published the previous year. Also in 1989 the coffee-table

book *Barcelona modernista* (Nouveau Barcelona), written with his sister, Museum of Modern Art curator Cristina Mendoza, and lavishly illustrated with photographs of Catalan art and architecture nouveau, was published.

In August 1990, inspired by nineteenth-century novels that had been serialized first in daily newspapers, Mendoza agreed to publish the comic novel *Sin noticias de Gurb* (No Word from Gurb) in installments in Spain's largest daily newspaper, *El País*. The work was published in book form by Seix Barral the following year. Gurb is an extraterrestrial who has landed just outside Barcelona and proceeds to describe a contemporary Catalonia for which his alien leaders had imperfectly prepared him.

Because Mendoza's formal education with the Marist Brothers and his childhood home had both operated in Spanish, Mendoza was not adept at writing in Catalan when he first returned to Barcelona in the early 1980s. Moreover, he had missed the transition to democracy, and with it, the Catalan process of linguistic *normalització* (normalization). Although the author had visited Barcelona during the UN years, and although he spoke Catalan fluently in given situations, he needed to spend additional time living in the language before writing in it. In 1990, after seven years in normalized Catalonia, Mendoza's first major work in Catalan, the play *Restauració* (Restoration), premiered at the Teatro Romea in Barcelona. Mendoza himself prepared the Spanish-language version shown in Madrid the same year. The play was also published in both languages by Seix Barral. Mendoza has explained that Catalan theater influenced him in a much more direct way than Catalan novels, and that he genuinely feels himself part of both the Spanish novelistic tradition and the Catalan stage heritage. Another play, *Gloria*, has been published only on his website.

*El año del diluvio* (translated as *The Year of the Flood*, 1995), set in a Catalan village in the 1950s, came out in 1992; the following year the French translation won a readers' popularity prize in *Elle* magazine. Constanza Briones is a nun filled with good intentions and little practical knowledge of the world. The local Falangist landowner, Aixelà de Collbató, becomes smitten with her and sets out to seduce her while pretending to help with one of her charitable good works. Other complications involve a group of maquis who have been in hiding, gradually losing their ideological direction since the end of the Spanish Civil War in 1939. The maquis in the book are drawn from historical reality, but they also echo and allude to the complicated maquis who frequent the works of Mendoza's friend and contemporary Marsé. Mendoza's maquis are likewise drawn in complicated shades of gray. Eventually, the stories in

Mendoza's book intertwine into an unhappy climax symbolized by the flood referred to in the title.

From 1995 to 2001 Mendoza taught at the Universitat Pompeu Fabra in Barcelona in the School of Translation and Interpretation. At roughly the same time, Mendoza became involved in a polemic that grew out of proportion. Some offhand comments to the press and a speech the author gave at the prestigious summer course at the Universidad Menéndez y Pelayo in Santander set off a dispute that Mendoza later wryly described as his failed attempt at literary suicide. The remarks recycled a weary postmodern cliché that Mendoza probably repeated only partly in earnest, namely that the novel was dead. Of the heat his statements generated, Mendoza wrote in 1999 in an article for the Seix Barral catalogue:

> Cuando dije lo que entonces dije (y enseguida repetiré) no pensé que mis palabras fueran a provocar ninguna reacción. Ni mi inserción en el campo de la teoría literaria (inexistente) ni los argumentos que entonces esgrimí (ninguno) justificaban, a mi modo de ver, al que fueran interpretadas como otra cosa que una opinión personal expresada en el curso de una entrevista. Sin embargo la reacción se produjo, y de un modo continuado y en diversos medios: informativos y académicos.

> (When I said what I said [and what I am about to repeat], I didn't think my words would cause such a commotion. Neither my insertion into the field of literary theory [nonexistent] nor the arguments I wielded at the time [not a one], justified, to my way of thinking, that my words should be interpreted as anything but a personal opinion expressed during an interview. Nevertheless, the reaction happened, and in a manner that was continued and in diverse media: both news and academic.)

For the second half of the decade Mendoza found himself answering questions on the subject in interviews and even in public spaces such as train stations and theaters. The essay that came out in the Seix Barral catalogue was intended to put the matter to rest. Mendoza commented, "Para los antiguos egipcios una momia no era una persona viva, pero tampoco definitivamente muerta. Quizás ésta sea ahora la situación de la novela" (For the ancient Egyptians, a mummy wasn't a live person, but neither was it definitively dead. Maybe this is the situation of the novel today).

In 1996 Mendoza found enough life left in the moribund novel genre to publish *Una comedia ligera* (translated as *A Light Comedy*, 2001), the story of Catalan playwright Carlos Prullàs, whose once-popular comedies of manners are beginning to creak with age as their inventor struggles with male menopause. In the summer of 1950 Prullàs attempts to prepare his comeback production, *¡Arrivederci, pollo!* (Goodbye, Chicken!), in the hopes of reviving public interest in his work, which also includes titles such as *Un puñal de quita y pon* (A Rubber Dagger) and *Todos los muertos se llaman Paco* (All Corpses are Called Paco). At the same time, a silly romantic dalliance with a comely but untalented actress in the company plunges Prullàs into a murder investigation and even a plot to overthrow Franco and put Juan Carlos de Borbón on the throne. Marta E. Altisent compares Prullàs with Mendoza's other businessmen characters:

> Prullàs no longer enjoys the expansionist and speculative fantasies of Onofre Bouvila, which gave Barcelona its entrée into European society with the international expositions of 1888 and 1929. Nor does he need, like the industrialist Savolta, to defend himself against the beggars and anarchists of the turbulent Barcelona of 1917–19. Unlike his predecessors, he is a hero, "sin otro futuro que la nostalgia" [with no other future but nostalgia].

*Una comedia ligera* was well received by critics and public alike, and in 1998 it won a prize in France as best foreign book.

In 1999 the movie version of *La ciudad de los prodigios* premiered, a French-Spanish-Portuguese co-production directed by Mario Camus. That year Jaime Chávarri announced that he would begin filming *El año del diluvio* with Fanny Ardant in the role of Consuelo (as Constanza is called in the movie) and with a script by himself and Mendoza. The movie was released in 2004.

In 2000 Mendoza quit his job at the Universitat Pompeu Fabra. In January 2001 a third volume in his Ceferino picaresque detective saga appeared and became an immediate best-seller. *La aventura del tocador de señoras* (The Adventure of the Ladies' Dressing Table) finds Ceferino, like many sufferers of mental illness, abruptly put out on the street with no preparation for the real world and no visible means of survival. Ceferino, like the good picaro he is, manages to survive by his slightly addled wits.

That same year Mendoza repeated his successful experiment in novel serialization with the debut in *El País* in August of *El último trayecto de Horacio Dos* (The Last Voyage of the Horace II). The story revolves around the picaresque adventures of the bumbling commander of the intergalactic spaceship *Horacio Dos* and his crew of bizarre extraterrestrial fauna. Passengers are divided into "los Delincuentes" (The Criminals), "las Mujeres Descarriadas" (The Wayward Women), and "los Ancianos Improvidentes" (The Unprepared Oldsters), but passengers and crew all act much like familiar earthlings in poli-

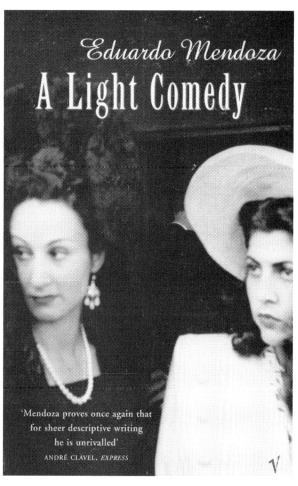

Cover for the 2003 paperback edition of the English translation
(2001) of Mendoza's novel Una comedia ligera (1996),
about a Catalan playwright who tries to revive his career
while having an affair with an actress and becoming
entangled in a murder investigation
(Richland County Public Library)

tics and government. Like Jonathan Swift's Lilliputians, Brobdingnagians, Houyhnhnms, and Yahoos, Mendoza's extraterrestrials are almost more human than humans are. The episodes were collected and published by Seix Barral in 2002.

Also in 2001 Mendoza published a biographical essay on one of his literary masters, Baroja. In the introduction, Mendoza claims to be motivated by what he perceives as Baroja's unique situation in the world of letters: "Baroja ocupa un sitial entre los grandes escritores, pero nadie consigue explicar muy bien por qué" (Baroja occupies a seat of honor among the great writers, but no one has managed to explain exactly why). Mendoza argues that the Basque writer's down-to-earth, spare style largely makes critical apparatus and scholarly footnotes unnecessary, and that his readabil-

ity makes him current, drawing contemporary nonacademic readers to "find out what happens." This quality, Mendoza claims, Baroja shares only with Clarín among Spanish novelists.

Although several of Mendoza's novels have been translated into English, he is not widely known to the American reading public. Mendoza's readers in this country largely fall into three groups: American college Hispanists, Spaniards living in the United States, and serious mystery fans. One of the most visible entries marking the attention of the first group was Joan Ramon Resina's 1992 article in *PMLA* about *City of Marvels.* Resina views historical theory as the most important quality in this novel and others by Mendoza. Several other American academic readers have weighed in with more positive analyses of *La ciudad de los prodigios,* in particular, and of Mendoza's work in general. The other part of Mendoza's reading public seems to appreciate him most for his sense of humor in the detective and science-fiction short novels, or for his wealth of historical detail and charming retelling of Barcelona's past in the historical ones.

In his home country of Spain, and within its smaller autonomous region, Catalonia, Mendoza is significantly more prominent. His books have all been runaway best-sellers by Spanish standards, with edition after edition of each of his works printed. He has received a comfortable number of important literary prizes and is invited to public participation in television round tables, newspaper interviews, book presentations, and other official cultural events with much more frequency than he accepts the invitations. Several significant book-length studies of Mendoza's work have appeared in Spain, and with the premiere of *Restauració* in Catalan, many who criticized him for being "too Spanish" relented as well.

In *Post-Totalitarian Spanish Fiction* (1996) Robert C. Spires writes:

> Mendoza's *La verdad sobre el caso Savolta* was instrumental in bestowing artistic credibility on the genre. Given the tradition of novelistic conformity that crystallized with neorealism in the 1950s and continued with the "new novel" of the 1960s and the self-referential fiction of the 1970s, Mendoza deserves major credit for providing an alternative mode of novelistic expression.

Concluding with what he recognizes as an oxymoron, Spires defines Mendoza's contribution to the twentieth-century Spanish novel as "innovative conventionality." On the one hand, Mendoza returns to the essential telling of a story, calling in all the skills honed by such writers as Charles Dickens, Honoré de Balzac, or Clarín. On the other hand, says Spires, Mendoza displays "a postmodernist distrust for the totalizing picture."

In what was for many years the ultimate authority on Spanish fiction, Francisco Rico's *Historia y crítica de la literatura española* (1980–1983, 1991–2000), Eduardo Mendoza is little more than a name in a long list of people publishing between 1975 and 2000, or an easy target for first declaring the death of the novel and then selling so many of them. Still, it is clear that the Spanish reading public holds him in high esteem. Although Mendoza has frequently declared himself to be finished with publishing comic detective fiction, as Miguel Rodrigo wryly observed in 1982 after interviewing the author, "Y sin embargo . . . Millares de noctívagos devoradores de serie Negra acechan. ¿Logrará Eduardo Mendoza evadirse de su presión? La solución, mañana" (And nevertheless . . . Thousands of nightowl gobblers of detective fiction lie in wait. Will Eduardo Mendoza be able to escape their pressure? The answer, tomorrow).

## Interviews:

Amparo Tuñón, "Eduardo Mendoza: La otra verdad," *Mundo,* 1861 (18 September 1976): 51–52;

Miguel Rodrigo, "El caso Mendoza," *Cambio 16,* 535 (1 March 1982): 89–90;

Gérard Cortanze, "Eduardo Mendoza: Les Mysteres de Barcelone," *Magazine Litteraire,* 408 (April 2002): 98–103.

## References:

Santos Alonso, *La verdad sobre el caso Savolta, Eduardo Mendoza* (Madrid: Alhambra, 1988);

Marta E. Altisent, "Theater and Life in Eduardo Mendoza's *Una comedia ligera,*" in *Multicultural Iberia: Language, Literature, and Music,* edited by Dru Dougherty and Milton M. Azevedo (Berkeley: University of California Press/University of California International and Area Studies Digital Collection, 1999), pp. 134–153;

Juan Benet, "La novela de los prodigios," *SABER/leer,* 1 (January 1987): 4;

Constantino Bértolo, "Introducción a la narrativa española actual," *Revista de Occidente,* 98–99 (1989): 29–60;

Amy Carder, "*El laberinto de las aceitunas:* Mendoza's Parodic, Postmodern Reworking of Crisis of Literatures," *Torre de Papel,* 7 (Summer 1997): 45–64;

José F. Colmeiro, "Eduardo Mendoza y los laberintos de la novela policíaca," in his *La novela policíaca española: Teoría e historia crítica* (Barcelona: Anthropos, 1994), pp. 194–206;

Antonia Ferriol-Montano, "De la paranoia a la ternura: Ironía y humor en la novela española posmoderna de los años ochenta: Eduardo Mendoza, Cristina Fernández Cubas y Luis Landero," dissertation, Pennsylvania State University, 1998;

Margarita Garbisu Buesa, "El juego realidad-ficción en *La ciudad de los prodigios* de Eduardo Mendoza," *Espéculo: Revista de Estudios Literarios,* no. 16 (November 2000–February 2001) <http://www. ucm.es/info/especulo/numero16/mendoza. html>;

Franklin García Sánchez, "*El laberinto de las aceitunas:* Reflexiones entorno a la parodia posmoderna," *España Contemporánea,* 6 (Fall 1993);

María José Giménez Micó, *Eduardo Mendoza y las novelas españolas de la transición* (Madrid: Pliegos, 2000);

Meriwynn Ford Grothe, "City of Memory: Barcelona in the Novels of Juan Marsé and Eduardo Mendoza," dissertation, Johns Hopkins University, 2000;

Agnieszka Gutthy, "El humor en las novelas de Eduardo Mendoza," *Cincinatti Romance Review,* 14 (1995): 132–137;

Patricia Hart, "Barcelona, Prodigious Protagonist of Eduardo Mendoza's *La ciudad de los prodigios,*" *Ideas '92* (October 1991): 109–121;

Hart, "Eduardo Mendoza," in her *The Spanish Sleuth: The Detective in Spanish Fiction* (Cranbury, N.J.: Fairleigh Dickinson University Press, 1977), pp. 101–108;

Miguel Herráez, *La estrategia de la posmodernidad en Eduardo Mendoza* (Madrid: Ronsel, 1997);

Herráez, "Lo histórico como signo de una ficción y la ficción como manifestacion de lo histórico: El caso de Eduardo Mendoza," in *La novela histórica a finales del siglo XX,* edited by José Romera Castillo, Francisco Gutiérrez Carbajo, and Mario García-Page Sánchez (Madrid: Visor, 1996), pp. 75–79;

Leo Hickey, "Deviancy and Deviation in Eduardo Mendoza's *Enchanted Crypt,*" *Anales de la Literatura Española Contemporánea,* 15, nos. 1–3 (1990): 51–63;

David Knutson, "Exploring New Worlds: Eduardo Mendoza's *Sin noticias de Gurb,*" *Monographic Review/Revista Monográfica,* 12 (1996): 228–236;

Knutson, *Las novelas de Eduardo Mendoza: La parodia de los márgenes* (Madrid: Pliegos, 1999);

Knutson and Jeffrey Oxford, eds., *Eduardo Mendoza: A New Look* (New York: Peter Lang, 2002);

Kalen Royce Oswald, "Eduardo Mendoza's Barcelona," dissertation, University of Arizona, 2001;

Joan Ramon Resina, *El cadáver en la cocina: La novela criminal en la cultura del desencanto* (Barcelona: Anthropos, 1997);

Resina, "Money, Desire, and History in Eduardo Mendoza's *City of Marvels*," *PMLA* (1992): 951–968;

Ascención Rivas-Hernández, "Picaresca, crítica y humor en *La aventura del tocador de señoras*," *Ínsula*, 652 (2001): 27–29;

Joaquín Roy, "*La ciudad de los prodigios* de Eduardo Mendoza: Una meditación cultural sobre Barcelona," *Hispanic Journal*, 12 (Autumn 1991): 231–248;

Isidora Rubio-López, "Eduardo Mendoza y Edgar Doctorow: Verdad histórica/verdad ficticia," dissertation, University of Kansas, 1998;

Eduardo Ruiz Tosaus, "De la manipulación histórica en *La ciudad de los prodigios*," *Espéculo: Revista de Estudios Literarios*, no. 17 (March–June 2001) <http://www.ucm.es/info/especulo/numero17/ciudad.html>;

Elena Santos Botana, "La narrativa de Eduardo Mendoza y la posmodernidad: Un análisis textual," dissertation, Universitat Autónoma de Barcelona, 1997;

Robert C. Spires, *Post-Totalitarian Spanish Fiction* (Columbia: University of Missouri Press, 1996);

Cathy Sweeney, "Nivel y voz en *La verdad sobre el caso Savolta* de Eduardo Mendoza," *Caligrama*, 3 (1991): 143–161;

José Valles Calatrava, *El espacio en la novela: El papel del espacio narrativo en* La ciudad de los prodigios *de Eduardo Mendoza* (Almería: Grupo de Investigación de Teoría de la Literatura y Literatura Comparada, Universidad de Almería, 1999);

Caragh Wells, "The City of Words: Eduardo Mendoza's *La ciudad de los prodigios*," *Modern Language Review*, 96 (July 2001): 715–722;

Chung-ying Yang, "The Detective Genre in the Narrative of Eduardo Mendoza," dissertation, Ohio State University, 1998.

# José María Merino

*(5 March 1941 –    )*

**Antonio Candau**
*Case Western Reserve University*

BOOKS: *El sitio de Tarifa* (Madrid: Helios, 1972);

*Cumpleaños lejos de casa* (León: Instituto Fray Bernardino de Sahagún, 1973);

*Parnasillo provincial de poetas apócrifos,* by Merino, Agustín Delgado, and Luis Mateo Díez (Madrid: Endymion, 1975);

*Novela de Andrés Choz* (Madrid: Magisterio Español, 1976);

*Ja Díez,* by Merino, Díez, and Delgado (Madrid: Servicio de Publicaciones del Ministerio de Educación y Ciencia, 1977);

*Los caminos del Esla,* by Merino and Juan Pedro Aparicio (Madrid: Everest, 1980);

*El caldero de oro* (Madrid: Alfaguara, 1981);

*Cuentos del reino secreto* (Madrid: Alfaguara, 1982);

*León, traza y memoria,* by Merino, Díez, Antonio Gamoneda, and Félix de Cárdenas (León: Antonio Machón, 1984);

*Mírame, Medusa y otros poemas* (Madrid: Ayuso, 1984);

*La orilla oscura* (Madrid: Alfaguara, 1985);

*Las cenizas del fénix,* by Merino, Aparicio, and Díez, as [collectively] Sabino Ordás (León: Diputación Provincial, 1985);

*El oro de los sueños* (Madrid: Alfaguara, 1986); translated by Helen Lane as *The Gold of Dreams* (New York: Farrar, Straus & Giroux, 1992);

*La tierra del tiempo perdido* (Madrid: Alfaguara, 1987); translated by Lane as *Beyond the Ancient Cities* (New York: Farrar, Straus & Giroux, 1994);

*Cumpleaños lejos de casa: Obra poética completa* (Madrid: Endymion, 1987)–includes *El sitio de Tarifa, Cumpleaños lejos de casa,* and *Mírame, Medusa y otros poemas;*

*Artrópodos y hadanes* (Madrid: Almarabú, 1987);

*Cuentos de la Calle de la Rúa,* by Díez, Merino, and Aparicio (Madrid: Editorial Popular, 1989);

*Las lágrimas del sol* (Madrid: Alfaguara, 1989);

*El viajero perdido* (Madrid: Alfaguara, 1990);

*El centro del aire* (Madrid: Alfaguara, 1991);

*Las palabras del mundo y otros relatos* (Madrid: Compañía Europea de Comunicación e Información, 1991);

*José María Merino ( from <www.educared.org.ar/guiadelertras/ archivos/merino_jose_maria>)*

*Los trenes del verano (No soy un libro)* (Madrid: Siruela, 1992);

*Las crónicas mestizas* (Madrid: Alfaguara, 1992);

*Cuentos del Barrio del Refugio* (Madrid: Alfaguara, 1994);

*La edad de la aventura* (Madrid: Altea, 1995);

*Las visiones de Lucrecia* (Madrid: Alfaguara, 1996);

*El cuaderno de hojas blancas* (Madrid: Anaya, 1996);

*Regreso al cuaderno de hojas blancas* (Madrid: Anaya, 1997);

*Bestiario,* by Merino and others (Madrid: Siruela, 1997);

*Cuentos* (Madrid: Alianza, 1997);

*Cincuenta cuentos y una fábula* (Madrid: Alfaguara, 1997);

*Adiós al cuaderno de hojas blancas* (Madrid: Anaya, 1998);

*Intramuros* (León: Edilesa, 1998);

*Silva leonesa* (León: Instituto Leonés de Cultura, 1998);

*La casa de los dos portales y otros cuentos,* edited by Ignacio Soldevila Durante (Barcelona: Octaedro, 1999);

*Cuatro nocturnos* (Madrid: Alfaguara, 1999)–comprises "El mar interior," "El misterio Vallota," "La dama de Urz," and "El hechizo de Isis";

*Los martes, cuento* (Cádiz: Ayuntamiento de San Roque, 1999);

*La memoria tramposa* (León: Edilesa, 1999);

*Los narradores cautivos,* by Merino, Jesús Felipe Martínez, and Antonio Martínez Menchén (Madrid: Alfaguara, 1999);

*Cuentos* (Madrid: Castalia, 2000);

*Los invisibles* (Madrid: Espasa-Calpe, 2000);

*Novelas del mito* (Madrid: Alfaguara, 2000)–includes *El caldero de oro, La orilla oscura,* and *El centro del aire;*

*Días imaginarios* (Barcelona: Seix Barral, 2002);

*El heredero* (Madrid: Alfaguara, 2003);

*Cuentos de los días raros* (Madrid: Alfaguara, 2004);

*Ficción continua* (Barcelona: Seix Barral, 2004).

OTHER: *Cien años de cuentos (1898–1998): Antología del cuento español en castellano,* edited by Merino (Madrid: Alfaguara, 1998);

*Los mejores cuentos españoles del siglo XX,* edited by Merino (Madrid: Alfaguara, 1998);

*Leyendas españolas de todos los tiempos: Una memoria soñada,* edited by Merino (Madrid: Temas de Hoy, 2000).

José María Merino's literary reputation is seldom described as revolutionary or groundbreaking; yet, his trajectory shows that he is one of the most independent, versatile, and pioneering authors of his generation. Merino started his writing career in the post-Franco era, with early success, and the quality of his production has continued as his novels and short stories have received wide public and academic recognition.

Merino was born on 5 March 1941 to Bonifacio Merino, a lawyer, and María Estrella Merino in the northwestern city of Coruña; he has two younger siblings, Roberto and Margarita. Merino grew up in León, the home of two of his most important literary contemporaries: Luis Mateo Díez and Juan Pedro Aparicio. Following a path not uncommon for their generation, the three writers went to Madrid to attend college. After completing his law degree at the Universidad Complutense de Madrid in 1964, Merino settled in the capital and obtained the first of several posts with the government, working mainly in the areas of education and culture.

Upon completing college, Díez and Aparicio also settled permanently in Madrid; however, León remained an important source of inspiration for this group of young authors. When the three writers began achieving their first literary successes in the early 1980s, they were sometimes referred to as "El grupo leonés" (The León Group). These years were known as "la transición," the transition from General Francisco Franco's dictatorship, which ended in 1975, to a more democratic system. One of the political issues was the administrative reorganization of Spain. In what was referred to as "autonomic fever," nearly every region in the country claimed historical rights and privileges, almost inevitably presenting a long list of grievances against the central government. On the positive side of this regionalist resurgence were many valuable anthropological, geographical, and historical works devoted to areas traditionally excluded from study. However, the grouping of the three provinces of Old León's kingdom with those of Castile in the autonomous region of Castile and León represented for many a new instance of a familiar gesture: subsuming León's geographical and cultural peculiarities under the "Castilian" label, which did not satisfy the most combative "leonesistas," such as Aparicio, who published an historical essay in 1981 documenting some of the issues of the region.

The provincial capital, the city of León, had been established by the Romans in an area rich with precious minerals, and it reached its high point during the Middle Ages, as the capital of the first Christian kingdom engaged in the fight against the Arabs, with one of the best-preserved Gothic cathedrals in Spain. However, León's traditional aristocracy was soon eclipsed by the low nobility from Castile. Later, during the nineteenth century and most of the twentieth, León was one of many languishing Spanish provincial cities. Although the grim reality of provincial León is covered more thoroughly by Aparicio and especially by Díez, Merino chronicled this period indirectly through the "biographies" of the many fictitious writers included in *Parnasillo provincial de poetas apócrifos* (1975, Provincial Parnassus of Apocryphal Poets), a poetry anthology he created with Díez and Agustín Delgado.

Merino's first published works were books of poetry, *El sitio de Tarifa* (1972, The Siege of Tarifa) and *Cumpleaños lejos de casa* (1973, Birthday away from Home), which he later included in the 1987 volume *Cumpleaños lejos de casa: Obra poética completa* (Birthday away from Home: Complete Poetic Works). These poems are mostly narratives of fairly simple structure that share some traits with the so-called poetry of experience, which became one of the major directions of Spanish poetry in the 1980s and early 1990s.

In 1976, with his first novel, *Novela de Andrés Choz* (Andrés Choz's Novel), Merino won the Premio Novelas y Cuentos, a comparatively modest award in economic terms but with a solid reputation among writers and publishers. *Novela de Andrés Choz* is a metafictional work with a strong science-fiction component. A writer diagnosed with cancer goes to a remote village on the northern coast of Spain to try to complete a novel; this story line alternates and later connects with the narrative of a boy of mysterious origins who might have been left on Earth by aliens. The mixture of popular genres with literary concerns, the interest in space and places, the reflections on identity, and, especially, the hybrid quality of the text became dominant traits throughout Merino's fiction.

In 1980 Merino collaborated with Aparicio on *Los caminos del Esla* (Esla's Ways), a travel book that recounts their trip through the landscapes, history, and contemporary life of the three-hundred-kilometer course of the Esla River. With text and photographs, the authors convey the beauty and rich history of the area, from pre-Roman times until the "invasion" of nuclear power plants. The course of the river brings forth symbolically both the simultaneity and the passage of places and time. Merino later explained in an unpublished interview that this trip and this book were behind his first major novel, *El caldero de oro* (1981, The Golden Bowl).

The main theme of *El caldero de oro* is the search for identity through the exploration of one's ancestral origins. The novel was published as part of the "Nueva ficción" (New Fiction) series, an important editorial effort by the publishing house Alfaguara. Works by Aparicio and Díez also appear in this series, the success of which established Alfaguara as one of the major publishers of narrative in Spain and Latin America. Merino has explained in unpublished interviews that during the years of his literary formation, he felt isolated between the two rigid narrative styles dominant in Spain: a neorealism concerned primarily with social and political realities, and an experimental narrative engaged for the most part in language and literary games. Franco's death and the end of censorship did not produce the anticipated outpouring of manuscripts, but it did have a liberating effect on Spanish letters. Without explicitly rejecting either narrative direction, Merino and others resisted any limitation on style and topics and were able to express a passion for narration, good storytelling being their only guide.

*El caldero de oro* is a complex and demanding work, with changes in narrative voice and an intricate temporal structure, but it is also a great framework tale

Cover for a 1993 paperback edition of Merino's first novel (1976, *Andrés Choz's Novel*), about a writer with cancer trying to complete a book and a boy who may be a space alien (Richland County Public Library)

of many stories. The narrator recalls his life and the lives of many of his ancestors, connecting his search for origins with his quest for the "golden bowl" of the title, a legendary treasure buried for generations. A symbol of earth, family history, the land, and roots threatened by the construction of a nuclear power plant, the golden artifact also symbolizes people's need to tell stories to others and to themselves, always constructing identity and searching for connections that will give meaning to their present condition. Merino effectively re-creates rural and urban spaces, past and contemporary, and he convincingly plots the ways in which those spaces trigger many conscious and unconscious narratives.

In 1982 Merino published a collection of short stories, *Cuentos del reino secreto* (Tales from the Secret Kingdom). Set in urban and rural areas of León and northwestern Spain in different historical periods, the collection is representative of one of the author's main interests, the short-story genre and its history. Most of the stories incorporate fantastic events, such as figurines who come to life, groups of people who disappear, persons who become animals, and several real and false hidden treasures. Geographical and human spaces—rivers, land, museums, churches, and old country homes—are in many stories the triggers of the fantastic events.

In 1984 Merino collaborated with Díez, Antonio Gamoneda, and Félix de Cárdenas on *León, traza y memoria* (León, Design and Memory), a volume devoted to the city as seen by these writers and artists. The poetry volume *Mírame, Medusa y otros poemas* (Medusa, Look at Me and Other Poems) appeared also in 1984 and was later included in the 1987 *Cumpleaños lejos de casa*. Most of the poems are narrative pieces dealing with the writer's biography.

In 1985 Merino published perhaps his most accomplished novel, *La orilla oscura* (The Dark Shore). It received the National Critics' Award for narrative. Once again space plays an important role in the characters' imaginations and feelings as well as in the plot twists, which are full of intrigue and surprises, anagnorisis, and disappearances. The "dark shore" of the title refers to the realm of dreams, memory, and fiction. A large part of the novel takes place in the urban and jungle settings of Central America, where an unnamed Spanish professor who works in the United States is traveling before going on to Spain for the rest of his vacation. The most immediate realities of travel—jet lag, sights, smells, sounds, and faces that remind one of other places—as well as the powerful settings of Tegucigalpa and the jungle trigger several interplays between conscious and unconscious memory, desire and reality, fiction and history, and dream and waking life. Those spaces and fictions construct and deconstruct the identities of people from the different but related "shores" of Spain and Latin America.

The text of the novel creates another "shore" where all those separate states of mind and geographical territories converge, in constant flux because of the plot twists. During the first chapters, the professor arrives in Honduras and starts having strange experiences that he initially attributes to jet lag and lack of sleep. At the same time, the traces of Spanish presence in Latin America play tricks on him, in a variation of déjà vu, making him think he recognizes establishments, faces, and names that he has in fact never seen. He has this sensation when he is led to a meeting with a distant relative living in the capital. The two characters meet and separate, but the professor has replaced the relative as an unwilling double unrecognized by the relative's wife. At this point several stories join together,

creating correspondences among various characters: a soldier who returns home, a "lizard god," and the professor, as a child, remembering a strange encounter with an iguana.

The protagonist and his wife take a trip through the forest, following the course of a river. The pilot of the boat becomes a new narrator whose long tale intersects with the previous ones. As a young man in Madrid, the pilot became interested in the work of the writer Pedro Palaz. With his girlfriend, Susana, a French painter who was traveling as a pilgrim through the "Camino de Santiago," he went to visit the writer and was received by Anastasio Marzán, supposedly a cousin of Palaz. Marzán told them that, in fact, Palaz was only his fictional creation; but later, the pilot was visited by a man claiming to be Palaz. They became friends, but one day Palaz disappeared with Susana. The pilot started seeing another woman, Nonia, who was interested in a story from the "Camino de Santiago" about an illicit love affair between a woman and a monk. The pilot and Nonia traced Marzán, who told them that their lives were similar to those of some characters in Palaz's fiction. Nonia's legend about the monk then connects with the other stories in *La orilla oscura*. The novel seems to explain all the threads as dreams and imaginations taking place in the professor's mind, until the last chapter, when upon his return to Spain, the apparently organized reality is unsettled once again as fiction and reality converge.

*La orilla oscura,* the ultimate mestizo text, joined the settings and stories of Spain and Latin America, two shores that had not frequently appeared together in Spanish fiction during the previous two centuries. In addition, it did so at a time when a good number of Spanish novelists were locating their novels in different European countries, partly, perhaps, as a sign of the modernization of a Spain quite different from that of Merino's childhood, a country now a member of the European Community and of NATO.

In 1985 Merino published another collaborative volume with Díez and Aparicio, *Las cenizas del fénix* (The Phoenix's Ashes), a project that, while belonging to the renewed concern for regionalism in post-Franco Spain, also focuses on three of Merino's narrative concerns: identity, the porous limits between fiction and reality, and the connections between America and Spain. The volume includes previously published articles by "Sabino Ordás," a fictitious personality created by the authors; he is an old professor who has returned to Spain after living and working in America during Franco's dictatorship. Ordás is an "apocryphal figure" who addresses some of the most immediate and concrete cultural, political, and social concerns of his creators, which are usually related to León and to the changing times of Spain under democracy.

In 1986 Merino published *El oro de los sueños* (translated as *The Gold of Dreams,* 1992), the first in a trilogy of novels–the *Crónicas mestizas* (Mestizo Chronicles)–dealing with the early colonial times in key areas of Central and South America: Mexico after Hernan Cortés's conquest and Peru during the Spaniards' civil wars. The three novels are intended for teenage readers and were inspired in part by Merino's travels through Latin America and his readings of the "Cronistas de Indias." The *Crónicas mestizas* became some of Merino's most popular novels, and the first two have been translated into English. Clever plots, substantial construction, and interesting characters make these texts accessible to young adults while introducing them to important chapters in Spanish and American history. The identity of the narrator-protagonist, a mestizo boy of Aztec and Spanish blood named Miguel Villacé Yólotl, allows Merino once again to incorporate different traditions, histories, and worldviews in his narrative. Without avoiding the destruction of the indigenous cultures brought about by the Spaniards, the stories present some of the other fruits of the clash of worlds opened by the arrival of Christopher Columbus in the Americas. Central to the novels are the issues of identity present in other Merino texts. In the mestizo and *aindiado* (those who adopt the Indian way of life) characters, readers see different results of the mix of blood and civilizations, such as adjustment, loss, rebellion, enrichment, and confusion.

*El oro de los sueños* presents the character of Miguel and his first adventure: he is a "personal assistant" of a noble lady who, with her fiancé, is looking for a city like El Dorado. At first, the trip is for Miguel a fulfillment of his dreams of adventure, forged from the stories he has heard and read in chivalry books. The expedition, by land and sea along the Yucatán Peninsula, encounters many dangers. Plot elements include betrayals by some of the informants; Spaniards who reveal their disregard for human dignity and their voracious appetite for gold; a true friendship with a young woman who travels as a boy; and a shocking discovery about Miguel's deceased father. The end of the novel brings Miguel back to his village, having learned the vanity and the true human cost of the dreams of gold.

The second novel of the trilogy, *La tierra del tiempo perdido* (The Land of Lost Time; translated as *Beyond the Ancient Cities,* 1994) was published in 1987. Miguel is writing this adventure as he lives it and, in a Cervantean twist, his manuscript is discovered by a French pirate who reads about himself and is not satisfied with his depiction in the story. The pirate decides to gain some relevance in Miguel's story by executing several

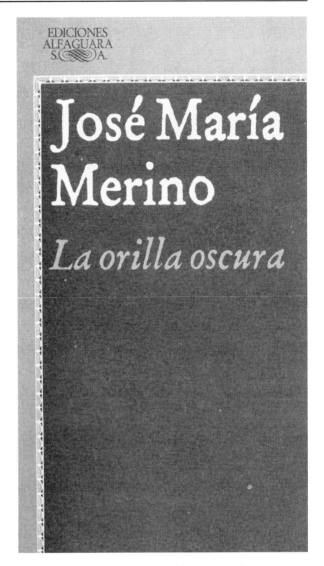

Cover for Merino's 1985 novel (The Dark Shore), about the phantasmagoric experiences of a professor traveling in Central America (Thomas Cooper Library, University of South Carolina)

prisoners. He promises Miguel and his companions he will let them go if he approves of the completed manuscript. Merino deals in this novel with two key issues connected with Spanish American colonial history: the mix of literature and history present in most of the chronicles, and the different conceptions of time held by Spaniards and by some of the natives they encounter. Whereas the Europeans see time as an arrow moving forward, several indigenous cultures see time and history as a circle, in which different eras are repeated.

In 1989 Merino published the last novel of the trilogy about colonial Latin America. *Las lágrimas del sol* (The Sun's Tears) follows Miguel during his journey to Peru, in the days of the ferocious fighting between the

*Dust jacket for the English translation (1992) of the first novel in
Merino's* Crónicas mestizas *(Mestizo Chronicles) trilogy for
teenage readers,* El oro de los sueños *(1986),
about a search for a lost city in the Yucatán
(Richland County Public Library)*

two factions of Spanish conquistadors, the *almagristas*
(followers of Diego de Almagro) and the *pizarristas* (followers of Francisco Pizarro). The novel describes the
fighting and concludes with the quest to find the Incas'
treasure. In a dream, Miguel sees the place where the
treasure is hidden and discovers that the way to that
place is "written" in *quipus,* a series of threads in which
different types and sequences of knots tell Miguel and
his friends, and also his pursuers, what steps to take in
order to reach it.

*El viajero perdido* (The Lost Traveler) from 1990 is
a volume of short stories in which several characters
attempt to recover their roots by connecting, in different ways, with domestic spaces of their childhood. A
concern for the roles of spaces, of language, and of fiction in human lives is a common denominator of the
stories.

Merino's childhood city, León, is the main setting
of his next novel, *El centro del aire* (1991, The Center of

the Air). The impossibility of returning to one's origins
and the fictive nature of all origins are explored in the
lives of three characters, Bernardo, Magdalena, and
Julio. The mythical character Heidi, their childhood
friend, and the legendary patio where the three played
as children appear to be part of a work written by Julio,
a novelist. With this novel, Merino brings his fiction
back to a more realistic realm, separating himself from
metafictional and fantastic elements. Those elements
are suggested as a possible direction at one point in the
story, but they are later abandoned in favor of an interest in character development and an exploration of the
failure of fiction to recapture the past.

Merino's next novel for young readers, *Los trenes
del verano (No soy un libro)* (1992, The Trains of Summer
[I Am Not a Book]), is a more ambitious book, truly
innovative in its use of the typographic presentation as
part of the fantastic-metafictional story. The science-
fiction plot involves a struggle between aliens and
humans centering in the book itself, a "machine" that
needs the reader's efforts to work and liberate the protagonist. This book was awarded the National Prize of
Literature for Children and Young Adults for 1992.
Merino had also ventured into science fiction with
*Artrópodos y hadanes* (1987, Arthropods and Adams), a
narrative that describes the characteristics, activities,
and histories of two different types of fantastic beings.
The 1994 collection of short stories *Cuentos del Barrio del
Refugio* (Stories from the "Refugio" Neighborhood) sets
Merino's narrative interest in the fantastic in a contem-
porary Madrid neighborhood.

Merino retired from the Department of Education
in 1996. With the novel that earned him the Miguel
Delibes Prize for Narrative in 1997, *Las visiones de Lucrecia* (1996, Lucrecia's Visions), he took his work in
another direction. A thoroughly researched historical
novel, it is a fictionalized account of the extraordinary
and little-known case of a late-sixteenth-century Spanish
woman whose strange dreams and visions arouse the
interest of politicians, advisers, and religious leaders.
They interpret her visions as forecasts for the eventual
fall of Spain's imperial dominance, while some of the
officials of the Inquisition consider these visions diaboli-
cal. The novel skillfully presents the institutions and
intrigues of the period and the evolution of the protagonist. *Las visiones de Lucrecia* deals with superstition,
dreams, and stories; the book is concerned with the
powers of imagination in a particular country during a
specific time, Spain in the 1500s, a land dominated by
censorship and fear of prosecution.

Merino has also written a three-book series for
younger readers, ages nine to twelve: *El cuaderno de hojas
blancas* (1996, The White Page Notebook), *Regreso al
cuaderno de hojas blancas* (1997, Return to the White Page

Notebook), and *Adiós al cuaderno de hojas blancas* (1998, Goodbye to the White Page Notebook). These books, illustrated by the author, incorporate metafictional and fantastic elements to depict the homework troubles of a boy named Santi. In 1997 Merino collaborated with five other writers on another fantastic project, *Bestiario* (Bestiary), a book on legendary animals.

In *Intramuros* (1998, Within the City) Merino describes the dark and limited atmosphere of 1950s León–a provincial town like many others during a period of political repression, in an internationally isolated country just out of a bloody civil war–and also explores the powers of fiction to construct identity in the present and to invent the past. It is an autobiographical account of how the childhood of a writer helps him to develop his literary worldview at that particular time, in the particular setting of León.

Merino next published *Silva leonesa* (1998, Leónese Miscellany), a volume of articles about León; *Cuatro nocturnos* (1999, Four Nocturnos), a collection of four novellas dealing with the ways in which dreams and fictions cover dark desires and memories; *La memoria tramposa* (1999, Memory, the Cheater), a short tale about false recognitions; and *Los martes, cuento* (1999, If It's Tuesday, It's Story-Time), a volume of short fiction. In addition, as a result of Merino's interest in the short story as a genre, he edited in 1998 two volumes of selected works from twentieth-century Spain. In 2000 he edited an anthology of Spanish legends from all periods. In these works Merino demonstrates his vast knowledge of the subject matter and his passion as a reader of good stories, regardless of the period, region of origin, or style. A fan of modern science fiction, he reveals his enthusiasm as well for the early Spanish narratives incorporated in the most primitive ballads. He also participated in another collaborative effort in 1999: the novel *Los narradores cautivos* (The Captive Narrators), an update on *Arabian Nights* in which a group of writers is kidnapped by terrorists and must use their storytelling abilities to escape.

Fantasy and metafiction reappear in the novel *Los invisibles* (2000, The Invisible Ones), which tells the story of Adrián, a young man who, upon touching a strange flower, becomes invisible. This fate, he discovers, is shared by many other people. They try to live normal lives, although they are threatened by a character called "The Hunter." Later, Adrián addresses Merino directly, begging the author to write his story and communicate his fate to the reading public. *Días imaginarios* (2002, Imaginary Days) includes fictional "mini stories" and brief commentaries on current events, derived from presentations by the author on a national radio program, "Los martes, cuento," on Radio Punto in the fall of 1999.

Dust jacket for the English translation (1994) of the second novel in the Crónicas mestizas trilogy, La tierra del tiempo perdido *(1987, The Land of Lost Time), in which the narrator is captured by a French pirate who does not approve of the way he is being portrayed in the story (Richland County Public Library)*

In the novel *El heredero* (2003, The Heir), Merino incorporates in new ways his interest in fictions–both oral and written–and in the connections between Spain and America, with sequences set in the mythical house of Isclacerta in northern Spain; in Puerto Rico, where some of the ancestors of protagonist Pablo Tomás lived; and in the United States, where Tomás worked on his dissertation on the nineteenth-century Spanish writer Benito Pérez Galdós. Tomás's search for the secrets in his family's past and in his own life takes the narrative back and forth between Spain and America in an adventure that seems to replicate the life of his great-grandfather. The novel covers the stories of four generations and incorporates many of Merino's topics of interest throughout his career.

*Ficción continua* (2004, Continuous Fiction) collects published and unpublished essays and reviews about storytelling in many different periods, styles, and media, from Miguel de Cervantes to J. K. Rowling and from oral narratives to movies, comics, and electronic books. The first part deals with general questions about storytelling, while the second part comments on specific texts and movies. Some of these pieces appeared previously in the journal *Revista de Libros* (Review of Books), in which Merino has a column reviewing literature and movies.

Merino is married to Carmen Norverto, a professor and vice provost at the Universidad Complutense de Madrid. Their older daughter, María, is a professor of constitutional law at the Universidad Juan Carlos I in Madrid; their younger daughter, Ana, is an award-winning poet in Spain and a professor of Spanish at Dartmouth College. Since his retirement, Merino has visited the United States on several occasions, and he has incorporated in his work the academic and urban settings where his daughter studied and worked, such as Pittsburgh and rural North Carolina. *El oro de los sueños* was dedicated to his newly born grandson, Pablo.

A review of José María Merino's production, looking at all the changes in Spanish cultural life during those years, makes clear that he has always followed the path of creative independence. He has often surprised the establishment and the readers by his original choices of topics and genres, often against the fashions in vogue and against expectations. By doing so, he has opened doors in the Spanish literary field to authors, genres, settings, characters, and topics that were previously forgotten or unexplored.

**References:**

Santos Alonso, "José María Merino," in his *Literatura leonesa actual: Estudio y antología de 17 escritores* (Valladolid: Junta de Castilla y León, 1986), pp. 303–322;

Alonso, "La perspectiva tetraédrica, José María Merino y la escritura fantástica," *Anthropos,* 154–155 (1994): 141–144;

Alonso, "Un renovado compromiso con el realismo y con el hombre," *Ínsula,* 464–465 (1985): 9–10;

Luis Alonso Girgado, "Tríptico de la conquista, de José María Merino," *Ínsula,* 525 (1990): 17–18;

Irene Andres-Suárez, Ana Casas, and Inés d'Ors, eds., *José María Merino: Coloquio internacional, 14–16 de mayo de 2001* (Neuchâtel: Centro de Investigación de Narrativa Española, Universidad de Neuchâtel / Madrid: Ministerio de Educación y Cultura, Dirección General del Libro, Archivos y Bibliotecas, 2001);

Antonio Candau, *La obra narrativa de José María Merino* (León: Diputación Provincial, 1992);

Judith Drinkwater, "Place, Memory and Death in José María Merino, *El caldero de oro,* and *Cuentos del Barrio del Refugio,*" in *The Scripted Self: Textual Identities in Contemporary Spanish Narrative,* by Drinkwater, Ruth Christie, and John Macklin (Warminster, U.K.: Aris & Philips, 1995), pp. 49–62;

Angeles Encinar, "*El caldero de oro* de José María Merino," in her *Novela española actual: La desaparición del héroe* (Madrid: Pliegos, 1990), pp. 167–179;

Encinar, "José María Merino: hacia una reconquista de las crónicas americanas," in *España y América en sus literaturas,* edited by Encinar (Madrid: Cultura Hispánica, 1993), pp. 141–150;

Encinar and Kathleen Glenn, eds., *Aproximaciones críticas al mundo narrativo de José María Merino* (León: Edilesa, 2000);

Carlos Javier García, *La invención del grupo leonés: Estudio y entrevistas* (Madrid: Júcar, 1995);

Eugenio García de Nora, "Historia y creación novelesca en José María Merino: Las visiones de Lucrecia y la ruina de la Nueva Restauración," *Ínsula,* 595–596 (1996): 20–21;

Kathleen Glenn, "Reflections on the Writing of a Fantastic Narrative," in *Reflections on the Fantastic,* edited by Michael R. Collins (New York: Greenwood Press, 1986), pp. 51–58;

Vance Holloway, *El posmodernismo y otras tendencias de la novela española (1967–1995)* (Madrid: Fundamentos, 1999);

Antonio Martínez Menchén, "La doble orilla de José María Merino," *Cuadernos Hispanoamericanos,* 439 (1987): 115–121;

Randolph Pope, "La oscura orilla de la fuente de la edad: Visión de América de José María Merino y Luis Mateo Díez," in *España y América en sus literaturas,* edited by Angeles Encinar (Madrid: Cultura Hispánica, 1993), pp. 103–126;

Gonzalo Sobejano, "Sobre la obra de José María Merino," *España Contemporánea,* 5, no. 2 (1992): 93–103;

Ignacio Soldevila Durante, "La fantástica realidad. La trayectoria narrativa de José María Merino y sus relatos breves," *España Contemporánea,* 9, no. 2 (1996): 89–106.

# Juan José Millás

*(31 January 1946 –   )*

Carter E. Smith
*University of Wisconsin–Eau Claire*

BOOKS: *Cerbero son las sombras* (Madrid: Espejo, 1975);

*Visión del ahogado* (Madrid: Alfaguara, 1977);

*El jardín vacío* (Madrid: Legasa, 1981);

*Papel mojado* (Madrid: Anaya, 1983);

*Letra muerta* (Madrid: Alfaguara, 1984);

*El desorden de tu nombre* (Madrid: Alfaguara, 1988); translated by Allison Beely as *The Disorder of Your Name* (London: Allison & Busby, 2000);

*La soledad era esto* (Barcelona: Destino, 1990); translated by Beely as *That Was Loneliness* (London: Allison & Busby, 2000);

*Volver a casa* (Barcelona: Destino, 1990);

*Primavera de luto y otros cuentos* (Barcelona: Destino, 1992);

*Ella imagina: Y otras obsesiones de Vicente Holgado* (Madrid: Alfaguara, 1994);

*Tonto, muerto, bastardo e invisible* (Madrid: Alfaguara, 1995);

*Algo que te concierne* (Madrid: El País/Aguilar, 1995);

*Cuentos a la intemperie* (Madrid: Acento, 1997);

*La viuda incompetente y otros cuentos* (Barcelona: Plaza & Janés, 1998);

*Tres novelas cortas* (Madrid: Santillana, 1998);

*El orden alfabético* (Madrid: Alfaguara, 1998);

*No mires debajo de la cama* (Madrid: Alfaguara, 1999);

*Cuerpo y prótesis* (Madrid: El País, 2000);

*Articuentos* (Barcelona: Alba, 2001);

*Números pares, impares e idiotas* (Barcelona: Alba, 2001);

*Dos mujeres en Praga* (Madrid: Espasa, 2002);

*Cuentos adúlteros desorientados* (Barcelona: Lumen, 2003);

*Todo son preguntas* (Barcelona: Península, 2005).

*Juan José Millás (photograph by Anna Löscher; from the cover for* La soledad era esto, *1990; Thomas Cooper Library, University of South Carolina)*

Juan José Millás belongs to a group of Spanish writers whose literary production began to bloom in the late 1960s and early 1970s, other members of the group include Luis Goytisolo, Eduardo Mendoza, Rosa Montero, and Julio Llamazares. Critics have also included Millás in the so-called Generation of '68. Characteristic of these novelists is a reaction against the social realism of the preceding literary generation and the belief that the literary production of social realism could not achieve the political successes for which it hoped. Millás and his "generation" argued that this literature led to artistic poverty, since it sacrificed form in favor of content intended to be both politically and socially revolutionary.

Millás successfully combines fiction and journalism. Since the beginning of the 1990s he has been a frequent contributor of articles to several Spanish newspapers, including *El País*. In the fictional worlds he creates, characters struggle with barriers to communication, isolation and loneliness, and the relationships between reality and fantasy and between language and

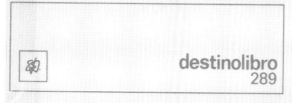

*Cover for Millás's 1977 novel (Vision of the Drowned Man), in which
the protagonist tries to escape after stabbing a policeman at
a Madrid subway station (Thomas Cooper Library,
University of South Carolina)*

identity. He creatively brings together a journalist's ability to gather and comment on the details of everyday life with a novelist's desire to question the veracity of "reality" and the fiction of "fantasy."

The fourth of nine siblings, Millás was born on 31 January 1946 in Valencia, to middle-class parents, Vicente Millás and Cándida García Millás. When he was six, his family moved to Madrid as part of the post–Civil War migration from rural to urban areas. The family settled into one of the poorer suburbs, where Millás began his schooling and later found a job at a post office. After one year at the Universidad Complutense of Madrid, a university he considered "franquista y vieja" (pro-Franco and old), he abandoned his studies in philosophy to dedicate himself to reading and writing. Madrid plays a significant role in Millás's liter-

ary production: not only does it provide the setting for all of his works, but it frequently takes on the importance of a character.

Millás's first novel, *Cerbero son las sombras* (1975, Cerberus Are the Shadows), opens with a long, morose epistle written by the anonymous narrator to his father: "Querido padre: es posible que en el fondo tu problema, como el mío, no haya sido más que un problema de soledad" (Dear Father: it's possible that in the end your problem, like mine, has been nothing more than a problem of loneliness). Through the extensive use of flashbacks the narrator, who lives in a dank and dirty basement apartment, explains how he and his family fled their home near the sea and came to Madrid. The reader is introduced to the family's dark, gloomy home in the city and witnesses their oppressive and tragic experiences in the capital.

Millás sets his narrative in a confined, stifling space to emphasize the characters' alienation from the repressive society in which they live. There are no concrete references to any specific historical period; nonetheless, the family's move from their rural home to an urban environment and the constant threat of political persecution suggest the immediate post–Civil War period. In refusing to link his plot to history, however, Millás endows the novel with a universal character. Millás received the Premio Sésamo literary award for *Cerbero son las sombras* in 1975.

The death of the dictator Francisco Franco in November 1975 and the subsequent transition toward a democratic society are reflected in Millás's second novel, *Visión del ahogado* (1977, Vision of the Drowned Man). The setting is Madrid in the 1960s and 1970s, a period of great social and political changes, although the action takes place during one morning in which the reader follows the erratic and delirious flight of Luis after he stabs a policeman at a subway stop. He is estranged from his wife, Julia, who now lives with Jorge, Luis's former classmate and friend. As Luis attempts to elude the police, the omniscient narrator gradually reveals Jorge and Julia's violent and disintegrating relationship while relating, through flashbacks, how these three people came together.

The novel opens with an epigraph: "Fue de nosotros de quienes aprendieron el secreto de la vida: hacerse viejo sin hacerse mejor" (They learned from us the secret of life: getting older without getting better). This statement introduces the central theme of the work, the political and social degradation of a generation of Spaniards. The emotional and intellectual disintegration of the relationships of the couples in the novel is a metaphor for the general degradation of societal norms at the time. The characters are representative of many couples from the 1960s and 1970s whose unions

216

were based on opposition to the Franco regime. As the demise of the dictatorship drew near, their reasons for being together began to disintegrate. The basic story line—the police hunt for the fugitive—then serves as the occasion for the introspection and self-reflection of each character. The story moves between the real, exterior persecution of the criminal and the equally real interior persecution within the conscience of each character.

In Millás's 1981 novel, *El jardín vacío* (The Empty Garden), official history and personal memory collide. In an obsessive search for his identity in the dark corners of his past, the protagonist returns to his childhood neighborhood and home to visit his mother, who is old, rather senile, and barely able to recognize her son, to find out "al cabo de los años, a quién me parezco más, si a mi padre o a ti" (after all these years, who I resemble most, you or my father). An omniscient narrator leads the reader through the labyrinth of memory that corresponds to the labyrinthine streets of a decrepit Madrid neighborhood where the houses are burned, empty, and deteriorating like "el jardín vacío." Memory is presented as something already elaborated, established, empty, and imposed on the characters, who struggle with their personal memories against the backdrop of a larger, communal history. In a 1980 interview with José María Marco, Millás stated that "la función más importante de la memoria es la de encubrir lo verdaderamente importante" (the most important function of memory is to cover up what is truly important). This obsession with memory is more readily understood when one considers that in 1981 Spain was struggling to leave behind almost forty years of dictatorship and was working through the transition to a democratic society. Millás's novel attempts to subvert the concealing nature of "official" memory and confront it with the personal, the individual stories of the past.

In 1983 Millás published a detective novel, *Papel mojado* (Wet Paper), which the Anaya publishing house had commissioned for a series for young readers. A literary study of the classic detective novel, this work provides the reader with the first glimpse of a narrative technique that occupies Millás in many of his later novels. His interest in writing about writing is, however, most completely developed in *El desorden de tu nombre* (1988; translated as *The Disorder of Your Name*, 2000). Julio Orgaz, a divorcé in his forties, is an executive in a publishing house. Leaving his psychoanalyst's office, Julio meets Laura, a married woman, in a nearby park. During continuing meetings the two fall in love. Their relationship leads them to murder her husband, Carlos Rodó, Julio's psychoanalyst. They commit what they believe to be a perfect crime and are free of suspicion. Julio is then promoted in spite of, or perhaps because of, having impeded the publication of a book of short

Cover for Millás's 1981 novel (The Empty Garden), about a man's obsessive search for identity in his memories (Thomas Cooper Library, University of South Carolina)

stories by a brilliant young writer, Orlando Azcárate. Azcárate's stories, secretly admired by Julio, stimulate Julio to write something of his own and to "vivir escribiendo (o escribir viviendo)" (live though writing [or write by living]).

Julio imagines an "other Julio" who seems to write these short stories behind his back. One of the stories, "El desorden de tu nombre," brings the novel to a conclusion. Indeed, the life Julio and the other characters experience is the one being mysteriously written by another. Millás places the existential question of the self first and invites the reader to think about who or what is writing his or her life. The novel comes to be about creating one's self through writing.

The success of *El desorden de tu nombre* changed Millás from a cult figure with average sales but critical success to an established, best-selling novelist. Further

*Cover for Millás's 1988 novel (translated as* The Disorder of Your Name, *2000), about a publisher who kills his psychoanalyst after falling in love with the man's wife (Thomas Cooper Library, University of South Carolina)*

commercial and critical success followed with his next work. The novel *La soledad era esto* (translated as *That Was Loneliness*, 2000), for which Millás received the prestigious Premio Nadal in 1990, continues his quest to delve into questions of identity and agency. Elena Rincón is a woman in her forties whose mundane existence is characterized by boredom, hashish, and a cheating husband. A few days after her mother's death, Elena finds the mother's diaries and discovers symmetries between mother and daughter of which she had not been aware. Two narratives—the diaries and the reports sent to Elena by a detective she has hired to investigate her husband's affair—allow the protagonist to discover herself, just as her mother relates in her diaries how she was forced to reevaluate her life after discovering a cancerous lump in her breast.

The discovery of cancer brings the first part of the novel to a disquieting close. In the second part Elena decides to keep her own diary, reduces her consumption of hashish, and begins an existential crisis in complete "soledad" (solitude). She leaves her husband and asks the detective to begin spying on and writing about her. In addition to revisiting themes of loneliness, solitude, and problematic communication, the novel, by emphasizing the metamorphosis of the main character, highlights the theme of the "other" in a manner different from that of *El desorden de tu nombre*. The search for a self that one can recognize through others is essential to the process of self-realization and development. The presence of multiple narrative voices in the novel—the narrator, Elena, her mother, and the detective—serves both to emphasize the state of loneliness and the separation from a society of innumerable voices and also to strengthen the hope that one might use them to reflect on and build a truer sense of self.

*Tonto, muerto, bastardo e invisible* (1995, Dumb, Dead, Illegitimate, and Invisible), one of Millás's most explicitly political novels, is narrated by Jesús, who loses his position as an executive in a state-run paper company and descends into insanity. This process is manifested through an escape from daily reality in search of an existence he considers more profound, that of his "true" identity. The character serves as a critique of the Socialist Party, which ruled Spain during the 1990s, through the repeated use of symbolic motifs throughout the novel. Jesús's constant obsession with body parts, especially female ones, hints at a desire to exploit. References to prosthetics—a fake mustache, for example, that allows Jesús to assume another identity—underscore a willingness to represent himself as someone other than who he really is. In addition, the reader encounters constant references to paper. Such references are related to the narrator's job but also to writing—writing one's life or the life one would rather live—and to the second Spanish meaning of *papel,* the "role" one plays in life.

Toward the end of the novel Jesús comes to the conclusion that all of his life up to this point—his career, his politics, his family life—has been like prosthetics or artificial organs: it is all as false as the supposed moral and political values of his society. The reader finds a clear reference to political activities of the *progresistas* (progressives) who fought during the 1960s and 1970s against Franco and who, by the mid 1990s, were ensconced in the seats of political and economic power. Jesús's transformation into an ambitious, egotistical, and exploitative man mirrors the concomitant evolution of the Socialist Party toward ever more conservative socio-economic policies. Millás suggests that the inhabitants of Western capitalist democracies are at once victims and executioners. Satisfying their physical and economic needs makes them accomplices in a market system that ultimately marginalizes and subjugates. *Tonto, muerto, bastardo e invisible* criticizes the corrupting effects of power and the oppressive nature of a capitalist economic system and society as it questions the sociopolitical direction of Spain in the mid 1990s.

In *El orden alfabético* (1998, The Alphabetical Order) Millás experiments with the fantasy genre. The young narrator, Julio, rebels against his father by refusing to take an interest in the family's cherished encyclopedia collection. The father warns that if the boy persists in his refusal to read, one day all of the books in the house will take flight like birds, and the family will be left without words. Julio discovers a parallel universe where the printed word is disappearing from homes, schools, hospitals, and street signs. Classes are canceled; people get lost driving around a city without street signs; and patients are unable to read drug prescriptions. After a few days all printed material begins to decompose, causing the loss of certain letters and eventually of complete words. People experience difficulty in expressing ideas since they are unable to pronounce words whose physical representations no longer exist.

The first half of the novel ends with Julio traveling back and forth between his world of words and the decaying universe where language and, therefore, the ability to name and understand reality are being lost. In the second part Julio is replaced by an omniscient narrator who describes Julio's present situations: he is grown up and is living once again in a world of books. Julio is obsessed with the knowledge that his reality is nothing more than a world created for him. The experiences he had in his youth taught him how easy it is to manipulate language and how intimately involved it is in the creation of one's identity. He is thus all too aware of the machines of popular culture and the arbitrary habits of consumption they produce. Unable to bear this manipulation of reality, he seeks refuge in the logical, alphabetical order of his father's encyclopedia collection. It is a world in stark contrast to the arbitrary order of his (or the reader's) world. In the alphabetical order one has *dinner* before *lunch,* and *lingerie* is not found in a dresser drawer but between *linger* and *lingo.* It is, more importantly, an order that names everything and in which everything named exists.

*Dos mujeres en Praga* (Two Women in Prague), the recipient of the Premio Primavera de Novela in 2002, is narrated by a journalist and writer who tells the story of a young novelist searching for the other half of his identity. The novelist's search begins when he meets a mysterious woman who wants him to write her biography, though she invents all of the stories she relates to

Cover for Millás's 1990 novel (translated as That Was Loneliness, 2000), about a woman whose life is transformed after she finds her deceased mother's diary (Thomas Cooper Library, University of South Carolina)

him in her own attempt to create an identity. The main themes of the novel are incomplete communications based on multiple narratives (reliable or not), the human condition of loneliness, and a questioning of what is real and what is fiction (biographies, novels, newspaper articles, and television interviews). The themes and characters of this novel are as universal as they are specific to their place and time.

Juan José Millás is as readily recognized for his weekly newspaper articles as for his novels and short stories. In a 1996 interview with John R. Rosenberg, Millás stated that "la literatura es un modo de conocimiento. . . . Uno escribe para saber" (literature is a means of learning. . . . One writes in order to learn). His fiction addresses the symbolic and the real that combine to constitute human communication, the relationship between reality and fantasy, and the relationship between language and identity.

**Interviews:**

José María Marco, "En fin . . . Entrevista con Juan José Millás," *Quimera*, 81 (1980): 20–26;

John R. Rosenberg, "Entre el oficio y la obsesión: Una entrevista con Juan José Millás," *Anales de la literatura española contemporánea*, 21 (1996): 143–160;

Pilar Cabañas, "Materiales gaseosos: Entrevista con Juan José Millás," *Cuadernos Hispanoamericanos*, 580 (October 1998): 103–120;

Guillermo Saavedra, "Entrevista con Juan José Millás: Entre lo cómico y lo siniestro," *Suplemento Cultural La Nación*, 6 June 1999, p. 4.

**References:**

Yaw Agawu-Kakraba, "Desire, Psychoanalysis, and Violence: Juan José Millás' *El desorden de tu nombre*," *Anales de la Literatura Española Contemporánea*, 24, nos. 1–2 (1999): 17–34;

Agawu-Kakraba, "*La soledad era esto* and the Process of Subjectivity," *Forum for Modern Language Studies*, 35 (January 1999): 81–94;

Carlos Ardavin, "Dialogía y heterobiografía en *Cerbero son las sombras* de Juan José Millás," *Mester*, 26 (1997): 71–83;

Robert Baah, "Ficción, historia y autoridad: Juan José Millás y el narrador inconstante en *Letra muerta*," *Mester*, 33 (Spring 1993): 9–18;

Baah, "Teoría de la extrapolación: La novela contemporánea y la reflexión teórica," *Thesaurus: Boletín del Instituto Caro y Cuervo*, 49 (January–April 1994): 77–91;

Jean-François Carcelen, "Le Brouillage des frontières génériques dans l'oeuvre de Juan José Millás," in *Postmodernité et écriture narrative dans l'Espagne contemporaine*, edited by Georges Tyras (Grenoble: Centre d'études et de recherches hispaniques Université Stendhal, 1996), pp. 197–208;

Esther Cuadrat, "Una aproximación al mundo novelístico de Juan José Millás," *Cuadernos Hispanoamericanos: Revista Mensual de Cultura Hispánica*, 541–542 (July–August 1995): 207–216;

Thomas Franz, "Envidia y existencia en Millás y Unamuno," *Revista Canadiense de Estudios Hispánicos*, 21 (Fall 1996): 131–142;

Edward Friedman, "Defining Solitude: Juan José Millás's *La soledad era esto*," *Romance Languages Annual*, 9 (1997): 492–495;

Barbara Gordon, "Doubles and Identities in Juan José Millás's *Cerbero son las sombras*," *Romance Languages Annual*, 6 (1994): 486–491;

Fabián Gutiérrez, *Cómo leer a Juan José Millás* (Madrid: Júcar, 1992);

Rebeca Gutiérrez, "Teorías que cohabitan con la ficción: Síntomas posmodernos en *El desorden de tu nombre* de Juan José Millás," *Romance Languages Annual*, 9 (1997): 526–528;

Vance Holloway, "The Pleasures of Oedipal Discontent and *El orden de tu nombre* by Juan José Millás," *Revista Canadiense de Estudios Hispánicos*, 18 (Fall 1993): 31–47;

Dale Knickerbocker, "Búsqueda del ser auténtico y crítica social en *Tonto, muerto, bastardo e invisible* de Juan José Millás," *Anales de la Literatura Española Contemporánea*, 22 (1997): 211–233;

Knickerbocker, "Identidad y otredad en *Primavera de luto* de Juan José Millás," *Letras Peninsulares*, 13 (Fall 2000–Winter 2001): 561–579;

Knickerbocker, *Juan José Millás: The Obsessive-Compulsive Aesthetic* (New York: Peter Lang, 2003);

Knickerbocker, "La reiteración de motivos en *Tonto, muerto, bastardo e invisible* de Juan José Millás," *Revista Hispánica Moderna*, 51 (June 1998): 147–160;

Ignacio Javier López, "Novela y realidad: En torno a la estructura de *Visión del ahogado* de Juan José Millás," *Anales de la Literatura Española Contemporánea*, 13, nos. 1–2 (1988): 37–54;

Javier Marías, "La huella del animal," *Vuelta*, 19 (March 1995): 43–45;

María Pilar Martínez-Latre, "Juan José Millás y la estrategia narativa de *Papel mojado*," *Mester*, 16 (Spring 1987): 5–15;

Martínez-Latre, "Técnicas narrativas en *Letra muerta* de Juan José Millás: Una relación equívoca con un autor ideal," *Mester*, 16 (Fall 1987): 3–17;

Martha Isabel Miranda, "El lenguaje cinematográfico de la acción en la narrativa de Juan José Millás," *Revista Hispánica Moderna*, 47 (December 1994): 526–542;

Françoise Peyrègne, "Espacio urbano, espacio íntimo en la novela de Juan José Millás," in *Historia, espacio e imaginario*, edited by Jacqueline Covo (Villeneuve d'Ascq, France: Presses Universitaires de Septentrion, 1997), pp. 71–77;

Carter Smith, "Between Two Chronotopes: Space and Time in Juan José Millás's *Visión del ahogado*," *Romance Languages Annual*, 9 (1997): 697–703;

Gonzalo Sobejano, *Juan José Millás, fabulador de la extrañeza* (Madrid: Alfaguara, 1995).

# Gabriel Miró

*(28 July 1879 – 27 May 1930)*

Marta E. Altisent
*University of California Davis*

BOOKS: *La mujer de Ojeda: Ensayo de novela,* preface by Luis Pérez Bueno (Alicante: Tipografía Carratalá, 1901);

*Hilván de escenas* (Alicante: Esplá, 1903);

*Del vivir: Apuntes de parajes leprosos* (Alicante: Esplá, 1904);

*Nómada (de la falta de amor): Novela* (Madrid: El Cuento Semanal, 1908);

*La novela de mi amigo* (Alicante: Esplá, 1908);

*La palma rota: Novela* (Madrid: Los Contemporáneos, 1909);

*El hijo santo* (Madrid: Los Contemporáneos, 1909);

*Amores de Antón Hernando: Novela* (Madrid: Los Contemporáneos, 1909); enlarged as *Niño y grande* (Madrid: Atenea, 1922);

*Las cerezas del cementerio* (Mexico City: Ballescá / Barcelona: Doménech, 1910);

*Del huerto provinciano* (Barcelona: Doménech, 1912);

*La señora, los suyos y los otros* (Madrid: Los Contemporáneos, 1912);

*Los amigos, los amantes y la muerte* (Barcelona: López, 1914);

*El abuelo del rey* (Barcelona: Ibérica, 1915);

*Dentro del cercado y La palma rota* (Barcelona: Doménech, 1916);

*Figuras de la pasión del Señor,* 2 volumes (Barcelona: Doménech, 1916, 1917); translated by Charles J. Hoghart as *Figures of the Passion of Our Lord* (London: Chapman, 1924; New York: Knopf, 1925);

*Libro de Sigüenza: Jornadas de un caballero levantino* (Barcelona: Doménech, 1917);

*El humo dormido: Tablas del calendario* (Madrid: Atenea, 1919);

*El ángel, el molino, el caracol del faro: Estampas rurales y de cuentos, estampas de un león y una leona, estampas del faro* (Madrid: Atenea, 1921);

*Niño y grande* (Madrid: Atenea, 1922);

*Nuestro Padre San Daniel: Novela de capellánes y devotos* (Madrid: Atenea, 1921); translated by Charlotte Remfry-Kidd as *Our Father San Daniel: Scenes of Clerical Life* (London: Benn, 1930);

*Frontispiece for* Obras escogidas, *edited by María Alfaro, 1955; Thomas Cooper Library, University of South Carolina)*

*Señorita y sor* (Madrid: Prensa Gráfica, 1924);

*El obispo leproso* (Madrid: Biblioteca Nueva, 1926);

*Años y leguas* (Madrid: Biblioteca Nueva, 1928);

*Figuras de Bethlem: La conciencia mesiánica de Jesús* (Buenos Aires: Losada, 1961);

*Siguenza y el mirador azul y prosas de* El Ibero: *El último escrito (inédito) de Gabriel Miró y algunos de los primeros,* edited by Edmund L. King (Madrid: Ediciones de La Torre, 1982).

**Editions and Collections:** *Obras completas: Edición Conmemorativa,* 12 volumes (Barcelona: Altés, 1932–1949)–comprises volume 1, *Del vivir: La novela de mi amigo,* prologue by Azorín (pseudonym of José Martínez Ruiz) (1932); volume 2, *Las cerezas del cementerio,* prologue by Miguel de Unamuno (1932); volume 3, *Dentro del cercado, La palma rota, Los pies y los zapatos de Enriqueta,* prologue by Gregorio Marañón (1933); volume 4, *El abuelo del rey, Nómada,* prologue by Augusto Pí Sunyer (1934); volume 5, *Figuras de la Pasión del Señor,* prologue by Ricardo Baeza (1935); volume 6, *Figuras de la Pasión del Señor, II. Bethlém. Los tres caminantes. La conciencia mesiánica de Jesús,* prologue by Baeza (1935); volume 7, *Libro de Sigüenza,* prologue by Pedro Salinas (1936); volume 8, *El humo dormido, El ángel, el molino, el caracol del faro,* prologue by Oscar Esplá (1941); volume 9, *Niño y grande, Corpus y otros cuentos,* prologue by Dámaso Alonso (1943); volume 10, *Nuestro padre San Daniel,* prologue by Salvador de Madariaga (1945); volume 11, *El obispo leproso,* prologue by Gerardo Diego (1947); and volume 12, *Años y leguas,* prologue by Duque de Maura (1949);

*Obras completas de Gabriel Miró,* edited by Clemencia Miró (Madrid: Biblioteca Nueva, 1943);

*Glosas de Sigüenza,* edited by Clemencia Miró (Buenos Aires & Mexico City: Espasa-Calpe, 1952);

*Obras escogidas,* edited by María Alfaro (Madrid: Aguilar, 1955);

*El humo dormido,* edited by Edmund L. King (New York: Dell, 1967);

*Novelas cortas,* edited by Victor Oller (Madrid: Felmar, 1976);

*El humo dormido,* edited by Vicente Ramos (Madrid: Cátedra, 1978);

*El obispo leproso: Segunda parte de Nuestro padre San Daniel,* edited by Carlos Luis Silva (Madrid: Ediciones de la Torre, 1984);

*Obras completas de Gabriel Miró,* 8 volumes published (Alicante: Instituto de Estudios "Juan Gil-Albert," Diputación Provincial de Alicante y Caja de Ahorros de Alicante y Murcia, 1986– )–comprises volume 5, *Novelas cortas,* edited by Miguel Ángel Lozano Marco (1986); volume 11, *Libro de Sigüenza,* edited by Ricardo Landeira (1990); volume 12, *El humo dormido,* edited by Edmund L. King (1991); volume 8, *El abuelo del rey,* edited by Gregorio Torres Nebrera (1992); volume 9, *Dentro del cercado,* edited by Kevin Larsen (1992); volume 16, *El obispo leproso,* edited by Ian R. Macdonald (1993); volume 15, *Nuestro padre San Daniel: Novela de capellanes y devotos,* edited by King (1994); volume 7, *Corpus y otros cuentos,* edited by Torres Nebrera (1995);

*La narrativa breve de Gabriel Miró y antología de cuentos,* edited by Marta E. Altisent (Barcelona: Anthropos, 1988);

*Huerto de cruces,* edited by Francisco Márquez Villanueva (Barcelona: Edhasa, 1991);

*Los artículos de Gabriel Miró en la prensa barcelonesa, 1911–1920,* edited by Altisent (Madrid: Pliegos, 1992);

*El abuelo del rey,* edited by Gregorio Torres Nebrera (Alicante: Caja de Ahorros del Mediterráneo, Instituto de Cultura Juan Gil-Albert, Diputación Provincial de Alicante, 1992);

*El obispo leproso,* edited by Ian R. Macdonald (Alicante: Caja de Ahorros del Mediterráneo, Instituto de Cultura Juan Gil-Albert, Diputación Provincial de Alicante, 1993).

TRANSLATIONS: Alfred von Hedenstjerna, *El señor de Halleborg* (Barcelona: Doménech, 1910);

Henry Lavedan, *Su majestad* (Barcelona: Doménech, 1911);

Ramón Turró, *Filosofía crítica* (Madrid: Atenea, 1919).

Gabriel Miró is one of Spain's quintessential "lyrical novelists," together with Juan Ramón Jiménez, Ramón del Valle-Inclán, Azorín, and Ramón Gómez de la Serna. He stands out for the quality of his prose, his sensual depictions of his native landscape of Alicante, and his re-creation of biblical stories. Miró's abundant imagery, his fragmented style, his preference for nouns rather than verbs, and the musical cadence of his prose make plot and causal sequence secondary elements of his novels, which are similar in that respect to the experiments conducted by modernist novelists such as Hermann Hesse, Virginia Woolf, and Marcel Proust. The prose poet of his native land, Miró fused the transient states of the physical world with the moods, musings, and memories of his characters, bringing past and present into a continuous time line akin to Henri Bergson's concept of interior time, or *dureé.* Miró has also been linked to the phenomenologists through his acquaintance with the doctrines of Catalan philosopher Ramón Turró, one of whose works he translated in 1919.

Miró was not a prolific writer. He published only thirteen novels, three collections of short stories, and articles that appeared in the main Spanish newspapers of his day: *La Publicidad, Los Lunes del Imparcial, Diario de Barcelona, La Vanguardia, La Nación,* and *El Sol.* Indeed, the most original part of his work is the book-length compilations of sui generis literary forms, such as *glosas* (commentaries), *estampas* (impressions), *viñetas* (vignettes), *jornadas*, (diary entries), *tablas*, (sketches), and *figuras* (figures), which resist categorization and clear genre demarcation. They combine elements of autobiography, journalistic chronicle, prose poem, biography, travelogue, political gossip, folktale, animal fable, description of local festivities and traditions, and biblical and hagiographic stories, thus exhibiting the archaic flavor and at the same time modern quality of his writing.

Miró's career spanned two literary generations, the Generation of '98 and the Generation of 1914, but he was not a part of either group. He did not share the preoccupation of the Generation of '98 writers with the decline of the colonial past brought about by the Spanish-American War. Nor was he involved in politics, as was the group of writers around the philosopher José Ortega y Gasset, later labeled the Generation of 1914, who laid the groundwork for the founding of the Second Republic in April 1931. Miró's aesthetic and ideological distance from the Generation of '98 writers can be explained by his affinity for the nineteenth-century masters Clarín (Leopoldo Alas), Juan Valera, José María Pereda, and Benito Pérez Galdós; his "aestheticism"; and the regional settings he chose for his fiction. The imaginary cities of Oleza, immortalized in *Nuestro Padre San Daniel: Novela de capellánes y devotos* (1921, Our Father St. Daniel: Novel of Chaplains and Pious People; translated as *Our Father San Daniel: Scenes of Clerical Life*, 1930) and *El obispo leproso* (1926, The Leper Bishop), and Serosca, the setting of *El abuelo del Rey* (1915, The King's Grandfather), portray a world in decline, closer to the Restoration years (1875–1898) than to the twentieth century. They reflect Spain's reluctant but unavoidable entry into the industrial age as trains, automobiles, and engineering projects erupt in the countryside and end its historical isolation.

Miró was not indifferent to recent history and the turbulent political developments of his time, as he made manifest in his newspaper columns. He enjoyed the friendship, protection, and respect of political figures such as Enric Prat de la Riba, Antonio Maura, Antonio Canalejas, and José Francos Rodríguez and was awarded official honors and recognition. He was not spared, however, the insidious effects that the Miguel Primo de Rivera dictatorship had exerted on intellectuals such as Valle-Inclán and Miguel de Unamuno. The conservative Catholic faction relentlessly attacked Miró for his unconventional approach to the life of Jesus in his *Figuras de la pasión del Señor* (1916, 1917; translated as *Figures of the Passion of Our Lord*, 1924) and for his controversial portraits of the Jesuit order. His entry into the Royal Academy of Letters was boycotted in 1927 and

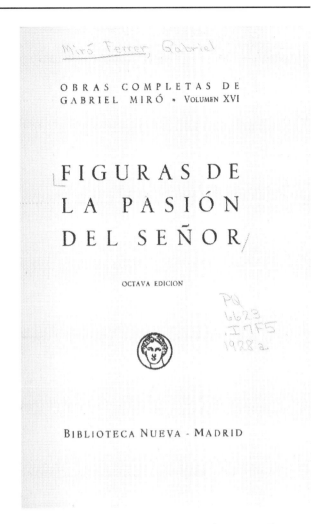

*Cover for a collected edition of Miró's work (translated as* Figures of the Passion of Our Lord, *1924), originally published in two volumes in 1916 and 1917, in which he takes an unconventional approach to the life of Christ (Thomas Cooper Library, University of South Carolina)*

in 1929, in spite of the support of its president and its most prestigious members.

The metaphorical density and intertextual richness of Miró's oeuvre mark him as a minority writer by European standards and by those of the Spanish literary critics of the time who questioned his talent as a novelist. As Ian R. Macdonald demonstrates in his *Gabriel Miró: His Private Library and His Literary Background* (1975), Miró was an avid reader of the classics and of modern European writers and thinkers. Miguel de Cervantes; the Romantics Johann Wolfgang von Goethe and Stendhal; the Spanish realists Pérez Galdós, Valera, and Clarín; and the symbolists, naturalists, and decadents Emile Zola, Gustave Flaubert, Edmond and Jules de Goncourt, Rubén Darío, and Gabriel D'Annunzio were significant influences in his early works and inspired his own version of self-conscious *Modernismo* (modernism). He later experimented with avant-garde trends akin to the Proustian explorations of memory and time, stream of consciousness, and slow tempo, showing stronger affinities to the artistic prose of Jiménez, Valle-Inclán, and Azorín than to the more direct language of the Generation of '98 writers. In addition, he employed impressionist techniques, integrating imagery and literary allusions into the organic development of the plot and increasing reticence and metaphoric condensation. Miró's dictum "No agotar los episodios; decir las cosas por insinuación" (Do not exhaust the episode; say things by insinuation) was perfected in his last novels, considered among the most accomplished Spanish twentieth-century fiction. At the end of his life Miró's work was better understood and appreciated by younger poets such as Federico García Lorca and Jorge Guillén, who recognized in him a precursor of their avant-garde experimentation with language.

Gabriel Miró Ferrer was born in Alicante on 28 July 1879 to Juan Miró Moltó, a public-works engineer from Alcoy, and Encarnación Ferrer Ons, the daughter of a well-to-do family of orange growers in Orihuela (Murcia). He had one brother, Juan, six years his elder, with whom he maintained a strong connection all his life. Juan's energetic and extroverted nature contrasted with Miró's hypersensitive personality. Miró grew up in the Benalúa neighborhood near the harbor and attended the school of Francisco Alemany until he was nine. He was then sent to boarding school at the prestigious Jesuit Colegio de Santo Domingo in Orihuela, where Juan was a student. Although Miró had visited his brother on many occasions, the prolonged separation from his parents traumatized him. The bleak and stifling institutional atmosphere, the need to comply with the austere rule of the Jesuit education system, and the spartan student life resulted in a psychosomatic pain in the knee. Thus, Miró was kept from sports and from exerting himself outdoors. Many of the bittersweet recollections of these moments of solitude and homesickness are captured in his autobiographical novella *Amores de Antón Hernándo* (1909, Loves of Antón Hernándo), as well as in *Libro de Sigüenza: Jornadas de un caballero levantino* (1917, Sigüenza's Book: Journals of a Levantine Gentleman) and *El humo dormido: Tablas del calendario* (1919, The Sleepy Haze: Sketches Devoted to Days of the Liturgic Calendar and Other Annual Feasts). *Niño y grande* (Boy and Man), the enlarged version of *Amores de Antón Hernándo* published in 1922, is a coming-of-age story about an impressionable adolescent who submits his first sensual and erotic yearnings for a classmate's sister to the moral scrutiny of Catholic doctrine. The consequences of sexual repression are dramatically

depicted in *El hijo santo* (1909, The Son Who Would Be Saint), a naturalistic novella in which a young priest's unfulfilled desires for a foreign widow and his guilt feelings lead to a stroke that leaves him prematurely aged, disfigured, and full of regret.

Miró left the boarding school at fourteen when his father was transferred to Ciudad Real in La Mancha. Miró welcomed the freedom afforded by the public school but was struck by the poverty and desolation of the Castillian *páramo* (barren plane) surrounding Ciudad Real. His impressions of the area found their way into his first book-length work, *Paisajes tristes* (Sad Lands), which was serialized in the literary newspaper *El Ibero* from 6 September 1901 to 16 February 1902). Miró later repudiated the work and did not want it republished (it was included in a 1982 collection edited by Edmund L. King).

After obtaining his high-school diploma in Alicante in 1896, Miró began to study law at the University of Valencia. After a year, he became homesick and decided to continue his career as an open university student, attending the University of Granada only for final exams. In Alicante he alternated his law studies with reading literature and with the company of intellectual friends such as Francisco Figueras Pacheco and Oscar Esplá. He received his degree in 1900.

On 16 January 1901 Miró married his childhood playmate and adolescent sweetheart, Clemencia Mignon, daughter of the French consul in Alicante. A few months later, his first novel, *La mujer de Ojeda: Ensayo de novela* (Ojeda's Wife: A Novel), was published. The work is clearly indebted to Valera's *Pepita Jiménez* (1874) in form and content but exhibits Miró's gift for psychological analysis and his penchant for portraying illicit passions. The novel, which he later rejected, was followed by *Hilván de escenas* (1903, Yarn of Scenes), a collection of sketches loosely connected by a turbulent and doomed love affair and a common setting, the Badaleste Valley, a fictionalized version of the village of Guadalest in the coastal range of Alicante), presided over by the palace-monastery belonging to the heirs of Eusebio Bermúdez. The majestic landscape clashes with the greed, cruelty, and monotony of the peasants' lives but even more with the harsh rule of Trinidad Bermúdez, the last survivor of a feudal order and a landowning matriarch in the tradition of Pérez Galdós's doña Perfecta in the 1876 novel of the same name, Valera's doña María in *Juanita la Larga* (1895), and García Lorca's Bernarda Alba in the play *La casa de Bernarda Alba* (1944; translated as *The House of Bernarda Alba*, 1947).

Miró's next work, *Del vivir: Apuntes de parajes leprosos* (1904, Of Living: Scenes of Leper Sites), attains greater coherence of design and content because of the consistent position of the narrator, the unifying theme of leprosy, and the rural setting of Parcent. The novel sprang from a trip Miró had taken with Esplá and his father's friend, Próspero Lafarga, in 1903 to explore the interior of the province by car. As in *Hilván de escenas,* he does not spare anti-idyllic notes of brutish and bleak peasant life conjured up by the presence of the biblical disease that afflicted remote areas of southeast Spain until it was contained and treated at the Sanatorium of Fontilles in 1920.

In *Del vivir* Miró presents his alter ego, Sigüenza, for the first time. The itinerant and meditative narrator traverses several mountain villages in the company of the rural doctor Don Hermenegildo, who acts as his guide and source of inspiration, since the doctor's resilience remains the only solace in his patients' quest for human contact. As an observer from the city, Sigüenza tries to reconcile the natural beauty with the solipsistic alienation of people whose fates personify unimaginable tales of pain and solitude. He laments the lack of compassion both for and among the needy, as well as the desolation of the sick who are condemned to a life of reclusion and marginalization. As in Miró's previous novels, antithesis is a structural device that further emphasizes this solitude. The main contrasts, according to Ernest Elwood Norden, are those between the exultant landscape and the degenerative bodily disease, and between the segregation, yet intimate nexus, between the sick and the healthy. Miró depicts the connectedness without fear of contamination between spouses at night; a mother's longings to watch her baby from a window in order to spare him the disease; and the desire of an infected boy to join in his friends' game. In one of the most poignant scenes he paints a cruel simulacrum of furtive love: a young leper swimming by moonlight in the river is raped by a foreign vagrant, who disappears without noticing her discolored skin.

The lepers are confined to houses on the outskirts of the villages during the day but free to roam at night. A village celebration serves as a counterpoint to the sorrow of the patients, who have learned to flee at the sight of others in order to be spared the horror reflected in their faces. Some, such as Baptiste, show more resilience than others. He grows illegal tobacco to survive, thus achieving a prosperity that allows him to joke and discuss politics with his customers. The grotesque qualities of the sick contrast with the insensitiveness of the healthy, who relish the thought of being free from the disease.

For the most part, *Del vivir* is a journey of self-discovery. The narrator feels empathetic but powerless, compulsively curious yet ashamed of his desire to contemplate human ugliness and suffering. Only nature appears as a dynamic and vigorous force in the face of human decay and cruelty. Sigüenza's ambivalent position as an intellectual and as an aesthete who finds solace in the majestic landscape but comes into conflict with suffering people is a central motif in the Sigüenza trilogy. In *Libro de Sigüenza* and *Años y leguas* (1928, Years and Leagues) Miró further exploits the device of the soft-hearted narrator to tell his tale. As an unobtrusive observer, this alter ego faces many of the author's own contradictions and feelings of guilt stemming from his privileged upbringing and hypersensitive nature. Vicente Ramos, Macdonald, and Richard López Landeira have shown how the alter ego became a favorite ironic device to come to terms with Miró's false humility and to establish a distance between his intimate persona and the world.

By 1906 Miró was the father of two daughters, Olympia, born on 5 October 1903, and Clemencia, born on 30 December 1905, and felt the need for a more lucrative profession. He submitted himself to the fiercely competitive state examinations for the position of judge, but after two years of unsuccessful attempts, he abandoned the pursuit.

In 1908 Miró was awarded the prestigious prize offered by the publishers of the magazine *El Cuento Semanal* (The Weekly Story) for his novella *Nómada (de la falta de amor)* (Nómada [of the Absence of Love]), which is based on a true story. The generous mayor of Jijona, don Diego, embittered by the deaths of his daughter and wife, escapes the stifling company of a pious sister, squanders his fortune, and lives in dissipation. He roams through France and the United States and returns, an old and disfigured beggar, to the sordidness and stupidity of his native land. When his only desire is to die in peace in a corner of his sister's mansion, the townspeople shave his head to give the prodigal son a more decent appearance.

The award from *El cuento semanal* provided Miró with national recognition and visibility among a sophisticated readership that included the most prominent writers of the Generation of '98, three of whom—Valle-Inclán, Pío Baroja, and Felipe Trigo—had been on the selection board. The honor led to a job promotion as the official chronicler of Alicante, a position offered by the Diputación Provincial that allowed him more time to complete the novellas *La novela de mi amigo* (1908, My Friend's Novel), *La palma rota* (1909, The Broken Palm), *El hijo santo, Amores de Antón Hernando,* and the novel *Las cerezas del cementerio* (1910, The Cemetery Cherries). All of these works have melodramatic plots, in which platonic and illicit passion and unrequited love are part of the heroes' self-discovery.

*Las cerezas del cementerio* represents the pinnacle of Miró's erotic themes. The story, charged with Freudian overtones, deals with the love of young Félix for his godmother, Beatriz, an attractive woman who had been

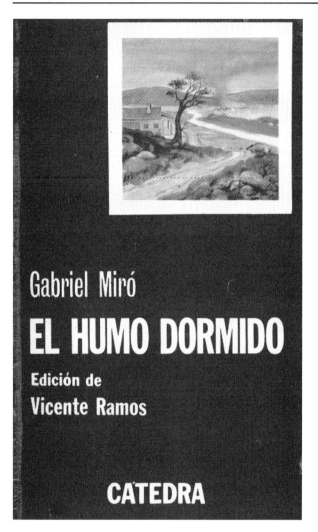

*Cover for a 1978 paperback edition of Miró's memoirs (The Sleepy Haze), originally published in 1919 (Thomas Cooper Library, University of South Carolina)*

the lover of Félix's deceased Uncle Guillermo. The idyll, enhanced by an atmosphere of summery exuberance, has incestuous connotations beneath the mystical and Eucharistic love imagery. The awakening of sensuality and desire in Félix leads to degenerative heart disease, a manifestation of his sexual frustration and psychological impotence in filling his uncle's role as a virile lover. Memories of his uncle haunt Félix, and his Oedipal conflict is resolved only by his own destruction. As Félix nears death, his love for Beatriz recedes to the devotion of a godson, since he desires only her motherly embrace; and he becomes an affectionate brother figure to her adolescent daughter, who is infatuated with him. The title alludes to a last love rite conducted by mother and daughter: they eat the fruit of the cherry tree that shades Félix's grave, thereby joining in the natural cycle of regeneration.

Miró's most autobiographical and powerful novella is *La novela de mi amigo.* The painter Federico Urios is left inconsolable by his failed quest for artistic fulfillment, his joyless marriage, and the death of his twelve-year-old daughter, Lucita. Named after Federico's younger sister, Lucita replicates her aunt's fate: the elder Lucita burned to death as a child while trying to retrieve a piece of bread from the fireplace as Federico looked on, unable to save her. Ridden with guilt and grief, the painter throws himself naked into the moonlit sea. As Norden notes, "the beauty of the scene in which the suicide takes place suggests nothing of defeat. Through this act Federico asserts the god-like power he has sought throughout his life. By remaining rebellious, solitary, and irreducible, he chooses to die free with dignity."

In 1910 Miró began to entertain the idea of moving to Barcelona. On several visits from 1911 to 1913 he established contacts with editors and writers associated with *La Veu de Catalunya;* (The Voice of Catalonia); one of these people, Joan Maragall, introduced Miró to the editors of the *Diario de Barcelona* (Diary of Barcelona), to which he contributed from 1911 to 1916. He also met the poets Josep Carner, Jaume Bofill i Mates, and Joaquim Ruyra; the playwright Josep María de Sagarra; the philosophers Turró and Eugenio d'Ors; the composer Enrique Granados; and the newly elected president of the Generalitat (autonomous government) of Catalonia, Prat de la Riba.

The move to Barcelona did not come until September 1914. Barcelona was an artistically vibrant city where turn-of-the-century modernism was being replaced by *Noucentisme* (1900-Style), a neo-Hellenistic and scholarly literary movement that preceded the avant-garde artistic innovations of the 1920s in the art of Pablo Picasso, Antoni Gaudí, Joan Miró, and Salvador Dalí. Although Miró felt estranged from the emerging nationalist euphoria, he established lifelong friendships with kindred spirits such as Maragall, Ruyra, and Granados, while maintaining a more reserved attitude toward the Catalonian *Noucentistes* clustered around the imposing personality of d'Ors.

In Barcelone Miró took an accounting job at La Casa de la Caridad (The House of Charity). Working only in the mornings gave him the opportunity to devote more time to literary endeavors, and he accepted the position of editor of the *Enciclopedia Católica Sagrada* (Sacred Catholic Encyclopedia) for the publisher Vecchi y Ramos. After Miró had invested more than a year of research in biblical and ecclesiastical history, however, the economic recession following World War I drove the publisher into bankruptcy. The encyclopedia project was canceled, and its contributors were left uncompensated. The biblical, hagiographical, and liturgical erudition Miró had accumulated changed the direction of his fiction. He incorporated much of the data into his writing, supplementing his imagination with accurate historical details. Soon after, he composed *Figuras de la Pasión del Señor* and *Figuras de Bethlem: La conciencia mesiánica de Jesús* (1961, Figures of Bethlehem: The Messianic Conscience of Jesus), two collections of stories dealing with key episodes of the Old and New Testaments, that were originally published in installments in *La Vanguardia* between March 1915 and 1917. The second set of the *figuras,* part of a more ambitious collection Miró intended to call "Estampas viejas" (Old Stamps), transports the reader to Palestine before the birth of Jesus. It is a mosaic in which the tales of Ruth, Naomi and Boaz, Solomon and the Shulamite, Joseph and Mary, and Herod and the Magi come alive through the eyes of childhood as Miró recaptures the emotions he had felt when these stories were first told to him.

The *figuras* were conceived of as "landscapes with figures," scenes molded by their physical locale, which in turn molds their characters' emotional traits. Western Alicante, with its parched hills, olive orchards, rugged rock formations, and pine-covered granite cliffs, fed Miró's illusion that ancient Palestine could be superimposed on the landscape of eastern Spain. More than a decorative background, this rural environment is a living organism. The tragedies and joys of its inhabitants become interchangeable with those of the peoples of Galilee. The sensuality of the evocations, the archaeological exactness of customs and objects, and the psychological immediacy of the introspections set these pieces apart from conventional Bible stories. For Edmund L. King, Miró's gift for sensory writing had dual origins in the doctrines of Lorenzo Casanova as well as those of Ignatius Loyola: "not the doctrine the Jesuits intended to teach," he writes in his introduction to the 1967 edition of *El humo dormido,* "but evidently the one Miró learned from." In 1917 the reprint of a chapter of *Figuras de la Pasión del Señor,* "Mujeres de Jerusalén" (Women of Jerusalem), in the Gijón newspaper *El Noroeste* on Good Friday resulted in the imprisonment of the editor, Valdés Prida, for publishing a blasphemous depiction of Jesus Christ.

The Mirós' apartment in Paseo de la Bonanova was damp and dilapidated. In the winter of 1914–1915 their daughter Clemencia, who had a congenital bone-marrow disease, fell ill with typhoid fever. The typhoid epidemic also afflicted the Granados household. The children's recovery at Christmas was celebrated by both families with a musical play, "La cieguecita de Belén" (The Blind Little Girl of Bethlehem). Miró wrote the lyrics for music composed by Granados, and the play was performed by the children. The Mirós later rented a spacious apartment in

the Ensanche, at Diputación 339, across from a convent where in the springtime the writer could hear the nuns' chants through his window, as he recalls in *El humo dormido.* Granados and his wife died on 24 March 1916 when the French steamer *Sussex* was sunk in the English Channel by a German torpedo. The impact of this loss was artistically rendered in Miró's "Estampas del faro" (1921, Scenes of the Lighthouse) in a description of the remains of a passenger liner shipwrecked on a magical sunny beach.

Miró used Alicante for the setting of two more novels: *El abuelo del rey* and *Dentro del cercado* (1916, Inside the Fence). The first is a three-generation saga set in turn-of-the-century Serosca (a fictional version of Alcoy), a city divided into conservative and progressive factions. In *Dentro del cercado* Luis, a quintessential seducer, allows himself to be adored by his wife, Librada; loved by her cousin Laura; and admired from a distance by his neighbor Agueda. Luis and Laura's affair ends in renunciation: when Luis returns to his wife, Laura overcomes guilt, jealousy, psychosomatic illness, and sexual frustration and serenely accepts her sacrifice for Librada's sake. Librada's maternal powers are associated with the reassuring light of dawn, while Laura's incandescent but fruitless beauty is compared to the eerie and mysterious moonlight.

Some of Miró's newspaper columns for *El Diario de Barcelona* were collected in 1917 in *Libro de Sigüenza* as stories loosely joined by a first-person narrator. The pieces include local customs, parables, anecdotes, and existential meditations about life, memory, and time. In 1919 Miró published his memoirs, *El humo dormido.* As King notes in his introduction to the 1967 edition of the book, "For Miró the very act of naming the objects of his experience completes their existence, and it is this act, not informative, not utilitarian, but celebrative, that we participate in when we read him."

In 1920 Miró moved to Madrid, where his friend, Prime Minister Maura, had guaranteed him a government post in the Ministry of Labor. There he wrote the "Oleza novels," *Nuestro Padre San Daniel* and its sequel, *El obispo leproso.*

The rigid moral code of Oleza stands in sharp contrast to the exuberant and aphrodisiac landscape of orange orchards and palm gardens of the fertile surrounding valley. This agricultural wealth is exported to enrich a few landowners and the Jesuit order. Miró draws a dichotomy, between those who celebrate life and those who distrust humankind and despise their own carnality: the sensuous and good-natured chaplain don Magín extends his influence to kindred spirits

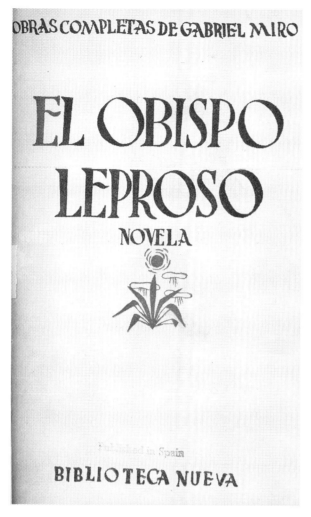

OBRAS COMPLETAS DE GABRIEL MIRO

EL OBISPO LEPROSO

NOVELA

Published in Spain

BIBLIOTECA NUEVA

*Cover for a 1928 paperback edition of Miró's 1926 novel (The Leper Bishop), in which he criticizes the rigid moral code imposed by the Jesuits on the fictional city of Oleza (Thomas Cooper Library, University of South Carolina)*

such as Paulina and her son Pablo, María Fulgencia, Purita, and doña Corazón; in contrast, the sadistic father Bellod, the somber don Alvaro, and the repressed doña Elvira personify the harsher aspects of religion. *Nuestro Padre San Daniel* centers on two major events: the nomination of the new bishop and the marriage of Paulina and don Alvaro. *El obispo leproso* follows Pablo's first seventeen years of life, with particular attention to the boy's infatuation with María Fulgencia and their separation when she is sent to Murcia by her tutor to rejoin her husband of convenience, don Amancio. In an epilogue, Paulina returns to her father's estate after fourteen years in an oppressive marriage, and Pablo departs from Oleza in a step in the direction of maturity.

After the publication of the Oleza novels in 1921 and 1926, the church and the official cultural establishment kept Miró from being considered for important literary honors because of the unfavorable light in which they thought he had portrayed the Jesuit order. They failed to see that Miró's critique of the religious establishment was counterbalanced by the Christian compassion of the main characters, Bishop Daniel and don Magín, whose pastoral care of and tenderness toward the most vulnerable supplied the Christian values that were lacking in the self-righteous Catholics of the city. Miró did not target Catholicism as such but exposed the dangers of theocracy. That the feudal order Miró depicted was still alive is evidenced by the fact that some of the offended readers thought that they saw themselves portrayed in the novels.

Spanish critics also misunderstood these novels, classifying them as decadent and baroque, either too emphatic or too vague to fit the demands of the conventional novel. In his review in the Madrid newspaper *El Imparcial* (27 February 1927) Luis Astrana Marín labeled Miró's self-conscious discourse "estilo leproso" (leper style) and included him among the heterodox and "effeminate" writers of modernism. More painful for Miró were the comments from admirers such as Ortega y Gasset, who objected in the Madrid newspaper *El Sol* (9 January 1927) to the "estática, paralítica" (static, paralytic) qualities, lack of dramatic suspense, and incongruous and spectral nature of the characters of *El Obispo leproso*. The label "novela deshumanizada" (dehumanized novel), a term Ortega had coined in his essay *La deshumanización del arte* (1925, The Dehumanization of Art) to describe the self-consciousness and formal detachment of the modern novel, seemed to him to be applicable to Miró's art.

In 1927 Miró left the Ministry of Labor for the Ministry of Education, where Maura had created the position of secretary of national artistic contests and commemorations specifically for him. He was put in charge of organizing celebrations in Seville of the tricentennial of the death of the baroque poet Luis de Góngora. Because of this responsibility he met a generation of younger poets, such as Guillén, García Lorca, Pedro Salinas, Benjamín Jarnés, and Dámaso Alonso, who were involved in the preparations for the tribute. The event, which took place in the Athenaeum of Seville that same year, strengthened the poets' friendship, giving them coherence as a literary group. All of these poets had read Miró's works and were awed by the dense texture of his lexicon. Miró's linguistic perfectionism, manifested in his quest for the most expressive and exact word, struck a special chord in Guillén and Salinas, who had learned to concentrate and distill the suggestive powers of language from Miró and from Miró's admirer Jiménez.

Despite the fact that his works were widely read and appreciated, Miró failed to be nominated to the Spanish Royal Academy of Letters in 1927 and again in 1929. He attributed his rejection to the hypocrisy of the conservative establishment that, since the incident of "Mujeres de Jerusalén," had discredited his literary reputation.

After turning fifty, Miró became reclusive and avoided major literary events. He spent every summer in a rented house in the town of Polop de la Marina in Alicante with his wife; his daughters; his son-in-law, Emilio Luengo; his grandson, Emilio, who was born on 1 November 1925; and some friends. There he finished his last novel, *Años y leguas,* during the summers of 1924 and 1925; it was serialized in the Barcelona newspaper *La Publicidad* and published in book form in 1928. In *Años y leguas* Sigüenza leaves the city behind. The coastal and mountain regions offer a wide range of Mediterranean earthly delights, from the fertile and green orchards of La Marina to the rocky formations of the inland sierras of Aitana. Sigüenza is now an older man, preoccupied with mortality and his legacy. He meditates on the consistency of his sense of himself by contemplating the familiar landscape that mirrors his younger soul. He also converses with the locals, such as the memorable grave-digger Gasparo, immortalized in the chapter "Huerto de cruces" (Orchard of Crosses). Gasparo shows Sigüenza a "geology of bones," recalling the lives of the dead townspeople as he relentlessly disinters their remains to make room for the newly deceased.

In 1930 Miró's melancholy and his disappointment in failing to become financially independent come across in letters to his longtime friend José Guardiola Ortíz. His withdrawal from literary events did not prevent him from making a last public appearance to celebrate Unamuno's return from exile on 3 May. When he arrived home after the banquet, he began suffering from flu-like symptoms. Two days later he underwent an appendectomy. Although the operation was successful, Miró felt that death was near and reassured his loved ones that he was well prepared for "el próximo viaje" (the next journey). He died of peritonitis on 27 May 1930 and was buried in La Almudena Cemetery in Madrid on 29 May. Miró's "inteligencia era la forma suprema de su bondad" (intelligence was the supreme form of his goodness), Unamuno stated in a condolence letter to his widow. In *Gabriel Miró, remembranza* (1980, Gabriel Miró, Remembrance) Juan Gil-Albert noted his honesty and generosity and said: "No era un hombre de lucha, como todo artista puro, y sin embargo, como hombre puro también, como hombre recto y consciente, en su intimidad se debatían las crisis agudas de nuestro siglo" (He was not a fighter, as is any genuine art-

ist, yet as a man of conscience and integrity, he debated in his soul all the profound crises of our time).

The legend that Miró led a life of failure, obscurity, and deprivation is not completely accurate. Guardiola Ortíz, Ramos, King, and Gil-Albert have described his witty personality and the many interests and joys that enriched his life. These interests range from the art lessons given to him by his uncle, the impressionist painter Lorenzo Casanova, and his friend Abelardo Parrilla, to the evening music recitals he shared with the composers Granados and Esplá. Miró's friend Sagarra describes in his *Memòries* (2000) the writer's sybaritic tastes and penchant for pastries and gourmet foods, which led him to discover many of the gastronomic marvels of Barcelona.

In the twenty-first century writers such as Salvador Espriu, Vicente Risco, Ricardo Baeza, Alonso Zamora Vicente, Francisco Umbral, and Pere (Pedro) Gimferrer consider Miró a major source of inspiration. The Mexican poet and novelist José Emilio Pacheco has recognized Miró's influence on writers of the previous generation such as Agustín Yañez, Ricardo Garibay, Alfonso Reyes, Francisco Pina, and José Enrique Moreno de Tagle. On the other hand, two of Miró's illustrious contemporaries, Ortega y Gasset and Jorge Luis Borges, considered his dense and metaphorical descriptions difficult to grasp, suggesting that Miró's style was eccentric even for modernist writers.

Scholarly interest in Gabriel Miró revived in the 1960s among Hispanists inside and outside of Spain. Nobel laureate Guillén ranked Miró's works among the five most exquisite examples of Spanish letters in his essay *Language and Poetry* (1961). The centennial of his birth in 1979 brought about a new recognition of his position in the Spanish canon parallel to that of Azorín and Ramón Pérez de Ayala.

## Letters:

José Guardiola Ortíz, *Biografía íntima de Gabriel Miró (el hombre y su obra) autógrafos inéditos, anécdotas, bibliografía* (Alicante: Guardiola, 1935);

Jorge Guillén, *En torno a Gabriel Miró: Breve epistolario* (Madrid: Arte y Bibliofilia, 1969).

## Bibliographies:

*Gabriel Miró (1879–1930): Vida y obra-bibliografía-antología* (New York: Instituto de Las Españas en Estados Unidos, 1936);

Ricardo López Landeira, *An Annotated Bibliography of Gabriel Miró (1900–1978)* (Manhattan, Kans.: Society of Spanish and Spanish-American Studies, 1978).

## Biographies:

Adolfo Lizón Gadea, *Gabriel Miró y los de su tiempo* (Madrid: Gredos, 1944);

Vicente Ramos, *Vida y obra de Gabriel Miró* (Madrid: Artes Gráficas CIM, 1955);

Oscar Esplá, *Evocación de Gabriel Miró* (Alicante: Caja de Ahorros del Sureste de España, 1961);

Joaquín Fuster Pérez, *Gabriel Miró en Polop* (Alicante: Caja de Ahorros Provincial, 1975);

Ramos, *Gabriel Miró* (Alicante: Instituto de Estudios Alicantinos, 1979);

Juan Gil-Albert, *Gabriel Miró, remembranza* (Madrid: La Torre, 1980);

Heliodoro Carpintero, *Gabriel Miró en el recuerdo: Con un epistolario inédito de Miró,* prologue by Julián Marías (Alicante: Universidad de Alicante y Caja de Ahorros Provincial de Alicante, 1983).

**References:**

Azorín, (pseudonym of José Martínez Ruiz), "Gabriel Miró (1879–1930): In memoriam," in his *Obras completas,* volume 6, edited by Ángel Cruz Rueda (Madrid: Aguilar, 1948);

Mariano Baquero Goyanes, "¿Azorín y Miró?" in his *Perspectivismo y contraste: (De Cadalso a Pérez de Ayala)* (Madrid: Gredos, 1963), pp. 83–160;

Teresa Barbero, *Las figuras femeninas en la obra de Gabriel Miró* (Alicante: Instituto de Estudios Alicantinos, Diputación Provincial de Alicante, 1981);

Alfred W. Becker, *El hombre y su circunstancia en las obras de Gabriel Miró* (Madrid: Revista de Occidente, 1958);

Marian G. R. Coope, *Reality and Time in the Oleza Novels of Gabriel Miró* (London: Tamesis, 1984);

*Cuadernos de Literatura contemporánea,* special Miró issue, nos. 5–6 (1942);

Frances T. Fields, *El paisaje en la obra de Gabriel Miró* (Guatemala City: Universidad de San Carlos de Guatemala, 1963);

Carlos Enrique García Lara, *Gabriel Miró y las figuras del deseo* (Alicante: Universidad de Alicante, 1999);

Juan Gil-Albert, *Gabriel Miró, el escritor y el hombre* (Valencia: Cuadernos de Cultura, 1931);

Jorge Guillén, "Gabriel Miró: Lenguaje suficiente," in his *Lenguaje y poesía* (Madrid: Revista de Occidente, 1962), pp. 185–232;

María del Carmen Hernández Valcárcel and Carmen Escudero Martínez, eds., *La narrativa lírica de Azorín y Miró* (Alicante: Caja de Ahorros de Alicante y Murcia, Obras Sociales, 1986);

James H. Hoddie, *Unidad y universalidad de la ficción modernista de Gabriel Miró* (Madrid: Orígenes, 1992);

Roberta Johnson, *El ser y la palabra en Gabriel Miró* (Madrid: Fundamentos, 1995);

Edmund L. King, *Gabriel Miró y "El mundo según es"* (Madrid: Palma de Mallorca, 1961);

C. A. Longhurst, *Gabriel Miró:* Nuestro Padre San Daniel *and* El obispo leproso (London: Grant & Cutler, 1994);

Richard López Landeira, *Gabriel Miró: Trilogía de Sigüenza* (Chapel Hill: Department of Romance Languages, University of North Carolina, 1972);

López Landeira, ed., *Critical Essays on Gabriel Miró* (Manhattan, Kans.: Society of Spanish and Spanish-American Studies / Ann Arbor, Mich.: University Microfilms International, 1979);

Ian R. Macdonald, "Caminos y lugares: Gabriel Miró's *El obispo leproso," Modern Language Review,* 77 (1982): 606–617;

Macdonald, *Gabriel Miró: His Private Library and His Literary Background* (London: Tamesis, 1975);

Francisco Márquez-Villanueva, ed., *Harvard University Conference in Honor of Gabriel Miró (1879–1930),* Harvard Studies in Romance Languages, no. 39 (Cambridge, Mass.: Department of Romance Languages and Literatures of Harvard University / Lexington, Ky.: French Forum, 1982);

Yvette E. Miller, *La novelística de Gabriel Miró* (Madrid: Códice, 1975);

Ernest Elwood Norden, *The Development of Imagery and Symbol in the Works of Gabriel Miró,* dissertation, University of California, Berkeley, 1974;

Antonio Porpetta, *El mundo sonoro de Gabriel Miró* (Alicante: Fundación Caja del Mediterráneo, 1996);

Jacqueline van Praag-Chantraine, *Gabriel Miró ou Le visage du Levant, terre d'Espagne* (Paris: Nizet, 1959);

Vicente Ramos, *El mundo de Gabriel Miró* (Madrid: Gredos, 1964);

José L. Román del Cerro and others, eds., *Homenaje a Gabriel Miró: Estudios de crítica literaria en el centenario de su nacimiento, 1879–1979* (Alicante: Caja de Ahorros Provincial, 1979);

Josep María de Sagarra, *Memòries* (Barcelona: Edicions 62, 1999), pp. 608–609;

Carlos Sánchez Gimeno, *Gabriel Miró y su obra* (Valencia: Castalia, 1960);

Raymond Vidal, *Gabriel Miró: Le Style, les moyens d'expresion* (Bordeaux: Féret, 1964);

Dario Villanueva, ed., *La novela lírica I: Azorín, Gabriel Miró* (Madrid: Taurus, 1983);

Francisco Marquez Villanueva, *La esfinge mironiana y otros estudios de Gabriel Miró* (Alicante: Instituto de Cultura "Juan Gil-Albert," Diputación Provincial, 1990).

**Papers:**

A collection of Gabriel Miró's papers is in the Biblioteca Nacional in Madrid.

# Rosa Montero

*(3 January 1951 –    )*

## Alma Amell
*Pontifical College Josephinum*

BOOKS: *España para tí para siempre* (Madrid: A.Q. Ediciones, 1976);

*Crónica del desamor* (Madrid: Debate, 1979); translated by Cristina de la Torre and Diana Glad as *Absent Love: A Chronicle* (Lincoln: Nebraska University Press, 1991);

*La función Delta* (Madrid: Debate, 1981); translated by Kari Easton and Yolanda Molina Gavilán as *The Delta Function* (Lincoln: Nebraska University Press, 1991);

*Cinco años de País* (Madrid: Debate, 1982);

*Te trataré como a una reina* (Barcelona: Seix Barral, 1983);

*Amado amo* (Madrid: Debate, 1988);

*Temblor* (Barcelona: Seix Barral, 1990);

*El nido de los sueños* (Madrid: Siruela, 1991);

*Bella y oscura* (Barcelona: Seix Barral, 1993);

*La vida desnuda: Una mirada apasionada sobre nuestro mundo* (Madrid: El País/Aguilar, 1994);

*Historias de mujeres* (Madrid: Alfaguara, 1995);

*Entrevistas* (Madrid: El País/Aguilar, 1996);

*Las barbaridades de Bárbara* (Madrid: Alfaguara, 1996);

*La hija del caníbal* (Madrid: Espasa, 1997);

*El viaje fantástico de Bárbara* (Madrid: Alfaguara, 1997);

*Bárbara contra el doctor Colmillos* (Madrid: Alfaguara, 1998);

*Amantes y enemigos* (Madrid: Alfaguara, 1998);

*Pasiones: Amores y desamores que han cambiado la Historia* (Madrid: Aguilar, 1999);

*El corazón del Tártaro* (Madrid: Espasa, 2001);

*Estampas bostonianas y otros viajes* (Barcelona: Península, 2002);

*La loca de la casa* (Madrid: Alfaguara, 2003);

*Historia del rey transparente* (Madrid: Alfaguara, 2005).

PLAY PRODUCTION: *El cristal de agua fría,* libretto by Montero, music by Marisa Manchado, Madrid, Centro Nacional de Artes Escénicas, 12 April 1994.

PRODUCED SCRIPTS: *Media naranja,* television, twelve episodes, Televisión Española, 1986.

OTHER: "Paulo Pumilio," in *Doce relatos de mujeres,* edited by Ymelda Navajo (Madrid: Alianza, 1982), pp. 69–93;

"El puñal en la garganta," in *Relatos urbanos* (Madrid: Alfaguara, 1994);

*Las madres no lloran en Disneylandia* (Madrid: Relato, 1999);

"Parecía un infierno," in *Cuentos del mar* (Madrid: Ediciones B, 2001).

Rosa Montero has been one of Spain's best-selling fiction writers since her first novel, *Crónica del desamor* (translated as *Absent Love: A Chronicle,* 1991), was published in 1979. She is one in a long line of Spanish authors whose main preoccupations are love, death, and Spain's history and society. Her humorous style in presenting these themes is reminiscent of Miguel de Cervantes, Francisco de Quevedo, and Mariano José de Larra, as well as the contemporary writer Francisco Umbral. Because of the universal nature of her themes, she is one of the most widely read Spanish authors abroad; her books have been translated into English, German, French, Portuguese (in Portugal and in Brazil), Greek, Italian, Russian, Polish, Romanian, Slovenian, Croatian, Serbian, Dutch, Chinese, Korean, Turkish, Danish, Swedish, and Norwegian.

Rosa María Montero Gayo was born in Madrid on 3 January 1951 to Pascual Montero and Amalia Gayo Montero. Her father was a *banderillero* (bullfighter's aide) who retired and started a brick factory when Rosa was five. Because of long-term illnesses (tuberculosis and anemia) and the fact that her only brother was five years older and spent most of his time with his friends, Montero created an imaginary world of her own. She loved to read and write but did not have access to children's books. Her uncle brought her adventure stories from his library, so Montero read and wrote about cowboys and Indians, crime stories, and everything else that this supply of books and her own imagination provided. She did not go to school until she was nine; she entered the Instituto Beatriz Galindo

*Rosa Montero (photograph by Pablo Juliá; from the cover for* El nido de los sueños, *1991;*
*Thomas Cooper Library, University of South Carolina)*

for girls, which she remembers as a "brutal" experience. She did not start reading the conventional books for children until she was ten. Even then, adventure stories, such as the William Brown series by Richmal Crompton, were her favorite.

As she grew older, Montero lost her confidence in her ability to create stories and felt that she did not have enough to tell that would fill a book. She still loved to write, however, so she decided to study journalism and also ventured into psychology, while collaborating with independent theater groups in Madrid, such as Tábano and Canon. At seventeen she enrolled in the Facultad de Filosofía y Letras (School of Philosophy and Literature) of the Universidad Complutense in Madrid. The next year, 1969, she started studying journalism.

In 1969 Montero started to work as a journalist and in the course of seven years wrote for publications such as *Teleradio, Pueblo, Arriba, Contrastes, Garbo, Telesiete, Jacaranda, El Indiscreto, Mundo Diario, Posible, Fotogramas,* and *Hermano Lobo.* She also wrote the scripts for the twelve-episode television series *Media naranja* (Half Orange), which was aired in 1986 by National Spanish Television and later in Argentina, where it received the 1988 Martín Fierro Award for best foreign production.

In 1976 Montero published her first book, *España para tí para siempre* (Spain for You, Always), a collection

of interviews from the different media in which she had collaborated. That same year her journalistic career was firmly established when she became a columnist for one of Spain's most influential newspapers, *El País.* In 1978 she earned the Manuel del Arco Award for interviews; it was the first time that a woman had received this prize. As a freelance journalist she has conducted and written more than two thousand interviews.

One of the consequences of her recognition as a skilled interviewer was that in 1979 Debate Publishers asked her to compile a collection of interviews with women. She accepted and signed the contract but soon realized that, instead of producing yet another series of interviews, she would prefer to try her luck at story writing again. After months of indecision and with the deadline approaching, she sat down at her typewriter and began to write. What emerged was a narrative about the daily lives and social struggles of young women during the transition of Spain from a forty-year dictatorship to a democracy after the death of Francisco Franco in 1975. She handed it to the publisher, who liked it and published it as the novel *Crónica del desamor.* Ana, the protagonist, works for a magazine publisher, but unlike Montero she does not succeed in obtaining a permanent position.

In spite of the enormous success of her first novel–which went through twenty-one editions in the thirteen years after its appearance—Montero was not satisfied with her narrative technique. She felt that *Crónica del desamor,* rather than being a novel, was more like the diary of a young woman and almost a factual description of Spain in the late 1970s. In 1980 she earned the National Journalism Award for her newspaper and literary articles and became the first female editor in chief of the Sunday magazine for *El País.* Encouraged by both the reception of her first novel and the recognition of her literary talents, she wrote *La función Delta* (1981; translated as *The Delta Function,* 1991). The title of this novel is the name that the protagonist's lover gives to a phenomenon of short duration and infinite intensity. The novel is the diary of a sixty-year-old woman, Lucía, a movie director and former writer of television commercials, who is lying in a hospital bed dying of a brain tumor and recalls the most memorable and important week in her life, which occurred thirty years earlier. Montero shows significant progress in developing her fiction from a narrative chronicle mixed with dialogue to a narrative that, though framed within a chronicle structure, is innovative in its switching back and forth between a futuristic present (2010) and the past, without creating confusion, by alternating past and present specific days of the week. The characters in this novel are also much better developed than those in *Crónica del desamor.*

In 1982, on the occasion of the fifth anniversary of Spain's post-Francoist parliamentary government, Montero was asked to compile a collection of the most significant interviews that she had conducted from 1977 to 1981. The result was *Cinco años de País* (Five Years of *Nation*), the title of which points to the history of the country as well as of the newspaper.

Montero's third novel, *Te trataré como a una reina* (I Will Treat You Like a Queen), was published in 1983. She opens the book with an article from a tabloid-type magazine about a nightclub singer, Isabel López, who has pushed her boss, Antonio Ortiz, out of a window. Although the article calls Isabel "the murderess," it turns out that Antonio is alive and recovering from multiple fractures and several reconstructive surgeries on his face. The victim's statements about the incident and its consequences for him do not appear until nearly the end of the book.

In 1988 Montero won the Mundo Award for her interviews and the Martín Fierro Award for her scripts for *Media naranja* in Argentina and published her next novel, *Amado amo* (Beloved Boss). In this work Montero elaborates on a theme that was present in her previous novels: the abuse of power by those who rank above others in the social system. The title of the book refers to the enslavement of people to their jobs and superiors. The employees of the Golden Line advertising agency

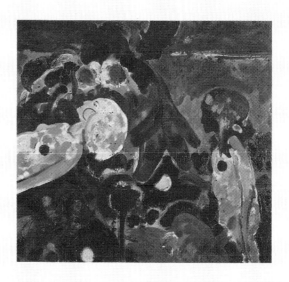

# THE DELTA FUNCTION
## ROSA MONTERO

Translated and with an afterword by Kari Easton and Yolanda Molina Gavilán

*Dust jacket for the English translation (1991) of Montero's 1981 novel,* La función Delta, *in which a sixty-year-old woman dying of a brain tumor looks back thirty years to the most important week in her life (Thomas Cooper Library, University of South Carolina)*

are aware that if they do not perform to the complete satisfaction of their superiors, they will be demoted, fired, or given early retirement. Under this pressure they become enemies and traitors to one another. The protagonist, César, is forced to betray his best friend to guarantee his continued employment.

*Temblor* (1990, Tremor) followed *Amado amo* in a logical sequence. It takes the lust for and fear of power to a new level in which the actions of a few almighty individuals have enveloped the world in an all-absorbing, annihilating mist. Instead of money, crystals are the objects of everyone's desire and give power and prestige to those who possess them. The fear of death, amply discussed in all the previous novels and confronted by Lucía in *La función Delta,* is represented by

*Cover for Montero's first children's book (The Nest of Dreams, 1991),*
*about a girl who becomes trapped in one of her imaginary worlds*
*(Thomas Cooper Library, University of South Carolina)*

the terror of seeing a mist submerge all things and beings in nothingness. The story unfolds several centuries after some apocalyptic event has destroyed everything on earth. The sole survivors were people who lived in spaceships with their families and animals—like Noah and his ark—and started a new life on earth after it cooled off from the disaster. They are forced to regress to a primal form of existence. In addition, the protagonist, Agua Fría, in her search for a way to dissolve the mist, travels through several eras and civilizations, all the way to a Stone Age community. Thus, in this novel, Montero has significantly expanded the narrative world in which events unfold. Likewise, her characters range from resourceful and persevering to fascinating creatures such as Pecado Doble, a hermaphroditic prostitute, and Torbellino, a spirited and intelligent Lilliputian woman with a sixth sense, who helps Agua Fría save the world from annihilation by the mist.

Montero's first work for children, *El nido de los sueños* (1991, The Nest of Dreams), was the fulfillment of a promise to write a book for her niece and nephew. The protagonist, Gabi, prefers being alone to playing with her ten siblings and school friends. Her favorite game is to invent a fantastic world called Balbalú where she is the heroine of many adventures. One day she cannot find her way out of this world of talking animals, surprises, and dangers. But when, at the end, she suddenly appears back home, she immediately starts dreaming of escaping to new imaginary worlds.

In *Bella y oscura* (1993, Beautiful and Dark), a novel for adults, Montero portrays the world from another girl's perspective. Her name, Baba, is similar to the one that Gabi assumed for her fantasy world; but Baba's world is a painfully realistic one. Like Agua Fría of *Temblor,* Baba has lost her mother at a young and vulnerable age. Her world is limited first to an orphanage and later to the house and neighborhood where she lives with the dysfunctional family consisting of her uncle, aunt, cousin, and grandmother. Baba waits patiently for her father, who is in prison but who she hopes will come home soon and take her away. A Lilliputian character named Airelai appears on the family's doorstep and remains with them until Baba's father arrives. Airelai, like Torbellino in *Temblor,* expresses both the darkness and beauty of the world. The depraved, depressing world of *Te trataré como a una reina* and the magical one of *Temblor* come together in Baba's daily surroundings and Airelai's enchanting stories. Airelai offers the girl an escape from bleak reality; but ultimately she flees with Baba's father, leaving Baba behind.

*La vida desnuda: Una mirada apasionada sobre nuestro mundo* (1994, Naked Life: A Passionate Look at Our World) is a collection of articles that Montero wrote for *El País* between 1983 and 1993. Its subtitle explains what these articles have in common. In February 1994 Montero received a journalism award, the Premio Correo, for her interview with the Basque secretary of the interior, José María Atutxa, in the newspaper *El correo Español/El Pueblo Vaseo.*

Two months later, the opera *El cristal de agua fría* (Cold Water Crystal), for which Montero wrote the libretto based on her novel *Temblor,* premiered in Madrid. In 1996 Montero published the first in a series of children's stories about the adventures of Bárbara, another child with a vivid imagination. The rest of this series came out in 1997 and 1998.

Montero published *La hija del caníbal* (The Cannibal's Daughter) in 1997. In this work, under the guise of a mystery novel, human existence is contemplated and experienced through three characters, representing three stages in life. Lucía is a middle-aged woman whose husband, Ramón, disappears from the bathroom of an airport while they are waiting for a flight. In the search for her husband she receives help and companionship from two neighbors: Adrián, who is twenty-one and becomes Lucía's lover, and Félix, an eighty-year-old former bullfighter who joined the Spanish anarchists when he was young. The events related to the search for Ramón are interwoven with the memories of Félix, whose stories relate historical facts–tinged with some fiction–about the anarchists' activities in Spain and Mexico; bullfighting is an additional theme. The author manipulates fiction and reality in the account of Lucía, who intentionally changes certain details of her story and sometimes appears in the first person and at other times in the third person. The novel won the Primavera Award. Antonio Serrano directed and wrote the screenplay for a 2003 movie version of *La hija del caníbal* (titled *Lucía, Lucía* in the United States and Mexico), starring Cecilia Roth.

After *La hija del caníbal* Montero published two collections about love relationships: *Amantes y enemigos* (1998, Lovers and Enemies), a volume of short stories; and *Pasiones: Amores y desamores que han cambiado la Historia* (1999, Passions: Loves and Unloves that Changed History), a collection of essays on famous couples ranging from Hernán Cortés and La Malinche to John Lennon and Yoko Ono. One of the short stories in *Amantes y enemigos,* "Paulo Pumilio," written in 1981, was the seed of *Bella y oscura.*

The interplay of fiction and reality that was playfully present in *La hija del caníbal* is taken to a more sophisticated level in Montero's 2001 novel, *El corazón del Tártaro* (The Heart of the Tartar). It is the heartrending story of a young woman, Sofía Zarzamala, whose abusive father and manic-depressive mother died when she was young. Since their older sister went away to live her own life, Zarza, as Sofía was nicknamed, and her brother were left to fend for themselves and also had to take care of their mentally handicapped younger brother. They both became addicted to heroin and started robbing banks to support their habit. When they were caught and imprisoned, Zarza received a lighter sentence in exchange for testifying against her brother, who now seeks revenge and haunts her. Incorporated in this story is that of *El caballero de la rosa* (The Knight of the Rose), a book that Zarza is preparing for the publisher for whom she works. The narrator says that the book "una edición de lujo . . . de la hermosa leyenda escrita en el siglo XII por Chrétien de Troyes y descubierta por casualidad, en los años setenta, por un joven medievalista inglés llamado Harris entre los manuscritos de un viejo monasterio" (is a luxury edition . . . of the beautiful legend written in the twelfth century by Chrétien de Troyes and discovered by coin-

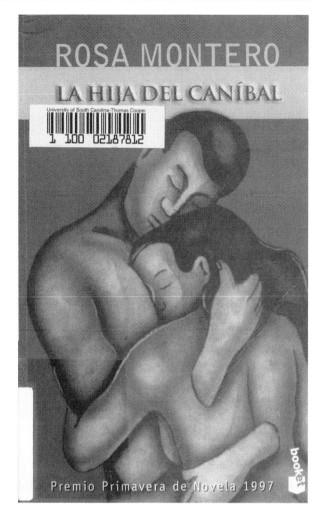

*Cover for a 1993 paperback edition of Montero's 1997 novel (The Cannibal's Daughter), about a woman whose husband disappears from the airport where they are waiting for a flight (Thomas Cooper Library, University of South Carolina)*

cidence, in the seventies, by a young English medievalist named Harris, among the manuscripts of an old monastery). Montero became a victim of her own intrigue when reviewers of the manuscript for her novel thought that *El caballero de la rosa* really existed. She had to think of a way to make the reader doubt its veracity without breaking the spell of the mystery surrounding the origin of the story. She does so at the end of the book by pointing out the insecurity of life, the inaccuracy of human memories, and the subjectivity of people's views of the world. Along these lines, she says that maybe the Knight of the Rose existed, or maybe he was an invention of Harris, or even Harris may have been an invention.

Since the beginning of her journalistic career, Montero has traveled to many countries and lived on several continents. The fruit of these experiences is *Estampas bostonianas y otros viajes* (2002, Bostonian Impressions and Other Journeys), a collection of her travel articles from *El País*. In 2003 she published *La loca de la casa* (The Madwoman of the House), which is part essay, part fiction, and part autobiography. The work received the 2003 Qué Leer Prize (a readers' award) for books in Spanish and the 2005 Grinzane Cavour Prize for Foreign Literature published in Italy. In September 2005 she published the novel *Historia del Rey transparente* (Story of the Transparent King), an adventure story with fantastic, historical, and pseudo-historical elements set in twelfth-century France; she has called it the most ambitious book she has ever written and has said that it took eight years to complete. The novel narrates ten years in the life of a peasant girl, Leola, who at fifteen is left to fend for herself in a war-torn world. To survive, she takes a dead soldier's armor and disguises herself as a man. Through all her tribulations Leola continually sees on the horizon the island of Avalon, which is ruled by a wise and beautiful queen; only women live there, death does not exist, and it is always spring. The image gives Leola courage and symbolizes hope for a better future.

Rosa Montero continues the tradition of writing to entertain as well as to stir the consciousness of her contemporaries, drawing their attention to both the deficiencies and beauty of daily existence. As a successor of Cervantes, Quevedo, and Larra, she feels that it is the writer's task to shake the public out of its complacent material existence and self-centeredness. Even though she is successful at exploring different and advanced narrative techniques, the themes of love, death, and survival in an increasingly dehumanized world will always be present in her novels.

**References:**

Haydée Ahumada Peña, *Poder y género en la narrativa de Rosa Montero* (Madrid: Pliegos, 1999);

Concha Alborg, "Metaficción y feminismo en Rosa Montero," *Revista de Estudios Hispánicos,* 22 (January 1988): 67–76;

Alma Amell, "La narrativa de Rosa Montero, crónica de la marginación," *Letras femeninas,* 18 (1992): 74–82;

Amell, "El personaje masculino en las novelas de Rosa Montero," *España Contemporánea,* 5, no. 2 (1992): 105–110;

Amell, *Rosa Montero's Odyssey* (Lanham, Md.: University Press of America, 1994);

Joan Lipman Brown, "Rosa Montero: From Journalist to Novelist," in *Women Writers of Contemporary Spain: Exiles in the Homeland,* edited by Brown (Newark: Delaware University Press, 1991), pp. 240–257;

Catherine Davies, *Contemporary Feminist Fiction in Spain: The Work of Montserrat Roig and Rosa Montero* (Oxford & Providence, R.I.: Berg, 1994);

Elena Gascón Vera, "Rosa Montero ante la escritura femenina," *Anales de la Literatura Española Contemporánea,* 15, no. 13 (1990): 275–283;

Kathleen W. Glenn, "Reader Expectations and Rosa Montero's *La función Delta,*" *Letras Peninsulares,* 1, no. 1 (1988): 87–96;

Glenn, "Victimized by Misreading: Rosa Montero's *Te trataré como a una reina,*" *Anales de la Literatura Española Contemporánea,* 12, no. 1–2 (1987): 191–202;

Javier González Escudero, "*Bella y oscura,* de Rosa Montero: Entre el resplandor y la muerte," *Anales de la Literatura Española Contemporánea,* 24, no. 1–2 (1999): 85–101;

González Escudero, "Rosa Montero ante la creación literaria: 'Escribir es vivir,'" *Arizona Journal of Hispanic Cultural Studies,* 4 (2000): 211–224;

Mary C. Harges, *Synergy and Subversion in the Second Stage Novels of Rosa Montero* (New York: Peter Lang, 2000);

Vanessa Knights, *The Search for Identity in the Narrative of Rosa Montero* (Lewiston, N.Y.: Edwin Mellen Press, 1999);

Emilio de Miguel Martínez, *La primera narrativa de Rosa Montero* (Salamanca: Ediciones Universidad de Salamanca, 1983);

Francisco Umbral, "Spleen de Madrid: Rosa," *El País,* 18 November 1983, p. 31;

Javier Villán, "Rosa Montero," *La Nueva España,* 8 December 1983, p. 23.

# Antonio Muñoz Molina

*(10 January 1956 –   )*

María del Mar López-Cabrales
*Colorado State University*

BOOKS: *Beatus Ille* (Barcelona: Seix Barral, 1986);

*Diario del Nautilus* (Granada: Diputación Provincial de Granada, 1986);

*El invierno en Lisboa* (Barcelona: Seix Barral, 1987); translated by Sonia Soto as *Winter in Lisbon* (London: Granta, 1999);

*El Robinson urbano* (Pamplona: Pamiela, 1988);

*Las otras vidas* (Madrid: Mondadori, 1988);

*Beltenebros* (Barcelona: Seix Barral, 1989); translated by Peter Bush as *Prince of Shadows* (London: Quartet, 1993);

*El jinete polaco* (Barcelona: Planeta, 1991);

*Córdoba de los Omeyas* (Barcelona: Planeta, 1991);

*La verdad de la ficción* (Seville: Renacimiento, 1992);

*Los misterios de Madrid* (Barcelona: Seix Barral, 1992);

*Nada del otro mundo* (Madrid: Espasa-Calpe, 1993);

*Por qué no es útil la literatura? La realidad de la ficción y Sostener la Mirada,* by Muñoz Molina and Luis García Montero (Madrid: Hiperión, 1993);

*El dueño del secreto* (Madrid: Ollero & Ramos, 1994);

*Las apariencias* (Madrid: Santillana, 1995);

*Ardor guerrero: Una memoria militar* (Madrid: Alfaguara, 1995);

*Picasso, 1923: Arlequín con espejo y La flauta de Pan,* by Muñoz Molina, Pierre Daix, and Tomàs Llorens (Madrid: Fundación Colección Thyssen-Bornemisza, 1995);

*La huerta del Edén: Escritos y diatribas sobre Andalucía* (Madrid: Ollero & Ramos, 1996);

*Escrito en un instante* (Palma de Mallorca: Calima, 1997);

*Plenilunio* (Madrid: Alfaguara, 1997);

*El Roto,* by Muñoz Molina, Andrés Rábago, and Felipe Hérnandez Cava (Seville: Diputación Provincial, 1997);

*Pura alegría* (Madrid: Alfaguara, 1998);

*La colina de los sacrificios* (Madrid: Ollero & Ramos, 1998);

*Carlota Fainberg* (Madrid: Alfaguara, 1999);

*Unas gafas de Pla* (Madrid: Aguilar, 2000);

*En ausencia de Blanca* (Madrid: Alfaguara, 2001);

*Sefarad: Una novela de novelas* (Madrid: Alfaguara, 2001); translated by Margaret Sayers Peden as *Sepharad* (Orlando, Fla.: Harcourt, 2003);

*Antonio Muñoz Molina (photograph by Elvira Lindo; from the dust jacket for* Sepharad, *2003; Richland County Public Library)*

*José Guerrero: El artista que vuelve* (Granada: Diputación Provincial de Granada, 2001);

*La vida por delante* (Madrid: Alfaguara, 2002);

*Ventanas de Manhattan* (Barcelona: Seix Barral, 2004).

**Collection:** *La huella de unas palabras: Antología de textos de Antonio Muñoz Molina,* edited by José Manuel Fajardo (Madrid: Espasa, 1999).

SELECTED PERIODICAL PUBLICATION–UNCOLLECTED: "25 años de literatura en democracia," *Babelia: Suplemento literario de El País,* 27 May 2000, p. 8.

On 16 June 1996, at the age of forty, Antonio Muñoz Molina became the youngest member of the Real Academia Española de la Lengua (Royal Academy of the Spanish Language). A prolific author, he has published two dozen books since the mid 1980s, from collections of newspaper articles such as *Diario del Nautilus* (1986, Journal of the Nautilus) to best-selling novels.

Muñoz Molina was born in Úbeda, Jaén, on 10 January 1956, into a lower-class family. His parents were Francisco Muñoz and Antonia Molina; he has a sister, Juana, who was born in 1962. He expressed an interest in literature early, writing imitations of Gustavo Adolfo Bécquer, Pablo Neruda, Federico García Lorca, Jorge Luis Borges, Adolfo Bioy Casares, William Faulkner, Juan Carlos Onetti, and Gabriel García Márquez. He went to Madrid to study journalism. He did not finish his degree and in 1974 returned to Andalusia, where he majored in art history at the University of Granada.

Muñoz Molina is part of a generation of leftist writers who lived through the Spanish transition to democracy and started to publish in the 1980s. On various occasions, he has been depicted as a person who is ideologically socialist but whose political commitment has certain limits. When he was studying in Madrid, Muñoz Molina was detained by the police and was jailed for forty-eight hours. He left saying that Francisco Franco's regime could last two hundred years but that he would not return to jail for his political convictions. This attitude is associated with his general shyness and timidity, characteristics that have marked him for his entire life. In an interview with his friend, the painter José Manuel Fajardo, included in *La huella de unas palabras: Antología de textos de Antonio Muñoz Molina* (1999, The Footprint of Some Words: Anthology of Texts of Antonio Muñoz Molina), he said that "Esa cobardía, ese retraerse ante la expectativa heróica, a mí me devuelve a mi propia infancia, a mi miedo a los niños mayores, a los demás, al mundo. Al modo en que cualquiera me podía hacer daño. Eso, de pequeño me marcó mucho" (This cowardice, this withdrawal from heroic expectations returns me to my own childhood, to my fear of older children, people, the world, and to the fact that anyone could hurt me. This marked me a great deal, since I was little). This sensation of not totally pertaining to a group also can be traced to the end of his adolescence. In the same interview Muñoz Molina explained how he lost friends because of his alienation from the drug culture and sexual revolution of the 1970s.

After receiving his degree from the University of Granada in 1979 and serving in the military in San Sebastián in 1979–1980, Muñoz Molina worked as a municipal employee at the Granada city hall and for area newspapers, including the *Ideal*. His first published writings were newspaper articles from this period. These early articles were collected in 1988 as *El Robinson urbano* (The Urban Robinson).

In 1982 Muñoz Molina married Marilena Vico. They had three children: Antonio, Arturo, and Elena. Muñoz Molina published his first novel, *Beatus Ille* (Latin for "Beautiful Place"), in 1986. It received the Premio Icaro (Icarus Prize) given by *Diario 16* to promising writers for a first novel, and the Premio Crisol (Crucible Prize). The novel follows an investigation undertaken by a student named Minaya to recuperate the life and works of a forgotten writer from the Generation of '27 named Jacinto Solana.

Plots involving Minaya, Solana, and vivid experiences in the mansion of Minaya's uncle Manuel are intertwined with a plot involving a criminal inquiry into the search for the identity of the person who killed Manuel's wife on their wedding night. Here, as in the literary works of García Márquez, Juan Rulfo, and Faulkner, Muñoz Molina introduces an imaginary city, Mágina, which he has continued to develop in later texts. Mágina is a fictional construction of Muñoz Molina's hometown of Úbeda. The young Minaya returns to Mágina to escape political problems and research Solana, who was a personal friend of Manuel's. The action takes place at the end of the 1960s; the murder of Manuel's wife, Mariana, occurred in 1937; and Solana died ten years later, in 1947.

One of the many successes of *Beatus Ille* is the use, as in the majority of Muñoz Molina's texts, of a first-person narrative voice. Here, the narrator is mostly hidden, presenting himself only intermittently in an objective manner that is nearly omniscient. At the end of the novel, the identity of this strange narrator is revealed: it is Solana, who has not died but instead lives in anonymity. The intent of Minaya to investigate Solana results in a maze in which Minaya does not find the truth, or at least what he would like the truth to be. This final paradox is consistent with what Muñoz Molina said to Fajardo: "no hay ningún empeño humano que en el fondo no sea fútil. Si la literatura tiene que ser revelación, continuamente tiene que estar incurriendo en paradojas. . . . la literatura te hace saber como ningún otro sistema de conocimiento que las cosas son memorables, pero que al mismo tiempo no son nada. . . . eso de nuevo tiene una profunda dimensión moral: hay que hacer las cosas aun cuando pueda suponerse que son inútiles. Porque la inutilidad es la gran coartada de los conformistas" (there is no human undertaking that at its core is not futile. . . . literature has to be a revelation, always having to take place in paradoxes. . . . literature makes you understand like no other system of understanding that things are memorable, but at the same time that they are nothing: one has to do things when one can, knowing that they might be useless, because uselessness is a great alibi for conformists).

Muñoz Molina's second novel, *El invierno en Lisboa* (1987; translated as *Winter in Lisbon,* 1999), made him famous both nationally and internationally. For it, he won in 1987 both the Premio Nacional de Narrativa (National Literature Prize for Narrative) and the Premio de la Crítica (Critic's Prize). *El invierno en Lisboa* begins with the main character, Santiago Biralbo, recalling the story while in a Madrid nightclub. Biralbo is a jazz pianist who is in love with Lucrecia, the wife of Malcolm, who is an illegal art exporter. Intrigue grows from the belief of those who are pursuing Malcolm that Biralbo is his collaborator. Biralbo's recollections carry the reader to another music club in San Sebastián and then to Lisbon, the city where the plot develops until Biralbo escapes to avoid prison. Biralbo's relationship with Lucrecia develops in a series of encounters shaped by the romantic and mysterious atmosphere of the novel. The narrator is a good friend of Biralbo.

Muñoz Molina has said that Biralbo is a romantic hero, adding that this novel is a testament to this period of his life when everything—including bourbon, jazz, and cinema—was idealized. As he told Fajardo,

> Yo escribí *El invierno en Lisboa* así porque no sabía hacerla de otro modo. No escribí una novela policíaca porque me apeteciera, es que fue la única manera en que supe hacerlo, porque yo pensaba escribirla como una novela mucho menos romántica, sin elementos mitológicos, y pensaba incluso que se desarrollara en Granada. Pero no funcionaba. ¿Cómo lo resolví? Trasladándola al plano del romanticismo de la novela de intriga, que era coherente porque el romanticismo formaba parte tanto de la materia novelesca como de mi propia percepción del mundo.

> (I wrote *El invierno en Lisboa* the way I did because I did not know how to do it any other way. I did not write a police novel because it appealed to me; it was the only way I knew how to do it. I thought about writing it as a much less romantic novel, without the mythological elements, and I even thought about having it take place in Granada. But it did not work. How did I resolve it? I made the novel into a romantic mystery. It was coherent because romanticism was such an important part of the fictional material as well as my own perception of the world.)

Muñoz Molina also said that when he wrote this novel, he thought he was writing something totally realistic. The image the reader has of Biralbo at the end of the novel is based on a combination of distinct perspectives. Muñoz Molina suggests that such a cubist portrait

Cover for a 1996 paperback edition of Muñoz Molina's 1989 novel (translated as Prince of Shadows, 1993), about a Communist secret agent sent back to Spain from exile in Britain to kill a traitor to the organization (Thomas Cooper Library, University of South Carolina)

is more accurate than any possible objective description of the pianist himself.

In 1988 Muñoz Molina published a collection of short stories, *Las otras vidas* (The Other Lives). A year later, his third novel, *Beltenebros* (translated as *Prince of Shadows,* 1993), appeared, which in 1992 was adapted into a movie by the director Pilar Miró. *Beltenebros* marks the beginning of a series of novels based in Madrid, including *Los misterios de Madrid* (1992, The Mysteries of Madrid) and *El dueño del secreto* (1994, The Owner of the Secret). Gonzalo Navajas, in his *Teoría y práctica de la novela española* (1994, Theory and Practice of the Spanish Novel), considers *Beltenebros* a postmodern novel because it demonstrates the inability to control what it means to be human within a contradictory, disintegrated, and nearly chaotic society. Salvador

Oropesa, in his *La novelística de Antonio Muñoz Molina: Sociedad civil y literatura lúdica* (1999, The Novels of Antonio Muñoz Molina: Civil Society and Ludic Literature), asserts that Muñoz Molina's postmodern techniques are necessary to tell clearly the story of an historical-psychological absurdity: "Los luchadores por la libertad son personas que no creen en la libertad y que en última instancia luchan por imponer otro sistema de faltas de libertades" (The fighters for liberty are people who do not believe in liberty and that in the end, fight to impose another system that lacks freedom).

In *Beltenebros* the main character, Darman, is a secret agent and skilled Communist Party organizer who is exiled in Britain. He is sent to Spain to kill a traitor to the organization, Andrade, who has already disappeared. At a nightclub show, the woman onstage, Rebeca Osorio, makes Darman remember a trip to Madrid at the end of World War II when he was in pursuit of another traitor, Walter, who became a police informant after having been a party organizer. On his earlier trip, Darman had killed Walter, and Rebeca was Darman's lover. Darman's memories of the case involving Walter begin to mix with the current one involving Andrade. Gradually, he becomes convinced of the innocence of Andrade, who ends up dying at the hands of Luque, a leftist political activist. Through a series of coincidences Darman learns that a mysterious person, Ugarte, is responsible for everything in this case. He discovers that Ugarte is actually the activist Valdivia, who, after faking his death, has lived in hiding. Valdivia ultimately falls to his death in an old and abandoned movie theater.

Muñoz Molina has said that *Beltenebros* is a bitter, but not dishonest, book. Among other things, Darman is always fighting against the false image that others have of him as hero, which condemns him to be something that he does not want to be. *Beltenebros* is a novel full of heartless characters, which is somewhat unusual in the works of Muñoz Molina. Only Andrade is treated kindly in the novel.

In the 1990s Muñoz Molina became one of the best-selling novelists in Spain. In 1991 he published two books: *Córdoba de los Omeyas* (Cordoba during the Omeyas), a travel book with novelistic elements, and his influential fourth novel, *El jinete polaco* (The Polish Rider). In *Córdoba de los Omeyas* Muñoz Molina offers a literary landscape of a city whose mosaics and whitewashed walls on houses, palaces, and cathedrals are testimonies to a period of splendor in Spain, when Córdoba was the cultural capital of the Western world. As he relates, "Cada mañana, cada uno de los días de mi breve viaje, yo buscaba a Córdoba en Córdoba y me habituaba al deslumbramiento y a la quieta aventura de encontrar lo inesperado y lo desconocido al mismo tiempo que lo presentía. Era como si la ciudad fuese creciendo ante mí y se multiplicara ante mis pasos" (Every morning, every one of the days of the brief trip, I searched for Córdoba in Córdoba, and I became accustomed to the glare and the motionless adventure of encountering the unexpected and the unknown, while at the same time presenting it. It was as if the city were growing in front of me and multiplying before my steps). For the author, Córdoba represents the discovery of perspective and the duality of the historic moment. The mosque exists in "la sombra de las naves y la claridad del patio, la selva aritmética de las columnas y la arquitectura vegetal de los naranjos y las palmeras" (the shadow of the naves and the clarity of the patio, the mathematical forest of columns and vegetable architecture of the oranges and palms).

*El jinete polaco* was a popular and critical success in Spain. It became a best-seller and won the Premio Planeta (Planet Prize) and the Premio Nacional de Narrativa (National Literature Prize for Narrative) in 1992. In the novel, Muñoz Molina presents the need to remember as an essential path for assuming one's identity. Manuel and Nadia, two people without roots, fulfill their needs to rediscover themselves through a long night of love and dialogue in New York. Manuel's marginal condition grows from his separation from his family, while Nadia's is a result of her father's forced exile to North America during the Franco regime. Their memories are linked to the city of Mágina and its streets and people.

The novel explores the importance of memories in three parts. In the first part, "El reino de las voces" (The Kingdom of the Voices), Manuel looks through a trunk that Nadia's father, the commander Galaz, took with him to New York. The trunk contains a manuscript of recollections written by the subcommander Florencio Pérez. It was rescued by Lorencito Quesada, a local journalist that Muñoz Molina uses in many of his novels that take place in Mágina. This part of the novel introduces characters from Mágina such as Mercurio, the doctor; Otto Zenner, the old German photographer; and *la guardesa,* an incorruptible woman in the town.

The second part, "Jinete en la tormenta" (Riders on the Storm), the title of which comes from a song by the Doors, focuses on Manuel's and Nadia's ups and downs as students at the Instituto de Enseñanza Media high school, where they both attend without noticing each other. One plot concerns Nadia's relationships with Praxis, who is an admired and rebel professor, and her friends Serrano, Martín, Felix, and Marina. The section pays the most attention, however, to Manuel's family, people from the country who sell fruit in the plaza, whose desires, such as Manuel's to go to Madrid and to break with the destiny that ties him to his small town, are frustrated.

The third part, "El jinete polaco," takes its title from a Rembrandt painting. In this section Muñoz Molina examines the present moment and the passion that devours, and at the same time reinvigorates, Manuel and Nadia.

After the publication of *El jinete polaco* and its broad recognition, Muñoz Molina was invited in 1993 to spend a semester as writer in residence at the University of Virginia. The invitation was a great honor for him because Faulkner had once held the same position. In "Conversación con Antonio Muñoz Molina" (1994, Conversation with Antonio Muñoz Molina), Elizabeth Scarlett recalls her acquaintance with the author in Virginia: "Ano se le escapaba nada a su mirada, una mezcla de cejas lorquianas con ojos de búho salido de la sierra de Mágina. . . . Al cruzar el umbral de una puerta que daba a una taberna rústica o a una noche charlottesviliana de luna llena, era frecuente oirlo exclamar 'Qué ambientazo!' . . . uno sabía que este ambiente ya quedaba grabado para infundir alguna narrativa futura" (Nothing escaped his gaze, a mixture of eyebrows like Lorca with eyes of an owl emerging from the mountains of Mágina. . . . Upon entering a rustic tavern under a full moon in Charlottesville, you frequently heard him exclaim, 'What ambiance!' . . . and you knew that the ambiance had already been recorded for a future narrative).

In 1997 Muñoz Molina published *Escrito en un instante* (Written in an Instant). It follows the example and tradition of many great Spanish opinion writers such as Mariano José de Larra, Clarín (Leopoldo Alas), and many authors from the Generation of '98 such as José Ortega y Gasset and Corpus Barga. The first part of the book is a collection of short articles, all less than fifteen lines, that he was assigned to write in February 1988 for the newspaper *Diario 16*. In the second part of *Escrito en un instante,* Muñoz Molina includes assignments from the Radio Nacional in 1992 telling about both true and fictitious walks.

Muñoz Molina's 1999 short novel, *Carlota Fainberg,* was influenced by his brief stay in the United States. This short novel had its origin in 1994 when, on assignment for a newspaper, Muñoz Molina wrote a story related to Robert Louis Stevenson's *Treasure Island* (1883). *Carlota Fainberg* tells of the chance acquaintance of two Spaniards in the Pittsburgh airport. Claudio is an untenured professor of Spanish literature at a North American university who is traveling to Buenos Aires for a conference. Marcelo is an extroverted executive who is going to Miami and who tells the story of a secret love he once had in a Buenos Aires hotel. Claudio highlights the story Marcelo is narrating by inter-

jecting poststructuralist jargon, English sayings, and words and expressions in English that do not translate into Spanish. In this way, Muñoz Molina makes clear that while he believes that literary criticism is necessary, he rejects the cheap analyses of literary works and the cryptic jargon used in them that often has nothing to do with the work that is being considered. In *Carlota Fainberg* the writer satirizes the Spanish departments of American universities and parodies leaders of the postmodern and poststructuralist schools of thought such as Jacques Lacan, Jacques Derrida, Michel Foucault, and Julia Kristeva.

In addition to this criticism of academia, *Carlota Fainberg* presents two types of Spaniards. Marcelo represents the macho Iberian who talks about his sexual escapades, while Claudio, as Muñoz Molina told Alfieri in 2000, is "el gardo más desaforado de la sofisticación intelectual, . . . universitario americano, o americanizado, para el cual la narración ya ha desaparecido y en su lugar sólo queda el laberinto, proposiciones teóricas, narratología" (the most outrageous grade of intellectual sophistication, . . . at an American university, fully Americanized, for whom the narrative has all but disappeared and in its place all that remains is a labyrinth of theoretical propositions).

In reference to the presence of English words in *Carlota Fainberg,* Muñoz Molina has denied that he was commenting on the changes that appear in one's native language after living in another country as a result of linguistic mixing. The author was criticizing, nonetheless, the ignorance and elitism that characterize many people who fill their language with English phrases to make themselves sound more important.

Juan José López Cabrales, in his 2000 essay "Las tres (cuatro) tesis de Carlota: De cuan fácilmente nacen fantasmas en la mente de un investigador erudito. Estudio en catorce páginas" (The Three [Four] Theses of Carlota: On How Easily Ghosts Are Born in the Mind of an Erudite Investigator. Study in Fourteen Pages), argues that there are fundamentally three theses in the novel. First, it is not the emptiness of erudite discourse but the emotion of love (as the greatest representation of mystery) that really gives meaning to life. Second, a false love causes one to lose contact with reality and will lead only to disaster. Third, the university and the academic world are devouring academics such as Claudio.

At the end of *Carlota Fainberg* Marcelo's story is revealed to be a fantasy. In Buenos Aires, Claudio enters the hotel at which Marcelo claimed to have stayed–now scheduled for demolition–and finds that Carlota had died long before Marcelo's trip to Argentina.

Between the publication of *El jinete polaco* in 1991 and his next major novel, *El dueño del secreto,* in 1994, Muñoz Molina published several other works. In 1992

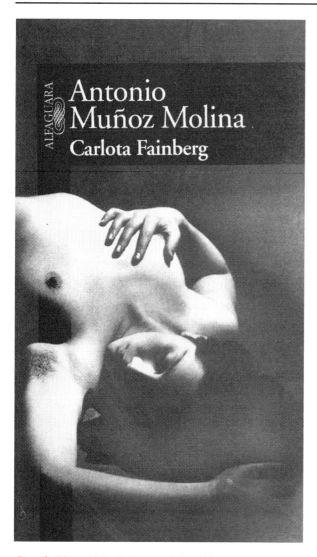

*Cover for Muñoz Molina's 1999 novel, in which he uses a conversation in the Pittsburgh airport between a professor of Spanish literature and a business executive to parody poststructuralist literary theory (Thomas Cooper Library, University of South Carolina)*

he published the detective novel *Los misterios de Madrid*, which explores Madrid in the early 1990s through Lorencito Quesada's investigation of the disappearance of the Santo Cristo de la Greña (a religious statue of Jesus).

Muñoz Molina's marriage ended in divorce in 1992. In 1993 his collection of stories *Nada del otro mundo* (Nothing from the Other World) appeared. It comprises stories the author published between 1983 and 1993, including the title story, the first and longest in the collection. Also in 1993, Muñoz Molina collaborated with the Granadan poet Luis García Montero on *Por qué no es útil la literatura? La realidad de la ficción y Sostener la Mirada* (Why Is Literature Not Useful? The Reality of Fiction and Sustaining the Gaze).

*El dueño del secreto* is a story of sentimental education, irony, and the nostalgia that unites the generation that lived through the final years of the Franco regime. In this novel, like many others, Muñoz Molina views remembering as the only possible salvation from the forgetfulness of life. Set in Madrid just before the death of Franco, the novel follows a young Andalusian journalism student, Manuel, through a series of complicated events. Manuel is poor and lives in a hostel. To make a living, he is a typist for his relative Ataúlfo Ramírez. Ramírez is a prestigious lawyer and an opportunist who earned a small fortune during the final years of the Franco regime. He is also secretary of a clandestine anarchist association that is planning a coup d'état. Manuel is involved in this plot because he is the association's messenger. Ultimately, the plot to overthrow the regime falters, and the association is dismantled because Manuel (to whom the title of the novel refers) is unable to keep the secret.

In 1994 Muñoz Molina married Elvira Lindo, the author of a series of children's books featuring the character Manolito Gafotas. The following year he published one of his most intense and popular novels, *Ardor guerrero: Una memoria militar* (1995, Warrior Ardor: A Military Memory). Based largely on his experiences in the military, it is a horrifying story of life in the barracks in 1979, when pictures of Franco were still on the walls and the ghosts of thirty-six years of dictatorship still hung over Spain. The title refers to a verse from an infantry hymn. *Ardor guerrero* offers a detailed portrayal of the Spanish youth who completed their obligatory military service during the transition to democracy. It opens with a quotation, translated into Spanish, from Michel de Montaigne: "Así pues, lector, yo mismo soy la materia de mi libro" (So, reader, I am the material of my book). On the cover of the first edition of the book is a photo of the author at age twenty-three in his soldier's uniform, smoking a cigarette with an air of resignation.

While some critics have suggested that Muñoz Molina judges too harshly the character based on himself in the novel, Lourdes Franco Bagnouls, in her *Los dones del espejo: La narrativa de Antonio Muñoz Molina* (2000, The Gifts of the Mirror: The Narrative of Antonio Muñoz Molina), writes that

> Muñoz Molina mira por el espejo de la ficción al joven dubitativo e inexperto que alguna vez fue él mismo, vestido de militar por fuera y de terror por dentro. Se mira con amor, con una ternura no exenta de lástima, pero también de orgullo porque más allá de la literatura él sabe cuánto, desde aquel entonces ha crecido y madurado y progresado aquel joven desmañado que aparece en la contraportada del libro con un grito de soledad y desvalimiento en la mirada.

(Muñoz Molina looks into the mirror of fiction at an uncertain and inexperienced youth who once was him, dressed like a soldier on the outside and filled with terror on the inside. He looks at him with love, with a kindness but not pity, but also pride because beyond literature, he knows how much he has grown and matured and progressed from the clumsy youth that appears on the back of the book with a shout of loneliness and helplessness in his gaze.)

Muñoz Molina has responded that the protagonist in *Ardor guerrero* is analyzed not only from the outside but also from the inside, in keeping with the writer's duty to examine his conscience before writing in the confessional genre: "Si uno hace un relato de no ficción, en lugar de una novela, tiene la responsabilidad de tratarse mal a veces, de hacer examen de conciencia. Y ay de aquel que haga un examen de conciencia en el que no reconozca sus errores" (If one writes a nonfiction story instead of a novel, one has the responsibility to treat oneself badly at times, to make oneself examine one's conscience. And pity the person who examines his conscience and does not recognize his errors).

The protagonist of the novel is a young man who dreams of becoming a writer but who, on beginning his obligatory military service in the Basque Country in 1979, must forget his desires and leave his identity behind. While the rest of Spain has a new democratic constitution and a new flag representing liberty, he lives in Francoist military barracks with photos of the caudillo on the walls and the old fascist Spanish flag. The novel follows the protagonist through the daily and often mundane reality of military service during this period.

While the Francoist hero is destroyed in this novel, there is nostalgia for the hero that Muñoz Molina makes references to in interviews, as in his conversation with Fajaro: "hay que pensar como un héroe para comportarse en la vida diaria simplemente con decencia. . . . Uno tiene que estar evaluándose y juzgándose continuamente, a no ser que se caiga en la indulgencia psicoanalítica de explicarlo y justificarlo todo. En el momento en el que se cae en esa tentación, el juicio moral queda suspendido" (you have to think like a hero to behave simply and with decency in everyday life. . . . One has to be continually evaluating and judging himself, unless he decides to indulge himself in psychoanalysis to explain and justify everything. At the moment when one gives in to this temptation, moral judgment is suspended).

In 1995 Muñoz Molina also published *Las apariencias* (The Appearances), a collection of articles he wrote from 1988 to 1991 that were originally published in the culture and opinion sections of the newspapers *ABC* and *El País*. In the introduction to the book Lindo argues that *Las apariencias* includes many ideas that later found their ways into novels and other books by her husband. One example is "Soldados" (Soldiers), which was first published in 1990 and is essentially a summary of *Ardor guerrero*, which appeared five years later. Lindo says that "Este libro contiene muchas cosas, entre otras el futuro del escritor, que está escrito en algunas de sus páginas, siguiendo aquella suerte de maldición de Graham Greene que decía que hay que tener cuidado con lo que se inventa porque la literatura se nutre de recuerdos del pasado pero también del futuro" (This book contains many things, among them being that the author's future is written on some of its pages, following Graham Greene's observation that one has to be careful with that which he invents because literature nourishes memories of the past and the future). Another book of articles, *La huerta del Edén: Escritos y diatribas sobre Andalucía* (1996, The Garden of Eden: Writings and Diatribes about Andalusia), comprises newspaper articles Muñoz Molina wrote about the region. A year later he published two books, the novel *Plenilunio* (Full Moon) and the collection *Escrito en un instante*.

Muñoz Molina published a collection of his speeches, *Pura alegría* (Pure Joy), in 1998. It is based on various speeches and essays from throughout his life on diverse topics, including authors (Miguel de Cervantes, Max Aub), literary themes (memory, invention, the reality of fiction), and prologues he wrote for editions of books by Faulkner and Onetti. In the introduction, he expresses his passion for writing books that are both intellectually engaging and reach a broad audience. Pointing out that many people make literature seem to be more confusing and difficult than it actually is in order to give it added importance, Muñoz Molina asserts: "Yo sé que la oscuridad tiene más prestigio intelectual que la transparencia, y la confusión que la serenidad, pero también sé que . . . las mejores obras de la literatura pueden ser entendidas y disfrutadas por cualquiera, sin otra condición que un dominio solvente de la lectura y un poco de atención" (I know that obscurity has more intellectual prestige than transparency, and confusion more than serenity, but I also know that . . . the best works of literature can be understood and enjoyed by anyone, with no other requirement than an adequate mastery of reading and a little attention).

In the last chapter of *Pura alegría,* Muñoz Molina explains the origins of *Plenilunio*. Several years before writing the novel, he saw an article about a trial in an American newspaper with a photo of a delinquent,

una cara de perfecta bondad, un hombre joven, con traje y corbata, con el pelo corto, con las manos cruzadas, tan pulcramente que parecía más bien que estaba en una iglesia y no en la sala de un juicio, sobre todo si uno no se fijaba en que las manos estaban esposadas. . . . me dio por imaginar onettianamente a un inspector de policía que mira una plaza tras los cristales de un bal-

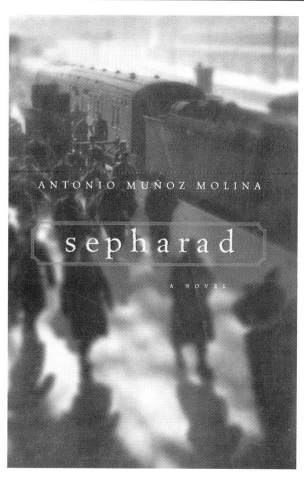

*Dust jacket for the English translation (2003) of Muñoz Molina's*
Sefarad *(2001), a collection of sixteen short stories about odd
characters who are persecuted for being different
(Richland County Public Library)*

cón, y que buscando a un asesino de niños va por las tardes a las salidas de los colegios y a los parques donde andan los pederastas.

(with a face of perfect goodness, a young man with a suit and tie, short hair and crossed hands. His hands were crossed so neatly that he looked more like he was in a church than in a courtroom, even more so if you did not notice that he was in handcuffs. . . . Later I imagined in the style of Onetti a police inspector who watches a plaza through balcony windows, searching for a child killer, and who goes to school gates and parks in the afternoons because that is where the pedophiles are.)

Muñoz Molina soon began to visit a psychiatric residence run by nuns. He also talked with police, lawyers, judges, and witnesses as research.

*Plenilunio,* like other works by Muñoz Molina—particularly *Beltenebros*—insists on the existence of evil and the necessity of fighting it. The story centers around a police inspector who is finally returning to southern Spain, where he and his wife are from, after living in the Basque Country for fourteen years. After the years of fear and uncertainty related to her husband's profession and threats against him from the Euzkadi Ta Askatasuna (ETA), the Basque separatist group, his wife is mentally ill and living in a psychiatric home, where the inspector visits her daily. In the south the unnamed inspector becomes obsessed with resolving the case of a five-year-old girl, Fátima, who was killed in a forest near Mágina, where he now lives.

The media, as Oropesa argues, are harshly criticized in this novel. After symbolically murdering Fátima a second time by forgetting about her after her burial, they also publicize the inspector's appearance and thus identify him to the ETA, which nearly kills him in Mágina. The inspector walks through the streets of Mágina searching for the killer by looking into people's eyes, much like the priest Orduña, one of his teachers at school, walked down the rows of students looking directly into their eyes and could immediately identify the guilty ones.

Muñoz Molina's conception of literature has become more realist as his career has progressed. In "25 años de literatura en democracia" (2000, Twenty-five Years of Literature and Democracy) he comments that "Antes, lo que me importaba era resaltar lo literario de la literatura, es una tentación a la que nadie se resiste. A lo que aspiro ahora es a que la literatura se note lo menos posible, aspiro a ser un escritor realista sobre todo. Claro que esto hace unos años no se podía decir. Creo que el resultado final de toda literatura es el realismo" (Before, what was important to me was to highlight the literary aspects of literature, it is a temptation that no one can resist. What I aspire to now, is to pay as little attention to literature as possible, I aspire to be a realist writer about everything. Clearly, I could not say this years ago. I think that the final result of all literature is realism).

Muñoz Molina's *Sefarad* (2001; translated as *Sepharad,* 2003) includes sixteen short stories about marginalized characters who are persecuted for their differences. It is full of people who represent various points of view and relate fantastic stories. For example, the short story that gives the volume its title is about an American who bought a great deal of art and antiques in Spain for practically nothing at the beginning of the twentieth century and created a museum in the Bronx. The museum is a desolate place that no one visits, but it houses Diego Velázquez's painting *Retrato de una niña* (1640–1642, Portrait of a Girl).

Muñoz Molina's novel *En ausencia de Blanca* (2001, In Absence of Blanca) is based on an idea from a text by Giovanni Papini, in which a man returns home and finds that his wife has changed and is another woman. In *En ausencia de Blanca* Mario López is a young man who works for the regional government in Jaén and is completely dedicated to his wife, Blanca. He is presented as a man in love with the simplicity and tranquillity of his home. Yet, Blanca is from a higher social class, and before marrying Mario she lived a tumultuous life with her friends and lovers. Mario pulled her from a depression and gave her a relaxed and stable existence, but he lives in constant fear that he is with a woman he does not deserve and who will, at any moment, abandon him, which she does. Blanca is attracted to a world and sophistication that Mario cannot offer her. She returns, nonetheless, to Mario, but she is no longer the same. The novel ends ambiguously, leaving open whether the woman Mario finds is actually Blanca or not.

Antonio Muñoz Molina presently resides in Madrid with his wife and their children from their previous marriages—three from Muñoz Molina's and one from Lindo's. Muñoz Molina's literary accomplishments as a novelist, journalist, and social critic are impressive for their breadth and depth. With each new publication, this versatile writer challenges his readers to look inside their own consciences to face the complexities and paradoxes of life. The atmosphere of intrigue and mystery he creates constitute his notion of writing, as he indicates in *Escrito en un instante:* "Writing is to dare persecution and capture and to descend to this hidden place guarded by the reader, the only reader, with secret treasures of happiness and guilt. The actual reader is a shadow that is always waiting to come alive and live in the gaze of the writer whose only desire is to draw his profile, to know him one day."

**Interviews:**

Juan Francisco Martín Gil, "El que habita en la oscuridad: Entrevista con Antonio Muñoz Molina," *Quimera,* 83 (1988): 24–29;

Víctor Alonso Troncoso, "En Córdoba de los Omeyas con Antonio Muñoz Molina," *Cuadernos hispanoamericanos,* 501 (1992): 33–51;

Elizabeth Scarlett, "Conversación con Antonio Muñoz Molina," *España Contemporánea,* 7, no. 1 (1994): 69–82;

Alan Smith, "Entrevista con Antonio Muñoz Molina," *Anales de la literatura española,* 12 (1995): 233–239;

Carlos Alfieri, "Entrevista con Muñoz Molina," *Cuadernos hispanoamericanos,* 600 (2000): 91–98.

**References:**

Lourdes Franco Bagnouls, *Los dones del espejo: La narrativa de Antonio Muñoz Molina* (Mexico City: Universidad Nacional Autónoma de México/Plaza & Valdés, 2000);

Carlos Javier García, "*Beltenebros:* Una misión incierta," *España Contemporánea,* 12, no. 2 (1999): 7–20;

María-Teresa Ibáñez Pastor de Ehrlich, ed., *Los presentes pasados de Antonio Muñoz Molina* (Frankfurt am Main: Vervuet / Madrid: Iberoamericana, 2000);

Juan José López Cabrales, "Las tres (cuatro) tesis de Carlota: De cuan fácilmente nacen fantasmas en la mente de un investigador erudito. Estudio en catorce páginas," in *Actas del VIII Simposio Internacional sobre narrativa hispánica contemporánea "Novela y ensayo"* (El Puerto de Santa María: Fundación Goytisolo, 2000), pp. 109–120;

Alicia Molero de la Iglesia, *La autojustificación en España: Jorge Semprúm, Carlos Barral, Luis Goytisolo, Enriqueta Antolín y Antonio Muñoz Molina* (Frankfurt am Main: Peter Lang, 2000);

Gonzalo Navajas, *Teoría y práctica de la novela española* (Barcelona: Del Mall, 1994);

Salvador Oropesa, *La novelística de Antonio Muñoz Molina: Sociedad civil y literatura lúdica* (Jaén: Universidad de Jaén, 1999);

Margarira Pillado-Miller, "Sobre la adaptación cinematográfica de *Beltenebros,*" *Ojaancano,* 11 (1996): 21–36;

Joan Ramón Resina, ed., *Disremembering the Dictatorship: The Politics of Memory in the Spanish Transition to Democracy* (Amsterdam: Rodopi, 2000);

Lawrence Rich, *The Narrative of Antonio Muñoz Molina: Self-Conscious Realism and "El Desencanto"* (New York: Peter Lang, 1999);

Fátima Serra, *La nueva narrativa española: Tiempo de tregua entre ficción e historia* (Madrid: Pliegos, 2000);

William Sherzer, "Antonio Muñoz Molina's *Carlota Fainberg:* An Ironic Manifesto," *Romance Notes,* 38, no. 3 (1998): 287–293;

Ignacio Soldevila, "Historias sobre la puta mili: Guerreros sin reposo," *Quimera,* 134 (1994): 56–58;

Andrés Soria Olmedo, "Fervor y sabiduría: La obra narrativa de Antonio Muñoz Molina," *Cuadernos hispanoamericanos,* 458 (1988): 107–111.

# Lourdes Ortiz

*(24 March 1943 –    )*

Ángeles Encinar
*Saint Louis University, Madrid Campus*

BOOKS: *Luz de la memoria* (Madrid: Akal, 1976);
*Comunicación crítica* (Madrid: Pablo del Río, 1977);
*Picadura mortal* (Madrid: Sedmay, 1979);
*Conocer Rimbaud y su obra* (Barcelona: DOPESA, 1979);
*Las murallas de Jericó: Farsa en tres actos y un prólogo* (Madrid: Peralta, 1980);
*En días como estos* (Madrid: Akal, 1981);
*La caja de lo que pudo ser* (Madrid: Altea, 1981);
*Urraca* (Madrid: Puntual, 1982);
*Arcángeles* (Barcelona: Plaza y Janés, 1986);
*Los motivos de Circe* (Madrid: Ediciones del Dragón, 1988); revised as *Los motivos de Circe; Yudita* (Madrid: Castalia, 1991);
*Camas* (Madrid: Temas de Hoy, 1989);
*Antes de la batalla* (Madrid: Planeta, 1992);
*Electra-Babel* (Madrid: ADE 25, 1992);
*La fuente de la vida* (Madrid: Planeta, 1995);
*El cascabel al gato* (Ciudad Real: Ñaque, 1996);
*El sueño de la pasión* (Madrid: Planeta, 1997);
*Fátima de los naufragios* (Madrid: Planeta, 1998);
*El local de Bernardeta A.* (Madrid: Acotaciones 1, 1998);
*La liberta: Una mirada insólita sobre Pablo y Nerón* (Barcelona: Planeta, 1999);
*Aquiles y Pentesilea; Rey loco* (Alicante: IX Muestra de Teatro Español Contemporáneos, 2001);
*Jardín, convento, capirote . . . pena* (Madrid: Cuadernos escénicos 3, 2001);
*Cara de niño* (Madrid: Planeta, 2002).

E-BOOK: *La guarida* (1999) <http://www.caoseditorial.com/libros/ficha.asp?lg=en&id=16>.

PLAY PRODUCTIONS: *Penteo,* Madrid, Real Escuela Superior de Arte Dramático, 1982;
*Fedra,* Seville, Teatro Lope de Vega, 1984;
*Yudita,* Madrid, Círculo de Bellas Artes, 1988;
*Pentesilea,* Mérida, Anfiteatro romano, 1991;
*El local de Bernardeta A.,* Madrid, Sala Galileo, 1995;
*El cascabel al gato,* Madrid, Sala Ensayo 100, 1996.

*Lourdes Ortiz ( from the cover for* La liberta: Una mirada insólita sobre Pablo y Nerón, *1999; University of Georgia Library)*

OTHER: Mariano José de Larra, *Artículos políticos,* edited by Ortiz (Madrid: Ciencia Nueva, 1967);
"Paisajes y figuras," in *Doce relatos de mujeres,* edited by Ymelda Navajo (Madrid: Alianza, 1982), pp. 111–125;
"Alicia," in *Cuentos eróticos* (Barcelona: Grijalbo, 1988), pp. 95–107;
"Charla de Lourdes Ortiz," in *Seis calas en la narrativa española contemporánea* (Alcalá de Henares: Fundación Colegio del Rey, 1989), pp. 126–130;
"Y te lo hace en 3D," in *Los pecados capitales* (Barcelona: Grijalbo, 1990), pp. 15–30;
"Las nalgas: La confesión," in *Verte desnudo* (Madrid: Temas de Hoy, 1992), pp. 110–126;

"El espejo de las sombras," in *Cuento español contemporáneo,* edited by Ángeles Encinar and Anthony Percival (Madrid: Cátedra, 1993), pp. 227–231;

"El inmortal," in *Cuentos de este siglo,* edited by Encinar (Barcelona: Lumen, 1995), pp. 171–180;

"El inocente," in *El libro de la inocencia* (Madrid: Fundación Inocente, 1997), pp. 57–62;

"El sabueso," in *Historias de detectives,* edited by Encinar (Barcelona: Lumen, 1998), pp. 83–115;

"Danae 2000," in *Vidas de mujer,* edited by Mercedes Monmany (Madrid: Alianza, 1998), pp. 55–63;

"Adagio," in *Cuentos solidarios* (Madrid: Perfiles, 1999), pp. 103–107;

"Crucigrama," in *De Madrid . . . al cielo,* edited by Rosa Regás (Madrid: Muchnik, 2000), pp. 105–115;

"Asco," in *Daños colaterales: Hazañas antibélicas,* edited by Carlo Fabretti (Madrid: Lengua de trapo, 2002), pp. 41–47.

TRANSLATIONS: Charles Morazé, *La lógica de la historia* (Madrid: Siglo XXI, 1967);

Anne-Marie Rocheblave Spenlé, *Lo masculino y lo femenino en la sociedad contemporánea* (Madrid: Ciencia Nueva, 1968);

Georges Bataille, *La literatura y el mal* (Madrid: Taurus, 1971);

Gustave Flaubert, *Las tentaciones de San Antonio* (Madrid: Akal, 1974);

Marquis de Sade, *Historia de Sainville y de Leónidas* (Madrid: Fundamentos, 1974);

Jean Jolivet, *La filosofía medieval en Occidente* (Madrid: Siglo XXI, 1974);

Michel Tournier, *Viernes o los limbos del Pacífico* (Madrid: Alfaguara, 1986);

Tournier, *El urogallo* (Madrid: Alfaguara, 1988).

From the early days of her literary career in the late 1960s, Lourdes Ortiz has maintained an ethical and aesthetic line untrammeled by the editorial fashions of the moment and the heavy marketing bent that the Spanish publishing industry has assumed in the late twentieth century. The quality of her works and the confidence with which she explores a variety of subgenres—realism, the police novel, the historical novel, metaliterary forms—establish Ortiz as an essential point of reference in any discussion of contemporary Spanish narrative.

Lourdes Ortiz Sánchez was born on 24 March 1943 in Madrid, at the height of the post–Spanish Civil War years. The eldest of three children of Daniel Ortiz and Alicia Sánchez, Ortiz lived throughout her childhood in the vicinity of Madrid's Puerta de Sol, the heart of the city. Her home offered a literary and artistic atmosphere: her grandfather fre-

quented the literary circles of the Círculo de Bellas Artes, while her father, a liberal thinker, journalist, and literature enthusiast, was a regular at the Café Gijón, a gathering place for writers and intellectuals. At four Ortiz contracted a pulmonary disease, and her confinement led her to a passionate and lifelong predilection for reading.

In 1961 Ortiz enrolled at the Universidad Complutense de Madrid, where she earned a degree in geography and history. Her attraction to these subjects eventually led to her exploration of historical events in two of her best-known novels, *Urraca* (1982) and *La liberta: Una mirada insólita sobre Pablo y Nerón* (1999, The Freedwoman: An Uncommon Look at Paul and Nero). During her student years, she took an active part in youth groups opposed to General Francisco Franco's regime. They exchanged prohibited books by Spanish and foreign authors and participated in cutting-edge cultural trends through theater and political groups. Looking back on those years in "Charla de Lourdes Ortiz" (1989, Chat of Lourdes Ortiz), Ortiz recalled her rejection of the nineteenth-century realist novel that was so deeply ingrained in the Spanish tradition, and she mentioned some of the authors she admires: Louis-Ferdinand Céline, Michel Butor, William Faulkner, John Dos Passos, James Joyce, Alejo Carpentier, Italo Svevo, Robert Musil, Ernesto Sábato, Malcolm Lowry, Julio Cortázar, and Mario Vargas Llosa. The influence of these authors and the impact of a key 1960s Spanish novel–Luis Martín-Santos's *Tiempo de silencio* (1961; translated as *Time of Silence,* 1964)–enabled Ortiz to broaden her literary horizons and discover other points of view. As she wrote in "Charla de Lourdes Ortiz," "para entender la evolución hay que tener en cuenta también la influencia de las teorías del psicoanálisis e incluso de Foucault: la realidad no era una sino múltiple. El 'Yo' férreo se descomponía. Aparecían los muchos 'Ayos.' Abordarlo era encontrar la 'forma' adecuada para dar cuenta de esa multiplicidad" (to understand evolution you must also bear in mind the influence of the theories of psychoanalysis and that of Foucault: reality was not one but multiple. The ironclad "I" was breaking down. Many "I"s were emerging. To address this was to find the appropriate "form" to recognize that multiplicity).

In 1962 Ortiz married the poet and publisher Jesús Munárriz; their only child, Jaime, was born on 30 August 1963. After witnessing the Soviet invasion of Prague and the events of May 1968 in France, Ortiz abandoned her political militancy, though she held onto an ideology committed to leftist thinking. Ortiz and her husband separated in 1972.

# LOURDES
# ORTIZ
### URRACA

### 🌐 Planeta

*Title page for a 2005 edition of Ortiz's 1982 novel, in which the title character, the imprisoned twelfth-century queen of Castile and León, tells the story of her life (University of Georgia Library)*

Ortiz has combined writing with a teaching career, first as a history teacher in a high school and later as a college professor of the sociology of art. From 1976 to 2003 she was professor of the theory and history of art at the Real Escuela Superior de Arte Dramático of Madrid. Throughout her career, she has contributed opinion columns on political and social matters to journals and newspapers, including *El País, El Mundo,* and *Diario 16.* She also has participated in radio and television debate shows.

Ortiz's first novel, *Luz de la memoria* (1976, Light of Memory) takes its title from a verse by Luis Cernuda, the Sevillian poet of the Generation of 1927– "Tu rosa del silencio, tú, luz de la memoria" (your rose of silence, you, light of memory)–that precedes the text and points to the process of reminiscence that the protagonist undergoes. Epigraphs by Isidore

Lucien Ducasse, comte de Lautréamont; Novalis; John Keats; and Arthur Rimbaud frame the narrative, set the lyrical tone that permeates the novel, and give a glimpse into the four parts of its plot. The protagonist, Enrique García Alonso, age twenty-nine, married and separated from his wife after two years together, is shut away in a psychiatric hospital because of a violent episode stemming from his aggressive schizoid tendencies. The narrator presents García Alonso's autobiographical remembrances from first-, second-, and third-person points of view, as perspectives that emanate from himself and relate current and past events interspersed with the views of others. His memories are supplemented with reports made by his father, his mother, and his estranged wife; the psychiatrist gives him these statements as a means of providing insight and as a possible path to recovery. These different perspectives allow the reader a full understanding of García Alonso's life. The social and personal determinants that have led him to his current situation include frustration with family, participation in the clandestine Communist Party, identity crisis, and feelings of failure and emptiness regarding his professional future.

The character's "I" emerges in disintegrated form throughout the text, not only in his family environment, where his choice of studying literature is seen as effeminate, but most especially in his various secret political activities, the ultimate consequence of which is his arrest at the end of 1967 and subsequent two-year imprisonment. The multiplicity of García Alonso's "I's" becomes more evident once he is out of the psychiatric hospital, when the coexistence of the many roles he takes on becomes a troublesome aspect of his personality. His return to normal life is dominated by monotony and disinterest, leading him to seek refuge in drugs and alcohol. In the end, death seems to him a liberation, and–perhaps deliberately, perhaps not–he commits suicide.

In *Luz de la memoria* Ortiz reflects the sexual and political repression of the Spanish youth of the late 1960s, an educated generation that felt the need to fight for certain ideals and change the world but most urgently to overthrow Franco's dictatorship. They failed, however, in their attempts, finding themselves oppressed by the difficult political and social situation and by their own ambivalences. As the author points out in "Charla de Lourdes Ortiz," the novel "es el reflejo de aquella realidad universitaria que había vivido con todas sus contradicciones y entusiasmos" (is a reflection of a university situation that I had experienced as a college student, with all of its contradictions and enthusiasms). This generational portrait is painted from multiple perspectives and also leaves open the possibility that the entire narration is part of a novel being written by García Alonso. The innovative, multilayered narrative structures led the book to be regarded as, in the words of Ricardo Gullón (*Ínsula,* 1979), "la más impresionante primera novela de los últimos diez años" (the most impressive first novel of the past ten years).

*Picadura mortal* (1979, Mortal Sting), Ortiz's second novel, takes a different approach in its playful, parodic mode. She set herself the challenge of imitating the American detective novel, and this intentional mimicry gives the text its quick dialogues and witty language. The heroine, Bárbara Arenas, the first woman detective in Spanish fiction, is commissioned with unraveling the mysterious disappearance of Ernesto Granados, an influential Canary Island industrialist. Bárbara's beauty and determination surprise the islanders, and, despite their attempts to dissuade her from her investigation using a variety of methods, she persists and discovers the landowner's dirty business, his political and social control, and the entangled family infighting of the supposed heirs.

In *En días como estos* (1981, In Days Like These) Ortiz delves into the theme of violence and friendship as seen through the eyes of two young Basque terrorists, Toni and Carlos. The lack of concrete space/time references gives the story more universally relevant values. In the first of the three sections of the novel Toni is fleeing with his comrades in the mountains. In the second he returns to his family's home, where he is arrested. In the final section Toni is freed from jail by his cohorts, who intend to force him to continue with their struggle. The narrative pace is dominated by constant action, conveying the anxiety of the fugitives. This anxiety arises from the irrational acts of violence to which they are compelled by their terrorist group, from which they are unable to break free. The use of an objective third-person narration and of cinematographic techniques distances the readers from the narrated facts.

Ortiz's most critically acclaimed novel, *Urraca,* appeared in 1982. Queen Urraca of Castile and León, frequently used as an inspiration for historical novels and plays, is presented in this work from her own inner perspective. Imprisoned in the monastery of Valcabados in 1123 on orders of her son and Bishop Diego Gelmírez, both of whom are greedy for power, she sets out to write her own chronicle to give her people a view other than the official story. The narration is offered through her retrospective monologues and the dialogues she conducts with Brother Roberto, the young monk who accompanies her during her imprisonment and who becomes her ideal interlocutor, confidant, and lover. Maintaining an intimate, confessional

tone, Urraca reminisces on the key moments of her life, such as her triumphal entry into Toledo with her father, Alfonso VI; his death; the battle of Uclés against the Moors in 1108; her strife-filled marriage to her second husband, Alfonso I of Aragon; and the coronation of her son, Alfonso VII. At all times, the acknowledged version of history is juxtaposed with her personal, and occasionally differing, view. Ortiz also uses free association of ideas and erotic involuntary memories to trigger flashbacks into the most meaningful periods of Urraca's life.

The novel has a circular structure. The first part portrays the road taken by Urraca to attain the throne; the second shows the queen at the peak of her splendor, wielding full power; and the last depicts the monarch's decline as she approaches her death. The leitmotiv that threads the entire story is the desire for power, giving the novel a universal, timeless message. It portrays the never-ending struggle of men or women to obtain and to hold onto power.

A marked feature of the novel is its metafictional theme, a reflection on the process of writing as part of the fiction itself. This dimension is present in *Luz de la memoria,* when García Alonso fantasizes about himself as the protagonist of a novel, and it recurs in Ortiz's later work. In *Urraca,* the queen takes it upon herself to become her own chronicler; and the self-consciousness of her writing is a recurring motif throughout the text. Writing about her lost kingdom becomes a refuge and a cause for her survival. Faced with the premonition of her imminent death, she ends up making Roberto the heir to her task and admonishes him to be meticulous and precise: "Una derrota puede ser gloriosa si se sabe emplear el adjetivo adecuado, si se comunica la acción, gracias al sucederse ritmado de los versos" (A defeat can be glorious if one knows how to use the right adjective, if the action is conveyed, thanks to the rhythmic succession of the verses).

Ortiz is using an intensely denigrated figure of Spanish official history to make a claim for feminism. Urraca is portrayed in multiple roles—as a mother, as a daughter, as a wife, as a queen, and as a lover—to enable the reader to evaluate each of these roles and the motivations behind her deeds. Ortiz spent more than two years searching historiographical sources to re-create a profoundly documented character, and wherever she found ambiguity and uncertainty she replaced it with meditated fiction.

*Arcángeles* (1986, Archangels) Ortiz's fifth novel, is decidedly experimental. It takes place in the Madrid of the 1980s and is narrated by an unnamed writer who alternates his work-in-progress with the constant companionship of Gabriel, an elusive young man who

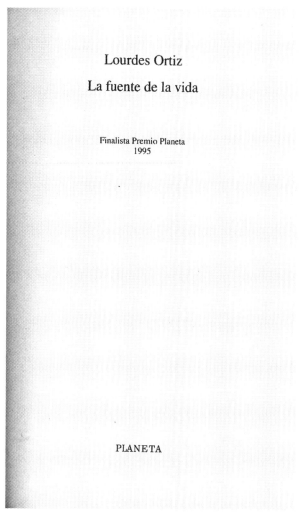

Lourdes Ortiz

La fuente de la vida

Finalista Premio Planeta
1995

PLANETA

*Title page for Ortiz's 1995 novel (The Fountain of Life), about the
kidnapping of children for the purposes of illegal adoption
and organ trafficking (Jean and Alexander Heard
Library, Vanderbilt University)*

functions as a reflection or spokesman of the diverse young lives that populate the novel. The metaliterary game begins with the first line as Gabriel tells the narrator, "en vez de una novela deberías hacer una película, un video" (instead of a novel you should do a movie, a video), and is underlined in its closure, "creo que ya encontré el final" (I think I already found the ending). The book that the narrator sets out to write and the one that the reader is holding differ widely from a conventional novel. Ortiz favors a technique that aims to capture instant images, fragmentary sensations, and the free flow of ideas, giving *Arcángeles* a video-like quality. This open form adjusts well to her purpose of uncovering the disenchantment of a Spanish consumerist society, with its ailments of youth unemployment, drugs and alcohol, ethnic intolerance, and violence toward the weakest.

Ortiz's first volume of short stories, *Los motivos de Circe* (Circe's Motives), was published in 1988. The author had already contributed other stories to anthologies such as the well-known *Doce relatos de mujeres* (1982, Twelve Stories by Women), which brought together the most important female writers of the time and has become a reference point for fiction written by women. In "Charla de Lourdes Ortiz" Ortiz calls *Los motivos de Circe* "quizá el único libro feminista que he hecho sin pretenderlo" (perhaps the only feminist book I have written without trying to). The collection includes six portraits of biblical, Homeric, and Renaissance heroines re-created from unexpected angles. Each of the six stories–"Eva," "Los motivos de Circe," "Penélope," "Betsabé," "Salomé," and "Gioconda"– and the two-act play "Cenicienta" (Cinderella, replaced in a subsequent edition by the dramatic monologue *Yudita* [1991, Judith], which was more attuned to the rest of the stories) demythologize these famous and infamous women by humanizing them. Ortiz gives them a voice, allowing them to retell their stories based on their own experiences, thus giving rise to new perspectives. For example, in the story of the faithfulness of Ulysses' wife, Penelope, what is highlighted is not her extreme virtue but the frustration she has suffered for so many years and the feeling of time lost. This story was later included in the anthology *Rainy Days: Short Stories by Contemporary Spanish Women Writers* (1997), with an introduction by Montserrat Lunati.

Throughout the 1980s and 1990s Ortiz combined fiction writing with playwriting. Her first drama, *Las murallas de Jericó* (The Walls of Jericho), was published in 1980 but was never produced; since then Ortiz has published and staged more than fourteen plays, one of which, *La guarida* (1999, The Lair), has been made available for purchase on-line. *Fedra* (Phaedra) was first performed at the Teatro Lope de Vega in Seville in 1984, directed by the author, who had also staged *Penteo* (Pentheus) in 1982. *Yudita*, under the direction of Francisco Ortuño, premiered at Madrid's Círculo de Bellas Artes in 1988. Other plays include *El local de Bernardeta A.* (Bernardeta's Place), which premiered at the Sala Galileo in Madrid in 1995, and *Aquiles y Pentesilea* (Achilles and Penthesilea), published together with *Rey loco* (Mad King) in 2001. These titles show the writer's preference for a return to antiquity. She models her characters on mythical figures in order to destroy the old, stereotypical image and replace it with a vision based on feminine intelligence and survival tactics. *El local de Bernardeta A.* is a parody of Federico García Lorca's tragedy *La casa de Bernarda Alba* (1945; translated as *The House of Bernarda Alba*, 1947), and Ortiz unveils a no less bitter reality of

Spanish contemporary women. In this play and others, the author is concerned with the plasticity of language, adapting the wit of high and popular speech to the characters through a distinctively personal style. In "Mito e historia en el teatro de Lourdes Ortiz" (2001, Myth and History in the Theater of Lourdes Ortiz) Fernando Doménech defines her dramas as "teatro poético" (poetic theater) because of the abundance of "los monólogos narrativos o explicativos, los coros, la inserción de textos poéticos propios o ajenos, los momentos de efusión lírica que se expresan por medio de símbolos y metáforas de amplio desarrollo" (narrative or explanatory monologues, choruses, the insertion of poetic texts of her own or by others, moments of lyrical effusion expressed through broadly developed symbols and metaphors). These plays, as those of Fernando Arrabal and Fernando Nieva, are rooted in universal paradigms of classical and Spanish Golden Age tragedy as well as in the twentieth-century absurdist tradition.

*Antes de la batalla* (1992, Before the Battle) is a generational chronicle that expands on *Luz de la memoria,* following former anti-Franco activists and documenting their contemporary sense of failure and voluntary embrace of amnesia after their dissent ended up equalized and commodified by the system. Despair has given way to nostalgia for the revolutionary aims of the past. The disillusioned college students are now in their mid forties and have either fallen into the routine of their civil-service jobs or spent their energies climbing the power ladder. Madrid is the setting that only the protagonist, Ernesto, deserts, fleeing to Greece and Egypt. The objective narration, focused occasionally on Ernesto's thoughts, manifests the emptiness and falsehood of these middle-aged citizens who have made the unscrupulous exercise of power and money their life goal, their absolute nihilism.

Ortiz's next novel, *La fuente de la vida* (1995, The Fountain of Life), was a finalist for the lucrative Planeta Prize and had a print run of sixty thousand copies for the first edition (the usual number is three to five thousand). *La fuente de la vida* depicts the abduction of children in Peru and Romania for the purposes of illegal adoption and organ trafficking, a practice that earned close scrutiny by the press a few months after release of the novel. Ortiz had anticipated that a scandal would erupt and be dissected at length by the media; she stated in an unpublished 2003 interview that "la literatura atrapa la realidad y se adelanta" (literature traps reality and moves ahead of it).

The nineteen chapters of the novel are split into two fundamental narrative lines: one takes place in the city of Cuzco, where a young Spanish wife is determined to leave Peru and return to Spain to give birth to her first child, as she has heard rumors of child abduction and fears the unsanitary conditions of the city. The second plot takes place in Bucharest, where the couple of Ródika and Valeriu carry out their shady adoption business in a clandestine nursery house where they raise "bought" children. The connection between these plots is carried out through a third plot, featuring Esteban, a professional journalist who is preparing an investigative article on illegal adoptions in Madrid. As he follows his leads to Romania and becomes an eyewitness to what is actually happening, Ortiz portrays the causes of child abduction as well as the misunderstandings among Spanish, Latin American, and Anglo American cultures (Nelly, a U.S. citizen, seems to be responsible for the disappearance of the children in Peru). The impoverished social, political, and economic situations faced by the Third World and the former Eastern bloc countries are a constant factor: "Sabía que Valeriu no se equivocaba. Y ella no tenía remordimientos: Niños que nacen para . . . los había visto abandonados en las cunitas del hospital con sus grandes tripas hinchadas. Era una obra de caridad para los niños y para las madres" (I knew that Valeriu was not wrong. And she felt no remorse: Children that are born to . . . she had seen them abandoned in the hospital cradles with their big, distended bellies. It was an act of charity for the children and for their mothers). At the end Esteban is conscious of the crime he is involved in, but, incapable of reacting, he opts to accept the horrid reality rather than to risk denouncing it. His apathy points a finger at the uncommitted and financially comfortable Spanish middle class that has forgotten the underdevelopment and retrograde attitudes of Spain's recent past.

There is a testimonial quality in Ortiz's second volume of short stories, *Fátima de los naufragios* (1998, Fatima of the Shipwrecked). The eponymous heroine of the title story is the survivor of the wreck of a small boat in which, along with several other would-be North African immigrants, her husband and her ten-year-old son lose their lives. For four years the woman lives on the beach, heartbroken and cast away, awaiting the impossible return of her loved ones. The reader can hear the collective voice of the townsfolk in the form of a chorus when, amazed by Fatima's perseverance, the neighbors come to support and revere her, giving her names such as "Moreneta" (Black Virgin) "Virgen de las pateras" (Virgin of the Small Boats), and "Macarena" (Dark Girl). Fantasy and reality are closely intertwined without diminishing the tragic dimensions of the message: the hardships that African immigrants carry or have to face once they have overcome the perils of the sea. In "La piel de Marcelinda" (The Skin of Marcelinda), the cocky,

**Lourdes Ortiz
La liberta**

*Una mirada insólita sobre Pablo y Nerón.*

PLANETA

*Cover for Ortiz's 1999 novel (The Freedwoman: An Uncommon Look
at Paul and Nero), narrated by a freed female slave who is the
lover of the Roman emperor Nero and an admirer of the
apostle Paul (University of Georgia Library)*

aggressive language of the narrator lends verisimilitude to the tragic love of the foreign prostitute Marcelinda for her pimp/protector, El Chano. The setting of the Casa de Campo in Madrid is a recognizable real-life stage for encounters of this sort. In stark contrast with the dramatic mood of these stories stands the irony and humor of "El vuelo de la mariposa" (The Flight of the Butterfly). In this novella, the first-person narrator reports on his odd encounter with a stranger and the surprising change his life has undergone since the occurrence. The common thread through all the stories is the solitude of the protagonists, who yearn for a better life that continues to elude them.

With *La liberta* Ortiz returned to the historical novel from a revisionist feminine perspective, re-creating the Roman Empire as a frame for the figures of Nero and St. Paul. Linked by the narrator,

Acté, these two opposing figures go through a process of humanization. As Acté states, "Escribo para que alguien algún día pueda encontrar estas notas y lograr que la verdad resplandezca al fin entre tanta mentira" (I write so that someone some day may find these notes and make the truth finally shine among so many lies). Like Queen Urraca she is resolute to rewrite history, within her own perspective. Acté is a freedwoman who has been educated by Seneca to enter into the service of Claudius and later Nero, thus becoming the latter's lover and companion. She also admires St. Paul and his new doctrine and is an occasional savior to both as they flee from Roman persecution. The oral dimension of the text is underpinned by the inclusion of multiple voices forming a chorus that helps to reconstruct the Roman and Judeo-Christian worldviews. These immediate points of reference are transcended by this timeless chorus and its variegated reflections on ambition, power, pain, lust, deception, and the quest for truth.

*Cara de niño* (2002, Face of a Child), Ortiz's next detective novel, denounces the unscrupulousness and hypocrisy of the Spanish medical establishment. The disappearance of the young homosexual Marcial is investigated by one of his friends and by the three owners of a marriage-counseling agency, Mami, Lola Carmela, and Lorenza. The emerging facts take them to Marcial's partner, Manolo, a renowned physician who is blackmailed by his medical partners to force him to continue running fraudulent businesses such as beauty clinics and a pharmaceutical laboratory where the export of expired drugs is being considered. The pervasive intolerance of homosexuality and the falseness of impeccable professionals is presented obliquely, by means of selective multiple perspectives that the omniscient narrator orchestrates, pointing to the mind-set that moves modern Spanish materialistic values.

Ortiz has not neglected the genre of the essay. In early books she analyzed the works of the Spaniard Mariano José de Larra and the Frenchman Rimbaud, two nineteenth-century authors who had turbulent lives and created works of great brilliance. Her later collections offer a more festive tone. *Camas* (1989, Beds), subtitled "An Irreverent Essay," gives voice to the beds used by the most famous historical and literary lovers. *El sueño de la pasión* (1997, The Dream of Passion) analyzes the meaning of passion in the literary and musical realm. Its chapters cover Tristan and Isolde, Abelard and Héloise, Romeo and Juliet, Calixto and Melibea, Charlotte and Werther, and other fictional Spanish women, such as Carmen and Ana Ozores, sworn to vehement and illicit love.

The writings of Lourdes Ortiz cover more than a quarter of a century. All of her fiction has been characterized by a rich, lyrical, and precise language oriented toward the description of the conflicting feelings and experiences of a generation that assimilated the revolutionary spirit of 1968 and grew to see its lost possibilities as Franco was succeeded by Juan Carlos I. Her novels and short stories have drawn resources from Lacanian feminism, metalanguage, and stream of consciousness, as well as a relentless social denunciation of greed and ambition. The various types of narration she has utilized—realist, testimonial, historical, and detective—have delved repeatedly, from highly diverse perspectives, into certain subjects: ambition, violence, metafiction, the struggle for power, and the difficult balance between ideology and action.

## Interviews:

Gregorio Morales Villena, "Entrevista con Lourdes Ortiz," *Ínsula*, 479 (1986): 1, 10;

Phoebe Porter, "Conversación con Lourdes Ortiz," *Letras femeninas*, 16 (1990): 139–144.

## References:

John C. Ackers, "The Generation of Spanish Novelists After Franco," *Review of Contemporary Fiction*, 8 (1988): 292–299;

Concha Alborg, "Cuatro narradoras de la transición," in *Nuevos y novísimos: Algunas perspectivas críticas sobre la narrativa española desde la década de los sesenta*, edited by Ricardo Landeira and Luis T. González del Valle (Boulder: Society of Spanish and Spanish-American Studies, 1987), pp. 11–27;

Santos Alonso, "La transición hacia una nueva novela," *Ínsula*, 512–513 (1989): 11–12;

Isolina Ballesteros, *Escritura femenina y discurso autobiográfico en la nueva novela española* (New York: Peter Lang, 1994), pp. 63–86;

María del Carmen Bobes Naves, "Novela histórica femenina," in *La novela histórica a finales del siglo XX*, edited by José Romera Castillo, Francisco Gutierrez Carbajo, and Mario García-Page (Madrid: Visor, 1996), pp. 39–54;

Biruté Ciplijauskaité, "Historical Novel from a Feminine Perspective: *Urraca*," in *Feminine Concerns in Contemporary Spanish Fictions by Women*, edited by Roberto C. Manteiga, Carolyn Galerstein, and Kathleen McNerney (Potomac, Md.: Scripta Humanística, 1987), pp. 29–42;

Ciplijauskaité, "Lyric Memory, Oral History, and the Shaping of Self in Spanish Narrative," *Forum for Modern Language Studies*, 28 (1992): 390–400;

Ciplijauskaité, *La novela femenina contemporánea (1970–1985): Hacia una tipología de la narración en primera persona* (Madrid: Anthropos, 1988), pp. 123–164;

Rafael Conte, "En busca de la novela perdida," *Ínsula*, 464–465 (1985): 1, 24;

Fernando Doménech, "Federico en el burdel," *Acotaciones*, 1 (1998): 57–62;

Doménech, "Mito e historia en el teatro de Lourdes Ortiz," *Teatro español contemporáneo*, 13 (2001): 5–8;

Ángeles Encinar, "Luz de la memoria de Lourdes Ortiz," in her *Novela española actual: La desaparición del héroe* (Madrid: Pliegos, 1990), pp. 112–127;

Encinar, "La sexualidad y su significación en la novelística española actual," *Asclepio*, 42 (1990): 63–74;

Encinar, "*Urraca*: Una recreación actual de la historia," *Letras femeninas*, 20 (1994): 87–99;

Celia Fernández Prieto, *Historia y novela: Poética de la novela histórica* (Pamplona: EUNSA, 1998);

Alicia Giralt, *Innovaciones y tradiciones en la novelística de Lourdes Ortiz* (Madrid: Pliegos, 2001);

Ricardo Gullón, "La novela española del siglo XX," *Ínsula*, 396–397 (1979): 1, 28;

Patricia Hart, "The Picadura and the Picardía of Lourdes Ortiz," in *The Spanish Sleuth: The Detective in Spanish Fiction* (Rutherford, N.J.: Fairleigh Dickinson University Press, 1987), pp. 172–181;

Anjouli Janzon, "*Urraca*: Un ejemplo de metaficción historiográfica," in *La novela histórica a finales del siglo XX*, pp. 265–273;

Montserrat Lunati, introduction to *Rainy Days: Short Stories by Contemporary Spanish Women Writers* (Warminster: Aris & Phillips, 1997), pp. 109–113;

Roberto Manteiga, "From Empathy to Detachment: The Author-Narrator Relationship in Several Spanish Novels by Women," *Monographic Review*, 8 (1992): 19–35;

Nina L. Molinaro, "Resistance, Gender, and the Meditation of History in Pizarnik's *La condesa sangrienta* and Ortiz's *Urraca*," *Letras femeninas*, 19 (1993): 45–54;

Jesús Moreno Moreno, "Lourdes Ortiz: La voz del lenguaje," in *Seis calas en la narrativa española contemporánea* (Alcalá de Henares: Fundación Colegio Rey, 1989), pp. 131–136;

Gonzalo Navajas, "Narrativa y género: La ficción actual desde la mujer," *Ínsula*, 589–590 (1996): 37–39;

Elizabeth J. Ordóñez, "Inscribing Difference: L'écriture Feminine and New Narrative by Women," *Anales de la literatura española contemporánea*, 12 (1987): 45–58;

Ordóñez, "Reading Contemporary Spanish Narrative by Women," *Anales de la literatura española contemporánea*, 7 (1982): 237–251;

Ordóñez, "Writing 'Her/story': Reinscriptions of Tradition in Texts by Riera, Gómez Ojea and Ortiz," in her *Voices of Their Own: Contemporary Spanish Narrative by Women* (Lewisburg, Pa.: Bucknell University Press, 1991), pp. 127–148;

Janet Pérez, "Characteristics of Erotic Brief Fiction by Women in Spain," *Monographic Review,* 7 (1991): 173–195;

Pérez, *Contemporary Women Writers of Spain* (Boston: Twayne, 1988), pp. 165–167;

Amalia Pulgarín, "La necesidad de contar por sí misma: *Urraca* de Lourdes Ortiz," in her *Metaficción historiográfica: La novela histórica en la narrativa hispánica postmodernista* (Madrid: Fundamentos, 1995), pp. 153–201;

María José Ragué-Arias, "Penélope, Agave y Fedra, personajes femeninos griegos, en el teatro de Carmen Resino y Lourdes Ortiz," *Estreno,* 15 (1989): 23–24;

Santos Sanz Villanueva, "Generación del 68," *El Urogallo,* 26 (1988): 28–31;

Gonzalo Sobejano, "Ante la novela de los años setenta," *Ínsula,* 396–397 (1979): 1, 22;

Sobejano, "La novela poemática y sus alrededores," *Ínsula,* 464–465 (1985): 1, 28;

Robert C. Spires, "Lourdes Ortiz: Mapping the Course of Postfrancoist Fiction," in *Women Writers of Contemporary Spain: Exiles in the Homeland,* edited by Joan L. Brown (Newark: University of Delaware Press, 1991), pp. 198–216;

Spires, "A Play of Difference: Fiction after Franco," *Letras Peninsulares,* 1 (1988): 285–298;

Luis Suñén, "Escritura y realidad," *Ínsula,* 464–465 (1985): 5;

Lynn K. Talbot, "Lourdes Ortiz' *Urraca:* A Re-Vision/Revision of History," *Romance Quarterly,* 38 (1991): 437–448;

Juan Tébar, "Novela criminal española de la transición," *Ínsula,* 464–465 (1985): 4;

Maruja Torres, "Un cadáver en la bañera," *El País Semanal,* 240 (15 November 1981): 19–23;

Darío Villanueva, "La novela, 1976," in *El año literario español 1974–1979* (Madrid: Castalia, 1980), pp. 331–345;

Juan Villarín, "Viaje por nuestra ignorada novela policiaca," *Alfoz,* 86 (1992): 123–126.

# Ramón Pérez de Ayala

*(9 August 1880 – 5 August 1962)*

José Ramón González
*Universidad de Valladolid*

BOOKS: *La paz del sendero* (Madrid: Fernando Fé, 1904); enlarged as *La paz del sendero; El sendero innumerable* (Madrid, 1915);

*Tinieblas en las cumbres* (Madrid: Fernando Fé, 1907);

*A.M.D.G.* (Madrid: Prieto, 1910);

*La pata de la raposa* (Madrid: Renacimiento, 1911); translated by Thomas Walsh as *The Fox's Paw: A Novel of Spanish Life* (New York: Dutton, 1924);

*Troteras y danzaderas* (Madrid: Renacimiento, 1912);

*Prometeo; Luz de domingo; La caída de los Limones: Novelas poemáticas de la vida española* (Madrid: Imprenta Clásica Española, 1916); translated by Alice P. Hubbard and Grace Hazard Conkling as *Prometheus; The Fall of the House of Limon; Sunday Sunlight: Poetic Novels of Spanish Life* (New York: Dutton, 1920);

*Herman encadenado: Notas de un viaje a los frentes del Isonzo la Carnia y el Trentino* (Madrid: Imprenta Clásica Española, 1917);

*Las máscaras: Ensayos de crítica teatral,* 2 volumes (Madrid: Imprenta Clásica Española, 1917, 1924);

*Política y toros: Ensayos* (Madrid: Saturnino Calleja, 1918);

*El sendero andante: Momentos, modos, ditirambos, doctrinal de vida y naturaleza, poemas* (Madrid: Saturnino Calleja, 1921);

*Belarmino y Apolonio: Novela* (Madrid: Saturnino Calleja, 1921); translated by Murray Baumgarten and Gabriel Berns as *Belarmino and Apolonio* (Berkeley: University of California Press, 1971; London: Quartet, 1990);

*Luna de miel, luna de hiel: Novela* (Madrid: Imprenta Helénica, 1923);

*Los trabajos de Urbano y Simona: Continuación de Luna de miel, luna de hiel* (Madrid: Mundo Latino, 1923);

*El ombligo del mundo: Novelas* (Madrid: Renacimiento, 1924);

*Bajo el signo de Artemisa: Novelas* (Madrid: Renacimiento, 1924);

*Tigre Juan: Novela* (Madrid: Pueyo, 1926);

*El curandero de su honra (segunda parte de Tigre Juan): Novela* (Madrid: Pueyo, 1926);

*Ramón Pérez de Ayala ( from* Obras completas, *volume 1, 1964; Thomas Cooper Library, University of South Carolina)*

*El libro de Ruth: Ensayos en vivo,* edited by Francisco Agustín (Madrid: Páez, 1928);

*5 ensayos sobre don Juan con un prólogo de Américo Castro,* by Pérez de Ayala, Gregorio Marañón, Ramiro de Maeztu, José Ingenieros, and Azorín (Santiago, Chile: Nueva época, 1933);

*Ramoneo* (London: Méndez & Altolaguirre, 1935);

*Poesías completas* (Buenos Aires & Mexico City: Espasa Calpe Argentina, 1942);

*Principios y finales de la novela* (Madrid: Taurus, 1958);

*Divagaciones literarias,* edited by José García Mercadal (Madrid: Biblioteca Nueva, 1958);

*El país del futuro: Mis viajes a los Estados Unidos (1913–1914, 1919–1920),* edited by García Mercadal (Madrid: Biblioteca Nueva, 1959);

*Más divagaciones literarias,* edited by García Mercadal (Madrid: Biblioteca Nueva, 1960);

*Fábulas y ciudades,* edited by García Mercadal (Barcelona: Destino, 1961);

*Amistades y recuerdos,* edited by García Mercadal (Barcelona: Aedos, 1961);

*El raposín* (Madrid: Taurus, 1962);

*Tabla rasa,* edited by García Mercadal (Madrid: Bullón, 1963);

*Tributo a Inglaterra,* edited by García Mercadal (Madrid: Aguilar, 1963);

*Pequeños ensayos,* edited by García Mercadal (Madrid: Biblioteca Nueva, 1963);

*Ante Azorín,* edited by García Mercadal (Madrid: Biblioteca Nueva, 1964);

*Obras completas,* 4 volumes, edited by García Mercadal (Madrid: Aguilar, 1964–1969);

*Nuestro Séneca y otros ensayos,* edited by García Mercadal (Barcelona: EDHASA, 1966);

*Escritos políticos,* edited by Paulino Garagorri (Madrid: Alianza, 1967);

*Viaje entretenido al país del ocio: (Reflexiones sobre la cultura griega),* edited by García Mercadal (Madrid: Guadarrama, 1975);

*Apostillas y divagaciones,* edited by García Mercadal (Madrid: Ediciones de Cultura Hispánica, 1976);

*Las terceras de "ABC,"* edited by José Luis Vázquez-Dodero (Madrid: Prensa Española, 1976);

*Crónicas londinenses,* edited by Agustín Coletes Blanco (Murcia: Universidad de Murcia, 1985; enlarged and corrected, 1988);

*Artículos y ensayos en los semanarios* España, Nuevo Mundo *y* La Esfera, edited by Florencio Friera (Oviedo: Universidad de Oviedo, Servicio de Publicaciones, 1986);

*Trece dioses: Fragmentos de las memorias de Florencio Flórez,* edited by Geraldine M. Scanlon (Madrid: Alianza, 1989);

*Ramón Pérez de Ayala y las artes plásticas: Escritos sobre arte,* edited by Friera and José Tomás Cañas Jiménez (Granada: Fundación Rodríguez-Acosta/Caja General de Ahorros, 1991);

*Obras completas,* 5 volumes, edited by Javier Serrano Alonso (Madrid: Fundación José Antonio de Castro, 1998–2003);

*Cartas Manchegas y otros artículos en* El Sol, edited by Friera (Oviedo: KRK, 2002).

**Editions and Collections:** *Selections from Pérez de Ayala,* edited by Nicholson B. Adams and Sterling A. Stoudemire (New York: Norton, 1934);

*Las novelas de Urbano y Simona: 1. Luna de miel, luna de hiel; 2. Los trabajos de Urbano y Simona,* edited by Andrés Amorós (Madrid: Alianza, 1969);

*La pata de la raposa,* edited by Amorós (Barcelona: Labor, 1970);

*Tinieblas en las cumbres,* edited by Amorós (Madrid: Castalia, 1971);

*Belarmino y Apolonio,* edited by Amorós (Madrid: Cátedra, 1978);

*Tigre Juan; y, El curandero de su honra,* edited by Amorós (Madrid: Castalia, 1980);

*Troteras y danzaderas,* edited by Amorós (Madrid: Castalia, 1982);

*A.M.D.G.,* edited by Amorós (Madrid: Cátedra, 1983);

*Tigre Juan: El curandero de su honra,* edited by Miguel Ángel Lozano Marco (Madrid: Espasa Calpe, 1990);

*El ombligo del mundo,* edited by Ángeles Prado (Madrid: Cátedra, 1998);

*Tigre Juan; El curandero de su honra,* edited by Prado (Madrid: Cátedra, 2001);

*El espíritu liberal: Antología de ensayos,* edited by Amorós (Madrid: Biblioteca Nueva, 2004);

*Ramoneo,* edited by Amorós (Seville: Point de Lunettes & Los papeles mojados de Río Seco, 2005).

**Editions in English:** "The Assistant Professor," translated by Warre Bradley Wells, in *Great Spanish Short Stories Representing the Work of the Leading Spanish Writers of the Day,* translated by Wells (Boston & New York: Houghton Mifflin, 1932);

*Tiger Juan,* translated by Walter Starkie (New York: Macmillan, 1933); republished as *Tigre Juan* (London: Cape, 1933)—comprises translations of *Tigre Juan* and *El curandero de su honra;*

*Honeymoon, Bittermoon; The Trials of Urbano and Simona,* translated by Barry Eisenberg (Berkeley: University of California Press, 1972); republished as *Honeymoon, Bittermoon* (London: Quartet, 1990).

OTHER: Juan José Domenchina, *Del poema eterno, 1898–1959,* foreword by Pérez de Ayala (Madrid: Imprenta Clásica Española, 1917);

Alberto Guillén, *La linterna de Diógenes,* prologue by Pérez de Ayala (Madrid: Editorial-América, 1921);

Julio Cejador y Frauca, *Recuerdos de mi vida (obra póstuma),* prologue by Pérez de Ayala (Madrid: Imprenta Radio, 1927);

Pablo Abril de Vivero, *Ausencia: Poemas,* prologue by Pérez de Ayala (Paris: Editorial Paris-America, 1927);

"Ensayo liminar," in *Tres ensayos sobre la vida sexual,* by Gregorio Marañón (Madrid: Biblioteca Nueva, 1927);

Luis de Tapia, *Luis de Tapia: Sus mejores versos,* prologue by Pérez de Ayala (Madrid: Gráfica Unión, 1929);

Luis Santullano, *Paxarón o la fatalidad: Novela,* prologue by Pérez de Ayala (Madrid: Biblioteca Nueva, 1932);

William F. Stirling, *Orange Groves,* introductory poem by Pérez de Ayala (London: Mathews & Marrot, 1934);

Vicente Solórzano Sagredo, *Tratado de papiroflexia superior: Manualidades del papel,* prologue by Pérez de Ayala (Buenos Aires: Guión, 1945);

Julia Helena Acevedo de Martinez de Hoz, *Itinerario de mis flores,* prologue by Pérez de Ayala (Buenos Aires: El Bibliófilo, 1945);

"'Clarín' y don Leopoldo Alas," in *A. Leopoldo Alas, "Clarín" (1852–1901)* (Oviedo: Universidad de Oviedo, 1952), pp. 5–21;

Solórzano Sagredo, *Papiroflexia zoomorfica: Construcción geometrica de los seres con papel plegado,* prologues by Peréz de Ayala, Ángel Cabrera, and Tomas Lara (Valladolid: El Autor, Talleres de la Editorial Sever-Cuesta, 1962);

Enrique de Mesa y Rosales, *Antología poética,* preliminary essay by Pérez de Ayala (Madrid: Espasa Calpe, 1962).

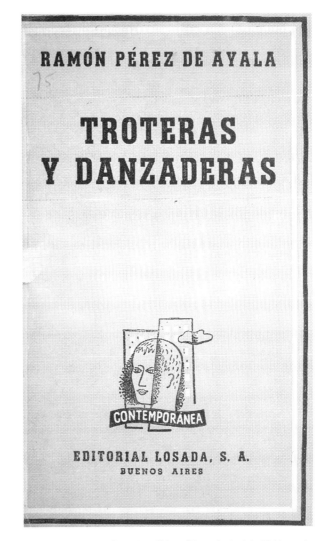

Cover for a 1942 Argentine edition of Pérez de Ayala's 1912 novel (Trotters and Dancers), about writers and intellectuals in the Madrid bohemia of the early twentieth century (Thomas Cooper Library, University of South Carolina)

Popular and critical reception of Ramón Pérez de Ayala's fiction progressed through several clearly marked stages during the twentieth century. Widespread recognition of his novels during the 1920s and 1930s in Spain was followed by a relative silence owing to his self-imposed exile with the outbreak of the Civil War in 1936. Neither the presence of his name in literary histories nor his permanent return to Madrid in 1954 revitalized his image in the 1940s and 1950s. This situation began to change in the 1960s, and today Pérez de Ayala is considered one of the most important innovators of the Spanish novel in the first quarter of the twentieth century. Following the path opened by such fin de siècle writers as Miguel de Unamuno, Pío Baroja, and Ramón del Valle-Inclán, Pérez de Ayala wrote novels that do not adhere to the formulas of realism and naturalism. Furthermore, one cannot fully understand Pérez de Ayala's fiction—especially his later works—without taking its ethical purpose into account. He regarded writing as part of his civic responsibility; his novels never offer explicit morals but allow readers to reflect on the way they should lead their lives within their society.

Ramón Pérez Fernández was born in Oviedo on 9 August 1880 to Cirilo Pérez Ayala and Carmen Fernández Viña. His father and his father's brother owned a fabric store. He had an older brother, Cirilo, and a younger sister, Asunción. At nine he entered the Jesuit school San Zoil in Carrión de los Céspedes, Palencia; two years later he transferred to another Jesuit school, the Colegio de la Inmaculada Concepción, in Gijón. In 1895 he entered the University of Oviedo, where he studied science before switching to law in his second year. There he met some of the leading figures of the pedagogic revolution then taking place in Spain, most of whom were heirs of the Krausist movement that supported social reform. The ideas of the post-Kantian German philosopher Karl Christian Friedrich Krause had been introduced into Spain in the mid nineteenth century by Julián Sanz del Río, a professor of philosophy at the University of Madrid. Under Sanz del Río and his followers, Krausism was transformed from a philosophical doctrine into a guide for a rational way of life. From this experience he gained, he later said, a "passion for justice, truth, and freedom." He received his degree in 1901 and began writing for the local press. In 1902 the Republican newspaper *El Progreso de Asturias* published his first novel, *Trece dioses: Fragmentos de las memorias de Florencio Flórez* (Thirteen Gods: Fragments of Memoirs by Florencio Flórez). Lost for almost eighty years, the work was recovered and republished in book form in 1989; it shows that Pérez de Ayala was influenced by the aesthetic decadence of Valle-Inclán.

In 1902 Pérez de Ayala began course work for a doctorate in law at the University of Madrid—he never completed it—and started publishing reviews, translations, poems, and essays in Madrid journals such as *Revista Ibérica* and *Alma Española*. In 1903 he, Juan Ramón Jiménez, Pedro González Blanco, and Gregorio Martínez Sierra founded the journal *Helios,* which became one of the most important vehicles of the incipient Spanish modernism. In 1904 his first book, the poetry collection *La paz del sendero* (The Peace of the Pathway), appeared; it evinces a melancholic tone and a symbolist orientation. It was favorably reviewed by Rubén Darío, and the positive reception helped to popularize Pérez de Ayala's name. Pérez de Ayala included the review as the foreword to the second edition (1915) of *La paz del sendero*—which was enlarged with the addition of another collection of poems, "El sendero innumerable" (The Numberless Path)—and it has appeared in all subsequent editions.

In 1907 Pérez de Ayala went to England as a correspondent. For several months he sent reports to the Madrid newspaper *Los Lunes de El Imparcial;* in January 1908 his articles began to appear in the daily national newspaper *ABC,* the Vigo journal *El Faro,* and the Buenos Aires newspaper *La Nación.* In February 1908 the family business went bankrupt, and his father committed suicide. At this point Pérez de Ayala decided to pursue a literary career. In the next six years, while continuing to contribute to newspapers and journals, he published four long autobiographical novels in which he is represented by the character Alberto Díaz de Guzmán. Taken together, the novels constitute a bildungsroman about a young artist in a hostile contemporary Spain.

The first novel in the series, *Tinieblas en las cumbres* (1907, Darkness at the Top), combines a naturalistic description of bohemian life with a symbolic subtext in which Pérez de Ayala establishes a set of thematic and stylistic contrasts—purity/lust, spirit/matter, humor/seri-

ousness, and triviality/momentousness—that highlight the protagonist's alienation. Alberto Díaz de Guzmán, a bohemian would-be artist, sets out with a group of friends and some prostitutes for Pinares Pass to watch a solar eclipse. Detailed descriptions of comic and salacious episodes along the way are meant to shock Pérez de Ayala's bourgeois readers. One of the girls, Rosina, had run away from home and become a prostitute after being seduced and impregnated by a circus strongman who had abandoned her after their one night together. The love story of Alberto and Rosina moves inexorably toward a tragic climax that stands in stark counterpoint to the light tone of the preceding narrative and that forces Alberto to acknowledge the absurdity of life and the need to search for meaning.

The title of the second novel in the tetralogy, *A.M.D.G.* (1910), stands for the motto of the Society of Jesus, *Ad Maiorem Dei Gloriam* (To the Greater Glory of God). Pérez de Ayala explains Alberto's apathy, abulia, and feeling of helplessness by returning to his childhood and describing his education in a Jesuit school. Alberto's problems are revealed to have been caused by the Jesuits' rejection of the body, denial of the principles of individual development, and use of ridicule as a pedagogical method.

In the third novel, *La pata de la raposa* (1911; translated as *The Fox's Paw,* 1924), Alberto seeks self-discovery in practical experience and meditation. In a series of epiphanies he imagines various ways of life in poems in which animals represent Christian resignation (dog), epicurean hedonism (cat), utilitarianism (ant), and skepticism, egocentrism, and sheer vanity (rooster). He ultimately decides to embrace the Horatian ideal of *aurea mediocritas* (the Golden Mean), while opening himself up to others through compassion and love.

The final novel in the series, *Troteras y danzaderas* (1912, Trotters and Dancers), is set in the bohemian Madrid of the early twentieth century and includes allusions to some of the prominent intellectual figures of the epoch, including Valle-Inclán, José Ortega y Gasset, Azorín (pseudonym of José Martínez Ruiz), and Manuel García Morente. Alberto is relegated to a minor role; the spotlight falls on characters such as Teófilo Pajares, a modernist poet whose romantic experiences oscillate between the sublime and the grotesque. Scholarly attention has focused on passages in which Pérez de Ayala points out the need for an aesthetic education that would develop one's imaginative capacity to empathize with others without sacrificing one's own individuality. This notion reflects the aesthetic theories of Teodor Lipps and Wilhelm Orringer, whom Pérez de Ayala had met in 1911 when he was in Germany on a scholarship from the Junta de Ampliación de Estudios (Board of Broadening of Studies).

In 1913 Pérez de Ayala traveled to the United States, where he visited New York City; Allentown, Pennsylvania; and Asbury Park, New Jersey. On 1 September he married an American, Mabel Darknell Rick, in Allentown; they had met in Florence, Italy, in 1911. In 1914 the couple settled in Madrid, where Pérez de Ayala obtained a position in the Ministerio de Instrucción Pública y Bellas Artes (Ministry of Public Instruction and Fine Arts). They had two sons. In 1914 he and Ortega y Gasset cofounded the Liga de Educación Política Española (Spanish League of Political Education).

In 1916 Pérez de Ayala published *Prometeo; Luz de domingo; La caída de los Limones: Novelas poemáticas de la vida española* (translated as *Prometheus; The Fall of the House of Limon; Sunday Sunlight: Poetic Novels of Spanish Life*, 1920). An innovation in these three novels is the inclusion of poems at the beginning of each chapter, forcing the reader to establish a connection between the prose and the verse. The works address societal obstacles to individual development. Marco, the protagonist of "Prometeo," longs to became a nobler sort of human being—a Nietzschean "superman"—but resigns himself to becoming the father of a new Prometheus. His son, however, turns out to be physically and mentally defective. The lovers Castor and Balbina in "Luz de domingo" flee their hometown after Balbina is raped by some of Castor's political enemies, and they die in a shipwreck on the way to America. In "La caida de los Limones" Arias, the spoiled heir of an aristocratic family in Guadalfranco, becomes a murderer because of his inability to sublimate his sexual desires.

During World War I, in which he favored the Allies, Pérez de Ayala served as a war correspondent in Italy. His reports were collected as *Herman encadenado: Notas de un viaje a los frentes del Isonzo la Carnia y el Trentino* (1917, Herman in Chains: Notes of a Journey to the Fronts of Isonzo la Carnia and Trentino). His theater reviews for various newspapers were collected in two volumes as *Las máscaras: Ensayos de crítica teatral* (1917, 1924, The Masks: Essays in Theatrical Criticism). His newspaper essays on political theory were gathered as *Política y toros* (1918, Politics and Bulls).

Pérez de Ayala returned to the United States in 1919 on another grant from the Junta de Ampliación de Estudios; he remained there for ten months, again visiting New York City and Allentown. His memoirs of the two trips were published years later as *El país del futuro: Mis viajes a los Estados Unidos (1913–1914, 1919–1920)* (1959, The Future Country: My Journeys to the United States [1913–1914, 1919–1920]).

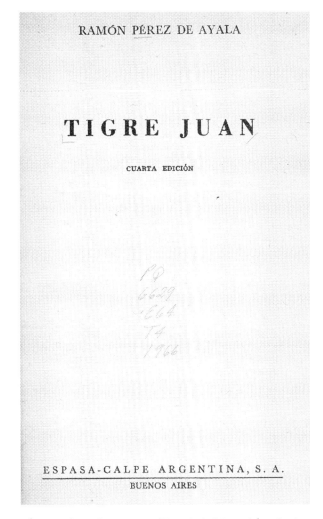

RAMÓN PÉREZ DE AYALA

# TIGRE JUAN

CUARTA EDICIÓN

ESPASA-CALPE ARGENTINA, S. A.
BUENOS AIRES

*Title page for the fourth edition of Pérez de Ayala's novel (translated as Tiger Juan, 1983), first published in 1926, about a man who is forced by his wife's betrayal to question the code of honor that would require him to kill her (Thomas Cooper Library, University of South Carolina)*

In 1921 Pérez de Ayala published a book of poetry, *El sendero andante: Momentos, modos, ditirambos, doctrinal de vida y naturaleza, poemas* (The Walking Pathway: Moments, Modes, Dithyrambs, Doctrinal on Life and Nature, Poems), and a novel, *Belarmino y Apolonio* (translated as *Belarmino and Apolonio*, 1971). In the latter work the title characters are opposites who ultimately reconcile their differences: Belarmino is a philosopher who examines reality through abstractions, and Apolonio is a playwright who lives reality as a constant drama. Two years later he published the two-part novel *Luna de miel, luna de hiel* (Honeymoon, Bittermoon) and *Los trabajos de Urbano y Simona: Continuación de Luna de miel, luna de hiel* (The Labors of Urbano and Simona: Continuation of Honeymoon, Bittermoon; translated together as *Honeymoon, Bittermoon; The Trials of Urbano and Simona*, 1972), in which he advocates an erotic pedagogy to prepare young people for sexuality instead of keeping them in an illusory paradise of innocence and ignorance until natural impulses prevail over artificially imposed morality.

The last of Pérez de Ayala's long novels is another two-part work: *Tigre Juan* (1926, Tiger John) and *El curandero de su honra (segunda parte de Tigre Juan)* (1926, The Healer of His Honor [Second Part of Tiger John]; translated together as *Tiger Juan*, 1933), for which he received the Premio Nacional de Literatura (National Literary Award) in 1927. When Tigre Juan's wife commits adultery with his adopted son, he is forced to question the validity of the code of honor that would require him to kill her.

In 1928 Pérez de Ayala was elected to the Real Academia de la Lengua (Royal Academy of the Language). In 1931 he, Ortega y Gasset, and Gregorio Marañón drew up the *Agrupación al Servicio de la República* (Gathering for the Service of the Republic), a manifesto advocating a change from monarchy to a republican form of government. After the Second Republic was established in April of that year, Pérez de Ayala was elected to the parliament, appointed director of the Prado Museum, and named ambassador to Great Britain. He resigned his ambassadorship in 1936 because of disagreement with government policy and went into voluntary exile in Buenos Aires. He never wrote another novel, or even a short story; aside from articles for the Buenos Aires newspaper *La Prensa*, he wrote only occasional poems that were published posthumously in the second volume of his *Obras completas* (1964–1969, Complete Works) under the title "El sendero ardiente" (The Burning Pathway). He visited Spain several times before returning permanently in 1954. He died in Madrid on 5 August 1962.

The novels of Ramón Pérez de Ayala's mature period, beginning with *Prometeo; Luz de domingo; La caída de los Limones,* are highly complex linguistic experiments. In these works he is unconcerned with causal and temporal consistency in his plots or with maintaining the reader's "suspension of disbelief"; he exploits mechanisms such as symmetries, contrasts, paradoxes, and the tension between appearance and reality to compel the reader's total commitment to the act of reading.

**Letters:**

*Cincuenta años de cartas íntimas a su amigo Miguel Rodríguez-Acosta (1904–1956),* edited by Andrés Amorós (Madrid: Castalia, 1980).

**Bibliography:**

Marigold Best, *Ramón Pérez de Ayala: An Annotated Bibliography of Criticism* (London: Grant & Cutler, 1980).

**Biographies:**

Francisco Agustín, *Ramón Pérez de Ayala: Su vida y obras* (Madrid: Imprenta de G. Hernández y Galo Sáez, 1927);

Miguel Pérez Ferrero, *Ramón Pérez de Ayala* (Madrid: Fundación Juan March/Guadarrama, 1973); republished as *Las mocedades de Ramón Pérez de Ayala* (Oviedo: GEA, 1992);

Jesús-Andrés Solís, *Vida de Ramón Pérez de Ayala* (Candás: Privately printed, 1979).

**References:**

Andrés Amorós, *La novela intelectual de Ramón Pérez de Ayala* (Madrid: Gredos, 1972);

Amorós, *Vida y literatura en* Troteras y danzaderas (Madrid: Castalia, 1973);

María del Carmen Bobes Naves, *Gramática textual de* Belarmino y Apolonio (Barcelona: Cupsa, 1977);

Agustín Coletes Blanco, *Gran Bretaña y los Estados Unidos en la vida de Ramón Pérez de Ayala* (Oviedo: Instituto de Estudios Asturianos, 1984);

Coletes Blanco, *La huella anglonorteamericana en la novela de Pérez de Ayala* (Murcia: Universidad de Murcia, 1987);

Coletes Blanco, *Pérez de Ayala, bajo el signo de Britannia* (Valladolid: Universidad de Valladolid, 1997);

Thomas Feeny, *The Paternal Orientation of Ramón Pérez de Ayala* (Valencia & Chapel Hill, N.C.: Hispanófila, 1985);

Pelayo H. Fernández, *Estudios sobre Ramón Pérez de Ayala* (Oviedo: Instituto de Estudios Asturianos, 1978);

Fernández, *Ideario etimológico de Ramón Pérez de Ayala* (Madrid: Porrúa Turanzas, 1982);

Florencio Friera Suárez, *Pérez de Ayala y la historia de Asturias (1880–1908)* (Oviedo: Instituto de Estudios Asturianos, 1986);

Friera Suárez, *Ramón Pérez de Ayala, testigo de su tiempo* (Gijón: Fundación Alvargonzález, 1997);

Víctor García de la Concha, "Pérez de Ayala y el compromiso generacional," *Cuadernos del Norte,* 2 (1980): 34–39;

García de la Concha, *Los senderos poéticos de Ramón Pérez de Ayala* (Oviedo: Universidad, 1970);

José Ramón González, *Ética y estética: Las novelas poemáticas de la vida española de Ramón Pérez de Ayala* (Valladolid: Universidad de Valladolid, 1992);

González, *Ramón Pérez de Ayala* (Madrid: Júcar, 1993);

José Manuel González Calvo, *La prosa de Ramón Pérez de Ayala* (Salamanca: Universidad de Salamanca, 1979);

Margarita de Hoyos González, *El mundo helénico en la obra de Ramón Pérez de Ayala* (Oviedo: Real Instituto de Estudios Asturianos, 1994);

Leon Livingstone, "The Theme of the 'Paradoxe sur le comedien' in the Novels of Ramón Pérez de Ayala," *Hispanic Review,* 22 (1954): 208–233;

Miguel Ángel Lozano Marco, *Del relato modernista a la novela poemática: La narrativa breve de Ramón Pérez de Ayala* (Alicante: Universidad de Alicante, 1983);

John J. Macklin, *The Window and the Garden: The Modernist Fictions of Ramón Pérez de Ayala* (Boulder, Colo.: Society of Spanish and Spanish-American Studies, 1988);

Julio Matas, *Contra el honor: Las novelas normativas de Ramón Pérez de Ayala* (Madrid: Seminarios y Ediciones, 1974);

Mac Gregor O'Brien, *El ideal clásico de Ramón Pérez de Ayala en sus ensayos en* La Prensa *de Buenos Aires* (Oviedo: Instituto de Estudios Asturianos, 1981);

Ángeles Prado, "Las novelas poemáticas de Ramón Pérez de Ayala," *Cuadernos Hispanoamericanos,* 367–368 (1981): 41–70;

Juan Ramón Prieto Jambrina, *El humanismo armónico de Ramón Pérez de Ayala* (Alicante: Universidad de Alicante, 1999);

Marguerite C. Rand, *Ramón Pérez de Ayala* (New York: Twayne, 1971);

K. W. Reinink, *Algunos aspectos literarios y lingüísticos de la obra de don Ramón Pérez de Ayala* (El Haya: Publicaciones del Instituto de Estudios Hispánicos, Portugueses e Hispanoamericanos de la Universidad Estatal de Utrecht, 1959);

Maruxa Salgues de Cargill, *Los mitos clásicos y modernos en la novela de Pérez de Ayala* (Jaén: Instituto de Estudios Giennenses, 1972);

Margaret Pol Stock, *Dualism and Polarity in the Novels of Ramón Pérez de Ayala* (London: Tamesis, 1988);

Sara Suárez Solís, *Análisis de "Belarmino y Apolonio"* (Oviedo: Instituto de Estudios Asturianos, 1974);

Norma Urrutia, *De* Troteras *a* Tigre Juan: *Dos grandes temas de Ramón Pérez de Ayala* (Madrid: Insula, 1960);

Miguel Viñuela, *Desmitificación y esperanza en la novela de Pérez de Ayala* (Oviedo: Instituto de Estudios Asturianos, 1991);

Frances W. Weber, *The Literary Perspectivism of Ramón Pérez de Ayala* (Chapel Hill: University of North Carolina Press, 1966).

**Papers:**

Ramón Pérez de Ayala's manuscripts and some letters received by the author are in the Archivo Pérez de Ayala in the Biblioteca de Asturias Ramón Pérez de Ayala in Oviedo.

# Arturo Pérez-Reverte
## (24 November 1951 –   )

Jeffrey Oxford
*University of Wisconsin–Milwaukee*

BOOKS: *El húsar* (Madrid: Akal, 1986);

*El maestro de esgrima* (Madrid: Mondadori, 1988); translated by Margaret Jull Costa as *The Fencing Master* (New York: Harcourt Brace, 1998; London: Harvill, 1999);

*La tabla de Flandes* (Madrid: Alfaguara, 1990); translated by Costa as *The Flanders Panel* (New York: Harcourt Brace, 1994; London: Harvill, 1994);

*El club Dumas* (Madrid: Alfaguara, 1993); translated by Peter Bush as *Dumas Club* (London: Harvill, 1995); translated by Sonia Soto as *The Club Dumas* (New York: Harcourt Brace, 1996);

*La sombra del águila* (Madrid: Alfaguara, 1993);

*Territorio comanche: Un relato* (Madrid: Ollero & Ramos, 1994);

*Cachito: Un asunto de honor* (Madrid: Santillana/Alfaguara, 1995);

*La piel del tambor* (Madrid: Santillana, 1995); translated by Soto as *The Seville Communion* (New York: Harcourt Brace, 1998; London: Harvill, 1998);

*Los héroes cansados: El demonio, el mundo, la carne,* edited by José Belmonte Serrano (Madrid: Espasa-Calpe, 1995);

*Las aventuras del capitán Alatriste* (Madrid: Alfaguara, 1996); translated by Margaret Sayers Peden as *Captain Alatriste* (New York: Putnam, 2005; London: Weidenfeld & Nicolson, 2005);

*Limpieza de sangre* (Madrid: Alfaguara, 1997); translated by Peden as *Purity of Blood* (New York: Putnam, 2006);

*El sol de Breda* (Madrid: Alfaguara, 1998);

*Patente de corso: 1993–1998,* edited by José Luis Martín Nogales (Madrid: Alfaguara, 1998);

*Sobre cuadros, libros y héroes* (Madrid: Ollero & Ramos, 1998);

*El oro del rey* (Madrid: Alfaguara, 2000);

*La carta esférica* (Madrid: Alfaguara, 2000); translated by Peden as *The Nautical Chart* (New York: Harcourt, 2001; London: Picador, 2002);

*Con ánimo de ofender, 1998–2001* (Madrid: Alfaguara, 2001);

*Arturo Pérez-Reverte ( photograph by Jerry Bauer; from the dust jacket for* The Fencing Master, *1998; Richland County Public Library)*

*La reina del sur* (Madrid: Alfaguara, 2002); translated by Andrew Hurley as *The Queen of the South* (New York: Putnam, 2004; London: Picador, 2004);

*El caballero del jubón amarillo* (Madrid: Alfaguara, 2003);

*Cabo Trafalgar: Un relato naval* (Madrid: Alfaguara, 2004).

**Collection:** *Obra breve* (Madrid: Santillana, 1995)— includes *El húsar; La pasajera del San Carlos; La sombra del águila; Un asunto de honor;* and *Sobre cuadros, libros y héroes.*

PRODUCED SCRIPTS: *Territorio comanche,* video, Videoteca Foco 2001, 1997;

*Camino de Santiago,* television, Antena 3 Televisión, 1999;

*Gitano,* motion picture, Sogepaq, 2000.


Arturo Pérez-Reverte, one of the leading detective-fiction writers of contemporary Spain, has successfully built a career since 1986 with a style that harks back to the historical and pamphlet novels of the nineteenth century. He is also one of the most widely known and read writers outside of Spain. Often compared, particularly in France, to Alexandre Dumas *pére,* Pérez-Reverte's works have been translated into more than thirty languages, adapted for the cinema, anthologized, and honored with multiple awards in various countries. Pérez-Reverte himself, however, considers his fictions to be simply a rewriting of the many books that he has read and loved in his life, manipulating them in a manner that details the historical implications and cultural influences on the modern world.

In a 1999 interview with Alix Wilber, Pérez-Reverte stated that he never really wanted to be a writer but that he began to write books after traveling abroad and feeling a desire to bring a sense of order to his world. This desire is also reflected in the characters within his works, characters who cling to their memories or culture in order to survive better in a world that they do not like. While some critics argue that Pérez-Reverte writes historical novels, this claim is true only in the sense that he uses history to expound upon the present-day conflicts he has witnessed as a journalist. As he stated in an interview with Ron Hogan: "The person who sees in my novels simple detective stories is making a mistake, as is the reader who sees them as historical novels." As José Belmonte Serrano writes, "En la olla mágica sigue cociéndose . . . la Historia, el arte y la novela gótica" (In the magical pot he continues cooking . . . History, art, and the gothic novel).

Pérez-Reverte was born on 24 November 1951 in Cartagena. His childhood on the Mediterranean coast, in the province of Murcia, has had a profound and continual impact on his life and writings, a fact demonstrated through his strong interest in scuba diving and long-term stays on his private sailboat, where he spends time composing his novels. Another childhood interest that he still maintains is reading; during his youth he read a book every two to three days. Between the ages of nine and eighteen he read thousands of books, with an abiding interest in the Spanish Golden Age of the sixteenth and seventeenth centuries as well as the Spanish novel of the nineteenth century, a time period and genre present in many of his own narratives.

After obtaining his undergraduate degree in political science and journalism, Pérez-Reverte worked on oil tankers in the early 1970s in order to see the world; his time at sea also allowed him to follow to a certain degree in the footsteps of his father and grandfather, both of whom had been employed in the merchant marine. After only a few years, however, he switched professions, working from 1973 to 1985 as a reporter for the Spanish newspaper *Pueblo,* specializing in terrorism, illegal trafficking, and armed conflict. During his more than twenty years as a journalist–from 1985 to 1994 he worked for Televisión Española–he covered wars in Cyprus, Lebanon, the Western Sahara, Equatorial Guinea, El Salvador, Nicaragua, the Falkland Islands, Chad, Libya, the Sudan, Angola, Mozambique, Croatia, and Sarajevo, as well as the coup in Tunisia, the Romanian Revolution, and the Gulf War. Twice he disappeared and was presumed dead: once in Western Sahara in 1975, and once in Eritrea in 1977. In the interview with Wilber, Pérez-Reverte commented that war "was a fascinating, passionately interesting adventure for a 20-year-old youth. I discovered horror later, when I started to see that war was not an adventure."

Almost all of Pérez-Reverte's novels have war as a backdrop to a critical examination of both Spanish society and human nature in general. His first published novel, dealing with the Spanish War of Independence, appeared in 1986 under the title *El húsar* (The Hussar). *El maestro de esgrima* (1988; translated as *The Fencing Master,* 1998) is, however, the first novel he wrote. Set in the fall of 1868, shortly before the ouster of Queen Isabel II, the plot centers on the fencing expert don Jaime Astarloa, who, having fallen in love with doña Adela de Otero, a mysterious Italian woman desirous of learning don Jaime's unstoppable fencing thrust, is soon swept up in the world of politics, secrecy, and betrayal. In this novel the author is portraying the society and day of 1868 Spain but embellishing that history with the events that he witnessed as a war correspondent in places such as Beirut, Sarajevo, Eritrea, and El Salvador.

Between the time of publication of *El maestro de esgrima* and *La tabla de Flandes* (1990; translated as *The Flanders Panel,* 1994), Pérez-Reverte served as a war correspondent covering the Romanian Revolution, the war in Mozambique, and the Gulf War. In *La tabla de Flandes* chess is used as an analogy for the complications, scheming, and intrigue of life, tying together Renaissance and late-twentieth-century Spanish society and mentality. The story revolves around Julia, hired to clean the fifteenth-century painting "La tabla de Flandes," in which the duke of Ostenburg and his knight Roger de Arras are playing a game of chess while Beatrice of Burgundy, the duke's wife and Roger's lover, is

*Dust jacket for the U.S. edition (1998) of the English translation of
Pérez-Reverte's novel* El maestro de esgrima *(1988), about a
nineteenth-century teacher of swordsmanship who falls in love
with a mysterious Italian student and is soon swept up in
the world of politics, secrecy, and betrayal
(Richland County Public Library)*

dressed in black, sitting and watching in the background. While cleaning the painting, Julia discovers a hidden Latin inscription: "Quis necavit equitem? (Who killed the knight?). During the unraveling of the mystery, she discovers that the scenario portrayed in the painting parallels the events occurring with her acquaintances and the chess expert she has consulted to solve the mystery. Pérez-Reverte's social commentary on 1990s Spain as a manipulative and egocentric society becomes most obvious through these cross-cultural and historical parallels.

In 1991, Pérez-Reverte covered the Gulf War and the war in Croatia. From 1992 to 1994 he was a war correspondent to Sarajevo, experiencing many of the events that he later placed in *Territorio comanche: Un relato* (1994, Comanche Territory: A Report), published shortly after he left his full-time job at Televisión Española. His departure from journalism was not unex-

pected; as early as March 1993, Pérez-Reverte was taking a cynical view of his life as a reporter and show host, once stating at the onset of the *Código uno* (Code One) program that he hosted: "Hoy van a ver un programa realmente sangriento, con todo el horror que puedan imaginar y más. Es tan asqueroso que me niego a verlo. Adiós" (Today you are going to see a really bloody program with all the horror that you can imagine and even more. It is so disgusting that I refuse to watch it. Goodbye), at which point he walked off the set. By this time the author-journalist had already become something of a celebrity. On 19 January 1993 he had received the Asturias-92 de Periodismo prize for his coverage of the civil war in Yugoslavia, and on 3 November 1993 he received the Premio Ondas for his *La ley de la calle* (The Law of the Street), a five-year Radio Nacional de España program on marginalized members of society. Additionally, in March the movie version of *El maestro de esgrima* won the Goya Prize for best adapted screenplay and best original music. Also in 1993, he was selected by the French magazine *Lire* as one of the ten best foreign novelists.

In May 1993 Pérez-Reverte's *El club Dumas* (translated as *Dumas Club*, 1995) was published and awarded the French Gran Prix de la littérature policière (Grand Prize for Detective Literature). As the title insinuates, the writer Dumas, as well as his novel *Les trois mousequetaires* (1844, The Three Musketeers), is present throughout Pérez-Reverte's work. The novel, however, is more than simply a metaliterary rewriting of its French inspiration, characters, and plot, although at times entire paragraphs in the two novels are parallel; it also includes bits of Pérez-Reverte's family history. For example, in *El club Dumas* "Boris Balkan toma entre sus manos el libro titulado *El caballero del jubón amarillo*, de Lucus René, y lee sólo el inicio" (Boris Balkan takes in his hands the book titled *The Horseman of the Yellow Tunic*, by Lucus René, and reads only the beginning). Lucus René was the pseudonym used by Pérez-Reverte's father, the author of an unedited novel with the same title, lines of which are reproduced in *El club Dumas*. When further questioned by Wilber about the autobiographical element of *El club Dumas*, Pérez-Reverte resorted to a comparison between that novel and his earlier *El maestro de esgrima*. The main character of *El club Dumas*, Lucas Corso, "may be precisely the character that most incarnates my perspective. If I had to compare Jaime Astarloa, the fencing master, to Lucas Corso, I might say that the fencing master is that older man that I might have wanted to be. And Lucas Corso is the man that life has made me."

*El club Dumas* is perhaps more intertextual than any other of the author's works. Pérez-Reverte noted to Wilber that "some students from the University of Salamanca did a paper on the implicit and explicit literature in *The club Dumas,* and there were about 500 titles, some of which are cited expressly, others not quoted but indirectly referred to. . . . I must confess there were some that even I had not foreseen. But I will say that there were others I knew were there, and that nobody caught." This novel is not the only instance of the author's incorporation of other texts into his own stories. Books and reading have been a lifelong love of Pérez-Reverte's, and their entrance into his narratives enriches his own texts as well as provides alternative readings of those canonical works.

In November 1993, *La sombra del águila* (The Shadow of the Eagle) appeared in print; this novel, the main characters of which are Spanish prisoners in the French army in 1812, had previously been serialized in *El País* during August of the same year. The prisoners, in fact, are "volunteers" in the French army attempting to desert to the Russian army. Napoleon, supposing them to be sacrificing themselves in a deadly military advance, honors them for heroic actions and offers another insight into the military debacles of the French general.

In May 1994 Pérez-Reverte announced his departure from Televisión Española in order to write novels full-time, although he continued to write a Sunday editorial for *El Semanal,* a supplement to various Spanish newspapers with a circulation of some 1.5 million copies. This work, however, he denies as being true journalism, telling Félix Linares in a 2002 interview that it is a type of personal exercise in which he shares a laugh with certain people or enrages others.

*Territorio comanche,* a recounting of Pérez-Reverte's experiences as a war correspondent in Bosnia, was published later in 1994. The author commented to Diego Barnabé in 2000 that the intent behind the work was to narrate the war as he saw it, not in sound bites but as "Cosas que se te quedan, miradas, recuerdos, sensaciones, olores, sentimientos, soledad" (Things that remain with you, looks, memories, sensations, smells, feelings, solitude). In this sense, the novel is an examination of the serious physical, psychological, and moral consequences of war and is more realistically achieved through autobiography. Barnabé concluded, quoting the novelist, that more than in any other of Pérez-Reverte's works, *Territorio comanche* displays the author playing an integral part in the narrative: Barlés, the main character, "es siempre, y en todos los casos, Arturo Pérez-Reverte. . . . no hay nada de ficción" (is always, and in all cases, Arturo Pérez-Reverte. . . . there is nothing fictitious).

*Cachito: Un asunto de honor* (Cachito: A Matter of Honor), Pérez-Reverte's little-known fairy tale of love featuring Prince Charming, was published in 1995. In

*Dust jacket for the U.S. edition (1994) of the English translation of Pérez-Reverte's novel* La tabla de Flandes *(1990), in which an art restorer discovers clues to a mystery in a fifteenth-century painting she is cleaning (Richland County Public Library)*

November of the same year, *La piel del tambor* (The Drum Skin; translated as *The Seville Communion,* 1998) appeared. The novel received the Best Book of Fiction Award from *Elle* magazine and the Jean Monnet Prize of European Literature in 1997 and remained on the best-seller lists for more than eleven months. The plot revolves around Father Lorenzo Quart, an emissary from the Vatican sent to Seville to determine the identity of the hacker into the Vatican computer system. The hacker has left a message for the Pope to save Our Lady of the Tears, a baroque church in downtown Seville scheduled for razing. During the course of his investigation, Father Quart faces both physical dangers and conflicts between his spiritual duty as a priest and his carnal desires. The Catholic Church, in this novel, turns out to be less than the stable, unchanging institution it claims to be, especially in Spanish society.

In 1996 Pérez-Reverte published *Las aventuras del capitán Alatriste* (translated as *Captain Alatriste,* 2005), the

*Dust jacket for the U.S. edition (1996) of the English translation of Pérez-Reverte's novel* El club Dumas *(1995), which combines passages from Alexandre Dumas* pére's *novel* The Three Musketeers *with incidents from Pérez-Reverte's family history and references to at least five hundred other literary works (Richland County Public Library)*

first of a series of novels based on Diego Alatriste, a soldier in the early-seventeenth-century battles between Spain and the Netherlands, and his charge, the orphaned Iñigo Balboa. In a 1999 interview with Juan Cruz, Pérez-Reverte explained this popular series: "Es evidente que detrás está toda la literatura española del Siglo de Oro . . . Cervantes, a Lope, a Calderón, a Quevedo, a Pellicer, no sólo los de primera fila y con todo eso destilado, de ahí sale Alatriste" (It is evident that behind it is all the Spanish Golden Age literature . . . Cervantes, Lope, Calderon, Quevedo, Pellicer, not only the first-rate writers, and from distilling all that out comes Alatriste). Alatriste portrays not only the literature of Golden Age Spain but also the society and culture of the time period; much of the historical

background research was completed by Pérez-Reverte's daughter Carlota. The seventeenth-century culture is evident in both the chivalry and gallantry of the male society and the violence inherent in the emphasis on swordsmanship and the Inquisition. All of the novels are narrated by Iñigo.

With this descriptive technique prevalent throughout the entire series, alongside Pérez-Reverte's constant social commentary of present-day Spain, the author deftly shows how little removed contemporary Spain is from the decadent society that witnessed the end of the Spanish Empire. In a 1999 interview with Gabriel Contreras, Pérez-Reverte stated: "Está muy claro que no estoy hablando sólo del siglo XVII. . . . Yo estoy hablando del ahora, del español de hoy, de lo español. . . . la piltrafa que todavía somos" (It is very clear that I am not talking only about the seventeenth century. . . . I am talking about now, about the Spaniard of today, about everything Spanish . . . the losers that we still are).

In 1997 *Limpieza de sangre* (translated as *Purity of Blood,* 2006), the second in the Alatriste series, was published. In this novel Alatriste is persuaded to join an attempt to kidnap don Vicente's daughter from a convent where a libertine is in charge. Iñigo is captured by the Inquisition, and Alatriste attempts to save him, the plot ending with a surprising revelation that the inquisitor himself has Jewish blood in his lineage. As is the case in the majority of Pérez-Reverte's narratives, and particularly in the other novels, the author plays with intertextuality by quoting poems or other pieces of literature from important writers of seventeenth-century Spain and using historical figures such as Luis de Góngora or Francisco de Quevedo as characters.

Pérez-Reverte published two books in 1998: *Patente de corso: 1993–1998* (Corsican Patent: 1993–1998), a compilation of articles from *El Semanal,* and *El sol de Breda* (The Sun of Breda), the third novel in the Alatriste series. In this work, Iñigo must try to survive a battle by getting close enough to his enemy to kill him with his sword. In the process he witnesses the surrender of Breda, an event he later recounts to his friend Velázquez, which inspires the latter's famous painting *La rendición de Breda* (The Surrender of Breda). In 1999 Pérez-Reverte saw the production of the motion-picture adaptation of *El club Dumas* as *The Ninth Gate;* that year he wrote the script for the three-part *Camino de Santiago* (1999, Road to Santiago) series for Antena 3 Televisión and the screenplay for the movie *Gitano* (2000, Gypsy).

In April 2000 Pérez-Reverte's *La carta esférica* (translated as *The Nautical Chart,* 2001) was published. This story, deriving from his experiences at an auction of maritime objects, is both autobiographical and intertextual, affording him an opportunity to write a novel incorporating elements from books about the sea. The sailor protagonist, Coy, returns to Cartagena and meets Tánger Soto, a female employee of the Naval Museum in Madrid obsessed with finding the sunken ship *Dei Gloria*. Realizing that Coy may aid her, she manipulates him into falling in love with her and thereby gains his assistance. As in the author's other "historical novels," this one as well combines the ancient with the contemporary in a blend that proves to be an examination of the history of maritime navigation as well as a commentary on the nature of the sea and womankind. Pérez-Reverte's portrayal of women is fairly constant: they are both mysterious and seductive.

Betrayal by a female lover is also part of *El oro del rey* (2000, The King's Gold), the fourth novel of the Alatriste series. Alatriste returns from Flanders and undertakes, in Seville, the mission of recruiting a group of swordsmen to help save the gold being brought from the Americas from smugglers and corrupt customs employees. Iñigo, assisting in the endeavor, is betrayed by Angelica, a woman he loves, and Alatriste rescues him at the last moment from being killed by Alatriste's enemy Malatesta.

An interactive game version of *Las aventuras del capitán Alatriste,* intended as an educational tool for high-school students, was released in 2001. In the same year, *La carta esférica* won the Premio Mediterráneo from the Goncourt Academy and Pérez-Reverte published *Con ánimo de ofender, 1998–2001* (With a Desire to Offend, 1998–2001), a compilation of newspaper articles with a biting tone evocative of the nineteenth-century author Mariano José de Larra's essays regarding the perennial flaws of Spain.

In January 2002, *Las aventuras del capitán Alatriste* was adapted in a comic-book format, and *La carta esférica* was awarded a medal from the French Maritime Academy. In addition, *La reina del sur* (translated as *The Queen of the South,* 2004) was published later in the year. This novel is a deviation from the author's general use of historical settings or contemporary military conflicts in favor of the context of the *narcocorridos* (drug ballads) of underground Mexico. This narrative is also innovative for the author because of its focus on women in a more positive fashion—depicting particularly their struggle to survive in a masculine world—and on the drug culture of another country, Mexico. The main character, Teresa Mendoza, narrates her life story as the girlfriend of a drug runner; after his assassination, she eventually becomes the leader of an internationally feared gang. Another, perhaps greater, innovation with this novel was Pérez-Reverte's invention of a slang that would both represent the underground of the Mexican drug society and be understood by the author's Iberian Spanish readers.

The fifth of six planned installments of the Alatriste series appeared in November 2003 with the publication of *El caballero del jubón amarillo,* named after his father's unpublished work. In this novel, Alatriste has a relationship with the actress María de Castro, King Phillip IV's lover. A palace conspiracy to kill the king is uncovered, and the blame falls on Alatriste. Iñigo, now somewhat older and more experienced, once again narrates the events.

In 2003 Arturo Pérez-Reverte was elected a member of the Real Academia Española, ending his independence from and indifference toward the literary establishment. While his novels have been widely accepted and read by the general public, until that honor was bestowed on him, few academicians outside of Spain had embraced him; such scholarly disinterest, however, is changing. His novels are distinct in their introduction of the reader to Golden Age Spain and offer a critical commentary of contemporary Spain understandable only in light of the historical antecedents of the day exposed in the narratives. At the same time, however, the acceptance of his work in multiple countries, languages, and cultures is evidence that his examination of human nature and foibles is not merely distinctive to the Spanish mentality—it is universal, as well.

## Interviews:

Diego Barnabé, "De corresponsal de guerra a escritor de best-sellers," *Radio El Espectador, Uruguay* (26 November 1996) <http://www.espectador.com/text/pglobal/reverte.htm>;

Alix Wilber, "The Accidental Author: A Conversation with Arturo Pérez-Reverte," *Amazon.com* (1999) <http://www.amazon.com/exec/obidos/ts/feature/7786/104-6291053-3982311>;

Gabriel Contreras, "Entrevista con Arturo Pérez-Reverte," *Espéculo,* 11 (June 1999) <www.ucm.es/info/especulo/numero11/perezrev.html>;

Juan Cruz, "Entrevista," *Revista Crisol* (Winter 1999/2000) <www.alatriste.inicia.es/arturo/entrevista2.htm>;

Barnabé, "El español Arturo Pérez-Reverte presenta 'La carta esférica,' su última novela," *Radio El Espectador, Uruguay* (16 May 2000) <http://www.espectador.com/text/pglobal/reverte1.htm>;

Félix Linares, "Transcripción de la conversación entre Arturo Pérez-Reverte y Félix Linares el 13 de junio de 2002," *El Correo digital* (13 June 2002) <http://www.canales.elcorreodigital.com/auladecultura/reverte2.html>;

Carolyn A. Durham and John P. Gabriele, "Entrevista con Arturo Pérez-Reverte: Deslindes de una novela globalizada," *Anales de la Literatura Española Contemporánea,* 28, no. 1 (2003): 233–245;

Ron Hogan, "Arturo Pérez-Reverte," *Beatrice Interview* <http://www.beatrice.com/interviews/perez-reverte> [accessed 16 September 2005];

Javier Rioyo, "Entrevista a Arturo Pérez-Reverte" <www.alatriste.inicia.es/arturo/entrevista3.htm> [accessed 16 September 2005].

**References:**

"Author of the Hour: Arturo Pérez-Reverte," *Criticas,* 2 (November/December 2002): 8;

José Belmonte Serrano, *Arturo Pérez-Reverte: La sonrisa del cazador (La novela y su didáctica)* (Murcia, Spain: Nausícaä Edición Electrónica, 2002);

Belmonte Serrano, "Un paseo por Revertelandia; La obra narrativa de Arturo Pérez-Reverte," *Murgetana,* 101 (1999): 115–129;

Belmonte Serrano and José Manuel López de Abiada, eds., *Sobre héroes y libros: La obra narrativa y periodística de Arturo Pérez-Reverte* (Murcia, Spain: Nausícaä Edición Electrónica, 2003);

Juan Cruz-Mendizabal, "El arte del siglo XV, al servicio de la literatura de suspense del siglo XX: *La tabla de Flandes,* de Arturo Pérez-Reverte," *Murgetana,* 92 (1996): 77–87;

Carolyn A. Durham, "Books beyond Borders: Intertextuality in Arturo Perez Reverte's *El club Dumas,*" *Anales de la Literatura Española Contemporánea,* 26, no. 2 (2001): 61–77;

Pablo Gil Casado, "*La piel del tambor:* Testimonio al modo posmoderno," in *LA CHISPA '99: Selected Proceedings,* edited by Gilberto Paolini and Claire J. Paolini (New Orleans: Tulane University, 1999), pp. 61–68;

Philippe Merlo-Morat, "El folletín moderno: El regreso de un género decimonónico," *Revista de Filología Hispánica,* 16, no. 3 (2000): 607–624;

Elisa Silió, "Elmer Mendoza explora los efectos del narcotráfico en la cultura mexicana en 'El amante de Janis Joplin,'" *El País,* 18 February 2003, p. 38;

Guy H. Wood, "*El maestro de esgrima* y el canon hollywoodiano," *Cine-Lit, II: Essays on Peninsular Film and Fiction,* edited by Wood, George Cabello Castellet, and Jaume Martí-Olivella (Portland, Ore.: Portland State University Press / Corvallis, Ore.: Oregon State University / Portland, Ore.: Reed College, 1995), pp. 117–129.

# Juan Manuel de Prada
## *(1970 –   )*

### Toni Dorca
*Macalester College*

BOOKS: *Un mundo especular y otros relatos* (Valencia: Gráficas Marí Montañana, 1991);

*Coños* (Madrid: Valdemar, 1995);

*El silencio del patinador* (Madrid: Valdemar, 1995);

*Las máscaras del héroe,* 2 volumes (Madrid: Valdemar, 1996);

*La tempestad* (Barcelona: Seix Barral, 1997); translated by Paul Antill as *The Tempest* (London: Sceptre, 2000; Woodstock, N.Y.: Overlook, 2003);

*La vida en el mar: A favor, en contra* ([Spain]: Sociedad Estatal Lisboa, 1998);

*Reserva natural* (Gijón: Llibros del Pexe, 1998);

*Las esquinas del aire: En busca de Ana María Martínez Sagi* (Barcelona: Planeta, 2000);

*Animales de compañía* (Madrid: SIAL Ediciones, 2000);

*Desgarrados y excéntricos* (Barcelona: Seix Barral, 2001);

*La vida invisible* (Madrid: Espasa Calpe, 2003).

*Juan Manuel de Prada (photograph © Gonzalo Cruz; from the dust jacket for* The Tempest, *translated by Paul Antill, 2003; Richland County Public Library)*

During the 1990s in Spain a group of young novelists came to the fore who succeeded in connecting to an adolescent audience by paying attention to its most immediate concerns. Their narratives, written in a colloquial style that includes frequent dialogues and references to popular culture, deal with the troubled existence of young men and women in postindustrial Spain. Critics have usually resorted to the label "Generation X" to describe this new vogue of realism that focuses on the loss of ideals of the protagonists and their difficult transition to adulthood. Another salient feature of this movement is its disavowal of canonical literature, which is surrendered to other types of intertextuality, such as television, rock music, cult movies, and pulp fiction.

In stark contrast to his Generation X contemporaries, Juan Manuel de Prada seeks to rescue literature from a cultural climate that privileges lowbrow forms of expression. Prada thus presents himself as a man of letters who conceives of his art as a profession rather than as dilettantism. In an age of technological advances that threaten to diminish the value of the printed page, Prada's works stand in defiance of the contention by cultural critics that a novel or a poem is a textual artifact like a comic strip, a rap, or a World Wide Web painting. Instead, the lives of both Prada and the characters he portrays are heavily determined by the all-pervasive influence of literature.

Born in 1970 in the Basque town of Baracaldo, Prada spent most of his childhood and adolescence in Zamora before moving to Salamanca. Since 1998 he has resided in Madrid. While he holds a law degree, writing has been his only professional occupation. In barely two years, from 1995 to 1997, he went from being unknown to winning the Planeta Prize, Spain's most celebrated literary award. Recently chosen by *The New Yorker* as one of the six most important young European authors, Prada has evolved into a public figure. His regular contributions to the newspaper *ABC*, on whose editorial board he sits, have established his reputation as a social commentator. He has gathered his articles into two collections, *Reserva natural* (1998, Natural Reserve) and *Animales de compañía* (2000, Pets).

Prada's *Coños* (1995, Pussies), pleased the majority of critics with its ingenious combination of eroticism, humor, and delightful prose. A generic indeterminacy presides over the fifty-four illustrated vignettes, centered on the celebration of the female sex organ. In his prologue, Luis García Jambrina comments on the impossible task of categorizing such a work: "A pesar de su título, estos *Coños* no tienen género conocido. La única etiqueta que les cuadra es la de libro insólito—a mitad de camino entre lo narrativo y lo lírico, el cuento y la poesía" (Despite its title, these *Coños* do not partake of a known genre. The only label that befits them is that of an unusual book—halfway between the narrative and the lyrical, the short story and the poem). *Coños* can also be read as an exercise in experimentation following in the steps of Ramón Gómez de la Serna's *Senos* (1917, Breasts). The brevity of the form allows for a minimally developed plot and a means for Prada to display his crafted prose.

*El silencio del patinador* (1995, The Silence of the Skater) is a collection of short stories including most of the recurrent themes in Prada's narrative. Notorious among these is a metafictional meditation upon literature as a human enterprise doomed to failure and oblivion, as in "Noches galantes" (Gallant Nights), "Las noches heroicas" (Heroic Nights), and "Gálvez" (Gálvez). In searching for literary fame, the protagonists of these stories usually move from the province to the capital only to witness the collapse of their careers. Prada's penchant for self-referential discourse touches also on the mysteries surrounding the creative act, as in his tribute to Jorge Luis Borges, "El gallito ciego" (The Blind Little Rooster). Additionally, Prada's obsessions include memory and a nostalgia for the past, as in "Señoritas en sepia" (Girls in Sepia). He also focuses on the rite of passage from childhood to adolescence, an apprenticeship fraught with disillusionment reminiscent of a baroque aesthetics, as in "Sangre azul" (Blue Blood).

Prada's short story "Gálvez" was expanded into *Las máscaras del héroe* (1996, The Masks of the Hero). A monumental novel both in length and scope, it fuses imagination into history in reconstructing Spain's social, artistic, and political arena between 1900 and the breakout of the Civil War in 1936. In Prada's words, *Las máscaras del héroe* ought to be considered historical

fiction, since "no aspira a la verdad, sino a la recreación de la verdad" (it does not aim at the truth, but at the recreation of the truth). The novel is presented as an autobiographical account of Fernando Navales (a fictional character) published posthumously by a nameless editor. The memoirs also devote considerable space to the haphazard existence of Pedro Luis de Gálvez, the poet-turned-revolutionary who is Fernando's nemesis throughout the story.

The first part of *Las máscaras del héroe*, "De profundis," is a letter written by Gálvez to the director of the Ocaña jail where he is serving time for allegedly slandering King Alfonso XIII during a public speech. In the letter, Gálvez resorts to the devices of the picaresque novel, whereby the narrative of one's life turns into an act of self-justification that ultimately seeks the empathy of the reader or, in Gálvez's case, his freedom. Parts 2 and 3, "Museo de espectros" (Museum of Specters) and "La dialéctica de las pistolas" (The Dialectic of the Pistols), comprise Fernando's memoirs proper, conveniently organized and selected with the consent of Soledad Blanco Navales, Fernando's sole heir. The editor includes a coda recounting both Gálvez's courageous last days in jail before being killed by a Francoist firing squad on 30 April 1940 and Fernando's impending hysteria, which ends in suicide two years later.

Prada's hybrid novel alternates between a pseudo-autobiography and a biography of lesser-known Andalusian poet Pedro Luis de Gálvez. Fernando begins by telling the reader that his origins in an impoverished aristocratic family have forced him to make a living on his own. Anxious to rise above his station, he soon manages to become the right-hand assistant of the director of a successful theater company in Madrid. Even though he enjoys the privileges of a comfortable position in society, Fernando yearns for wider recognition in the literary field. Since he suffers from chronic writer's block, he does not hesitate to steal and plagiarize Gálvez's unpublished poems as a means to achieve glory. At the onset of the 1936 military uprising, Fernando is arrested by Republican forces and sentenced to capital punishment, but his life is spared by Gálvez in the most climatic moment of the novel. Yet, despite having survived the war, Fernando's failed pursuit of love and celebrity finally get the better of him as he decides to take his own life in desperation. His name then sinks into total oblivion.

The title of the novel refers not to Fernando but to the complex and multifaceted personality of his alter ego, Gálvez. A representative of the art for art's sake attitude of early-twentieth-century modernism, Gálvez epitomizes the bohemian artist's desperate efforts at circumventing the conventions of bourgeois society. An irreconcilable mixture of opposite traits, Gálvez appears simultaneously as a villain and a hero, a con artist and a committed revolutionary, an unfaithful and a devoted husband. His ultimate triumph over Fernando lies in having his poems left to posterity: his name will not be forgotten by future generations. Though Gálvez was miserably poor and neglected during his lifetime, the publication of Fernando's memoirs has promoted him to the "cielo intacto de las mitologías" (intact heaven of mythologies).

Las máscaras del héroe encompasses a crucial period in Spain's oft-interrupted quest for modernity. In his attempt to re-create those years accurately, Prada has conducted thorough research that has yielded impressive results, in particular the rediscovery of Gálvez and other secondary figures of the time. But as Prada himself admits in the foreword of the novel, "el respeto minucioso por el pasado es una coartada que emplean quienes necesitan ocultar su mala prosa" (the minute respect for the past is an alibi employed by those who need to hide their bad prose). He thus allows himself considerable latitude in the characterization of icons such as Borges, Carmen de Burgos, Ramón Gómez de la Serna, Luis Buñuel, Federico García Lorca, and José Antonio Primo de Rivera. In general, Las máscaras del héroe underscores that Prada is more concerned about the self-referential dimension of literature than he is about realistic illusion.

Prada was the recipient of the Planeta Prize for his next novel, La tempestad (1997; translated as The Tempest, 2000). Set in contemporary Venice, La tempestad can be read as a detective fiction that reflects on the nature of the artistic experience and its effects upon the audience. The story concerns Alejandro Ballesteros, a young art-history professor who arrives in Venice on a fellowship to complete his dissertation on The Tempest, the painting by the Renaissance artist Giorgione displayed at one of the city museums. After witnessing the murder of Fabio Valenzin, a notorious art dealer and forger, Alejandro decides to investigate the motives behind the killing. In the process, he becomes sentimentally involved with Chiara Gabetto, a painting restorer and former lover of Valenzin. Upon the final revelation that it was Chiara who killed Valenzin in order to retrieve The Tempest, stolen from the museum, Alejandro decides to leave Venice and return to Spain.

Like other Prada protagonists, Alejandro realizes that his youth has been wasted on futile enterprises. His commitment to resolving the crime stems from his need for Chiara's love, which would cure his solitude. Alejandro does not succeed in having Chiara give up Venice and move to Spain with him. In the end he is bereft of consolation, while coping with an increasing and incurable misanthropy. Only the indelible memory of Chiara, at once painful and soothing, provides some

*Dust jacket for the U.S. edition (2003) of the English translation of Prada's novel* La tempestad *(1997), in which a Spanish professor of art history becomes involved in a murder mystery in Venice (Richland County Public Library)*

relief to the life of celibacy to which he has resigned himself. Underlying this plot characteristic of detective stories, La tempestad provides a metafictional commentary on the perception of art based upon "la religión del sentimiento" (the religion of sentiment). This doctrine emphasizes the emotional component inherent in the appreciation of a painting at the expense of the higher role usually attributed to intelligence and reason.

A familiar awareness of the porosity between historical research and literary imagination reappears in Las esquinas del aire: En busca de Ana María Martínez Sagi (2000, The Corners of the Air. In Search of Ana María Martínez Sagi). In the prologue Prada advocates the practice of an "escritura ebria en libertad" (writing drunk with liberty) that does away with genre conventions. He adds, though, that he has fused elements of traditional biography, literary essay, documentary, and memoirs into a final product presented "de manera novelesca" (in the fashion of a novel). He calls this commingling of genres a "quest," a term he translates freely as "biografía detectivesca" (detective biography).

*Las esquinas del aire* is a first-person account of a nameless narrator's hunt for Ana María Martínez Sagi, a multifaceted Catalan poet, athlete, Republican union leader, war correspondent, and forerunner of feminism. After making a name for herself during the 1920s and 1930s, she vanished from the public arena while in exile in France and the United States, from 1939 to 1969. Prada's efforts at retrieving a forgotten writer attest once again to his interest in "los desheredados de la literatura" (the disinherited of literature), who enjoy a brief period of celebrity before falling into oblivion.

The narrator's curiosity is stirred by the reading of an interview with Martínez Sagi conducted years earlier by César González Ruano. With the help of an eccentric bookstore owner and a discreet young woman, he embarks upon a quest for Martínez Sagi that barely disguises the search for his own identity: "la convicción supersticiosa de que, al reivindicar su figura, estaba también afirmando la mía" (the superstitious conviction that, upon vindicating her figure, I was also asserting mine). Near the end of section 1, "Un laberinto de presencias" (A Labyrinth of Presences), the narrator and his peers find out that Martínez Sagi has returned from exile and is living in a small town near Barcelona. She agrees to meet with them provided that they do not subject her to a formal interview but rather allow her to unravel her memories at will. In part 2, "El hilo de Ariadna" (Ariadne's Thread), the narrative voice of Martínez Sagi takes over in order to fill in the gaps and complete the story of her life. The first narrator reappears in the epilogue to inform the reader about the worsening condition of Martínez Sagi, which culminates in her death on 2 January 2000, just a few hours after the conclusion of the book. Finally, the last section includes an anthology of her poems, "La voz sola" (The Solitary Voice), selected and edited by the narrator.

In *Las esquinas del aire* the narrator's goal is to reveal the real woman emerging from what were no more than quasi-fictional traits at the beginning. She embodies a new generation of Spanish women trying to free themselves from the constraints of a patriarchal society. Yet, notwithstanding the modern attitude espoused by Martínez Sagi, *Las esquinas del aire* cannot be read as a feminist manifesto. When the narrator claims that he is writing "una biografía del corazón" (a biography of the heart), he suggests that readers should look beyond the events of the story to delve into the psychology of the protagonist and ultimately understand her life in retrospect. The young, free-spirited, and extroverted Martínez Sagi turns into a solitary individual as a result of two life-transforming experiences. The first is her intimate relationship with the writer

Elisabeth Mulder, which culminates in a trip together to Mallorca during Easter 1932 and ends tragically when her partner decides not to risk her reputation any more. The intensity of Martínez Sagi's passion is such, though, that she remains forever loyal to the memory of her congenial soul, to whom she devotes the final words of her testimony. The second experience is the defeat of the Republicans at the hands of Franco's troops, which forces her to leave Spain for France, where she becomes part of the Resistance against the German invaders in World War II. Upon France's liberation, however, she slides into incurable melancholy, "que sería mi condena perpetua hasta hoy" (which would be my perpetual condemnation until today).

Like Alejandro in *La tempestad,* Martínez Sagi has grown increasingly devoid of love and companionship save for her faithful remembrance of Elisabeth Mulder. Only her relentless dedication to poetry has sustained her during all these years of seclusion, allowing her to sublimate her deepest anxieties and frustrations in "otra realidad donde la poesía triunfase sobre la monótona crueldad de los días" (another reality where poetry triumphed over the monotonous cruelty of the days). In the end, she is granted the opportunity to redeem herself by telling her life, after which she dies at peace with herself.

*Desgarrados y excéntricos* (2001, Lacerated and Eccentric People) is a collection of fifteen portraits of writers whose short-lived fame has not led to their inclusion in the Spanish literary canon. They are Armando Buscarini, Gálvez, Fernando Villegas Estrada, Mario Arnold, Silverio Lanza, Nicasio Pajares, Iván de Nogales, Xavier Bóveda, Gonzalo Seijas, Pedro Boluda, Pedro Barrantes, Vicente Massot, Eliodoro Puche, Daja-Tarto, and Margarita de Pedroso. Prada's recovery of historical facts serves as a starting point for a process of fictionalization that blurs the lines between biography and novel. His compilation of "hechos reales perfectamente documentados" (perfectly documented real facts) aims nonetheless at outlining "personajes que parecen fabulosos y no pocas veces fantásticos" (characters who seem imaginary and at times fantastic).

Prada's novel *La vida invisible* (2003, The Invisible Life) was awarded the Espasa Calpe Primavera Prize. The title refers to mysterious forces that rise to the surface and determine the behavior of the characters under their spell. Such an occurrence is what befalls the protagonist, writer Alejandro Losada. In the first part, "El guardián del secreto" (The Guardian of the Secret), Alejandro's trip to Chicago in the wake of the 11 September 2001 terrorist attacks in New York becomes a life-transforming experience. While there, he makes the acquaintance of two people who forever change his outlook on life. The first is Elena Salvador, a deranged young woman with whom he has an affair that fills him with remorse soon afterward. The second is Tom Chambers, a Vietnam War veteran who introduces Alejandro to unknown facts about Fanny Riffel. A famous pinup girl in the 1950s, Fanny ended up in an asylum after brutally murdering one of her former abusers. Having confessed to Alejandro how he harassed Fanny years ago, Chambers provides Alejandro with all the documentation he has gathered over years of looking after her so that his friend may write "la vida invisible de Fanny Riffel" (Fanny Riffel's invisible life).

The second section of the novel, "Guía de lugares imaginarios" (Guide of Imaginary Places), narrates retrospectively that Alejandro and his fiancée, Laura, had known each other ever since their adolescence. Destiny brings them together again when they meet unexpectedly at the National Library in Madrid and resume their friendship. This friendship gradually evolves into romance and, ultimately, into a promise of marriage.

The third section, "La vida invisible" (The Invisible Life), alternates between two narratives. The first deals with Fanny Riffel's life as told by Alejandro at the instigation of his friend Chambers. The second continues in the present, when Elena follows Alejandro to Madrid in an attempt to claim his love for her and have him acknowledge that he is the father of her unborn baby. Having accepted his share of responsibility in Elena's madness, Alejandro rescues her from a prostitution ring and assists her in delivering her son. Finally, the epilogue brings Alejandro and Elena together, while leaving open what will happen with his commitment to Laura.

*La vida invisible* explores the redemption of one's guilt through pain and sacrifice. In this respect, Chambers and Alejandro resemble each other in their decision to atone for their crimes through an act of reparation. Such a reparation entails the awakening of Alejandro's moral conscience, which in turn transforms him, like Chambers, into "un hombre nuevo" (a new man). These parallel stories (Chambers/Fanny and Alejandro/Elena) both involve decisive moments in which a character discovers his or her true self as revealed in another person.

In Juan Manuel de Prada's first works, most notably *Las máscaras del héroe,* the futility of ambition, along with tainted relations among human beings, leads inevitably to despair, solitude, and death. In *Las esquinas del aire* and *La vida invisible,* however, pessimism has given way to hope and an ethical stance. As a result of this evolution, Prada is becoming a mature writer capable of conveying a transcendental message to his readers. His writing has moved beyond the use of highly elaborate prose to reach universal truths about the human condition.

*Cover for Prada's 2003 novel,* La Vida Invisible *(The Invisible Life), about a Spanish writer who visits Chicago in 2001 and becomes intrigued with the story of a 1950s American pinup girl who went insane after murdering a man who abused her (Gorgas Library, University of Alabama)*

**References:**

Rubén Castillo Gallego, "Dos aspectos de una novela: *Las máscaras del héroe,* de Juan Manuel de Prada," *Versants: Revue Suisse des Littératures Romanes/Rivista Svizzera di Letterature Romanze/Schweizerische Zeitschrift für Romanische Literaturen,* 36 (1999): 153–163;

Luis Alberto de Cuenca, "La narrativa de Juan Manuel de Prada," *Ínsula,* 591 (1996): 9–11;

Toni Dorca, "Juan Manuel de Prada o el arte de la biografía," *Symposium,* 58, no. 4 (2004): 108–121;

Ottmar Ette, "Mit Haut und Haar? Korperliches und Leibhaftiges bei Ramón Gómez de la Serna, Luisa Futoransky und Juan Manuel de Prada: Jenseits binarer Oppositionen," *Romanistische Zeitschrift für Literaturgeschichte/Cahiers d'Histoire des Littératures Romanes,* 25, nos. 3–4 (2001): 429–465;

Luis García Jambrina, "En torno a *Las máscaras del héroe, de* Juan Manuel de Prada," *Ínsula,* 605 (1997): 11–13;

García Jambrina, "La narrativa española de los Noventa: El caso de Juan Manuel de Prada," *Versants: Revue Suisse des Littératures Romanes/Rivista Svizzera di Letterature Romanze/Schweizerische Zeitschrift für Romanische Literaturen,* 36 (1999): 165–176;

María Asunción Gómez, "*Las máscaras del héroe* de Juan Manuel de Prada: Una reescritura del esperpento," *Anales de la Literatura Española Contemporánea,* 26, no. 2 (2001): 115–232;

Edward T. Gurski, "*La Tempestad:* A Renaissance Painting by Giorgione Intersects with a Twentieth-Century Thriller by Juan Manuel de Prada," in *La Chispa '99. Selected Proceedings,* edited by Gilbert Paolini and Claire J. Paolini (New Orleans: Tulane University Press, 1999), pp. 167–176;

Marco Kunz, "Autorretrato de un escritor joven: La poetología de Juan Manuel de Prada en *Reserva natural," Versants: Revue Suisse des Littératures Romanes/Rivista Svizzera di Letterature Romanze/Schweizerische Zeitschrift für Romanische Literaturen,* 36 (1999): 177–187;

Carlos Moreno Hernández, "La biografía novelada como ejercicio de estilo(s): *Las máscaras del héroe* de J. M. de Prada," in *Biografías literarias (1975–1997),* edited by José Romera Castillo and Francisco Gutiérrez Carbajo (Madrid: Visor, 1998), pp. 537–547;

Francisco Ernesto Puertas Moya, "La autocompasión y el escarnio: Un ajuste de cuentas de Juan Manuel de Prada con la biografía de un escritor fracasado," in *Biografías literarias (1975–1997),* pp. 609–621.

# Soledad Puértolas

*(3 February 1947 –   )*

Cintia Santana
*Claremont McKenna College*

BOOKS: *El Madrid de La lucha por la vida* (Madrid:
  Helios, 1971);
*El bandido doblemente armado* (Madrid: Legasa, 1980);
*Una enfermedad moral* (Madrid: Trieste, 1982);
*El recorrido de los animales* (Gijón: Jucar, 1986);
*Burdeos* (Barcelona: Anagrama, 1986); translated by
  Francisca González-Arias as *Bordeaux* (Lincoln:
  University of Nebraska Press, 1998);
*La sombra de una noche* (Madrid: Anaya, 1986);
*Todos mienten* (Barcelona: Anagrama, 1988);
*Queda la noche* (Barcelona: Planeta, 1989);
*Imagen de Navarra* (Madrid: El País/Aguilar, 1991);
*Días del Arenal* (Barcelona: Planeta, 1992);
*La corriente del golfo* (Barcelona: Anagrama, 1993);
*La vida oculta* (Barcelona: Anagrama, 1993);
*Si al atardecer llegara el mensajero* (Barcelona: Anagrama,
  1995);
*Recuerdos de otra persona* (Barcelona: Anagrama, 1996);
*La vida se mueve: A pesar de las convenciones, los prejuicios y la
  desigualdad* (Madrid: El País/Aguilar, 1996);
*Una vida inesperada* (Barcelona: Anagrama, 1997);
*A través de las ondas* (Madrid: Ollero & Ramos, 1998);
*Gente que vino a mi boda* (Barcelona: Anagrama, 1998);
*La rosa de plata* (Madrid: Espasa-Calpe, 1999);
*La señora Berg* (Barcelona: Anagrama, 1999);
*Adiós a las novias* (Barcelona: Anagrama, 2000);
*Con mi madre* (Barcelona: Anagrama, 2001);
*Como el sueño* (Saragossa: Gobierno de Aragón, 2004).

*Soledad Puértolas (photograph © Thomas Mattil; from the cover
for* El bandido doblemente armado, *1995; Thomas
Cooper Library, University of South Carolina)*

The work of Soledad Puértolas, one of the foremost contemporary Spanish writers, derives its force from what it suggests rather than what it asserts. Puértolas's work often relies on the juxtaposition of images and scenes, which are discontinuous both temporally and spatially. Through this structure, Puértolas's words reveal what lies outside the sum of juxtaposed parts. While motion pictures as well as the detective novel influence Puértolas's work, her observations of real life provide the basis for much of her writing. The larger mysteries at the center of her works are people, enigmas that resist revealing themselves in their entirety.

Through her ability to sound the depths of human nature, Puértolas conveys palpable psychological truths. This talent for revealing the inner workings of her characters is perhaps the quality that most captures the attention of her readers.

Puértolas is primarily considered a novelist, although she has also published four short-story collections and several autobiographical works. She has written extensively for newspapers; a selection of her pieces was gathered in *La vida se mueve: A pesar de las convenciones, los prejuicios y la desigualdad* (1996, Life Moves On:

275

Despite Conventions, Prejudices, and Inequality). Puértolas has written two children's books: *El recorrido de los animales* (1986, The Animals' Trip) and *La sombra de una noche* (1986, The Shadow of a Night), as well as an Arthurian tale, *La rosa de plata* (1999, The Silver Rose), populated by damsels, fairies, knights, sorcerers, and kings. She currently resides in Pozuelo de Alarcón on the outskirts of Madrid.

Puértolas was born on 3 February 1947 in Saragossa into a middle-class family; she was the second of three daughters. Her paternal grandparents and aunt lived in the same building as the Puértolas family. Summers were spent in Pamplona with her maternal grandparents. Whereas her father's family was unassuming and took pride in honesty and sincerity, her maternal relatives were, in Puértolas's words in her *La vida oculta* (1993, The Hidden Life), "un poco snobs" (slight snobs), taking pride in their physical beauty and their dress. These radically different households intrigued Puértolas, offering her two worlds that came to inform the settings and the characters of much of her fictional work. Through her movement between the two households, Puértolas developed an outsider's perspective. The quality of a distant observer characterizes many of her first-person narrators. The contrasts, she says in *La vida oculta,* were a source of lessons allowing her to "vislumbrar que los honestos pueden, por ejemplo, ser insensibles y hasta crueles; que los elegantes a veces son generosos" (discern that honest people could, for example, be insensitive and even cruel; that elegant people are sometimes generous). This type of nuance is precisely the kind of quality that brings her fictional characters to life.

The family's move to Madrid when Puértolas was fourteen constituted a dramatic rupture in her early adolescence and situated her as an observer once again. Madrid became the setting for the majority of her works. In Madrid she obtained a degree in journalism and took a job as a magazine editor. At the age of twenty-one, Puértolas married Leopoldo Pita, an industrial-engineering student. Shortly after the wedding, they moved to Trondheim, Norway, where her husband continued his studies. Puértolas's first experience living abroad over the next eight months proved a formative one that appears in both her fictional and autobiographical work. While in Trondheim, she and her husband rented a room in a house in the mountains. The distance from the house to town, coupled with the winter cold, exacerbated Puértolas's feelings of linguistic and cultural isolation. She describes experiencing acute loneliness, a feeling that has become one of the hallmark themes of her work.

After briefly returning to Spain, Puértolas and her husband moved to California. Their son, Diego, was born in 1971. In 1974 Puértolas completed a master's degree in Spanish literature at the University of California, Santa Barbara. The following year, she traveled to Portugal to study the work of Fernando Pessoa, then returned to Madrid, where she was present during the period immediately following Francisco Franco's death. In 1976 she wrote her first novel. It and her second novel were rejected by publishers.

Puértolas's third manuscript, *El bandido doblemente armado* (The Two-Armed Bandit), earned her the 1979 Sésamo Award and was published in 1980. *El bandido doblemente armado* is named for a problem in decision theory and serves as a metaphor for two approaches to life: continually placing the same bet, and continually switching. The nameless narrator of the novel is an emerging writer who recounts his interrupted associations over time with members of the atypical Lennoxes, a North American family living in Madrid. The narrator's episodic recollections are an attempt to decipher the enigmatic household to which he was privy and yet from which he was distanced, a mystery that continues to resist entirely yielding itself throughout his narrative. As Puértolas explains in her prologue, the writing of *El bandido doblemente armado* coincided with her rereading novels by Raymond Chandler and Dashiell Hammett. All of the Lennox children's names are taken from Chandler's *The Long Goodbye* (1953) as an homage to his work. *El bandido doblemente armado,* like other Spanish literary works at the end of the twentieth century, reveals the growing influence of the United States on Spanish life, an influence that increased even more with the end of Franco's regime and the subsequent rise of visual culture in Spain.

In 1982 Puértolas published her first collection of short stories, *Una enfermedad moral* (A Moral Illness). As the title suggests, the stories feature protagonists who suffer from a diversity of moral ills. Most of the stories are set in indeterminate locations, with the exception of two stories, "La vida oculta" and "La orilla del Danubio" (The Bank of the Danube), which take place in seventeenth-century Naples and along the Danube, respectively. The setting for the story "El origen del deseo" (The Origin of Desire) is drawn from Puértolas's maternal grandmother's house. The second story that appears in the collection, "La indiferencia de Eva" (Eva's Indifference), has been widely anthologized.

The publication of Puértolas's third book, *Burdeos* (1986; translated as *Bordeaux,* 1998), confirmed her as an astute observer of human nature. The three interrelated novellas are narrated from the omniscient third-person point of view. The featured protagonists have managed to sidestep maturity for much longer than is conventional. In the first story, an older woman, Pauline, has foregone marriage, children, and an occupation, having chosen instead to live a life of habit alongside her father. His death subsequently leaves her unmoored. A neighbor's request for help involves Pauline in a minor situation of intrigue tinged with blackmail and adultery. Through her role in this bourgeois plot, which involves her maid, her neighbor's maid, and her neighbor's husband, Pauline discovers the ability to take action in her own life. The tensions between distance and proximity, stagnation and change are effectively revealed. In the second story, the reappearance of René Dufour's mother, who abandoned him many years before, gives rise to René's inner turmoil. The protagonist of the third novella, Lillian Skalnick, is forever on the move, without direction. Commissioned with an important report on Europe, Lillian's fragmented personal life and her disparate observations of Europe are the raw material to which she struggles to bring order and meaning. *Burdeos* displays Puértolas's ability to unfold and inhabit the lives of minor characters, then develop them as protagonists in the succeeding novellas. The novellas are imperfectly superimposed, so that by the end of the brief volume Puértolas has skillfully rendered entire lives through juxtaposition and interstice.

In contrast to Puértolas's previous works, in which the time and place of the action are incidental, the late-Franco-era Madrid setting is essential to *Todos mienten* (1988, Everyone Lies). The novel initiates a period in Puértolas's writing that is characterized by exploration of Spanish life. She returns to the use of a male narrator, Javier Arroyo, whose chronicle also centers around a family, although this time the family is his own. History functions as a background to the characters, whose ideology is in keeping with their lifestyle. While recovering from hepatitis, Javier narrates how he and his brother were raised by their young widowed mother whose days were spent reminiscing with her female friends about her deceased husband, who had been a promising playwright. Javier is also subject to the influence of his conservative paternal grandparents and his nouveau riche uncle, Ernesto, who returns to Madrid after having made his fortune in Mexico. Javier's account illustrates his resistance to engaging fully in life, a life that, as so many of those around him demonstrate, involves deceit. *Todos mienten,* one of Puértolas's most ironic takes on a sector of the Spanish upper class, manages to avoid derision, thus rescuing the characters from stereotype.

Puértolas's novel *Queda la noche* (1989, The Night Remains) was awarded the Planeta Prize. The narrator, Aurora, lives life on the margin in Madrid, where the novel is primarily set; her passivity renders her incapable of envisioning a more fulfilling life. A summer trip to India gives rise to intrigue that increasingly envelops

SOLEDAD PUÉRTOLAS

*El bandido doblemente armado*

**ANAGRAMA**
Narrativas hispánicas

*Cover for a 1995 edition of Puértolas's 1980 novel (The Two-Armed Bandit), influenced by the works of Raymond Chandler and Dashiell Hammett, in which a writer recounts his association with a mysterious North American family living in Madrid (Thomas Cooper Library, University of South Carolina)*

her despite her resistance. Upon her return to Madrid, she begins to make connections between the people she met during her travels and an international spy ring. *Queda la noche* plays out two mysteries, one of which is solved, while the other narrative direction resists being fully understood. Aurora oscillates between the safety of the observer and the risk that comes with action; her narration is itself the attempt to control and explain events that resist being grasped. The loose ends of the narrative are a struggle against any continuity. The role of chance is highlighted in this novel and leads to an ending reminiscent of the detective genre.

With her next novel, *Días del Arenal* (1992, Days of the Arenal), Puértolas returns to a narrative told from the third-person point of view. The action of the novel, which is divided into four sections, is set in Madrid and in a fictional small town named El Sauco.

Antonio Cardús, an elderly man who has lived his life almost entirely within the narrow confines of his neighborhood, remembers his affair with a married woman, Gracia. The affair proved to be the only period in his life when he dared to live life fully. Several years after Gracia ends the affair, her death is communicated to Antonio in a letter by Gracia's sister, Herminia. The letter serves as a segue into the second section of the novel, which narrates Herminia's life in El Sauco. A small-town wife and mother, Herminia is also a poet who has not come to terms with the tension between her art and her life. Although Olga Francines, an editor from Madrid, "discovers" her, Herminia is unable to transcend her despair and commits suicide.

Olga Francines's stepson, Guillermo Aguiar, is the main character of the third section of the novel. On the day of his father's funeral, Guillermo's mother reveals an anecdote from her life that causes Guillermo to rethink the trajectory of his own life. Guillermo's story serves to illustrate the ways in which people construct the meaning of their lives based on memory. Torn by his mother's disclosure, Guillermo has a one-night affair with a model named Covadonga. While Covadonga takes on a larger role in the fourth section of the novel, the narrative circles back to Antonio Cardús, who, on taking action when Covadonga is brutally beaten, finds the ability to become a participant in life once again.

If *Burdeos* can be read as the imperfect superimposition of three stories, *Días del Arenal* follows a circular superimposition; the ripple effect of people's actions on those around them are revealed to the reader, even as they remain unknown to the characters themselves. *Días del Arenal* is filled with counterpoint and panoramic vision: life in the city, as viewed from El Sauco, gives way to life in El Sauco as viewed from Madrid. Loneliness plagues both men and women in these rural and urban settings, but unexpected complicity and contiguities between people are everywhere.

Puértolas's tripartite collection of essays about the writing life, *La vida oculta,* was awarded the Anagrama Prize for essay in 1993. The first section, "El pañuelo de seda azul" (The Blue Silk Handkerchief), attempts to elucidate the mysteries behind the writing impulse and the obstacles that are encountered. Many of Puértolas's observations respond to questions that she has been asked in interviews and at conferences. In part 2, "Afinidades" (Affinities), Puértolas looks at those writers in whose work she has identified her own concerns and who have provided her with a sense of accompaniment in her life and in her work. The list includes Miguel de Cervantes, Stendhal, Anton Chekhov, Gustave Flaubert, and Virginia Woolf, as well as less celebrated or obvious identifications such as Jean Rhys,

Dino Buzzati, and S. E. Hinton. The third section, "La vida novelada" (Life, Fictionalized), describes the thin line that separates life and fiction in Puértolas's work as she recounts formative people, places, and occupations from which she has created fictional characters and situations.

Puértolas published a second collection of short stories, *La corriente del golfo* (The Gulf Stream), in 1993. The title story is based on Puértolas's time in Trondheim and refers to the Gulf Stream that tempers the waters of the Norwegian coast. Throughout her stay, the townspeople assured her of their great fortune in having the Gulf Stream grace their coast. Puértolas could not imagine a colder climate, and the townspeople's feelings of good fortune mystified her. The narrator does not begin to comprehend how graced is her own life until a last-minute discovery on the eve of her departure. In these twelve narratives, the indeterminate flow of life takes on the form of the Gulf Stream. When regarded from a distance in the future, "el vacío, la nada, el dolor, la soledad, el error, el amor, la inconsciencia, la juventud, son inesperada y dulcemente acariciados, y todo cobra la forma de un preludio, repentinamente hermoso preludio de una vida por hacer" (emptiness, nothingness, pain, loneliness, error, love, irresponsibility, and youth, are unexpectedly and tenderly caressed, and everything takes on the form of a prelude, a suddenly lovely prelude to a life about to begin).

With her next novel, *Si al atardecer llegara el mensajero* (1995, If the Messenger Were to Arrive at Dusk), Puértolas takes a leap away from the realism that is characteristic of her work. Set in a world in which human beings know the date of their death, God's cosmic arbitrator sends an angel-like being, Tobias Kaluga, on a mission to Earth in order to investigate the lives of men in this new situation. The novel consists of a series of reflections, organized fundamentally around Kaluga and his series of interlocutors. The structure of this novel also constitutes a departure from Puértolas's earlier work. While much of her fiction crafts situations immediately before or after a revelation, the structural elements in this novel are thematic: death, illness, love, art, and time.

*Recuerdos de otra persona* (1996, Memories of Another Person) constitutes Puértolas's first explicitly autobiographical narrative. The work is a collection of memories that provides glimpses into the life of a young Puértolas, a largely different person than the older author on whom the telling relies. *Recuerdos de otra persona,* which documents many details of Spanish life during the 1950s and 1960s, also explores the role of memory, a recurring theme in Puértolas's work. Memory, the thread by which Puértolas and many of her characters have come to define themselves, is fraught with ambiguities. *Recuerdos de otra persona* is a personal account of the contradictions, lapses, and idiosyncratic assertions of memory. As in her fiction, Puértolas here, too, refrains from imparting a definitive meaning on the series of events described. The remembrances are no more certain and unambiguous than was the life recalled at the time it was lived.

Puértolas returns to the use of a nameless narrator in her novel *Una vida inesperada* (1997, An Unexpected Life). The narrator is a woman who moves between two poles: swimming and her job as the director of a library. The sustained monologue revisits incidents in her life during several nights of insomnia. Memories of a childhood friend, Olga Francines (a character first introduced in *Días del Arenal*), for whom the narrator felt a mix of admiration and hate, unify her reflections. *Una vida inesperada,* while positing loneliness as a given element of the human condition, asks how loneliness can be useful to the narrator rather than a condition that will extinguish her.

The following year Puértolas published her third collection of short stories, *Gente que vino a mi boda* (People Who Came to My Wedding). The collection demonstrates the ease with which the author narrates both male and female points of view; of the seventeen stories, all of which are told in the first person, nine are narrated by a male character. In the title story a seamstress looks back on her wedding day, paying special attention to the wedding pictures and what they reveal. The disparity between her private memories and the public memory captured in the pictures serves to make problematic her role at her own wedding.

In keeping with *El bandido doblemente armado* and *Todos mienten,* Puértolas's ninth novel, *La señora Berg,* (1999, Mrs. Berg), is narrated from the point of view of a man attempting to decipher the mysteries that people have constituted in his life. Mario, an architect in his forties, revisits his encounters with Marta Berg, the mother of an old school friend and the object of Mario's adolescent crush. Marta weaves in and out of Mario's life over the years; each encounter serves as a measuring stick with which Mario takes stock of his life. The character of Marta can be read as representing that which is unattainable, beautiful, and fleeting and through which the mysterious designs of life are glimpsed.

As the title of Puértolas's fourth short-story collection, *Adiós a las novias* (2000, Goodbye to the Brides), indicates, the stories gathered in this volume bid farewell to youth. Most of the twenty-one stories share as their point of departure a moment in which the protagonists, both men and women, look back upon their lives in order to question and make sense of events, having

SOLEDAD
PUERTOLAS

*Burdeos*

Narrativas hispánicas
Editorial Anagrama

*Cover for a 1988 edition of Puértolas's 1986 collection (translated as* Bordeaux, *1998), which comprises three interrelated novellas with female protagonists (Thomas Cooper Library, University of South Carolina)*

been unable to do so at the time. The collection was awarded the NH Story Prize.

Puértolas's mother died at eighty-two on 26 January 1999. In an attempt to come to terms with her sense of loss, Puértolas wrote *Con mi madre* (2001, With My Mother). Through the memory of moments shared with her mother, she strives to understand her mother's life. The account simultaneously sheds light on Puértolas's own identity as a mother and her continued sense of herself as a daughter. In this way, death, which was initially introduced as the absolute ending to the narrative of her mother's life, is, over the course of Puértolas's exploration, "opened."

Soledad Puértolas's work belongs to a current of post-Franco, postmodern, transnational literature in which Spanish place and history are secondary to the individual's sense of personal place and history. Similarly, Puertolas's fiction cannot be categorized as "women's writing," although gendered situations are not absent from her work. Rather, Puértolas's writings demonstrate her dexterity at narrating both male and female individuals' quest for meaning.

**Interviews:**

Miguel Riera, "Los vacíos del tiempo: Entrevista con Soledad Puértolas," *Quimera: Revista de Literatura,* 72 (1987): 42–48;

Lynn K. Talbot, "Entrevista con Soledad Puértolas," *Hispania: A Journal Devoted to the Teaching of Spanish and Portuguese,* 71, no. 4 (1988): 882–883;

Katica Urbanc, "Soledad Puértolas: 'He vuelto a la realidad de otra manera . . . ,'" *Espéculo: Revista de Estudios Literarios,* 8 (1998).

**References:**

Wang Jun Albolote, *El mundo novelístico de Soledad Puértolas* (Granada: Comares, 2000);

Eduardo Barraza, "Escenas de la vida provisional: *Todos mienten* de Soledad Puértolas," in *Literatura femenina contemporanea de España: VII simposio internacional,* edited by Juana Arancibia, Adrienne Mandel, and Yolanda Rosas (Northridge: California State University, Northridge / Westminster, Cal.: Instituto Literario y Cultural Hispánico, 1991), pp. 179–187;

Frieda H. Blackwell, "Conventions of Detective Fiction and Their Subversion in 'A través de las ondas' and *Queda la noche* de Soledad Puértolas," *Letras Femeninas,* 26, nos. 1–2 (2000): 171–183;

Tomás Camarero Arribas, "Lógica de una narrativa en *Una enfermedad moral* de Soledad Puértolas," *Ventanal: Revista de Creación y Crítica,* 14 (1988): 133–157;

Marguerite DiNonno Intemann, *El tema de la soledad en la narrativa de Soledad Puértolas* (Lewiston, Pa.: Mellen University Press, 1994);

Darcy Donahue, "The Narrator in Soledad Puértolas's *Todos mienten,*" *Letras Femeninas,* 20, nos. 1–2 (1994): 101–108;

Elena Gascón-Vera, "Un lenguaje solidario: América en España en los 80," in *España y América en sus literaturas,* edited by María Ángeles Encinar (Madrid: Cultura Hispánica, 1993), pp. 53–71;

Estelle Irizarry, "Aventura y apertura en la nueva novela española: *Queda la noche* de Soledad Puértolas," in *Studies in Honor of Donald W. Bleznick,* edited by Delia V. Galván, Anita K. Stoll, and Philippa Brown Yin (Newark, Del.: Juan de la Cuesta, 1995), pp. 59–74;

Sonia Mattalia, "Entre miradas: Las novelas de Soledad Puértolas," *Ventanal: Revista de Creación y Crítica,* 14 (1988): 171–192;

Mercedes Mazquiarán de Rodríguez, "Beyond Fiction: Voicing the Personal in Soledad Puértolas's *La vida oculta,*" in *Spanish Women Writers and the Essay: Gender, Politics, and the Self,* edited by Kathleen M. Glenn and Mazquiarán de Rodríguez (Columbia: University of Missouri Press, 1998), pp. 231–249;

Charlene Merithew, "Silencios poderosos: El tema de la quietud en los ensayos de Soledad Puértolas," *Monographic Review/Revista Monografica* (2000);

Jesús Pérez Magallón, "*Todos mienten:* Crónica del desencanto y sublimación de la diferencia," *Salina,* 10 (1996): 183–189;

Randolph D. Pope, "Misterios y epifanías en la narrativa de Soledad Puértolas," in *La novela española actual: Autores y tendencias,* edited by Alfonso de Toro and Dieter Ingenschay (Kassel, Germany: Reichenbcrgcr, 1995), pp. 271–301;

Akiko Tsuchiya, "Language, Desire, and the Feminine Riddle in Soledad Puértolas's 'La indiferencia de Eva,'" *Revista de Estudios Hispánicos,* 25, no. 1 (1991): 69–79.

# Carme Riera
*(12 January 1948 –   )*

Sandra J. Schumm
*Baker University*

BOOKS: *Te deix, amor, la mar com a penyora* (Barcelona: Laia, 1975);

*Jo pos per testimoni les gavines* (Barcelona: Laia, 1975);

*Palabra de mujer: Bajo el signo de una memoria impenitente* (Barcelona: Laia, 1980)—comprises selected stories from *Te deix, amor, la mar com a penyora* and *Jo pos per testimoni les gavines,* translated into Spanish by Riera;

*Una primavera per a Domenico Guarini* (Barcelona: Ediciones 62, 1980); translated into Spanish by Luisa Cotoner as *Una primavera para Domenico Guarini* (Barcelona: Montesinos, 1981);

*Gairebé un conte: La vida de Ramon Llull* (Barcelona: Ajuntament de Barcelona, 1980);

*Epitelis tendríssims* (Barcelona: Ediciones 62, 1981);

*Els cementiris de Barcelona: Una aproximació* (Barcelona: Edhasa, 1981);

*La obra poética de José Agustín Goytisolo* (Barcelona: Llibres del Mall, 1987);

*La Escuela de Barcelona: Barral, Gil de Biedma, Goytisolo. El núcleo poético de la generación de los 50* (Barcelona: Anagrama, 1988);

*Qüestió d'amor propi* (Barcelona: Laia, 1988); translated into Spanish by Riera as *Cuestión de amor propio* (Barcelona: Tusquets, 1988);

*La molt exemplar història del gos màgic i la seva cua* (Barcelona: Empúries, 1988);

*Joc de miralls* (Barcelona: Planeta, 1989); translated into Spanish by Riera as *Por persona interpuesta* (Barcelona: Planeta, 1989); translated by Cristina de la Torre as *Mirror Images* (New York: Peter Lang, 1993);

*La obra poética de Carlos Barral* (Barcelona: Península, 1990);

*Hay veneno y jazmín en tu tinta: Aproximación a la poesía de J. A. Goytisolo* (Barcelona: Anthropos, 1991);

*Contra l'amor en companyia i altres relats* (Barcelona: Destino, 1991); translated into Spanish by Riera as *Contra el amor en compañía y otros relatos* (Barcelona: Destino, 1991);

*Dins el darrer blau* (Barcelona: Destino, 1994); translated into Spanish by Riera as *En el último azul* (Madrid: Alfaguara, 1996; Barcelona: Círculo de Lectores, 1997);

*Temps d'una espera* (Barcelona: Columna, 1998); translated into Spanish by Riera as *Tiempo de espera* (Barcelona: Lumen, 1998);

*Cap al cel obert* (Barcelona: Destino, 2000; revised, 2002); translated into Spanish by Riera as *Por el cielo y más allá* (Madrid: Alfaguara, 2001);

*Mallorca, imatges per la felicitat,* text by Riera, photographs by Climent Picornell (Palma de Mallorca: Edicions de Turisme Cultural, Illes Balears, 2000); translated into Spanish by Riera as *Mallorca, imágenes para la felicidad* (Palma de Mallorca: Edicions de Turisme Cultural, Illes Balears, 2000);

*El gos magic* (Barcelona: Planeta, 2003); Spanish version published as *El perro mágico* (Barcelona: Planeta, 2003);

*El meravellos viatge de Maria al pais de les tulipes* (Barcelona: Destino, 2003);

*Llengües mortes: Selecció de contes,* edited by Carles Cortés (Barcelona: Destino, 2003);

*La meitat de l'ànima* (Barcelona: Proa, 2004); translated into Spanish by Riera as *La mitad del alma* ([Madrid]: Alfaguara, 2004);

*El Quijote desde el nacionalismo catalán, en torno al tercer centenario* (Barcelona: Destino, 2005);

*El Quijote y Barcelona,* by Riera and others (Barcelona: Lunwerg, 2005).

**Editions in English:** "Some Flowers" and "The Knot, the Void," translated by Alberto Moreiras, and "A Cool Breeze for Wanda" and "Miss Angel Ruscadell Investigates the Horrible Death of Mariana Servera," translated by Eulàlia Benejam, in *On Our Own Behalf: Women's Tales from Catalonia,* edited by Kathleen NcNerney (Lincoln: University of Nebraska Press, 1988), pp. 129–135;

"The Report," translated by Julie Flanagan, in *The Origins of Desire: Modern Spanish Short Stories,* edited by

*Carme Riera (photograph © Colita; from the cover for* Cuestión de amor propio, *1988; Thomas Cooper Library, University of South Carolina)*

Juan Antonio Masoliver (London: Serpent's Tail, 1993), pp. 55–63;

*A Matter of Self-Esteem and Other Stories,* translated by Roser Caminals-Heath and Holly Cashman (New York: Holmes & Meyer, 2001).

OTHER: Carlos Barral, *Poesía,* edited by Riera (Madrid: Cátedra, 1991);

Barral, *Los diarios, 1957–1989,* edited by Riera (Madrid: Anaya, 1993);

Gabriel de Henao, *Rimas,* edited by Riera (Valladolid: Fundación Jorge Guillén, 1997);

José Agustín Goytisolo, *Poesía,* edited by Riera (Madrid: Cátedra, 1999);

*Partidarios de la felicidad: Antología poética del grupo catalán de los 50,* edited by Riera (Barcelona: Círculo de Lectores, 2000);

*Antología de poesía catalana femenina,* edited by Riera (Barcelona: Mediterrània, 2003).

Carme Riera's bilingual upbringing in Spanish and Catalan has significantly influenced her writing. Born in Majorca on 12 January 1948 to a Catalan mother, Carmen Guilera Vallhonrat, and a Majorcan father, Eusebio Riera Estada, a philosophy professor, Riera was schooled in Castilian (Spanish), but her family spoke Catalan and its Majorcan dialect at home—

especially her grandmother, whose stories served as a catalyst for Riera's imagination and writing. While Riera's academic works are mainly in Spanish, she publishes her fiction in Catalan, often later translating them herself into Castilian. Her personal conviction to write in Catalan is a testimony to her belief in the importance of freedom of expression after the dictator Francisco Franco's ban of the use of the Galician, Catalan, and Basque languages throughout Spain. Her patronage of Catalan language and culture is related to her sympathetic support of other minority issues in her works as well, with empathy for Jews, women, blacks, and homosexuals often appearing in her writing. Ideas in her work of doubling and searching for identity are also connected to the influence of her bifurcated linguistic and cultural heritage.

Growing up in Majorca, Riera received her primary education from the Sagrado Corazón (Sacred Heart) school, where nuns stressed the importance of women's comportment in society and skills of refinement, especially the ability to produce elegant correspondence. The emphasis on the latter influenced the epistolary style of many of Riera's stories and novels. She then studied at the Joan Alcover Institute in Majorca, where one of her teachers encouraged her to write in Catalan. After beginning her studies at the University of Barcelona in 1965, Riera participated in several hippie demonstrations, particularly in resistance to the war in Vietnam. She also became interested in feminist concerns after reading the works of such writers as Simone de Beauvoir, Virginia Woolf, and Annie Leclerc. Riera's support of women's issues is another theme evident in her writing. In 1970 she received a degree in Spanish philology from the University of Barcelona with a special interest in the Golden Age literature of Spain. The next year she was hired to teach classes at the university. That same year she married Francesc Llinás, a physics professor she had met at the Joan Alcover Institute before beginning her studies. In 1972 their first child, Ferrán, was born.

In 1973 Riera won the Ramón Llull prize for her short story "¿Que hi és n'Àngela?" (Is Angela There?), a story about a lonely woman who calls random telephone numbers asking to speak to Àngela until someone named Àngela answers, thinking the caller is her friend Maria. Àngela promises to visit Maria, who expectantly waits in vain, since she never relocates the number she called. The nostalgia and sense of loss of this story, included in Riera's first published book, *Te deix, amor, la mar com a penyora* (1975, I Leave You, My Love, the Sea as a Token), winner of the Francesc Puig i Llensa Prize in 1974, fits well with the rest of the collection. The stories, the narrators of which are often women of various social classes, explore the human personality and the intimate essence of the individual, often through first-person narrators in epistolary, confessional, or interlocutory forms. The title story, for example, is a long letter from a young woman to her former lover. The sea serves as a nostalgic symbol of their prohibited relationship. The writer reassures the recipient of her letter that she has no hard feelings about the love expressed between them when she was fifteen and the lover was her professor. Only at the end of the letter does the reader discover that the professor's name is Maria, an unexpected twist to the seductive story of a past love.

Riera's second book of stories, *Jo pos per testimoni les gavines* (1975, I Call on the Seagulls as Witness), serves as an elaboration and continuation of the themes of the first. In the first story, which has the same title as the book, the female narrator writes to Carme Riera, telling Riera that the story "Te deix, amor, la mar com a penyora" was so familiar to her that it seemed to be a chronicle of her life, but that she would like to tell her version. The narrator's story includes a student, Marina, who also fell in love with her professor (the narrator herself). But Marina, instead of marrying and having a child, committed suicide by drowning herself in the sea and thus merged with Pluto's underwater realm. The narrator begins by asking Riera if she minds her using Riera's words to begin "nuestra historia–suya, porque la ha escrito y mía porque la viví" (our story–yours, because you wrote it and mine because I lived it). In this way, Riera refers to her own story from the first book, again employing the epistolary form and themes of lesbian love, nostalgia, and the sea. Other stories in *Jo pos per testimoni les gavines* also utilize first-person narration, nostalgic memories, and nested stories and letters that reveal intimate secrets about the lives of the protagonists. Many stories denounce the exploitation of women in society.

The idea that *Jo pos per testimoni les gavines* is a continuation of *Te deix, amor, la mar com a penyora* is reinforced by two different Spanish translations that combine many of the stories of both books in a single volume. *Palabra de mujer: Bajo el signo de una memoria impenitente* (1980, Woman's Word: Under the Sign of an Unrepentant Memory) is Riera's own translation and revision of many of the stories included in her first two books. Several critics have commented that Riera's Castilian versions of her writing include so many changes that they constitute a rewriting, rather than a translation, of her original work. *Te dejo el mar* (1991, I Leave You the Sea), on the other hand, also includes many of the stories from both books, but Luisa Cotoner has translated them from their original Catalan versions.

Riera's first novel, *Una primavera per a Domenico Guarini* (1980, A Primavera for Domenico Guarini), which won the Prudenci Bertrana Prize, also deals with a woman's problems in society, notably the pregnancy of an unwed woman just after the end of Franco's dictatorship, but the novel fits within the genre of detective fiction as well. Riera uses second-person stream-of-consciousness narration to reveal the thoughts of a young journalist, Clara, as she travels from Barcelona to Florence to report on the trial of Domenico Guarini, a man accused of vandalizing Sandro Botticelli's 1482 painting *Primavera* (Spring). Clara's investigation of Guarini's actions and motives is played against her personal decision of whether to abort her pregnancy. Riera alternates Clara's narration with her journalistic accounts of the Guarini investigation and a professor's academic explanation of Botticelli's painting, which Clara symbolically links with her own life and Guarini's.

*Gairebé un conte: la vida de Ramon Llull* (1980, Almost like a Story: The Life of Ramon Llull) is a biography of Catalan writer Ramon Llull. Another nonfiction work Riera published soon after is *Els cementiris de Barcelona: Una aproximació* (1981, The Cemeteries of Barcelona: An Approximation). The book includes photographs taken by Pilar Aymerich. *Epitelis tendríssims* (Most Tender Epithelia), a book of short stories not yet

*Cover for the Spanish translation (1981) of Riera's Catalan-language novel* Una primavera per a Domenico Guarini *(1980, A Primavera for Domenico Guarini), about a journalist covering the trial of a man accused of defacing a painting by the Renaissance master Sandro Botticelli (Thomas Cooper Library, University of South Carolina)*

translated into Spanish or English, was also published in 1981. In this book Riera experiments with erotic literature, accentuating the humorous aspects of eroticism, a theme that unifies the stories. Irony and seduction, an art that Riera often links with writing, intertwine in seven stories introduced in a prologue by a fictitious author, Aina Maria Sureda. One story, "Estimat Thomas" (Dear Thomas), consists of nine sensual letters signed by the same person, Montse, declaring her love. At the end the reader discovers that Thomas is a dog, a revelation that gives the story a humorous twist.

A second child, Maria, was born to Riera and her husband in 1987. Although Riera's publications halted briefly during the time she was completing her doctoral thesis, in 1988 she won the seventeenth Ana-

grama Essay Prize for *La Escuela de Barcelona: Barral, Gil de Biedma, Goytisolo. El núcleo poético de la generación de los 50* (1988, The School of Barcelona: Barral, Gil de Biedma, Goytisolo. The Poetic Nucleus of the Generation of the 50s), a book based on her dissertation. Riera investigates whether these Catalan poets fit within the parameters of the idea of a literary "generation" between 1959 and 1965. Two subsequent scholarly publications exploring more deeply the poetry of some of these writers are *La obra poética de Carlos Barral* (1990, The Poetic Works of Carlos Barral) and *Hay veneno y jazmín en tu tinta: Aproximación a la poesía de J. A. Goytisolo* (1991, There Is Venom and Jasmine in Your Ink: Approaching the Poetry of J. A. Goytisolo).

Also published in 1988 were *La molt exemplar història del gos màgic i la seva cua* (The Most Exemplary Story of the Magic Dog and His Tail), a book for children, and *Qüestió d'amor propi* (translated as "A Matter of Self-Esteem," 2001), a short novel. *Qüestió d'amor propi* consists of a long letter from Àngela, a published author, to her Danish friend Ingrid, explaining why she has not written in more than a year. After being betrayed by another writer, Miquel, with whom she had a brief affair, Àngela solicits Ingrid's help to get revenge on Miquel by giving him erroneous information for a book he is writing. According to some critics, Àngela's letter is also an attempt to seduce Ingrid and the reader to come around to Àngela's way of thinking. Riera has stated that all writing is a form of seduction, and her character Àngela declares that "Qualsevol escriptura és una carta d'amor" (All writing is a love letter). The epistolary style of this novel is complicated by many references to other works of literature by Catalan, Spanish, and other European writers, but the English translation includes helpful explanatory notes.

The novel *Joc de miralls* (1989; translated as *Mirror Images,* 1993) exemplifies the theme of doubling that critics have noted in many of Riera's works. The first part of this political detective novel consists of a journal written by Teresa Mascaró, a young woman working on her doctoral dissertation about Pablo Corbalán, a Latin American author and former political prisoner. Teresa's first-person journal entries, beginning with her reaction to meeting Corbalán in Barcelona on the way to a peace conference shortly before his suspicious "suicide," are interspersed with third-person accounts of Bettina Bretano's meeting and infatuation with author Johann Wolfgang von Goethe. As Teresa investigates Corbalán's death, the reader learns from her letters to her literary agent that Corbalán's identity has been confused with that of Antonio Gallego, another writer and a political prisoner. An epilogue informs the reader that Teresa died in a fire along with Gallego's sister Constanza in the Gallego family home. The doubling in the novel–the confusing of the identities of Gallego and Corbalán–is emphasized even more by Gallego's having plastic surgery to assume Corbalán's identity and to finish his last novel, and by the burying of Gallego's body in Barcelona under the name of Corbalán, his former rival. Riera's fascination with identity formation and the use of masks to conceal the self are evident in this book.

In the prologue to *Temps d'una espera* (1998, A Time of Waiting) Riera relates that in 1996, during a conference about literature, autobiography, and memory, she publicly mentioned for the first time the journal entries she had written from the fall of 1986 through the spring of 1987 while she was pregnant with her second child. After thinking about the similarities between gestation of a child and that of a text and that few works are written about pregnancy, Riera decided to organize her journal entries into a book. The entries date from 23 September, when Riera's pregnancy was confirmed, until the second of May, just before the birth of her child Maria. The entries begin as Riera's notations to herself, but she soon begins to address her unborn child in the writings and expresses herself even more intimately after learning the child is female. Riera writes, "Ahora que sé que eres una niña . . . estas notas cobran un sentido mayor" (Now that I know that you're a girl . . . these notes acquire a greater meaning). She explains that although she would have loved a boy as well, the connection is different, because her relationship with a son "se basaría en la diferencia, no en la semejanza . . ." (would be based on difference, not on similarity . . . ), and she rejoices in a feeling of sisterhood with her unborn daughter.

In 1998 Riera published *Contra l'amor en companyia i altres relats* (Against Love in Company and Other Stories), a book with stories unified by the theme of writing and by texts that mix truth and fiction. In the story "La seducció del geni" (Seduction of Genius), for example, Juanita Chamorro writes a letter to Carmen Balcells, Riera's real-life literary agent, asking Balcells to introduce her to some male writers. Juanita, who was formerly Juan Chamorro, explains that, after being told he had no literary talent, he had wanted to marry a writer in order to observe the creative process. But since so many female writers refused him, Juan underwent operations to become a woman in order to entice a male writer as a spouse. In "Letra d'angel" (Letter from an Angel), an older man receives letters advertising a book, but he thinks that writer Olga Macià is trying to communicate with him. The company later reveals that Olga really does not exist, a truth that seriously disillusions the older man: her name was invented as an advertising technique. The

stories, like those of *Epitelis tendríssims*, often demonstrate ironic or poignant humor. Several are included in *A Matter of Self-Esteem and Other Stories.*

Riera's novel *Dins el darrer blau* (1994, In the Furthest Blue) has won five literary prizes: the Josep Pla Prize, the Creixell Prize, the Lletra d'Or in 1994, and the National Prize for Literature in 1995 (the first novel written in Catalan to receive the National Prize). It was also awarded the 2000 Elio Vittorini Prize in Italy for its Italian translation. *Dins el darrer blau* takes place in Majorca between 1687 and 1691; it focuses on the intimate and conflicted thoughts of several different characters involved in the Inquisition. The first part of the novel concentrates on Rafael Cortés, a Jewish convert to Catholicism who betrays his friends for financial reasons by revealing to his priest confessor that they are continuing to practice Judaism secretly. In hopes of furthering his position in the Church, the priest takes the information to the Inquisition and thus hastens the Jews' already planned attempt to escape by sea to Livorno, Italy. After their capture and detention in prison, the novel focuses principally on the thoughts of Gabriel Valls, the patriarch of the crypto Jews (those still secretly practicing Judaism), who had encouraged and helped to plan their aborted escape. Some other interesting characters whose thoughts are exposed include La Coixa, a prostitute who tries to help Gabriel's son escape; Sara dels Olors, a Catholic mystic who is also burned; the morally corrupt viceroy of Majorca; and the widow of Sampol, one of the Spanish Jews living in Livorno.

The conclusion of the novel reveals the distress of the Jews waiting in Livorno, the political machinery of the Inquisition, and the despair of the captured as they hear their sentences and await death. Although João Peres travels from Livorno in a final attempt to bribe the Inquisition to spare the lives of the condemned, his quest is to no avail. As he witnesses their execution, his only desire is to return to his ship so that it can set sail and "se pierda . . . deprisa, muy deprisa, en la distancia infinita del último azul" (rapidly, very rapidly, lose itself in the infinite distance of the furthest blue).

*Cap al cel obert* (2000, Toward the Open Sky), winner of the 2001 Crítica Serra d'Or Prize and the 2001 National Literature Prize of the Generalitat of Catalonia, takes place in Cuba in the nineteenth century between 1850 and 1860, and its characters are descendants of Isabel Tarongí, one of the crypto Jews burned by the Inquisition in the previous novel. Many of the incidents in the novels are based on historical events, including the immigration of many Majorcans to Cuba, a card game that required the wealthy loser to

*Paperback cover for Riera's Spanish translation of her Catalan-language epistolary novel* Qüestió d'amor propi *(1988; translated as "A Matter of Self-Esteem," 2001), in which a writer tries to persuade her friend to help her get revenge on a former lover who betrayed her (Thomas Cooper Library, University of South Carolina)*

marry and produce heirs, and the flight of a hot-air balloon.

While Riera's previous novel focused on many characters, Maria Forteza is the principal character of *Cap al cel obert*. Maria travels from Majorca to Cuba with her sister, Isabel, who is engaged to Miguel Fortaleza, a cousin she has never met. A game of chance with his brother Gabriel had awarded Miguel the unwanted duty of marrying to produce an heir, but the seductive love letters between Miguel and Isabel are secretly written by Maria and by Miguel's sister, Ángela, continuing another sort of game. The exchange of letters between Maria and Ángela also continues Riera's emphasis on epistolary fiction and obscured identity. The masked identity continues even further when an outbreak of the plague sickens both sisters, and Isabel slips her engagement ring on Maria's finger, hoping that her sister can take her place and

marry Miguel. After arriving barely alive in Cuba, Maria inspires Miguel's disgust but later marries his father—a wealthy landowner with slaves—and becomes the victim of a political plot to usurp her husband's wealth and power. After he is murdered, she is convicted of treason and sentenced to die. But the appearance of a hot-air balloon over her execution site encourages many onlookers to believe that she has magically escaped death.

While *Dins el darrer blau* emphasizes the unfair treatment of Jews in Majorca, *Cap al cel obert* reveals the abuse and fear of slaves in Cuba. Maria, who sympathizes with the slaves, is also discriminated against because she is a woman and because she is descended from Jews, qualities the authorities use to convict her of treason. Both novels express the wish to erase the persecution of cultures discriminated against in history, but they are also linked by their endings that emphasize inaccessible beauty. Just as João Peres, the Jew from Livorno, while watching the bonfire of the Inquisition, only wants to flee into the blueness of the sea, hopeful observers believe that Maria averts death by rising with the balloon "deprisa, muy deprisa hasta perderse por el cielo y más allá" (quickly, very quickly, until she disappeared in the sky and beyond). These words describing Maria's ascent through the blueness of the sky echo almost exactly those expressing João Peres's wish to sail rapidly into the furthest blue of the sea. From her earliest stories to the most recent novels, Riera often represents hope and unattainable beauty or desire with the color blue or the sea, drawing inspiration from the sea surrounding her homeland, Majorca. She has also written descriptions of Majorca for the board of tourism in *Mallorca, imatges per la felicitat* (2000, Majorca, Images for Happiness). In 2000 the Generalitat (autonomous government) of Catalonia presented Riera with the Saint George Cross for her writing.

In 2003 Riera published *Antología de poesía catalana femenina* (Anthology of Catalan Poetry by Women) and two books for children: *El gos magic* (The Magic Dog) and *El meravellos viatge de Maria al pais de les tulipes* (Maria's Marvelous Voyage to the Land of Tulips). Also that year Carles Cortés edited an anthology of Riera's stories, *Llengües mortes: Selecció de contes* (Dead Languages: An Anthology of Stories).

*La meitat de l'ànima* (2004, Half of the Soul) resumes the identity theme prevalent in Riera's early writing, imbuing the search for self with mystery. The protagonist, C, receives a folder from an unknown man while she is signing books at a book fair. The folder contains letters written by her mother, Cecília Balaguer, who had died in an accident when C was a girl, as well as photographs. The materials suggest that Cecília had an affair with a Frenchman and that he is C's biological father. After she discovers that the man was probably the writer Albert Camus and that her mother may have been a spy or double agent, knowing the truth about her heritage becomes the focus of C's life. Because the people who could help in her investigation are dead, C needs the assistance of the stranger, whose name and address she has lost. She writes a book about her pursuit in which she appeals to her readers to help her find him so that she can clarify her foggy memories of her mother and resolve the question of her identity: "Per a mi la memòria és imprescindible, sense memòria som morts. La memòria és l'ànima de les persones i tal vegada és per això que jo seguesc cercant la meitat de la meva ánima" (For me memory is essential; without memory we are dead. Memory is the soul of people, and perhaps because of that I continue searching for half of my soul). By including her readers, C extends her quest from the individual to the collective sphere. *La meitat de l'ànima* won the Sant Jordi Prize.

In 2005, in honor of the four-hundredth anniversary of the first part of Miguel de Cervantes's *Don Quijote* (1605, 1615), Riera published *El Quijote desde el nacionalismo catalán, en torno al tercer centenario* (The Quijote and Catalan Nationalism, on the Threshold of the Third Centennial) and *El Quijote y Barcelona* (The Quijote and Barcelona), which also includes essays by other specialists on Cervantes. That year she received the Jaume Fuster Prize for literature written in Catalan.

The critical acclaim, popularity, and depth of Carme Riera's latest novels, as well as her expertise in literary criticism, ensure that her writing will become even more recognized worldwide. Although only a few of her works have English translations, many have been translated into German, Italian, Greek, Dutch, Hebrew, and Russian. Riera has repeatedly stated that she cannot help but write, and she told Kathleen M. Glenn: "my best work is the one I am writing in my head."

## References:

Francesco Ardolino, "La ficció epístolar de Carme Riera," *Journal of Catalan Studies/Revista Internacional de Catalanística* (2000) <http://www.uoc.edu/jocs/3/articles/ardolino4/index.html> [accessed 17 October 2005];

Emilie L. Bergmann, "Letters and Diaries as Narrative Strategies in Contemporary Catalan Women's Writing," in *Critical Essays on the Literatures of Spain and Spanish America,* edited by Luis González-del-Valle and Julio Baena (Boulder, Colo.: Society of Spanish and Spanish-American Studies, 1991), pp. 19–28;

María Camí-Vela, *La búsqueda de la identidad en la obra literaria de Carme Riera* (Madrid: Pliegos, 2000);

Luisa Cotoner, ed., *El espejo y la mascara: Veinticinco años de ficción narrativa en la obra de Carme Riera* (Barcelona: Destino, 2000);

Kathleen M. Glenn, Mirella Servodidio, and Mary S. Vásquez, eds., *Moveable Margins: The Narrative Art of Carme Riera* (London: Associated University Press, 1999);

Roberta Johnson, "Voice and Intersubjectivity in Carme Riera's Narratives," in *Critical Essays on the Literatures of Spain and Spanish America,* pp. 153–159;

Geraldine Nichols, *Des/cifrar la diferencia: Narrativa femenina de la España contemporánea* (Madrid: Siglo veintiuno, 1992);

Elisabeth Ordóñez, *Voices of Their Own: Contemporary Spanish Narrative by Women* (Lewisburg, Pa.: Bucknell University Press, 1991), pp. 129–135;

Janet Pérez, *Contemporary Women Writers of Spain* (Boston: Twayne, 1988), pp. 194–196;

Sandra Schumm, *Reflection in Sequence: Novels by Spanish Women, 1944–1988* (Lewisburg, Pa.: Bucknell University Press, 1999), pp. 142–158.

# Mercè Rodoreda
## (10 October 1908 – 13 April 1983)

### Jaume Martí-Olivella
*University of New Hampshire*

BOOKS: *Sóc una dona honrada?* (Barcelona: Llibreria Catalonia, 1932);

*Del que hom no pot fugir* (Barcelona: Clarisme, 1934);

*Un dia en la vida d'un home* (Badalona: Proa, 1934);

*Polèmica* (Barcelona: Clarisme, 1934)—includes *Delfí Dalmau;*

*Crim!* (Barcelona: La Rosa dels Vents, 1936);

*Aloma* (Barcelona: Institució de les Lletres Catalanes, 1938; revised edition, Barcelona: 62, 1969); translated into Spanish by J. F. Vidal Jové as *Aloma* (Madrid: AL-BORAK, 1971);

*Vint-i-dos contes* (Barcelona: Selecta, 1958); translated into Spanish by Ana María Moix as *Veintidós cuentos* (Madrid: Mondadori, 1988);

*La plaça del Diamant* (Barcelona: El Club dels Novel·listes, 1962); translated into Spanish by Enrique Sordo as *La plaza del diamante* (Madrid: Edhasa, 1965); translated by Eda O'Shiel as *Pigeon Girl* (London: Deutsch, 1967); translated by David H. Rosenthal as *The Time of the Doves* (New York: Taplinger, 1980);

*El carrer de les Camèlies* (Barcelona: El Club dels Novel·listes, 1966); translated into Spanish by José Batlló as *La calle de las Camelias* (Barcelona: Planeta, 1970); translated by Rosenthal as *Camellia Street* (Saint Paul, Minn.: Graywolf Press, 1993);

*Jardí vora el mar* (Barcelona: El Club dels Novel·listes, 1967); translated into Spanish as *Jardín junto al mar* (Barcelona: Planeta, 1975);

*La meva Cristina i altres contes* (Barcelona: 62, 1967); translated into Spanish by Batlló as *Mi Cristina y otros cuentos* (Barcelona: Poligrafa, 1969); translated by Rosenthal as *My Christina and Other Stories* (Port Townsend, Wash.: Graywolf Press, 1984);

*Mirall trencat* (Barcelona: El Club dels Novel·listes, 1974); translated into Spanish by Pere Gimferrer as *Espejo roto* (Barcelona: Seix Barral, 1978);

*Semblava de seda i altres contes* (Barcelona: 62, 1978); translated into Spanish as *Parecía de seda* (Barcelona: Edhasa, 1981);

*Tots els contes* (Barcelona: 62, 1979);

*Mercè Rodoreda ( from the cover for* Isabel y Maria, *1992; Thomas Cooper Library, University of South Carolina)*

*Viatges i flores* (Barcelona: 62, 1980); translated into Spanish by Clara Janés as *Viatges i flors* (Barcelona: 62, 1980);

*Quanta, quanta guerra* (Barcelona: El Club dels Novel·listes, 1980); translated into Spanish by Moix as *Cuánta, cuánta guerra* (Barcelona: Edhasa, 1982);

*Contes de guerra i revolució* (Barcelona: Laia, 1981);

*Cartes a l'Anna Muriá (1939–1956)* (Barcelona: La Sal, 1985);

*La mort i la primavera* (Barcelona: El Club dels Novel·listes, 1986); translated into Spanish by

Sordo as *La muerte y la primavera* (Barcelona: Seix Barral, 1986);

*Isabel i Maria* (Valencia: Climent, 1991); translated into Spanish by Basilio Losada as *Isabel y Maria* (Barcelona: Seix Barral, 1992).

**Editions and Collections:** *Obres Completes,* volume 1 (1936–1960), volume 2 (1960–1966), and volume 3 (1967–1980) (Barcelona: 62, 1976–1984);

*Una campana de vidre; antologia de contes* (Barcelona: Destino, 1984);

*Gallines de Guinea: antologia de contes* (Barcelona: Abadia de Montserrat, 1989);

*La brusa vermella i altres contes* (Barcelona: Barcanova, 1990);

*El torrent de les flors* (Valencia: Climent, 1993)–includes *La senyora Florentina i el seu amor Homer, La casa dels gladiols, Maniquí 1, Maniquí 2, L'hostal de les tres camèlies,* and *Un dia.*

On 23 January 1939, only two days before the arrival of General Francisco Franco's troops in Barcelona, Mercè Rodoreda, together with many other Catalan writers and artists, went into exile. By then, she had already published four novels and received a respectable amount of critical attention. She had spent the war years (1936–1939) working for the Institució de les Lletres Catalanes (Catalan Literature Institute) and for the Generalitat (Catalan Autonomous Government), in its Comissariat de Propaganda (Propaganda Office). Privately, she had recently separated from her husband and was undergoing what she referred to as a revolution of her own. The collapse of the Catalan cultural and political scene and the deep trauma brought about by the defeat of the Spanish Republic was only magnified by the direct experience of the Nazi occupation of France, which Rodoreda, unlike most of her fellow Catalan exiles, who initially decided to immigrate to Central or South America, endured in its totality. War and exile became the historical and personal parameters of her entire life as an adult writer. And yet, the direct portrayal of those two crucial experiences was not what turned her work into the best-known narratives to emerge from Catalonia in the twentieth century. On the contrary, Rodoreda's claim to posterity was established by her creation of a series of fictional characters who combined a rare sense of inner exile and stubborn resilience, most notably seen in Natàlia/Colometa, the female protagonist of *La plaça del Diamant* (1962; translated as *Pigeon Girl,* 1967), a novel translated into more than twenty languages and considered by Gabriel García Márquez to be the most beautiful published in Spain after the Civil War. With the publication of *La plaça del Diamant,* Rodoreda broke a novelistic publishing silence that had lasted since 1938. During those

years of exile she had only been able to publish in Catalonia *Vint-i-dos contes* (1958, Twenty-two Stories), a volume that gathered most of the realistic stories she wrote in Paris and Bordeaux during World War II. Publicly, Rodoreda was virtually unknown in the still highly suppressed world of Catalan culture. The remarkable popular and critical success of her novel marked the turning point of her career. Yet, Rodoreda still remained partly exiled in Geneva, where she had lived since 1954. Not until 1975, the year of Franco's death, did Rodoreda finally decide to resettle in Catalonia, in her newly built house in the small village of Romanyà de la Selva, in the mountain landscape of the Gavarres region, just a few miles inland from the Costa Brava seashore. Five years later, Rodoreda was the first woman ever to receive the Premi d'Honor de les Lletres Catalanes (Honorary Prize for Catalan Literature), Catalonia's most prestigious literary award.

Rodoreda was born on 10 October 1908 in a small house in Sant Gervasi de Cassoles, a neighborhood newly added to the city of Barcelona, which had six hundred thousand inhabitants at the time and was growing fast. She was the only child of Andreu Rodoreda and Montserrat Gurgui. Their house had been bought by Pere Gurgui, Rodoreda's grandfather, who had made a living as an antiques dealer. When Gurgui and his partner parted ways, they distributed the remaining antiques between them, and many of those pieces ended up filling the crammed house. Rodoreda's father was an accountant who loved literature and who, like her grandfather, was a devoted follower of Jacint Verdaguer's literary work. Verdaguer was, in fact, the emblematic figure of the Catalan literary Renaixença (Renaissance), the neo-Romantic movement that had prefigured the modern development of a Catalan political consciousness. At the time of Rodoreda's birth Catalonia was experiencing the effervescence of the Solidaritat Catalana (Catalan Solidarity) and the Mancomunitat de Catalunya (Catalonia's Self Rule), the first two political formations of modern Catalan nationalism. Half seriously, half in jest, Rodoreda recounted later that as a child she had listened to all of Verdaguer's works while on her father's or grandfather's lap. Such a familiar devotion found its iconic illustration in the little monument that Gurgui had erected to honor the famous poet-priest and that presided over the garden that became a literary landmark in Rodoreda's fiction.

Rodoreda's grandfather occupied a privileged position as the refuge of her childhood and as the source of her literary inspiration. Her grandfather's illness, however, prevented her from receiving a formal education. Because of the scarce financial resources of the household, when Gurgui fell ill, Rodoreda was

Cover for a 1993 Buenos Aires paperback edition of the Spanish translation of Rodoreda's Catalan-language novel La plaça del Diamant (1962, The Plaza of the Diamond; translated as Pigeon Girl, 1967), which the Colombian Nobel laureate Gabriel García Márquez called the most beautiful novel published in Spain after the Civil War (Thomas Cooper Library, University of South Carolina)

asked to stay home to take care of him. She was ten and had spent only three full years attending school. When Gurgui died two years later, Rodoreda felt what she later had some of her characters say: "Tots ens aturem de viure als dotze anys" (We all stopped living at twelve). She was never sent back to school. Cooking and sewing were her only formal occupations. (Later, during her initial years in exile, she made a living by means of her sewing abilities.)

At this time Rodoreda began her most persistent condition—solitude. One of Rodoreda's most beloved fictional characters was Mila, the protagonist of *Solitud* (1909, Solitude), a novel by Víctor Català (pseudonym of Caterina Albert). Mila managed to fend for herself

alone in the mountains after having been ravaged by male greediness and sexual violence. At the end of her life Rodoreda, like Mila, remained alone in her mountain house at Romanyà de la Selva—although Rodoreda had the comfort of a house and a garden of her own.

Rodoreda's solitary youth ended with the arrival of Joan Gurgui, her *oncle d'Amérique* (uncle from America). He was her mother's younger brother who had been sent off to Buenos Aires, Argentina, at the age of fifteen. Like many other Catalan migrants to Latin America, Joan had the dream of all *indianos:* to return home with a sizable fortune, settle down, and start a family. Gurgui felt deceived because the money he had been sending to Rodoreda's mother had not only not earned him the solid foundations to build a new house but was all gone, while the family house was mortgaged. He took it upon himself to clear the mortgage and pay off the family debts. He moved in with Rodoreda and her parents. Soon he and Rodoreda started a sexual relationship. On the day Rodoreda turned twenty, they were married. Jordi, their only son, was born in 1929. By 1931, Rodoreda realized that her marriage was a mistake. The couple had moved to a nearby apartment, but Rodoreda felt even more isolated and stifled than before and often returned to the old *colomar* (dovecote) at her parents' house to find the peace of mind to write. She had already found her literary vocation, and her husband was seemingly interested only in making money. Her sense of having broken an incest taboo always came back to haunt her—especially in the last years of her life, when Jordi was institutionalized with an incurable mental illness.

Rodoreda turned the experiences of her early life into one of the most quietly dramatic and life-asserting fictional worlds ever to emerge from a Catalan writer. Every critical account of her work coincides in stating the extraordinary poetic breadth of her work. Joaquim Molas, a leading scholar and critic of the Catalan postwar generation, has written, "Rodoreda sap transformar-ho tot en un món d'una prodigiosa riquesa poètica. I, aquí, en definitiva, resideix el secret més profund del seu art" (Rodoreda knows how to turn everything into a world of a prodigious poetic richness. And this is, ultimately, where the deepest secret of her art lies). Rodoreda chose George Meredith's epigraph "My dear, these things are life" to frame her best-known and most moving story, *La plaça del Diamant,* told by Natàlia/Colometa in an unflinching poetic monologue that constitutes the most enduring flashback to the survival of an entire culture. Rodoreda's deep metamorphosis of historical detail into poetic prose turns Natàlia's innocence into the bearer of Catalonia's own collective memory. To do so, Rodoreda returned to her own memories, her most private experiences. This intimate connection between life and work helps explain why Rodoreda later rejected her first four novels. They were, according to her, exercises in style, derivative imitating gestures.

In *Sóc una dona honrada?* (Am I an Honest Woman?), her first published novel, Rodoreda is already toying fictionally with her own life. By 1932, when the novel was published, she was in search of a public persona that would pave the way for her personal and literary emancipation. Implicit in the question of the title is Rodoreda's questioning of the social limitations imposed on married women at the time. Her choice to become an independent journalist and writer in a literary world dominated by males was not only her first true gesture of rebellion but also an answer to the initial question of her novel. Formally, the novel uses artificial wordplay and a rather static structure based on the two protagonists' diaries. Thematically, it is the story of a conventional bourgeois marriage and the desired liberation from it. Teresa, the female protagonist, stops short of that desire and remains within the boundaries of her imaginative escapes. The publication of the novel was financed by Rodoreda's husband.

Personal experience reappears in Rodoreda's second novel, *Del que hom no pot fugir* (1934, That from Which One Cannot Escape). A young orphan woman leaves behind the city where she has had an unhappy relationship with an older married man who had been her father's friend and is now her tutor. In the country she is raped and endures an extremely painful childbirth. Conceived as an homage to Albert and her melodramatic *drames rurals* (rural dramas), the title of this novel, in the words of Carme Arnau (1992), a leading Rodoreda scholar, "és gairebé premonitori en la vida de Mercè Rodoreda" (is almost a premonition of Mercè Rodoreda's life). But despite frequent bouts of despair, Rodoreda never followed the path of madness and suicide taken by the protagonist of her second novel.

Rodoreda, who was already writing regularly for various Catalan magazines, such as *Clarisme* and *Mirador,* published another novel in 1934. *Un dia en la vida d'un home* (One Day in a Man's Life) was printed by Edicions Proa, one of Catalonia's leading publishing houses. A bitter criticism of urban and conventional bourgeois life, Rodoreda's third novel, arguably her most stylistically unfinished work, was the one that opened her path into the literary meetings of the Club dels Novel·listes (The Novelists Club), a collective of writers mostly responsible for the many translations of contemporary European fiction also published by Proa. Many of these novelists became known as the Grup de Sabadell (Sabadell's Group), since most of them came from that industrial city a few miles northwest of Barcelona. Francesc Trabal and Joan Prat (generally known

by his pen name Armand Obiols) were prominent figures in the group and became two of the central influences on Rodoreda's life and work. In a rather self-conscious way, *Un dia en la vida d'un home* followed the iconoclastic humor of Trabal's work, especially *Hi ha homes que ploren perquè el sol es pon* (There Are Men Who Cry Because the Sun Sets), published the year before. Trabal's work had become the most fashionable expression of a new urban novelistic style that did away with neo-Romantic and melodramatic plots, such as the one Rodoreda herself had used in her second book.

The last of the rejected novels was *Crim!* (Crime!), a mock thriller that Rodoreda published in 1936. This work was her response to the call for the creation of urban narratives by Carles Riba in "Una generació sense novel·la?" (1925, A Generation without a Novel?), an essay in which the poet and translator of Greek classics into Catalan stated the need for a new novelistic readership if Catalan literature was to survive in the twentieth century.

*Aloma* (1938) is generally accepted as the beginning of Rodoreda's literary career. A sensitive girl living in a low-income Catalan household, Aloma cannot afford to go to the beach or to dance halls and has to rely on local cinemas and hidden books for her lonely imaginative escapades. Later, she has a love affair with an older relative and becomes a single mother. She kept the finished novel in the drawer for more than a year; in a 1966 interview she told Baltasar Porcel: "Em feia por ensenyar-la. Tenia la sensació que al donar-la a llegir em descobria massa jo" (I was afraid to show it to anyone. I had the feeling that by having it read I would be revealing too much of myself). The advice of several of her newfound friends and colleagues from the Club dels Novel·listes and the Institució de les Lletres Catalanes, especially that of Trabal, was required to overcome Rodoreda's apprehensions. They persuaded her to enter the novel in the contest for the Premi Crexells, the most prestigious award for Catalan narrative at the time. The novel won the prize in 1937 and was published the following year.

*Aloma* chronicles the years that led to the proclamation of the Second Republic in 1931 and the start of the Civil War in 1936 in a restrained and direct narrative prose that prefigures Rodoreda's best style. Each chapter is framed by epigraphs that are revealing of the author's life and readings. The first epigraph is "I bé, tot m'apareix en la forma més grollera, més repugnant" (Well, everything appears to me in the crudest, ugliest way). These words are uttered by Anna Karenina in the Catalan translation of Leo Tolstoy's 1878 novel by Rodoreda's friend, the writer and political activist Andreu Nin. Despite that defining epigraph, *Aloma* captures the beauty of Barcelona in the years when politi-

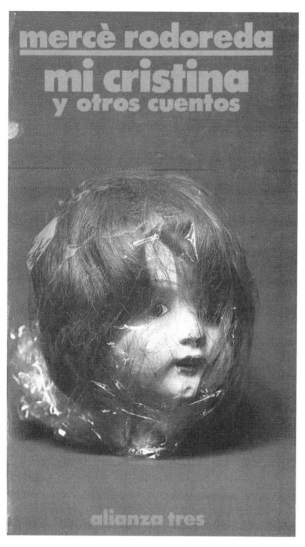

*Cover for a 1988 paperback edition of the Spanish translation (1969)
by José Batlló of Rodoreda's Catalan-language collection* La
meva Cristina i altres contes, 1967; translated as
My Christina and Other Stories, 1984), *which
deals with symbols of death and rebirth (Thomas
Cooper Library, University of South Carolina)*

cal violence could not prevent a feeling of social and
cultural renewal. Laws passed after the arrival of the
Republic included a progressive divorce law and, for
the first time, universal voting rights for women in Catalonia and Spain. Rodoreda herself was no longer the
shy and secluded young woman who had jumped from
adolescence to a married life. She was on the brink of
separating from her uncle/husband and had created a
public persona as a modern and independent woman.

But Rodoreda's hopes for a new life were put to a
severe test during the Civil War. The experience of loss
started with Nin's assassination in 1937. Since the beginning of the war, Nin had been in charge of the Justice
Department in the Generalitat as the leader of the
Workers Party of Marxist Unification. After the confrontations in the streets of Barcelona of May 1937
between pro-Soviet parties and anarchist groups, events
recorded by George Orwell in his *Homage to Catalonia*
(1938), Nin was kidnapped, tortured, and killed by
Soviet agents; no one else knew of his fate at the time,
and no voice was raised against his brutal demise. For
Rodoreda, whose friendship with Nin was based on literary kinship and personal appeal, it became a dramatic
sign of an inner split: the Catalan family was divided not
only along class and gender lines but also along lines of
political fear. Her second loss of the war years was that
of her father, who died in an aerial bombardment by the
Francoist forces. Rodoreda found strength in her writing
and in her public service as secretary of the Institució de
les Lletres Catalanes and as a member of the Comissariat de Propaganda of the Generalitat. As part of her cultural work, Rodoreda traveled with Francesc Trabal to
Prague in 1938 to attend the thirteenth International
PEN Club Conference. Rodoreda and Trabal became
lovers during that trip. In the spring of 1939 a group of
Catalan writers and artists who had fled the incoming
Francoist troops was sent by the French government to
a youth hostel in Roissy-en-Brie. In April, Trabal and
Rodoreda joined the group at Roissy-en-Brie. There
Rodoreda fell in love with Obiols, Trabal's brother-in-
law, and a crisis ensued. The refugees divided themselves among those who tolerated or supported the relationship and those who opposed it. The opponents
moved to another youth hostel in Saint-Cyr-sur-Morin
in August. A few weeks later, with the beginning of
World War II, Obiols and Rodoreda decided to stay in
France, while most of the refugees seized any available
opportunity to sail to Latin America.

David Rosenthal's preface to his translation of
Rodoreda's *La plaça del Diamant* offers one of the clearest and most compelling interpretations of the meaning
of exile in Rodoreda's life and work: "Catalans were on
the losing side in the Spanish Civil War, and immediately afterwards were forbidden to speak their language
outside the home. For writers like Rodoreda, who did
not reestablish her residence in Spain until 1979, the
fate of Catalan was a matter of artistic survival. . . .
Thus, as with many Catalan authors, her personal
story is of a kind of death followed by a recent and partial rebirth." All of Rodoreda's work written in exile is
marked by the archetypes of death and rebirth.
Whether under the guise of the realistic portrayal of
Colometa's attempt to kill herself and her two children
in the middle of the war, or via the fantastic metamorphoses in "La salamandra" and "La meva Cristina," or
through the ritual underwater passages of *La mort i la*

*primavera* (1986, Death and Spring), these motifs become a recurrent presence. Rodoreda told Porcel that "The prewar world seemed unreal to me, and I still haven't reconstructed it. And the time I spent! Everything burned inside, but imperceptibly it was becoming a little anachronistic. And perhaps this is what hurt most. I couldn't have written a novel if they'd beaten it out of me. I was too disconnected from everything, or maybe too terribly bound up with everything, though that might sound like a paradox." Rodoreda and Obiols lived through many harrowing moments as they fled the advancing German armies. Those moments were transformed into some of Rodoreda's most realistic short stories: "Orléans 3 kilòmetres," "Nocturn," and "Nit i boira" (Night and Fog).

At the end of the war Rodoreda and Obiols went to Limoges for two years, then to Bordeaux, and in 1948 to Paris. In the early postwar years Rodoreda resorted almost entirely to writing poetry and painting to express the turmoil through which she had lived. Her poems involve mythical female figures such as Eve and Judith and Calypso and Nausica. Her work received poetry prizes in the Jocs Florals (Literary Contests) of the Catalan Diaspora: in London in 1947, Paris in 1948, and Montevideo in 1949. The poems create a symmetrical, almost classical, rendering of her suffering, as in the last three verses of "Plany de Calipso" (Calypso's Complaint): "Ara voldria ésser lleó que juga i mata / o l'olivera inmòbil en son furor i retort / però al pit m'agonitza un escorpí escarlata" (Now I would like to be the lion that plays and kills / or the still olive tree in its retorted fury / but in my chest the scarlet scorpion is dying).

The years in Paris were clouded by uncertainties regarding her future with Obiols, who had thought about returning to his wife, and the pressure she was receiving from her mother from Barcelona to reunite with Gurgui and their son. Rodoreda visited her husband and son in Catalonia on several occasions but never regained the desire to live with them. During these years she suffered psychosomatic symptoms that prevented her from being able to sustain any long-term writing project. Her visual work consisted of almost a hundred drawings of the female figure. Paul Klee, Wassily Kandinski, Pablo Picasso, and Joan Miró were the clearest influences on Rodoreda's artwork.

In 1954 Rodoreda and Obiols moved to Geneva, where Obiols took a job as translator at the headquarters of the United Nations Educational, Scientific, and Cultural Organization (UNESCO). In 1957 Rodoreda entered *Vint-i-dos contes,* a selection of realistic short stories written in France during the war, in the contest for the Víctor Català Prize for Catalan narrative, which had been reinstated in 1953. It won, and the book was

published by Editorial Selecta the following year. From 1959 to 1961 she worked on four novels at the same time. She finished two of them—*Jardí vora el mar* (1967, Garden by the Sea) and *La plaça del Diamant;* left an almost complete first draft of *La mort i la primavera;* and wrote several chapters of *Mirall trencat* (1974, Broken Mirror). All these novels share the symbolic function given to the most essential private spaces—the house and the garden. These spaces have a quasi-mythical status associated with Rodoreda's childhood in the house with the little garden in Sant Gervasi de Cassoles.

In the early 1960s the literary juries of the Joanot Martorell and the Sant Jordi Prizes consecutively rejected *Jardí vora el mar; Colometa,* the initial title she gave to *La plaça del Diamant;* and *La mort i la primavera.* Those rejections, especially the first one, stimulated her writing and provide an explanation for her contemporaneous creation of four novels and the thematic continuities found in them despite their diverse literary registers. The mythical role attributed to gardens brings together *Jardí vora el mar* and *Mirall trencat,* initially titled "Una casa abandonada" (An Abandoned House). In these novels the garden is an expression of both a real and an imagined space—Rodoreda's childhood garden and the one of which she had always dreamed. Both novels, on the other hand, also chronicle the decay of a familiar household. Rodoreda's alter ego may be seen in Eugeni, the professional gardener who takes care of the spacious garden by the sea in *Jardí vora el mar,* and in Teresa Goday, the protagonist of *Mirall trencat,* who evokes days gone by from the vantage point of her lonely old years. The two novels constitute the clearest illustration of the cleansing "death-by-water" motif that permeates Rodoreda's work. By then Rodoreda had learned the necessity of what a novelist she greatly admired, Franz Kafka, summarized in the title of his famous story: metamorphosis. As Arnau (1979) says, "La metamorfosi acostuma a produir-se en dues substàncies lligades estretament a la producció de Mercè Rodoreda i a la seva vida, també—, dues primeres matèries, que simbolitzen la mort i el renaixement: l'aigua i la vegetació" (The metamorphosis tends to happen inside two substances that are very tied to Mercè Rodoreda's production and also to her life—, two primary materials that symbolize death and rebirth: water and vegetation).

That archetypal rebirth is dramatically portrayed in the stories collected in *La meva Cristina i altres contes* (1967; translated as *My Christina and Other Stories,* 1984) and in the mesmerizing primitive world described in *La mort i la primavera.* Early on in this novel is a harrowing account of a young man in hiding who witnesses his father's disinterment from a hollow tree that ultimately becomes his tomb. This most brutal and direct inscrip-

Cover for a 1989 paperback edition of the 1986 Spanish translation by
Enrique Sordo of Rodoreda's Catalan-language novel La mort i la
primavera (1986, Death and Spring), in which a man is
killed by being sealed inside a hollow tree (Thomas
Cooper Library, University of South Carolina)

tion of traumatic loss is the beginning of a series of ritu-alized gestures that constitute the core of social activity of the primitive people inhabiting the fantastic and terrible world of Rodoreda's least realistic work. The use of the tree, a traditional symbol of life, as the marker of death, on the other hand, exemplifies the poetic double articulation that, according to Jaume Martí-Olivella (1995), is the literary device that links all of Rodoreda's production. *La mort i la primavera* also constitutes the clearest illustration of Rodoreda's parodic use of the Eden myth, since the characters get to know the secret of the "forbidden tree" while placing themselves in a state of prelapsarian innocence that allows them to play amid the dead.

Contemporary feminist criticism has identified the use of literary forms of metamorphosis as a strategy of resistance for historical women submerged in or marginalized by a male-dominated world. This concept is clearly illustrated in *La meva Cristina i altres contes,* especially in the title story, in which Rodoreda retells the biblical tale of Jonah's watery exile in the belly of the great fish. The shipwrecked sailor who survives by eating away the body of Cristina, the whale, ends up finding himself back home under the guise of a pearl. His body has been symbiotically altered, and he no longer resembles a human being. Neither surgery nor the final recovery of his identity papers is enough to give the sailor a sense of belonging in his homeland. The story ends with his lonely longing for Cristina, the mother-whale who has become the defining experience of his life. Geraldine Clearly Nichols offers an insight into the rich symbolic layering of the story:

> The model of exile proposed in "My Christina" is that of symbiosis, a sustained but finite relationship of mutual dependency that is figured in three fluid but well determined metaphorical levels. One level is the fantastic (sailor in the belly of a whale); another level is particular (expatriate in a foreign culture or inner exile in a hostile homeland); and, the other level is universal (fetus in the maternal uterus).

In 1966 the jury of the Sant Jordi Prize gave the award to Rodoreda's *El carrer de les Camèlies* (1966; translated as *Camellia Street,* 1993), a dark sequel to *La plaça del Diamant.* Rodoreda thought that the award was a way to compensate for failing to recognize *Colometa* in 1960. In any case, the prize helped promote a novel that, read together with *La plaça del Diamant,* is an example of what the Chicano writer Sandra Cisneros wrote in the preface to Rosenthal's English translation: "Rodoreda writes about feelings, about characters so numbed or overwhelmed by events they have only their emotions as a language. I think it's because one has no words that one writes, not because one is gifted with language. It is this precision at naming the unnameable that attracts me to Rodoreda." Among the many qualities shared by Cecília Ce and Natàlia/ Colometa, the survivors who are the lead characters in *El carrer de les Camèlies* and *La plaça del Diamant,* respectively, is a struggle against the fear of language, since, as Natàlia states, "A casa vivíem sense paraules i les coses que jo duia per dintre em feien por perquè no sabia si eren meves" (At home we used to live without words and I was afraid of the things I had inside me because I didn't know if they were mine).

The last three works published by Rodoreda were *Semblava de seda i altres contes* (1978, It Looked Like Silk and Other Stories), *Viatges i flores* (1980, Travels and Flowers), and *Quanta, quanta guerra* (1980, So, So Much War). The last two books were each awarded the Serra d'Or critics' prize. In 1980 Rodoreda's entire production was honored with Catalonia's most important literary award, the Premi d'Honor de les Lletres Catalanes. Her last three books showed Rodoreda's sustained capacity to transform a painful life into poetic prose. Thus, "Semblava de seda" dramatically portrays the sense of intimate betrayal Rodoreda felt in 1971 when, after Obiols's death in Vienna, she discovered that he had fallen in love with a young woman. By collecting that story with "Nit i boira," "Paràlisi" (Paralysis), and other stories written during the hard times of the German occupation of France, Rodoreda is once more linking past and present, public and private. With *Viatges i flores,* moreover, she combines an old collection of poetic vignettes titled "Flors de debò" (True Flowers), written during the early years of her stay in Geneva, with a series of ironic and fantastic narrative sketches titled "Viatges a uns quants pobles" as a *divertimento* (diversion) to rest from *Quanta, quanta guerra* and *La mort i la primavera,* the novel she was trying to finish when she died on 13 April 1983. In *Quanta, quanta guerra* Rodoreda found her most poetic "separate peace." In this final retelling of the Eden myth Eva and Adrià are able to see each other anew, and in their gaze they mirror all the beauty of the world: "Els ulls violeta em miraven com si miressin el món, tot el que de bo té el món, i aquest pensament em va fer pujar una onada de vergonya a les galtes. Em va dir que, mirant-me, se li havia quedat el cor tranquil" (Her violet eyes were looking at me as if they were looking at the world, at all that is good in the world, and this thought made me blush in a wave of shame. She told me that by looking at me her heart had found peace).

The richness and depth of Mercè Rodoreda's work is still being analyzed and documented by critics and scholars around the world. This analysis has placed a special emphasis on the diverse literary works that Rodoreda bequeathed to the Institut d'Estudis Catalans (Catalan Studies Institute) after her death. From this material, two texts deserve special attention: *Un dia,* a play staged in 1993 as part of the *Barcelona Grec,* the popular summer festival of the Catalan capital and published in 1993 in *El torrent de les flors* (The Flower Creek), a volume that gathers all of Rodoreda's previously unpublished plays; and the unfinished novel *Isabel i Maria* (1991, Isabel and Maria). Both texts seem to have had a dormant existence throughout Rodoreda's life. They are early formulations of her two most acclaimed novels—*La plaça del Diamant* and *Mirall trencat*—and point to the crucial importance of the absent mother figure in the author's life and work. Ultimately, even if Rodoreda dismissed feminism as "un xarampió" (the measles), her work

*Paperback cover for the Spanish translation (1992) by Basilio Losada of Rodoreda's unfinished Catalan-language final novel,* Isabel i Maria *(Isabel and Maria), published in 1991 (Thomas Cooper Library, University of South Carolina)*

has become the most enduring representation of any Catalan feminine subject to date.

**Interviews:**

Baltasar Porcel, "Mercè Rodoreda o la força lírica," *Serra d'Or* (March 1966): 231–235;

Montserrat Roig, "L'alè poètic de Mercè Rodored," in her *Retrats Paral·lels,* volume 2 (Barcelona: Abadia de Montserrat, 1975).

**Bibliography:**

Maria Isidra Mcncos, "Mercè Rodoreda and the Criticism of Her Work: Analysis and Selected Bibliography," in *Voices and Visions: The Words and Works of Mercè Rodoreda,* edited by Kathleen McNerney (Selinsgrove, Pa.: Susquehanna University Press, 1999), pp. 240–270.

**Biographies:**

Montserrat Casals, *Mercè Rodoreda: Contra la vida, la literatura* (Barcelona: 62, 1991);

Mercè Ibarz, *Mercè Rodoreda* (Barcelona: Empúries, 1991);

Carme Arnau, *Mercè Rodoreda* (Barcelona: 62, 1992).

**References:**

Carme Arnau, *Introducció a la narrativa de Mercè Rodoreda; el mite de la infantesa* (Barcelona: 62, 1979);

Arnau, "Mercè Rodoreda o la força de l'escriptura," in *Literatura de dones: Una visió del món*, by Arnau, Isabel Segura, and others (Barcelona: La Sal, 1988), pp. 81–96;

Arnau, *Miralls tràgics: Aproximació a l'última narrativa de Mercè Rodoreda* (Barcelona: 62, 1990);

Arnau, "Mort et métamorphose: *La meva Cristina i altres contes* de Mercè Rodoreda," *Revue des Langues Romanes*, 93 (1989): 51–60;

Emilie L. Bergmann, "Flowers at the North Pole: Mercè Rodoreda and the Female Imagination in Exile," *Catalan Review*, 2 (1987): 83–99;

Bergmann, "Reshaping the Canon: Intertextuality in Spanish Novels of Female Development," *Anales de la literatura española contemporánea*, 12, nos. 1–2 (1987): 141–157;

Maryellen Bieder, "Cataclysm and Rebirth: Journey to the Edge of the Maelstrom. Mercè Rodoreda's *Quanta, quanta guerra*," in *Actes del Tercer Col·loqui d'Estudis Catalans a Nord-Amèrica* (Barcelona: Abadia de Montserrat, 1983), pp. 227–237;

Bieder, "The Woman in the Garden: The Problem of Identity in the Novels of Mercè Rodoreda," in *Actes del Segon Col·loqui d'Estudis Catalans a Nord-Amèrica, Yale, 1979* (Barcelona: Abadia de Montserrat, 1982), pp. 353–364;

Loreto Busquets, "El mito de la culpa en *La plaça del Diamant*," *Cuadernos Hispanoamericanos: Revista Mensual de Cultura Hispánica*, 420 (1985): 117–140;

Busquets, "The Unconscious in the Novels of Mercè Rodoreda," *Catalan Review*, 2 (1987): 101–117;

Maria Campillo and Marina Gustà, *Mirall trencat de Mercè Rodoreda* (Barcelona: Les Naus d'Empúries, 1985);

Maria Aurèlia Capmany, "Mercè Rodoreda o les coses de la vida," *Serra d'Or*, 104 (1968): 415–417;

Neus Carbonell, *La plaça del Diamant de Mercè Rodoreda* (Barcelona: Les Naus d'Empúries, 1994);

Montserrat Casals, "La ciutat, una casa, un trenca-closques," *El temps*, 586 (1995): 1–8;

Casals, "El *Rosebud* de Mercè Rodoreda," *Catalan Review*, 2 (1987): 27–47;

Mona Fayad, "The Process of Becoming: Engendering the Subject in Mercè Rodoreda and Virginia Woolf," *Catalan Review*, 2 (1987): 119–129;

Gabriel García Márquez, "Sabe usted quién era Mercè Rodoreda?" *El País*, 18 May 1983;

Kathleen M. Glenn, "Muted Voices in Mercè Rodoreda's *La meva Cristina i altres contes*," *Catalan Review*, 2 (1987): 131–142;

Glenn, "*La plaza del Diamante:* The Other Side of the Story," *Letras Femeninas*, 12, nos. 1–2 (1986): 60–68;

Glenn, "Rare Birds and Hardy Flowers: Mercè Rodoreda's *La senyora Florentina i el seu amor Homer*," *Catalan Review*, 8, nos. 1–2 (1994): 193–201;

Josefina González, "*Mirall trencat:* Un umbral autobiográfico en la obra de Mercè Rodoreda," *Revista de Estudios Hispánicos*, 30, no. 1 (1996): 103–119;

Giuseppe Grilli, "Estructures narratives a l'obra de Mercè Rodoreda," *Serra d'Or*, 155 (1972): 39–40;

Grilli, "A partir d'*Aloma*," *Catalan Review*, 2 (1987): 143–158;

Jaume Martí-Olivella, "Bachelardian Myth in Rodoreda's Construction of Identity," in *Imagination, Emblems and Expressions: Essays on Latin American, Caribbean and Continental Culture and Identity*, edited by Helen Ryan-Ramson (Bowling Green, Ohio: Popular Press, 1993), pp. 315–328;

Martí-Olivella, "Death and Spring or Mercè Rodoreda's Semiotic Chora," *Romance Quarterly*, 42 (1995): 154–162;

Martí-Olivella, "Foreword," *Catalan Review*, 2 (1987): 9–15;

Martí-Olivella, "The Witches' Touch: Towards a Poetics of Double Articulation in Rodoreda," *Catalan Review*, 2 (1987): 159–169;

Carmen Martín-Gaite, "Los lazos desatados," *El País*, 15 April 1983;

Kathleen McNerney, "La identitat a *La plaça del Diamant:* supressió i recerca," in *Actes del Quart Col·loqui d'Estudis Catalans a Nord-Amèrica* (Barcelona: Abadia de Montserrat, 1985), pp. 297–302;

McNerney, "Masks and Metamorphoses, Dreams and Illusions in Mercè Rodoreda's *Carnaval*," *Catalan Review*, 7, no. 1 (1993): 71–77;

McNerney, ed., *Voices and Visions: The Words and Works of Mercè Rodoreda* (Selinsgrove, Pa.: Susquehanna University Press, 1999);

McNerney and Nancy Vosburg, eds., *The Garden across the Border: Mercè Rodoreda's Fiction* (Selinsgrove, Pa.: Susquehanna University Press, 1994);

Maria Isidra Mencos, "Mercè Rodoreda: La mirada transgressora en *La meva Cristina i altres contes*," in *Actes del Setè Col·loqui d'Estudis Catalans a Nord-*

*Amèrica, Berkeley 1993* (Barcelona: Abadia de Montserrat, 1996), pp. 167–174;

Joaquim Molas, "Mercè Rodoreda i la novel·la psicològica," *El Pont,* 31 (1969): 12–17;

Murià, "Mercè o la vida dolorosa," *Catalan Review,* 2 (1987): 17–26;

Gonzalo Navajas, "La microhistoria y Cataluña en *El carrer de les Camèlies* de Mercè Rodoreda," *Hispania,* 74, no. 4 (1991): 848–859;

Geraldine Clearly Nichols, "Exile, Gender, and Mercè Rodoreda," *Modern Language Notes,* 101 (1986): 405–417;

Nichols, "El exilio y el género en Mercè Rodoreda," in *Des/cifrar la diferencia Narrativa femenina de la España contemporánea* (Madrid: Siglo XXI de España Editores, 1992), pp. 114–132;

Nichols, "Mitja poma, mitja taronja: génesis y destino literarios de la catalana contemporánea," in *Literatura catalan de dones: una visió del món* (Barcelona: La Sal, 1988), pp. 121–155;

Nichols, "Sex, the Single Girl, and Other Mésalliances in Rodoreda and Laforet," *Anales de la Literatura Española Contemporánea,* 12, nos. 1–2 (1987): 123–140;

Nichols, "Writers, Wantons, Witches: Woman and the Expression of Desire in Rodoreda," *Catalan Review,* 2 (1987): 171–180;

Janet Pérez, "Metamorphosis as a Protest Device in Catalan Feminist Writing: Rodoreda and Oliver," *Catalan Review,* 2 (1987): 181–198;

Pérez, "Presence of the Picaresque and the Quest-Romance in Mercè Rodoreda's *Quanta, quanta guerra!*" *Hispania,* 76, no. 3 (1993): 428–438;

Pérez, "Time and Symbol, Life and Death, Decay and Regeneration: Vital Cycles and the Round of Seasons in Mercè Rodoreda's *La mort i la primavera,*" *Catalan Review,* 5, no. 1 (1991): 179–196;

Joaquim Poch, "El fet femení en els textos de Mercè Rodoreda (una reflexió des de la psicoanàlisi)," *Catalan Review,* 2 (1987): 199–224;

Poch and Conxa Planas, *Dona i psicoanàlisi a l'obra de Mercè Rodoreda: Un estudi del narcissime femení* (Barce-

lona: Promociones Publicaciones Universitarias, 1987);

Randolph Pope, "Mercè Rodoreda's Subtle Greatness," in *Women Writers of Contemporary Spain: Exiles in the Homeland,* edited by Joan L. Brown (Newark: University of Delaware Press, 1991), pp. 116–135;

Joan Ramon Resina, "The Link in Consciousness: Time and Community in Rodoreda's *La plaça del Diamant,*" *Catalan Review,* 2 (1987): 225–246;

Maria A Roca Mussons, *Construuzioni simboliche nel romanzo di Mercè Rodoreda: La plaça del Diamant* (Sassari: Centro Stampa, 1986);

Anna Maria Saludes, "Una passió secreta de Mercè Rodoreda: El teatre," *Revista de Catalunya,* 76 (1993): 121–129;

Saludes, "Suggestioni Lulliane in Mercè Rodoreda's *Aloma,*" *Annali Instituto Universitario Orientale,* 34, no. 1 (1992): 433–443;

Elizabeth A. Scarlett, "Mercè Rodoreda," in her *Under Construction: The Body in Spanish Novels* (Charlottesville & London: University Press of Virginia, 1994);

Josep Miquel Sobrer, "L'artifici de *La plaça del Diamant,* un estudi lingüístic," in *In Memoriam Carles Riba,* edited by Institut d'Estudis Catalans (Esplugues de Llobregat: Ariel, 1973), pp. 363–375;

Joan Triadú, *La novel·la catalana de postguerra* (Barcelona: 62, 1982);

Triadú, "Una novel·la excepcional: *La plaça del Diamant* de Mercè Rodoreda," in her *Llegir com viure* (Barcelona: Fontanella, 1963);

Alejandro Varderi, "Mercè Rodoreda: Més enllà del jardí," *Catalan Review,* 2 (1987): 263–271;

Marie-Claire Zimmeman, "La reconstruction romanesque du lien familiel dans *La plaça del Diamant* de Mercè Rodoreda," *Iberica,* 1 (1992): 187–198.

## Papers:

The Institut d'Estudis Catalans in Barcelona has Mercè Rodoreda's manuscripts and letters.

# Montserrat Roig
### (13 June 1946 – 10 November 1991)

Emilie L. Bergmann
*University of California, Berkeley*

BOOKS: *Molta roba i poc sabó . . . i tan neta que la volen* (Barcelona: Selecta, 1971); translated by Mercedes Nogués as *Aprendizaje sentimental* (Barcelona: Argos Vergara, 1981);

*Ramona, adéu, 1894–1969* (Barcelona: 62, 1972); translated into Spanish by Joaquim Sempere as *Ramona, adiós* (Barcelona: Argos Vergara, 1980);

*Los hechiceros de la palabra* (Barcelona: Martínez Roca, 1975);

*Retrats paral·lels,* 3 volumes (Barcelona: Abadia de Montserrat, 1975–1978);

*Rafael Vidiella: L'aventura de la revolució* (Barcelona: Laia, 1976);

*Els catalans als camps nazis* (Barcelona: 62, 1977); translated as *Noche y niebla: Los catalanes en los campos nazis* (Barcelona: Península, 1978);

*El temps de les cireres* (Barcelona: 62, 1977); translated into Spanish by Enrique Sordo as *Tiempo de cerezas* (Barcelona: Argos Vergara, 1978);

*Personatges: Segons el programa del mateix títol emès per TVE* (Barcelona: Pòrtic, 1978);

*L'hora violeta* (Barcelona: Edicions 62, 1980); translated by Sordo as *La hora violeta* (Barcelona: Argos Vergara, 1980);

*Personatges: Segona sèrie* (Barcelona: Pòrtic, 1980);

*¿Tiempo de mujer?* (Esplugues de Llobregat: Plaza & Janés, 1980);

*Mujeres en busca de un nuevo humanismo* (Barcelona: Salvat, 1981); republished as *El feminismo* (Barcelona: Salvat, 1986);

*Mi viaje al bloqueo: 900 días de la lucha heróica de Leningrado* (Moscow: Progreso, 1982);

*L'òpera quotidiana* (Barcelona: Planeta, 1982); translated into Spanish by Sordo as *La ópera cotidiana* (Barcelona: Planeta, 1983); selections translated by Kathleen McNerney as "The Everyday Opera," in *On Our Own Behalf: Women's Tales from Catalonia,* edited by McNerney (Lincoln: University of Nebraska Press, 1988), pp. 203–234;

*L'agulla daurada* (Barcelona: Edicions 62, 1985); translated into Spanish as *La aguja dorada* (Esplugues

*Montserrat Roig ( from the cover for* Ramona, adiós, *1993; Thomas Cooper Library, University of South Carolina)*

de Llobregat: Plaza & Janés, 1985); selection translated by Deborah Bonner as "The Golden Needle," *Catalan Writing,* 3 (October 1989): 34–40;

*Isabel Clara Simó, Montserrat Roig,* by Roig and Isabel Clara Simó (Barcelona: Ajuntament de Barcelona/Laia, 1985);

*Barcelona a vol d'ocell,* by Roig and Xavier Miserachs (Barcelona: 62, 1987);

*La veu melodiosa* (Barcelona: 62, 1987); translated into Spanish by José Agustín Goytisolo as *La voz melo-*

*diosa* (Esplugues de Llobregat: Plaza & Janés, 1987);

*100 pàgines triades per mi* (Barcelona: La Campana, 1988);

*El cant de la joventut* (Barcelona: 62, 1989); translated into Spanish by Sempere as *El canto de la juventud,* Barcelona: Península, 1990);

*Pau Vila: He viscut! Biografia oral,* by Roig and Bru Rovira (Barcelona: La Campana, 1989);

*L'autèntica història de Catalunya: Una petita nació situada al nord-est d'Espanya i de com sobreviu després d'una guerra civil, una dictadura feixista interminable, una fràgil transició i, també, de com viu, avui, sota una democràcia* (Barcelona: 62, 1990);

*Melindros* (Barcelona: Ediciones B/Grupo Zeta, 1990);

*Digues que m'estimes encara que sigui mentida: Sobre el plaer solitari d'escriure i el vici compartit de llegir* (Barcelona: 62, 1991); translated into Spanish by Antonia Picazo as *Dime que me quieres aunque sea mentira: Sobre el placer solitario de escribir y el vicio compartido de leer* (Barcelona: Península, 1992);

*Un pensament de sal, un pessic de pebre: Dietari obert, 1990– 1991* (Barcelona: 62, 1992); translated into Spanish by Jordi Domènech as *Ultima crónica: Diario abierto* (Barcelona: Península, 1994);

*Reivindicació de la senyora Clito Mestres, seguit de El mateix paisatge* (Barcelona: 62, 1992);

*Mémoires de Barcelone,* by Roig and Annie Goetzinger, translated by Victor Mora (Sèvres, France: La Sirène, 1993);

*Breu història sentimental, i altres contes* (Barcelona: 62, 1995);

*De Veu a veu: Contes i narracions,* by Roig and Maria Aurèlia Capmany (Barcelona: Cercle de Lectors, 2001);

*La lluita contra l'oblit: Escrits sobre la deportació=La lucha contra el olvido: Escritos sobre la deportación* (Barcelona: Amical de Mauthausen i altres camps de concentració nazis, 2001).

**Collection:** *De com s'inicia l'educació sentimental de la Mundeta Claret i altres contes* (Barcelona: 62, 1998).

PLAY PRODUCTION: *Reivindicació de la senyora Clito Mestres,* Barcelona, Teatre Romea, 1991.

PRODUCED SCRIPTS: *Tot art,* television, TVE Catalunya, 1975;

*Personatges,* television, TVE Catalunya, 1977–1978;

*Líders,* television, TVE Catalunya, 1981.

OTHER: Eugeni Castells, *El derecho a la contracepción: Los métodos anticonceptivos y sus indicaciones,* introduction by Roig (Barcelona: Rol, 1978);

Antonina Rodrigo, *Mujeres de España (Las silenciadas),* prologue by Roig (Esplugues de Llobregat: Plaza & Janés, 1979);

"Mar," in *Carnets de mujer: Autoras de nueve paises cuentan lo que significa ser mujer hoy, con ternura, crueldad, humor,* translated by Mireia Bofill, Pilar Giralt, and Enrique Sordo (Barcelona: Argos Vergara, 1981), pp. 11–35; translated by Helen Lane in *Sex and Sensibility: Stories by Contemporary Women Writers from Nine Countries* (London: Sidgwick & Jackson, 1981), pp. 179–212; original Spanish version revised and republished in Catalan, in *El cant de la joventut* (Barcelona: 62, 1989);

Maksim Gor'ky, *Els fills del sol,* translated by Roig and Ricard Sanvicente (Barcelona: Societat Cooperativa Teatre Lliure, 1984);

Rodrigo, *Mujeres para la historia: La España silenciada del siglo XX,* prologue by Roig (Madrid: Compañía Literaria, 1996).

Montserrat Roig's choice of Catalan as a literary language was integral to her feminism and her concern for cultural and historical memory. For her, Spanish was the language of "power and domination, while the language of love and affection" was Catalan. Because the dictatorship of Francisco Franco suppressed publication and teaching in Catalan, the ironic, expressive vitality of Roig's prose style had to be adapted from great Catalan prose writers such as Narcís Oller, Josep Plá, and Mercè Rodoreda. In post-Franco Barcelona, where Catalan was taught in school but no longer spoken on the street, Roig created storytelling women characters whose voices bring the Catalan language to life in her work. She was a lifelong resident of the neighborhood she drew upon as her "myth," the quintessentially bourgeois Barcelona district called the Eixample (Extension), dating from a period of mid-nineteenth-century urban expansion, but she belonged to the politically active generation of students who defied the political restrictions of the central government. Roig's Catalan-language fiction, journalism, and television interviews were instrumental to the reconstruction of Catalonian culture during the transition to democracy and regional autonomy in the 1970s.

In a trilogy of novels, *Ramona, adéu, 1894–1969* (1972, Goodbye, Ramona, 1894–1969), *El temps de les cireres* (1977, Season of Cherries), and *L'hora violeta* (1980, The Violet Hour), Roig wrote with insight and compassion of the inner lives of three generations of women, including those of her own generation, with their struggles for personal autonomy. She cast a critical eye on the social and political move-

*Cover for a 1993 edition of Joaquim Sempere's Spanish translation
(1980) of Roig's novel* Ramona, adéu, 1894–1969 *(1972,
Goodbye, Ramona, 1894–1969), about three generations
of women named Ramona (Thomas Cooper Library,
University of South Carolina)*

ments with which she was affiliated: feminism, the anti-Franco Left, and Catalan nationalism. For her sharp observation of women's objectification and the fraying relationships between women and men in the male-dominated Partit Socialista Unificat de Catalunya (PSUC, Unified Socialist Party of Catalonia), Roig has been compared to Doris Lessing. Although she wrote almost exclusively in Catalan, her "mother tongue," her novels also became best-sellers in Spanish translation and were translated into Portuguese, Italian, French, German, Dutch, Hungarian, and Chinese; selections from her stories and novels have been translated into English.

Montserrat Roig i Fransitorra was one of seven children born to Tomàs Roig i Llop, a Barcelona lawyer whose career as a writer was curtailed by Franco's repression of Catalan culture, and Albina Fransitorra i

Aleñà, who at age fifty-eight embarked on university training to become a professor of Catalan. Roig was educated at the nearby school of the Divina Pastora until the age of thirteen, when she enrolled at the Institut de Secundària Montserrat. Her sister Glòria was an actress, and at the age of sixteen Roig became a student at the Escola de Arte Dramático Adrià Gual, where the dramatist Maria Aurèlia Capmany became her teacher and lifelong friend.

In 1963 Roig enrolled in the University of Barcelona, where she completed her undergraduate degree in philosophy and letters in 1968, followed by two terms of doctoral study. She was an active member of the Sindicato Democrático de Estudiantes (Democratic Students' Union). In March 1966, together with other Catalonian students and intellectuals, Roig participated in the Caputxinata, the anti-Franco occupation of a Capuchin monastery, a watershed in her generation's demonstration of political commitment. Her marriage to an architect in July of that same year lasted only four years. Also in 1966 she won a prize in the Catalan literary competition Jocs Florals (Floral Games) in Caracas, Venezuela, for her story "La Falç" (The Scythe). In 1968 she joined the then-clandestine PSUC but left the party two years later, critical of the rigid Stalinism that continued to dominate it. She was divorced soon after the birth of her son in June 1970. Her husband was a political prisoner during the years of their marriage. She worked as an editor of the *Gran enciclopèdia catalana* (1969–1983, Great Catalan Encyclopedia) from 1968 to 1971 and of the *Diccionari de la literatura catalana* (1979, Dictionary of Catalan Literature) in 1971. She taught as a lecturer at the University of Bristol from 1973 to 1974 and as a visiting professor at the University of Strathclyde in Glasgow in 1983. Roig's career as a journalist included prizewinning reporting on her generation for the magazine *Serra d'Or,* with photography by her friend and longtime collaborator Pilar Aymerich. Roig directed the Catalan literature and criticism section of the newspaper *Tele-eXprés* from 1970 to 1973 and wrote a weekly column in the newspaper *Mundo diario* from 1974 to 1978. In addition, she was a contributor to the Catalan-language journals *Oriflama, El Pont, Preséncia, L'Avenç, Els Marges, El Món, Cavall Fort,* and *El Temps* and an editor of the journals *Arreu, Triunfo,* and *Vindicación Feminista.* In 1972 she began a relationship with Joaquim Sempere, who translated *Ramona, adéu, 1894–1969* and the story collection *El cant de la joventut* (1989, The Song of Youth); their son, Jordi, was born in 1975. As director of the PSUC journal *Treball,* Sempere wrote under the pseudonym of Ernest Martí, and Roig, once again aligned with the party, wrote as Capitá Nemo. On her Catalan television programs *Personatges* (1977–1978) and *Líders* (1981), Roig's perceptive interviews gave important exposure to Catalonian literary and political figures during the period of transition to democracy and Catalan political autonomy.

While participating in the student occupation of the abbey of Montserrat in 1970, Roig learned that she had received the prestigious Premi Víctor Català (Víctor Català Prize) for the manuscript for her first collection of short stories, *Molta roba i poc sabó . . . i tan neta que la volen* (1971, Lots of Laundry and Little Soap . . . and They Want It Really Clean). The lengthy titles of the stories parody nineteenth-century popular fiction, while the collection displays the range and fine-tuning of Roig's stylistic registers, with characters ranging from staid middle-class matrons to student political activists to Andalusian immigrants for whom Catalan is a second language. Three generations of women named Ramona and the embattled, womanizing PSUC leader Jordi Soteres, characters whose complexities are developed further in Roig's novels, appear for the first time in these stories of the unfulfilled desires of women of earlier generations, the marginalization of the elderly, the exploitation of Andalusian immigrants in Barcelona, and the conflicts between Stalinism and new developments on the Left. "Breu història sentimental d'una madama Bovary barcelonina nascuda a Gràcia i educada segons els nostres millors principis i tradicions" (Brief Emotional History of a Madame Bovary Born in Gràcia and Brought Up According to Our Best Values and Traditions) alternates between an ironic twentieth-century account of an elderly woman's death and burial and a series of letters that interweave her disappointing marriage with historical events, including the anarchist bombing of the Gran Teatre de Liceu in 1893 and the "Setmana Tràgica" (Tragic Week) of strikes and violent police reprisals in July 1909. Roig's admiration for the works of Rodoreda is evident in her use of the epistolary mode and female narrators who are unaware of the historical significance of the events they relate. The monologue "De com una criada de l'eixample intenta d'escarxofar-se a la nostra estimada Barcelona" (How a Servant in the Eixample Tries to Take a Break in Our Beloved Barcelona) revisits Rodoreda's parody of Andalusian pronunciation in "Zerafina" (1967). Roig takes Rodoreda's underlying theme of lost innocence and sexual exploitation one step further: the servant presents her "case history" of seduction, abandonment, and illegal abortion to her new employer; the setting of her storytelling is part of the routine sexual exploitation of Andalusian immigrant women. With both irony and compassion Roig examines the disillusionment of a student leader nostalgic for the moral clarities of 1966 in "Jordi Soteres reclama l'ajut de Maciste" (Jordi Soteres Asks for Help from Maciste); Maciste is the mythical hero of a series

of Italian "sword-and-sandal" movies of the early 1960s. This story won the prize in short fiction awarded by the literary journal *Recull* in 1970, when it was published under the title "Aquella petita volta blava" (That Little Tent of Blue), a line taken from Oscar Wilde's *The Ballad of Reading Gaol* (1898), cited in the epigraph of the story.

The central themes of *Ramona, adéu, 1894–1969,* the first novel in Roig's trilogy, are family secrets and the lack of communication among generations of women and between women and men. The novel interweaves third-person narrative with diary entries to highlight the silencing of women's inner desires and struggles. The name Ramona, shared by three generations of women, suggests that little has changed for Catalan women from one generation to the next. The mother and grandmother construct facades of devotion to their husbands, while the youngest Ramona displays a sexual bravado that belies her desire for a more committed relationship with her lover, the student political leader Jordi Soteres. The historical status of the Catalan language is a recurring theme: the first Ramona's husband is named Francisco, not the Catalan version of the name, Francesc, and he courts her with a trite poem in Spanish. She finds the Catalan verses sent to her by a young student far more romantic. A short story in *Molta roba i poc sabó . . . i tan neta que la volen* features her daughter among Catalan poets meeting clandestinely in 1953: "Ramona Ventura és convidada en un tec de germanor i admira com els lletraferits de l'any de la fam es fan la llesca mútuament" (Ramona Ventura is invited to a feast of brotherhood and admires how the literati in the year of hunger slice each other up). The characters' flowery names allude to the awards given at the literary contests called Jocs Florals, which originated with the troubadours of fourteenth-century Languedoc and were revived in the mid-nineteenth-century Catalan *Renaixença* (Renaissance). Roig parodies the mediocre poetry celebrated in this clandestine festivity, but she also recaptures the barely articulated desire for linguistic and political freedom inspired by such gatherings in the repressive conditions of the Franco dictatorship.

To the puzzlement of her daughter Ramona–nicknamed Mundeta–the highlight of the second Ramona's married life was a terrifying day during the Spanish Civil War when, despite her pregnancy, she searched for her husband, Joan Claret, amid the wreckage of a bombed cinema and came into contact with classes of people and political concepts she had not known before. She also discovered her husband's clandestine business dealings, destined to be concealed by the family's facade of bourgeois respectability. Mundeta, like Roig a student participant in the 1966 Caputxinata,

Cover for a 1993 edition of Enrique Sordo's Spanish translation
(1978) of Roig's novel El temps de les cireres (1977,
Season of Cherries), about a photographer who returns
from exile in England to Spain during the final years
of Francisco Franco's dictatorship (Thomas Cooper
Library, University of South Carolina)

struggles for sexual and political liberation, unaware of
the passions and disappointments of her foremothers.

The title of the second novel of the trilogy, *El
temps de les cireres,* awarded the 1976 Premi Sant Jordi
(Sant Jordi Prize), refers to a song by Jean-Baptiste Clément, "Les Temps des cerises," the anthem of the Paris
Commune of 1871. The characters' allusions to the
song, recorded by Yves Montand in the late 1950s,
imply that love will continue to cause sorrow, even in
the summer of plenitude and political liberation. The
narrative is framed by two events in the grim history of
Francoist reprisals against political dissidents: the execution of communist leader Julian Grimau in 1963, just
after the main character, Natàlia Miralpeix, goes into
exile, and the brutal garroting of Catalonian anarchist
Salvador Puig Ántic on the eve of her return from exile

in England in 1974. While Natàlia pays the price for
defying both sexual and political repression, the passive
adaptation of her father, Joan Miralpeix, to the political
climate has led to his loss of self. Natàlia regards her
father as a coward for abandoning his Republican sympathies and complying with the dictatorship, but she is
also aware that the clandestine efforts of communists
and anarchists are ineffectual and plagued by betrayal
and factionalism. She has returned to an uncertain political future in Spain as the aging dictator's health
declines, and she is about to discover a series of family
secrets, including her father's descent into madness.

During her years of exile in England, Natàlia has
become a professional photographer, and the camera
rather than a diary structures the narrative of *El temps de
les cireres.* In contrast to the focus in *Ramona, adéu, 1894–
1969* on mothers and daughters, *El temps de les cireres*
explores a richer fabric of relationships among aunts,
nieces, nephews, sisters-in-law, mentors, students,
employers, servants, friends, lovers, and spouses.
Natàlia's mother, Judit, was a pianist whose health
forced her to abandon the concert stage after her marriage. She became increasingly reclusive after her flam-
boyantly liberated friend Kati committed suicide in
1939, and a stroke left her completely paralyzed and
mute when Natàlia was in her teens. Sílvia Claret, the
oldest daughter of Ramona Ventura Claret, abandoned
her promising career in ballet after she married
Natàlia's brother Lluís; now, her obsessive consumerism distracts her from her husband's infidelities.
Natàlia's independent painting teacher, Harmonía
Carreras, blames women themselves for their oppression. Her formative years in the freedom of the Second
Republic gave her "prou defenses com per a suportar
les crítiques de déu I sa mare" (adequate defenses
against the criticism of God and her mother), and her
art sustains her in the "exili interior" (interior exile) of
the dictatorship.

References to the rich heritage of Catalan poetry
are interwoven throughout *El temps de les cireres,* and the
novel is divided into six parts, with titles derived from
the works of Catalan poets. The brief depictions of sexual pleasure are outweighed by the grotesque and
humiliating processes of the body's aging and disability.
In the first section, "Gorgs" (Whirlpools), Natàlia is
reunited with Harmonía, Sílvia, and her Aunt Patrícia,
the widow of the poet Esteve Miràngels. She also recalls
her mother's devotion to Pere, Natàlia's other brother,
born with Down's syndrome, a devotion that led to the
neglect of Natàlia and Lluís. The second section of the
novel, "Aroma de tardor" (Scent of Autumn), is narrated from the perspective of Patrícia, who drinks at
night and complains to her fifty-two-year-old Andalusian maid, Encarna, about her husband's infidelities.

She omits her greatest disappointment: finding her husband in bed with another male poet. In the third section of *El temps de les cireres,* "Corns de caça" (Hunting Horns), Natàlia's recollection of her sexual initiation is inseparable from her education in leftist politics and feminism. Most instructive were her lover's abandoning her while both were in prison after a demonstration and her illegal abortion, which resulted in life-threatening septicemia and a break with her family. Male passivity and impotence shape the fourth section, "Quietud" (Silence), with Joan Miralpeix's recollection of how his wife, Judit, cured him of impotence. Before the Civil War he was an idealistic architect, but he was shattered by his experience as a prisoner of war. He made his fortune with a construction firm responsible for a disastrous hotel fire. Judit's devotion to "fetitxes" (knickknacks) is emblematic of the paralysis that empties her body of its sensuality and transforms her into a mute, Sphinx-like figure. The female body is rendered grotesque in the fifth section of the novel, "Becaines d'àngels custodis" (Sleep of Guardian Angels), which depicts Encarna's raucous wedding reception and a Tupperware party given by Natàlia's sister-in-law, Sílvia. Natàlia leaves the latter just before the guests' impersonation of schoolgirls and nuns degenerates into a guilt-ridden lesbian orgy. Joan Miralpeix's dementia provides the narrative perspective for the final section, "Només somnis" (Only Dreams), in which he dresses in his dead wife's clothing. His transvestism seems a logical development of his passivity and excessive identification with his late wife. Similarly, Miràngel's sexual relationship with his fellow poet Gonçal Rodés is revealed only after Rodés's return from the trauma of war and brutal treatment as a political prisoner. Roig frames male homosexuality, transvestism, and voyeurism in terms of sexual repression and emotional trauma in *El temps de les cireres, L'hora violeta,* and the short story "Abans que no mereixi l'oblit" (Before Becoming Worthy of Oblivion), from *El cant de la joventut.*

Roig's concern for the suffering of political prisoners led to her rigorously documented historical study *Els catalans als camps nazis* (1977, Catalans in Nazi Concentration Camps), which received the Premi Crítica Serra d'Or (Serra d'Or Critics' Prize) in 1978. The interviews she conducted for this volume brought her into contact with the untold stories of Catalans who had fled to France after the Civil War and were later deported to the Mauthausen concentration camp in Austria. Although Roig referred to her interviews and her novels as separate projects, the character Norma in *L'hora violeta* has just completed a book identical to Roig's oral history, and she struggles with the profoundly disturbing impact of the survivors' unspeakable suffering. The text of *Els catalans als camps nazis* is illustrated with haunting photographs of Catalan survivors by Roig's collaborator, Aymerich.

Women's writing and the photographer's lens are brought together in the third novel of Roig's trilogy, *L'hora violeta,* in the figures of the photographer Natàlia and her friend Norma, a novelist and journalist. The three central female characters, Natàlia, Norma, and Agnès, are unconnected by family ties and belong to the same generation. All three have had relationships with the recurring figure of Soteres, and they struggle with the archetypal female roles suggested in the opening section, in which Natàlia reads the *Odyssey* on an island in the Mediterranean. After a six-year relationship, Natàlia, like Calypso in Homer's epic, is about to be abandoned as Soteres returns to Agnès, the mother of his two sons, only because he expects the Penelope-like Agnès to tolerate his new relationship with a younger woman. Natàlia regards her friend Norma as a Circe-like enchantress or the druid priestess in Vincenzo Bellini's opera *Norma* (1831). The depiction of women in these traditional roles prompted Spanish feminist Lidia Falcón to attack *L'hora violeta* as antifeminist, but the novel represents a courageous engagement with questions of sexuality, politics, and female friendship, as well as a confrontation with the radical feminist theories of the 1970s.

*L'hora violeta* is divided into four sections. In a brief introduction Norma explains that Natàlia has asked her to write a novel about the wartime friendship between Natàlia's mother, Judit, and Judit's friend Kati, who also appears in *El temps de les cireres.* The first section, "L'hora perduda: La Natàlia i l'Agnès" (The Lost Hour: Natàlia and Agnes), consists of Natàlia's long farewell letter to Soteres, interwoven with a third-person narrative of Agnès's process of healing from his abandonment. The second section consists of the novel "L'hora violeta," which Norma writes for Natàlia using Judit's diaries and Natàlia's Aunt Patrícia's memoirs. In this section Norma attempts to imagine the relationship between Kati and Judit in order better to understand her own friendship with Natàlia. The denouement of this story is already given in *El temps de les cireres:* Kati committed suicide in 1939 after her married Irish lover, Patrick, was killed in battle and she realized that the fledgling Second Republic was doomed. She tells Judit that she cannot survive in Nationalist Spain and suggests, "Per qué no ens n'anem ben lluny?" (Why don't we go far away?). Judit responds that she must stay in Barcelona with her children, awaiting the return of her husband, Joan, a prisoner of war. The crisis of masculinities in the PSUC during the transition to democracy is the focus of the third section of the novel, "L'hora dispersa (Ells i la Norma)" (The Scattered Hour [Men and Norma]). Soteres, once a hero of the clandestine

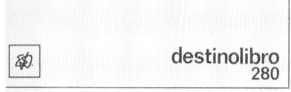

*Cover for a 1989 paperback edition of Sordo's Spanish translation (1983) of Roig's novel* L'òpera quotidiana *(1982; excerpts translated as "The Everyday Opera," 1988), in which a young cleaning woman's outlook is shaped by the fantasies and distortions of older characters (Thomas Cooper Library, University of South Carolina)*

PSUC, has been sidelined as Stalinism is eclipsed by Eurocommunism. Norma's husband, Ferrán, a writer once unjustly accused of cowardice, is unable to grieve for the death of his childhood friend, the hypermasculine Germinal, who died in a traffic accident typical of his risk-taking behavior. In the brief final section, "L'hora oberta" (The Open Hour), the long-suffering Agnès rejects the role of Penelope, having learned to thrive without Soteres.

Love and friendship between women are at the center of *L'hora violeta,* as well as of Roig's "Mar," a story published in Spanish in 1980 and revised and republished in Catalan in *El cant de la joventut.* Two of the

most significant lesbian narratives of twentieth-century Spanish literature had been published by the time Roig began working on *L'hora violeta* in 1978: Carme Riera's story "Te deix, amor, la mar com a penyora" (1975, I Leave You, Love, the Sea as a Token) and Esther Tusquets's novel *El mismo mar de todos los veranos* (1978, The Same Sea as Every Summer). In *L'hora violeta* and "Mar," Roig struggles to represent the possibility of passionate commitments between heterosexual women. At a time when Natàlia's and Norma's relationships with men are breaking up, both women affirm their heterosexuality while referring to a passage from Lessing's *The Golden Notebook* (1962) in which the protagonist, Anna Wulf, observes that women's awakening consciousness of their unsatisfying relationships with men "can turn them bitter, or Lesbian, or solitary." Their friendship, strong enough for Norma to write a novel in response to Natàlia's request, has been tempered by years of conflict, admiration, envy, and disagreement, and it makes them skeptical of lesbian-feminist claims about relationships free from domination and objectification.

Although the narrator of "Mar" is unnamed, the story expands on Natàlia's brief, disapproving narrative of Norma's "adolescent" infatuation with Mar in *L'hora violeta.* In "Mar," Norma struggles to write about her relationship with the title character two years after her violent death, possibly by suicide. Norma's and Mar's reiterated denial of the label "lesbian" is undermined by the affirmation, denial, and rewording of the erotic and emotional bonds between the women. There is, however, more to the story than a transparent process of disavowal. In "Mar" and *L'hora violeta,* Roig highlights the problem of legal inequality that is missing from feminist arguments based on gender difference. Norma is attracted to Mar's lack of possessiveness, but when Mar opts out of a custody battle with her vindictive husband, Ernest, insisting that children do not belong to anyone, she sacrifices them to her husband's irrational jealousy and possessiveness.

In 1980, the year in which she broke with the PSUC for the second and last time, Roig was invited to the Soviet Union for two months to carry out research for a book about the 1941–1944 Siege of Leningrad. She published an account of the heroism of the people of Leningrad, *Mi viaje al bloqueo: 900 días de la lucha heróica de Leningrado* (1982, My Journey to the Blockade: 900 Days of the Heroic Fight of Leningrad), in Spanish. Three years later Roig presented a substantially different view in the Catalan text *L'agulla daurada* (1985, The Golden Needle), awarded the Premi Nacional de Literatura Catalana (National Prize of Catalan Literature) in 1986. The social and political problems of the Soviet Union, as well as Roig's love for the people of Leningrad (now St. Petersburg), are evident in this lively, personal travel narrative.

*L'òpera quotidiana* (1982) is a novel conceived in terms of opera, with an "overture," "duets, cavatinas, and recitativos," and a final "chorus." The four central characters tell stories, and the youngest, Mari Cruz, is shaped by the older characters' fantasies and distortions of history. She cleans for Natàlia's Aunt Patrícia and reads Emily Brontë's *Wuthering Heights* (1847) to Senyora Altafulla, a retired secretary who lives in a fantasy world based on an imaginary relationship with a Civil War–era army officer, Colonel Saura. Patrícia rents a room to a retired butcher, Horaci Duc, and she listens each morning to his stories about his wife, Maria, an Andalusian immigrant whom he educated in Catalan language, history, and culture. To Horaci's dismay, Maria has become more committed to Catalan nationalism than he is, and he accuses her of adultery with a heroic member of the Catalan resistance, Pagés. An unreliable narrator, Horaci revises his story to suggest that he was responsible for Pagés's arrest and death from torture in prison and that he pushed Pagés's wife and daughter under an oncoming train. Mari Cruz's illegitimate birth, symbolized by her lack of a surname, and her childhood experience of sexual molestation while in an orphanage compel her to search for a father figure; she makes the unwise choice of Horaci, and, like most opera heroines, she ends badly.

The mythic atmosphere and the male protagonist of Roig's last novel, *La veu melodiosa* (1987, The Melodious Voice), represented a new direction in her fiction. The title is taken from a poem by the medieval Catalan poet Ausias March–"car, si l'hom és a mals aparellat, / la veu de la mort li és melodiosa" (for the man who is prepared for misfortune, / the voice of death is melodious)–and Roig's epigraphs from the Book of Job point to suffering of biblical intensity. The protagonist is a young man with the humiliating nickname Espardenya (canvas sandal) whose grandfather protects him from painful historical and social realities by educating him in isolation and concealing from him his incestuous origins and his physical ugliness. Like Buddha, Espardenya inevitably discovers the suffering and injustice of the outside world and seeks to alleviate it. At the university he is drawn to a political group that includes Soteres and Mundeta from Roig's trilogy. Having no real sympathy for the poor, Espardenya's comrades treat him as a buffoon and later as a scapegoat, after he proves unable to withstand torture in prison and betrays them. The police, however, regard Espardenya as far more dangerous than his comrades because he is motivated by compassion and humility rather than a political platform; by teaching homeless women to read, he is raising their social consciousness. The epilogue,

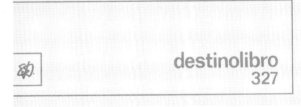

Cover for a 1991 paperback edition of the Spanish translation by José Agustín Goytisolo (1987) of Roig's novel La veu melodiosa (1987, The Melodious Voice), about a naive young idealist who tries to alleviate suffering and injustice (Thomas Cooper Library, University of South Carolina)

ostensibly written twenty years later by Espardenya's university friend Virginia, reveals that he has become a poet, while Virginia has become disillusioned with politics.

Despite the title of Roig's second collection of short stories, *El cant de la joventut,* several of the stories focus on death. In the title story a song barely remembered from her youth by a dying woman brings up memories of a sexual encounter with demonic overtones reminiscent of Rodoreda's stories "Una carta" (1967, A Letter) and "La salamandre" (1967, The Salamander). The longest stories in the collection are the revised "Mar" and "Abans que no mereixi l'oblit," a narrative of voyeurism reminiscent of Vladimir Nabokov.

During a visiting professorship at the University of Arizona in 1990, Montserrat Roig wrote several prose pieces, collected in *Digues que m'estimes encara que sigui mentida: Sobre el plaer solitari d'escriure i el vici compartit de llegir* (1991, Tell Me You Love Me Even If It's a Lie: On the Solitary Pleasure of Writing and the Shared Vice of Reading), in which she explores her vocation as a writer, her love of words, and the topics of photography, movies, and historical memory. Two collections with culinary titles bring together her newspaper columns: *Melindros* (1990, Ladyfingers), her Spanish-language columns for the daily *Periódico de Catalunya*, written from 1984 to 1988; and the posthumously published *Un pensament de sal, un pessic de pebre: Dietari obert, 1990–1991* (1992, A Bit of Salt, a Pinch of Pepper: Open Diary, 1990–1991), her daily columns written for *Avui* from September 1990 to 9 November 1991, the day before her death from cancer.

## References:

Pilar Aymerich and Marta Pessarrodona, *Montserrat Roig: Un retrat* (Barcelona: Institute Català de la Dona/Generalitat de Catalunya, 1994);

Catherine G. Bellver, "Montserrat Roig and the Creation of a Gynocentric Reality," in *Women Writers of Contemporary Spain: Exiles in the Homeland,* edited by Joan L. Brown (Newark: University of Delaware Press, 1991), pp. 217–239;

Emilie L. Bergmann, "When Norma Met Mar: Thelma and Louise on the Costa Brava," in *Women's Narrative and Film in Twentieth-Century Spain: A World of Difference(s),* edited by Ofelia Ferrán and Kathleen M. Glenn (New York: Routledge, 2002), pp. 168–183;

Ana María Brenes-García, "El cuerpo matrio catalán como ideologema en *Ramona, adéu* de Montserrat Roig," *Anales de la literatura española contemporánea,* 21, nos. 1–2 (1996): 13–26;

Brenes-García, "La representación de la comunidad xarnega en *La ópera cotidiana* de Montserrat Roig: La textualización de una colonia interna," *Textos: Works and Criticism,* 4, no. 2 (1996): 27–32;

Anne Charlon, *La condició de la dona en la narrativa femenina catalana (1900–1983),* translated by Pilar Canal (Barcelona: Edicions 62, 1990);

Catherine Davies, *Contemporary Feminist Fiction in Spain: The Work of Montserrat Roig and Rosa Montero* (Oxford & Providence, R.I.: Berg, 1994);

Cristina Dupláa, *La voz testimonial en Montserrat Roig: Estudio cultural de los textos* (Barcelona: Icaria, 1996);

Kathleen M. Glenn, "First Person Singular: Montserrat Roig and the Essay," *Catalan Review,* 9, no. 1 (1995): 81–90;

Stewart King, "Role-Playing and the (De)construction of Catalan Identities in Montserrat Roig's *L'òpera quotidiana,*" *Catalan Review,* 12, no. 2 (1998): 37–48;

Jaume Martí-Olivella, ed., "Woman, History, and Nation in the Works of Montserrat Roig and Maria Aurèlia Capmany," *Catalan Review,* 7, no. 2 (1993): 117–198;

Geraldine C. Nichols, "Montserrat Roig," in her *Escribir, espacio propio: Laforet, Matute, Moix, Tusquets, Riera y Roig por sí mismas* (Minneapolis: Institute for the Study of Ideologies and Literature, 1989), pp. 147–185;

Elizabeth S. Rogers, "Montserrat Roig's *Ramona, adiós:* A Novel of Suppression and Disclosure," *Revista de Estudios Hispánicos,* 20, no. 1 (1986): 103–122;

Akiko Tsuchiya, "Montserrat Roig's *La ópera cotidiana* as Historiographic Metafiction," *Anales de literatura española contemporánea,* 15 (1990): 145–159;

Helen Wing, "Deviance and Legitimation: Archetypal Traps in Roig's *La hora violeta,*" *Bulletin of Hispanic Studies,* 72, no. 1 (1995): 87–96.

# Rafael Sánchez Ferlosio

*(4 December 1927 –    )*

Jeremy S. Squires
*University College Dublin*

BOOKS: *Industrias y andanzas de Alfanhuí* (Madrid: Gráficas Cíes, 1951; enlarged edition, Barcelona: Destino, 1961); translated by Ruth M. Danald as *Alfanhui* (West Lafayette, Ind.: Purdue University Press, 1975);

*El Jarama* (Barcelona: Destino, 1956); translated by J. M. Cohen as *The One Day of the Week* (London & New York: Abelard-Schuman, 1962); translated by Margaret Jull Costa as *The River* (Sawtry, U.K.: Dedalus, 2004);

*Efemérides hidrológica y fervorosa,* by Sánchez Ferlosio and Rafael Couchoud Sebastiá (Madrid: S. Aguirre, 1965);

*Las semanas del jardín,* 2 volumes (Madrid: Nostromo, 1974)–comprises volume 1, *Liber scriptus proferetur,* and volume 2, *Splendet dum frangitur;* republished in 1 volume (Madrid: Alianza, 1981);

*El huésped de las nieves* (Madrid: Alfaguara, 1982);

*El escudo de Jotán* (Madrid: Alfaguara, 1983);

*El testimonio de Yarfoz* (Madrid: Alianza, 1986);

*Homilía del ratón* (Madrid: El País, 1986);

*Mientras no cambien los dioses, nada ha cambiado* (Madrid: Alianza, 1986);

*Campo de Marte: 1. El ejército nacional* (Madrid: Alianza, 1986);

*Ensayos y artículos,* 2 volumes (Barcelona: Destino, 1992);

*Vendrán más años y nos harán más ciegos* (Barcelona: Destino, 1993);

*Esas Yndias equivocadas y malditas: Comentarios a la historia* (Barcelona: Destino, 1994);

*El alma y la vergüenza* (Barcelona: Destino, 2000);

*La hija de la guerra y la madre de la patria* (Barcelona: Destino, 2002);

*Non olet* (Barcelona: Destino, 2003);

*El geco: Cuentos y fragmentos* (Barcelona: Destino, 2005);

*Glosas castellanas y otros ensayos: (Diversiones)* (Alcalá de Henares: Universidad de Alcalá / Madrid: Fondo de Cultura Económica, 2005).

**Editions in English:** *Adventures of the Ingenious Alfanhuí,* translated by Pat Sabatini (Madrid: Iberia, 1986);

*Rafael Sánchez Ferlosio (Stringer/AFP/Getty Images/#51815321)*

*The Adventures of the Ingenious Alfanhuí,* translated by Margaret Jull Costa (Sawtry, U.K.: Dedalus, 2000).

TRANSLATIONS: Lucien Malson and Jean Itard, *Los niños selváticos, Memoria e informe sobre Victor de l'Aveyron* (Madrid: Alianza, 1973);

Itard, *Memoria e informe sobre Victor de l'Aveyron* (Madrid: Alianza, 1982).

OTHER: "Dientes, pólvora, febrero," in *Antología de cuentistas españoles contemporáneos (1939–1958),* edited by Frederico García Pavón (Madrid: Gredos, 1959), pp. 361–368;

Carlo Collodi, *Las aventuras de Pinocho,* prologue by Sánchez Ferlosio (Madrid: Alianza, 1972), pp. 7–16.

SELECTED PERIODICAL PUBLICATIONS–UNCOLLECTED: "El juego," *La hora,* 6 (1948): 15;

"Niño fuerte," *Revista Española,* 1 (May–June 1953): 39–48;

"Hermanos," *Revista Española,* 4 (November–December 1953): 400–405;

"De cinco a seis," *Ateneo,* 72 (December 1954): 18–19.

The novels of Rafael Sánchez Ferlosio confirm the dictum that important works either create new genres or dissolve existing ones. Sánchez Ferlosio's tactic of probing the edges of the novel form is at once disconcerting and releasing. His digressive manner, unorthodox use of time, unwillingness to subordinate character and dialogue to the exigencies of plot, and delight in the material and the mundane for their own sakes, all challenge the reader's expectations. His untraditional novels offer an antidote to what Walter Benjamin once identified as the atrophy of experiential truth at the heart of Western living: Sánchez Ferlosio is above all a writer who seeks to repair human sensibility–to allow readers to feel and reflect upon what is uniquely their own.

Although Sánchez Ferlosio has chosen to publish only a portion of his writings, their quality and originality have earned him a privileged place in the world of Spanish letters. Winner of the Nadal Prize in 1955, the author's second novel, *El Jarama* (1956, The River Jarama; translated as *The One Day of the Week,* 1962), drew international critical praise and propelled the still relatively young author into a limelight from which he thenceforth appeared ready to withdraw. An autodidact, he wrote and researched constantly but published only sporadically until the appearance in 1973 of his annotated translations of works on feral children, learning, and cognition, followed in 1974 by *Las semanas del jardín* (The Garden Weeks), a study of narrativity. In 1986 a long-awaited third novel, *El testimonio de Yarfoz* (The Testimony of Yarfoz), emerged alongside two substantial essays and a collection of journalism. The fact that the author had agreed grudgingly to his publisher's request for fiction on the grounds that a novel would help the other books to sell was clear indication of the direction in which his interests had evolved since he first made his mark in the 1950s. The relative lack of commercial and critical success for the third novel has dissuaded him from publishing a fourth. He has, however, not been discouraged from publishing nonfiction.

Since Spain's transition to democracy following the death of Francisco Franco in 1975, Sánchez Ferlosio has written regularly for *El País* on a range of political and cultural topics. Typically, these articles are demanding, often stinging, sometimes hilarious, yet always springing from deep humanitarian impulses. His stance on many matters is comparable to that of Theodor W. Adorno or Noam Chomsky.

One of five children, Sánchez Ferlosio was born on 4 December 1927 to Rafael Sánchez Mazas and Liliana Ferlosio Vitali in Rome, where his father, an important Falangist writer and ideologue, worked as cultural attaché to the Spanish embassy. Sánchez Ferlosio is half Italian and spent long periods of his childhood in his country of birth. After receiving his secondary education at the Jesuit school of Villafranca de los Barros, he pursued various courses of study, none of them to completion, at the universities of Salamanca and Madrid, followed by a brief spell in the newly formed Escuela Oficial de Cinematografía (Official School of Cinematography) before he became immersed in the literary scene of the capital. In Madrid, as both an editor and contributor, he collaborated on the short-lived literary magazine *Revista Española* (1953–1954, Spanish Review), and he established important friendships with other young writers such as Ignacio Aldecoa, Jesús Fernández Santos, Alfonso Sastre, and Carmen Martín-Gaite, whom he married in 1953.

The publication of the writer's first novel, *Industrias y andanzas de Alfanhuí* (1951, Skills and Rambles of Alfanhuí; translated as *Alfanhuí,* 1975), was financed by his mother. The work is remarkable for its poetry, wit, and invention. The fact that this novel is not particularly well known may be attributed to its surface resemblance to children's literature and to its having been eclipsed by *El Jarama.* Many readers, nonetheless, consider *Industrias y andanzas de Alfanhuí* the author's most satisfying work. Sánchez Ferlosio, who in later years grew notoriously scornful of *El Jarama,* has remained moderately well disposed toward its predecessor.

Alfanhuí is an apprentice of the mind. His demeanor of intelligent curiosity pervades the entire novel, and in pursuing his inquiries, he and his world are transformed. In part 1, Alfanhuí and his mentor, the Master, stringently adhere to the scientific method in their probings of natural phenomena, but with extraordinary results. The peculiarity of these initial episodes lies more in the oddness of Alfanhuí's world than in the method he uses to explore it. His experiments with a chestnut tree, in which liquid light is used to produce a variegated canopy of leaves, and with a new species of asymmetrical vegetable bird created by crossing eggs with seeds, are thus as plausible in their results as they are alien to everyday understandings of reality. Sánchez

Ferlosio provokes a great deal of humor in this way, deploying the authoritative discourse of the natural sciences to evoke a powerful sense of verisimilitude while invariably presenting nonsensical or amoral results, such as when the remains of a cat are recycled into clock parts, a handy pelt groomer, and a small drum. Similarly, he toys with the reader's subliminal memory of traditional plotlines. This distortion can disorient and delight in equal measure.

In part 2, which follows the death of the Master, Alfanhuí, in an echo of the picaresque genre, journeys to Madrid, and the text begins to brim with social types and vignettes of local customs. An inner journey continues as well, a key milestone of which is the confrontation with the brilliant but cynical puppet don Zana, who in some ways is a caricature of Alfanhuí himself. The omega to the hero's alpha, Zana is an egotist and a charlatan, someone who curtails growth and experience, so Alfanhuí's rejection of him represents a fresh avowal of the Master's quiet, imaginatively receptive attitude to life. It can be seen as an attempt, if only partially successful, to retrieve a sense of primal sympathy with the world.

While part 1 depicts a fantasy world ruled by strict principles of observation and deduction, and part 2 ventures into a domain governed by moral quandaries and the inwardness associated with the onset of maturity, part 3 introduces the reader into a world that is much more conventionally real—where fantasy is confined to the realms of story and imagination. Using the familiar metaphor of life as a journey, the author conveys, through the exploits of his hero, a universal motion of the human mind as it moves from seeing the world first and foremost as a physical enigma to becoming gradually attuned to a form of reality that is more socially, morally, and narratively based. A central paradox of this novel is that the first part, where hard-headed materialism prevails, is also the most fantastic, whereas the later parts, where reality acquires a more metaphoric dimension, are more realistic. Hence, with the appearance of a rainbow in the final chapter, the hero, remembering the Master, achieves an epiphany via the poetic medium of color. In the initial chapters, by contrast, color and light are akin to chemical substances, whereas now they incite emotion. The reader is left to ponder whether Alfanhuí's symbolic sensitivity to the hue of light, culminating in the vision of the rainbow, can be explained in purely psychological terms (he has achieved emotional maturity and is rendered capable of love), or whether it hints at something more spiritual.

*Industrias y andanzas de Alfanhuí* has been regarded as a rejection by Sánchez Ferlosio of paternal influences; as a parable of the life of Man in which a child hero journeys through a land of Jungian archetypes; as a parody of pre-Enlightenment science; and as an intuitive exploration of the processes involved in child cognition and learning. There are important similarities between *Industrias y andanzas de Alfanhuí* and the opinions expressed by Sánchez Ferlosio in the commentaries in his translation of Jean Itard's study of the feral child known as Victor de L'Aveyron. There, he asserts that goal-oriented activity is antipedagogical; that human nature is plastic, yet basically irreversible once formed; and that people's perceptions run along linguistic lines.

In Sánchez Ferlosio's second novel, *El Jarama,* set in the early 1950s, eleven working-class youths escape from the city heat to spend their Sunday relaxing, chatting, and bathing on the banks of the river Jarama, just outside Madrid. Meanwhile, a set of older characters who experienced the Civil War as adults forms a second conversational nucleus centered on Mauricio's bar. The author uses the generation gap between these groups to convey a sense of historical rupture within Spanish society as a whole. In this sense the youngsters are implicitly recoiling not only from the dreary weekday world but from the internecine trauma of their country's recent history, as well. It seems that nothing worthy of a novel in the traditional sense is going to occur until, late in the day and toward the end of the text, one of the youngsters, Lucita, goes for a swim and is drowned. For critics, the effect, or underlying intent, of this event has constituted a principal point of discussion about the novel. For instance, is the death in any way heralded?

There are significant differences between *Industrias y andanzas de Alfanhuí* and *El Jarama*. Whereas the former narrates the evolution of a psyche, a development that is itself inscribed in a changing reality, the latter presents a world that is neutral, passive, and alien to the vision that human beings might have of it. In *El Jarama,* narrative slows to the pace of dialogue; the eye is superseded by the ear; and personal history is replaced by the collective moment.

For all its pursuit of typical life, however, *El Jarama* is not a complete negation of the first novel, nor is it a depiction of Spanish youth made dull and defeatist by the imposition of Francoist culture. Released from the daily rounds of bosses, money, and family politics, the eleven young adults spend their time in easy conversation, provoking, conciliating, pondering each other's motives, discussing their relationships, and reacting with intelligence, wit, and feeling to the ephemera of their immediate surroundings. The river is a place where people can unwind. It is that rare place in Francoist society where seminakedness is publicly acceptable. On the banks of the Jarama, parts of society that normally are kept apart may come together. People

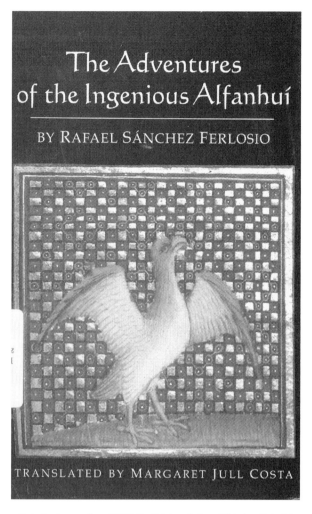

*Paperback cover for a 2000 English translation of Sánchez Ferlosio's first novel,* Industrias y andanzas de Alfanhuí *(1951, Skills and Wanderings of Alfanhuí), a picaresque work about an early scientist (Richland County Public Library)*

from town and country, the old and the young, male and female, all mix freely (at the factory where one of the characters works, by contrast, the sexes are segregated). Furthermore, the characters appear to be freed from their more customary state of anxiety about time. The novel is an ellipsis in which, for one day of the week at least, real conversational exchange can flourish.

As Randolph D. Pope has observed, a text in which free dialogue is permitted to burgeon forth is in itself a notable affront to a regime bent on imposing a stultifying discourse of officialese that obliged citizens to live permanently within themselves. Only toward the close of the day, as they become aware of the impending weekly routine, do the young friends try to exploit their few remaining hours of freedom with a sense of urgency. More meditative than rational, the river of dialogue, which makes up some nine-tenths of the text,

is not simply idle prattle, for it gravitates continually toward matters of intimacy. The group dynamic is one of tolerant self-regulation. Everyone instinctively holds the indolent Miguel in high regard, and not even Daniel, in his state of self-imposed exile, is deemed an outcast.

At the same time, however, something is missing; a potential is left untapped. Alfanhuí and his world are marvelously integrated, and time is always on his side. In *El Jarama,* workaday tasks do not inspire the youths, and the deeper waters of politics, history, and culture remain uncharted or taboo even during their moments of private relaxation.

The resurgence of realism in the post–Civil War Spanish novel has been accounted for in diverse ways. The critic José María Castellet, a decisive influence on the school as a whole if not on Sánchez Ferlosio himself, viewed this trend as the outcome of modern developments in philosophy, movies, and physics, in essence as the inevitable evolution in aesthetics toward purely representational models of narrative. *El Jarama* fulfills an important testimonial role as a rich source of sociological and historical information. It is also possible that the phenomenon of Spanish objectivism was a response to local cultural conditions, in particular to the regime's heavy censorship of news and print media. Thus, the author of *El Jarama* turns censorship against itself by excising overt criticism of Francoism yet naming his novel not only for the river but also after a famously bloody and indecisive Civil War battle fought in the vicinity (to prevent the encirclement of Madrid by Nationalist forces), in such a way that it inevitably raises large and potentially subversive questions in the reader's mind about the intent of the novel.

*El Jarama* is the work that both made Sánchez Ferlosio's reputation as a novelist and constituted the high-water mark of the objectivist movement among Spanish writers of the 1950s and early 1960s. Drawing especially on his Italian background–he is a fluent speaker of Italian and has translated works into and out of the language–Sánchez Ferlosio's first two novels are in spirit with the genial verismo of Italian neorealist writers and moviemakers such as Cesare Zavattini and Vittorio De Sica, whose fascination with formal innovation he shares. The peculiar plotlessness of the novel, with its strict adherence to the spatial and temporal frame of the eyewitness–a technique that greatly enhances the tragedy of Lucita's accidental death–is crucial to the impact of the work. As Edward C. Riley remarks, *El Jarama* "is about time, life and death–in particular the utter incredibility of sudden death." Patrick Gallagher plausibly suggests in a 1990 article that Sánchez Ferlosio was present when a real drowning took place on the Jarama in the summer of 1952.

In the context of the drowning, the title of the novel assumes special resonance, suggesting an association between the present victim and those who fell during the Civil War battle at the river. Accordingly, the novel tacitly confronts the anesthetizing myth at the heart of Francoist propaganda. In harping on a triumphalist reading of history, the regime had evacuated the past of lived experience and authentic memory. *El Jarama* is such a powerful evocation of loss that it reverses this process and prompts the reader to question official historiography.

During his protracted silence after *El Jarama,* Sánchez Ferlosio became a quasi-mythical figure. He was said to be devoting himself almost monomaniacally to linguistics, and soon he developed a reputation for reclusiveness and eccentricity. By his own admission, his wife was a lifeline: "she is like a widow," he once remarked, "with the deceased living at home." In reality, financial security, the pleasures of fatherhood (his daughter, Marta Sánchez-Martín, was born in 1956), and his wide-ranging reading habits were merely conspiring to produce a long period of literary gestation. Although his friend Sastre believed that the great critical success of *El Jarama* destroyed Sánchez Ferlosio's development as a writer, Sánchez Ferlosio's renunciation of fiction was neither immediate nor absolute. Several unpublished novels from those years remain among his private papers—away from the public eye, the writing of narrative continued.

An indication of the direction in which Sánchez Ferlosio's interests were leading him was provided with the publication in 1966 of his essay "Personas y animales en una fiesta de bautizo" (People and Animals at a Christening) in *Revista de Occidente.* Here he vehemently denounced what he identified as a generalized and anonymous instinct in society that makes adults wish to blunt the cognitive autonomy of the child through the manipulation of language. The author's fascination with pedagogy, language, and the child's vision of the world culminated in 1973 in his annotated translation of Lucien Malson's *Les enfants sauvages* (1964, Savage Children). In the early 1970s Sánchez Ferlosio separated from his wife after eighteen years of marriage, but he continued to live in Madrid.

A two-volume analysis of the vices and virtues of narrativity, reading, and spectatorship, *Las semanas del jardín,* appeared in 1974, a work the author himself described as a delirium tremens and which, owing to its apparent incoherence and incompletion, added little to Sánchez Ferlosio's reputation. The death of his twenty-nine-year-old daughter in obscure circumstances in the mid 1980s dealt the writer his severest blow. Both the breakup of his marriage and the loss of his daughter were followed by periods of increased publication. In

1986 he published not only a new novel but also two long essays: *Mientras no cambien los dioses, nada ha cambiado* (While the Gods Remain Unchanged, Nothing Has Changed), which attacks modern mythologies of history and progress as the purveyors of cruelty and suffering; and *Campo de Marte: 1. El ejército nacional* (Field of Mars: 1. The National Army), in which he suggests that obligatory military service is one way of deterring the army from intervening in politics, both at home and abroad.

The bulk of Sánchez Ferlosio's imaginative third novel, *El testimonio de Yarfoz,* was written in 1970 and 1971; it is a fragment of a much larger, unpublished work comprising the fictional chronicles of the Barcialean wars, waged in an elaborate imaginary world of the author's creation. Critics have identified the interpenetration of fiction and history as a central theme. The narrator, Yarfoz, a hydrologist in the service of his beloved Prince Nébride, relates the story of his employer's self-imposed exile following the murder by Prince Obnelobio and Prince Caserres (Nébride's father and uncle) of Espel, the benevolent ruler of the Atánidas people. Abandoning his country the very day he receives news of the assassination, Nébride begins a journey of exile that lasts approximately seven years. For two and a half years he and his entourage enjoy the hospitality first of Prince Rodoresio of the Atánidas people, then of the king of the Iscobascos, before once more venturing forth beyond the towering cliff face of the Meseged into the lower reaches of the Barcial River. Entirely unrecognized, Nébride spends the remainder of his days among the emigrant peoples of the Camino-del-Mar. There, his life begins anew at the Great Necropolis of Gromba Feceria, where he takes a job as an obituarist responsible for expressing in words the sentiments of those who have lost friends and relatives. At this point Nébride's tale—that of an unhurried journey without a final destination, or as David K. Herzberger expressed it in a 1987 article, "a run-on of digressions"—comes to an end. Yarfoz, who has accompanied Nébride into exile, has fulfilled his stated aim of bearing witness and closing a gap in the historical record. Now he must reconstruct what follows from alternative sources. His narrative is therefore no longer a *testimonio;* the fragile thread of lived experience has been broken.

In this second part of the novel the focus shifts to Nébride's son, Sorfos. Because the end of the joint reign of Caserres and Obnelobio (owing to the former's sudden death) leaves the Grágidos people without an heir, a search party is dispatched to locate Nébride and thereby fill a dangerous power vacuum. Sorfos, however, deftly substitutes his own candidacy, using surprise tactics both to further his own claim and to

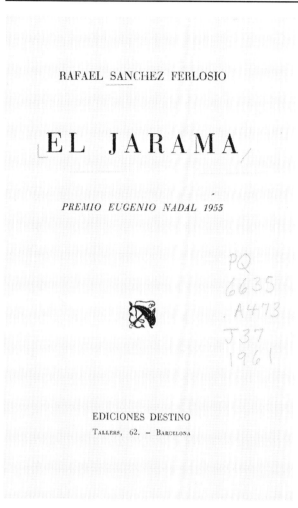

RAFAEL SANCHEZ FERLOSIO

EL JARAMA

PREMIO EUGENIO NADAL 1955

EDICIONES DESTINO
TALLERS, 62. — BARCELONA

*Title page for an edition of Sánchez Ferlosio's 1956 novel (The River
Jarama; translated as* The One Day of the Week, *1962),
in which a group of young people converse freely on a riverbank
on the one day each week when they are able to escape
Francoist repression (Thomas Cooper Library,
University of South Carolina)*

guarantee his father's continued anonymity. Indeed, having lost his centrality, Nébride plays no further part in the novel, except as a thematic foil to what ensues. There is little doubt that the course on which his son is embarked will displease him, for it is leading inexorably to war and the pursuit of power. Even before Caserres's death, relations between father and son are strained because Sorfos, gifted with natural dexterity, is drawn to a life of military prowess. The novel ends ominously on a discordant simile that compares the arm of the five-year-old Glea, Sorfos's son and heir, to that of a warrior. The reader has prior knowledge that the adult Glea will be guilty of at least one murder—namely, that of the hermit Trasfaz, who first brought word to Nébride of Espel's death and thereby set in train Nébride's peripatetic journey. Hence, the novel depicts

contrasting personal itineraries: the one centrifugal, life-affirming, and conciliatory, the other centripetal, self-affirming, and confrontational.

The figure on whom the testimony hinges is an unobtrusive and diminishing presence in the novel, one who fades into the background. Temperate, honorable, and magnanimous, Nébride is an essentially creative figure, with special enthusiasm for public works and architecture of the type that harmoniously weds human resourcefulness to the inherent qualities of the natural world. His attitude to his surroundings, as toward others, is essentially interactive. At the Necropolis, he commences a career as a writer-counselor, displaying tact and delicacy of feeling toward his clients. Like his namesake, Nebridius, St. Augustine's cherished friend, who abhorred short responses to large matters, Nébride's mind is of a deeply philosophical cast, fond of embarking upon speculative digressions that parallel the roving momentum of his exile. His decision to leave his homeland for a crime for which he bears no personal responsibility signals a positive orientation toward the world, not a proud rejection of it. Accordingly, the narrative form of the novel is one of shifting centers and multiplying horizons, at least until the story of Sorfos takes over. Throughout, however, the river is a unifying presence—a Heraclitean symbol of stasis in the midst of change.

Critics have identified in *El testimonio de Yarfoz* many of the qualities that Sánchez Ferlosio extolled in *Las semanas del jardín.* He removes traditional plot intrigue from this novel, just as he did with the two that precede it. *El testimonio de Yarfoz* is richly inlaid with parables and cautionary tales belonging firmly to the traditions of the storyteller. Yet, by divesting the main narrative of dramatic interest, Sánchez Ferlosio diverts the readers' curiosity toward the nature of the invented world he holds before them. In his nonfiction writings, Sánchez Ferlosio has often sought to decry a trait he sees as characteristic of the age: namely, "el fetichismo de la identidad" (the fetish of identity). That is, whereas many have stressed that contemporary individuals play host to a plural and fluid sense of personhood, Sánchez Ferlosio contends that the commodified world in contrast encourages the creation of identities that are assertive and narcissistic. Nébride's quality of receptivity affords a fictional solution to both predicaments.

Through a wealth of sociological and anthropological detail *El testimonio de Yarfoz* implies that virtue is as much institutional as it is individual. Similarly, in his nonfiction Sánchez Ferlosio has, for example, decried neoliberal efforts to privatize all areas of the public arena. While Nébride's son is neither demonic nor self-seeking, his actions emanate from a typicality of character at the public level. The novel espouses a civic model of ethics, though one in which the institutional and the individual have equal stature, so that society remains civilized and pliable to the human will. Sorfos is seduced by institutional patterns of thought, but he is no more beyond the redemptive power of reason than are the institutions themselves. Sánchez Ferlosio has often maintained that human life at its fullest entails the acknowledgment of free will. The characters in *El testimonio de Yarfoz* exhibit a form of pre-Christian, or Hellenic, belief in the freedom and autonomy of the mind. Their faith in the dignity of the spoken word betokens a world that is freshly made and always renewable. As Santos Sanz Villanueva observes in a 1988 article, the novel affords "una especie de visión de una naturaleza humana ideal" (a sort of idealized vision of human nature).

Sánchez Ferlosio has continued to publish widely on an assortment of national, international, and philosophical themes. He criticized the quincentenary celebration of Columbus's discovery of America, the 1992 Olympics in Barcelona, and the Gulf War. He has also written at length on religion, terrorism, and money. A respected literary and intellectual figure, he received honorary doctorates in 1992 and 2002 from the University of Rome and the Universidad Autónoma in Madrid, respectively. In 2004 he received the prestigious Premio Cervantes (Cervantes Prize). He has also remarried; his second wife is Demetria Chamorro.

Rafael Sánchez Ferlosio's novels are ill served by descriptions of them in terms of their content. Foremost among their themes is the enrichment and impoverishment of human experience. His journalism aside, Sánchez Ferlosio's nonfiction is highly cerebral, yet often lacks the sort of system building one normally associates with sustained intellectual endeavor. He prefers to argue either synecdochically in chains of numbered paragraphs, or to accumulate aphorisms, which he terms *pecios* (flotsam or wreckage). Although his prose is rich, his syntax sophisticated, and his range of references broad, Sánchez Ferlosio has a tendency to shun definitive conclusions. He is aware of this apparent shortcoming, being, he suggested in an interview with Arcadi Espada, like someone who knows how to knit but is unable to make a jersey. The remark is characteristic of one of the most whimsical and retiring of contemporary Spanish writers.

## Interviews:

Miguel Pérez Ferrero, "Rafael Sánchez Ferlosio, Premio Nadal 1955, interpretado por su padre, Rafael Sánchez Mazas," *ABC,* 8 January 1956, p. 52;

Mauro Muriz, "*El Jarama*: una novela hecha con cálculo infinitesimal," *Estafeta Literaria,* 41 (1956): 4;

Pedro Mario Herrero, "Rafael Sánchez Ferlosio: Un escritor con musa de Renacimiento," *La Hora,* 41 (1957): 6–17;

Juan Luis de Suárez Granda, "De un encuentro con Rafael Sánchez Ferlosio," *Cuadernos del Diálogo,* 21 (1983): 40–45;

Juanjo Fernández, "Un galeón en el Jarama," *Quimera,* 63 (1986): 24–26;

Blanca Berasátegui, "Sánchez Ferlosio: así en su piso como su alma," *ABC Literario,* 29 November 1986, p. 8;

Igor Reyes-Ortiz, "La creatividad de la ira: cuatro nuevos libros de Rafael Sánchez Ferlosio," *El País,* 4 December 1986, pp. 3–4;

Miguel Angel Trenas, "Sánchez Ferlosio: Treinta años después de *El Jarama*," *La Vanguardia,* 7 December 1986, p. 11;

J. M. Plaza, "Ferlosio: 'Nunca debí escribir *El Jarama*,'" *Diario 16,* 10 December 1986, p. 46;

Miguel Angel del Arco, "Rafael Sánchez Ferlosio, un novelista irritado," *Tiempo,* 327 (1988): 94–96;

Alfonso Armado, "Soy un hombre sin experiencia," *El País,* 1 June 1992, pp. 3–4;

Arcadi Espada, "Rafael Sánchez Ferlosio: 'El pueblo americano pedía venganza y la ha tenido,'" *El País Babelia,* 4 May 2002.

## References:

Nancy Allen, "Alfanhuí y su cartilla intacta," *Revista Hispanoamericana,* 30 (1964): 126–135;

Salvador Bacarisse, "Rafael Sánchez Ferlosio: Literature *sub specie ludi*," *Forum for Modern Language Studies,* 7 (1971): 52–59;

Karen E. Breiner-Sanders, "*Industrias y andanzas de Alfanhuí*: Incorporación mítica del rito de iniciación," *Actas del VIII Congreso Internacional de Hispanistas,* 1 (1986): 263–274;

Luis Cañizal de la Fuente, "Recostarse y arregostarse a la última novela de Ferlosio," *Ínsula,* 496 (1986): 13;

Pedro Carrero Eras, "Mendoza y Ferlosio: dos hitos en el 86," *Cuenta y Razón,* 26 (1987): 122–129;

José María Castellet, "Notas para una iniciación a la lectura de *El Jarama*," *Papeles de Son Armadans,* 1 (1956): 205–217;

Anthony H. Clarke and Shirley Clarke, introduction to *Industrias y andanzas de Alfanhuí* (London: Harrap, 1969), pp. 9–28;

Miguel Delibes, "Rafael Sánchez Ferlosio," in his *España 1936–1950: Muerte y resurrección de la novela* (Barcelona: Destino, 2004), pp. 73–80;

Roberto Echavarren, "*Las semanas del jardín* de Sánchez Ferlosio: Narratividad y sujeto," *Cuadernos Hispanoamericanos,* 128 (1982): 660–677;

Luis Miguel Fernández Fernández, *El neorrealismo en la narración española de los años cincuenta* (Santiago: Santiago de Compostela, 1992);

Medardo Fraile, "El Henares, el Jarama, y un bautizo: La obra unitaria de Rafael Sánchez Ferlosio," *Revista de Occidente*, 40–41 (1973): 125–147;

Patrick Gallagher, "Moonrise to Moonset: A Reading of *El Jarama*," in *Essays on Hispanic Themes in Honour of Edward C. Riley*, edited by Jennifer Lowe and Philip Swanson (Edinburgh: University of Edinburgh, 1989), pp. 228–250;

Gallagher, "Sánchez Ferlosio y el Jarama: Los hechos," *Diario 16*, 17 March 1990, p. 2;

Francisco García Sarrià, "*El Jarama:* Muerte y merienda de Lucita," *Bulletin of Hispanic Studies*, 53 (1976): 323–337;

Alicia de Gregorio, "Mujer y palabra en *El Jarama:* Una nueva perspectiva del lenguaje en la novela de Sánchez Ferlosio," *Cincinnati Romance Review*, 14 (1995): 103–108;

Ricardo Gullón, "Recapitulación de *El Jarama*," *Hispanic Review*, 43 (1975): 1–23;

Gullón, "Relectura de *Alfanhuí*," in *Philologica Hispaniense in honorem Manuel Alvar*, volume 4 (Madrid: Gredos, 1987), pp. 225–237;

Rafael Gutiérrez Girardot, "El arte de la excepción," *Quimera*, 65 (1986): 61–65;

Luis Alberto Hernando Cuadrado, *El español coloquial en "El Jarama"* (Madrid: Playor, 1988);

David K. Herzberger, "*El testimonio de Yarfoz*, by Rafael Sánchez Ferlosio," *Anales de la Literatura Española Contemporánea*, 12 (1987): 433–435;

Gonzalo Hidalgo Bayal, *Camino de Jotán (la razón narrativa de Ferlosio)* (Badajoz: Ediciones del oeste, 1994);

Margaret E. W. Jones, *The Contemporary Spanish Novel, 1939–1975* (Boston: Twayne, 1985);

Barry Jordan, *Writing and Politics in Franco's Spain* (London & New York: Routledge, 1990);

Danilo Manera, introduction to *Industrias y andanzas de Alfanhuí* (Barcelona: Destino, 1996);

Gregorio Martín, "Juventud y vejez en *El Jarama*," *Papeles de Son Armadans*, 229 (1975): 9–33;

Inés d'Ors, "Nombre, rostro e identidad: Rafael Sánchez Ferlosio, teoría y práctica narrativa,"

*Anales de Literatura Española Contemporánea*, 23 (1998): 623–639;

d'Ors, *El testimonio de Yarfoz, de Rafael Sánchez Ferlosio, o los fragmentos del todo* (Kassel: Reichenberger, 1995);

Jesús Pérez-Magallón, "*Alfanhuí:* Marginalidad y reescritura de la picaresca," *Bulletin of Hispanic Studies*, 73 (1996): 165–177;

Randolph D. Pope, "Narrative in Culture, 1936–1975," in *The Cambridge Companion to Modern Spanish Culture*, edited by David T. Gies (Cambridge: Cambridge University Press, 1999), pp. 134–146;

Harold Reynolds, "Archetypal Perception in Rafael Sánchez Ferlosio's *Alfanhuí*," *Bulletin of Hispanic Studies*, 53 (1976): 215–224;

Edward C. Riley, "Sobre el arte de Sánchez Ferlosio: Aspectos de *El Jarama*," *Filología*, 9 (1963): 201–221;

Antonio Risco, "Una relectura de *El Jarama* de Sánchez Ferlosio," *Cuadernos Hispanoamericanos*, 288 (1974): 700–711;

María A. Salgado, "Fantasía y realidad en *Alfanhuí*," *Papeles de Son Armadans*, 116 (1965): 140–152;

Santos Sanz Villanueva, "Ferlosio y Alfanhuí: el placer de narrar," *Camp de l'Arpa*, 100 (1982): 33–37;

Sanz Villanueva, "El regreso de Sánchez Ferlosio," *Cuadernos Hispanoamericanos*, 453 (1988): 119–125;

José Schraibman and William T. Little, "La estructura simbólica de *El Jarama*," *Philological Quarterly*, 51 (1972): 329–342;

Gonzalo Sobejano, "Retrovisión de *El Jarama:* El día habitado," in *Entre la cruz y la espada: En torno a la España de posguerra. Homenaje a Eugenio de Nora*, edited by J. M. López de Abiada (Madrid: Gredos, 1984), pp. 327–344;

Jeremy S. Squires, *Experience and Objectivity in the Writings of Rafael Sánchez Ferlosio* (Lewiston, Pa.: Edwin Mellen Press, 1998);

José Luis Suárez Granda, *Guía de lectura de "Industrias y andanzas de Alfanhuí"* (Madrid: Akal, 1986);

Mónica Rector Toledo Silva, "El adjetivo de *color* en Rafael Sánchez Ferlosio," *Boletín de Filología Española*, 40–41 (1971): 3–8;

Darío Villanueva, *"El Jarama" de Sánchez Ferlosio: Su estructura y significado* (Santiago: Universidad de Santiago de Compostela, 1973).

# Ramón J. Sender

*(3 February 1901 – 16 January 1982)*

Stephen Hart
*University College London*

and

Francis Lough
*University of Birmingham*

BOOKS: *El problema religioso en Méjico: Católicos y cristianos* (Madrid: Cenit, 1928);

*América antes de Colón* (Valencia: Cuadernos de Cultura, 1930);

*Imán* (Madrid: Cenit, 1930; translated by James Cleugh as *Earmarked for Hell* (London: Wishart, 1934); translation republished as *Pro Patria* (Boston: Houghton Mifflin, 1935);

*O.P. (Orden público)* (Madrid: Cenit, 1930);

*El verbo se hizo sexo: Teresa de Jesús* (Madrid: Zeus, 1931);

*Teatro de masas* (Valencia: Orto, 1931);

*Siete domingos rojos* (Barcelona: Balagué, 1932); translated by Sir Peter Chalmers-Mitchell as *Seven Red Sundays* (New York: Liveright, 1936; London: Faber & Faber, 1936); Spanish version revised (Buenos Aires: Proyección, 1970; revised again, 1973);

*Casas Viejas* (Madrid: Cenit, 1933); revised and enlarged as *Viaje a la aldea del crimen: Documental de Casas Viejas* (Madrid: Juan Pueyo, 1934);

*La noche de las cien cabezas: Novela del tiempo en delirio* (Madrid: Pueyo, 1934);

*Madrid-Moscú: Notas de viaje, 1933–1934* (Madrid: Pueyo, 1934);

*Carta de Moscú sobre el amor: A una muchacha española* (Madrid: Pueyo, 1934);

*Proclamación de la sonrisa: Ensayos* (Madrid: Pueyo, 1934);

*El secreto: Drama en un acto* (Madrid: Tensor, 1935); translated as *The Secret, International Literature,* 4 (1936): 51–59;

*Míster Witt en el Cantón* (Madrid: Espasa-Calpe, 1936); translated by Chalmers-Mitchell as *Mr. Witt among the Rebels* (London: Faber & Faber, 1937; Boston: Houghton Mifflin, 1938);

*Crónica del pueblo en armas (Historias para niños)* (Madrid & Valencia: Ediciones Españolas, 1936);

*Ramón J. Sender ( from Charles L. King,* Ramón J. Sender, *1974; Thomas Cooper Library, University of South Carolina)*

*Counter-Attack in Spain,* translated by Chalmers-Mitchell (Boston: Houghton Mifflin, 1937); republished as *The War in Spain: A Personal Narrative* (London: Faber & Faber, 1937); Spanish version published as *Contraataque* (Madrid: Nuestro Pueblo, 1938);

*El lugar del hombre* (Mexico City: Quetzal, 1939); translated by Oliver La Farge as *A Man's Place* (New York: Duell, Sloan & Pearce, 1940; London: Cape, 1941); Spanish version revised as *El lugar de un hombre* (Mexico City: CNT, 1958);

*Proverbio de la muerte* (Mexico City: Quetzal, 1939); revised as *La esfera* (Buenos Aires: Siglo Veinte, 1947; translated by Felix Giovanelli as *The Sphere* (New York: Helman, Williams, 1949; Manchester, U.K.: Grey Walls, 1950);

*Hernán Cortés: Retablo en dos partes y once cuadros* (Mexico City: Quetzal, 1940);

*Mexicayotl: Viñetas de Darío Carmona* (Mexico City: Quetzal, 1940);

*Crónica del alba* (Mexico City: Nuevo Mundo, 1942); translated by Willard R. Trask as *Chronicle of Dawn* (Garden City, N.Y.: Doubleday, Doran, 1944; London: Cape, 1945);

*Epitalamio del Prieto Trinidad* (Mexico City: Quetzal, 1942); translated by Eleanor Clark as *Dark Wedding* (Garden City, N.Y.: Doubleday, Doran, 1943; Manchester, U.K.: Grey Walls, 1948);

*El rey y la reina* (Buenos Aires: Jackson, 1948); translated by Mary Low as *The King and the Queen* (New York: Vanguard, 1948; London: Grey Walls, 1949);

*El verdugo afable* (Santiago, Chile: Nascimiento, 1952); translated by Florence Hall as *The Affable Hangman* (London: Cape, 1954; New York: Las Américas, 1963);

*Mosén Millán* (Mexico City: Aquirre, 1953); republished in a bilingual edition as *Réquiem por un campesino español / Requiem for a Spanish Peasant,* translated by Elinor Randall (New York: Las Américas, 1960);

*Hipogrifo violeto* (Mexico City, 1954); translated by F. Hall Sender as "Violent Griffin," in *Before Noon: A Novel in Three Parts* (Albuquerque: University of New Mexico Press, 1957; London: Gollancz, 1959), pp. 153–284;

*Unamuno, Valle-Inclán y la dificultad de la tragedia* (Mexico City: De Andrea, 1955); revised as *Valle Inclán y la dificultad de la tragedia* (Madrid: Gredos, 1965);

*Bizancio* (Mexico City: Diana, 1956);

*La Quinta Julieta* (Mexico City: Costa-Amic, 1957); translated by F. Hall Sender as "The Villa Julieta," in *Before Noon: A Novel in Three Parts,* pp. 285–405;

*Los cinco libros de Ariadna* (New York: Ibérica, 1957);

*El diantre: Tragicomedia para el cine según un cuento de Andreiev* (Mexico City: De Andrea, 1958);

*Emen Hetan (Aquí estamos)* (Mexico City: Libro Mex, 1958);

*Los laureles de Anselmo: Novelas dialogada* (Mexico City: Atenea, 1958);

*Las imágenes migratorias: Poesía* (Mexico City: Atenea, 1960);

*La llave* (Montevideo: Alfa, 1960);

*El mancebo y los héroes* (Mexico City: Atenea, 1960);

*Examen de ingenios: los noventayochos: Ensayos críticos* (New York: Las Américas, 1961; revised and corrected edition, Mexico City: Aguilar, 1971);

*Novelas ejemplares de Cíbola* (New York: Las Américas, 1961); translated by Hall and others as *Tales of Cíbola* (New York: Las Américas, 1964);

*La luna de los perros* (New York: Las Américas, 1962);

*La tesis de Nancy* (Mexico City: Atenea, 1962);

*Carolus Rex* (Mexico City: Mexicanos Unidos, 1963);

*Los tontos de la Concepción: Crónica misionera* (Sandoval, N.M.: Coronado, 1963);

*La aventura equinoccial de Lope de Aguirre* (New York: Las Américas, 1964);

*Jubileo en el Zócalo* (New York: Appleton-Century-Crofts, 1964);

*El bandido adolescente* (Barcelona: Destino, 1965);

*Cabrerizas Altas* (Mexico City: Mexicanos Unidos, 1965);

*El sosia y los delegados* (Mexico City: Costa-Amic, 1965);

*Ensayos sobre el infringimiento cristiano* (Mexico City: Mexicanos Unidos, 1967);

*Las gallinas de Cervantes y otras narraciones parabólicas* (Mexico City: Mexicanos Unidos, 1967);

*La llave y otras narraciones* (Madrid: EMESA, 1967);

*Tres novelas teresianas* (Barcelona: Destino, 1967);

*Las criaturas saturnianas* (Barcelona: Destino, 1968);

*El extraño señor Photynos y otras novelas americanas* (Barcelona: Delos-Aymá, 1968);

*Don Juan en la mancebía: Drama litúrgico en cuatro actos* (Mexico City: Mexicanos Unidos, 1968);

*Comedia del Diantre y otras dos* (Barcelona: Destino, 1969);

*Tres ejemplos de amor y una teoría* (Madrid: Alianza, 1969);

*En la vida de Ignacio Morel* (Barcelona: Planeta, 1969);

*Nocturno de los 14* (New York: Iberama, 1969);

*Novelas del otro jueves* (Mexico City: Aguilar, 1969);

*Ensayos del otro mundo* (Barcelona: Destino, 1970);

*Relatos fronterizos* (Mexico City: Mexicanos Unidos, 1970);

*Tánit* (Barcelona: Planeta, 1970);

*Zu: El ángel anfibio* (Barcelona: Planeta, 1970);

*La antesala* (Barcelona: Destino, 1971);

*El fugitivo* (Barcelona: Planeta, 1972);

*Donde crece la marihuana: Drama en cuatro actos* (Madrid: Escelicer, 1973);

*Túpac Amaru* (Barcelona: Destino, 1973);

*Una virgen llama a tu puerta* (Barcelona: Destino, 1973);

*Cronus y la señora con rabo* (Madrid: Akal, 1974);

*Libro armilar de poesía y memorias bisiestas* (Mexico City: Aguilar, 1974);

*La mesa de las tres moiras* (Barcelona: Planeta, 1974);

*Las Tres Sorores* (Barcelona: Destino, 1974);

*El futuro comenzó ayer: Lecturas mosaicas* (Madrid: CVS, 1975);

*Ramón J. Sender: Obra pictórica* (Madrid: Galería Multitud, 1975);

*Arlene y la gaya ciencia* (Barcelona: Destino, 1976);

*La efemérides* (Madrid: Sedmay, 1976);

*El pez de oro* (Barcelona: Destino, 1976);

*El alarido de Yaurí* (Barcelona: Destino, 1977);

*El mechudo y la llorona* (Barcelona: Destino, 1977);

*Adela y yo* (Barcelona: Destino, 1978);

*Solanar y lucernario aragonés* (Saragossa: Heraldo de Aragón, 1978);

*El superviviente* (Barcelona: Destino, 1978);

*La mirada inmóvil* (Barcelona: Argos Vergara, 1979);

*Por qué se suicidan las ballenas: Bajo el signo de Sagitario* (Barcelona: Destino, 1979);

*Una hoguera en la noche: Bajo el signo de Aries* (Barcelona: Destino, 1980);

*Luz zodiacal en el parque: Bajo el signo de Acuario* (Barcelona: Destino, 1980);

*Monte Odina* (Saragossa: Guara, 1980);

*La muñeca en la vitrina: Bajo el signo de Virgo* (Barcelona: Destino, 1980);

*Ramú y los animales propicios* (Barcelona: Argos Vergara, 1980);

*La saga de los suburbios: Bajo el signo de Escorpión* (Barcelona: Destino, 1980);

*Ver o no ver: Reflexiones sobre la pintura española* (Madrid: Heliodoro, 1980);

*La cisterna de Chichén-Itzá* (Barcelona: Acervo, 1981);

*Memorias bisiestas: Bajo el signo de Sagitario* (Barcelona: Destino, 1981);

*Orestiada y los pingüinos: Bajo el signo de Piscis* (Barcelona: Destino, 1981);

*El Oso Malayo: Bajo el signo de Leo* (Barcelona: Destino, 1981);

*Segundo solanar y lucernario* (Saragossa: Heraldo de Aragón, 1981);

*Chandrío en la plaza de la cortes: Fantasía evidentísima* (Barcelona: Destino, 1981);

*Album de radiografías secretas* (Barcelona: Destino, 1982);

*El jinete y la yegua nocturna: Bajo el signo de Capricornio* (Barcelona: Destino, 1982);

*La kermesse de los alguaciles: Bajo el signo de Géminis* (Barcelona: Destino, 1982);

*Epílogo de Nancy: Bajo el signo de Tauro* (Barcelona: Destino, 1982);

*Los cinco libros de Nancy* (Barcelona: Destino, 1984);

*Hughes y el once Negro* (Barcelona: Destino, 1984);

*Toque de queda* (Barcelona: Plaza & Janés, 1985);

*Literatura y periodismo en los años veinte: Antología,* edited by José Domingo Dueñas Lorente (Saragossa: Edizions de l'Astral, 1992);

*Primeros escritos (1916–1929),* edited by Jesús Vived Mairal (Huesca: Instituto de Estudios Altoaragoneses, 1993);

*Rimas compulsivas: Antología poética,* edited by Francisco Carrasquer Launed (Ferrol: Sociedad de Cultura Valle-Inclán, 1998).

**Editions and Collections:** *Páginas escogidas,* edited by Marcelino C. Peñuelas (Madrid: Gredos, 1972);

*Obra completa,* 3 volumes (Barcelona: Destino, 1976–1981);

*Míster Witt en el Cantón,* edited by José María Jover (Madrid: Castalia, 1987);

*Réquiem por un campesino español,* edited by Patricia McDermott (Manchester, U.K.: Manchester University Press/New York: St. Martin's Press, 1991);

*Imán,* edited by Francisco Carrasquer Launed (Huesca: Instituto de Estudios Altoaragoneses, 1992);

*El lugar de un hombre,* edited by Donatella Pini (Huesca: Instituto de Estudios Altoaragoneses / Barcelona: Destino, 1998);

*Siete domingos rojos,* edited by José Miguel Oltra Tomás (Saragossa: Prensas Universitarias de Zaragoza, 2004).

**Edition in English:** *Requiem for a Spanish Peasant,* translated by Bernard Molloy (Madrid: Ibéria, 1986).

Ramón J. Sender is regarded as one of the most important Spanish novelists of the twentieth century. He was certainly one of the most prolific, publishing some seventy novels and thirty more volumes of drama, poetry, and essays, as well as countless articles in newspapers spanning more than sixty years. The sheer scale and range of Sender's output makes him an extremely difficult writer to know completely. There are significant constants in his work, however, in spite of the changes wrought by time and experience.

The third of nineteen children, of whom ten survived infancy, Ramón José Sender was born on 3 February 1901 in Chalamera de Cinca, a village in northern Spain, to José Sender Chavanel and Andrea Garcés Laspalas. He grew up in Alcolea de Cinca, a neighboring village, and in Tauste, Reus, and Saragossa. Always headstrong and seeking independence from his father, Sender ran away to Madrid at the age of seventeen, only to be brought back to Huesca. By then he had had time to savor the political and cultural atmosphere of the capital, which became his permanent home a few years later.

Although Sender enrolled at the University of Madrid, he never completed any studies, preferring to dedicate himself to a career as a journalist, essayist, and novelist. His passion for writing began at an early age—he wrote several books before the age of twenty, although none of them were published until many years

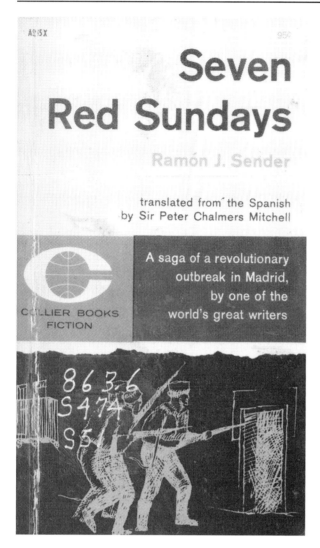

Seven
Red Sundays

Ramón J. Sender

translated from the Spanish
by Sir Peter Chalmers Mitchell

COLLIER BOOKS
FICTION

A saga of a revolutionary
outbreak in Madrid,
by one of the
world's great writers

*Cover for a 1961 edition of the English translation (1936) of Sender's
novel* Siete domingos rojos *(1932), about an anarchist uprising
(Thomas Cooper Library, University of South Carolina)*

politics, Spanish and other European writers—he regularly reviewed fiction and nonfiction—and the geography and customs of his native Aragón.

In the intense political climate that dominated Spain between the end of World War I and the outbreak of the Spanish Civil War, Sender's political stance was heavily influenced by anarchist and Marxist thinkers. In 1926, during the dictatorship of Miguel Primo de Rivera, Sender was imprisoned while investigating a story for *El Sol;* on other occasions he had to go into hiding from the police. Sender was an admirer of Pyotr Kropotkin and Rosa Luxemburg; his fundamental beliefs were always closer to those of the anarchists, although after the Civil War political urgency gave way to a more mystical approach to life that had always been a part of his thinking. In the 1930s, exasperated by the anarchists' failure to organize their activities effectively, Sender was regarded as a fellow traveler of the communists, until he began to criticize their role in Spain and in the Civil War in particular. By the end of the war, Sender had turned completely against communism; his novel *Los cinco libros de Ariadna* (1957, The Five Books of Ariadne) combines historical and autobiographical elements and is a satire directed at both Francisco Franco and Stalinist Russia. After the Civil War, Sender never lost his interest in political issues, although he ceased to be actively engaged in action of a political nature. While his views became much less radical with time, he always retained his admiration for the independent spirit that characterized his anarchist friends.

Sender's first published novel, *Imán* (1930, Magnet; translated as *Earmarked for Hell,* 1934), was a huge success in many countries. Translations appeared in German, Portuguese, French, Russian, Yiddish, and English. For this novel Sender drew heavily on his experience in Morocco during the war; the ideology of the novel was sharply critical of the war itself and Spanish colonial politics. His next novel, *O.P. (Orden público)* (1930, Public Order), focuses on political prisoners in a Madrid jail and was based on Sender's own experiences in prison in 1926. As a result of these two novels Sender began to establish his name as a writer with a social conscience. In 1931 he published *El verbo se hizo sexo: Teresa de Jesús* (The Word Became Sex: Teresa of Jesus), a provocatively titled fictional biography of St. Teresa of Ávila that he later transformed into *Tres novelas teresianas* (1967, Three Novels about Teresa).

In his 1932 novel, *Siete domingos rojos* (1932; translated as *Seven Red Sundays,* 1936), Sender continued to show his interest in social reform. The novel follows the activities of revolutionaries in an anarchist uprising, portraying not only their political ideologies but also the moral principles that underlay them. In general,

later, with revisions that inevitably corresponded to new ways of thinking. Sender's early experience was as a freelance journalist, when he published articles, poems, and short stories, sometimes using pseudonyms. In the early 1920s he became editor of the Huesca newspaper *La Tierra* (The Earth). After serving with the Spanish army in Morocco in 1923, he returned to Spain to work on the staff of the prestigious daily newspaper *El Sol* (The Sun), which was published in Madrid. In the 1930s he wrote for the anarchist newspaper *Solidaridad Obrera* (Workers Solidarity) and the Republican daily *La Libertad* (Liberty). Sender's articles in *El Sol* and *La Libertad* particularly give a good sense of the issues that informed his novels. In addition to writing commentaries on the political events of the day, his articles dealt with Spanish history, Latin American

while expressing Sender's admiration for the anarchists, the novel is critical of their failings as revolutionaries. *Siete domingos rojos* was translated into eight languages. The year after its publication the highly regarded Spanish novelist Pío Baroja declared: "Tenemos entre los jóvenes un poeta: García Lorca. Y un novelista: Sender" (Among our young [writers] we have one poet: [Federico] García Lorca. And one novelist: Sender).

From the early days, Sender's work concerned itself with his own life experiences, Spanish history, and, in particular, the notion of social justice. As both novelist and journalist he strove to expose the injustice that he saw at the heart of Spanish society. This commitment often led him to distance himself from the capitalist system, which, following a standard revolutionary reasoning quite common at the time (the 1930s were radical times throughout Europe), he saw as divisive and exploitative. His political concerns are revealed clearly in much of his journalism. In 1933 he went to Casas Viejas in Andalusia to report on the brutal repression by the security forces of a small anarchist uprising, which ended in eight people being burned to death in a small house. His series of articles for *La Libertad* were first collected in book form as *Casas Viejas* (1933). A year later, with more information, some of it taken from the report of a parliamentary commission set up to investigate the affair, an updated version of the original book was provocatively titled *Viaje a la aldea del crimen: Documental de Casas Viejas* (1934, Journey to the Village of the Crime: Documentary of Casas Viejas).

The first major recognition of Sender's talents came with the novel *Míster Witt en el Cantón* (1936; translated as *Mr Witt among the Rebels*, 1937), which was awarded the Premio Nacional de Literatura (National Prize for Literature). The book was based on an uprising that took place in Cartagena in 1873 during the First Spanish Republic. This novel was Sender's first historical work, and it gives some idea of the approach he took in later historical novels written after the Civil War. Sender was interested in the Cartagena uprising because he saw in the circumstances of the insurrection and the failure of the rebel movement a parallel of Spanish society and the political situation during the Second Republic in the 1930s. *Míster Witt en el Cantón* was written shortly before the outbreak of the Spanish Civil War, when a right-wing coalition was gearing itself up for war. Key players in this coalition were military officers, landowners disillusioned with the government's agrarian-reform program, high-ranking church officials who were alarmed by the rise of secularism and republicanism, and sections of the urban upper and upper-middle classes. Sender's rather gloomy diagnosis of the way in which sections of society become locked

into a conflict proved to be near the truth when the war did actually break out. Witt is a conservative Englishman living in Cartagena, whose Spanish wife supports the rebel cause. The contrast in positions held by the husband and wife provide the framework for a detached view of the passions and aspirations of the separatist rebels.

The Spanish Civil War brought Sender's work into sharp focus. The war broke out in mid July 1936 and was the result of a military revolt against the Republican government, supported by conservative elements within the country. The Nationalists, as the rebels were called, received aid from Fascist Italy and Nazi Germany. The Republicans—on whose side all extreme left-wing parties fought—received support from the Soviet Union, as well as the International Brigades, an army of volunteers who came from other European countries and the United States to counter what they saw as a threat to European stability caused by the rise of fascist ideologies. The governments of important European countries such as France and Britain, however, favored a policy of nonintervention, which worked in the favor of the Nationalists. The war was the outcome of a polarization of Spanish life and politics that had been building up over previous decades. On one side were most of the Roman Catholic Church in Spain, important elements of the military, most landowners, and many businessmen. On the other side were urban workers, most agricultural laborers, and many of the educated middle class—a coalition of Republicans and all left-wing factions in a fight against fascism in their own country. Discontent among the conservative elements of Spanish society had begun to grow from 1931 onward when the Second Republic was declared and King Alfonso XIII was forced into exile. This polarization came to a head when Franco, along with other prominent right-wing generals, rebelled against the government, seizing strategic cities in the south and north of the country. The Civil War, which the rebels believed would be over within a few months, dragged on for three years and was a bitter struggle in which about one million people died. It ended in the spring of 1939 when Barcelona, the last Republican stronghold, fell, and the Republican government was forced to flee over the border into France.

Within weeks of the outbreak of war Sender signed up for the Spanish Republican army—an inevitable choice, given his strong left-wing sympathies—and served as an officer. His wife, Amparo Barayón, was killed by the Nationalist forces. (The date of their marriage in a civil ceremony is uncertain. They had a son, Ramón, born on 29 October 1934, and a daughter, Andrea, born on 3 February 1936.) The experience was something Sender never forgot and was tied to feelings

*Cover for a 1947 edition of Sender's 1942 autobiographical novel (translated as* Chronicle of Dawn, *1944), a fictionalized depiction of his childhood in Aragón (Thomas Cooper Library, University of South Carolina)*

of guilt that lived with the author for the rest of his life, a theme that pervades much of his work after the Civil War. *Los cinco libros de Ariadna* treats this idea. Sender later explained, somewhat cryptically, the reference to Ariadne in the title, saying that Barayón had laid the thread that led him out of the labyrinth. Sender's brother Manuel, who had been mayor of Huesca, was also shot by the Nationalists.

In the middle of the conflict Sender wrote an account of his war experiences, *Contraataque,* which was published in the United States as *Counter-Attack in Spain* in 1937 before being published in Spanish in Madrid the following year. The book was intended to win support for the Republicans, and it was successful in doing so. It recounts Sender's everyday life in the trenches and gives a compelling view of what life was like during the war. At the same time it offers a critique of the role of the communists and anarchists in the conflict.

With the victory of the Nationalist forces, Sender, like hundreds of thousands of Spaniards, was forced to go into exile to avoid imprisonment and most likely execution; being a prominent intellectual of the Left, he was immediately identified as one of the most wanted members of the Republican community. Sender also believed for a long time that he was being pursued by his former communist colleagues. He fled first to France and then to Mexico—where he visited the exiled Leon Trotsky shortly before he was assassinated in 1940—before eventually settling in the United States in 1942. Sender became a U.S. citizen in 1946. While in the United States he held various university teaching positions. He taught Spanish literature at Amherst College in Massachusetts in 1943–1944. From 1947 until 1963 he was employed by the University of New Mexico, and he taught at the University of Southern California from 1965 until 1973. Sender often talked of going back to settle in Spain, a possibility that seemed to be open to him toward the end of Franco's regime, but he refused to do so while many of his works were still banned there—his works did not begin to be published in Spain again until 1965. In May 1974, eighteen months before Franco's death, he made the first of three brief visits to his homeland. None of these journeys proved to be entirely satisfactory. Sender was welcomed and celebrated by many who had begun to read his work again, or in many cases, for the first time; he had been awarded the prestigious Premio Planeta (Planeta Prize, from the publisher of that name) in 1969 for his novel *En la vida de Ignacio Morel* (1969, In the Life of Ignacio Morel). For many others, however, the man did not match the myth of the great revolutionary who had fought against Franco and continued to live in voluntary exile. Sender had changed, Spain had changed, but some still held onto old loyalties and looked upon the author with disappointment. The gap was particularly noticeable when, at a lecture in Barcelona, Sender avoided all political subjects, choosing to speak on the topic of Atlantis. In spite of everything, Sender was indeed happy that his works were once again being read in Spain and, although he never went back to live in his native country, he regained his Spanish nationality in 1980 so that he could die a Spaniard.

The Spanish Civil War and the long experience of exile had a deep and lasting effect on many writers, including Sender. Some of his greatest works, such as *Réquiem por un campesino español* (originally published as *Mosén Millán,* 1953; translated as *Requiem for a Spanish Peasant,* 1960), were inspired by the Spanish Civil War on several levels: the politics of the conflict, the cultural and moral values that underlay the politics, and a nostalgia for the Spain, more precisely his native Aragón, that he was forced to leave behind.

Between the end of the war and his arrival in the United States, Sender led an unsettled life. Nevertheless, he continued to write and publish his works with regularity. His first four novels published after the Civil War, *El lugar del hombre* (1939; translated as *A Man's Place,* 1940), *Proverbio de la muerte* (1939, Proverb of Death), *Crónica del Alba* (1942; translated as *Chronicle of Dawn,* 1944), and *Epitalamio del Prieto Trinidad* (1942; translated as *Dark Wedding,* 1943), provide insight into the many areas that interested him and the direction his fiction took from that point on.

*El lugar del hombre* combines Sender's attachment to Aragón, his sense of justice, and his philosophical and epistemological concerns relating to man's place in the world. The title was later changed definitively to *El lugar de un hombre* (1958), with a connotative shift from "man's place" to "a man's place." The novel is based on a miscarriage of justice that Sender had investigated as a reporter for *El Sol* in 1926. Two men had spent twelve years in prison convicted of the murder of a young peasant man. The error came to light when it was eventually discovered that the supposed victim, who had simply left home unannounced to go and live in another part of the country and who knew nothing of the consequences of his action, was alive and well. Sender's tale paints a picture of corrupt rural politics and police brutality combined with a nostalgic evocation of the rural Spain he knew as a child. In the novel, the young peasant, Sabino, is portrayed as a simpleton who, tired of the taunts of the villagers, decides to take off and live in the hills. He is mistaken for a wild beast and eventually captured. Far from being an animal, however, Sabino knowingly fled social contact to prevent himself from committing acts of violence against his tormentors. During his years in the wilderness, his skin becomes scaly, hard, and mineral-like—an indication of his becoming one with his environment—but Sabino maintains intact his moral values and his love for his wife. The monster the villagers think they have captured is far less monstrous than the society in which they live and from which Sabino had chosen to exile himself. The title alludes to the idea that every man has his place in society. Even though Sabino may have seemed an insignificant character, his decision to remove himself from the village has dreadful consequences.

*Proverbio de la muerte* is one of the many texts that Sender rewrote at a later stage in his life, in this case as *La esfera* (1947; translated as *The Sphere,* 1949). One of the author's most complex works, *Proverbio de la muerte* explores the psychological effects of exile on the protagonist Saila as he flees Spain at the end of the Civil War with thoughts of committing suicide. The disintegration of his personality is clearly associated with the collapse of the Republican movement, the end of the war, and the loss of his native land: "si España llegaba a desnaturalizarse por completo, si 'la perdía' ¿a dónde iría aquel amor en el que se sentía arder lentamente? . . . Todo era imposible lejos de España. . . . Todo era, fuera de España, infecundo y estéril" (if the nature of Spain is changed completely, if he "lost her," where could he direct that love within which he could feel himself slowly burning? . . . Everything was impossible far from Spain. . . . Outside Spain, everything was barren and sterile). Saila does not kill himself in the end, but he emerges from his deliberations as he reaches South America alienated from his companions and from the occurrences of everyday life. He rejects the idea of continuing the fight against fascism and compensates for the loss of his beloved native land by retreating into a detached world in which he feels a metaphysical union with nature and that parallels the physical union portrayed through Sabino in *El lugar de un hombre:* he has "sueños de carbonato de calcio o de manganeso y sobre todo de lava, de roca volcánica" (dreams of calcium carbonate and of magnesium and above all of lava, and volcanic rock). This metaphysical strand was evident in Sender's first novel, *Imán,* and underlies all of his work. The magnet of the title of that work represents love as the unifying force in all of nature, as Sender explained in an interview with Marcelino C. Peñuelas: "el amor, por decirlo así, inorgánico, el amor de los minerales; el amor por lo cual la aguja magnética apunta hacia el norte. Esa voluntad de lo inorgánico a la que se refiere Schopenhauer" (inorganic love, one might say, the love of minerals; the love that makes the needle of the compass point to the north. That will of inorganic matter to which Schopenhauer refers). This idea of a natural, intuitive, love defines the character of many of Sender's protagonists, simple men who are instinctively good such as Viance in *Imán,* Sabino in *El lugar de un hombre,* and Paco in *Réquiem por un campesino español.* They have something in common with the idea of the noble savage. In Sender's terminology such characters are dominated by their "hombría" (manliness), where man is understood as relating to the species and not to the male gender. *Hombría* is a human expression of this inorganic love, as opposed to the "persona" (from the Greek for *mask*), which represents the manifestation of a self-centered approach to life. In the early days, revolution was presented as the victory of *hombría* over man's persona, the latter manifesting itself in bourgeois individualism and self-interest. In later years, when the hope of revolution had faded, *hombría* became associated with a utopian ideal to which man could aspire even though he know he could never create a perfect world.

ramón
j. sender:
la esfera

destinolibro
240

Cover for a 1985 edition of Sender's 1947 novel (translated as
The Sphere, 1949), about a Republican supporter who flees
to South America after the Nationalist victory in the
Spanish Civil War (Thomas Cooper Library,
University of South Carolina)

In *Epitalamio del Prieto Trinidad* the representatives of this love are Niña Lucha and Darío, who escape together from a world of violence, which can be read as an allegory of the Spanish Civil War and World War II. Unlike most of Sender's previous novels, the positive ending suggests the possibility of a better future. In this case the two lovers return to the world of "monsters" from which they have fled. They are motivated by a belief that although life may be full of such evil, one has to confront rather than avoid it: "parece que no hay más remedio que recibir la sangre de los otros, o hacer caer sobre ellos la nuestra. Y si no queremos ni lo uno ni lo otro debemos renunciar a vivir la vida entre los hombres" (it seems as though we have no choice but to receive the blood of others, or to let ours fall on them.

And if we do not want either of these options we must give up the idea of living among men). This novel clearly defines the view of life that dominates Sender's fiction after the Civil War. Niña Lucha is a symbol of love, but her name combines the idea of childhood and innocence (*niña,* or young girl) with the idea of struggle *(lucha)*. Life is a struggle, an idea first entertained in *Imán,* and no revolution will change that circumstance. Darío's relationship with Niña Lucha indicates that he inhabits the same metaphysical space as Saila and so feels marginalized to some degree. At the same time, however, he feels as if he is at the center of life and needs to confront the reality of human conflict rather than flee from it. Consequently, he decides to take action, even though he knows it is dangerous and may not lead to radical change.

This seemingly paradoxical understanding of life, of the individual feeling marginalized and central at the same time, parallels the key element of Arthur Schopenhauer's metaphysics. It is a view already present in *Imán,* in which the protagonist, Viance, feels that he is both an insignificant part of a grander nature (an awareness of his *hombría*) and, through his own self-conscious, the center of the universe (an awareness of himself as persona). In one of his later novels, *Las Tres Sorores* (1974, The Three Sisters), a complete rewrite of *Siete domingos rojos,* the protagonist defines himself as an "extremista del centro" (an extremist of the center).

In the 1930s Sender sought to convince himself that many of the evils in the world were man-made and a result of the corrupting influence of bourgeois society. The political revolution required to change the world would entail also a moral revolution. With the failure of the Republican movement and, in his view, the increasing evidence in Russia of a betrayal of the principles of the revolution of 1917, Sender's basic understanding of man's condition remained constant, but he began to believe that evil was unavoidable. Man has the choice of running away from it, marginalizing himself from society, or confronting it. This confrontation involves a dual approach, viewing the whole from the margins but continuing to take an active part in life to change it for the better even though it cannot be made perfect. Sender described this change in his work as a shift from writing "una literatura de combate" (a combative literature) to writing "una literatura de iluminación" (a literature of illumination). One of his most significant novels on this theme is *El verdugo afable* (1952; translated as *The Affable Hangman,* 1954). The motivation behind the plot in this novel is the desire of a journalist who has just attended the execution of a convicted criminal to understand what made the protagonist, Ramiro, want to become state executioner, a role that society demands but that, because of what it entails, marginalizes him and forces him to lead a solitary existence. The journalist interviews Ramiro, whose life history is framed around a rewriting of some of Sender's key texts from the 1930s: *O.P., Viaje a la aldea del crimen,* and *La noche de las cien cabezas: Novela del tiempo en delirio* (1934, The Night of the One Hundred Heads: A Novel of Time in Delirium). The rewriting involves a change of emphasis that subordinates political concerns to issues relating to morality and man's nature. Ramiro becomes involved in political action but is not a political activist, as was the case of Sender and the protagonists in the earlier texts—a similar role is played by the protagonist of *Las Tres Sorores.* All of his experiences during peacetime and war teach him that killing, the worst of all evils, is inevitable, and so he decides that the only honorable stance is to adopt the lowly position of executioner, one who kills in the name of society. The moral justification for this decision lies in his reading of the Spanish quietist Miguel de Molinos, who believed in the moral superiority of the man who immerses himself in the miseries of life and awaits salvation from God. This novel is perhaps one of Sender's most pessimistic, as it ends with an image of Ramiro content with his role that places him at the heart of society because of his function but that segregates him from his fellowman because of their distrust and suspicion of someone who kills for a living.

The fourth novel Sender published in the immediate aftermath of the Civil War, *Crónica del alba,* was the first in a series of nine autobiographical novels that also took *Crónica del alba* as its general title. The series depicts Sender's early life and experiences through the politically charged 1930s and the Civil War. The popularity of the first volume owed to the lyrical evocation of his childhood in Aragón and the presentation of an idyllic vision of this mountainous region. The novel emphasizes the protagonist's friendship with his sweetheart, Valentina, a fictionalized version of a real companion from Sender's youth, Valentina María de Sancho Abarca Ventura Peñalba.

These four novels indicate an increasing interest in moral and metaphysical issues based on an essentialist view of life. As the political struggle is left behind, life for Sender becomes a battle between good and evil. His optimism is still evident, however, in his idealistic belief in love as a force that operates on several levels—personal, social, and metaphysical—and can be exploited to counter evil. This idealism is matched by a continuing belief in the capacity of simple men to realize man's full moral potential. The novels also reveal a developing nostalgia for the author's lost youth and native land and a preoccupation with the Civil War as an expression of his sense of exile.

During this same period, Sender published *Mexicayotl: Viñetas de Darío Carmona* (1940, Mexicayotl: Vignettes of Darío Carmona), a collection of short stories inspired by the legends and geography of Mexico, which captivated Sender during his short stay in that country. The stories reflect personal concerns expressed in other novels. Sender saw Mexico as "un país donde la naturaleza [habla] tan alto y tan fuerte y [ofrece] tantos caminos a la emoción de lo 'primario universal'" (a country where nature speaks so loudly and with such strength and which offers so many pathways to the emotion of what is "universally fundamental"). Sender's other work from the same year is an historical play, *Hernán Cortés: Retablo en dos partes y once cuadros* (Hernán Cortés: Altarpiece in Two Parts and Eleven Pictures), which traces the activities of the Spanish conquistador. This text, later reformulated as a novel, *Jubileo en el Zócalo* (1964, Jubilee in the Square), reveals Sender's fascination for the Americas and his interest in historical themes.

In addition to *Míster Witt en el Cantón* and, to some degree, *El verbo se hizo sexo,* Sender's key historical novels include *Bizancio* (1956, Byzantium), *Los tontos de la Concepción: Crónica misionera* (1963, The Fools from La Concepción: Missionary Chronicle), *Carolus Rex* (1963), *La aventura equinoccial de Lope de Aguirre* (1964, The Equinoctial Adventure of Lope de Aguirre), *Las criaturas saturnianas* (1968, Saturn's Children), and *El pez de oro* (1976, The Golden Fish). Sender's interest in these novels is less in historical accuracy than in capturing the spirit of the characters as representatives of his own ideas on human nature.

*Bizancio* is set between 1302 and 1304 and charts the exploits of Roger de Flor in Constantinople in defense of the Byzantium Empire, his assassination, and the revenge taken on the Turks by his Catalan and Aragonese compatriots. The action of *Los tontos de la Concepción* takes place between 1778 and 1781 and revolves around the mission of La Concepción. The protagonist is the good-intentioned if ill-fated Spanish missionary and ethnographer Father Francisco Garcés, who attempted to help the indigenous people of what is now New Mexico. *Carolus Rex* depicts the wedding of King Charles II of Spain, his marriage to Maria Luisa de Orleans, and the political intrigue that ensues within the palace when no heir is born. *La aventura equinnocial de Lope de Aguirre* is based on Lope de Aguirre's voyage along the Amazon in 1561 in an attempt to find the fabled city of El Dorado. While all of these novels are centered on some aspect of Spanish history, two of them reflecting the role of Spain as a colonizer of the Americas, *Las criaturas saturnianas*—which includes the 1958 text *Emen Hetan (Aquí estamos)* (Here We Are)— and *El pez de oro* are inspired by Russian themes. *Las criaturas saturnianas* traces the battles of succession in late-eighteenth-century Russia—the dethroning of Peter III by Catherine the Great with the help of her lover, Grigory

*Dust jacket for Sender's 1952 novel (translated as* The Affable
Hangman, *1954), in which the title character explains
to a journalist why he decided to become the public
executioner (Thomas Cooper Library,
University of South Carolina)*

Orlov—before focusing on the adventures of Elizabeth
Petrovna (Lizaveta), her imprisonment by Orlov, and
her travels through Europe in the company of Count
Alessandro di Cagliostro. *El pez de oro* concerns Alexander I, the grandson of Catherine the Great and
emperor of Russia from 1801 until his death in 1825.
Alexander died in mysterious circumstances after having become increasingly interested in mysticism.
Sender's interest in tsarist Russia is perhaps the eventual result of his years spent denouncing communism.
These two novels offer protagonists who, in a manner
similar to Saila in *Proverbio de la muerte,* opt to turn their
back on social affairs to concentrate on their own personal survival.

More generally, Sender's historical novels deal
with issues that arise in many of his other works: for
example, an exploration of the dichotomy between
what is primitive and what is civilized through an
encounter between two cultures. This theme is often
connected to an interest in the natural world. The novels also include graphic descriptions of the cruelties of
war or torture alongside episodes of intense lyricism.
Such passages reflect, on the one hand, Sender's interest
in man's capacity for evil and, on the other, an enduring faith in good. The latter is often reflected in the
instinctive nature of key characters, particularly young
women. Underlying all of these themes is a preoccupation with an ineffable dimension to reality that takes on
metaphysical, mystical, or magical qualities. Love in
one form or another also plays its part and is manifest
in a variety of forms—paternal, erotic, and mystical or
metaphysical.

Of all of Sender's novels, however, the best
known is *Réquiem por un campesino español,* which was first
published under that title in 1960. It is the story of a
young man, Paco el del Molino (Paco the Miller), who
fights an absent landowner for the rights of the poor
and the homeless in Spain in the 1930s—a conflict that
culminates in the Civil War. *Réquiem por un campesino
español* is a cleverly constructed novel that manages to
put its political point over effectively in an indirect way.
It does not, for example, present its message in such a
way that the reader instinctively knows he is reading
propaganda. Instead it focuses on the life of one individual, Paco el del Molino, who becomes a symbol of
the Republican cause. This identification encourages
the reader, by dint of a variety of strategies, to sympathize fully with his plight. The closing sections of the
novel, in which Paco is executed by the Nationalists,
thus provoke a sense of outrage.

The novel is, first, a chronicle of the main events
of Paco's life, including his birth, his baptism party, and
the time he spends as an altar boy, all of which is portrayed in careful detail. Young Paco is presented as
thoughtful and socially concerned. These qualities are
most evident when he feels compassion for those in the
village who, because of their extreme poverty, are
forced to live in caves, without light, water, or any type
of heat; he is concerned that nothing is being done for
them. Paco's nascent sense of social justice is expressed
when he tries to persuade the dog not to fight with the
cat, arguing that the cat has as much right to live as the
dog.

Paco takes a more political path, becoming a
councillor and deciding to fight against the local duke,
an absent landlord who is becoming rich at the expense
of the farmhands and laborers who work his land for a
pittance. He becomes the spokesperson for the five
local villages in their dispute with the duke, informing
the duke's representative, don Valeriano, that they will
not pay rent until the tribunal commissioned to decide

on the validity of seignorial rights has reached its decision. Finally, Paco is appalled by the events of the Spanish Civil War, particularly by the senseless murder of innocent people. He hides from the Nationalists in the fens outside the village–the Pardinas–only to be betrayed by the local priest, Mosén Millán of the original Spanish title, who effectively delivers him up to the Nationalist troops.

Although formally a third-person narrative, the events of *Réquiem por un campesino español* are often filtered through the memories of Mosén Millán. The narrative time of the novel elapses as he is sitting in the sacristy, waiting for the parishioners to arrive for the requiem mass he has prepared in memory of Paco's soul. So, even when events are presented in an objective narrative style, they are invariably revealed through the frame of the priest's memories. Given this perspective, it is difficult for the reader to see *Réquiem por un campesino español* as a biased, Republican account of the war, since the events have necessarily been filtered by the right-wing lens of the priest's consciousness. What, finally, is masterful about this short novel is that it is able to allow the truth of what really happened–a rural community was destroyed in the opening months of the Civil War as a result of the collusion of the local priest with the Nationalist army along with the rich landowners–to emerge from the mouth of the person who is hostile to the Republican cause. The events of the novel, in a sense, speak for themselves, and in this way the novel is a defense of human dignity and social justice first, and of the Republican cause second. Mosén Millán is overcome with guilt for the role that he played in Paco's downfall and, despite his attempts to sweep it all under the rug the truth comes out. His guilt is underlined by his feeling, even though a year has passed since the events, that Paco's blood is still on his cassock.

The novel reverses Francoist ideology by suggesting that the Nationalists–including the Catholic Church–far from being involved in a crusade to rid Spain of antinational elements, are actually destroying the Spanish nation. In fact they are shown to be the equivalent of a Judas betraying the Spanish people. Sender reinforces this message by presenting Paco as something of a Christ figure. He feels compassion for the poor people whom he sees living in barbaric conditions when he accompanies Mosén Millán on his visit to the caves in order to give last rites to a dying man. Mosén Millán, in contrast, is indifferent to the sorrow experienced by the cave people and wants to hurry through the rites so he can go home. Paco's struggle for the political and social rights of the villagers is presented in terms of the compassion that he maintains even when it puts him in personal danger. In an ironic

scene toward the end of the novel, Mosén Millán offers him the chance to confess his sins, and Paco does not understand; though Paco has apparently been traumatized by what he has witnessed, Sender is also emphasizing his blameless nature. The parallel is further underlined when Paco asks that the two men who are about to be executed with him should be spared, echoing the Gospels' account of Jesus' crucifixion. Further, Paco's colt, which roams the village streets now that his owner is dead, suggests the mount Jesus requested of his disciples for his entry into Jerusalem. The colt disrupts the solemnity of the church before the requiem service that the priest guiltily holds to honor Paco.

Whenever Francoist ideology is introduced into the story, it is presented as mumbo jumbo. Toward the end of the novel, for example, the "well-to-do foreigners" hold a ceremony in the main square in which they declaim a series of speeches upholding the values of "el imperio" (the empire), "el destino inmortal y el orden" (immortal destiny and order), as well as "la santa fe" (Holy Faith), although the villagers have no idea what they are talking about. The villagers are far more at home in their rural Aragonese world–characterized by the rituals of popular culture and by the use of Aragonese dialect–than in the world of violence, the city, and Castilian. The contrast between these worlds is, indeed, at the center of Sender's vision of what Franco had done to Spain. The invasion of the Nationalist troops, according to *Réquiem por un campesino español,* far from being a crusade to bring back to life the ancient empire, spread only terror and destruction. For an audience attuned to the religious resonance of Sender's attack–and a Spanish audience in the 1950s would have been aware of what he was hinting at–*Réquiem por un campesino español* was an outspoken rebuttal of Francoist ideology.

Since 1942 Sender had published several articles in the likes of *Books Abroad,* the *New Mexico Quarterly,* and the *New Leader.* In 1953, the same year *Réquiem por un campesino español* was published, he returned to regular journalism after being invited by Joaquín Maurín to contribute articles on a weekly basis to the American Literary Agency (ALA), which Maurín had founded in 1948. The arrangement became the basis of a long-lasting friendship and working relationship, as indicated by the collection of Sender and Maurín's correspondence published in 1995. Sender contributed regularly to the ALA until shortly before his death in 1982, covering literature in general and whatever other topics interested him. His prolific journalistic output is a significant part of his body of work. It is generally believed that his literary style was forged during his early years as a journalist, before the publication of his first novel. In his later years there was also a strong

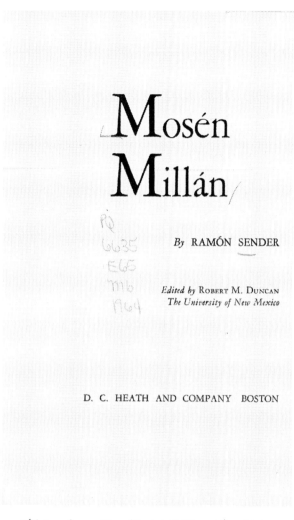

Mosén Millán

*By* RAMÓN SENDER

*Edited by* ROBERT M. DUNCAN
*The University of New Mexico*

D. C. HEATH AND COMPANY BOSTON

*Title page for an edition of Sender's 1953 novel (translated as*
Requiem for a Spanish Peasant, *1960), about a priest
who betrays a young man to the Nationalists during
the Civil War (Thomas Cooper Library,
University of South Carolina)*

overlap between his fiction and his articles or essays as his novelistic style tended at times to become increasingly discursive. For some readers this shift, together with Sender's growing interest in ideas of a more mystical and esoteric kind derived from his basically monistic philosophy, marks a decline in the quality of his literary output. In reality, however, Sender's later writing is not sufficiently well known or studied. Critics have tended to pay the most attention to those works that have a significant autobiographical element, such as *Monte Odina* (1980), *Album de radiografías secretas* (1982, Album of Secret X-rays), and the posthumously published *Toque de queda* (1985, Last Post).

In addition to these three works, the last years of Sender's life were dominated by a flurry of publications, including *Solanar y lucernario aragonés* (1978, Aragonese

Sunshine and Starlight) and *Segundo solanar y lucernario* (1981, Second Aragonese Sunshine and Starlight), two collections of essays on his native Aragón previously published in newspapers; he also wrote a series of novels each with a subtitle referring to a sign of the zodiac, although Sender wrote in a letter to his editor that the subtitles are arbitrary, capricious, and poetic rather than an indication of the content. Three of these novels—*La saga de los suburbios: Bajo el signo de Escorpión* (1980, Saga of the Suburbs: Under the Sign of Scorpio), *Una hoguera en la noche: Bajo el signo de Aries* (1980, A Bonfire at Night: Under the Sign of Aries), and *Orestiada y los pingüinos: Bajo el signo de Piscis* (1981, Orestiada and the Penguins: Under the Sign of Pisces) are texts that Sender first drafted between the ages of fourteen and sixteen. While some books in the series are conventional narratives, many are in the form of essays in which Sender ranges freely over his many interests.

The circumstances that surrounded Ramón J. Sender's emergence as a writer in Spain, his exile, and his political development after the Civil War inevitably limited and influenced the reception of his work in Spain during Franco's regime, a time when he was much better known abroad. In 1981 a group of friends and colleagues presented him unsuccessfully as a candidate for the Nobel Prize. Although there was much backing in Spain, the proposers did not find support from the Spanish Royal Academy. Nonetheless, when he died on 16 January 1982, shortly before his eighty-first birthday, Sender had found his place as an important literary figure in his native land once more. By 1980 most of his works were being printed—and reprinted—in Spain in paperback editions (excluding, however, some key texts dating from before the Civil War) and all his new works were routinely being published there. It is fitting that in his native Aragón, in Huesca, the Instituto de Estudios Altoaragoneses (Institute of Upper-Aragonese Studies) has established the Centro de Estudios Senderianos (Center for Sender Studies) to promote the study of his life and works.

**Letters:**

*Correspondencia Ramón J. Sender–Joaquín Maurín (1952–1973),* edited by Francisco Caudet (Madrid: De la Torre, 1995).

**Interviews:**

Marcelino C. Peñuelas, *Conversaciones con Ramón J. Sender* (Madrid: EMESA, 1970).

**Bibliographies:**

Charles L. King, *Ramón J. Sender: An Annotated Bibliography* (Metuchen, N.J.: Scarecrow Press, 1976);

Elizabeth Espadas, *A lo largo de una escritura: Ramón J. Sender. Guía bibliográfica* (Huesca: Instituto de Estudios Altoaragoneses, 2002).

**Biographies:**

Luz C. Watts, *Veintiún días con Sender en España* (Barcelona: Destino, 1976);

Jesús Vived Mairal, *Ramón J. Sender: Biografía* (Madrid: Páginas de Espuma, 2002).

**References:**

Juan Carlos Ara Torralba and Fermín Gil Encabo, eds., *El lugar de Sender: Actas del Primer Congreso sobre Ramón J. Sender: Huesca, 3–7 de abril de 1995* (Huesca: Instituto de Estudios Altoaragoneses / Saragossa: Institución Fernando el Católico, 1997);

Peter A. Bly, "A Confused Reality and Its Presentation: Ramón Sender's *Réquiem por un campesino español,*" *International Fiction Review,* 5 (1978): 96–102;

Francisco Carrasquer, *Imán y la novela histórica de Ramón J. Sender: Primera incursión en el realismo mágico senderiano* (Zaandijk, Netherlands: Heijnis, 1968);

Carrasquer, *Ramón J Sender: El escritor del siglo XX* (Lleida: Milenio, 2001);

Carrasquer, *La verdad de Ramón J. Sender* (Leiden: CINCA, 1982);

José Luis Castillo Puche, *Ramón J. Sender: El distanciamiento del exilio* (Barcelona: Destino, 1985);

Patrick Collard, *Ramón J. Sender en los años 1930–1936: Sus ideas sobre la relación entre literatura y sociedad* (Ghent: University of Ghent, 1980);

José Domingo Dueñas Lorente, *Ramón J. Sender (1924–1939): Periodismo y compromiso* (Huesca: Instituto de Estudios Altoaragoneses, 1994);

Dueñas Lorente, ed., *Sender y su tiempo: Crónica de un siglo: Actas del II congreso sobre Ramón J. Sender. Huesca, 27–31 de marzo de 2001* (Huesca: Instituto de Estudios Altoaragoneses, 2001);

Luis Antonio Esteve Juárez and Gemma Mañá Delgado, *Ramón J. Sender "Réquiem por un campesino español"* (Madrid: Alhambra Longman, 1995);

Stephen Hart, *Réquiem por un campesino español: Critical Guide* (London: Grant & Cutler, 1990; revised, 1996);

Robert Havard, "The Romance in Sender's *Réquiem por un campesino español,*" *Modern Language Review,* 79 (1984): 88–96;

David Henn, "The Priest in Sender's *Réquiem por un campesino español,*" *International Fiction Review,* 1 (1974): 106–111;

Charles L. King, *Ramón J. Sender* (New York: Twayne, 1974);

Francis Lough, *Politics and Philosophy in the Early Novels of Ramón J. Sender, 1930–1936: The Impossible Revolution* (Lewiston, N.Y.: Edwin Mellen Press, 1996);

José Carlos Mainer, ed., *Ramón J. Sender, In memoriam: Antología crítica* (Saragossa: Diputación General de Aragón, 1983);

Patricia McDermott, "Ramón Sender: 'Un gran recuerdo típico,'" *Romance Studies,* 3 (1983): 47–59;

José Luis Negre Carasol, "Aragonesismos en *Réquiem por un campesino español,*" *Alazet,* 1 (1988): 273–284;

Michiko Nonoyama, *El anarquismo en las obras de Ramón J. Sender* (Madrid: Playor, 1979);

Marcelino C. Peñuelas, *La obra narrativa de Ramón J. Sender* (Madrid: Gredos, 1971);

José Manuel Pérez Carrera, *Guía de lectura de Réquiem por un campesino español* (Madrid: Akal, 1988);

Donatella Pini Moro, *Ramón José Sender tra la guerra e l'esilio* (Alessandria: Edizioni dell'Orso, 1994);

Josefa Rivas, *El escritor y su senda: Estudio crítico-literario sobre Ramón J. Sender* (Mexico City: Mexicanos Unidos, 1967);

Marshall Schneider and Mary Vásquez, eds., *Ramón Sender y sus coetáneos: Homenaje a Charles L. King* (Davidson, N.C.: Davidson College / Huesca: Instituto de Estudios Altoaragoneses, 1998);

Raymond Skyrme, "On the Chronology of Sender's *Réquiem por un campesino español,*" *Romance Notes,* 24 (1983–1984): 116–122;

Anthony Trippett, *Adjusting to Reality: Philosophical and Psychological Ideas in the Post-Civil War Novels of Ramón J. Sender* (London: Tamesis, 1986);

Trippett, ed., *Sender 2001: Actas del congreso centenario celebrado en Sheffield* (Bristol, U.K.: HiPLAM, 2002);

Gilberto Triviños, *Ramón J. Sender: Mito y contramito de Lope de Aguirre* (Saragossa: Instituto Fernando el Católico, 1991);

Mary S. Vásquez, ed., *Homenaje a Ramón J. Sender* (Newark, Del.: Juan de la Cuesta, 1982);

Vásquez, ed., *Ramón J. Sender en su centenario 1901–2001 / Ramón J. Sender Centenal Issue 1901–2001,* special issue of *Letras Peninsulares,* 14 (Spring 2001).

**Papers:**

The Instituto de Estudios Altoaragoneses in Huesca has some of Ramón J. Sender's papers.

# Gonzalo Torrente Ballester

*(13 June 1910 – 27 January 1999)*

Frieda H. Blackwell
*Baylor University*

BOOKS: *El viaje del joven Tobías: Milagro representable* (Bilbao: Jerarquía, 1938);

*Las ideas políticas modernas: El liberalismo* (Barcelona: Editora Nacional, 1939);

*Antecedentes históricos de la subversión universal* (Barcelona: Editora Nacional, 1939);

*Lope de Aguirre, el peregrino: Biografía* (Madrid: Vértice, 1940);

*El casamiento engañoso* (Madrid: Escorial, 1941);

*República Barataria: Teomaquía en tres actos, el primero dividido en dos cuadros* (Madrid: Escorial, 1942);

*Seite ensayos y una farsa* (Madrid: Escorial, 1942);

*Javier Mariño* (Madrid: Editora Nacional, 1943);

*El retorno de Ulises* (Madrid: Editora Nacional, 1946);

*El golpe de estado de Guadalupe Limón* (Madrid: Ediciones Nueva Época, 1946);

*Minoridad de Don Enrique III el Doliente* (Madrid: Editora Nacional, 1947);

*Ifigenia* (Madrid: Aguado, 1950);

*Los gozos y las sombras,* 3 volumes (Madrid: Arión, 1957–1962)–comprises volume 1, *El señor llega* (1957); volume 2, *Donde da la vuelta el aire* (1960); and volume 3, *La pascua triste* (1962);

*España* (Madrid: Hispano-Argentina, 1959);

*Aprendiz de hombre* (Madrid: Doncel, 1963);

*Don Juan* (Barcelona: Destino, 1963);

*Off-side* (Barcelona: Destino, 1969);

*La saga/fuga de J. B.* (Barcelona: Destino, 1972);

*Cuadernos de La Romana* (Barcelona: Destino, 1975);

*El Quijote como juego* (Barcelona: Destino, 1975);

*Nuevos cuadernos de La Romana* (Barcelona: Destino, 1976);

*Acerca del novelista y de su arte: Discurso* (Madrid: Royal Academy of the Spanish Language, 1977);

*Fragmentos de apocalipsis* (Barcelona: Destino, 1977);

*Obra completa* (Barcelona: Destino, 1977);

*Las sombras recobradas* (Barcelona: Planeta, 1979);

*La isla de los jacintos cortados* (Barcelona: Destino, 1980);

*Diario de un vate vago* (Barcelona: Plaza y Janés, 1982);

*Ensayos críticos* (Barcelona: Destino, 1982);

*Teatro* (Barcelona: Destino, 1982);

*Gonzalo Torrente Ballester (photograph © Rafael Samano; from the cover for* Crónica del rey pasmado, *1996; Thomas Cooper Library, University of South Carolina)*

*Dafne y ensueños* (Barcelona: Destino, 1983);

*La princesa durmiente va a la escuela* (Barcelona: Plaza y Janés, 1983);

*Compostela y su ángel* (Barcelona: Destino, 1984);

*Quizá nos lleve el viento al infinito* (Barcelona: Plaza y Janés, 1984);

*La rosa de los vientos* (Barcelona: Plaza y Janés, 1985);

*Cotufas en el golfo* (Barcelona: Destino, 1986);

*Yo no soy yo, evidentemente* (Barcelona: Plaza y Janés, 1987);

*Hombre al agua* (Madrid: Almarabu, 1987);

*Filomeno, a mi pesar* (Barcelona: Planeta, 1988);

*Crónica del rey pasmado* (Barcelona: Planeta, 1989); translated by Colin Smith as *The King Amaz'd: A Chroni-*

*cle* (London: Everyman, 1992; Rutland, Vt.: Tuttle, 1996);

*Lo mejor de Gonzalo Torrente Ballester* (Barcelona: Seix Barral, 1989);

*Santiago de Rosalía de Castro: Apuntes sobre la vida en Compostela en tiempos de Rosalía de Castro* (Barcelona: Planeta, 1989);

*Las islas extraordinarias* (Barcelona: Planeta, 1991);

*Escenas amatorias* (Madrid: Temas de hoy, 1992);

*La muerte del decano* (Barcelona: Planeta, 1992);

*Proceso de la Creación narrativa: Teoría literaria* (Santander: Universidad de Catabría, 1992);

*Torre del aire* (La Coruña: Diputación Provincial del al Coruña, 1992);

*El cuento de Sirena* (Barcelona: Juventud, 1992);

*La novela de Pepe Ansuréz* (Barcelona: Planeta, 1994);

*Los mundos imaginarios* (Madrid: Espasa-Calpe, 1994);

*La boda de Chon Recalde* (Barcelona: Planeta, 1995);

*Fragmentos de memoria* (Barcelona: Planeta, 1995);

*Historias de humor para eruditos* (Barcelona: Planeta, 1995);

*Memoria de un inconformista* (Madrid: Alianza Tres, 1997);

*Los años indecisos* (Barcelona: Planeta, 1998);

*Doménica* (Madrid: Espasa-Calpe, 1999).

PLAY PRODUCTION: *¡Oh, Penélope!* 1986.

PRODUCED SCRIPTS: *Llegada de noche,* motion picture, Marta Films, 1949;

*El cerco del diablo,* motion picture, Guadalupe Films/Mercurio Films, 1952;

*Rebeldía,* motion picture, Aafa-Film/AG Imago/Osa Films, 1954;

*Los gozos y las sombras,* television miniseries, Televisión Española, October 1982.

OTHER: *Sor María de Agreda, correspondencia con Felipe IV.,* edited by Torrente Ballester (Madrid: Fé, 1942);

Rainer Maria Rilke, *Requiem: Las elegías de Duino,* edited and translated by Torrente Ballester (Madrid: Nueva Época, 1946);

*Literatura española contemporánea, 1898–1936* (Madrid: Aguado, 1949);

*Panorama de la literatura española contemporánea,* 2 volumes, edited by Torrente Ballester (Madrid: Castilla, 1956);

*Teatro español contemporáneo,* edited by Torrente Ballester (Madrid: Guadarrama, 1957).

Among Spanish writers of the twentieth century, Gonzalo Torrente Ballester is known both for the creativity of his narratives and for the richness of his scholarly output. Nevertheless, his narrative ability received scant critical and popular attention until the last two decades of his career. Torrente Ballester usually spurned the predominant Spanish literary styles of the 1950s, neorealism and objectivism, for a more imaginative and fantastic form of fiction. His concept of realism, developed from his reading of the works of Miguel de Cervantes Saavedra, held that the writer's task is to create new worlds through the evocative power of words. Torrente Ballester believed that achieving total objectivism within a work of fiction was impossible, since the writer always chooses the elements of reality he wishes to present. Thus, Torrente Ballester uses irony, parody, and fantasy to question assumptions about reality, history, and truth. His novels combine realism with fantasy, frequently with humor, and, occasionally, with whimsy.

The first child of Gonzalo Torrente Piñón, a lieutenant in the navy, and Ángela Ballester Friere, Torrente Ballester was born on 13 June 1910 in the home of his maternal grandparents, Eladio Ballester and Francisca Freire, in the Galician village of Os Corrás. Because his father was often absent, Torrente Ballester spent much time with his grandparents. The Galician countryside, with its medieval atmosphere, serves as the setting for several of Torrente Ballester's works. He commented in a 1997 interview with Elena Pita: "los gallegos falsificamos el castellano y lo hacemos sonoro, que no lo es" (we Galicians falsify the Castillian language and we make it musical, which it is not). He added that he had two voices inside him: the scientific and literary Torrente Ballester who conforms to prescriptive grammars, and "the Other," who has fantasies and a vivid imagination.

Torrente Ballester began elementary school at age four. He attended a high school run by the Fathers of the Order of Our Lady of Mercy (it is known today as the Tirso de Molina School). His early reading included William Shakespeare's *Hamlet* (circa 1604) and *Romeo and Juliet* (circa 1595) and works that his father had collected by French writers, including Claude-Henri de Saint-Simon, Jules-Amédée Barbey d'Aurevilly, Alfred de Musset, and Sidonie-Gabrielle Coletta. In high school he read works by more-modern–or what he considered vanguard–writers, such as Henrik Ibsen, Jean-Nicolas-Arthur Rimbaud, Paul Verlaine, and James Joyce, as well as the Spanish classics. He also attended the local theater in Jofre as frequently as possible. In 1921 his family discovered that Torrente Ballester suffered from severe myopia, which precluded him from following his boyhood dream of becoming a sailor like his father. On his twelfth birthday he received his first copy of Cervantes's *Don Quixote* (1605, 1615). At seventeen he wrote an imitation of a Western novel on a bet. A year later, his maternal grandfather

Cover for a 1985 edition of Torrente Ballester's 1946 novel
(Guadalupe Limón's Coup d'Etat), in which a small-time
South American politician is converted into a national
hero after being killed at the beginning of a war
(Thomas Cooper Library, University
of South Carolina)

died; Torrente Ballester asserted later that his grandfather, with whom he had long conversations on most afternoons, influenced his tendency toward rationalism and intellectual analysis. His grandmother, who died in 1934, created in him an awareness of the power of the oral traditions of Galicia and of storytelling in general.

Torrente Ballester graduated from high school in 1926. The following year the family moved to Oviedo in the Asturias region, next to Galicia. There Torrente Ballester came into contact with a group of aspiring writers who introduced him to the vanguard movements of the 1920s. His first publications were articles he contributed to a local newspaper. In 1928 his father was transferred to Vigo in Galicia. During this time Torrente Ballester often traveled to Madrid to take competitive national examinations, known as *oposiciones*, in hopes of acquiring a position in the National Tele-

graph Office. In Madrid he attended meetings of literary groups, including one led by Ramón del Valle-Inclán, the major Galician writer of the earlier Generation of 1898. He also contributed to *La Tierra,* an anarchist newspaper published by the National Workers' Party. In 1929 he began studying for a *licenciatura,* roughly equivalent to a master's degree in the United States, in philosophy and literature at the University of Santiago in Santiago de Compostela. He continued to travel back and forth between Galicia and Madrid until the paper ceased publication in 1930.

In 1931 Torrente Ballester's family moved to the town of Bueu in Pontevedra. In these years, Torrente Ballester began reading works by some of the novelists who had the greatest impact on his own literary production—including James Joyce, Marcel Proust, Miguel de Unamuno, and José Ortega y Gasset. Also during this period, at age twenty-two, Torrente Ballester was introduced to Charles-Pierre Baudelaire's works, which sensitized him to the importance of the artist's role in shaping the artistic work through narrative perspective and raised his consciousness of the artistic process. During one of his trips home to visit his family he met Josefina Malvido, who was completing her degree in education. They were married in 1932.

In 1933 Torrente Ballester and his wife had moved to the seaport town El Ferrol. He found a job as professor of grammar, Latin, and history at a high school, Rapariz Academy. At that point he decided to complete his education, graduating with degrees in philosophy and literature and in history *Premio Extraordinario* (with highest honors). He then joined the Partido Galeguista (Galician Party), a political party advocating rights for Galicia. He and his wife had their first child, María José, in 1934, followed by a son, Gonzalo, in 1935.

In 1936 Torrente Ballester passed the *oposiciones* for a position teaching ancient history at the University of Santiago and went to Paris with his family to do research for his doctoral dissertation. There he reread Joyce's works and had the opportunity to see Joyce in person. A friend who worked at Odeon Records mentioned that Joyce was making a recording of a reading from the manuscript for *Finnegans Wake* (1939) and invited Torrente Ballester to be present. Joyce was accompanied by his secretary, whom Torrente Ballester later learned was Samuel Beckett. Joyce's work became a significant influence on Torrente Ballester's writing, and for several years he kept a bound facsimile of Joyce's manuscript for *Ulysses* (1922) next to his chair in his study. In Paris, Torrente Ballester also reread Laurence Sterne's *The Life and Opinions of Tristram Shandy, Gentleman* (1760–1767), which led him back to the works of Cervantes. All of these influences were eventually combined in Torrente Ballester's own works.

On 18 July 1936 the Spanish Civil War broke out when troops in Spanish Morocco under General Francisco Franco and troops in the north under General Emilio Mola rose up in rebellion against the Republican government in Madrid. Torrente Ballester returned to Spain in October. On the advice of a priest he joined the Falange, the fascist political party of Franco's Nationalists. During the war he spent time in Pamplona, where he met Dionisio Ridruejo, an important Falangist intellectual, and in Burgos, the temporary Nationalist capital until Madrid fell into Nationalist hands. He became a member of a circle of young writers, later known as the "Burgos Group," which included Pedro Laín Entralgo, Luis Rosales, and Luis Felipe Vivanco. These connections proved useful to him when he began his literary career in the early years of the Franco dictatorship.

In 1938 Torrente Ballester and his wife had a daughter, Marisa. That same year Torrente Ballester published his first literary work, the play *El viaje del joven Tobías: Milagro representable* (The Trip of Young Tobias: Representable Miracle). Another son, Javier, was born in 1939. After the war ended that year, Torrente Ballester wrote propaganda for the Falange. His second play, *Lope de Aguirre, el peregrino: Biografía* (Lope de Aguirre, the Pilgrim: Biography) was published in 1940. His third play, *El casamiento engañoso* (1941, The Deceptive Marriage), won the National Prize for Sacramental Theater. He published one more play, *República Barataria* (1942, Baratarian Republic). None of these works was performed. Unable to support his family by his writing, Torrente Ballester secured a teaching position at the Instituto Rosalía de Castro in Santiago. In 1942 he moved back to Ferrol and began teaching at the Instituto Concepción Arenal. With the other members of the Burgos Group, he contributed to the Falangist literary magazine, *Escorial.*

The publication of *Javier Mariño* in 1943 began Torrente Ballester's career as a novelist. The story of a young man's coming of age, the novel is written as a realistic, biographical narrative. In spite of his Falangist connections, Torrente Ballester was forced by the Francoist censors to change the ending of the novel. His next two novels shift the focus from a central protagonist to the process of mythmaking. In *El golpe de estado de Guadalupe Limón* (1946, Guadalupe Limón's Coup d'Etat) Clavijo, a small-time politician, is killed at the beginning of a war in a South American country and is promptly converted into a hero-savior who has rescued the nation from nefarious forces. The novel is a roman à clef in which Clavijo represents José Antonio Primo de Rivera, the founder of the Falange Party, who was

*Cover for a 1983 edition of Torrente Ballester's 1972 novel (The Saga/Flight of J. B.), in which a scholar investigates the myth of the seven "J. B." figures who will return from beyond the Western Sea and save the inhabitants of a Galician village (Thomas Cooper Library, University of South Carolina)*

shot by the Republicans in Valencia in 1935 and made a national hero by Franco. Fortunately for Torrente Ballester, the censors failed to see the similarities to the contemporary political situation.

In 1947 Torrente Ballester became professor of universal history at the Naval War College in Madrid. The move to the capital allowed him to work as a theater critic for the newspaper *Arriba,* as well as for the National Radio of Spain. He also started writing scripts for the movie director José Antonio Nieves Conde. His next novel, *Ifigenia* (1950, Iphigenia), is, like *El golpe de estado de Guadalupe Limón,* a "demythifying" work: his retelling of the ancient Greek myth of the sacrifice of

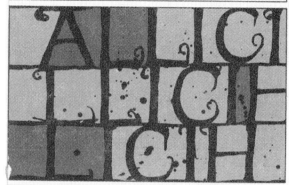

Cover for a 1982 edition of Torrente Ballester's 1977 novel (Fragments
of Apocalypse), in which Vikings, disguised as American Indians,
invade and destroy a Spanish village (Thomas Cooper
Library, University of South Carolina)

King Agamemnon's daughter reduces the heroes of the Trojan War to all-too-human dimensions. Even the goddess Aphrodite, provoked by a chance encounter with the girl, acts from base, trivial motives. Years later he explained to Joaquín Marco: "The only attitude tolerated in Franco's Spain was that of laud and praise for the regime, but anyone reading these works would surely have thought, Here is a man living in a situation with which he does not agree and is expressing it the only way he can." While the works received scant attention from the censors, who missed the ironic tone, they were also largely ignored by the reading public, who favored neorealistic works that purported to offer a "camera's-eye view" of contemporary Spain. Torrente Ballester began publishing works of literary criticism, including volumes on contemporary Spanish literature and theater.

Having had little success with fantasy and myth, Torrente Ballester turned to the realistic style of the nineteenth century with the trilogy Los gozos y las sombras (1957–1962, Joys and Shadows). A nobleman terrorizes the residents of a Galician village to maintain his power and to obtain sexual favors from the women. Carlos, a member of a prominent family, returns from studying and traveling abroad and challenges the tyrant. The first volume, El señor llega (1957, The Gentleman Arrives), received the Novel Award from the Juan March Foundation in 1959.

Torrente Ballester's wife died of complications from asthma, in January 1958, and his father died in February. To assuage his grief Torrente Ballester went to the island of Majorca, where he wrote the second part of his trilogy, Donde da la vuelta el aire (1960, Where the Air Turns Around). In 1960 he traveled to France and Germany. That same year he met and married Fernanda Sánchez-Guisande Camaño. They had seven children; the first was born in 1961, the year Torrente Ballester published the third part of his trilogy, La pascua tristes (The Sad Easter Holidays). The trilogy had modest sales.

When the Asturian miners went on strike in 1962, Torrente Ballester signed a declaration of support. As a result, he was ousted from his professorship and his positions as theater critic for the newspaper and the national radio. He survived by doing translation work. He published his next novel, Don Juan, in 1963, after an extended struggle with the censors that left him depressed and frustrated.

In Don Juan Torrente Ballester returns from the detailed realism of the trilogy to the retelling of well-known myths. The narrator, living in Paris, meets a man who claims to be the immortal don Juan. Don Juan informs the narrator that the 1622 play by Tirso de Molina (pseudonym of Gabriel Téllez), in which he went to hell for causing the death of doña Elvira, is inaccurate, as is José Zorrilla y Moral's 1844 Romantic version, in which he was saved by doña Inés's love and went to heaven. Actually, don Juan tells the narrator, he has been condemned to live for all eternity, fighting men and seducing women. He is tired of his role as the "great seducer" and would much prefer to spend his time collecting coins. Later, the narrator attends a play about don Juan and sees the man with whom he has been talking as one of the actors onstage; by the end of the performance he has come to believe that "don Juan" is simply a madman. But he remembers several inexplicable incidents that leave him wondering whether the literary figure has really come to life. Interpolated into the novel is "The Story of Adam and Eve," in which Torrente Ballester modernizes the biblical story of humanity's fall into sin in the Garden of Eden. In this version the serpent tempts Eve to keep all the pleasure to herself when she and Adam make love; she does, and selfishness causes a rupture in the perfect understanding between men and women. Torrente Ballester claimed that his retelling of the story was not intended to express disrespect for the Bible; he remained a devout Christian throughout his life, although the Spanish Catholic Church comes under harsh attacks in most of his works.

To provide for his family, which by this time included eight children, Torrente Ballester requested a position as a teacher in a middle school or high school in 1964. He received one at an *instituto* (which started at about eighth grade and went through high school) in Pontevedra, Galicia. In 1966 he accepted an invitation from the State University of New York in Albany to join the faculty as a distinguished visiting professor. In 1968 he was visited in Albany by several major Spanish literary figures, including Ridruejo, Ramón Piñeiro, and Dámaso Alonso.

In 1969 Torrente Ballester published *Off-side*, a long novel about a work by a well-known baroque painter that is put up for sale at a modest price at the Rastro, Madrid's flea market. Art critics and scholars try to determine the authenticity of the painting, which remains in doubt throughout the novel. Interwoven with the principal story line are those of other characters who are trying to gain seats on the Royal Academy of Art. One candidate is told that an artist needs at least a dissertation by some graduate student from the United States to give credibility to his artistic production. Behind the ironic humor of the scene lay Torrente Ballester's years of frustration with the Spanish academic and literary community, which refused to acknowledge any work not written in the dominant objectivist style.

Some critics—including Victor García de la Concha, Janet Pérez, and Carmen Becerra Suárez—contend that Torrente Ballester's *La saga/fuga de J. B.* (1972, The Saga/Flight of J. B.) is the most ambitious and significant Spanish novel of the twentieth century; they praise its synthesis of tradition and experimentation and compare it in scope and depth to Joyce's *Ulysses*. The title defies easy translation: *fuga* can mean "flight" or "escape" and can therefore refer to the event that both begins and ends the novel (like Joyce's *Finnegans Wake*, the novel ends where it began), when the Galician village of Castroforte is detached from its foundations and floats away into the morning sky because all of the inhabitants have become engrossed in thinking about a single problem; translated as "fugue," it can refer to the structure of the novel, which parallels that of the musical composition with its complex themes and variations. The village has built its life on the myth that an individ-

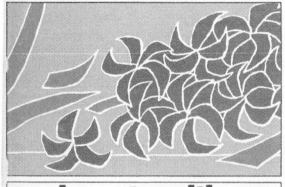

*Cover for a 1984 edition of Torrente Ballester's 1980 novel (The Island of Cut Hyacinths), in which Napoleon Bonaparte is shown to be an invented character rather than an historical personage (Thomas Cooper Library, University of South Carolina)*

ual with the initials J. B. will return from beyond the Western Sea and save the inhabitants (the myth imitates that of the return of the Portuguese monarch Sebastian, who died on a crusade in 1578). The town has had seven inhabitants with those initials, four of whom are dead. José Bastida, a small, unattractive scholar, decides to investigate the myth transmigrates through the personalities of the seven J. B.s to discover what "really" happened to each of them. When the town levitates into the morning air, Bastida and his lover, Julia, escape. (Torrente Ballester has said that he got the idea for the floating town when he saw a Francisco Goya painting in the National Gallery in Washington, D.C., and that the initials *J. B.* are those of his favorite brand of Scotch whiskey). Interwoven with the principal plotline is the story of the Holy Body of St. Eulalia, which the community venerates in competition with the neighboring village, which has a male saint's body. The relic is disintegrating, and community officials have to find a way to replace it. Furthermore, the eels, which provide an important source of income for the village, have disappeared from the river. Included in the novel are parodies of structuralism; the "Tubular Hommage," a circular railroad that goes nowhere; and various objects that seem to serve a variety of sexual functions simultaneously, although a closer examination reveals that they really do nothing.

*La saga/fuga de J. B.* employs the technique of realistic fantasy that the Colombian writer Gabriel García Márquez popularized in his novel *Cien años de soledad* (1967; translated as *One Hundred Years of Solitude,* 1970). Torrente Ballester has attributed the popularity of *La saga/fuga de J. B.*–which he has said is probably the least-read best-seller published in Spain in his century because of the challenges it offers readers–to his creation of an imaginary place, similar to García Márquez's Macondo, in which fantastic events occur. Spaniards wanted a novel that rivaled the Latin American work in breath and scope, and in *La saga/fuga de J. B.* they had it. Furthermore, the novel examines regionalism and central governments, the way history is remembered and written, and the difference between public figures and private personas. The novel won the 1972 Premio de la Crítica (Critics' Award) and Premio de Ciudad de Barcelona (Award of the City of Barcelona).

In 1972 Torrente Ballester returned to Spain. He took a teaching position in a high school in Vigo and began writing a column for the local newspaper; the columns were collected as *Cuadernos de la Romana* (1975, Notebooks of La Romana). Torrente Ballester began suffering from arthritis and decided to move to a dryer climate; in 1975 he began teaching at the Instituto Torres Villarroel Salamanca. That same year he was elected to the Royal Academy of the Spanish Language, occupying the chair left vacant by the death of Juan Ignacio Luca de Tena. The next year he suffered a heart attack. His eyesight worsened to the point that he could no longer see to write or type, and he began dictating his novels into a tape recorder; he could only read with the use of thick lenses and with the material inches from his face. His visual limitations in his later years contributed to an oral quality that began to emerge in his prose.

*Fragmentos de apocalipsis* (1977, Fragments of Apocalypse) was published two years after the death of Franco and the end of the dictatorship, although Torrente Ballester had begun writing it at the same time as *La saga/fuga de J. B. Fragmentos de apocalipsis* is set in Castroforte's rival town, Villasanta de la Estrella, a fan-

tastic version of Santiago de Compostela. The narrative consists of a novelist's notebook, with interpolated passages of the story that the novelist is in the process of writing. Throughout the work Torrente Ballester plays with the conventions of the novel and its creation of an internal reality. At the end of the opening section the narrator writes, "nada de lo que escribo ni de lo que he escrito tiene que ver con la realidad. Su espacio es mi imaginación, su tiempo el de mis pulsos. Si con ciertas palabras intento configurar imágenes, de hombres, es por seguir la costumbre, pero nadie lo tome en serio" (Nothing about which I write or about which I have written has anything to do with reality. Its space is my imagination, its time, that of my heartbeats. If with certain words I try to create images of men, it is in order to follow custom, but let no one take it seriously). He continually reminds the reader that what he or she is reading is fiction. Yet, the narrator notices that certain characters are altering his manuscripts in ways that he does not remember. The novel includes a negative portrait of the Catholic Church and an ugly dictator, "El Supremo" (The Supreme One), obviously based on Franco. At the end of the book the Vikings return disguised as American Indians and destroy Villasanta. *Fragmentos de apocalipsis* won the Premio de la Crítica in 1977. That same year Torrente Ballester was formally inducted into the Royal Academy.

Torrente Ballester collected some short stories he had written much earlier but that had been unpublishable because of the Francoist censorship as *Las sombras recobradas* (1979, The Shadows Recollected). He retired from his teaching position in 1980. His novel *La isla de los jacintos cortados* (1980, The Island of Cut Hyacinths), which explores the "myth" that Napoleon Bonaparte actually existed, won the National Literary Prize in 1981.

In 1982 Torrente Ballester became a household name in Spain when Televisión Española broadcast a ten-part miniseries based on *Los gozos y las sombras* directed by Rafael Moreno Alba; Torrente Ballester helped to write the script for the series, which aired both in Spain and in Latin America. Torrente Ballester began receiving prizes and critical attention for his entire literary production. In 1982 he was awarded the Prince of Asturias Award in Letters by the king and queen of Spain. He was named "Favorite Hometown Son" by Ferrol in 1983 and "Adopted Son of Salamanca" in 1984. During this time he published four novels: *Dafne y ensueños* (1983, Daphne and Dreams), based on his childhood memories of Galicia; *La princesa durmiente va a la escuela* (1983, Sleeping Beauty Goes to School), a retelling of the fairy tale with an unhappy ending, which he had written during the 1950s; *Quizá nos lleve el viento al infinito* (1984, Perhaps the Wind May Carry Us to Infinity), a spoof of the spy novel and science-fiction thriller; and *La rosa de los vientos* (1985, The Rosa of the Winds), a light-hearted blend of history and fantasy modeled after the memoirs of François-Auguste-René de Chateaubriand (1849–1850). In 1985 he was the first Spanish novelist to receive the Miguel de Cervantes Literary Prize. That same year his play *¡Oh, Penélope!*, which he had written in the 1930s, was produced. A series of articles he had written for the Madrid newspaper *ABC* were collected in 1986 as *Cotufas en el golfo* (Tidbits in the Gulf). In 1987 he received an honorary doctorate from the University of Salamanca, and the next year he received honorary doctorates from the Universities of Santiago de Compostela and Dijon and the Knight of Honor of Arts and Letters from France. His novels *Yo no soy yo, evidentemente* (I Am Not I, Evidently), a spoof of detective fiction, and *Filomeno, a mi pesar* (Filomeno, Much to My Regret), about a youth moving between Galicia and London, were published in 1987 and 1988, respectively. The latter work won the Planeta Award, which is equivalent to the Pulitzer Prize for the novel in the United States.

In 1989 Torrente Ballester published *Crónica del rey pasmado* (translated as *The King Amaz'd: A Chronicle*, 1992). The humorous novel describes the efforts of a young seventeenth-century Spanish monarch, probably based on Felipe IV, to see his queen nude after he has seen a courtesan in that state. The request sets the court in an uproar, as Church officials question its morality and courtiers speculate on whether the king will achieve his goal. Torrente Ballester's son Gonzalo Torrente Malvido and Juan Potau wrote the script for a 1991 movie based on the novel. Also in 1989 Torrente Ballester published *Santiago de Rosalía de Castro: Apuntes sobre la vida en Compostela en tiempos de Rosalía de Castro* (Santiago of Rosalía de Castro: Notes on Life in Compostela during the Time of Rosalía de Castro), a study of the nineteenth-century Galician poet and her hometown. That same year the Galician city of La Coruña instituted a literary award for narrative named after Torrente Ballester, and he underwent cataract surgery that improved his vision.

During the 1990s Torrente Ballester published the novels *Las islas extraordinarias* (1991, The Extraordinary Islands), *La muerte del decano* (1992, The Death of the Dean), *La novela de Pepe Ansúrez* (1994, The Novel of Pepe Ansúrez), *La boda de Chon Recalde* (1995, Chon Recalde's Wedding), and *Los años indecisos* (1998, The Indecisive Years), a semi-autobiographical work that pays tribute to his sailor father. He received an honorary doctorate degree from the University of Havana in 1992, the Azorín Award for the novel in 1994, the Castilla and León Award for Letters in 1996, the Rosalía de Castro Award in 1997, and the Knight of the Order of Santiago de la Espada, the highest award

*Cover for a 1996 edition of Torrente Ballester's humorous 1989 novel (translated as* The King Amaz'd: A Chronicle, *1992), about the efforts of a young seventeenth-century Spanish monarch to see his queen naked (Thomas Cooper Library, University of South Carolina)*

given by Portugal for accomplishments in literature, in 1998.

Torrente Ballester was hospitalized in 1997 for pneumonia and the next year for heart problems. He died of heart failure on 27 January 1999. Nobel laureate José Saramago called Torrente Ballester's death "a hard blow," and Camilio José Cela, another Nobel laureate, said that he was one of the truly important writers of the twentieth century. Other literary notables, the royal family, government officials, and actors sent messages of condolence to his family. His funeral was held at the Church of San Juan de Sahagún in Salamanca, and he was buried in the Galician parish of Sedantes. *Doménica* (1999), his only children's book, was published posthumously.

Gonzalo Torrente Ballester was one of the few writers identified in the early years of the Franco regime with the Falange who found widespread acceptance among younger readers who came of age during democracy. Asked about his affiliation with the Falange, Torrente Ballester explained that one does what is necessary to survive and to provide for one's family. A careful reading of his fiction reveals, however, that he was one of the many "internal exiles" in Spain during the Franco years; he expressed his disillusionment with the dictatorship through his irony and humor. While many of his works are much more accessible than *La saga/fuga de J. B.,* most critics believe that this work, above the others, will stand the test of time.

## Interviews:

Carmen Becerra Suárez, *Guardo la voz, cedo la palabra: Conversaciones con Gonzalo Torrente Ballester* (Barcelona: Anthropos, 1990);

Elena Pita, "Entrevista con Gonzalo Torrente Ballester," *La Revista de El Mundo,* 21 October 1997.

## References:

Frieda H. Blackwell, *The Game of Literature: Demythification and Parody in Novels of Gonzalo Torrente Ballester* (Valencia: Albatros, 1985);

John A. Crispin, "'Off-side' o Los espejos cambiantes de Gonzalo Torrente Ballester," *Cuadernos hispanoamericanos,* 248 (1970): 633–641;

Ignacio Francia and Victor García de la Concha, "Muere Torrente Ballester gran fabulador de misterios," *El País,* 28 January 1999, section 1, p. 37;

Alicia González Giménez González, *Torrente Ballester en su mundo literario* (Salamanca: Universidad de Salamanca, 1984);

Juan Carlos Lertora, *Tipología de la narración a propósito de Torrente Ballester* (Madrid: Pliegos, 1990);

Joaquín Marco, "Las narraciones de Gonzalo Torrente Ballester," in *Novela española actual,* by Lertora, Andrés Amoros, and others (Madrid: Fundación Juan March, 1977), pp. 63–130;

Janet Pérez, *Gonzalo Torrente Ballester* (Boston: Twayne, 1984);

Pérez and Stephen Miller, eds., *Critical Studies on Gonzalo Torrente Ballester* (Boulder, Colo.: Society of Spanish and Spanish-American Studies, 1989);

José A. Ponte Far, *Galicia en la obra narrativa de Torrente Ballester* (La Coruña: Tambre, 1994);

Sagrano Ruíz Baños, *Itinerario de la ficción en Gonzalo Torrente Ballester* (Murcia: University of Murcia, 1992);

Javier Villán, ed., *Gonzalo Torrente Ballester: Semana de autor sobre Gonzalo Torrente Ballester en el centro Cultural del Instituto de cooperación Iberoamericana de Buenos Aires (12–15 September 1988)* (Madrid: Ediciones de Cultura Hispánica, Agencia Española de Cooperación Internacional, 1990).

**Internet Sites:** <http://www.babab.com/no04/torrente_ballester.htm> [accessed 29 September 2005];

<http://www.gonzalotorrenteballester.com/primera.html> [accessed 29 September 2005].

## Papers:

Gonzalo Torrente Ballester's papers and a re-creation of his study are in the Gonzolo Torrente Ballester Foundation in Santiago de Compostela.

# Esther Tusquets
## (30 August 1936 –   )

### Barbara F. Ichiishi

BOOKS: *El mismo mar de todos los veranos* (Barcelona: Lumen, 1978); translated by Margaret E. W. Jones as *The Same Sea as Every Summer* (Lincoln: University of Nebraska Press, 1990);

*El amor es un juego solitario* (Barcelona: Lumen, 1979); translated by Bruce Penman as *Love Is a Solitary Game* (New York: Riverrun Press, 1985);

*Varada tras el último naufragio* (Barcelona: Lumen, 1980); translated by Susan E. Clark as *Stranded* (Elmwood Park, Ill.: Dalkey Archive Press, 1991);

*La conejita Marcela* (Barcelona: Lumen, 1980);

*Siete miradas en un mismo paisaje* (Barcelona: Lumen, 1981);

*Para no volver* (Barcelona: Lumen, 1985); translated by Barbara F. Ichiishi as *Never to Return* (Lincoln: University of Nebraska Press, 1999);

*La reina de los gatos* (Barcelona: Lumen, 1993);

*"La niña lunática" y otros cuentos* (Barcelona: Lumen, 1997);

*Con la miel en los labios* (Barcelona: Anagrama, 1997);

*Correspondencia privada* (Barcelona: Anagrama, 2001);

*"Orquesta de verano" y otros cuentos* (Barcelona: Plaza y Janés, 2002);

*Confesiones de una editora poco mentirosa* (Barcelona: RqueR, 2005).

OTHER: "Carta a la madre," in *Madres e hijas,* edited by Laura Freixas (Barcelona: Anagrama, 1996), pp. 75–93.

SELECTED PERIODICAL PUBLICATIONS–
UNCOLLECTED: "Olivia," *Penthouse,* 29 (August 1980): 57–60;

"La orilla de amar," *El País* (15 July 1987);

"Para salir de tanta miseria," *Taifa* (Barcelona), 1 (January 1988)–lecture delivered at Tulane University, University of North Carolina at Chapel Hill, Barnard College/Columbia University (October 1987).

*Esther Tusquets (from the dust jacket for* Stranded, *1991; Richland County Public Library)*

The Catalan author Esther Tusquets is one of the most innovative writers of twentieth-century Spain. The originality of her literary oeuvre lies in the way the subject matter and the form (narrative structure and style) work together to render her unique vision, a vision that is at once individual, distinctly feminine, and in the largest sense, universal. In Tusquets's writings the fictional and the autobiographical dimensions are closely allied. All of her works present configurations and reconfigurations of the same basic elements: characters, situations, and themes. And beneath the changing constellation of characters and plots, her books constantly spin the same underlying tale. While her novels and stories offer the reader important views of the social world that shaped her and other members of her generation, her primary focus is psychological and aesthetic: her narrative is a penetrating study of the inner emotional life. As she explores the inner labyrinth of the self in its relation to the other, her story ripples outward, yielding insights into women's experience and the nature of the human condition.

The constant theme of Tusquets's narrative is love, or human communion—the meaning of love and the impact of its presence or absence on the individual and on society as a whole. She sees the interrelatedness of various forms of love, from the primary bond linking mother and child to adult heterosexual, homosexual, and bisexual modes of attachment. For Tusquets love is the attempt to overcome one's basic solitude through intimate union with the other, thereby awakening to the wonder and meaning of life. In showing the beauty and importance of all forms of love, she offers a feminine perspective that is realized both in content and in style. Her vision of female erotic desire is inscribed through narrative structure and through her daring play with language. Tusquets has spoken in interviews about what is for her the indissoluble bond between woman's sexuality and her emotional life; in contrast to the experience of men, she believes that for most women there can be no sense of erotic completion without love. She has also explained that in her books she is not interested in simply describing the technical aspects of the sexual act but rather in "eroticizing" people by writing as she does. Through her long, winding sentences that follow the logic of feeling states, her fluid, musical style, her writing dissolves the barriers among different forms of sensuality and illuminates the tie between the erotic and the emotional life.

Tusquets was born in Barcelona on 30 August 1936 in an upper-middle-class Catalonian family. Her life began during the opening weeks of the Spanish Civil War, and she grew to adulthood under the repressive fascist regime of Francisco Franco. Both of these ordeals left a deep imprint on the girl, as they did on every member of her generation. Her family suffered hardship during the war, but with the end of the armed conflict in 1939 her father, Magín Tusquets, worked tirelessly to establish a successful medical practice, enabling him to provide for his wife, Guillermina Guillén, and their children, Esther and Oscar, a life of ease. Tusquets's parents were privileged members of Catalan society, but their daughter grew to reject the materialist values of her social class and to sympathize with the plight of the oppressed and the misunderstood. She attended the prestigious Colegio Alemán for her secondary schooling and went on to study philosophy and literature at the University of Barcelona, specializing in history. From her graduation in 1959 until her retirement in 2000 she directed a distinguished Barcelona publishing house, Lumen, which under her leadership developed a solid reputation for contemporary Spanish literature, translations of

foreign classics, and children's literature. Tusquets began writing late, publishing her first novel at age forty-two. She has produced five novels, one autobiographical work, one professional memoir, three collections of short stories, and two children's tales. She has also contributed articles on a wide range of subjects to the Barcelona newspapers and has been an active participant in Spanish cultural life.

Along with the external facts of Tusquets's biography, it is illuminating to trace the course of her inner emotional life as reflected in her most important relationships. She has discussed some of these relationships in articles and interviews and has described them at length in her 2001 memoir *Correspondencia privada* (Private Correspondence). There are three pivotal points of her emotional history as evidenced in her literary production. The first is her difficult relationship with her seductive but coldly rejecting mother. Tusquets describes her as a worldly, well-educated woman who dissipated her considerable gifts in a round of frivolous social activities. The mother was a gifted storyteller and passed on to her daughter her devotion to literature, theater, and the visual arts. Guillermina Guillén was, however, an unhappy woman who was incapable of giving love to those around her and denied her daughter the bonding she needed to believe in her own ability to sustain intimate attachments.

Tusquets's romantic relationships culminated in her love for the idealistic Esteban Busquets, the man she lived with for fourteen years and the father of her children, Milena and Nestór. In her autobiographical account she describes Busquets as a man who had lived a life of valor and social engagement, having supported the Republican cause in the Civil War and worked for the underground resistance during World War II. She met him in the early 1960s on his return from a long period of exile in Latin America, where he had taken refuge after suffering imprisonment and torture in Spain. To her he represented a world of nobility and sacrifice, far removed from the artificial values of her parents and their social set, and the years spent with him were the happiest period of her life. But for reasons that are not made explicit, the relationship eventually failed, leaving the devastated woman to raise their children and seek to reconstruct her life.

The third key attachment is her bond with a younger fellow writer, Ana María Moix. Aside from their well-known personal and professional friendship, they appear to maintain a dialogue throughout their fictional works. In the trilogy formed by Tusquets's first three novels Moix serves as the inspiration for the protagonist's adolescent lover, Clara, and she is also the model for characters in some of her later works. In Moix's interview of the author on the publication of her first novel, *El mismo mar de todos los veranos* (1978; translated as *The Same Sea as Every Summer,* 1990), the two women playfully re-created and alluded to the relationship that was the source of the plot.

Tusquets's fictional works are all intimately related, and in her successive books she plays the game of creating characters who are and are not the same person and plots that appear to differ but set up a chain of echoes in the mind of the reader. Some critics regard her books as autonomous works that offer different explorations of the same themes; others view them as a continuum and try to fathom the overall design. Tusquets herself has often referred to her first three novels as a trilogy, and in a 1988 interview she agreed with Stacey L. Dolgin that the fourth novel is a continuation of the series, forming a tetralogy. Critics who take the latter approach generally regard the first four novels as an extended developmental tale centering on the middle-aged female protagonist; Mirella d'Ambrosio Servodidio, for example, sees the narrative cycle as "a single gender-marked tale," while Catherine G. Bellver speaks of each of Tusquets's heroines as "a more mature version of the previous one." The continuity of the works is reinforced by the fact that all the protagonists' names begin with the letter *E:* those of the trilogy are all named Elia (in the first edition of *El mismo mar de todos los veranos* the main character was anonymous, but she was given the name in a later edition), and the protagonist of the fourth novel is named Elena. In each novel a middle-aged woman, a wife and mother, goes through a crisis involving the failure of love. This loss impels her on a journey inward and backward in time to solve the mystery of the course her life has taken and to find a path to psychic liberation and fulfillment. In conjunction with this developmental story is a strong critique of the author's social milieu of upper-middle-class Catalonia, which on a broader level appears to encompass the attitudes and norms of Western patriarchal society. Tusquets seeks to undermine the belief systems that surround her by showing what happens to people who grow up in a world without the life-affirming values of intimacy and love.

*El mismo mar de todos los veranos,* in its focus on the primary mother-daughter bond, is the point of departure for the series. It is the first person account of fifty year old Elia, who, stinging from the wounds she has received in the outer world, returns to her vacant childhood home as a kind of shelter in the storm. As she uncovers the old furniture and leafs through her beloved children's books, in every corner she finds pieces of the child self that she thought was lost but that has only been buried in the deepest layers of her mind. The specter of the tantalizingly cold maternal figure of forty years earlier brings to life the tale that marked her forever—the story of a child's unrequited love for her mother. A proud, fashionable high-society woman who takes little real interest in her daughter, the mother cannot offer her nurturing and acceptance but instead tries to mold the homely young girl into the Aryan

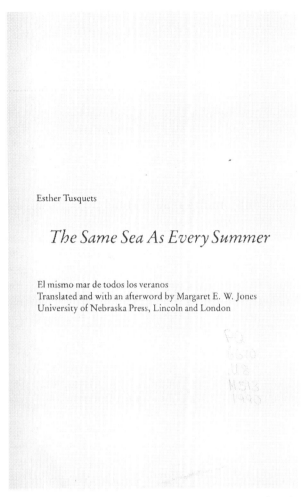

Esther Tusquets

*The Same Sea As Every Summer*

El mismo mar de todos los veranos
Translated and with an afterword by Margaret E. W. Jones
University of Nebraska Press, Lincoln and London

*Title page for the English translation of Tusquets's first novel (1978), in which the protagonist makes an imaginary journey into her past accompanied by a young female lover (Thomas Cooper Library, University of South Carolina)*

princess of her disappointed narcissistic desires. Unable to resist the mother's invasive control of her life, the child retreats into the inner world of fantasy, seeking in fairy tales and myths the bonding she cannot find in the real world. As Servodidio has observed, these literary texts both provide her with emotional sustenance and serve as guides to her understanding and expectations of life. But although she later finds the fairy-tale prince she has been awaiting in the form of the idealistic foreigner Jorge, the promise of rescue and deliverance through romantic love is shattered with Jorge's sudden unexplained suicide, a "desertion" that, in her mind, repeats and magnifies the early abandonment by the mother. Having lost all hope, she agrees to an arranged marriage to the eligible bachelor Julio, thus ensuring her enslavement to her mother and her parents' alien world.

Elia does not embark on her voyage of discovery alone but in the company of a Colombian student in her literature class named Clara. Although to the older woman the liaison with Clara begins as a frivolous game, she soon sees in the adolescent a mirror image of the impassioned, needy girl she once was and senses that Clara may be the rare individual who can understand and love her, enabling her to emerge from the abyss of her former life. As Clara accompanies her on her inner journey, the two act out all the stories, imaginary and real, that filled the woman's early life, mixing and interchanging the parts in a bid to undo the fixed cultural roles that have shaped their existence. In their lovemaking they arrive at a state of symbiosis, a blissful union in which each motherless child gives birth to the other, while each becomes mother/lover to herself. But while for Clara this transformative experience heralds a break from the past and a fresh beginning in which they will create their own life together, for Elia the weight of the past is too strong; she lacks the courage to translate the dream into reality. When her philandering husband summons her, she returns to her empty life of ease, knowing that in betraying Clara she is also betraying herself, unable to break out of the chain of abandonments that have governed her life.

In *El mismo mar de todos los veranos* form and content work together to express a woman's imaginary life–the yearning back to the lost mother and desire for psychic wholeness. The overall structure is circular, and within this frame the narrator's monologue continually moves back and forth from the present to key episodes in her past life. The writing is associative rather than linear and rational, organized according to feeling states, and it freely mixes and blurs the boundaries between past and present, self and other, the real and the imaginary, and memory and dream. Woven into Elia's text are elements of the fairy tales and myths she loved as a child. The writing abounds in female archetypal imagery from these tales (romantic heroines such as Sleeping Beauty, Rapunzel, the Little Mermaid, Ariadne, and Isolde) as well as imagery from the natural world suggestive of female eroticism (closed interior spaces evoking the womb as well as the unconscious mind, and imagery of the sea, long associated with many aspects of woman's erotic life). The long sentences (often extending to many pages) are incantational with their wordplay and fantasy, their musical rhythm and flow. Many critics see the prose style as a striking illustration of the French feminists' ideas about writing–in particular, Hélène Cixous's notion of a "feminine writing" that gives verbal form to woman's unconscious life of desire.

Tusquets's prizewinning second novel, *El amor es un juego solitario* (1979; translated as *Love Is a Solitary Game,* 1985), a work she first conceived as an erotic tale but then decided to incorporate into a trilogy of novels, is the darkest of her books. As the title suggests, the novel paints a world of false love or nonlove, where people are incapable of coming together to experience the joy of communion. Instead, they engage in frenetic sexual games in pursuit of pleasure and power over others with the aim of gratifying their obsessive instinctual needs. Unloved themselves as children, they cannot overcome this basic lack to be able to give love to those around them. Thus, because sex is not integrated with love, their couplings are to no avail; in the end they remain apart, each only living out his or her solitary story. Tusquets views this dismal situation as a societal failure: on the immediate level, the narrative mounts an attack on the values and modes of behavior of the postwar Catalonian upper-middle class, but on a larger level it can be seen as a condemnation of the value systems that give rise to cruelty and oppression everywhere. In the author's fictional realm, only children and adolescents really know how to love, to give freely of themselves to others, because they have not yet been tainted by the cold calculations of the adult world.

In this novel the cast of characters has grown from two to three, and the third-person omniscient narration is concentrated alternately in the mind of each. The "players" are Elia, a sophisticated thirty-year-old lady of leisure who feels detached from her life and from herself; the impoverished and emotionally deprived student poet Ricardo; and the innocent, needy adolescent Clara. Elia and Ricardo are drawn together because each views the other as an instrument to fill his or her insatiable psychic needs: the ambitious Ricardo wants the worldly older woman to initiate him into the pleasures of sex, thereby furnishing him with the tools–or weapons–he needs to conquer life, while the young man's proposal makes Elia feel young and desirable and renews the prospect of achieving the erotic "highs" that allow her a temporary escape from her inner emptiness and despair. Their "game" of love is governed by strict rules (such as the time and place of their meetings and the prohibition against really falling in love) and is modeled on the erotic literature they have read, showing the falsity of living life only "in the head," cut off from one's natural impulses and emotions. But their perfectly planned affair gets out of control when they decide to bring in a third party: Clara. By making love to Clara, Elia satisfies the girl's hunger for maternal bonding. Their union only serves as a prelude, however, to a nightmarish three-way sex scene staged by Ricardo for the purpose of seducing the unwilling Clara. In the climactic final episode Clara's horrified resistance to Ricardo's advances unleashes the instinctual drives of the other two, leading to a frenzied coupling unlike any experience they have ever known, the urge to unite fused with the urge to kill. The pretentious pair is seen for what they really are, humanity at its most abject, caught in a bestial mating devoid of any human contact. In showing the ultimate consequences of the "solitary game of love," the author reveals the dismal nature of a life without meaningful emotional ties–of a hollow, inauthentic existence.

There is a subtle but clear change in atmosphere from *El amor es un juego solitario* to the final work of the trilogy, *Varada tras el último naufragio* (1980, Stranded after the Final Shipwreck; translated as *Stranded*, 1991). While the characters of the second book appear to exist only in a static, frozen present and in an artificial world derived from their readings, in the third book one finds vibrant human beings engaged in their own struggles, joys, and sorrows. Forty-year-old Elia, in an emotional crisis caused by the sudden breakup with her husband, Jorge, joins their friends Eva and Pablo at the beach house they all share. The three are in turn joined by Eva's new protégée, the adolescent student Clara. Over the course of the summer each character goes through an emotional upheaval: Pablo's involves a midlife disillusionment in himself and his faded dreams, and the three women's involve the failure or loss of love. Despite their close and lasting ties, in their time of need each one feels alone because the others cannot understand his or her subjective experience. The characters' inner stories are woven together in the form of third-person unmarked segments, written from the viewpoint of each of the four in turn.

Elia's situation hearkens back to that of the Elia of *El mismo mar de todos los veranos*, since each woman has suffered the loss of a man named Jorge, the love of her life. Like the protagonist of the earlier book, this Elia undertakes an introspective journey into the past in search of understanding and inner peace. But unlike the earlier story with its fatalistic return to the point of departure, Tusquets's third novel records an emotional breakthrough as, after a long struggle, the heroine emerges from darkness into light. Elia achieves this transformation through self-analysis, aided by insights she gains from counseling with her psychiatrist friend Miguel, and through the lessons she learns from the experiences and perspectives of her friends. By the end of the summer she has come to a deeper understanding of self and world and has discovered two pathways into the future—her maternal love for her son, Daniel, and her writing. Elia's final monologue, addressed inwardly to her son on the drive to pick him up from camp, is the climax of the novel and of the trilogy. For the first time the narration shifts to the first person, signaling that Elia has regained her voice as a desiring subject. With the elimination of all punctuation marks, her twenty-two-page monologue expresses the excitement she feels at the prospect of making a fresh start together with her son. Everything she has experienced comes together in a wave of enlightenment as she follows the line of the same sea as all her summers on her way to a new life.

After completing the trilogy, Tusquets did not publish another novel for five years. During that time she wrote a collection of stories, *Siete miradas en un mismo paisaje* (1981, Seven Views of the Same Landscape). Each story consists of a remembered episode in the life of a girl

*Dust jacket for the English translation (1991) of Tusquets's novel* Varada tras el último naufragio *(1980, Stranded after the Final Shipwreck), in which characters gathered at a beach house go through various emotional upheavals (Richland County Public Library)*

named Sara, who is growing up in the years following World War II. Akin to the midlife protagonists of the novels, the Sara characters appear to be both the same and different: their superficial circumstances change, but they all maintain the same underlying viewpoint. They range in age from nine to eighteen, and their tales unfold in nonchronological order from 1945 to the mid 1950s. As Servodidio has noted, the stories taken together can be seen as a "pre-text" of the novels, recounting key episodes in the early life of the mature female protagonist. More embedded in the social/historical context than the novels, the tales provide a revealing picture of Francoist Spain as they show a girl's rites of passage from childhood to adulthood.

The innocent child Sara is fascinated by and drawn to the glittering milieu of her parents, the Catalonian upper-middle class that sided with Franco in the Spanish Civil War. But gradually she discerns the presence of a harsher reality that is hidden from view and realizes the hypocrisy and cruelty of her parents' inbred world. From an early age she feels like an outsider because of her attraction to the arts and her sensitivity and compassion in the face of human suffering. By the time she reaches adolescence, Sara rejects the superficial values of her social class and hopes that by allying herself with the marginalized, with idealistic rebels and artists, she can shed her past and forge a new life. In growing up, however, she, like her peers, assimilates the values of the adult world and thus cannot help but take part in the chain of betrayals that constitutes adult life.

In 1985 Tusquets returned to her novelistic project with the publication of *Para no volver* (translated as *Never to Return,* 1999). Fifty-year-old Elena falls into a deep depression brought on by her director husband Julio's trip with a younger woman to New York to celebrate the American premiere of his latest movie and by the departure of her grown sons to their own lives and relationships. Elena tries to deal with her problems by undergoing treatment with an Argentine psychoanalyst. Tusquets's protagonists appear to have a need to go over and over the same psychic story in a working-through process without end. The choice of a "scientific" approach such as psychoanalysis as the subject of the fourth novel suggests a determination to solve the problem by the most powerful means available. The title of the book is taken from a poem by Rubén Darío; like the poem, the novel expresses a romantic nostalgia for the loss of youth and love–but the phrase "para no volver," in addition to meaning "never to return," can also mean "in order not to return." Thus, the title condenses the basic conflict of Tusquets's work–the tension between the pull back to a mythical past and the urge forward into a new future, supported by a more sober, realistic view of life.

The narration focuses on Elena's experience of Freudian psychoanalysis as the vehicle for inner development. Its complexity lies in the narrator's ambivalence toward the analytic method. At times she mocks her analyst and the Freudian approach, while at other times she recognizes their possible effectiveness. The main premises of Freudian theory consign woman to a secondary position by setting up the male developmental model as the norm for all human development. The belief in female inferiority and weakness, which Elena has absorbed over the course of her life, is symbolically played out in her relationship with her analyst. Cold and distant, he exudes the mystique of the quintessential male authority figure, and she both feels dependent on him and longs to rebel against that dependence. She struggles against the rule of silence that denies the patient's need for a warm, empathic human response. She ridicules his search for her hidden "penis envy" and her "Oedipus complex." As Bellver has demonstrated, on one level she obeys the rules of the "talking cure," while on another she tries to undermine the process. Her behavior can be understood in one sense as part of the psychoanalytic processes of transference and resistance. But it can also be seen as an attempt to shed the rules of a rigid game to engage in a more genuine human encounter. Despite her ambivalence, Elena does grow through the analytic experience. She now questions her decision not to become a writer so as to devote herself to her husband's career and to raising their children. By the time Julio returns, the giants of her life have shrunk in size; she now sees her husband and friends in the light of their own human weakness and vulnerability. Julio and Elena's love does survive, but in a tarnished state; she will never return to the idealistic passion she once felt for him. Her new awareness of human frailty and of the limits imposed by aging and death leads Elena to a deeper acceptance of life and of herself. Tusquets leaves the ending of the story open: the obedient wife goes back to her errant husband, but her newfound confidence and decision to continue with the analysis may signal a path to self-creation.

The style of this book reflects a more mature viewpoint than that of Tusquets's earlier works. In contrast to the heightened life-and-death atmosphere of the trilogy, this narrative takes on a lighter tone. Elena uses ironic humor to distance and thereby free herself from the social discourses that have governed her life. The imagery and style are drier and less poetic than those of the early books. When compared with the beautiful erotic imagery and musical flow of the first novel, Elena's narration is cooler and more rational in tone, with a conscious downplaying of the erotic element.

After the publication of *Para no volver,* the author took a long break from writing fiction. Her fifth novel, *Con la miel en los labios* (The Taste of Honey), appeared in 1997. With this book Tusquets finally leaves behind the middle-aged female protagonist engaged in an intense review of her life story; in contrast, here both characters are young people setting out in life. Yet, the book also recalls her early work in that she again takes as her subject a lesbian love relationship. The main characters are students who meet at the university café–the competent and stable Inés, who is finishing her doctorate, and the seductive, child-like, and emotionally deprived undergraduate Andrea. At Andrea's instigation, the two embark on an affair that has great meaning for them both. But as in so many of Tusquets's works, the relationship seems doomed from the start because of the participants' different ways of experiencing it: Andrea sees their relationship as the great love of her life, while Inés sees it only as a beautiful but transient episode, to be followed by the compulsory return to heterosexuality and marriage to a man she does not love. *Con la miel en los labios* is a carefully constructed and well-written story, but in essence it is a replay of old themes. As Tusquets herself has observed, this third-person omniscient narration is a colder, more distanced book; it lacks the warmth and sympathy for the characters, the scenes of tender love-making and rich verbal eroticism of its counterpart, *El mismo mar de todos los veranos.* The most novel feature of the book is, perhaps, its portrayal of two social environments of the 1970s—the university student milieu, as seen in Inés's circle of friends, and the left-wing cultural elite represented by Andrea's architect father and his associates.

With her 2001 work, *Correspondencia privada,* the author appears to bring her narrative cycle to a graceful close. As she herself has affirmed, this book is almost purely autobiographical in content. It is made up of four chapters, each constituting an imaginary letter to one of the most important people in her life, now dead or dying, in which she reviews and meditates on her relationship with each and the role he or she has played in her story. The first letter is addressed to her mother. It shows at close range this overpowering woman—glamorous, arrogant, and clever—whose egoism and emotional shortcomings left an indelible imprint on her daughter. The second letter is to her high-school literature teacher, her first adolescent love. The third is to Eduardo, an iconoclastic young playwright in whose play she acted and with whom she had an ardent relationship during her university years. And the fourth letter is to Esteban, the culminating love of her life. The letters that compose this sentimental history have the lyrical flow of a private conversation in which one pours out one's thoughts and feelings to the chosen interlocutor in a quest for understanding. Each of these attachments represents one stage of her existence, and each letter likewise vividly evokes the era in which her personal drama was played out, showing how the country evolved from the repression and stagnation of the early Franco years, with their totalitarian social and religious indoctrination, their undercurrents of rebellion and unrest, to the prosperous and liberated Spain of the modern period. Together they show the interplay of the personal and the social over the forty-year course of Francoist Spain, as seen through the lens of a woman's inner world.

Where Tusquets's earlier works still looked to the future with determination and hope, this book is fully oriented to the past and the bittersweet joys of remembrance. The moving epilogue gives the author's final reflections on her life story. From her present vantage point, she sees the loss of love in one's life as a foreshadow of death, the final closure. She recounts that the termination of her relationship with Busquets was a watershed event, after which something fundamental changed. Since that occurrence she has been filled with a sense of transience and futility; as she explains it, where up to then she had been living "stories," from that time on she has only experienced "things," signifying the "end" of her emotional life. And yet, as Luis García Jam-

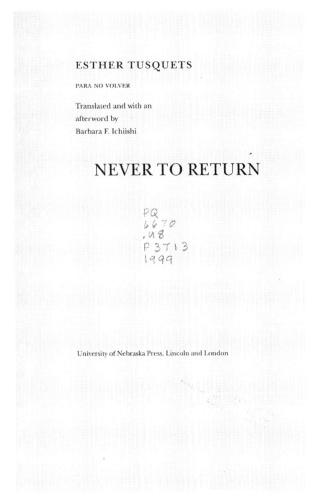

ESTHER TUSQUETS

PARA NO VOLVER

Translated and with an
afterword by
Barbara F. Ichiishi

**NEVER TO RETURN**

PQ
6670
.U8
P3713
1999

University of Nebraska Press, Lincoln and London

*Title page for the English translation of Tusquets's 1985 novel, about a middle-aged woman who undergoes psychoanalysis (Thomas Cooper Library, University of South Carolina)*

brina observes, from the moment when her life story apparently draws to a close the inverse process begins—the conversion of her life into literature.

In her writing Tusquets has both an artistic and a social mission, which are closely intertwined. By sharing with readers her experience, she hopes to help others who have suffered similar misfortunes and to effect social change. In a 1980 interview with Arantza Elu she declared, "El amor, la creación artística y la transformación de la sociedad son las tres únicas razones por las que creo merece la pena vivir" (Love, artistic creation, and transforming society are for me the three unique projects that make life worth living).

From a broad literary perspective, Esther Tusquets's narrative comes out of the European modernist tradition, established by such early-twentieth-century writers as Marcel Proust, James Joyce, and Virginia Woolf, who explored the interiorization of experience. In her Proustian search for lost time, she has produced a sizable body of work while drawing on a small store of material from the outer world. In a 1987 lecture at the University of North Carolina, Tusquets remarked that while it would seem better for novelists to dispose of a large variety of ingredients out of which to build their novels, "hay quienes se las han arreglado para construir algo magnífico a través de un champán y una lata de caviar, o utilizando hasta la obsesión una única y siempre repetida flor" (there are those who have managed to construct something magnificent with a bottle of champagne and a tin of caviar, or using to the point of obsession a unique, ever repeated flower). These words may well suggest the artistic credo of an author who, by plumbing every facet of her own experience, has created a fictional world not of breadth but of remarkable beauty, complexity, and depth.

## Interviews:

Vicente Verdu, "'Los adultos no sabemos amar,'" *Cuadernos para el diálogo* (10 June 1978): 52–53;

Ana María Moix, "Esther Tusquets: Madame Lumen para los amigos," *El viejo topo,* 24 (September 1978): 64–67;

Arantza Elu, "Esther Tusquets, amor y literatura para poder vivir," *Ere,* 36 (21–28 May 1980);

Montserrat Sala, "'La soledad es la ausencia del amor y el predominio de la muerte,'" *El noticiero universal* (Barcelona, 24 August 1981;

Stacey L. Dolgin, "Conversación con Esther Tusquets: 'Para salir de tanta miseria,'" *Anales de la literatura española contemporanea,* 13, no. 3 (1988): 397–406;

Mercedes Mazquiarán de Rodríguez, "Entrevista con Esther Tusquets," *Letras Peninsulares,* 13 (Fall 2000): 609–619.

## References:

Catherine G. Bellver, "Assimilation and Confrontation in Esther Tusquets's *Para no volver," Romanic Review,* 81 (May 1990): 368–376;

Bellver, "The Language of Eroticism in the Novels of Esther Tusquets," *Anales de la literatura española contemporanea,* 9, nos. 1–3 (1984): 13–27;

Stacey Dolgin Casado, *Squaring the Circle: Esther Tusquets' Novelistic Tetralogy (A Jungian Analysis)* (Newark, Del.: Juan de la Cuesta, 2002);

Hélène Cixous, "The Laugh of the Medusa," translated by Keith Cohen and Paula Cohen, in *New French Feminisms: An Anthology,* edited by Elaine Marks and Isabelle de Courtivron (Amherst: University of Massachusetts Press, 1980), pp. 245–264;

Cixous and Catherine Clément, *The Newly Born Woman,* translated by Betsy Wing, Theory and History of Literature, volume 24 (Minneapolis: University of Minnesota Press, 1986);

Rubén Darío, *Cantos de vida y esperanza* (Madrid: Espasa-Calpe, 1964);

Luis García Jambrina, "Cuatro cartas abiertas," *ABC Cultural* (2 June 2001): 11;

Barbara F. Ichiishi, *The Apple of Earthly Love: Female Development in Esther Tusquets' Fiction* (New York: Peter Lang, 1994);

Lucy Lee-Bonanno, "The Renewal of the Quest in Esther Tusquets' *El mismo mar de todos los veranos,*" in *Feminine Concerns in Contemporary Spanish Fiction by Women,* edited by Robert C. Manteiga, Carolyn Galerstein, and Kathleen McNerney (Potomac, Md.: Scripta Humanistica, 1988), pp. 134–151;

Nina L. Molinaro, *Foucault, Feminism, and Power: Reading Esther Tusquets* (Lewisburg, Pa.: Bucknell University Press, 1991);

Gonzalo Navajas, "Repetition and the Rhetoric of Love in Esther Tusquets' *El mismo mar de todos los veranos,*" in *Nuevos y novísimos: Algunas perspectivas críticas sobre la narrativa española desde la década de los 60,* edited by Ricardo Landeira and Luis T. González-del-Valle (Boulder, Colo.: Society of Spanish and Spanish-American Studies, 1987), pp. 113–129;

Elizabeth J. Ordóñez, "A Quest for Matrilineal Roots and Mythopoesis: Esther Tusquets' *El mismo mar de todos los veranos,*" *Crítica Hispánica,* 6 (Spring 1984): 37–46;

Marcel Proust, *A la recherche du temps perdu* (Paris: Gallimard, 1954);

Mirella d'Ambrosio Servodidio, "A Case of Pre-oedipal and Narrative Fixation: *El mismo mar de todos los veranos,*" *Anales de la literatura española contemporanea,* 12, nos. 1–2 (1987): 157–174;

Servodidio, "Esther Tusquets's Fiction: The Spinning of a Narrative Web," in *Women Writers of Contemporary Spain: Exiles in the Homeland,* edited by Joan L. Brown (Newark: University of Delaware Press, 1991), pp. 159–178;

Servodidio, "Perverse Pairings and Corrupted Codes: *El amor es un juego solitario,*" *Anales de la literatura española contemporanea,* 11, no. 3 (1986): 237–254;

Akiko Tsuchiya, "Theorizing the Feminine: Esther Tusquets's *El mismo mar de todos los veranos* and Hélène Cixous's *écriture féminine,*" *Revista de estudios hispánicos,* 26 (May 1992): 183–199;

Mary S. Vásquez, ed., *The Sea of Becoming: Approaches to the Fiction of Esther Tusquets* (Westport, Conn.: Greenwood Press, 1991);

Nancy B. Vosburg, "*Siete miradas en un mismo paisaje* de Esther Tusquets: Hacia un proceso de individuación," *Monographic Review,* 4 (1988): 97–106.

# Miguel de Unamuno

*(26 September 1864 – 31 December 1936)*

Julia Biggane
*University of Aberdeen*

See also the Unamuno entry in *DLB 108: Twentieth-Century Spanish Poets, First Series.*

BOOKS: *Paz en la guerra* (Madrid: Fernando Fé, 1897);

*De la enseñanza superior en España* (Madrid: Revista Nueva, 1899);

*Tres ensayos: Adentro! La ideocracia; La fe* (Madrid: B. Rodríguez Serra, 1900);

*En torno al casticismo* (Barcelona: Fernando Fé / Barcelona: A. López, 1902);

*Amor y pedagogía* (Barcelona: Heinrich, 1902; revised edition, Madrid: Espasa-Calpe, 1934);

*Paisajes* (Salamanca: Colón, 1902; enlarged edition, Madrid: Aguado, 1950);

*De mi país: Descripciones, relatos y artículos de costumbres* (Madrid: Fernando Fé, 1903);

*Vida de Don Quijote y Sancho según Miguel de Cervantes Saavedra, explicada y comentada* (Madrid: Fernando Fé, 1905); translated by Homer P. Earle as *The Life of Don Quixote and Sancho according to Miguel de Cervantes Saavedra, Expounded with Comment* (New York & London: Knopf, 1927);

*Poesías* (Bilbao: Rojas, 1907);

*Recuerdos de niñez y de mocedad* (Madrid: Suárez, 1908);

*Mi religión y otros ensayos breves* (Madrid: Renacimiento, 1910); translated by Stuart Gross as *Perplexities and Paradoxes* (New York: Philosophical Library, 1945);

*Por tierras de Portugal y de España* (Madrid: Renacimiento, 1911);

*Soliloquios y conversaciones* (Madrid: Renacimiento, 1911);

*Rosario de sonetos líricos* (Madrid: Imprenta Española, 1911);

*Contra esto y aquello* (Madrid: Renacimiento, 1912);

*El porvenir de España,* by Unamuno and Angel Ganivet (Madrid: Sociedad Anónima, 1912);

*Del sentimiento trágico de la vida* (Madrid: Renacimiento, 1912); republished as *Del sentimiento trágico de la vida en los hombres y en los pueblos* (New York: Las Americas, 1912); translated by J. E. Crawford

*Miguel de Unamuno (Collection of Cándido Ansede, Salamanca; from Margaret Thomas Rudd,* The Lone Heretic: A Biography of Miguel de Unamuno y Jugo, *1963; Thomas Cooper Library, University of South Carolina)*

Flitch as *The Tragic Sense of Life in Men and Peoples* (London & New York: Macmillan, 1921);

*El espejo de la muerte* (Madrid: Renacimiento, 1913);

*Niebla* (Madrid: Renacimiento, 1914); translated by Warner Fite as *Mist (Niebla): A Tragicomic Novel* (New York: Knopf, 1928);

*Ensayos,* 7 volumes (Madrid: Residencia de Estudiantes, 1916–1918); excerpts translated by Flitch as *Essays and Soliloquies* (London: Harrap, 1924; New York: Knopf, 1925);

*Abel Sánchez: Una historia de pasión* (Madrid: Renacimiento, 1917);

*Tres novelas ejemplares y un prólogo* (Madrid: Calpe, 1920); translated by Angel Flores as *Three Exemplary Novels and a Prologue* (New York: Boni, 1930);

*El Cristo de Velázquez* (Madrid: Calpe, 1920); translated by Eleanor L. Turnbull as *The Christ of Velázquez* (Baltimore: Johns Hopkins University Press, 1951);

*La Tía Tula* (Madrid: Renacimiento, 1921);

*Sensaciones de Bilbao* (Bilbao: Vasca, 1922);

*Andanzas y visiones españolas* (Madrid: Renacimiento, 1922);

*Teresa: Rimas de un poeta desconocido, presentadas y presentado por Miguel de Unamuno* (Madrid: Renacimiento, 1923 [i.e., 1924]);

*L'agonie du Christianisme,* translated into French by Jean Cassou (Paris: Rieder, 1925); translated by Pierre Loving as *The Agony of Christianity* (New York: Payson & Clark, 1928); original Spanish version published as *La agonía del cristianismo* (Madrid: Renacimiento, 1931);

*De Fuerteventura a París: Diario íntimo de confinamiento y destierro vertido en sonetos* (Paris: Excelsior, 1925);

*Cómo se hace una novela* (Buenos Aires: Alba, 1927);

*Romancero del destierro* (Buenos Aires: Alba, 1928);

*Dos artículos y dos discursos* (Madrid: Historia Nueva, 1930);

*El otro: Misterio en tres jornadas y un epílogo* (Madrid: Espasa-Calpe, 1931);

*El otro* [play version] (Madrid: Espasa-Calpe, 1932);

*San Manuel Bueno, mártir, y tres historias más* (Madrid: Espasa-Calpe, 1933);

*El hermano Juan; o, El mundo es teatro: Vieja comedia nueva* (Madrid: Espasa-Calpe, 1934);

*La ciudad de Henoc, comentario, 1933,* prologue by José Bergamín (Mexico City: Séneca, 1941);

*Antología poética,* edited by Luis Felipe Vivanco (Madrid: Escorial, 1942);

*Cuatro narraciones* (Barcelona: Tartessos, 1943);

*Cuenca Ibérica (lenguaje y paisaje)* (Mexico City: Séneca, 1943);

*Temas argentinos* (Buenos Aires: Institución Cultural Española, 1943);

*Almas de jóvenes* (Buenos Aires: Espasa-Calpe Argentina, 1944);

*Viejos y jóvenes* (Buenos Aires: Espasa-Calpe, 1944);

*El caballero de la triste figura* (Buenos Aires & Mexico City: Espasa-Calpe, 1944);

*La dignidad humana* (Buenos Aires & Mexico City: Espasa-Calpe Argentina, 1944);

*Paisajes del alma* (Madrid: Revista de Occidente, 1944);

*La enormedad de España* (Mexico City: Séneca, 1945);

*Soledad* (Buenos Aires: Espasa-Calpe Argentina, 1946);

*Algunas consideraciones sobre la literatura hispanoamericana* (Madrid: Espasa-Calpe, 1947);

*Visiones y comentarios* (Buenos Aires: Espasa-Calpe, 1949);

*Mi Salamanca,* edited by Mario Grande Ramos (Bilbao: Escuelas Gráficas de la Santa Casa de Misericordia, 1950);

*Madrid* (Madrid: Afrodisio Aguado, 1950);

*De esto y de aquello: Escritos no recogidos en libro,* 4 volumes, edited by Manuel García Blanco (Buenos Aires: Sudamericana, 1950–1954);

*Obras completas,* 16 volumes, edited by García Blanco (Madrid: Afrodisio Aguado, 1950–1959);

*Vida literaria* (Buenos Aires: Sudamericana, 1951);

*Cancionero: Diario poético,* edited by Federico de Onís (Buenos Aires: Losada, 1953); excerpts translated by Edita Mas-López as *The Last Poems of Miguel de Unamuno* (Rutherford, N.J.: Fairleigh Dickinson University Press, 1974);

*España y los españoles,* edited by García Blanco (Madrid: Aguado, 1955);

*Inquietudes y meditaciones,* edited by García Blanco (Madrid: Aguado, 1957);

*En el destierro: Recuerdos y esperanzas,* edited by García Blanco (Madrid: Pegaso, 1957);

*Cincuenta poesías inéditas,* edited by García Blanco (Madrid: Papeles de Son Armadans, 1958);

*Mi vida y otros recuerdos personales,* edited by García Blanco (Buenos Aires: Losada, 1959);

*Teatro completo,* edited by García Blanco (Madrid: Aguilar, 1959);

*La esfinge: Drama en tres actos original* (Madrid: Alfil, 1960);

*El pasado que vuelve: Drama en tres actos,* edited by García Blanco (Madrid: Alfil, 1960);

*Del diario poético,* edited by A. R. Vázquez (Buenos Aires: Losada, 1961);

*Cuentos,* 2 volumes, edited by Eleanor Krane Paucker (Madrid: Minotauro, 1961);

*Mi bochito,* edited by García Blanco (Bilbao: Arturo, 1965);

*El gaucho Martín Fierro,* preliminary study by Dardo Cúneo (Buenos Aires: Américalee, 1967);

*Diario íntimo* (Madrid: Alianza, 1970); selections translated by Martin Nozick as *The Private World* (Princeton: Princeton University Press, 1984);

*Desde el mirador de la guerra: Colaboración al periódico "La nacion" de Buenos Aires [agosto de 1914–diciembre de 1919]. Textos nuevos recogidos y presentados,* edited by

Louis Urrutia (Paris: Centre de recherches hispaniques, 1970);

*Escritos socialistas: Artículos inéditos sobre el socialismo, 1894–1922,* edited by Pedro Ribas, Biblioteca de textos socialistas, no. 11 (Madrid: Ayuso, 1976);

*Artículos olvidados,* edited by Christopher H. Cobb (London: Tamesis, 1976);

*Republica española y España republicana (1931–1936): Artículos no recogidos en las obras completas,* edited by Vicente González Martín, Colección Patio de escuelas, no. 11 (Salamanca: Almar, 1979);

*Poesía completa,* 4 volumes, edited by Ana Suárez Miramón (Madrid: Alianza, 1987–1989);

*Politica y filosofia: Articulos recuperados (1886–1924),* edited by Ribas and Diego Nuñcz (Madrid: Fundacion Banco Exterior, 1992);

*Artículos en* Las noticias de Barcelona *(1899–1902),* edited by Adolfo Sotelo Vázquez (Barcelona: Lumen, 1993);

*Artículos en "La nacion" de Buenos Aires, 1919–1924,* edited by Luis Urrutia (Salamanca: Ediciones Universidad de Salamanca, 1994);

*Prensa de juventud,* edited by Elías Amézaga (Madrid: Compañía Literaria, 1995);

*Obras completas,* 7 volumes, edited by Ricardo Senabre (Madrid: Turner, 1995–1996).

**Editions and Collections:** *Ensayos y sentencias de Unamuno,* edited by Wilfred A. Beardsley (New York: Macmillan, 1932);

*Prosa diversa,* edited by J. L. Gili (New York & Toronto: Oxford University Press, 1938; London: Dolphin Bookshop, 1938);

*Poesías místicas,* edited by Jesus Nieto Pena (Madrid: Patria, 1941);

*Páginas líricas,* edited by Benjamín Jarnés (Mexico City: Mensaje, 1943);

*Soliloquios y conversaciones* (Buenos Aires: Espasa-Calpe, 1944);

*Ensayos,* 2 volumes, edited by Bernardo G. de Candamo (Madrid: Aguilar, 1945);

*Obras selectas,* edited by Julián Marías (Madrid: Pléyade, 1946);

*Antología poética,* edited by José María de Cossío (Madrid: Espasa-Calpe, 1946);

*Por tierras de Portugal y de España: Andanzas y visiones españolas,* Colección Crisol, no. 157 (Madrid: Aguilar, 1953);

*Teatro: Fedra, Soledad, Raquel encadenada, Medea,* edited by Manuel García Blanco (Barcelona: Juventud, 1954);

*Almas de jóvenes,* Colección austral, no. 499 (Madrid: Espasa-Calpe, 1958);

*Autodiálogos* (Madrid: Aguilar, 1959);

*Obras completas,* 9 volumes (Madrid: Escelicer, 1966–1971);

*Poesías,* edited by Manuel Alvar (Barcelona: Labor, 1975);

*Crónica política española (1915–1923): Artículos no recogidos en las obras completas,* edited by Vicente González Martín, Colección Patio de escuelas, no. 3 (Salamanca: Almar, 1977);

*Política y filosofía: Artículos recuperados (1886–1924),* edited by Diego Nuñez and Pedro Ribas (Madrid: Fundación Banco Exterior, 1992);

*Miguel de Unamuno's Political Writings, 1918–1924,* 3 volumes, edited by G. D. Robertson (Lewiston, N.Y.: Edwin Mellen Press, 1996);

*Political Speeches and Journalism 1923–1929,* edited by Stephen G. H. Roberts (Exeter, U.K.: University of Exeter Press, 1996);

*De patriotismo espiritual: Artículos en "La nación" de Buenos Aires, 1901–1914,* edited by Víctor Ouimette (Salamanca: Ediciones Universidad de Salamanca, 1997);

*Alrededor del estilo,* edited by Laureano Robles (Salamanca: Ediciones Universidad de Salamanca, 1998);

*Paz en la guerra,* edited by Francisco Caudet (Madrid: Cátedra, 1999);

*Madrid, Castilla,* edited by Jon Juaristi, Letras madrileñas contemporáneas, no. 6 (Madrid: Consejería de Educación, Comunidad de Madrid/Visor Libros, 2001).

**Editions in English:** *Poems,* translated by Eleanor L. Turnbull (Baltimore: Johns Hopkins University Press, 1952);

*Abel Sánchez and Other Stories,* translated by Anthony Kerrigan (Chicago: Gateway/Regnery, 1956);

*San Manuel Bueno, mártir,* bilingual edition, translated by Francisco de Segovia and Jean Pérez (London: Harrap, 1957);

*Selected Works,* 7 volumes, edited by Kerrigan and others (Princeton: Princeton University Press, 1967–1984; London: Routledge & Kegan Paul, 1967–1984).

PLAY PRODUCTIONS: *La esfinge,* Las Palmas, Gran Canaria, Teatro Pérez Galdós, 24 February 1909;

*El pasado que vuelve,* Salamanca, Teatro Bretón, 10 February 1910;

*La difunta,* Madrid, Teatro de la Comedia, 27 February 1910;

*Fedra,* Madrid, Salón del Ateneo, 28 March 1918;

*La venda,* Salamanca, Teatro Bretón, 7 January 1921;

*Todo un hombre,* Madrid, Teatro Infanta Beatriz, 19 December 1925;

*Raquel encadenada,* Barcelona, Teatro Tivoli, 7 September 1926;

*Sombras de sueño,* Salamanca, Teatro del Liceo, 24 February 1930;

*El otro,* Madrid, Teatro español, 14 December 1932;

*Medea,* based on Lucius Anneas Seneca's *Medea,* Mérida, Anfiteatro Romano, 25 June 1933;

*Soledad,* Madrid, Teatro María Guerrero, 16 November 1953;

*La princesa doña Lambra,* Barcelona, Teatro Candilejas, November 1964.

Miguel de Unamuno is a crucially important figure in twentieth-century Spanish culture. Novelist, short-story writer, poet, playwright, teacher, and commentator on politics, culture, and literature, he was appointed professor of Greek philology at the University of Salamanca at twenty-six. By the age of fifty he was rector of the university and had published a study of the cultural politics of Spanish identity and nationalism; a proto-existentialist philosophical treatise; a study of the ontology of Miguel de Cervantes's *Don Quixote* (1605–1615); three novels, including the groundbreaking modernist work *Niebla* (1914; translated as *Mist [Niebla]: A Tragicomic Novel,* 1928); a collection of short stories; six plays; two collections of verse; half a dozen volumes of essays and memoirs; and hundreds of articles on Spanish and European political and cultural life. Dismissed from his rectorship and later imprisoned and exiled for his public criticisms of the monarchy and the government, he went on to publish a study of the politics and philosophy of Christianity, a complex metanovel of exile and identity, eight novels or novellas, many essays and articles, half a dozen plays, and four poetry collections. After a triumphant return to his native country, Unamuno remained a controversial figure: the Vatican placed his essay *L'agonie du Christianisme* (1925; translated as *The Agony of Christianity,* 1928) on the Index of Prohibited Books twenty years after his death.

Unamuno's major preoccupations include the self and its relation to the other, the nature of being, the limits of fiction and textuality, and questions of agency, determinism, and power. Unamuno has been read as a—sometimes anticipatory—interlocutor of thinkers as diverse as Georg Wilhelm Friedrich Hegel, Friedrich Nietzsche, Søren Kierkegaard, William James, Luigi Pirandello, Sigmund Freud, Bertolt Brecht, Henri Bergson, Fyodor Dostoevsky, Franz Kafka, André Gide, and Jean-Paul Sartre. Readings of Unamunian texts in relation to the work of Roland Barthes, Jacques Lacan, and Michel Foucault have cast new light on his representations of subjectivity and power.

Miguel de Unamuno y Jugo was born on 26 September 1864 in Bilbao, the major industrial city and port of the Basque region. Unamuno's father, Félix, a merchant, had married his niece Salomé de Jugo, and Miguel was the youngest of their four children who survived infancy. His father died shortly before Unamuno's sixth birthday. Unamuno later described himself as an introspective, bookish, physically weak, and fervently religious child. In 1874 he experienced the siege and bombing of Bilbao by the Catholic army during the Second Carlist War.

At sixteen Unamuno enrolled at the University of Madrid, where he studied philosophy, philology, Latin, Greek, Hebrew, Sanskrit, Arabic, Spanish history, and literature. Unfulfilled by his philosophy courses, he undertook independent study and became particularly interested in the ideas of Hegel and Immanuel Kant. Hegel's theory of the dialectic became an intellectual touchstone for Unamuno, albeit in a partial or reductive form: he turns time and again in his work to unresolved conflict, paradox, and dynamic, contradictory conclusions.

During his studies in Madrid, Unamuno was influenced by positivism; when his attempts to rationalize his religious beliefs according to positivist tenets failed, his formerly staunch faith waned. He frequented the Ateneo Científico, Literario y Artístico (Scientific, Literary and Artistic Athenaeum) where he listened to debates about contemporary politics, culture, and science. He also came into contact with Marxist and socialist thought.

Like most middle-class inhabitants of Bilbao, Unamuno had been raised in a Castilian-speaking household. But he had learned the Basque language informally during adolescence and undertook further study of it after graduating from the university in 1883. A year later, he successfully defended his doctoral thesis, a critique of previous histories of the Basque race and language. In his youth he briefly supported Basque nationalist aspirations, but later in his career he rejected the arguments for a separate Basque identity.

Unamuno returned to Bilbao in 1884 and supported himself by teaching Latin in schools and by giving private classes in Latin and Greek and instruction in the Castilian language for foreigners while applying unsuccessfully for various academic posts. He also contributed articles on Basque issues and poetry to local journals and newspapers and began working on his first novel, *Paz en la guerra* (1897, Peace in War). In 1891 he was appointed to the chair of Greek philology at the University of Salamanca. That same year he married Concepción Lizárraga, whom he had known since childhood. In 1894 he joined the Partido Socialista Obrero Español (Workers' Socialist Party of Spain). In the mid 1890s he began to contribute essays and articles to the national press on Spanish national identity, politics, and education. In a series of 1895 articles that were collected in 1902 as *En torno al casticismo* (On Spanish Authenticity) he discusses his concept of *intrahistoria* (intrahistory): continuities with the past that are experienced, mostly unconsciously, by ordinary people in everyday life. Comprising cultural memory, customs, ritualized and sacralized social practices and exchanges, and intimate relationships, *intrahistoria* is both deeply personal and fundamentally collective and underlies the mutability of specific political and historical events. Unamuno argues that traditional historiography has not sufficiently acknowledged the legitimacy of *intrahistoria* as an object of study. He asserts the importance of the phenomenon for the study of nationhood and nationalism, as it is the most powerful adhesive force binding a people through time and space. At the same time, because of the emotional, unconscious character of much intrahistorical experience, it transcends geography or ethnicity. For Unamuno, *intrahistoria* is nothing less than the basis of a common humanity. Gayana Jurkevich notes that *intrahistoria* has affinities with Carl Gustav Jung's roughly contemporaneous concept of the "collective unconscious." In the essays collected in *En torno al casticismo* he also discusses Spanish identity, the notion of a Spanish authenticity or purity, and the role of tradition, land, and literary culture in the formation of nation. Although he admits that people are shaped by their particular landscapes and traditions, he is concerned to seek an unchanging human universality beneath such local differences. There is an underlying commonality of knowledge and experience, even if it cannot be experienced or apprehended directly; given this commonality, the notion of *casticismo* (pure or authentic Spanishness), can and should assimilate ethnic and cultural differences. Unamuno argues that Spain should not seek to close itself off from progressive outside influence, or "Europeización," but should seek to be shaped by, and to shape, its neighbors.

The only historical novel Unamuno ever wrote, *Paz en la guerra* recounts the impact of the Second Carlist War of 1872 to 1876 on the inhabitants of the Basque Vizcaya region, from the besieged city of Bilbao to the Carlist guerrillas in the mountains. Unlike his subsequent fiction, this work shares several formal features with the nineteenth-century realist novel: it is set in a specific time and place and relates the experiences of several characters rather than centering on those of a single protagonist. Nevertheless, the novel is not merely a realist historical text: the characterization of two of the major figures, the young Carlist volunteer Ignacio Iturriondo and the studious Pachico Zabalbide, focuses on the complexities of male identity formation. War is a

*Unamuno at age twenty (from* Paz en la guerra, *edited by Francisco Caudet, 1999; Strozier Library, Florida State University)*

metaphorical as well as an actual conflict as both characters have to fight interior battles during their transition to adulthood.

Unamuno is also concerned in the novel to represent the *intrahistoria* of the Basques, which is an important emotional bulwark to the characters damaged by war. At the end of the novel Pedro Antonio Iturriondo, a veteran of the first Carlist conflict, has lost his wife, son, and livelihood; but the familiar, unchanging rituals of the Catholic Communion, at once privately felt and collective, provide him and others with great succor:

recojidos todos, soñolientos muchos, repetían las salutaciones marianas, sin parar la atención en ellas, por máquina, rumiando mentalmente cada uno sus cosas propias, sus preocupaciones domésticas . . . puesta la intención en el piadoso ejercicio y dejando vagar la mente. De aquella plegaria común, entretejida con las humildes preocupaciones de la vida de cada una, de aquella vaga música espiritual, a la que ponían sendas letras propias, brotaba íntimo efluvio de recogimiento, perfume de fraternidad de humildes y de sencillos.

(all were quiet; many were sleepy. They repeated the Ave Marias without paying attention to them, automat-

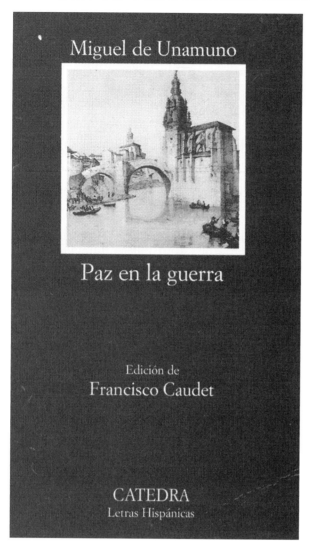

Miguel de Unamuno

Paz en la guerra

Edición de
Francisco Caudet

CATEDRA
Letras Hispánicas

*Paperback cover for a 1999 edition of Unamuno's first book (Peace in War), originally published in 1897, a novel about Basque fighters coming of age during the Second Carlist War of 1872 to 1876 (Strozier Library, Florida State University)*

ically, each congregant ruminating on his or her own thoughts, own domestic preoccupations . . . intentions fixed on the holy ritual, but minds wandering. Out of that common prayer, interwoven with the humble worries of life, out of that vague spiritual music, to which each added his or her own words, arose an intimate core of absorption, an essence of the fraternity of simple, humble people.)

This dynamic interweaving of the personal with the collective and of the vicissitudes of history with an unchanging transcendent humanity are central features of *Paz en la guerra*. The concern with the interior life and subjectivity of the characters, the perspectivism of the plural foci, and the engagement with history and nation demonstrate affinities both with broad currents of Euro-

pean modernism and with specifically Spanish debates about modernity, nationalism, and state. Although the novel is in some ways uncharacteristic of Unamuno's subsequent fiction, the attempt to transcend specific time and place, the dialectical interaction of social formations and individual agency, and the representation of the struggle for an adult self prefigure major preoccupations in his later work.

In 1897 Unamuno's infant son, Raimundo, was left severely disabled by meningitis. His anguish over his son, who died in 1903, contributed to a severe emotional crisis Unamuno suffered during this period. After overcoming its worst effects, he resumed religious observance and moderated his skepticism about Christian doctrines. Nevertheless, his attitude to Christianity remained ambivalent throughout his life. A private journal Unamuno kept during this crisis was published posthumously in 1970 as *Diario íntimo* (Intimate Diary; translated as *The Private World*, 1984).

Unamuno contrasted the "*ovíparo*" (oviparous) conception of *Paz en la guerra* with the "*vivíparo*" (viviparous) nature of his subsequent fiction. This contrast is most fully explored in his articles "De vuelta" (1902, On My Return) and "A lo que salga" (1904, Letting It Flow), both of which are collected in his *Obras completas* (1950–1959, Complete Works). An "oviparous" work is painstakingly predetermined, empirically researched, and written according to preexisting axioms or conclusions; a "viviparous" work comes into existence in a more improvised, "organic," and unpredictable manner. Unamuno's second novel, *Amor y pedagogía* (1902, Love and Pedagogy), is a contemporary tragicomedy. Despite his desire to conduct his life on a purely rational basis, Avito Carrascal falls in love with and marries the instinctive and romantic Marina. He raises and educates their son, Apolodoro, according to scientific methods in order to produce a genius, while Marina attempts to counteract Avito's severe rationalism. This dichotomous upbringing produces a confused, vulnerable, and socially inept adolescent. Although Avito enlists the aid of another pedagogical "expert," Don Fulgencio Entreambosmares, who champions the humanities over science, Apolodoro commits suicide after the novel he writes meets critical indifference and the woman he loves rejects him. Apolodoro's sister, the sickly Rosa, whom Avito did not consider a suitable candidate to be made into a genius, dies shortly before her brother, apparently of anemia despite Avito's last-minute attempts to cure her scientifically.

The tragedy of the work is mitigated by the characterizations. None of the characters is portrayed realistically; Avito and Fulgencio, in particular, are parodic embodiments of contemporary educational fads. The realism and affective capacity of the novel are also undermined by the playfulness of the various addenda to the work. The first edition included a preface in which Unamuno genially anticipates such criticisms of the faults of the novel as the wrongheadedness of the satire, the crude characterizations, and the careless style. He also specifies that the novel is intended for genuine "readers," rather than for those who buy books as decorative accessories for their homes and demand a standard size for their bookshelves. In an epilogue he says that his publisher has requested that, for marketing reasons, the novel should be exactly two hundred pages long. Unamuno laments the difficulty of this task at considerable length before reaching the requisite number of pages by appending a whimsical pseudo-scientific treatise on the study of origami birds. In a 1934 edition Unamuno adds an additional combined "prologue-epilogue" and a second appendix discussing the sexes of origami birds.

The antipositivist satire, undermining of realist conventions, ludic ironizing, and mockery of the commodification of literature for new mass readerships in *Amor y pedagogía* are typical characteristics of European modernism. The novel also raises questions about determinism and agency as Apolodoro struggles to establish an autonomous identity in the face of his father's attempts to mold his personality and intellect, and his suicide appears to be, paradoxically, his most successful act of free will. Unamuno discusses the status of his characters as "marionettes" in the prologue. While the explicit treatment of issues of authority and authorship are also a hallmark of literary modernism, the prominence and complexity of these unresolved questions throughout Unamuno's fiction suggest a sustained engagement that is not simply reducible to a decentering of political power or a questioning of the claims of religion in late modernity.

Unamuno's engagement with Spanishness, history, and identity in *Paz en la guerra* and the articles collected in *En torno al casticismo* allied him with the so-called Generación del 98 (Generation of 1898): a small, loose, heterogeneous group of essayists, poets, journalists, and novelists whose highly diverse output was, in part, a cultural response to the political decadence of late-nineteenth-century Spain that culminated in the *"Desastre"* (Disaster)—the Spanish-American War of 1898, in which Spain lost its last colonies. Introspective and often focused on Castile, the work of the Generación del 98 was bound together by a concern to examine Spain and Spanishness, sometimes nostalgically, sometimes critically. Their nonfiction often uses medical terminology to diagnose the metaphorical national "illnesses" that, in their opinion, led Restoration Spain to be mired in economic and social backwardness, corruption, and complacency. Various

political, social, and cultural cures are prescribed. A key concern of the Generación del 98 is the need for national *"regeneración"* (regeneration). Unamuno collaborated with Angel Ganivet to produce four epistolary articles outlining their respective views on the Spanish nation and its future possibilities. Published in 1898, the articles were collected in 1912 as *El porvenir de España* (The Future of Spain). Jo Labanyi argues that the Generación del 98 attempted to suppress awareness of the regionalist movements that had gained momentum in Catalonia, Galicia, and the Basque country: "By privileging the landscape of Castile as an image of the national soul, the 1898 writers are forging (in every sense of the word) a new brand of nationalist sentiment which proposes a supposed geographic uniformity as a way of naturalizing a belief in the need for cultural uniformity."

In 1900 Unamuno was appointed to the rectorship of the University of Salamanca and to the chair of Spanish and Latin philology. In 1905 he was awarded the Cross of the Order of Alfonso XII in recognition of his services to literature. He maintained his political and social commentaries in the press and became a renowned speaker at the Ateneo in Madrid. Notorious for his vocal hostility to the monarchy of Alfonso XIII, he was also highly critical of conservative clergy in Salamanca and Madrid.

During summer vacations Unamuno traveled widely around Spain, publishing his impressions in *Paisajes* (1902, Landscapes), *De mi país: Descripciones, relatos y artículos de costumbres* (1903, From My Country: Descriptions, Accounts and Customs), and *Por tierras de Portugal y de España* (1911, In the Lands of Spain and Portugal), as well as in national and local newspapers. In these years he also brought out four volumes of collected essays and articles on social, cultural, and religious questions: *Tres ensayos: Adentro! La ideocracia; La fe* (1900, Three Essays: Within! Ideocracy; Faith), *Mi religión y otros ensayos breves* (1910; My Religion and Other Brief Essays; translated as *Perplexities and Paradoxes,* 1945), *Soliloquios y conversaciones* (1911, Soliloquies and Conversations), and *Contra esto y aquello* (1912, Against This and That). He also published two volumes of often intensely personal and lyrical poetry, *Poesías* (1907, Poems) and *Rosario de sonetos líricos* (1911, Rosary of Lyrical Sonnets); and a memoir, *Recuerdos de niñez y de mocedad* (1908, Memories of Childhood and of Adolescence). In 1905 appeared *Vida de Don Quijote y Sancho según Miguel de Cervantes Saavedra, explicada y comentada* (translated as *The Life of Don Quixote and Sancho according to Miguel de Cervantes Saavedra, Expounded with Comment,* 1927), a rereading and rewriting of the Cervantes novel; Unamuno also uses *Don Quixote* as the basis for an examination of such issues as existence,

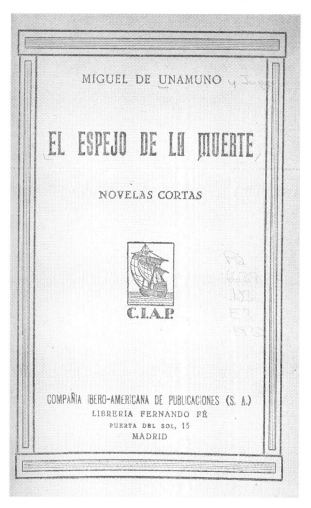

*Title page for a 1930 edition of Unamuno's 1913 collection of stories (The Mirror of Death: Short Fictions), in which parenthood is a major theme (Thomas Cooper Library, University of South Carolina)*

human life, Unamuno argues, arises from the irreconcilability of humankind's hunger for immortality with its certainty of death. The tension produces existential agony. The only solution is for each individual to "create" himself or herself and to seek immortality by influencing others. Unamuno also discusses how fame, religious faith, and personality are connected with the tragic sense of life.

Unamuno published no fiction between 1902 and 1913, although he completed the first draft of *Niebla* in 1907. He devoted much of his time to study of ancient and modern history, the new discipline of psychology, natural science, and Catholic and Protestant theology. In addition to the languages he had learned at the University of Madrid, he was able to read and write French, Italian, Portuguese, and English. He had a reading knowledge of other languages, including Danish, which he taught himself so that he could read the works of the forerunner of existentialist philosophy, Kierkegaard.

A collection of twenty-six short stories, *El espejo de la muerte* (The Mirror of Death), appeared in 1913. Parenthood is prominent in the pieces, and the theme of impotent anguish in the face of filial suffering is continued from *Paz en la guerra* and *Amor y pedagogía*. In the title story the hopelessness and insubstantiality felt by a young woman, Matilde, are manifested as an inability to eat. She is engaged to a man she loves, and there is no apparent reason for her feelings. Her mother is powerless to help and must watch her daughter become dangerously thin. Abandoned by her fiancé, who is frustrated by her unidentified malady, Matilde believes that she is ignored by other men—perhaps, she thinks, from unconscious fear of her emaciation. This apparent neglect exacerbates her feelings of insubstantiality and leads her to commit suicide. The individual's existential need to be noticed and to leave a mark on others in order to fashion a self was a central argument in *Del sentimiento trágico de la vida*. A happier resolution of this need is reached in "El sencillo Don Rafael: Cazador y tresillista" (The Simple Don Rafael: Hunter and Cardplayer). The aging bachelor Don Rafael leads a sterile, passive life until, by chance, he becomes first a surrogate father and then a real one. At the end of the story he dies peacefully, secure in the knowledge that he has left a lasting human legacy in the form of his ten children. Hermetic, twin-like relationships, whether amorous or fraternal, are featured in the stories "El semejante" (The Similar One), "Al correr los años" (With the Passing of the Years), "El amor que asalta" (Overwhelming Love), and "Las tijeras" (The Odd Couple). In these relationships the "other" may act as an existential mirror allowing the self to trace its own contours but is never sufficient to rescue the self from

personal identity, religious faith, and the relationship of author and character. The premiere of his first play, *La esfinge* (The Sphinx), took place in Gran Canaria in 1909; two further plays, *La difunta* (The Deceased Woman) and *El pasado que vuelve* (The Past That Returns), were staged the following year in Madrid and Salamanca, respectively. The reasons for Unamuno's increased productivity seem to have been partly economic: his academic salary was modest, and he and his wife had seven surviving children by 1900. By 1916 two more children had been born, and the family was complete.

In 1912 Unamuno published his major philosophical essay, *Del sentimiento trágico de la vida* (translated as *The Tragic Sense of Life in Men and Peoples,* 1921), which crystallizes some of the problems that had preoccupied him in earlier works. The tragedy underlying all

solitude, yearning, or death. The theme of the double became important in Unamuno's fiction over the next two decades. Not all of the stories in the collection share these preoccupations. "¡Viva la introyección!" (Long Live Introjection!), for example, is a satire of the ailing Restoration constitutional settlement. Politicians create a demand for a radical new order based on the people's right to an undefined "introyección." The new order is instituted by a popular revolution, and the story closes with an expectant member of the public wondering, "Y ahora bien; ¿qué es eso de introyección y con qué se come?" (Now then, what *is* this introjection, and what does one eat it with?). The final story, "Y va de cuento" (Let Me Tell You a Story), is a whimsical metafictional conceit that calls to mind the playful prologues and epilogues of *Amor y pedagogía*.

Unamuno continued to contribute political articles to the national press and to make speeches criticizing the government and the monarchy but rejected suggestions that he run for the senate, refusing to be identified with any group. When Spain declared neutrality in World War I, Unamuno, who, like many liberal intellectuals, supported the Allied cause, was not reticent in attacking the government's position, which was more sympathetic to Germany than its official stance suggested. In response he was removed from the university rectorship in 1914 on a transparently thin pretext. Though he retained the chair of Spanish and Latin philology, it was a humiliating demotion. Protests were held in Madrid, one of them led by the philosopher and cultural commentator José Ortega y Gassett.

Also in 1914 Unamuno's third novel, the structurally complex *Niebla,* was published; it is his most celebrated work of fiction. The well-educated and financially comfortable but passive and indecisive Augusto Pérez meets a piano teacher, Eugenia Domingo, and convinces himself that he is in love with her; the relationship gives his life purpose. He courts her clumsily, offering to pay her mortgage so that she can give up teaching, which she hates. Eugenia, who is already engaged, rejects Augusto's advances, then consents to marry him, only to abandon him shortly before the wedding to elope with her original fiancé. Shattered, Augusto decides to commit suicide. First, however, he travels to Salamanca to consult the writer, teacher, and philosopher Miguel de Unamuno, who explains that, as a fictional character, Augusto has no free will and cannot make the decision to kill himself: only the author can determine his fate. In his first truly assertive act Augusto challenges Unamuno's authority, arguing that fictional characters can be more real than their authors, achieving greater fame and living on through history; he cites Don Quixote as an example. Angered, Unamuno decides that he will kill Augusto in a manner

of his own choosing; Augusto remains determined to kill himself. Augusto does die at the end of the novel, but whether as a result of suicide or authorial homicide remains unclear. Further structural complexity is added by a prologue purportedly written by an unknown novelist, Victor Goti, who suggests that Unamuno's wishes were successfully resisted by Augusto. A threatening "post-prologue" by Unamuno counters Goti's interpretation and asserts his authorial omnipotence.

*Niebla* includes a discussion of an alternative to the novel called the "nivola." Its qualities are not clearly defined but seem to be the opposite of those of the conventional novel; for this reason *nivola* has been translated as "anti-novel" or "un-novel." Unamuno, keen to avoid what he saw as reductive taxonomies, used the largely undefined term *nivola* to refer to several of his longer prose narratives. Like *Amor y pedagogía,* but to a greater extent, *Niebla* undermines key tenets of the nineteenth-century realist novel; it displays many of the characteristics of high literary modernism, and the conceptual audacity of the plot allows it simultaneously to be an unhappy love story, a novel about existence and identity in an alienating world, and an antirealist text that parades its own fictionality. It also examines the complex relationships between language and ontology.

The semantic richness of *Niebla* has yielded a correspondingly rich critical response. David G. Turner, Carlos Blanco Aguinaga, Frances Wyers, Martin Nozick, and Paul R. Olson have explored the author figure as a trope for a determining causality in human life. No consensus exists, however, on whether this figure represents God, blind fate, parental influence, or environment. The nature of the existential "mist" that surrounds Augusto, clouding his ability to understand the purpose (or author) of his life, also remains uncertain. Turner argues that it represents both the annihilation threatening Augusto and his vague unconscious existence before he attains a greater degree of self-awareness and challenges his "author." Mario J. Valdés, Alison Sinclair, and Nicholas Round have examined the importance of language in the construction of subjectivity and reality for the characters in *Niebla.* For Valdés, Unamuno's exploration of the alienating effects of language anticipate the psychoanalytic work of Lacan by at least fifty years. Sinclair, Alexander A. Parker, and Geoffrey Ribbans have attended to questions of gender and sexuality, particularly to the way the novel questions the representation of "woman" as a homogenized collective "other" to Augusto. Thomas Franz and Malcolm K. Read argue for a political reading of the novel. Franz notes that the class relations of the characters parallel the ontological uncertainties and conflicts and concludes that "there is no material solution to the class conflict presented beneath the foregrounded philosoph-

*Paperback cover for Unamuno's celebrated 1914 work (translated as*
Mist [Niebla]: A Tragicomic Novel, *1928), in which a passive
and indecisive character is jilted by his fiancée and then engages
in a debate with his creator, Unamuno, over his right to
commit suicide (University of Georgia Library)*

ical/metafictional focus, but rather a surrender to an existentially structured discourse that posits the achievement of eternal life and social justice by means of a self-interested adherence to a co-created fiction or myth." Read interprets the politics of the text differently, arguing that the metafictional elements "preserve the notion of the work of art as something made and, accordingly, solicit the creative participation of the reader." Such participation, he maintains, counters the passivity and alienation resulting from capitalist consumer production. *Niebla* was published in three Spanish editions and translated into eleven languages during Unamuno's lifetime.

Unamuno's next novel, *Abel Sánchez: Una historia de pasión* (1917; Abel Sánchez: A Story of Passion; translated as "Abel Sánchez," 1956), also widely translated, is structurally much simpler and substantially shorter

than *Niebla*. It articulates some of the anxieties about the self-other relationship voiced in *El espejo de la muerte* and *Del sentimiento trágico de la vida*. Based partly on the biblical story of Cain and Abel, the novel recounts the intertwined fates of Joaquín Monegro and Abel Sánchez, childhood friends whose adult relationship is destroyed by betrayal and envy. Despite their reciprocal antipathy, Joaquín, a doctor, cares for Abel when the latter becomes seriously ill; he also provides a public encomium of Abel's artistic achievements. Abel's son becomes Joaquín's assistant and marries Joaquín's daughter. Envy flares again after the birth of a grandson: the two men argue over the child's affections, and Joaquín starts to strangle Abel. He removes his hands from Abel's throat almost immediately, but Abel dies of a heart attack. While he hates Abel passionately, Joaquín's behavior, thoughts, relationships, and sense of self are determined by this adversarial "other." Round, Sinclair, and A. Carlos Longhurst point out that the protagonists may be read as constituting complementary and conflicting or mirror aspects of a single character's subjectivity. Viewed this way, the text represents in the starkest terms the self's dependence on the other for its own realization and the threat to the possibility of selfhood that the other represents. Sinclair also outlines two possible historicizing readings. In the first, she notes that Unamuno's novel, like other works by the Generación del 98, presents Cain (Joaquín) in Byronic terms as a creative rebel figure in contrast with the submissive and jejune Abel. Cain, like the Generación del 98, embodies both the atavistic and the new; he is a destructive figure who also forges a new civilization. The novel can thus be read as a comment on the ambivalent nature of the Generación del 98's political project. In Sinclair's second reading, Joaquín represents Spain and Abel represents Latin America, allowing the reader to perceive "beneath the complex attitudes of '98 Spain to the thriving Latin American colonies, the mixture of envy and yet fierce retention of a feeling of superiority that characterizes the Cain of *Abel Sánchez*." The reworking of the Cain-Abel relationship as an illustration of the problematics of selfhood reappears in the 1932 play *El otro* (The Other) and, more obliquely, in the novella "Tulio Montalbán y Julio Macedo" (1920, Tulio Montalbán and Julio Macedo), which was dramatized as *Sombras de sueño* (Shadowy Dreams) in 1930.

After his removal as rector, Unamuno's criticisms of what he saw as the increasing absolutism of Alfonso XIII and of obtuse, divisive government policy became increasingly trenchant. Spain's neutrality in World War I had initially bolstered its economy, but by 1917 the country was in a precarious state fiscally and politically. Inflation soared; divisions between Left and Right were becoming more polarized; labor movements were increasingly militant in their demands for better working conditions and more rights; and new nationalist movements in the Basque country and Catalonia challenged centralized government. Civil unrest grew; it was violently suppressed. The two-party Restoration parliamentary system came under intolerable strain. Some constitutional rights were suspended, and the king temporarily dissolved the Cortes (Parliament). The situation then deteriorated even further as poverty, unrest, and military intervention grew yet more acute.

In 1920, after the publication of a particularly deprecatory article in a Valencia newspaper, Unamuno was arraigned on charges of defaming the king and sentenced to sixteen years' imprisonment. The sentence was widely condemned in Spain and abroad. Unamuno was paroled pending appeal; but his freedom of movement was curtailed, and he lived under threat of the sentence for a considerable time. He was nominated that same year as a parliamentary candidate by Basque republican and Madrid socialist constituencies. Although he did not reject the nominations, Unamuno refused to canvass for votes; he stated that his electoral manifesto was to be found in his *Del sentimiento trágico de la vida* and *Vida de Don Quijote and Sancho según Miguel de Cervantes Saavedra*. He was not elected.

Between 1916 and 1918 a seven-volume collection of Unamuno's essays was published in one of several public gestures of solidarity from liberal circles following his removal from the rectorship. In 1918 his version of the Phaedra myth, *Fedra,* premiered in Madrid. Unamuno was working on several literary projects, and in 1920 he published three of them. The novella "Tulio Montalbán y Julio Macedo" appeared in the mass-market periodical *La novela corta* (The Short Novel). *El Cristo de Velázquez* (translated as *The Christ of Velázquez,* 1951), a long poem written in tender address to Christ during the last stages of his Passion, also appeared. Unamuno's reading of Diego Velázquez's renowned painting *Cristo Crucificado* (1632, Christ on the Cross) is lyrical and precise.

The third work Unamuno published in 1920 was *Tres novelas ejemplares y un prólogo* (translated as *Three Exemplary Novels and a Prologue,* 1930). The prologue is partly a restatement of his ideas about the relationship of literary characters to their authors. Here, however, Unamuno places greater emphasis on the will ("*querer ser*") as a component of identity than he has previously, and the three stories illustrate the triumph of the will over biological, social, and ethical limitations and barriers. In "Dos madres" (translated as "Two Mothers") a childless widow persuades her lover to marry another woman and give their firstborn child to her. In "El marqués de Lumbría" (translated as "The Marquis of Lum-

bría") the protagonist succeeds in becoming recognized as the mother of the heir to the Lumbría estate by seducing her sister's husband and bearing his child illegitimately. The previously recognized heir, still a child himself, is supplanted without resistance from his father. In "Nada menos que todo un hombre" (Nothing Less Than All Man; translated as "A He Man") a man inspires love in a woman who has been forced to marry him. These stories develop some of the preoccupations of Unamuno's previous fiction, including the rivalry and envy of *Abel Sánchez* and the prominence of parenthood and complex struggles for power of *Niebla* and *Amor y pedagogía.* But they also represent a departure. In two of the stories the rivalry and power struggles are between female, rather than male, antagonists. The apparently strong and invulnerable characters are not haunted by a deficient sense of autonomy or reality, and the authenticity of proxy identities is explored. The triumph of the will, in all cases at a high human and ethical price, contrasts notably with texts such as *Niebla* and *Amor y pedagogía,* where the assertion of agency results in self-annihilation.

These issues are developed further in Unamuno's next novel, *La Tía Tula* (1921, Aunt Tula). Tula and Rosa are orphaned sisters. The dominant Tula adopts the role of surrogate mother to Rosa, and after she has prompted and overseen the marriage of Rosa and Ramiro, she becomes a zealous co-mother to their children. Tula insists that Rosa continue to have babies, even though she has become seriously debilitated by doing so, and she dies after giving birth again. Although Tula and Ramiro loved each other before Ramiro and Rosa's marriage, Tula rejects Ramiro's declarations of love after Rosa's death. The lonely Ramiro makes Manuela, the housemaid, pregnant; to their great humiliation, Tula compels them to marry and becomes proxy mother to their offspring. The cowed and miserable Manuela also dies after giving birth, and, following the death of Ramiro, Tula becomes the sole parent of all the children. Although at times tender and hugely self-sacrificing, Tula is also authoritarian, pitiless, perverse, and rigid. The motives for her complex behavior are not explained. The sheer force of Tula's willpower overcomes social and even biological obstacles, but at a high price both for her and those around her.

Sinclair points out that Tula's disgust at sexual relations, combined with her strong maternal instincts, may be read as an exaggerated embodiment of the traditional "ángel del hogar" (domestic angel), while Laura Hynes notes that she may also be seen as a radical protofeminist. Hynes, Ribbans, Longhurst, Carlos Feal, and Mary Lee Bretz argue that Tula is represented in a broadly positive light. Bretz concludes that Tula "is not

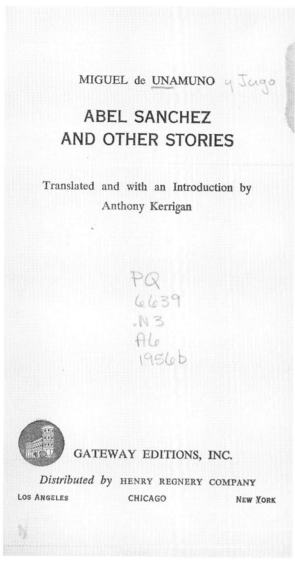

MIGUEL de UNAMUNO y Jugo

## ABEL SANCHEZ
## AND OTHER STORIES

Translated and with an Introduction by
Anthony Kerrigan

PQ
6639
.N3
A6
1956b

GATEWAY EDITIONS, INC.

*Distributed by* HENRY REGNERY COMPANY

LOS ANGELES          CHICAGO          NEW YORK

*Title page for a collection of translations of Unamuno's fiction. The title
work is the English version of his 1917 novel,* Abel Sánchez:
Una historia de pasión *(Abel Sánchez: A Story of Passion),
an updating of the biblical story of Cain and Abel (Thomas
Cooper Library, University of South Carolina).*

a fully realized model but an insinuation of a different and better social order."

Unamuno's female characters mostly exercise agency, power, and self-realization through proxy states. The maternal identity of Tula and of Raquel in "Dos madres" is not represented as less valid for not being biological or legal. Female characters are not subject to the ontological anguish and fear of lack of individuation that afflicts Augusto Pérez and Apolodoro Carrascal; indeed, several of Unamuno's female figures subjugate male characters ruthlessly. It is difficult to decide whether the female characters are protofeminists, gaining power wherever their limited opportunities allow them to, or whether they are merely less complex than the men and incapable of existential doubt. That women's strength appears achievable only at the cost of male subordination is a common anxiety in male writing of the period. Roberta Johnson and Lynette Seator read Unamuno's fiction as hostile to the burgeoning feminist movement in Spain in the first three decades of the twentieth century, while Feal, Hynes, and Bretz argue that his work challenges normative gender identities in various ways.

In 1921 Unamuno became dean of the faculty of philosophy and letters and acting rector of the University of Salamanca. In 1922 he published *Andanzas y visiones españolas* (Spanish Adventures and Visions), a collection of meditations on his travels around Spain since 1911. As the political situation deteriorated, Unamuno maintained his public criticism of Alfonso XIII's simultaneous authoritarianism and weak government. The king, wounded by these attacks, met with Unamuno, but the breach between the two men was irreconcilable. As the year progressed, the parliamentary system began to collapse; it was too weak to withstand the strain of the assassination of Prime Minister Eduardo Dato in 1921, a humiliating defeat of the armed forces in Morocco, and growing labor and republican unrest. A series of short-term governments and coalitions were unable to stabilize the country. In 1923 a coup d'état resulted in a military dictatorship under General Manuel Primo de Rivera. Unamuno continued his criticism of the king and added a further target: the unconstitutionality and tyrannical nature of Primo de Rivera's government and what Unamuno saw as its fatuous leadership. In February 1924, after Unamuno delivered a particularly censorious speech in Bilbao, he was stripped of his university positions and salary and sentenced to internal exile on the volcanic Canary Island of Fuerteventura. The loss of his salary meant that Unamuno's family could not accompany him in exile. Despite international condemnation of the punishment, Unamuno did not appeal his sentence and remained in Fuerteventura until the beginning of July, when he accepted an offer to help him escape to France. Coincidentally, he was pardoned by the dictatorship as part of an amnesty for dissidents. Unamuno learned of his permission to return home when he was en route to France; he decided to continue his journey, preferring self-imposed exile to any sort of dealings with the dictatorship. Exile would also allow him to wage verbal war on the regime with impunity. He settled in Paris at the end of the month.

Unamuno's only published work in 1924 was a curious collection titled *Teresa: Rimas de un poeta desconocido, presentadas y presentado por Miguel de Unamuno* (Teresa: Poems by an Unknown Poet, Presented by Miguel de

Unamuno). Another volume of poems appeared in 1925: *De Fuerteventura a París: Diario íntimo de confinamiento y destierro vertido en sonetos* (From Fuerteventura to Paris: An Intimate Diary of Confinement and Exile Cast in Sonnets). It included occasional verse about Spanish politics and history, meditations on the landscape and culture of Fuerteventura, and poems on exile and loneliness.

Shortly after his arrival in Paris, Unamuno had been commissioned to contribute an essay to a series of books on Christianity. Translated into French by Unamuno's friend Jean Cassou, the work appeared in 1925 as *L'agonie du Christianisme;* the original Spanish version, *La agonía del cristianismo,* was published in 1931. The ambiguity of the title–*agonía* can mean "death throes," as well as "struggle"–is deliberate. The essay is a reflection on Unamuno's complex relationship to Christianity both as an organized religion and as an intimate personal experience. He admitted that the work had been written in a febrile haste, and not all of his arguments cohere neatly. The essay rehearses further his diagnosis in *Del sentimiento trágico de la vida* of humanity's need for immortality and discusses some of the complexities of the relationships between religion and nation. It also includes harsh criticisms of the Jesuit order. Unamuno returns repeatedly to the irreconcilability of the aims of Christianity and society; yet, in his concluding remarks he notes that contemporary Spain and Christianity are in a state of connected "agonía."

Although Unamuno had been feted on his arrival in Paris, he was not easily integrated into French intellectual or literary life and had only a few friends in Paris. He lived alone; his health was not robust; and he despaired over whether he would ever be able to return to Spain. In August 1925, no longer able to endure the isolation and homesickness he felt in Paris, he traveled to Hendaye on the French-Spanish border. The area was similar to the region of Unamuno's birth, and he could see his native country across the frontier. He remained in Hendaye to await the downfall of Primo de Rivera, who was facing increasingly organized and effective dissent. The premiere of *Todo un hombre* (All Man), a dramatic adaptation of Unamuno's 1920 novella "Nada menos que todo un hombre," was staged in Madrid in December. Although Unamuno's name was removed from the theater posters, many of his friends and supporters attended as a gesture of solidarity and protest.

In 1927 Unamuno published *Cómo se hace una novela* (How to Write a Novel), a complex account of his first year outside Spain and a commentary on a novel he intended to write about his exile. Embedded within the discussion of this unwritten novel is an account of yet another novel, which, when read by the protagonist

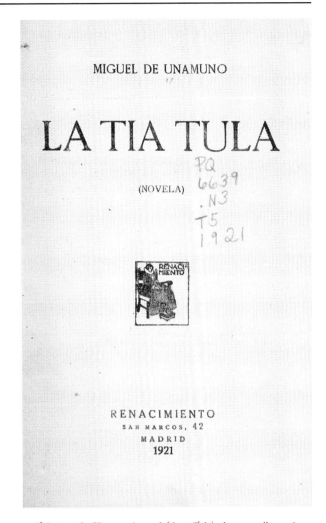

Title page for Unamuno's novel (Aunt Tula) about a well-meaning but domineering woman who ruins the lives of her sister, the sister's husband, and the husband's second wife
(University of Alabama Library)

of the first novel, will lead to his death. The book includes a profile of Unamuno by Cassou and a response by Unamuno. In 1928 Unamuno published *Romancero del destierro* (Ballads of Exile) and began working on an intimate diary in verse in which he records his day-to-day reflections on his exile, on Spain, and on identity and immortality. The "diary" formed the mainstay of Unamuno's literary activity for the rest of 1928 and all of 1929. Published posthumously in 1953 as *Cancionero: Diario poético* (Songbook: Poetic Diary; excerpts translated as *The Last Poems of Miguel de Unamuno,* 1974), the collection comprises an extraordinary 1,755 poems.

At the beginning of 1930 Primo de Rivera resigned and went into exile. Unamuno returned to Spain almost immediately and was received as a hero. He toured major cities, giving speeches on his experi-

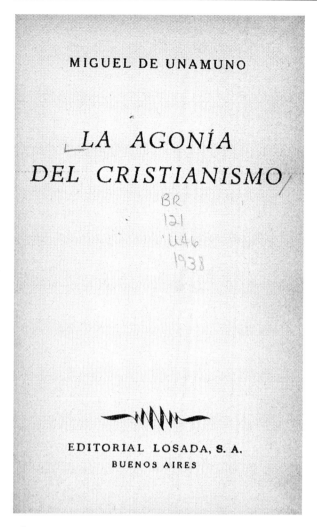

MIGUEL DE UNAMUNO

*LA AGONÍA
DEL CRISTIANISMO*

BR
121
.U46
1933

EDITORIAL LOSADA, S. A.
BUENOS AIRES

*Title page for a later edition of Unamuno's book-length essay (translated
as* The Agony of Christianity, *1928), originally published in
French translation in 1925 and in the original Spanish in 1931,
about the irreconcilability of the aims of Christianity and society
(Thomas Cooper Library, University of South Carolina)*

apart. The protagonist's anguish is not alleviated by murdering his brother, though: not only do the other characters still not know which twin he is, but his own identity has mutated. He is no longer "himself" but a nameless "Otro" (Other) who carries his dead twin inside. There is no escape from his lack of individuation.

In 1933 Unamuno published his last book of fiction, *San Manuel Bueno, mártir, y tres historias más* (St. Manuel the Good, Martyr, and Three other Stories). Written in 1930, just after Unamuno's return to Spain, the title novella is one of his best-known works. "San Manuel Bueno, mártir" (translated as "Saint Emmanuel the Good, Martyr," 1956) is narrated by Angela Carballino, a former parishioner of Don Manuel, the priest of the isolated village of Valverde de Lucerna. Angela, now in late middle age, recalls the influence the priest had on Valverde. His simple, tireless kindnesses and his material and pastoral support of the villagers led them to revere him as a saint, and news of his goodness spread beyond the village. Angela, however, was privy to secrets that Don Manuel kept from the rest of the villagers: he was unable to believe in life after death and was tormented by thoughts of suicide. Helping the humble parishioners to find earthly happiness was his only distraction from his anguish. He did not share his doubts with his parishioners or advocate political rights or education for them because, he said, "La verdad . . . es acaso algo terrible, algo intolerable, algo mortal; la gente sencilla no podría vivir con ella" (The truth . . . is perhaps something terrible, something intolerable and mortal; simple folk would not be able to live with it). After Don Manuel's death, the processes necessary for his beatification begin. At the end of Angela's account, which she calls a "confesión" (confession), Unamuno explains that her manuscript was sent to him by an unknown reader.

The text is notable for its ethical and narrative ambiguity. Don Manuel may be seen as heroic and tragic: unlike previous protagonists assailed by existential doubt and anguish about mortality, Don Manuel attempts to put aside his own suffering to give succor to others. On the other hand, since he himself fears that the religious succor he offers is based on false premises, and since he is hostile to truth that may upset his parishioners, he may be seen as hypocritical or as perniciously paternalistic. Furthermore, Longhurst and Wyers have argued that Angela's reliability as narrator is questionable. Critics are divided between those, such as Jurkevich, Johnson, and Julián Marías, who place the story of Don Manuel's life at the narrative center of the story, and those, such as Blanco Aguinaga (1974), Stephen J. Summerhill, Reed Anderson, and Pamela Bacarisse, who argue that Angela's mediating presence

ence in exile, on Spain's history, and on the country's future civic responsibilities. He continued his criticisms of the king. He resumed his chair in Latin and Spanish philology at Salamanca and was made professor of history and comparative philology, as well. In 1931, after the declaration of the Second Republic and the abdication of Alfonso XIII, Unamuno regained his rectorship. He was also elected to the Republic's parliament, the Cortes Constituyentes. Although an independent, he was associated with the Republican bloc.

In 1932 *El otro* was staged in Madrid and published. A man is driven to kill his identical twin out of rivalry but also because he cannot endure being unindividuated from him; even those with whom he is most intimate, including his wife, cannot tell the two men

*Unamuno at his home, no. 4 Bordadores Street, Madrid (Collection of Cándido Ansede, Salamanca; from Margaret Thomas Rudd,*
The Lone Heretic: A Biography of Miguel de Unamuno y Jugo, *1963;*
*Thomas Cooper Library, University of South Carolina)*

as narrator places her at the heart of the novella. A significant strand of criticism represented by Blanco Aguinaga, Wyers, Antonio Sánchez Barbudo, and Arturo Barea views Don Manuel's story as an autobiographical allegory of Unamuno's struggle with religious belief or with the burden of political faith placed on him by his supporters during and after Primo de Rivera's dictatorship. These critics explore the extent to which the text may be read as an apology for political quietism or pessimism or as evidence of a liberal fear of revolution. In contrast, Ricardo Gullón and Anthony N. Zahareas read the work as questioning or criticizing the Catholic Church's politics in early-twentieth-century Spain.

Another story in the collection, "La novela de Don Sandalio, jugador de ajedrez" (The Novel of Don Sandalio, Chess Player), which is epistolary in form, is also of indeterminate narrative reliability, and the mystery surrounding the enigmatic and solitary Don Sandalio is not solved satisfactorily. The story marks a return to questions about the epistemology and ontol-

ogy of the "other" discussed in *Vida de Don Quijote y Sancho según Miguel de Cervantes Saavedra* and *Niebla*. The other two stories, "Un pobre hombre rico, o el sentimiento cómico de la vida" (A Poor Rich Man, or the Comic Sense of Life) and "Una historia de amor" (A Love Story), are markedly less complex. "Una historia de amor," written in 1911, may be read as a simple Christian exemplary text in which spiritual love, attained through suffering, provides true communion between a couple whose secular love had failed to fulfill them.

In 1932 and 1933 Unamuno played a key role in overseeing public instruction in the Republic, and he continued to deliver speeches on literature, history, education, and politics. In 1934 his play *El hermano Juan; o, El mundo es teatro: Vieja comedia nueva* (Brother Juan; or, The World Is a Theater: Old New Comedy) was published. Based loosely on the Don Juan myth, the play presents the Lothario as an insubstantial, passive, and sterile figure beset by fundamental existential doubts.

The drama reworks the familiar Unamunian questions about identity, fame, and literal and figurative parenthood.

In 1934 Unamuno's wife died, and he retired from the University of Salamanca. He was paid public homage by the university and the republic and granted the rectorship for life, and a professorship was created in his name. Unamuno used his final university lecture to denounce the danger of the dissolution of the Spanish state as divisions among political groupings placed parliamentary democracy under severe strain. After his retirement, his preoccupation with the possibility of a catastrophic national cleavage became more acute. Barea notes that he directed ever more bitter criticism against "every sort of slogan, Right or Left, against Marxism, against urban mass movements, and against the new generation of Europeanizers. More vehemently than ever he extolled the 'Spanishness of Spain.'"

Unamuno initially welcomed General Francisco Franco's insurgency in 1936 for its attempt to save what Unamuno called the "Christian civilization" of Spain. But he rapidly became disillusioned with Franco's Falangist forces and began to speak out against them. On 12 October 1936, Spain's national day, he publicly challenged General José Millán Astray, Franco's most trusted military strategist. As a result, he was again stripped of his rectorship and placed under house arrest. He died at home of a stroke on the last day of 1936.

Miguel de Unamuno's contribution to twentieth-century Spanish culture was huge. He was in the vanguard of modernist experiment and reinvigoration of the possibilities of fictional narrative. His intellectual bravery allowed him to confront the most complex questions about existence and identity. If he tended to resort to paradox and inconclusiveness, it was a measure of the difficulty of the issues he was discussing and of his ethically informed desire to maintain debate and favor dynamic interrogation over premature conclusion. His intellectual courage was matched by his personal bravery and stamina. He played a key role in shaping the literary and political landscape of his country, and his legacy seems sure to continue well into the future.

## Letters:

*Epistolario y escritos complementarios: Unamuno-Maragall,* edited by Dionisio Ridruejo and Pedro Laín Entralgo (Madrid: Seminarios y Ediciones, 1971);

*Cartas 1903–1933,* edited by Luis de Zulueta and Carmen de Zulueta (Madrid: Aguilar, 1972);

*Cartas inéditas de Miguel de Unamuno,* edited by Sergio Fernández Larrain (Santiago, Chile: Zig-Zag, 1972);

*Epistolario completo Ortega-Unamuno,* edited by Laureano Robles and Antonio Ramos Gascón (Madrid: El Arquero, 1987);

*Epistolario inédito,* 2 volumes, edited by Robles (Madrid: Espasa-Calpe, 1991);

*El epistolario (1923–1935): José Bergamín–Unamuno,* edited by Nigel Dennis (Valencia: Pre-Textos, 1993);

*Unamuno y el Perú: Epistolario, 1902–1934,* edited by Wilfredo Kapsoli Escudero (Salamanca: Universidad de Salamanca, 2002);

*Unamuno: Cartas de Alemania,* edited by Pedro Ribas and Fernando Hermida de Blas (Madrid: Fondo de Cultura Economica, 2002).

## Bibliography:

Pelayo H. Fernández, *Bibliografía crítica de Miguel de Unamuno (1888–1975)* (Madrid: Porrúa Turanzas, 1976).

## Biographies:

J. B. Trend, *Unamuno, a Biographical Study* (Cambridge: R. I. Severs, 1951);

Margaret Thomas Rudd, *The Lone Heretic: A Biography of Miguel de Unamuno y Jugo* (New York: Gordian Press, 1963);

Emilio Salcedo, *Vida de don Miguel* (Salamanca: Anaya, 1964).

## References:

Reed Anderson, "The Narrative Voice in Unamuno's *San Manuel Bueno, mártir,*" *Hispanófila,* 50 (1974): 67–76;

Pamela Bacarisse, "Will the Story Tell? Unamuno's *San Manuel Bueno, mártir,*" in *Carnal Knowledge: Essays on the Flesh, Sex and Sexuality in Hispanic Letters and Film,* edited by Bacarisse (Pittsburgh: Ediciones Tres Rios, 1995), pp. 55–72;

Armand F. Baker, "Unamuno and the Religion of Uncertainty," *Hispanic Review,* 58 (1990): 37–56;

Arturo Barea, *Unamuno* (London: Bowyer & Bowyer, 1953);

R. E. Batchelor, *Unamuno–Novelist: A European Perspective* (Oxford: Dolphin Bookshop, 1972);

Carlos Blanco Aguinaga, *El Unamuno contemplativo* (Barcelona: Laia, 1975);

German Bleiberg and E. Inman Fox, eds., *Spanish Thought and Letters in the Twentieth Century: An International Symposium to Commemorate the Centenary of the Birth of Miguel de Unamuno* (Nashville, Tenn.: Vanderbilt University Press, 1966)—includes Geoffrey Ribbans, "The Structure of Unamuno's *Niebla,*" pp. 395–406;

Mary Lee Bretz, *Encounters across Borders: The Changing Visions of Spanish Modernism* (Lewisburg, Pa. & London: Bucknell University Press/Associated University Presses, 2001);

Bretz, "The Role of Negativity in Unamuno's *La Tía Tula*," *Revista Canadiense de Estudios Hispánicos*, 18 (1993): 17–30;

Carlos Clavería, *Temas de Unamuno* (Madrid: Biblioteca Románica Hispánica, 1953);

Jesús Antonio Collado, *Kierkegaard y Unamuno: La existencia religiosa* (Madrid: Gredos, 1962);

Emilia Doyaga, *Unamuno y la mujer* (Newark, N.J.: Washington Irving, 1969);

Carlos Feal, "Nada menos que toda una mujer: 'La Tía Tula' de Unamuno," in *Estelas, Laberintos, Nuevas sendas: Unamuno. Valle Inclán. García Lorca. La guerra civil*, edited by Angel G. Loureiro (Barcelona: Anthropos, 1988), pp. 65–80;

David W. Foster, *Unamuno and the Novel as Expressionistic Conceit* (Hato Rey: Inter American University Press, 1973);

Arturo A. Fox, *El edipo en Unamuno y el espejo de Lacan* (Lewiston, N.Y.: Edwin Mellen Press, 2001);

Thomas Franz, "The Discourse of Class in *Niebla*," *Revista de Estudios Hispánicos,* 29 (1995): 521–539;

Manuel García Blanco, *Don Miguel de Unamuno y sus poesías: Estudio y antología de textos poéticos no incluidos en sus libros* (Salamanca: Universidad de Salamanca, 1954);

D. Gómez Molleda, ed., *Actas del congreso internacional Cincuentenario de Unamuno Universidad de Salamanca 10–20 diciembre 1986* (Salamanca: Universidad de Salamanca, 1989)–includes María Elena Bravo Guerreira, "Algunos aspectos del problema de la genericidad en *La Tía Tula* de Miguel de Unamuno," pp. 409–416;

Jacinto Grau, *Unamuno: La España de su tiempo* (Buenos Aires: PHAC, 1943);

Ricardo Gullón, *Autobiografías de Unamuno* (Madrid: Gredos, 1964);

Laura Hynes, "La Tía Tula: Forerunner of Radical Feminism," *Hispanófila*, 117 (1996): 45–54;

Paul Ilie, "Language and Cognition in Unamuno," *Revista Canadiense de Estudios Hispánicos*, 11 (1987): 289–314;

Ilie, *Unamuno: An Existential View of Self and Society* (Madison: University of Wisconsin Press, 1967);

Roberta Johnson, *Gender and Nation in the Spanish Modernist Novel* (Nashville, Tenn.: Vanderbilt University Press, 2003), pp. 31–44, 70–76, 80–83, 141–142, 159–170, 198–204;

Gayana Jurkevich, *The Elusive Self: Archetypal Approaches to the Novels of Miguel de Unamuno* (Columbia: University of Missouri Press, 1991);

Francisco La Rubia Prado, *Alegorías de la voluntad: Pensamiento orgánico, retorical y deconstrucción en la obra de Miguel de Unamuno* (Madrid: Prodhufi, 1996);

Jo Labanyi, "Nation, Narration, Naturalization: A Barthesian Critique of the 1898 Generation," in *New Hispanisms: Literature, Culture, Theory*, edited by Mark Millington and Paul Julian Smith (Ottawa: Dovehouse, 1994), pp. 127–149;

Allen Lacy, "Censorship and *Cómo de hace una novela*," *Hispanic Review,* 34 (1966): 317–324;

Lacy, *Miguel de Unamuno: The Rhetoric of Existence* (The Hague: Mouton, 1987);

Jesús María Lasagabáster, ed., *El teatro de Miguel de Unamuno* (San Sebastián: Facultad de Filosofía y Letras, Universidad de San Sebastián, 1987);

José María López-Marrón, *Unamuno y su camino a la "individualizacion"* (New York: Peter Lang, 1998);

Julián Marías, *Miguel de Unamuno* (Buenos Aires: Espasa-Calpe, 1950);

Juan Antonio Marichal, *El designio de Unamuno,* edited by Julia Cela (Madrid: Taurus, 2002);

Alejandro Martínez, *Lenguaje y dialogía en la obra de Miguel de Unamuno* (Madrid: Pliegos, 1998);

Gonzalo Navajas, *Miguel de Unamuno: Bipolaridad y síntesis ficcional: una lectura posmoderna* (Barcelona: PPU, 1988);

Martin Nozick, *Miguel de Unamuno: The Agony of Belief* (Princeton: Princeton University Press, 1971);

Paul R. Olson, *The Great Chiasmus: Word and Flesh in the Novels of Unamuno* (West Lafayette, Ind.: Purdue University Press, 2003);

Victor Ouimette, *Reason Aflame: Unamuno and the Heroic Will* (New Haven: Yale University Press, 1974);

Malcolm K. Read, *Language, Text, Subject: A Critique of Hispanism* (West Lafayette, Ind.: Purdue University Press, 1992), pp. 137–148;

Geoffrey Ribbans, "A New Look at *La Tía Tula*," *Revista Canadiense de Estudios Hispánicos*, 11, no. 2 (1986–1987): 403–420;

Nicholas Round, "The Tragic Sense of *Niebla*," in *Hispanic Studies in Honour of Geoffrey Ribbans,* special issue of *Bulletin of Hispanic Studies,* edited by Ann L. Mackenzie and Dorothy S. Severin (Liverpool: Liverpool University Press, 1992), pp. 171–183;

Round, ed., *Re-reading Unamuno* (Glasgow: University of Glasgow Department of Hispanic Studies, 1989);

Antonio Sánchez Barbudo, *Estudios sobre Unamuno y Machado* (Madrid: Guadarrama, 1959);

Sánchez Barbudo, ed., *Miguel de Unamuno: El escritor y la crítica* (Madrid: Taurus, 1974)–includes Alexander A. Parker, "En torno a la interpretación de *Niebla*," pp. 203–225, and Carlos Blanco Aguinaga, "Sobre la complejidad de *San Manuel Bueno, mártir*," pp. 273–296;

Lynette Seator, "Unamuno: The Body and the Myth," in *Reading the Social Body,* edited by Catherine B. Burroughs (Iowa City: University of Iowa Press, 1993), pp. 185–201;

Seator, "Women and Men in the Novels of Unamuno," *Kentucky Romance Quarterly,* 27 (1980): 39–55;

Alison Sinclair, "Definition as the Enemy of Self-Definition: A Commentary on the Role of Language in Unamuno's *Niebla,*" in *Words of Power: Essays in Honour of Alison Fairlie,* edited by Dorothy Gabe Coleman and Gillian Jondorf (Glasgow: University of Glasgow Publications in French Language and Literature, 1987), pp. 187–225;

Sinclair, *Uncovering the Mind: Unamuno, the Unknown and the Vicissitudes of Self* (Manchester, U.K.: Manchester University Press, 2001);

Robert C. Spires, *Beyond the Metafictional Mode: Directions in the Modern Spanish Novel* (Lexington: University of Kentucky Press, 1984), pp. 34–44;

Stephen J. Summerhill, "San Manuel Bueno mártir and the Reader," *Anales de la Literatura Contemporánea,* 10 (1985): 61–79;

David G. Turner, *Unamuno's Webs of Fatality* (London: Tamesis, 1974);

Manuel María Urrutia, *Evolución del pensamiento político de Unamuno* (Bilbao: Universidad de Deusto, 1997);

Mario J. Valdés, *Death in the Literature of Unamuno* (Urbana: University of Illinois Press, 1966);

Valdés, "Requiem for Augusto Pérez: Alterity, Alienation and Identity," *Revista de Estudios Hispánicos,* 29 (1995): 505–519;

Valdés and María Elena Valdés, *An Unamuno Source Book* (Toronto: University of Toronto Press, 1973);

Frances Wyers, *Miguel de Unamuno: The Contrary Self* (London: Tamesis, 1976);

Wyers, "Unamuno and the Death of the Author," *Hispanic Review,* 58 (1990): 325–346;

Anthony N. Zahareas, "Unamuno's Marxian Slip: Religion as Opium of the People," *Journal of the Midwest Language Association,* 17 (1984): 16–37;

María Zambrano, *Unamuno,* edited by Mercedes Gómez Blesa (Barcelona: Debate, 2003);

Iris M. Zavala, *Unamuno y el pensamiento dialógico* (Barcelona: Anthropos, 1991);

Zavala, *Unamuno y su teatro de conciencia* (Salamanca: Universidad de Salamanca, 1963).

**Papers:**

An archive of Miguel de Unamuno's papers is at the Casa-Museo Unamuno in Salamanca.

# Ramón del Valle-Inclán

*(28 October 1866 – 5 January 1936)*

Leda Schiavo
*University of Illinois at Chicago*

See also the Valle-Inclán entry in *DLB 134: Twentieth-Century Spanish Poets, Second Series.*

BOOKS: *Femeninas: Seis historias amorosas* (Pontevedra: Andrés Landín, 1895);

*Epitalamio: Historia de amores* (Madrid: Marzo, 1897);

*Cenizas* (Pontevedra: Rodríguez & Perma, 1899);

*Sonata de otoño: Memorias del Marqués de Bradomín* (Madrid: Pérez, 1902);

*Jardín umbrío* (Madrid: Rodríguez Serra, 1903);

*Corte de amor: Florilegio de honestas y nobles damas* (Madrid: Marzo, 1903);

*Sonata de estío: Memorias del Marqués de Bradomín* (Madrid: Marzo, 1903);

*Sonata de primavera: Memorias del Marqués de Bradomín* (Madrid: Marzo, 1904);

*Flor de santidad: Historia milenaria* (Madrid: Marzo, 1904);

*Sonata de invierno: Memorias del Marqués de Bradomín* (Madrid: Archivos, Bibliotecas y Museos, 1905);

*Jardín novelesco: Historias de santos, de almas en pena, de duendes y de ladrones* (Madrid: Archivos, Bibliotecas y Museos, 1905; enlarged edition, Barcelona: Maucci, 1908);

*Aguila de blasón: Comedia bárbara dividida en cinco jornadas* (Barcelona: Granada, 1907);

*Aromas de leyenda: Versos en loor de un ermitaño* (Madrid: Villavicencio, 1907);

*Historias perversas* (Barcelona: Maucci, 1907);

*Romance de lobos: Comedia bárbara dividida en cinco jornadas* (Madrid: Pueyo, 1908); translated by Cyril Bertram Lander as *Wolves! Wolves! A Play of Savagery in Three Acts* (Birmingham, U.K.: Lander, 1957);

*Los cruzados de la causa* (Madrid: Balgañón & Moreno, 1908);

*Gerifaltes de antaño* (Madrid: Suárez, 1909);

*El resplandor de la hoguera: La guerra carlista* (Madrid: Pueyo, 1909);

*Cofre de sándalo* (Madrid: Suárez, 1909);

*Una tertulia de antaño* (Madrid: Cuento Semanal, 1909);

*Cuento de abril: Escenas rimadas de una manera extravagante* (Madrid: Pueyo, 1910);

*Ramón del Valle-Inclán (photograph by Roger Viollet/ Getty Images)*

*Las mieles del rosal* (Madrid: Marzo, 1910);

*Voces de gesta: Tragedia pastoril* (Madrid: Alemana, 1911);

*Obras completas,* 19 volumes, edited by Perlado Pácz (Madrid: Renacimiento, 1912–1928);

*El embrujado: Tragedia de tierras de Salnés* (Madrid: Izquierdo, 1913);

*La Marquesa Rosalinda: Farsa sentimental y grotesca* (Madrid: Alemana, 1913);

*La cabeza del dragón: Farsa* (Madrid: Perlado, Páez, 1914); translated by May Heywood Broun as *The Dragon's Head: A Fantastic Farce* (Boston: Badger, 1919);

*La lámpara maravillosa: Ejercicios espirituales* (Madrid: Helénica, 1916); translated by Robert Lima as *The Lamp of Marvels* (West Stockbridge, Mass.: Lindisfarne, 1986);

*Eulalia* (Madrid: Novela Corta, 1917);

*La media noche: Visión estelar de un momento de guerra* (Madrid: Clásica Española, 1917);

*Rosita* (Madrid: Novela Corta, 1917);

*Mi hermana Antonia* (Madrid: Blass, 1918);

*Cuentos, estética y poemas,* edited by Guillermo Jiménez (Mexico City: Cultura, 1919); translated by Robert Lima as *Autobiography, Aesthetics, Aphorisms* (University Park: Pennsylvania State University, 1966);

*La pipa de kif: Versos* (Madrid: Sociedad General Española de Librería, 1919);

*El pasajero: Claves líricas* (Madrid: Yagües, 1920);

*Farsa de la enamorada del rey: Dividida en tres jornadas* (Madrid: Sociedad General Española de Librería, 1920);

*Divinas palabras: Tragicomedia de aldea* (Madrid: Yagües, 1920); translated by Edwin Williams as *Divine Words: A Village Tragicomedy,* in *Modern Spanish Theatre: An Anthology of Plays,* edited by Michael Benedikt and George Wellwarth (New York: Dutton, 1968);

*Zacarías el cruzado* (Madrid: Artística Saez Hermanos, 1920);

*Farsa y licencia de la reina castiza* (Madrid: Artes de la Ilustración, 1922);

*Cara de Plata: Comedia bárbara* (Madrid: Renacimiento, 1923);

*La rosa de papel y La cabeza del Bautista: Novelas macabras* (Madrid: Prensa Gráfica, 1924);

*Luces de bohemia: Esperpento* (Madrid: Cervantina, 1924); translated by Anthony N. Zahareas and Gerald Gillespie as *Lights of Bohemia* (University Park: University of Pennsylvania Press, 1976);

*Cartel de ferias: Cromos isabelinos* (Madrid: Prensa Gráfica, 1925);

*Los cuernos de don Friolera: Esperpento* (Madrid: Cervantina, 1925); translated by Robin Warner and Dominic Keown as *The Grotesque Farce of Mr. Punch the Cuckold* (Warminster, U.K.: Aris & Phillips, 1991);

*Ecos de Asmodeo* (Madrid: Novela Mundial, 1926);

*El terno del difunto* (Madrid: Novela Mundial, 1926);

*Las galas del difunto* (Madrid: Rivadeneyra, 1926);

*Ligazón: Auto para siluetas* (Madrid: Novela Mundial, 1926);

*Tablado de marionetas para educación de príncipes* (Madrid: Rivadeneyra, 1926);

*Tirano Banderas: Novela de Tierra Caliente* (Madrid: Rivadeneyra, 1926); translated by Margarita Pavitt as *The Tyrant: A Novel of Warm Lands* (New York: Holt, 1929);

*La corte de los milagros* (Madrid: Rivadeneyra, 1927);

*Estampas isabelinas: La rosa de oro* (Madrid: Novela Mundial, 1927);

*La hija del capitán: Esperpento* (Madrid: Novela Mundial, 1927);

*Retablo de la avaricia: La lujuria y la muerte* (Madrid: Rivadeneyra, 1927);

*Fin de un revolucionario: Aleluyas de la Gloriosa* (Madrid: Moderna, 1928);

*Las reales antecámeras* (Madrid: Atlántida, 1928);

*Teatrillo de enredo* (Madrid: Moderna, 1928);

*Viva mi dueño* (Madrid: Rivadeneyra, 1928);

*Otra castiza de Samaria* (Madrid: Novela de Hoy, 1929);

*Claves líricas* (Madrid: Rivadeneyra, 1930);

*Martes de Carnaval: Esperpentos* (Madrid: Rivadeneyra, 1930);

*Flores de almendro* (Madrid: Bergua, 1936);

*Opera lírica* (Madrid: Rua Nueva, 1943);

*Obras completas de Don Ramón del Valle-Inclán,* 2 volumes (Madrid: Rivadeneyra, 1944);

*Publicaciónes periodísticas anteriores a 1895,* edited by William L. Fichter (Mexico City: Colegio de México, 1952);

*Baza de espadas* (Barcelona: AHR, 1958);

*Obras escogidas* (Madrid: Aguilar, 1958);

*Teatro selecto* (Madrid: Escelicer, 1969);

*El trueno dorado* (Madrid: Nostromo, 1975);

*Artículos completos y otras páginas olvidadas,* edited by Javier Serrano Alonso (Madrid: Istmo, 1987).

**Collections:** *El Marqués de Bradomín: Coloquios románticos* (Madrid: Pueyo, 1907); translated by May Heywood Brown and Thomas Walsh as *The Pleasant Memoirs of the Marquis de Bradomín: Four Sonatas* (New York: Harcourt, Brace, 1924);

*La guerra carlista,* 3 volumes (Madrid: Suárez, 1909).

**Editions in English:** *Savage Acts: Four Plays,* translated by Robert Lima (University Park, Pa.: Estreno, 1993);

*Three Plays: Divine Words, Bohemian Lights, Silver Face,* translated by María M. Delgado (London: Methuen Drama, 1993);

*Spring and Summer Sonatas: The Memoirs of the Marquis of Bradomín,* translated by Margaret Jull Costa (Sawtry, U.K.: Dedalus, 1997);

*Autumn and Winter Sonatas: The Memoirs of the Marquis of Bradomín,* translated by Costa (Sawtry, U.K.: Dedalus, 1998).

PLAY PRODUCTIONS: *Cenizas,* Madrid, Teatro Lara, 7 December 1899;

*El Marqués de Bradomín,* Madrid, Teatro de la Princesa, 25 January 1906;

*Aguila de blasón,* Barcelona, Teatro Eldorado, 3 March 1907;

*La cabeza del dragón,* Madrid, Teatro de la Comedia, 5 March 1910;

*Cuento de abril,* Madrid, Teatro de la Comedia, 19 March 1910;

*Voces de gesta,* Barcelona, Teatro Novedades, 18 June 1911;

*La Marquesa Rosalinda,* Madrid, Teatro de la Princesa, 5 March 1912;

*La cabeza del Bautista,* Madrid, Teatro del Centro, 17 October 1924;

*Ligazón,* Madrid, Teatro de Bellas Artes, 19 December 1926;

*Farsa y licencia de la reina castiza,* Madrid, Teatro Muñoz Seca, 3 June 1931;

*El embrujado,* Madrid, Teatro Muñoz Seca, 11 November 1931;

*Divinas palabras,* Madrid, Teatro Español, 16 November 1933.

Ramón del Valle-Inclán was one of the most controversial literary figures in Spain in the late nineteenth and early twentieth centuries. He was a reformer of the modern Spanish stage, an inventor of new narrative and dramatic modes, and a highly original re-creator of the Spanish language. Although Valle-Inclán wrote in Spanish, his ties to Galicia and the Galician language are discernible in the themes, vocabulary, and rhythms of his writings.

Ramón María del Valle-Inclán was born on 28 October 1866 into an illustrious, aristocratic, but impoverished family in Vilanova de Arousa, a village in the province of Pontevedra on the coast of the region of Galicia. An ancestor, Francisco del Valle-Inclán, was the founder of the first public library in Santiago de Compostela. The writer's father, Ramón del Valle Bermúdez, was the publisher of two regional newspapers, and his brother Carlos was a journalist and creative writer who achieved local fame. Valle-Inclán's mother, Dolores Peña Montenegro, and her ancestors provided the writer with the oddest characters in his fiction; one of them, Juan Manuel de Montenegro, appears in several of his books.

Valle-Inclán finished secondary school in Pontevedra and reluctantly began to study law at the University of Santiago de Compostela. When his father died in 1889, he abandoned his formal education and became an autodidact. The library that Jesús Muruais had established in Pontevedra was filled with European novelties that strongly influenced the young writer.

Toward the end of the nineteenth century, decadence and symbolism were the new literary tendencies in Europe; under their influence, the artistic movement *modernismo* (modernism) was flowering in the Spanish-speaking countries. During this period a fruitful interchange occurred between Spain and its former American colonies. In 1892 Valle-Inclán traveled to Mexico, where he became acquainted with the young practitioners of the new literary trend. He later became friendly with the modernist authors Rubén Darío of Nicaragua and Leopoldo Lugones of Argentina, with both of whom he shared an interest in occultism, spiritualism, and mysticism. Valle-Inclán designed most of his books using a concentric or circular pattern, in which there is a nucleus flanked by sections related by a rigorous symmetry. For example, the novel *Flor de santidad: Historia milenaria* (1904, Flower of Sanctity: Millenarian History) is divided into five parts called *estancias;* each *estancia* is subdivided into five chapters, except for the central *estancia,* which has six. The novel *Tirano Banderas: Novela de Tierra Caliente* (1926, Tyrant Banderas: Novel of Warm Lands; translated as *The Tyrant: A Novel of Warm Lands,* 1929) is divided into a prologue, seven parts, and an epilogue; six of the seven parts are further divided into three books each, and the central one, part 4, into seven. Book 4 of part 4 is thus the center of the novel. The epilogue continues directly from the events in the prologue, and every book in the first three parts has a counterpart in the latter three. The numerical symbolism and the symmetry may be interpreted in various ways, but the rejection of linear time is clearly part of Valle-Inclán's search for occult meanings and use of myths of reunification.

Valle-Inclán's first book, *Femeninas: Seis historias amorosas* (Feminines: Six Love Stories), appeared in Pontevedra in 1895 with a prologue by the respected Galician author Manuel Murguía. Following the publication of the book, Valle-Inclán moved to Madrid. There he became friends with Darío, Jacinto Benavente, Azorín (pseudonym of José Martínez Ruiz), Pío Baroja, and Miguel de Unamuno. In a simulated duel with another writer in 1899 Valle-Inclán's cufflink became embedded in his left wrist. An infection developed, and his arm had to be amputated. He took advantage of the accident by referring to himself as "the second great one-armed writer of Spain"–alluding to Miguel de Cervantes, whose left hand was maimed in the battle of Lepanto. Valle-Inclán's missing left arm, along with his witty and interminable talk in the café *tertulias* (literary circles), long beard, round spectacles, and thin physique, combined to make him an extravagant figure in the Madrid literary Bohemia.

*Clásicos castellanos*

Ramón del Valle-Inclán

DIVINAS PALABRAS
TRAGICOMEDIA
DE ALDEA

*Edición crítica de Luis Iglesias Feijoo*

*Espasa Calpe*

Cover for a 1991 edition of Valle-Inclán's 1920 play (translated as
Divine Words: A Village Tragicomedy, 1968), in which
strange happenings occur in a Galician village (Thomas
Cooper Library, University of South Carolina)

Between 1902 and 1905 Valle-Inclán published four volumes of *Sonatas,* each of which is related to a season and to a stage of manhood and bears the subtitle *Memorias del Marqués de Bradomín* (Memoirs of the Marquis of Bradomín): *Sonata de otoño* (1902; translated as "Autumn Sonata," 1924), *Sonata de estío* (1903; translated as "Summer Sonata," 1924), *Sonata de primavera* (1904; translated as "Spring Sonata," 1924), and *Sonata de invierno* (1905; translated as "Winter Sonata," 1924). Bradomín is described as an "ugly, catholic, and sentimental don Juan." *Sonata de otoño,* the best known of the quartet, is set in a decadent aristocratic manor house in Galicia and depicts the final sexual encounters between Bradomín, who here is past middle age, and a former lover. *Sonata de estío* is set in Mexico. *Sonata de primavera* is set in Italy, where Bradomín, a young man, is surrounded by priests and fanatical Catholics as he attempts to seduce a girl who is about to enter a con-

vent. *Sonata de invierno* combines historical and fictional characters in the cold Navarre winter, during the third Carlist war. Eroticism, violence, religion, sadism, masochism, and death are intertwined with irony and humor in this display of the most recurrent decadent topics. Valle-Inclán loved to erase the borders between fiction and real life: he gave the fictional Bradomín some of his own traits and adopted some of the character's. The novellas secured Valle-Inclán's reputation as a writer of modernist prose and a master of erotic fiction.

In 1904, between *Sonata de primavera* and *Sonata de invierno,* Valle-Inclán published *Flor de santidad,* a short, poetic novel set in nineteenth-century Galicia. He displays here, as in the *Sonatas,* all the new aesthetic traits of the modernist school, with the addition of a striking originality.

A controversial aspect of Valle-Inclán's life is his adherence to Carlism. The Carlists were a branch of the Bourbon dynasty who claimed the right to the Spanish throne and held the most conservative positions with regard to absolutism, Catholicism, and traditionalism. Although Valle-Inclán expressed his support for Carlism in many ways, some critics believe that his commitment to the cause was an aesthetic pose. The Carlist cause provides material for several of Valle-Inclán's works and is the most important theme of his *La guerra carlista* (The Carlist War) trilogy, comprising the novels *Los cruzados de la causa* (1908, Crusaders of the Cause), *Gerifaltes de antaño* (1909, Gerfalcons of Yore), and *El resplandor de la hoguera* (1909, The Glow of the Bonfire). In the first novel, which is set in Galicia, Bradomín is a committed Carlist trying to convey weapons to the soldiers. The following novels are set in the Basque and Navarre regions, where the hostilities actually took place. The unforgettable protagonist of *El resplandor de la hoguera,* the priest Santa Cruz, is a cruel warrior who is depicted as a fanatical and epic hero.

In 1907 Valle-Inclán married the actress Josefina Blanco; they had six children, one of whom died young. He joined his wife's troupe as artistic director and toured the provinces. He wrote three plays, inspired by his family history, about the decadent aristocrat don Juan Manuel Montenegro. The last two chronologically, *Aguila de blasón: Comedia bárbara dividida en cinco jornadas* (The Eagle Scutcheon: Barbaric Comedy in Five Acts) and *Romance de lobos: Comedia bárbara dividida en cinco jornadas* (Romance of Wolves: Barbaric Comedy in Five Acts; translated as *Wolves! Wolves! A Play of Savagery in Three Acts,* 1957), were published in 1907 and 1908, respectively; *Cara de Plata: Comedia bárbara* (Silver Face: Barbaric Comedy; translated as *Silver Face,* 1993), the first chronologically, was written in 1922 and published in 1923. The difficulties involved in presenting these plays in contemporary theaters were nearly insurmountable: changes of scene are frequent and complicated, and the cinematographic and expressionistic techniques he used were ahead of their time. Valle-Inclán's play for children, *La cabeza del dragón* (first produced in 1910; translated as *The Dragon's Head: A Fantastic Farce*, 1919), includes sarcastic comments about King Alfonso XIII and his flatterers. In 1910 the Valle-Incláns traveled to South America. The writer was acclaimed in Buenos Aires for his lectures on aesthetics and for the success of the premiere of his play *Cuento de abril* (April's Tale). His play *Voces de gesta: Tragedia pastoril* (1911) is an apology for Carlism. The actors in his *La Marquesa Rosalinda: Farsa sentimental y grotesca* (1912, The Marquise Rosalinda: Sentimental and Grotesque Farce) could manage neither the refined verses nor the literary sophistication of the play.

In 1916 Valle-Inclán published an aesthetic treatise, *La lámpara maravillosa: Ejercicios espirituales* (translated as *The Lamp of Marvels*, 1986), in which he expounds theories similar to those of the French symbolists. During World War I, Valle-Inclán supported the Allied cause and was invited by the French government to visit the front. Following the ideas developed in *La lámpara maravillosa*, he wrote a rather mystical account of his experience: *La media noche: Visión estelar de un momento de guerra* (1917, Midnight: A Starry Vision of a Moment of War). His play *Divinas palabras: Tragicomedia de aldea* (1920; translated as *Divine Words: A Village Tragicomedy*, 1968) is set in rural Galicia, where anything seems credible, from the sexual power of the devil to a subnormal boy's ability to change the life of his entire family.

In 1920 Valle-Inclán published in the periodical *España* an early version of his seminal *Luces de bohemia* (1924; translated as *Lights of Bohemia*, 1976), the first of his plays with the subtitle *Esperpento*. The protagonist, the blind poet Max Estrella, declares before dying: "The *esperpento* was invented by Goya. . . . The classic heroes have gone to stroll in the Callejón del Gato," a street in Madrid where it was possible to see oneself reflected in distorting mirrors. The *esperpento* is a grotesque tragicomedy, a denunciation of a broken social order and of the violence of power. The *esperpentos* are written in a broken Spanish filled with slang, dialect, interjections, and discordant elements; the dehumanized characters react mechanically in mean and vile ways.

Valle-Inclán's second *esperpento*, *Los cuernos de don Friolera* (1925; translated as *The Grotesque Farce of Mr. Punch the Cuckold*, 1991), consists of twelve scenes framed by a prologue and an epilogue. In the frame two intellectual characters, don Estrafalario and don Manolito, discuss aesthetics and popular taste and comment satirically on the singular qualities of Spain. *Los cuernos de don Friolera* is a parody of the honor plays of Pedro

*Clásicos castellanos*

**Ramón del Valle-Inclán**

## LUCES DE BOHEMIA
### ESPERPENTO

*Edición crítica de Alonso Zamora Vicente*

*Espasa Calpe*

Cover for a 1993 edition of Valle-Inclán's 1924 play (translated as Lights of Bohemia, 1976), about a blind poet. It is the first of his esperpentos, *grotesque tragicomedies written in a broken Spanish filled with slang, dialect, interjections, and discordant elements and in which dehumanized characters behave mechanically in cruel and vile ways (Thomas Cooper Library, University of South Carolina).*

Calderón de la Barca and also a satire of the military, while another *esperpento, Las galas del difunto* (1926, The Dead Man's Dress Suit), mocks the don Juan theme and is also a burlesque criticism of the Cuban war. After Alfonso XIII installed a military dictatorship headed by General Miguel Primo de Rivera in 1923, Valle-Inclán published *La hija del capitán* (1927, The Captain's Daughter), a savage satire of the monarchy, the army, and the Catholic Church; referring to Valle-Inclán as an "eminent writer and extravagant citizen," Primo de Rivera ordered the edition confiscated.

In 1926 Valle-Inclán published *Tirano Banderas*; the novel initiated a vogue for novels about dictators. Banderas is a dictator in a fictitious Latin American

*Clásicos castellanos*

Ramón del Valle-Inclán

TIRANO BANDERAS

*Edición crítica de Alonso Zamora Vicente*

*Espasa Calpe*

Cover for a 1993 edition of Valle-Inclán's 1926 novel (translated as The
Tyrant: A Novel of Warm Lands, *1929), about an uprising
against the dictator of a fictitious Latin American country (Thomas
Cooper Library, University of South Carolina)*

nation that synthesizes characteristics of several countries, including Spain and Mexico. An uprising against
the tyrant takes place during the Catholic festival of the
Day of the Dead on the first two days of November,
and Banderas dies after killing his daughter to save her
from falling into the hands of his enemies. The satire
falls not only on the imaginary country where the
action is set but also on the Spaniards who have colonized the region and continue to oppress the poor.

Valle-Inclán's last project was to be a cycle of
three trilogies of historical novels about Spain since the
liberal revolution of the nineteenth century; he completed only the first two novels. The first novel of the
first trilogy, "El ruedo ibérico" (The Iberian Ring), is *La
corte de los milagros* (1927, The Court of Miracles); it
shows Isabel II under the influence of a supposedly

miracle-working nun, Sor Patrocinio. The second
novel, *Viva mi dueño* (1928, Hurrah for My Owner),
deals with the uprising against the queen. The unfinished third novel, *Baza de espadas* (Military Tricks),
appeared in newspapers and was published posthumously in 1958. All of the novels are exhaustively documented with archival materials, books, newspapers,
and popular literature. The two completed novels have
a circular structure, indicating that Valle-Inclán did not
believe in historical progress but in the recurrence of
evil. It is a controversial argument, since Valle-Inclán
adhered to progressive ideas in the last decades of his
life and took more interest in the depiction of popular
misery than in the life of idealized aristocrats. Nothing
is univocal in Valle-Inclán's life or work, however, and
an array of possible interpretations have been posed by
his critics.

Valle-Inclán published three books of poetry over
the course of his career. *Aromas de leyenda: Versos en loor
de un ermitaño* (1907, Aromas of Legend: Verses in Praise
of a Hermit) and *El pasajero: Claves líricas* (1920, The
Passenger: Lyrical Clefs) were composed under the
influence of modernism. The 1919 collection, *La pipa de
kif* (The Hashish Pipe), anticipates the aesthetics of
*esperpento* that he developed in his novels.

Ramón del Valle-Inclán and his wife were
divorced in 1932. Valle-Inclán died of bladder cancer
on 5 January 1936. He had chosen to return to die in
Santiago de Compostela, where he had many friends,
and to be buried, rejecting Catholic rites, in its small
cemetery. Valle-Inclán's reputation grew in foreign
countries and in Spain during Francisco Franco's dictatorship from 1939 to 1975, even though censorship
kept the full meaning of his work from being known.
Since the political transition to democracy in the 1970s,
Valle-Inclán's work has increasingly attracted the attention of critics, translators, and the general public.

**Letters:**

Juan Antonio Hormigón, *Valle-Inclán: Cronología. Escritos
dispersos. Espistolario* (Madrid: Fundación Banco
Exterior, 1987).

**Interviews:**

Dru Dougherty, *Un Valle-Inclán olvidado: Entrevistas y con-
ferencias,* edited by Eugenio Suárez Galbán
(Madrid: Fundamentos, 1982);

Joaquín del Valle-Inclán, ed., *Entrevistas* (Madrid:
Alianza, 2000).

**Bibliographies:**

Javier Serrano Alonso and Amparo de Juan Bloufer,
*Bibliografía general de Ramón del Valle-Inclán* (Santi-

ago de Compostela, Spain: Universidade de Santiago de Compostela, 1995);

Serrano Alonso and Bloufer, "Anuario Valle-Inclán I," *Anales de Literatura Española Contemporánea* (2001);

Serrano Alonso and Bloufer, "Anuario Valle-Inclán II," *Anales de Literatura Española Contemporánea* (2002): 297–310;

Serrano Alonso and Bloufer, "Anuario Valle-Inclán III," *Anales de Literatura Española Contemporánea* (2003): 271–309.

## Biography:

Robert Lima, *Valle-Inclán: The Theatre of His Life* (Columbia: University of Missouri Press, 1988).

## References:

Manuel Bermejo Marcos, *Valle-Inclán: Introducción a su obra* (Salamanca: Anaya, 1971);

Rodolfo Cardona and Anthony Zahareas, *Visión del esperpento: Teoría y práctica en los esperpentos de Valle-Inclán* (Madrid: Castalia, 1970);

Gonzalo Díaz Migoyo, *Guía de Tirano Banderas* (Madrid: Fundamentos, 1985);

Dru Dougherty, *Guía para caminantes en Santa Fe de Tierra Firme: Estudio sistémico de "Tirano Banderas"* (Valencia: Pre-Textos, 1999);

Dougherty, *Palimpsestos al cubo: Prácticas discursivas de Valle-Inclán* (Madrid: Fundamentos, 2003);

Virginia Milner Garlitz, "El centro del círculo: 'La lámpara maravillosa' de Valle-Inclán," dissertation, University of Chicago, 1978;

Luis González del Valle, *La ficción breve de Valle-Inclán: Hermenéutica y estrategias narrativas* (Barcelona: Anthropos, 1990);

Sumner Greenfield, *Valle-Inclán: Anatomía de un teatro problemático* (Madrid: Fundamentos, 1972);

Germán Gullón, *La novela moderna en España (1885–1902): Los albores de la modernidad* (Madrid: Taurus, 1992);

Ricardo Gullón, ed., *Valle-Inclán Centennial Studies* (Austin: Department of Spanish and Portuguese, University of Texas, 1968);

John Lyon, *The Theatre of Valle-Inclán* (Cambridge & New York: Cambridge University Press, 1983);

Carol Maier and Roberta L. Salper, eds., *Ramón María del Valle-Inclán: Questions of Gender* (Lewisburg, Pa.: Bucknell University Press / London & Cranbury, N.J.: Associated University Presses, 1994);

María del Carmen Porrúa, *La Galicia decimonónica en las "Comedias bárbaras" de Valle-Inclán* (Sada: Ediciós do Castro, 1983);

José Rubia Barcia, *A Biobibliography and Iconography of Valle-Inclán, 1866–1936* (Berkeley: University of California Press, 1960);

Margarita Santos Zas, *Tradicionalismo y literatura en Valle-Inclán (1889–1910)* (Boulder, Colo.: Society of Spanish and Spanish-American Studies, 1993);

Leda Schiavo, *Historia y novela en Valle-Inclán: Para leer "El ruedo ibérico"* (Madrid: Castalia, 1980);

Verity Smith, *Ramón del Valle-Inclán* (New York: Twayne, 1973);

Emma Susana Speratti-Piñero, *La elaboración artística en "Tirano Banderas"* (Mexico City: Colegio de México, 1957);

Darío Villanueva, *En torno a Valle-Inclán* (Vigo: Galaxia, 1991);

Alonso Zamora Vicente, *La realidad esperpéntica: Aproximación a "Luces de Bohemia"* (Madrid: Gredos, 1974);

Zamora Vicente, *Las "Sonatas" de Valle-Inclán* (Madrid: Gredos, 1966);

Iris M. Zavala, *La musa funambulesca de Valle-Inclán: Poética de la carnavalización* (Madrid: Orígenes, 1990).

# Manuel Vázquez Montalbán

*(14 June 1939 – 18 October 2003)*

José F. Colmeiro
*Michigan State University*

See also the Vázquez Montalbán entry in *DLB 134: Twentieth-Century Spanish Poets, Second Series.*

BOOKS: *Informe sobre la información* (Barcelona: Fontanella, 1963; revised and enlarged, 1971; revised and enlarged again, 1975);

*Una educación sentimental* (Barcelona: El Bardo, 1967; enlarged, 1970);

*Reflexiones ante el neocapitalismo* (Barcelona: Cultura Popular, 1968);

*Antología de la "Nova Cançó" catalana* (Barcelona: Cultura Popular, 1968);

*Movimientos sin éxito* (Barcelona: Saturno, 1969);

*Recordando a Dardé y otros relatos* (Barcelona: Seix Barral, 1969);

*Manifiesto subnormal* (Barcelona: Kairós, 1970);

*Crónica sentimental de España* (Barcelona: Lumen, 1971);

*Cancionero general 1939–1971* (Barcelona: Lumen, 1972); revised and enlarged as *Cancionero general del franquismo 1939–1975* (Barcelona: Crítica, 2000);

*Yo maté a Kennedy: Impresiones, observaciones y memorias de un guardaespaldas* (Barcelona: Planeta, 1972);

*Joan Manuel Serrat* (Madrid: Júcar, 1972);

*El pequeño libro pardo del general,* anonymous (Paris: Ruedo Ibérico, 1972);

*100 años de deporte, del esfuerzo individual al espectáculo de masas,* by Vázquez Montalbán, Andrés Mercé Varela, and Joaquín Ibarz Ibars, 2 volumes (Barcelona: Difusora Internacional, 1973);

*Guillermotta en el país de las Guillerminas* (Barcelona: Anagrama, 1973);

*Coplas a la muerte de mi tía Daniela* (Barcelona: Saturno, 1973);

*A la sombra de las muchachas sin flor: Poemas del amor y del terror* (Barcelona: Saturno, 1973);

*La vía chilena al golpe de Estado* (Barcelona: Saturno, 1973);

*El libro gris de televisión española* (Madrid: Ediciones 99, 1973);

*Las noticias y la información* (Barcelona: Salvat, 1973);

*Cuestiones marxistas* (Barcelona: Anagrama, 1974);

*Manuel Vázquez Montalbán (photograph by Daniel Vázquez Sallés; from the cover for* Crónica sentimental de la transición, *1985; Thomas Cooper Library, University of South Carolina)*

*Happy End* (Barcelona: La Gaya Ciencia, 1974);

*Tatuaje* (Barcelona: José Batlló, 1974);

*La penetración americana en España* (Madrid: Cuadernos para el Diálogo, 1974);

*100 años de canción y Music Hall* (Barcelona: Difusora Internacional, 1974);

*1974: España se queda sola,* by Vázquez Montalbán, as Manolo V El Empecinado, and Jaime Perich, Lo mejor de Por Favor, no. 1 (Barcelona: Punch, 1974);

*1975: El año del ¡Ay, ay, ay!* by Vázquez Montalbán, as Manolo V El Empecinado, and Perich (Madrid: Sedmay, 1976);

*¿Qué es el imperialismo?* (Barcelona: La Gaya Ciencia, 1976);

*La soledad del manager* (Barcelona: Planeta, 1977); translated by Ed Emery as *The Angst-Ridden Executive* (London: Serpent's Tail, 1990);

*Cómo liquidaron el franquismo en dieciséis meses y un día* (Barcelona: Planeta, 1977);

*Imágenes y recuerdos, 1919–1930: La rebelión de las masas* (Barcelona: Difusora Internacional, 1977);

*Diccionario del franquismo* (Barcelona: Dopesa, 1977);

*L'art del menjar a Catalunya: Crónica de la resistència dels senyals d'identitat gastronòmica catalana* (Barcelona: Edicions 62, 1977); translated into Spanish as *La cocina catalana: El arte de comer en Cataluña* (Barcelona: Península, 1979);

*Los demonios familiares de Franco* (Barcelona: Dopesa, 1978; revised edition, Barcelona: Planeta, 1987);

*Los mares del Sur* (Barcelona: Planeta, 1979); translated by Patrick Camiller as *Southern Seas* (London: Pluto, 1986);

*La palabra libre en la ciudad libre* (Barcelona: Gedisa, 1979);

*Historia y comunicación social* (Barcelona: Bruguera, 1980; revised edition, Barcelona: Crítica/Mondadori, 1997);

*Asesinato en el Comité Central* (Barcelona: Planeta, 1981); translated by Camiller as *Murder in the Central Committee* (London: Pluto, 1984; Chicago: Academy Chicago, 1985);

*Las recetas inmorales* (Barcelona: Oh Sauce, 1981; revised edition, Madrid: Afanias, 1996);

*Praga* (Barcelona: Lumen, 1982);

*Los pájaros de Bangkok* (Barcelona: Planeta, 1983);

*Tres novelas ejemplares* (Barcelona: Bruguera, 1983)– includes "Recordando a Dardé," "Happy End," and "La vida privada del doctor Betriu";

*La rosa de Alejandría* (Barcelona: Planeta, 1984);

*Mis almuerzos con gente inquietante* (Barcelona: Planeta, 1984);

*El pianista* (Barcelona: Seix Barral, 1985); translated by Elizabeth Plaister as *The Pianist* (London & New York: Quartet, 1989);

*Crónica sentimental de la transición* (Barcelona: Planeta, 1985);

*Contra los gourmets* (Barcelona: Difusora Internacional, 1985);

*El matarife* (Madrid: Almarabú, 1986);

*El balneario* (Barcelona: Planeta, 1986);

*Las cenizas de Laura* (Madrid: Cambio 16, 1986);

*Desde los tejados* (Madrid: Cambio 16, 1986);

*Jordi Anfruns, sociólogo* (Madrid: Cambio 16, 1986);

*Aquel 23 de febrero* (Madrid: Cambio 16, 1986);

*Tiempo para la mesa* (Barcelona: Difusora Internacional, 1986);

*Memoria y deseo: Obra poética (1963–1983)* (Barcelona: Seix Barral, 1986); revised and enlarged as *Memoria y deseo (1963–1990)* (Barcelona: Mondadori, 1996);

*Los alegres muchachos de Atzavara* (Barcelona: Seix Barral, 1987);

*Historias de fantasmas* (Barcelona: Planeta, 1987);

*Historias de padres e hijos* (Barcelona: Planeta, 1987);

*Tres historias de amor* (Barcelona: Planeta, 1987);

*Historias de política ficción* (Barcelona: Planeta, 1987);

*Asesinato en Prado del Rey y otras historias sórdidas* (Barcelona: Planeta, 1987);

*Pigmalión y otros relatos* (Barcelona: Seix Barral, 1987);

*Barcelonas* (Barcelona: Empúries, 1987; revised, 1990); translated by Andy Robinson as *Barcelonas* (London & New York: Verso, 1992);

*Cuarteto* (Madrid: Mondadori, 1988);

*El delantero centro fue asesinado al atardecer* (Barcelona: Planeta, 1988); translated by Emery as *Off Side* (London & New York: Serpent's Tail, 1996);

*Rafael Ribó: L'optimisme de la raó* (Barcelona: Planeta, 1988); Spanish version published as *Rafael Ribó: El optimismo de la razón* (Barcelona: Planeta, 1988);

*Escritos subnormales* (Barcelona: Seix Barral, 1989);

*Las recetas de Carvalho* (Barcelona: Planeta, 1989);

*Barcelona: Fuente a fuente* (Madrid: Repsol, 1990);

*Galíndez* (Barcelona: Seix Barral, 1990); translated by Carol Christensen and Thomas Christensen as *Galíndez* (New York: Atheneum, 1992);

*La historia no es como la merecíamos* (Barcelona: Cambio 16, 1990);

*Moscú de la Revolución* (Barcelona: Planeta, 1990);

*El laberinto griego* (Barcelona: Planeta, 1991); translated by Emery as *An Olympic Death* (London: Serpent's Tail, 1992);

*Gauguin* (Paris: Flohic, 1991); translated by Plaister as *Gauguin & M. Vázquez Montalbán* (Paris: Flohic, 1991);

*25 años, 25 anuarios: Del apagón de Nueva York a la caída del muro de Berlín, pasando por la transición* (Barcelona: Difusora Internacional, 1991);

*¿Barcelona, cap a on vas? Diàlegs per a una ultra Barcelona,* by Vázquez Montalbán and Eduardo Moreno, transcribed by Xavier Garcia (Barcelona: Llibres de l'Index, 1991); Spanish version published as *¿Barcelona, a dónde vas? Dialogos para otra Barcelona* (Barcelona: Tempestad, 1991);

*Pero el viajero que huye* (Madrid: Visor, 1991);

*Autobiografía del general Franco* (Barcelona: Planeta, 1992);

*Sabotaje olímpico* (Barcelona: Planeta, 1993);

*El hermano pequeño* (Barcelona: Planeta, 1994);

*Roldán, ni vivo ni muerto* (Barcelona: Planeta, 1994);

*El estrangulador* (Barcelona: Mondadori, 1994);

*Felípicas: Sobre las miserias de la razón práctica* (Madrid: El País/Aguilar, 1994);

*Panfleto desde el planeta de los simios* (Barcelona: Crítica, 1995);

*Pasionaria y los siete enanitos* (Barcelona: Planeta, 1995);

*Les meves receptes de cuina catalana* (Barcelona: Edicions 62, 1995);

*Reflexiones de Robinsón ante un bacalao* (Barcelona: Lumen, 1995);

*El poder,* edited by Francisco J. Satué (Madrid: Espasa, 1996);

*El premio* (Barcelona: Planeta, 1996);

*Un polaco en la corte del rey Juan Carlos* (Barcelona: Alfaguara, 1996);

*Antes de que el milenio nos separe* (Barcelona: Planeta, 1997);

*Quinteto de Buenos Aires* (Barcelona: Planeta, 1997); translated by Nick Caistor as *The Buenos Aires Quintet* (London: Serpent's Tail, 2003);

*Ciudad* (Madrid: Visor, 1997);

*Elogis desmesurats* (Barcelona: Empúries, 1997);

*El escriba sentado* (Barcelona: Crítica, 1997);

*O César o nada* (Barcelona: Planeta, 1998);

*La literatura en la construcción de la ciudad democrática* (Barcelona: Crítica, 1998);

*Y Dios entró en La Habana* (Madrid: El País/Aguilar, 1998);

*El señor de los bonsáis* (Madrid: Alfaguara, 1999);

*Marcos: El señor de los espejos* (Madrid: Aguilar, 1999);

*El hombre de mi vida* (Barcelona: Planeta, 2000); translated by Caistor as *The Man of My Life* (London: Serpent's Tail, 2005);

*Ars Amandi: Poesía erótico amorosa (1963–2000)* (Madrid: Bartleby, 2001);

*Una educación sentimental y Praga,* edited by Manuel Rico (Madrid: Cátedra, 2001);

*Erec y Enide* (Barcelona: Random House Mondadori, 2002);

*Carvalho gastronómico,* 10 volumes (Barcelona: Ediciones B, 2002–2003);

*La aznaridad: Por el imperio hacia Dios o por Dios hacia el imperio* (Barcelona: Mondadori, 2003);

*Geometría y compasión* (Barcelona: Mondadori, 2003);

*Guerrero Medina* (Barcelona: March, 2004);

*Milenio Carvalho,* 2 volumes (Barcelona: Planeta, 2004)– comprises volume 1, *Rumbo a Kabul,* and volume 2, *En las antípodas;*

*Fútbol: Una religion en busca de un Dios,* edited by Daniel Vázquez Sallés (Madrid: Debate, 2005).

PLAY PRODUCTIONS: *Flor de nit,* text by Vázquez Montalbán, music by Albert Guinovart, Barcelona, Teatre Victoria, 3 April 1992;

*Antes de que el milenio nos separe,* Verem Rhizon, Germany, Schloss Theater Moers, 1995;

*Etre Dieu,* libretto by Vázquez Montalbán, score by Salvador Dalí, Figueres, Rambla de Figueres, 11 May 2005.

PRODUCED SCRIPTS: *Tatuaje,* screenplay by Vázquez Montalbán, J. J. Bigas Luna, and José Ulloa, motion picture, Profilmar, 1978;

*Las aventuras de Pepe Carvalho,* scripts by Vázquez Montalbán and Domenec Font, adapted by Adolfo Aristarain, television, Antenne-2 / Radio Televisión Española / Radio Télévision Luxembourgeoise / Télécip, 1986;

*El laberinto griego,* screenplay by Vázquez Montalbán and Rafael Alcázar, motion picture, Impala S.A. / Televisión Española / Trabala, 1993.

OTHER: *El libro de la pena de muerte,* prologue by Vázquez Montalbán (Madrid: Sedmay, 1976);

*Galicia,* edited by Vázquez Montalbán, Las cocinas españolas, volume 1 (Madrid: Sedmay, 1981);

*Valencia,* edited by Vázquez Montalbán, Las cocinas españolas, volume 2 (Madrid: Sedmay, 1981);

"Sobre la imposibilidad de la novela policiaca en España," in *La novela policiaca española,* edited by Juan Paredes Núñez (Granada: Universidad de Granada, 1989), pp. 49–62;

"La novela española entre el posfranquismo y el posmodernismo," in *La renovation du roman espagnol depuis 1975,* edited by Yvan Lissorgues (Toulouse: Presses Universitaires du Mirail, 1991), pp. 13–25.

SELECTED PERIODICAL PUBLICATIONS–UNCOLLECTED: "No escribo novelas negras," *El Urogallo,* 9–10 (1987): 26–27;

"Contra la novela policiaca," *Ínsula,* 512–513 (1989): 9.

Manuel Vázquez Montalbán has been one of the most influential intellectuals in contemporary Spanish culture. A novelist, essayist, poet, and playwright, he published prolifically in such diverse areas as detective fiction, mass communications, and Spanish popular culture. Among his varied works are political essays, cultural manifestos, songs for musicals, an opera libretto with the surrealist painter Salvador Dalí, and a series of cookbooks. In Spain alone he published more than eight thousand articles in thirty-seven newspapers and magazines. He also created one of the best-known fictional characters of twentieth-century Spanish literature, the Catalan detective Pepe Carvalho. Vázquez Montalbán's work blurs the boundaries of genres and subverts traditional categories of high and low culture, combining the fictional and the historical, the essay and the novel, and diverse topics such as food and eroticism, mass media and historical memory, or soccer and nationalism. An element in all of his work is the at times radical and provocative mix of irony and observation in his analysis of Spanish contemporary culture. Vázquez Montalbán was a frequent subject of newspaper and magazine articles and was interviewed many times on radio and television programs. He achieved best-seller status not only in Spain but also in other European and Latin American countries. Many of his novels and short stories have been adapted for movies and television in Spain and abroad.

Vázquez Montalbán's parents were poor immigrants who came to Barcelona in the early twentieth century; his father, Evaristo, a lower-level state worker for the Second Republic, was from the rural region of Galicia, and his mother, Rosa, was from the province of Murcia in southern Spain. They lived in the Fifth District, an underprivileged neighborhood near the port that was popularly known as the *barrio chino,* or red-light district, and was populated by other immigrants, port and factory workers, and gypsies. Such working-class neighborhoods were breeding grounds for anarchists, communists, socialists, and Catalan nationalists.

Vázquez Montalbán was born on 14 June 1939. General Francisco Franco's fascist troops had captured Barcelona three months earlier, putting an end to the Spanish Civil War and initiating a thirty-six-year-long period of repression. Vázquez Montalbán's father had gone into exile in France but returned to Spain when he heard that his son had been born. He was arrested at the border, sent to prison, and sentenced to death; the sentence was commuted to twenty years' imprisonment, of which he served only five. After his release, he worked as a collector for an insurance company.

Vázquez Montalbán attended San Luis Gonzaga School in the Fifth District, and at sixteen he started teaching the first-graders at the school. In 1956 he was admitted to the School of Philosophy and Letters at the University of Barcelona, a rare feat for students of his socio-economic background. Joaquim Marco, a professor and poet from Vázquez Montalbán's neighborhood, became his mentor and introduced him to the officially prohibited works of authors such as Antonio Machado and Federico García Lorca. At the university he came into contact with the organized student resistance against Franco, the Frente de Liberación Popular (commonly known as "Felipe").

In 1957 Vázquez Montalbán transferred to the journalism school at the university. In the spring of 1959 he participated in a campaign for the release of political prisoners. He studied at Madrid's Official School of Journalism in 1959–1960. On his return to Barcelona he joined the Partido Socialista Unificat de Catalunya (PSUC), the Catalan branch of the Commu-

Manuel Vázquez Montalbán
"Tatuaje"

PLANETA

*Title page for a 1997 edition of the first novel (1974, Tattoo) in Vázquez Montalbán's popular series about the cynical Barcelona private detective Pepe Carvalho (John W. Brister Library, Memphis State University)*

nist Party, and married Anna Sallés, a recent graduate in history.

Vázquez Montalbán's first job, beginning in 1960, was as a reporter and interviewer on the night shift at the newspaper *Solidaridad Nacional;* formerly the anarchist *Solidaridad Obrera,* the paper had been transformed into an official publication of Franco's Movimiento Nacional. He lost the position in 1962 because he did not have the obligatory membership in the party. On 11 May 1962 he was imprisoned for participating in demonstrations against the repression of miners' strikes in Asturias and was sentenced to three years in jail. In 1962–1963 he was in a prison in Lérida, where he and other political prisoners formed an intellectual circle.

During his incarceration Vázquez Montalbán began to elaborate his theory of "subnormality" and wrote his first books. He obtained an early release in

1963 when a partial amnesty was declared after Pope John XXIII's death. That year he published his first book, *Informe sobre la información* (Report on Information); combining elements of sociology and mass communications, it was assigned reading in Spain's schools of journalism for many years.

Vázquez Montalbán had great difficulty obtaining employment as a journalist because of his police record and lack of affiliation with the official party of the Movimiento Nacional. He worked in the archives for the Enciclopedia Larousse-Espasa in 1964 and was named editor of the new magazine *Siglo XX* in 1965, but the government closed the publication six months later. The following year his son, Daniel, was born. For the next three years he survived by writing about subjects such as decorating and gardening for general-interest magazines. He published a collection of poems, *Una educación sentimental* (A Sentimental Education), in 1967 and another poetry volume, *Movimientos sin éxito* (Unsuccessful Movements), in 1969, for which he received the Vizcaya de Poesía Prize of the Ateneo de Bilbao. His *Antología de la "Nova Cançó" catalana* (1968, Anthology of the Catalan "New Song") was the first study of the emergence of this important musical movement.

In 1969 *Triunfo*, a prestigious and widely read leftist cultural magazine, accepted an idea Vázquez Montalbán had submitted years earlier for a series of essays on Spanish postwar popular culture titled "Crónica sentimental de España" (Sentimental Chronicle of Spain). He completed the articles in two weeks, and they were published in September and October of that year. Vázquez Montalbán's humorous and lucid insights into popular music, soccer, radio, and cinema provide an analysis of Spanish postwar cultural identity. The essays were a great success and inaugurated a new kind of writing in Spain: the "sentimental chronicle," which occupies a space between the personal creative writing of New Journalism and the cultural-studies approach of the Frankfurt School. The essays were published in book form in 1971 to great acclaim and were republished several times thereafter.

In 1969 Vázquez Montalbán obtained a position teaching the history of communication at the School of Journalism of the University of Barcelona. That same year he published *Recordando a Dardé y otros relatos* (Remembering Dardé and Other Stories). The title story inaugurated Vázquez Montalbán's experiment with the new genre of "political fiction," characterized by the description of fictitious political events in a hypothetical setting. A satirical allegory of 1960s Spain caught between booming economic development and political dictatorship, the story portrays the industrialization of a Spanish rural community for the production of robots and the symbolic robotization of Spanish soci-

ety. "Recordando a Dardé" shows signs of the "subnormal" poetics that came to dominate Vázquez Montalbán's works: the subversion of traditional literary practices through the technique of collage, the transgression of narrative conventions, the mixing of genres, and the use of irony, parody, the surreal, and the absurd for social criticism.

Vázquez Montalbán's *Manifiesto subnormal* (1970, Subnormal Manifesto) is a highly experimental text that mixes essay, theatrical farce, Surrealist poetry, advertisement, pop-art visuals, and narrative collages. It is a theory of cultural expression, a critique of Spanish consumerist mass-media society, and a self-critique of intellectuals. The intellectual is situated in what Vázquez Montalbán calls a "subnormal" position: he or she fulfills a complementary function to normality and the established order. This position is particularly alienating for the intellectual living in a repressive society, subject to government control and censorship. Vázquez Montalbán's sense of alienation is intensified by his disillusionment with the unfulfilled promises of the 1968 revolutionary movements.

During Vázquez Montalbán's "subnormal" period, which extended roughly from 1968 to 1974, there was a pervading distrust of conventional literary forms. The traditional novel, in particular, had been declared a dead, bourgeois form by avant-garde writers and critics in the late 1960s. Vázquez Montalbán's novels of this period are experimental antinovels, intentionally subverting all narrative conventions and readers' expectations and creating new hybrid forms that owe as much to movies and advertisements as to poetry or political essays. *Yo maté a Kennedy: Impresiones, observaciones y memorias de un guardaespaldas* (1972, I Killed Kennedy: Impressions, Observations and Memories of a Bodyguard), written between 1967 and 1971, is a spoof of the spy novel with elements of the mystery novel, science fiction, Cold War movies, and the new genre of "political fiction." It introduces the character Pepe Carvalho, who narrates the story. Carvalho is a double agent who has infiltrated the Central Intelligence Agency and observes the inner workings of President John F. Kennedy's administration. Using caricature, poetry, songs, lists, schematics, and advertisements, Vázquez Montalbán creates a humorous but powerful critique of American imperialism and Spain's subservient role in the Cold War. Initially rejected by the censors, the work was published as part of a marketing campaign by two major Spanish publishing houses—the popular Planeta, which specialized in best-sellers, and the prestigious Seix Barral—to promote the New Spanish Novel. It failed to be recognized by critics or to attract a wide audience.

During the early 1970s Vázquez Montalbán was a columnist for several publications, including the cultural magazine *Triunfo* and the Barcelona daily *Tele-exprés,* and a prolific author of books; some of the latter were hastily written in a few weeks, while others were developed over several years. In 1973 he published two new books of poetry, *Coplas a la muerte de mi tía Daniela* (Couplets on the Death of My Aunt Daniela) and *A la sombra de las muchachas sin flor: Poemas del amor y del terror* (In the Shadow of Young Girls without Flowers: Poems of Love and Terror). Also in 1973, after several years of battling the censors, he published his first play, *Guillermotta en el país de las Guillerminas* (Guillermotta in the Country of the Guillerminas), which he had written for the Catalan actress and *nova cançó* singer Guillermina Motta. It is a highly experimental hybrid work that follows the "subnormal" aesthetic employed in his narratives. Production of the play was prohibited by the censors, and it has never been staged. In 1974 Vázquez Montalbán cofounded the satirical magazine *Por Favor* and wrote the libretto for Dalí's experimental opera *Etre Dieu* (2005).

Also in 1974 Vázquez Montalbán published his last experimental "subnormal" works. *Cuestiones marxistas* (Marxist Issues) is a highly theatrical, absurdist novel about the family reunion of the Marx Brothers, Groucho, Harpo, and Karl. The novel confronts the reader with the futility of all dogmas, the arbitrariness of language, and the impossibility of achieving utopia. *Cuestiones marxistas* was adapted for the stage by Guillermo Heras with the title *Se vive solamente una vez* and was performed by the independent theater company Tábano in Madrid in 1981. *Happy End* is an antinovel in dialogue form that reveals a strong skepticism toward all ideologies that defer their promised happy endings until the distant future; it also satirizes the conventional happy ending produced by Hollywood. Finding the earthly utopia is impossible, because the human condition always returns to the point of departure.

By this time Vázquez Montalbán had realized that while his work as journalist and cultural analyst reached a wide audience and had a direct impact on society, his avant-garde creative works were linguistic and intellectual exercises that did not reach beyond a small cultural elite. He decided that Pepe Carvalho of *Yo maté a Kennedy* would make an ideal protagonist. In two weeks he wrote *Tatuaje* (1974, Tattoo), in which he exploits, in a postmodern fashion, the narrative conventions of film noir and the hard-boiled detective novel in the vein of Dashiell Hammett and Raymond Chandler. There are abundant references to mass media and popular culture, including cinema, music (*Tatuaje* is also the title of a popular song by Conchita Piquer), food, and sports. There are also many literary self-references and

*Cover for the second edition (1978) of Vázquez Montalbán's 1977 Carvalho novel (*The Loneliness of the Manager*; translated as* The Angst-Ridden Executive, *1990), in which he provides critical portraits of the economic elite, right-wing political parties, and the police (William T. Young Library, University of Kentucky)*

metafictional reflections in a constant parody of generic conventions with humorous exaggerations and playful inversions. Carvalho is a former anti-Franco Communist militant and former Central Intelligence Agency operative who has become a skeptical and cynical private detective in Barcelona's *barrio chino.* A woman has been killed, and the case takes Carvalho through the slums of Barcelona and—because the censors would not permit a realistic or critical portrayal of the Spanish police—into the milieu of Spanish migrant workers in Amsterdam. In defiance of bourgeois conventionality, Carvalho's girlfriend, Charo, is a call girl, and his friends and associates are thieves and former prisoners. His disdain for elitist culture is reflected in the ritual burning of books in his fireplace, but he is a connoisseur of sexual pleasure as well as a gourmand. Recipes, erotic scenes, political and cultural reflections, songs, and poems create a multilayered collage that at times resembles the experimentalism of Vázquez Montalbán's previous novels, with the addition of a strong narrative line. *Tatuaje* was published in 1974 by a small press and failed to reach either the public or the critics.

Franco died in 1975. In 1977, a few months after the first democratic elections in Spain in more than forty years, Vázquez Montalbán's next Carvalho novel, *La soledad del manager* (The Loneliness of the Manager; translated as *The Angst-Ridden Executive*, 1990), was published by Planeta. Carvalho's investigation of the death of an executive of a multinational company based in Spain unravels a political mystery. The freedoms gained with the end of the dictatorship are clearly reflected in the explicit sex scenes, the realistic depictions of corruption, and the critical portrayals of the economic elite, right-wing political parties, and the police. The novel conveys the atmosphere of excitement, as well as confusion, surrounding the elections; negative social realities that fully emerged following Franco's death, such as the high levels of unemployment, drug use, and crime, are also reflected. Well received by the public and the critics, *La soledad del manager* was Vázquez Montalbán's first novel in his literary career to achieve some degree of success.

One of the most popular Carvalho novels with both the public and the critics, *Los mares del Sur* (1979; translated as *Southern Seas*, 1986) captures the sense of *desencanto* (disillusionment) that followed the initial euphoria over the end of the dictatorship. Instead of a revolutionary break with the past, Spain underwent a moderate transition to democracy and an agreement to forget about the crimes of the Franco regime. The story deals with the guilty conscience of an entrepreneur who became rich during the 1960s economic boom of *desarrollismo* (industrialization and economic development) by building substandard housing complexes for the rural immigrants who moved to working-class suburbs of the big cities. Undergoing a midlife crisis, he leaves behind his bourgeois comfort and moves into a slum he built in the southern part of Barcelona—only to be killed, in an instance of poetic justice, by one of the inhabitants of the monster he had created. Carvalho investigates his disappearance and death. Vázquez Montalbán achieves in this novel a balance of fast-paced action, introspection, and ironic social commentary, and it was one of the triggers for the boom in Spanish detective fiction, or *novela negra* (noir novel), during the Transition years.

Vázquez Montalbán received the coveted Planeta literary prize in 1979 for *Los mares del Sur*. The prize carries the largest monetary award in Spain, allowing the recipients to develop their literary projects more freely, and the prestige makes their works instant best-sellers. Vázquez Montalbán became a public personality and

one of only a handful of writers in Spain who could live comfortably from sales of their books. The reception of the work also changed the perception that his career as a novelist was secondary to that as a journalist; he became one of the novelists identified with the new democratic Spain.

*Los mares del Sur* was translated into French in 1980 under the title *Marquises, si vos rivages . . .* (Marquesas, If Your Beaches . . .); it was awarded the Prix International de la Littérature Policière (International Prize for Crime Literature) in 1981, and *Le Monde Littéraire* selected it as one of the most important books of the period 1975 to 1985. The enormous success of this novel with French critics and readers opened the door for Vázquez Montalbán's novels in France and the rest of Europe, making him one of the best-known contemporary Spanish novelists outside of Spain.

Throughout the 1980s Vázquez Montalbán was known primarily as the author of the Pepe Carvalho novels. In 1981 he published *Asesinato en el Comité Central* (translated as *Murder in the Central Committee*, 1984), a political "locked-room mystery novel" in which Carvalho travels from Barcelona to Madrid to investigate the assassination of the president of the Spanish Communist Party during a blackout in the middle of a Central Committee meeting. The decline of Eurocommunism and the general sense of confusion and disillusionment of the 1980s resonate throughout the novel, as do echoes of the political turmoil that spurred an attempted coup against the Spanish Parliament by Lieutenant Colonel Antonio Tejero that same year. In this novel Vázquez Montalbán, who had been a revisionist critic, a militant, and a member of the Central Committee at various times, settles his accounts with the party. *Asesinato en el Comité Central* was awarded the Premio Recalmare in Italy.

The background of Vázquez Montalbán's next novel, *Los pájaros de Bangkok* (1983, The Birds of Bangkok), is the political, economic, and cultural opening of Spain to the outside world after the victory in the 1982 general elections of the Spanish Socialist Party (which governed Spain for the next fourteen years). Carvalho goes to Thailand in search of a Spanish tourist who disappeared. The central theme of *La rosa de Alejandría* (1984, The Rose of Alexandria) is the impossibility of escape from the trappings of bourgeois culture. Parallel stories of the journeys of rural migrant workers, the romantic escapades of a respectable housewife, Carvalho's investigative travels, and a Spanish sailor trying to reach beyond the limits that confine his existence take place in the Caribbean islands, the remote province of Albacete, and aboard a cargo ship in the middle of the ocean but converge in Barcelona, which acts almost as a force of destiny. Using as a leitmotiv the popular song "La rosa de Alejandría," with its refrain "colorada de noche, blanca de día" (red by night, white by day), the novel chronicles the ambiguity, moral duplicity, and *desencanto* resulting from the awareness of individual and collective unfulfilled promises in Spanish society in the 1980s. The critical consensus is that Vázquez Montalbán is at his best in the Pepe Carvalho novels from *La soledad del manager* to *La rosa de Alejandría*.

In 1985 Vázquez Montalbán published *El pianista* (translated as *The Pianist,* 1989), his first novel in more than ten years unrelated to the extremely successful Carvalho series. From this point onward he alternated between the Carvalho novels and other works; all of his novels have in common, however, the objective of chronicling contemporary Spanish society. *El pianista* is the first of a trilogy of novels about "the ethics of resistance" in which Vázquez Montalbán reflects on the role of the artist and the intellectual and on the collective moral decline from the revolutionary spirit of resistance to yuppie conformity. The novel is divided into three parts, told in reverse chronological order to mimic the effects of memory and to highlight the connections between past and present. In the first part, set in contemporary Barcelona, a group of intellectual friends walk through the streets of the Fifth District where they grew up and reminisce about the past and how their revolutionary ideals have given way to bourgeois conventionality. The second part takes place in the Fifth District in 1942; Barcelona is recovering from the traumas of the recent Civil War, and a group of neighbors travels along the roof terraces, the only space of freedom available, in a surreal and poetic search for a piano to help a recently released political prisoner. The third part is set in Paris in 1936, at the beginning of the Civil War, and presents the varying responses to the war of a group of Spanish artists and intellectuals: some choose to stay in France, others to return to Spain to defend the Republic. The novel shows that conformist behavior is publicly acclaimed, while courageous acts of resistance encounter defeat and are forgotten. *El pianista* was received with great critical and public acclaim, was translated into many languages, and received the Premio Recalmare in Italy.

In 1986 Vázquez Montalbán published *El balneario* (The Spa) in the new Planeta "Serie Carvalho"— the first Spanish series devoted to a single fictional character. Carvalho is growing old, and there is less action and a great deal more caricature in this novel than in the earlier ones. In the context of Spain's recent entrance into the European Union, the novel is a satire of the comfort of the First World, the exclusive health club of rich nations. During a stay at an exclusive international spa, where he follows a strict diet, Carvalho

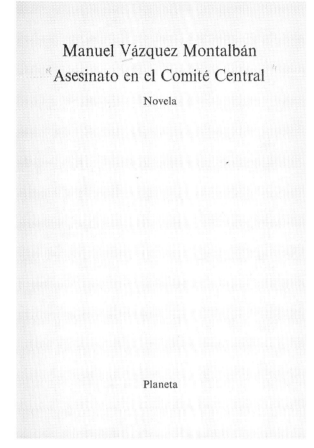

Manuel Vázquez Montalbán
*Asesinato en el Comité Central*

Novela

Planeta

*Title page for Vázquez Montalbán's 1981 novel (translated as*
Murder in the Central Committee, *1984), in which
Carvalho investigates the assassination of the president
of the Spanish Communist Party (John W. Brister
Library, Memphis State University)*

investigates several mysterious deaths. *El balneario* received the Deutscher Kritiker Preis (German Critics' Prize). In the next two years Vázquez Montalbán published five short novels and short-story collections in the Serie Carvalho; all are entertaining, but none is comparable in literary quality to the earlier Carvalho novels. Many of them were adapted for television in 1986 by the Argentine director Adolfo Aristain under the title *Las aventuras de Pepe Carvalho,* but the result was unsatisfactory to both Vázquez Montalbán and the viewers. Vázquez Montalbán took revenge in his 1987 novella "Asesinato en Prado del Rey" (Murder in Prado del Rey), in which the murder victim, Araquistain, had directed a series of detective stories written for television by Sánchez Bolín, a fictional stand-in for Vázquez Montalbán. He also published *El delantero centro fue asesinado al atardecer* (1988, The Center-Forward Was Murdered in the Afternoon; translated as *Off Side,* 1996), a Pepe Carvalho novel that has the energy of the early works. Set during Barcelona's drastic renovations for the 1992 Olympics, the novel deals with soccer, urban planning, and the erasure of collective memory. It received the Ciudad de Barcelona literary prize.

Works unrelated to Pepe Carvalho published during this period include the novellas *Cuarteto* (1988, Quartet) and *El matarife* (1986, The Slaughterman) and the novel *Los alegres muchachos de Atzavara* (1987, The Merry Boys of Atzavara). The latter, an ironic look at the contradictions of the Catalan bourgeoisie at the end of the dictatorship and at the incipient gay subculture narrated from multiple points of view, received the Boccaccio Prize in Italy.

In 1990 Vázquez Montalbán published *Galíndez* (translated, 1992), the second novel in his "ethics of resistance" trilogy. It is based on the disappearance on the streets of New York in 1956 of Jesús de Galíndez, a Basque nationalist representative to the United Nations, on the orders of the dictator Rafael Trujillo of the Dominican Republic. The novel indicates that Galíndez was murdered in retaliation for publishing an exposé of Trujillo's dictatorship. The investigation is reopened in the 1980s by an idealistic young American scholar who uncovers the involvement in Galíndez's disappearance and death of various intelligence agencies; the discovery leads her to suffer the same fate as Galíndez. The scholar's boyfriend, a young Basque working for the Madrid city government, investigates her disappearance and thus symbolically takes up her cause. Vázquez Montalbán mixes the suspense of the novel of investigation with essays, poems, and rigorous documentation in the form of interviews and letters. A deeply moving work, it offers a more optimistic look at the possibility of resistance than the hopelessness portrayed in *El pianista*. *Galíndez* received the National Prize of Literature in Spain and the European Literary Prize.

In 1992, the centennial of Franco's birth, Vázquez Montalbán published the third novel in the "ethics of resistance" trilogy, *Autobiografía del general Franco* (Autobiography of General Franco). More than six hundred pages long and including an exhaustive bibliography of secondary sources, *Autobiografía del general Franco* follows a long tradition of novels of dictatorship in twentieth-century Hispanic literature by such authors as Ramón del Valle-Inclán, Augusto Roa Bastos, Miguel Ángel Asturias, and Gabriel García Márquez. Rather than choosing the grotesque or the satiric mode as those authors had, Vázquez Montalbán opts for the postmodern strategy of creating "noise." The novel combines a fictional autobiography by Franco with a counterdiscourse by an anti-Franco intellectual who has been commissioned to ghost-write the book. He creates "noise" by correcting, supplementing, and refuting the

official account and, at the same time, writing the collective autobiography of the anti-Franco resistance. *Autobiografía del general Franco* was praised by Eduardo Haro Tecglén in *El País* (31 October 1992) as "an anti-Franco monument." Also in 1992 Vázquez Montalbán received the Raymond Chandler Prize in Italy for the totality of his literary work.

*El estrangulador* (1994, The Strangler) is a radical indictment of contemporary society as seen by a mental patient, an alienated intellectual who claims to be the Boston Strangler. Following the theories of Michel Foucault and the antipsychiatry movement, Vázquez Montalbán depicts madness as a cultural construction created to protect the social order. The novel, composed of the journal written by the patient as part of his medical therapy, deconstructs the social, political, and medical establishments that have imprisoned the narrator. *El estrangulador* was received by critics as one of Vázquez Montalbán's best and most ambitious novels and received the Spanish Premio de la Crítica in 1994. The following year Vázquez Montalbán was awarded the Premio Nacional de las Letras Españolas for his entire oeuvre.

Installments in the Pepe Carvalho series published in the 1990s include *El laberinto griego* (1991, The Greek Labyrinth; translated as *An Olympic Death*, 1992) and *Sabotaje olímpico* (1993, Olympic Sabotage), both of which use the 1992 Barcelona Olympics as backdrops. The novels are clearly caricatures, sometimes bordering on the surreal. The same is true of *Roldán, ni vivo ni muerto* (1994, Roldán, Neither Living Nor Dead), which includes comic-book illustrations and fictionalizes the capture of Luis Roldán, the director of the Spanish Civil Guard, who had fled the country after embezzling public funds. *El premio* (1996, The Prize) is a satiric roman à clef in which Vázquez Montalbán presents an iconoclastic settling of accounts with the Spanish literary establishment, including publishers, critics, and prizes.

In 1997 many public events were orchestrated by Planeta to commemorate the twenty-fifth anniversary of the Pepe Carvalho series, including the international "Jornadas Carvalho" (Carvalho Conference) in Madrid; the launching of a new edition of Vázquez Montalbán's novels under the rubric "Carvalho 25 Años" (Carvalho 25 Years), with prologues by distinguished authors; and the publication of a seven-volume commemorative work, including a new play by Vázquez Montalbán featuring Pepe Carvalho (*Antes de que el milenio nos separe* [Before the Millennium Separates Us]), photographic essays, and dedications and illustrations by many Spanish intellectuals and artists. Also in 1997 the novel *Quinteto de Buenos Aires* (translated as *The Buenos Aires Quintet*, 2003) was published; here Carvalho travels to Buenos Aires in the aftermath of the defeat of the military junta in 1983 to investigate the case of a distant uncle who has been "disappeared." In 1997 Vázquez Montalbán received an honorary doctorate from the Universitat Autonoma de Barcelona.

The title of Vázquez Montalbán's *O César o nada* (1998, Caesar or Nothing) is borrowed from a 1910 novel by Pío Baroja. On the surface it is an historical novel about the Machiavellian power struggles of the corrupt Borgias–Pope Alexander IV and his family– during the Renaissance, but it is actually a parable about political ambition, corruption, and terror in Spain in the 1990s.

The next installment of the Pepe Carvalho series, *El hombre de mi vida* (2000; translated as *The Man of My Life,* 2005), reunites Carvalho with his old girlfriend Charo, who is now running a hotel in Andorra. The novel *Erec y Enide* (2002, Eric and Enide) is a modern reinterpretation of the Arthurian tale of Eric and Enide, the courageous lovers and seekers of adventure in Chrétien de Troyes's *Erec et Enide* (circa 1165). It presents two parallel stories: an aged writer and medieval scholar is to receive an homage for lifetime achievement on the island of San Simón in the Bay of Vigo. While preparing his acceptance speech about Eric and Enide, he remembers his life and his relationship with his wife, who is leaving him. Meanwhile, their son and his girlfriend embark on an Eric-and-Enide adventure of their own as part of the organization Doctors Without Borders in the Mexican state of Chiapas. One of Vázquez Montalbán's most optimistic novels, *Erec y Enide* affirms the virtues of solidarity, love, and commitment to others in the face of adversity and injustice.

On 18 October 2003, on his way back to Barcelona from a series of lectures in Australia and New Zealand, Vázquez Montalbán suffered a fatal heart attack in the Bangkok airport. He had just finished the much-anticipated two-volume novel *Milenio Carvalho* (2004, Carvalho Millennium). This eight-hundred-page conclusion to the series mixes Miguel de Cervantes's *Don Quixote* (1605, 1615) and Jules Verne's *Le Tour du monde en quatre-vingts jours* (1873, Around the World in Eighty Days; translated as *A Tour of the World in Eighty Days,* 1873) as Carvalho and his assistant journey around the globe, witnessing terrorism and military intervention in the Middle East and the devastating impact of globalization on poor regions from Asia to Africa and South America. Vázquez Montalbán's death received much attention in the media, and he was remembered as one of the most influential and recognizable figures of post-Franco Spain. Even so, the fictional Pepe Carvalho largely surpassed his creator in public recognition.

Cover for Vázquez Montalbán's 1985 novel (translated as The Pianist, 1989), in which the events are told in reverse chronological order to mimic the effects of memory and to highlight the connections between past and present (Thomas Cooper Library, University of South Carolina)

Manuel Vázquez Montalbán was a respected opinion maker and had a multitude of devoted followers in Spain and abroad. Some critics have reproached him for his leftist leanings, others for what they consider his excessively prolific literary production, his reliance on the formulas of popular culture, and the lengthy political and cultural digressions in his fiction. For still others, however, these characteristics are some of the better qualities of his work: they praise the consistency of his commitment as an intellectual, the postmodern combining of high and low cultural forms, and the extent and profundity of his observations. In any case, as a result of his ability to depict and analyze the social and cultural events of the times, Vázquez Montalbán's novels are among the best chronicles of the last part of the twentieth century in Spain.

**Interviews:**

Federico Campbell, "Manuel Vázquez Montalbán o la mitología popular," in his *Infame turba* (Barcelona: Lumen, 1971), pp. 157–166;

Mary Mérida, "Manuel Vázquez Montalbán: 'Un país bastante decepcionante,'" *Reseña,* 66 (1973): 53–55;

Montserrat Roig, "Manolo Vázquez Montalbán, tras las rejas del sentimiento," in her *Los hechiceros de la palabra* (Barcelona: Martínez Roca, 1975), pp. 113–126;

Colectivo Lantaba, "Vázquez Montalbán: El desencanto y la lucidez," *Viejo topo,* 23 (1978): 48–50;

Víctor Claudín, "Entrevista: Manuel Vázquez Montalbán: Un escéptico activista," *Ozono,* 41 (1979): 5–8;

Miguel Bayón, "Vázquez Montalbán: No creer en las evidencias," *Triunfo,* 900 (1980): 56;

Angel S. Harguindey, "La importancia de vivir," *País Semanal* (Madrid), 27 December 1981, pp. 11–13;

Lola Díaz, "Vuelve Pepe Carvalho," *Cambio 16* (6 April 1984): 144–149;

Claudín, "Con Vázquez Montalbán, sobre su Carvalho," *Ínsula,* 462 (1985): 7;

Díaz, "Manuel Vázquez Montalbán, el futuro ya no es lo que era," *País Semanal* (Madrid), 15 April 1985, pp. 108–111;

José F. Colmeiro, "Desde el balneario: Entrevista con Manuel Vázquez Montalbán," *Quimera,* 73 (1988): 12–23;

Díaz, "'La justicia me da muchísimo miedo,'" *Cambio 16* (15 February 1988): 104–108;

Ernesto Ayala-Dip, "Manuel Vázquez Montalbán," *Urogallo,* 52–53 (1990): 12–17;

José Manuel Fajardo, "'La política es una obsesión que me sirve para escribir,'" *Cambio 16* (18 June 1990): 128–129;

Leonardo Padura Fuentes, "Reivindicación de la memoria: Entrevista con Manuel Vázquez Montalbán," *Quimera,* 108 (1991): 62;

Marie-Lise Gazarian-Gautier, "Manuel Vázquez Montalbán," in her *Interviews with Spanish Writers* (Elmwood Park, Ill.: Dalkey Archive, 1991), pp. 302–312;

Xavier Moret, "'El franquismo era feísimo; daba la impresión de que a todo el mundo le olían los calcetines,'" *País* (Madrid), 26 October 1992, p. 26;

Quim Aranda, *Qué pensa Manuel Vázquez Montalbán* (Barcelona: Dèria, 1995);

Colmeiro, "¿Qué pueden los intelectuales? Entrevista con Manuel Vázquez Montalbán," in *Spain Today: Essays on Literature, Culture, Society,* edited by Colmeiro (Hanover, N.H.: Dartmouth College, 1995), pp. 149–153;

William Nichols, "La novela negra en el mundo hispano: Entrevistas con Manuel Vázquez Montalbán y Paco Ignacio Taibo II," *Arizona Journal of Hispanic Cultural Studies,* 2 (1998): 197–231;

Georges Tyras, *Geometrías de la memoria: Conversaciones con Manuel Vázquez Montalbán* (Granada: Zoela, 2003).

**Biographies:**

Manuel Blanco Chivite, *Manuel Vázquez Montalbán* (Madrid: Grupo Libro 88, 1992);

Florence Estrade, *Manuel Vázquez Montalbán* (Barcelona: Ediciones de la Tempestad, 2004);

José V. Saval, *Manuel Vázquez Montalbán: El triunfo de un luchador incansable* (Madrid: Síntesis, 2004).

**References:**

Quim Aranda and others, *Manuel Vázquez Montalbán, Carvalho 25 años: El aniversario de un gran detective,* 7 volumes (Barcelona: Planeta, 1997);

Mari Paz Balibrea Enríquez, *En la tierra baldía: Manuel Vázquez Montalbán y la izquierda española en la postmodernidad* (Barcelona: El Viejo Topo, 1999);

Susana Bayo Belenguer, *Theory, Genre, and Memory in the Carvalho Series of Manuel Vázquez Montalbán* (Lewiston, N.Y.: Edwin Mellen Press, 2001);

Francie Cate-Arries, "Lost in the Language of Culture: Manuel Vázquez Montalbán's Novel of Detection," *Revista de estudios hispánicos,* 22, no. 3 (1988): 47–56;

Víctor Claudín, "Vázquez Montalbán y la novela policiaca española," *Cuadernos Hispanoamericanos,* 416 (1985): 157–166;

José F. Colmeiro, *Crónica del desencanto: La narrativa de Manuel Vázquez Montalbán* (Coral Gables, Fla.: University of Miami–North South Center, 1996);

Colmeiro, "Dissonant Voices: Memory and Counter-Memory in Manuel Vázquez Montalbán's *Autobiografía del General Franco,*" *Studies in Twentieth Century Literature,* 21, no. 2 (1997): 337–360;

Colmeiro, "La novela policiaca posmodernista de Manuel Vázquez Montalbán," *Anales de la literatura española contemporánea,* 14 (1989): 11–32;

Colmeiro, "La re-escritura de la historia o la verdad sobre el caso *Galíndez,*" in *Actas del XI Congreso de la Asociación Internacional de Hispanistas,* volume 4 (Irvine: University of California, 1994), pp. 211–222;

Malcolm Compitello, "De la metanovela a la novela: Manuel Vázquez Montalbán y los límites de la vanguardia española contemporánea," in *Prosa hispánica de vanguardia,* edited by Fernando Burgos (Madrid: Orígenes, 1986), pp. 191–199;

Compitello, "Spain's *nueva novela negra* and the Question of Form," *Monographic Review / Revista Monográfica,* 3, nos. 1–2 (1987): 182–191;

Luis F. Costa, "La nueva novela negra española: El caso de Pepe Carvalho," *Monographic Review / Revista Monográfica*, 3, nos. 1–2 (1987): 298–305;

John Cottam, "Understanding the Creation of Pepe Carvalho," in *Leeds Papers on Thrillers in the Transition: "Novela negra" and Political Change in Spain*, edited by Rob Rix (Leeds, U.K.: Trinity and All Saints College, 1992), pp. 123–135;

Domenec Font, "Sobre la novela policiaca de Vázquez Montalbán: Paisaje en ruinas," *Quimera*, 42 (1984): 54–55;

Thomas Franz, "*Collage* y *montage* en *Happy End* de Manuel Vázquez Montalbán," *Hispanic Journal*, 8, no. 2 (1987): 151–160;

Patricia Hart, "Manuel Vázquez Montalbán: Pepe Carvalho and the Probing of Pathos," in her *The Spanish Sleuth: The Detective in Spanish Fiction* (Rutherford, N.J.: Fairleigh Dickinson University Press, 1987);

Hado Lyra, *Il Viaggio en Italia: Omaggio del Premio Grinzane a Manuel Vázquez Montalbán* (Piacenza: Frassinelli, 2004);

John Macklin, "Realism Revisited: Myth, Mimesis and the *Novela Negra*," in *Leeds Papers on Thrillers in the Transition*, pp. 49–73;

Gonzalo Navajas, "Una estética para después del posmodernismo: La nostalgia asertiva y la reciente novela española," *Revista de Estudios Hispánicos*, 25, no. 3 (1991): 129–151;

Navajas, "Género y contragénero policiaco en *La Rosa de Alejandría* de Manuel Vázquez Montalbán,"
*Monographic Review / Revista Monográfica*, 3, nos. 1–2 (1987): 247–260;

Sandra Puvogel, "Pepe Carvalho and Spain: A Look at Manuel Vázquez Montalbán's Detective Fiction," *Monographic Review / Revista Monográfica*, 3, nos. 1–2 (1987): 261–267;

Joan Ramón Resina, "Desencanto y fórmula literaria en las novelas policiacas de Manuel Vázquez Montalbán," *Modern Language Notes*, 108, no. 2 (1993): 254–282;

Mario Vargas Llosa, "Un escritor numeroso: Manuel Vázquez Montalbán," *Revista de la Universidad de México*, 33, no. 12 (1979): 11–14;

Salvador Vázquez de Parga, "Hacia una novela policíaca literaria," in his *La novela policíaca en España* (Barcelona: Ronsel, 1993), pp. 208–223.

**Internet Sites:** *La página web sobre Manuel Vázquez Montalbán* <http://www.vespito.net/mvm> [accessed 5 October 2005];

*Las páginas negras de Pepe Carvalho* <http://www.msu.edu/~colmeiro/carvalho.html> [accessed 5 October 2005];

*Obra periodística: Manuel Vázquez Montalbán* (Universitat Pompeu Fabra) <http://www.upf.edu/periodis/mvm/presentacio.htm> [accessed 5 October 2005].

**Papers:**

An archive of Manuel Vázquez Montalbán's papers will be established at the University of Barcelona.

# Enrique Vila-Matas

## (31 March 1948 – )

### Wilfrido H. Corral
*California State University, Sacramento*

BOOKS: *Mujer en el espejo contemplando el paisaje* (Barcelona: Tusquets, 1973);

*La asesina ilustrada* (Barcelona: Tusquets, 1977);

*Al sur de los párpados* (Madrid: Fundamentos, 1980);

*Nunca voy al cine* (Barcelona: Laertes, 1982);

*Impostura* (Barcelona: Anagrama, 1984);

*Historia abreviada de la literatura portátil* (Barcelona: Anagrama, 1985);

*Una casa para siempre* (Barcelona: Anagrama, 1988);

*Suicidios ejemplares* (Barcelona: Anagrama, 1991);

*El viajero más lento* (Barcelona: Anagrama, 1992);

*Hijos sin hijos* (Barcelona: Anagrama, 1993);

*Recuerdos inventados: Primera antología personal* (Barcelona: Anagrama, 1994);

*Lejos de Veracruz* (Barcelona: Anagrama, 1995);

*El traje de los domingos* (Madrid: Huerga y Fierro, 1995);

*Para acabar con los números redondos* (Valencia: Pre-Textos, 1997);

*Extraña forma de vida* (Barcelona: Anagrama, 1997);

*El viaje vertical* (Barcelona: Anagrama, 1999);

*Bartleby y compañía* (Barcelona: Anagrama, 2000); translated by Jonathan Dunne as *Bartleby & Co.* (London: Harvill, 2004; New York: New Directions, 2004);

*Desde la ciudad nerviosa* (Madrid: Alfaguara, 2000);

*El mal de Montano* (Barcelona: Anagrama, 2002);

*Regreso al tapiz que se dispara en muchas direcciones* (Cuenca: Centro de Profesores y Recursos de Cuenca, 2002);

*París no se acaba nunca* (Barcelona: Anagrama, 2003);

*Extrañas notas de laboratorio* (Mérida, Venezuela: CELARG, 2003);

*Aunque no entendamos nada* (Santiago, Chile: J. C. Sáez, 2004);

*El viento ligero en Parma* (Mexico City: Sexto Piso, 2004);

*Doctor Pasavento* (Barcelona: Anagrama, 2005).

*Enrique Vila-Matas (photograph © Florencio Palencia; from the cover for* El viaje vertical, *2001; Mervyn H. Sterne Library, University of Alabama at Birmingham)*

Enrique Vila-Matas is one of the most prominent writers of the Spanish-speaking world. Some Spanish writers born toward the end of the 1940s and later have opted to retell the story of the Civil War years (1936 to 1939); others have used a minimal realism to depict the period of Francisco Franco's regime (1939 to 1975); and still others, especially since Franco's death in 1975, are determined to present Spain and its full reincorporation into European modernity with sophisticated narrative techniques. Vila-Matas belongs to the last group.

Vila-Matas was born in Barcelona on 31 March 1948 to Enrique and Tayo Vila-Matas. His father was in the real-estate business. Vila-Matas started writing at twelve; he studied law and journalism. In 1968 he went into self-exile in Paris, seeking greater intellectual freedom than was possible under the Franco regime. He rented a garret from the writer Marguerite Duras and supported himself by editing articles for popular magazines such as the movie journal *Fotogramas*. He returned to Spain after two years. In 1971 he directed two movie shorts, *Todos los jóvenes* (All the Sad Young Men) and *Fin de verano* (End of Summer), and wrote movie criticism for *Destino* magazine.

Vila-Matas's first novel, *Mujer en el espejo contemplando el paisaje* (Woman Watching the Landscape in a Mirror), was published in 1973. The story centers on mirror images of various characters: the narrator and Elena; the father and mother; and Rojas, a supporter of the Spanish Republic, and the owner of a yacht named *Victoria*. It is a tale about time and how the mind operates within frames that only allow oppositions: awareness and dream, reason and madness, and perception and representation. It was followed in 1977 by a police thriller, *La asesina ilustrada* (The Cultured Assassin). Both novels involve distortions of time, doubles, dream sequences, and the writing of letters, notes, and drafts. In 1978 he married Paula de Parma. In 1980 he published the novel *Al sur de los párpados* (South of the Eyelids), a false thriller that concentrates on the dream states of the characters. His short-story collection *Nunca voy al cine* (I Never Go to the Movies) appeared in 1982.

*Impostura* (1984, Imposture), Vila-Matas's next novel, is set in Barcelona in the 1950s. Dr. Vigil and his assistant, Barnaola, seek to discover the identity of an amnesiac madman who has been arrested for stealing funeral urns. Two women show up claiming to be the wife of the madman; one says that he is an illustrious Falangist (Francoist) professor, the other that he is an anarchist, liar, and thief. The stage is thus set for a comedy of errors, mistaken identities, and thematic cross-references. *Impostura* posits that writing itself is fakery and that narrators are a calculated farce or fraud.

In the mid 1980s Vila-Matas began to travel widely, particularly to Latin America, where he came into contact with younger prose writers. This period also brought a large influx of Latin American writers to Barcelona, where Vila-Matas befriended many of them.

In 1985 Vila-Matas published *Historia abreviada de la literatura portátil* (Brief History of Portable Literature). The prologue, ten brief essays, and "basic bibliography" deal with authors such as Tristan Tzara, Valery Larbaud, Lawrence Sterne, Louis-Ferdinand Céline, Maurice Blanchot, and Walter de la Mare and artists such as Man Ray, Paul Klee, and Georgia O'Keeffe. Vila-Matas designates them a secret society of "Shandys"–international nomads whose reason for existing was the abolition of all artistic conventions. *Historia abreviada de la literatura portátil* marked the start of Vila-Matas's international reputation; it received an especially enthusiastic reception in Latin America and still has a cult following in literary circles there.

The novel *Una casa para siempre* (1988, A House Forever) seems at first to be a series of disconnected tales, but about halfway through the book the reader realizes that they all have the same narrator, a ventriloquist. In one story a woman has to deal with the appearance of several men claiming to be her husband, who fled sometime before. In another tale a couple discovers an old infidelity after fifty years of marital harmony. Yet another story centers on a passion that leads to murder and the culprit's flight to a remote place. Critics noted the essayistic digressions in *Una casa para siempre* and pointed to such influences as Luigi Pirandello, Max Frisch, Wenceslao Fernández Flores, and James Joyce.

*Suicidios ejemplares* (1991, Exemplary Suicides) comprises ten stories of madness and suicide in which the only salvation is through writing. Reviewers spoke of perfection and maturity, especially in regard to "El coleccionista de tempestades" (The Storm Collector), "Los amores que duran toda una vida" (Loves that Last a Lifetime), and "Un invento muy práctico" (A Very Practical Experiment). Vila-Matas's popularity increased greatly after the publication of the collection.

Most of the essays in *El viajero más lento* (1992, The Slower Traveler) are literary notes that were originally published in Spanish and Latin American newspapers. The authors Vila-Matas celebrates include Franz Kafka, Augusto Monterroso, Vladimir Nabokov, Joseph Conrad, Fernando Pessoa, and Witold Gombrowicz. *Hijos sin hijos* (1993, Children without Children) is a collection of fourteen tales that relate Kafkaesque childhood traumas. The titles include the place and year of composition: for example, "Los de abajo (Sa Ràpita, 1992)" (The Underdogs [Sa Ràpita, 1992]) and "Azorín de la selva (Arive, 1989)" (Azorín of the Jungle [Arive, 1989]).

*Lejos de Veracruz* (1995, Far from Veracruz) is narrated by Enrique Tenorio, the youngest of three brothers. The older two have died when twenty-seven-year-old Enrique begins the story of his dysfunctional family: Antonio, a spoiled pedant and travel-book author, killed himself while writing a novel, "El descenso" (The Descent), that Enrique tries to complete; Máximo, a fragile painter, was murdered. Enrique travels to Barcelona, Majorca, the Caribbean, and Mexico to avoid the rest of his family; accompanied by the real-life Mexican novelist Sergio Pitol, he ends up drunkenly killing a person in Veracruz. The novel includes erotic games, sarcastic humor, songs, and parodies of and tributes to writers who have been the subjects of Vila-Matas's essays.

*El traje de los domingos* (1995, The Sunday Suit) is a collection of Vila-Matas's book reviews, newspaper columns, and prologues. *Para acabar con los números redondos*

ENRIQUE VILA-MATAS

*El viaje vertical*

**ANAGRAMA**
Narrativas hispánicas

*Cover for a 2001 edition of Vila-Matas's 1999 novel (The Vertical*
*Voyage), about a seventy-year-old Barcelona businessman*
*who sets out on a journey of self-discovery after his*
*wife rejects him on their fiftieth anniversary*
*(Mervyn H. Sterne Library, University*
*of Alabama at Birmingham)*

(1997, To Get Rid of Round Numbers) comprises fifty-two unorthodox biographies of authors including Conrad, Antonin Artaud, Joseph Roth, Graham Greene, Augusto Monterroso, Roland Barthes, Gustave Flaubert, Virginia Woolf, Georges Perec, Sigmund Freud, Georg Christoph Lichtenberg, Robert Walser, Guy de Maupassant, and Jorge Luis Borges. Vila-Matas's next novel, *Extraña forma de vida* (1997, Strange Form of Life), opens with a writer, Cyrano, waking up and realizing that during the next twenty-four hours he has to choose between his wife, Carmina, and his sister-in-law, Rosita. His decision must be made while he prepares a talk, "The Mythical Structure of the Hero," which he is to give that night to the sisters with the ultimate purpose of seducing Rosita. Cyrano decides to impress her by

talking about the permanent human need to spy, and the narrator "spies" on writers and artists in a tragic and comic fashion. Thus, the "strange form of life" of the title is the voyeuristic aspect implicit in creating lives, which in this novel comes to an unhappy end.

The protagonist of *El viaje vertical* (1999, The Vertical Voyage) is Federico Mayol, a distinguished seventy-year-old Barcelona businessman. On their fiftieth anniversary his wife asks him to leave because she wants to "find herself." Mayol sets out on a journey of soul-searching that takes him from Barcelona to Oporto, Lisbon, Madeira, and, finally, Atlantis. The voyage leaves him at peace with himself and eager to acquire the literary culture he never had time to obtain while living a purportedly "full" life during the Franco years. Fiction and reality and humor and tragedy alternate with digressions about the Spanish Civil War, exile, the ironies of life, and the therapeutic value of literature. At the end the manager of the hotel in which Mayol is staying finds in Mayol's story the material for a novel. *El viaje vertical* received the prestigious Venezuelan Rómulo Gallegos Prize.

*El viaje vertical* is the closest Vila-Matas has come to a conventional novel. His next work, the best-selling *Bartleby y compañía* (2000; translated as *Bartleby & Co.,* 2004), is a combination of essay and fiction about writers who have been forgotten by Western literary history. The narrator, Marcelo, decides to research what he calls the "literature of No"—the literature of stillness, passivity, and postponement. He calls his musings and summaries "notes without a text" and aims to show the impossibility of producing a conventionally coherent narrative. The eighty-six sections that make up *Bartleby y compañía* create a canon of authors who, like Herman Melville's protagonist in "Bartleby, the Scrivener" (1853), answer any request by saying that they "would prefer not to." *Bartleby y compañía* was awarded France's Prix du Meilleur Livre Etranger (Best Foreign Novel Prize) and the City of Barcelona Prize in 2002.

The articles, essays, tributes, newspaper notes, and criticism collected in *Desde la ciudad nerviosa* (2000, From the Nervous City) deal with neighborhood bars, television programs, word games, the lives of authors, the origin of Vila-Matas's vocation as a writer, and the composition and reception of *Bartleby y compañía*. The long third section, "Un tapiz que se dispara en muchas direcciones" (A Tapestry That Goes Off in Many Directions), was published separately in 2002 with a slightly different title.

*El mal de Montano* (2002, Montano's Disease) is an essayistic novel in the tradition of Joyce, Nabokov, Marcel Proust, Robert Musil, Hermann Broch, and Latin American novelists such as Augusto Roa Bastos, Alejandro Rossi, and Roberto Bolaño. The unnamed narrator writes a story titled "El mal de Montano." In that story he presents himself as a Spanish literary critic who travels to Nantes to visit Montano, his first wife's son. Obsessed with the future of literature and devoted to deciphering the diaries of his favorite authors, he goes back to Barcelona, where his second wife, Rosa, a movie director, suggests that he travel to Chile. The second part of *El mal de Montano,* "Diccionario del tímido amor a la vida" (Dictionary of the Timid Love of Life), is devoted to disproving the first part, which the narrator calls a *nouvelle.* He now says that he is not a literary critic; he is a writer whose pseudonym is Rosario Girondo, and he is suffering from writer's block. Montano does not exist, and Rosa is not a director but his literary agent. His descriptions of his travels through South America are interrupted by Tongoy, an actor, who periodically takes over the narration. The section "Teoría de Budapest" (Budapest Theory) is a hilarious parody of a scholarly talk in which Girondo re-creates his mother's secret diary; the real subject of the talk is his wife's affair with Tongoy. *El mal de Montano* received the Premio Herralde de Novela and the Premio de la Crítica in 2002.

*París no se acaba nunca* (2003, There Is Never Any End to Paris) is a fictionalized memoir of the two years Vila-Matas spent writing *La asesina ilustrada* in Paris. The novel begins with Vila-Matas finding on an airplane the manuscript for a book about the year the unknown author of the manuscript spent in Paris writing his first novel. A cat-and-mouse game ensues between the "real" Vila-Matas and the writer of the manuscript, with many hilarious episodes that include a digression about Vila-Matas's physical resemblance to Ernest Hemingway (ironic, since the resemblance is nonexistent), conversations with his parents about his future, meetings with eccentric Parisians, and writing lessons from Duras, who was never paid for the attic Vila-Matas rented from her. His editors appear, as do various Spanish, Spanish American, French, and American writers such as Perec, Juan Marsé, Copi (pseudonym of Raúl Damonte), Samuel Beckett, and William S. Burroughs Jr., as well as a transvestite, Vicky Vaporú, who turns out to be the only sensible character in the book. The pervading irony and the narrator's tendency to disappear into the background make this work quite different from its main source, the chapter "There Is Never Any End to Paris" in Hemingway's *A Moveable Feast* (1964). In 2003 Vila-Matas received the Spanish Premio Nacional de la Crítica and the French Prix Medicis-Etranger for the translation of *El mal de montano.*

The theme of the novel *Doctor Pasavento* (2005) is the loneliness of writers. The title character is a well-known psychiatrist and writer who disappears for

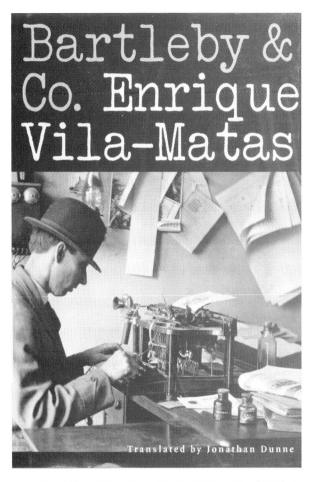

Dust jacket for the U.S. edition of the English translation (2004) of Vila-Matas's Bartleby y compañía (2000), a combination of essay and fiction about forgotten writers who practice "the literature of No" by saying, like the character in Herman Melville's story, "Bartleby, the Scrivener" (1853), that they "would prefer not to" (Richland County Public Library)

eleven days to devote himself exclusively to writing. Pasavento travels to Seville in December 2004, where he meets the Spanish author Bernardo Atxaga (whom Vila-Matas met under exactly the same conditions in December 2003). He goes on to Naples and then to Paris (where he stays in the hotel in which Vila-Matas's French publisher puts up authors). When no one wonders where he is or looks for him, Pasavento realizes that he is alone in the world. Pasavento admires Robert Walser, the German-Swiss modernist writer who, repulsed by literary power and greatness, put himself in the Waldau and then the Herisau mental hospitals, remaining in the latter until his death. Pasavento's adventure ends at Herisau when the real-life director, Dr. Bruno Kägi, refuses to accept him as a patient. The novel is divided into four sections; each section is composed of numbered vignettes in which mentions of the author's preferred readings and authors are intertwined with names of real-life critics and friends.

Enrique Vila-Matas has traveled to at least eighteen countries at the invitation of various institutions and universities. In 2005 he participated in FLIP (Fiesta Literaria Internacional de Paraty [International Literary Festival of Paraty]) in Paraty, Brazil, along with the writers Salman Rushdie, Michael Ondaatje, and Jon Lee Anderson. Vila-Matas has told interviewers that his books are "mental trips that, sometimes, are based on geographical voyages." He lives in Barcelona, where he continues to write fiction and to contribute monthly articles to the Mexican and Spanish editions of the prestigious periodical *Letras Libres,* as well as to France's monthly *Magazine littéraire.* Vila-Matas has been called the best Spanish metanovelist of his time, and his works have been described as passionately modern texts.

**Interviews:**

Ignacio Vidal-Folch, "Vila-Matas: Raro entre los raros," *Qué leer,* 4 (February 2000): 24–30;

Beatriz Berger, "Profesional de la mentira," *El Mercurio* (Santiago, Chile), 18 March 2000, Revista de Libros, pp. 1–3;

Alicia Adela Kohan, "Entrevista con Enrique Vila-Matas: El espía del mundo," *La Nación* (Buenos Aires), 18 February 2001, Suplemento Cultura, pp. 1–2.

**References:**

Irene Andrés-Suárez and Ana Casas, eds., *Enrique Vila-Matas: Actas del "Gran Séminaire" de Neuchatel, 2–3 de diciembre de 2002. Cuadernos de Narrativa, VII* (Saragossa: Póritoc, 2003);

Ángel Basanta and others, "Enrique Vila-Matas y *El viaje vertical,*" *Lateral,* 6 (September 1999): 42–43;

Rafael Conte and others, "Los mundos particulares de Enrique Vila-Matas y Miguel Sánchez-Ostiz," in *Historia y crítica de la literatura española,* volume 9: *Los nuevos nombres: 1975–2000,* edited by Jordi Gracia (Barcelona: Crítica, 2000), pp. 378–385;

Alvaro Enrigue, "Memorias: Pesimismo," *Letras Libres,* 7 (January 2004): 88–89;

*El Periódico,* special Vila-Matas issue, 36 (19 February 1999);

Ana Rodríguez Fischer, "Las novelas peligrosas de Enrique Vila-Matas," *Cuadernos Hispanoamericanos,* 635 (May 2003): 85–92;

Leonardo Valencia, "Silenciosa turba," *Lateral,* 6, no. 64 (April 2000): 14–15;

Fernando Valls, "Unas cuantas verdades fingidas," in his *La realidad inventada: Análisis crítico de la novela española actual* (Barcelona: Crítica, 2003), pp. 263–264, 275–278, 291–293, 302–305;

Stéphane Zékian, "Vila-Matas existe-t-il?" *Nouvelle Revue Française,* 99 (January 2003): 235–243.

# Checklist of Further Readings

Abellán, José Luis. *El exilio español de 1939,* volume 4. Madrid: Taurus, 1977.

Baquero Goyanes, Mariano. *Estructuras de la novela actual*. Barcelona: Planeta, 1970.

Basanta, Angel. *40 años de novela española,* 2 volumes. Madrid: Cincel-Kapelusz, 1979.

Basanta. *La novela española de nuestra época*. Madrid: Anaya, 1990.

Bergmann, Emilie L., and Paul Julian Smith. *¿Entiendes? Queer Readings, Hispanic Writings*. Durham, N.C.: Duke University Press, 2000.

Bértolo, Constantino. "Introducción a la novela española actual," *Revista de Occidente,* nos. 98–99 (1989): 29–60.

Blanco Aguinaga, Carlos, Julio Rodríguez Puértolas, and Iris M. Zavala. *Historia social de la literatura española (en lengua castellana),* 3 volumes. Madrid: Castalia, 1978–1979.

Brown, Gerald G. *The Twentieth Century*. London: Benn / New York: Barnes & Noble, 1972.

Brown, Joan Lipman. *Women Writers of Contemporary Spain: Exiles in the Homeland*. Newark: University of Delaware Press / London & Cranbury, N.J.: Associated University Presses, 1991.

Buckley, Ramón. *La doble transición: Política y literatura en la España de los años setenta*. Madrid: Siglo XXI, 1996.

Cardona, Rodolfo, ed. *Novelistas españoles de la posguerra*. Madrid: Taurus, 1976.

Carr, Raymond. *Modern Spain, 1875–1980*. Oxford & New York: Oxford University Press, 1980.

Ciplijauskaité, Biruté. *Novela femenina contemporánea (1970–1985): Hacia una tipología de la narración en primera persona*. Barcelona: Anthropos, 1988.

Colmeiro, José F. *La novela policiaca española: Teoría y historia crítica*. Barcelona: Anthropos, 1994.

Concha, Victor G. de la, and others, eds. *Epoca contemporánea, 1914–1939,* volume 7 of *Historia y crítica de la literatura española,* edited by Francisco Rico. Barcelona: Crítica, 1984.

Conte, Rafael. *La novela española del exilio*. Barcelona: Sopena, 1969.

Díaz-Diocaretz, Myriam, and Zavala, eds. *Breve historia feminista de la literatura española (en lengua castellana),* volume 2. Barcelona: Anthropos, 1993.

Encinar, Angeles. *La novela española actual: La desaparición del héroe*. Madrid: Pliegos, 1991.

Eoff, Sherman. *The Modern Spanish Novel: Comparative Essays Examining the Philosophical Impact of Science on Fiction*. New York: New York University Press, 1961.

Ferreras, Juan Ignacio. *Tendencias de la novela española actual, 1931–1969: Seguidas de un catálogo de urgencia de novelas y novelistas de la posguerra española*. Paris: Ediciones Hispanoamericanas, 1970.

Galerstein, Carolyn L., and Kathleen McNerney, eds. *Women Writers of Spain: An Annotated Bio-Bibliographical Guide*. New York & Westport, Conn.: Greenwood Press, 1986.

García Fernández, Javier. *Contrasentidos: Acercamiento a la novela española contemporánea*. Saragossa: Universidad de Zaragoza, Servicio de Publicaciones, 2002.

García González de Nora, Eugenio. *La novela española contemporánea,* 2 volumes. Madrid: Gredos, 1958, 1962.

Gould Levine, Linda, Ellen Engleson Marson, and Gloria Feiman Waldman. *Spanish Women Writers: A Bio-Bibliographical Source Book.* Westport, Conn.: Greenwood Press, 1993.

Goytisolo, Juan. *Problemas de la novela.* Barcelona: Seix Barral, 1959.

Gullón, Agnes, and Germán Gullón. *Teoría de la novela: Aproximaciones hispánicas.* Madrid: Taurus, 1974.

Gullón, Germán. *La novela moderna en España (1885–1902): Los albores de la modernidad.* Madrid: Taurus, 1992.

Gullón, Ricardo. *Espacio y novela.* Barcelona: Bosch, 1980.

Gullón, *La invención del 98 y otros ensayos.* Madrid: Gredos, 1969.

Gullón. *La novela española contemporánea: Ensayos críticos.* Madrid: Alianza, 1994.

Gullón. *La novela lírica.* Madrid: Cátedra, 1984.

Labani, Jo. *Myth and History in the Contemporary Spanish Novel.* Cambridge & New York: Cambridge University Press, 1989.

Landeira, Richard, and Luis González del Valle, eds. *Nuevos y novísimos: Algunas perspectivas críticas sobre la narrativa española desde la década de los sesenta.* Boulder, Colo.: Society of Spanish and Spanish-American Studies, 1987.

López Morillas, Juan. *Hacia el 98: Literatura, sociedad, ideología.* Barcelona: Ariel, 1972.

Mainer, José-Carlos. *De postguerra: 1951–1990.* Barcelona: Editorial Crítica, 1994.

Mainer. *La Edad de Plata (1902–1939): Ensayo de interpretación de un proceso cultural.* Madrid: Cátedra, 1981.

Mainer, ed. *Modernismo y 98,* volume 6 of *Historia y crítica de la literatura española.* Barcelona: Crítica, 1980.

Manteiga, Roberto C., Kathleen McNerney, and Carolyn Galerstein, eds. *Feminine Concerns in Contemporary Spanish Fiction by Women.* Potomac, Md.: Scripta Humanistica, 1988.

Marra-López, José R. *Narrativa española fuera de España, 1939–1961.* Madrid: Guadarrama, 1963.

Martínez Cachero, José María. *La novela española entre 1936 y 1980: Historia de una aventura.* Madrid: Castalia, 1985.

Navajas, Gonzalo. *Teoría y práctica de la novela española posmoderna.* Barcelona: Ediciones del Mall, 1997.

Nichols, Geraldine C. *Descifrar la diferencia: Narrativa femenina de la España contemporánea.* Madrid: Siglo XXI, 1992.

Nichols. *Escribir, espacio propio: Laforet, Matute, Moix, Tusquets, Riera y Roig por sí mismas.* Minneapolis: Institute for the Study of Ideologies and Literature, 1989.

Nora, Eugenio G. de. *La novela española contemporánea,* second edition. 3 volumes. Madrid: Gredos, 1973–1979.

Ordoñez, Elizabeth. "Inscribing Difference: 'L'Ecriture Fémenine' and New Narrative by Women," *ALEC,* 12, nos. 1–2 (1987): 45–58.

Ordoñez. *Voices of Their Own: Contemporary Spanish Narrative by Women.* Lewisburg, Pa.: Bucknell University Press / London & Cranbury, N.J.: Associated University Presses, 1991.

Paredes Náñez, Juan. *La novela policiaca española.* Granada: Universidad de Granada, 1989.

Pérez, Janet. *Contemporary Women Writers of Spain.* Boston: Twayne, 1988.

Pérez, ed. *Novelistas femeninas de la postguerra español.* Madrid: Porrúa, 1983.

Pope, Randolph. *Novela de emergencia: España, 1939–1954.* Madrid: Sociedad General Española de Librería, 1984.

Pozuelo Yvancos, José M. *Poética de la ficción.* Madrid: Síntesis, 1993.

Ramsden, Herbert. *The 1898 Movement in Spain: Towards a Reinterpretation with Special Reference to En torno al casticismo and Idearium español.* Manchester: Manchester University Press / Totowa, N.J.: Rowman & Littlefield, 1974.

Sanz Villanueva, Santos. *Historia de la novela social española (1942–1975).* Madrid: Alhambra, 1980.

Sanz Villanueva. *Tendecias de la novela española actual.* Madrid: Cuadernos para el Diálogo, 1972.

Scarlett, Elizabeth A. *Under Construction: The Body in Spanish Novels.* Charlottesville: University Press of Virginia, 1994.

Servodidio, Mirella, ed. "Reading for Difference: Feminist Perspectives on Women Novelists of Contemporary Spain," *Anales de la literatura española contemporánea,* 12, nos. 1–2 (1987): 11–115.

Shaw, Donald L. *The Generation of 1898 in Spain.* London: Benn / New York: Barnes & Noble, 1975.

Sobejano, Gonzalo. *Forma literaria y sensibilidad social (Mateo Alemán, Galdós, Clarín, el 98 y Valle-Inclán).* Madrid: Gredos, 1967.

Sobejano. *Novela española de nuestro tiempo (en busca del pueblo perdido),* revised edition. Madrid: Prensa Española, 1975.

Soldevila Durante, Ignacio. *Historia de la novela española, 1936–2000.* Madrid: Cátedra, 2001.

Soldevila Durante. *La novela desde 1936.* Madrid: Alhambra, 1980.

Spires, Robert C. *La novela española de posguerra: Creación artística y experiencia personal.* Madrid: Cupsa, 1978.

Spitzmesser, Ana María. *Narrativa posmoderna española: Crónica de un desengaño.* New York: Peter Lang, 1999.

Subirats, Eduardo. *La cultura como espectáculo.* Madrid: Fondo de cultura económica de España, 1988.

Tuñón de Lara, Manuel. *Historia de España,* 13 volumes. Barcelona: Labor, 1980–1983.

Tusell, Javier. *La transición española a la democracia.* Madrid: Historia 16, 1991.

Villanueva, Darío. *Espacio y tiempo reducido en la novela española contemporánea.* Valencia: Bello, 1977.

Villanueva. *Theories of Literary Realism,* revised edition, translated by Mihai I. Spariosu and Santiago García Castañón. Albany: State University of New York Press, 1997.

Villanueva, ed. *La novela lírica,* 2 volumes. Madrid: Taurus, 1983.

Villanueva and others, eds. *Los nuevos nombres, 1975–1990,* volume 9 of *Historia y crítica de la literatura española,* Barcelona: Crítica, 1992.

Villegas Morales, Juan. *La estructura mítica del héroe en la novela del siglo XX.* Barcelona: Planeta, 1973.

Ynduráin, Domingo, ed. *Época contemporánea, 1939–1980,* volume 8 of *Historia y crítica de la literatura española.* Barcelona: Crítica, 1981.

# Contributors

Yaw Agawu-Kakraba . . . . . . . . . . . . . . . . . . . . . . . .*Pennsylvania State University–Altoona College*

Marta E. Altisent . . . . . . . . . . . . . . . . . . . . . . . . . . . . . . . *University of California Davis*

Alma Amell . . . . . . . . . . . . . . . . . . . . . . . . . . . . . . . *Pontifical College Josephinum*

Emilie L. Bergmann . . . . . . . . . . . . . . . . . . . . . . . . . . . *University of California, Berkeley*

Julia Biggane . . . . . . . . . . . . . . . . . . . . . . . . . . . . . . . . . . *University of Aberdeen*

Frieda H. Blackwell . . . . . . . . . . . . . . . . . . . . . . . . . . . . . . . . . . .*Baylor University*

Antonio Candau . . . . . . . . . . . . . . . . . . . . . . . . . . . *Case Western Reserve University*

Richard A. Cardwell . . . . . . . . . . . . . . . . . . . . . . . . . . . . *University of Nottingham*

Lucile C. Charlebois . . . . . . . . . . . . . . . . . . . . . . . . . . . *University of South Carolina*

Rosemary Clark . . . . . . . . . . . . . . . . . . . . . . . . . . . . . . . *University of Cambridge*

José F. Colmeiro . . . . . . . . . . . . . . . . . . . . . . . . . . . . . . .*Michigan State University*

Wilfrido H. Corral . . . . . . . . . . . . . . . . . . . . . . .*California State University, Sacramento*

Pamela DeWeese . . . . . . . . . . . . . . . . . . . . . . . . . . . . . . . . . *Sweet Briar College*

Toni Dorca . . . . . . . . . . . . . . . . . . . . . . . . . . . . . . . . . . .*Macalester College*

Ángeles Encinar . . . . . . . . . . . . . . . . . . . . . . . . *Saint Louis University, Madrid Campus*

Sebastiaan Faber . . . . . . . . . . . . . . . . . . . . . . . . . . . . . . . . . . *Oberlin College*

José Ramón González . . . . . . . . . . . . . . . . . . . . . . . *Universidad de Valladolid*

Alexis Grohmann . . . . . . . . . . . . . . . . . . . . . . . . . . . . . *University of Edinburgh*

Germán Gullón . . . . . . . . . . . . . . . . . . . . . . . . . . . . . . .*University of Amsterdam*

Patricia Hart . . . . . . . . . . . . . . . . . . . . . . . . . . . . . . . . *Purdue University*

Stephen Hart . . . . . . . . . . . . . . . . . . . . . . . . . . . . . .*University College London*

Barbara F. Ichiishi . . . . . . . . . . . . . . . . . . . . . . . . . . . . . .*Columbus, Ohio*

Catherine Jaffe . . . . . . . . . . . . . . . . . . . . . . . . *Texas State University–San Marcos*

Roberta Johnson . . . . . . . . . . . . . . . . . . . . . . . . . . . . . .*University of Kansas*

Mercedes Juliá . . . . . . . . . . . . . . . . . . . . . . . . . . . . . . . *Villanova University*

Caridad R. Kenna . . . . . . . . . . . . . . . . . . . . . . . . . . . . . . *Stanford University*

Eva Legido-Quigley . . . . . . . . . . . . . . . . . . . . . . . *Letra Hispánica, Salamanca*

María del Mar López-Cabrales . . . . . . . . . . . . . . . . . . *Colorado State University*

Francis Lough . . . . . . . . . . . . . . . . . . . . . . . . . . . . . . *University of Birmingham*

Cristina Martínez-Carazo . . . . . . . . . . . . . . . . . . . . . . *University of California Davis*

Jaume Martí-Olivella . . . . . . . . . . . . . . . . . . . . . . . . . *University of New Hampshire*

Nelson R. Orringer . . . . . . . . . . . . . . . . . . . . . . . . . . .*University of Connecticut*

Jeffrey Oxford . . . . . . . . . . . . . . . . . . . . . . . . . . *University of Wisconsin–Milwaukee*

Janet Pérez . . . . . . . . . . . . . . . . . . . . . . . . . . . . . . . *Texas Tech University*

Randolph D. Pope . . . . . . . . . . . . . . . . . . . . . . . . . . .*University of Virginia*

Alison Ribeiro de Menezes . . . . . . . . . . . . . . . . . . . . . . . . . *University College Dublin*

391

Cintia Santana . . . . . . . . . . . . . . . . . . . . . . . . . . . . . . . . . . . . . . . . *Claremont McKenna College*

Elizabeth Scarlett . . . . . . . . . . . . . . . . . . . . . . . . . . . . *State University of New York at Buffalo*

Leda Schiavo . . . . . . . . . . . . . . . . . . . . . . . . . . . . . . . . . . . . *University of Illinois at Chicago*

Sandra J. Schumm . . . . . . . . . . . . . . . . . . . . . . . . . . . . . . . . . . . . . . . . *Baker University*

Carter E. Smith . . . . . . . . . . . . . . . . . . . . . . . . . . . . . . *University of Wisconsin–Eau Claire*

Jeremy S. Squires . . . . . . . . . . . . . . . . . . . . . . . . . . . . . . . . . . . *University College Dublin*

# Cumulative Index

*Dictionary of Literary Biography,* Volumes 1-322
*Dictionary of Literary Biography Yearbook,* 1980-2002
*Dictionary of Literary Biography Documentary Series,* Volumes 1-19
*Concise Dictionary of American Literary Biography,* Volumes 1-7
*Concise Dictionary of British Literary Biography,* Volumes 1-8
*Concise Dictionary of World Literary Biography,* Volumes 1-4

# Cumulative Index

**DLB** before number: *Dictionary of Literary Biography*, Volumes 1-322
**Y** before number: *Dictionary of Literary Biography Yearbook*, 1980-2002
**DS** before number: *Dictionary of Literary Biography Documentary Series*, Volumes 1-19
**CDALB** before number: *Concise Dictionary of American Literary Biography*, Volumes 1-7
**CDBLB** before number: *Concise Dictionary of British Literary Biography*, Volumes 1-8
**CDWLB** before number: *Concise Dictionary of World Literary Biography*, Volumes 1-4

# G

# N

ISBN 0-7876-8140-7

90000

9 780787 681401